Vision of Utopia	Some Leading Theorists	Key Strength	Key Weakness
Unconflicted psychosexual development, mature socialization of id instincts	S. Freud	Attention to unconscious influences, importance of sexual drives even in nonsexual spheres	Many ideas superseded by more modern research on the brain, speculations often unverified or unverifiable, influenced by sexist assumptions of the times
Mature self, adapted to the many situations to be faced	A. Adler, K. Horney, E. Erikson	Emphasis on the self as it struggles to cope with emotions and drives on the inside and the demands of others on the outside	Sometimes a hodgepodge of ideas from different traditions, difficult to test in rigorous manner
Improvement through medication of the brain and gene manipulation or selection, understanding how our biological inheritance affects society	I. Pavlov, R. Plomin, H. Eysenck, S. Scarr, M. Daly	Focuses on tendencies and limits imposed by biological inheritance, can be combined with other approaches	Tends to minimize human potential for growth and change, serious danger of misuse by politicians who oversimplify its findings
Conditioning and reinforcing of individual behaviors so the person wants to do what benefits society	B. F. Skinner, J. Dollard, N. Miller	Can force a more scientific analysis of the learning experiences that shape personality	May dehumanize unique human potentials through comparisons to rats and pigeons, may ignore advances from cognitive and social psychology
Rational decision making through understanding thought processes, computer simulation of personality	G. Kelly, A. Bandura	Captures active nature of human thought and uses modern knowledge from cognitive psychology	Often ignores unconscious and emotional aspects of personality
Understanding unity of each individual, accurate assessment of abilities	G. Allport, R. B. Cattell, H. Eysenck	Good individual assessment techniques	May reach too far in trying to capture individual in a few ways, may label people on the basis of test scores
Self-actualization, overcoming existential crises, love and dignity	A. Maslow, C. Rogers, E. Fromm	Appreciates the spiritual nature of a person, emphasizes struggles for self-fulfillment and dignity	May avoid quantification and scientific method needed for science of personality
Understanding how the individual creates and maintains appropriate or inappropriate roles and identities	H. Murray, H. S. Sullivan, W. Mischel	Understands that we are different selves in different situations	No good ways to define situations nor to study the many complexities of interactions

Personality

Personality

Classic Theories
and Modern Research

Howard S. Friedman
University of California, Riverside

Miriam W. Schustack
California State University, San Marcos

Allyn and Bacon

Boston ▪ London ▪ Toronto ▪ Sydney ▪ Tokyo ▪ Singapore

Vice President, Education and Social Sciences: Sean W. Wakely
Senior Editor: Carolyn Merrill
Series Editorial Assistant: Jessica Barnard
Marketing Manager: Joyce Nilsen
Senior Editorial Production Administrator: Susan McIntyre
Editorial Production Service: Andrea Cava
Composition Buyer: Linda Cox
Manufacturing Buyer: Megan Cochran
Cover Administrator: Linda Knowles
Text Design and Electronic Composition: Denise Hoffman
Photo Researcher: Sue C. Howard

Allyn & Bacon
160 Gould Street
Needham Heights, MA 02494
Internet: www.abacon.com

Library of Congress Cataloging-in-Publication Data

Friedman, Howard S.
    Personality: classic theories and modern research / Howard S.
  Friedman, Miriam W. Schustack.
        p.   cm.
    Includes bibliographical references and indexes.
    ISBN 0-205-13953-1 (alk. paper)
    1. Personality.   I. Schustack, Miriam W., 1952–   . II. Title.
  BF698.F44   1999
  155.2—dc21   98-28088
                                                          CIP

Printed in the United States of America

10 9 8 7 6 5 4 3 2 1   RRD   04 03 02 01 00 99 98

Photo Credits: Photo credits appear on page 565, which should be considered an extension of the copyright page.

For

Pearl and Bernard Friedman

Ada Lillian and Walter L. Schustack

Four striking personalities
and well over a century of marriage

Brief Contents

Contents

Part II   *Eight Basic Aspects of Personality*

Chapter 6   Behaviorist and Learning Aspects of Personality   183

Chapter 7   Cognitive Aspects of Personality   213

Chapter 8   Trait and Skill Aspects of Personality   249

Chapter 9   Humanistic and Existential Aspects of Personality   287

Chapter 10   Person–Situation Interactionist Aspects of Personality   317

Part III   Applications to Individual Differences

Chapter 11   Male–Female Differences   351

Chapter 12 Stress, Adjustment, and Health Differences   385

Chapter 13 Cultural and Ethnic Differences   417

Chapter 14 Love and Hate   449

Part IV   Conclusion and Outlook for the Future

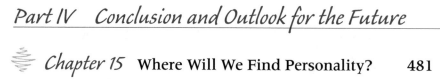

Chapter 15   Where Will We Find Personality?   481

 *Preface*

Although in one sense this volume involves a natural progression from previous personality texts, in another sense it is wholly new. Generations of students have been taught personality theories by venerable "theories" books, but many modern courses have abandoned the classics in favor of the new narrow, empirical look of personality. We have aimed to integrate the best of the old with the best of the new.

What distinguishes our book? We believe that seven features set this book apart. These features have guided its development as a distinctive choice in personality texts.

First, we have tried to make this an exceptionally well-written book, full of examples that pique students' interest. We believe that students learn best when fascinated with the material and that attention to literary style does not mean a sacrifice of scientific rigor. Indeed, many of the most influential theorists—Allport, Freud, Skinner, Rogers, May, and others—were successful in part because of their clear and powerful writing.

Second, this book strives for a coherence and balance that arises from viewing personality as having eight basic aspects. (These are the psychoanalytic, ego, biological, behaviorist, cognitive, trait, humanistic, and situational/ interactionist aspects). Our view is that human complexity derives from the various influences on development—including biological predispositions, early experiences, cognitive structures, reinforcements, situational demands, and self-actualizing motivations. It is not the case that one approach is always "right" and another is always "wrong"; each has insights to contribute. Thus we take an optimistic approach, focusing on what each approach has to offer, but also pointing out the weaknesses of each.

Third, this book integrates theory and basic research. Although the lives of personality theorists are often used as illustrations, the focus is on intellectual content rather than on biography. Dead-end approaches, of minor historical interest, are not included. Where available, the most modern research is integrated with the original theory. For example, the chapter on Freudian psychoanalytic approaches ends with a thorough discussion of modern cognitive approaches to the unconscious. Similarly, the work of Henry Murray and Harry Stack Sullivan is shown to lay the groundwork for modern interactionist approaches. The aim is to capture the brilliant insights of classical theorists and reveal how their ideas have been studied and sometimes realized in modern research. Throughout, we retain the focus of our title, *Personality: Classic Theories and Modern Research.*

Fourth, this book includes a substantial integration of cross-cultural and women's issues, topics traditionally neglected. The emphasis is on science and logic rather than political correctness. For example, the problems of test bias are emphasized, but without disparaging all testing. The cultural-boundedness of each theorist is noted, but without disdain; we are all blinded in part by our times and our cultures. These issues are integrated throughout the book, as well as considered in separate chapters.

Fifth, this book presents a general, connected, and opinionated approach to thinking about personality, in the spirit of Gordon Allport's and Henry Murray's books. In other words, evaluation and integration are emphasized as the text proceeds. This book strives to help students understand personality as relevant to important issues in their own lives and in society. For example, the implications of biological influences on personality are carefully evaluated. Just as important new developments in behavioral genetics and brain physiology cannot be ignored, the dangers of a modern eugenics movement must be carefully presented for student thought and discussion. The different perspectives on personality reflect, in part, the assumptions and values of their proponents, and we repeatedly urge students to think for themselves about what it means to be a person. This book tells a story about human character.

Sixth, this book concludes with several chapters on practical applications to individual differences. Personality theory and research are highly relevant to current societal thinking about gender differences, health differences, cultural differences, and love and hate. These chapters also serve to reinforce the lessons of the earlier chapters. These chapters may be selectively omitted in a short quarter (ten-week) course.

Seventh, this book endeavors to encourage *critical thinking about human nature.* Students are learning a specific content, but they are also learning how to evaluate theory and research. Do not be deceived: although this book seems easy to read, we hold to the highest scientific and intellectual standards. A goal, in all seriousness, is to have students return years later and say, "This course changed my life."

What does this book *not* do? Although it draws on the most current research, this book is not a compendium of current findings. This book is not a narrow, advanced text aimed at graduate students, nor is it an encyclopedia. This book is not an idiosyncratic sampling of personality issues, nor is it full of chatty hype. Rather it endeavors to be comprehensive yet engrossing. It has been extensively tested in real class settings.

In sum, the emphases are on being clear and articulate, coherent and balanced, theoretical yet empirically accurate, culturally sensitive yet scientific, integrated and opinionated, basic and applied, and promoting of critical thinking. These are ambitious goals, but we think our students deserve no less.

The emphasis on clarity is reflected in the structure—ten basic chapters and five applied chapters. Three types of boxed features appear in the chapters: Self-Understanding gives sample assessment techniques for students to try out, Famous Personalities illustrates select concepts using well-known, often contemporary, people such as Madonna, and Evaluating the Perspectives describes the main strengths and weaknesses of each theoretical approach. Other didactic aids include extensive use of real-world examples and applications to society, lists of key theorists and concepts, integrative chapter conclusions, and a comprehensive glossary. These reinforce textual material already geared toward learning and critical thinking. A complete Instructor's Manual also is available.

Acknowledgments

Our thanks and great appreciation to the many wonderful scholars and students who assisted us with this project: Dr. Nancy Lees, Dr. Leslie Martin, and Patricia Lee, for helping prepare and evaluate parts of the text. Dr. Kathy McCartney, Dr. Glenn Stanley, Dr. Dan Ozer, Dr. Steve Reise, and other colleagues who consulted on key points. And Mike Furr, Kathleen Clark, Jessica Dennis, Heidi Olson-Tinker, Tanya Taylor, Heather Asper, Kara and Lauren, and many, many other students and graduate students, who contributed in myriad ways. Since this book was student-oriented from its conception, it is fitting that students were involved throughout its development.

We also have had the benefit of great support from many at Allyn and Bacon, starting with terrific encouragement and ideas from Susan Badger and ending with the superb professionalism and insight of Sean Wakely and Carolyn Merrill.

We also thank the following reviewers for their significant advice: Joan B. Cannon, University of Masschusetts at Lowell; Nancy Dixon, Tennessee Technological University; Christina M. Frederick, Southern Utah University; Steven C. Funk, Northern Arizona University; Diane Henschel, California State University, Dominguez Hills; Ralph W. Hood, Jr., University of Tennessee at Chattanooga; David Korotkov, Memorial University (Canada); Mary Jo Litten, Pittsburg State University; Mitchell S. Nesler, Regents College; Leonard S. Newman, University of Illinois at Chicago; John W. Nichols, Tulsa

Community College; Jean Nyland, College of Notre Dame; Augustine Osman, University of Northern Iowa; Michael F. Shaughnessy, Eastern New Mexico University; and Brian H. Stagner, Texas A & M University.

We welcome feedback and suggestions for future editions from teachers and students.

Howard S. Friedman
Miriam W. Schustack

 *About the Authors*

Professor Howard S. Friedman teaches psychology at the University of California, Riverside, where he currently studies personality and health. In 1995, Dr. Friedman was awarded UCR's Distinguished Teaching Award. He is an elected Fellow of the Division of Personality and Social Psychology, and the Division of Health Psychology, of the American Psychological Association. An honors graduate of Yale University, Friedman received his Ph.D. from Harvard University.

Professor Miriam W. Schustack teaches psychology at the California State University in San Marcos (near San Diego), where she currently specializes in the use of computers in learning. She previously taught at Harvard University. An honors graduate of Princeton University, Schustack received her master's from Yale and her Ph.D. from Carnegie-Mellon University.

Personality

Chapter 1

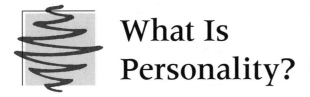

What Is Personality?

On leaving chemistry class, two nineteen-year-old college students saw their classmate Susan slip and take a nasty fall down the stairs. One of the watching students stood pale and trembling, paralyzed with fear; a weak smile crossed his face. The other student took charge of the situation, beginning first aid and ordering a passerby to call an ambulance. Why did the two students react so differently?

The first, fearful student— Michael—was a nervous, introverted but likable guy, studying computer programming. In a later interview, Michael reported that he had always been kind of shy, but that those feelings intensified at age seven when he was sexually molested by his uncle. The second,

1

take-charge student—Sara—was a friendly and vivacious honors student, studying to be a doctor. She was an officer in her sorority. As a member of an ethnic minority group, Sara had faced some discrimination in elementary school, but her parents raised her with a strong sense of moral values, and they vigorously encouraged her achievements.

Michael and Sara are both bright, affable college students, but when facing the same emergency situation, they reacted very differently. Could we have predicted which student would help Susan if we had gathered some information about their personalities? In most, but not all, cases, yes. If we know the right information about individuals, we can do a fairly accurate job of predicting their behavior and understanding the reasons for it, especially if we simultaneously consider the particular social situation.

As same-aged college students sharing a college class, Michael and Sara have a lot in common, but they are also each unique. We have given a brief description of some of their characteristics and behaviors, but what really makes them tick? What psychological forces make Michael who he is and Sara who she is? This book tells what psychologists think and know about personality.

*M*ost basically, personality psychology asks the question, *What does it mean to be a person?* In other words, How are we unique as individuals? What is the nature of the self? Personality psychologists answer these fascinating questions in terms of systematic observations about how and why individuals behave as they do. Personality psychologists tend to avoid abstract philosophical or religious musings and focus instead on the thoughts, feelings, and behaviors of real people. Personality is generally *not* studied in terms of nonpsychological concepts such as profits and losses, souls or spirits, or molecules and electromagnetism. Personality is a subfield of psychology.

Personality psychology can be defined as the scientific study of the psychological forces that make people uniquely themselves. To be comprehensive, we can say that personality has eight key aspects, which together help us understand the complex nature of the individual. First, the individual is affected by *unconscious aspects*, forces that are not in moment-to-moment awareness. For example, we might say or do things to others that our parents used to say or do to us, without recognizing that we are motivated by our desire to resemble our parents. Second, the individual is affected by so-called *ego forces* that provide a sense of identity or "self." For example, we often strive to maintain a sense of mastery and consistency in our behavior. Third, a person is a *biological being,* with a unique genetic, physical, physiological, and temperamental nature. Fourth, people are *conditioned and shaped* by the experiences and environments that surround them. That is, our surroundings sometimes train us to respond in certain ways, and we grow up in varying cultures. Fifth, people have a *cognitive dimension*, thinking about and actively interpreting the world around them. Different people construe the happenings around them in different ways.

Sixth, an individual is a collection of specific *traits, skills, and predispositions*. There is no denying that each of us has certain specific abilities and inclinations. Seventh, human beings have a *spiritual dimension* to their lives, which ennobles them and prompts them to ponder the meaning of their existence. People are much more than robots that are programmed by computers. Eighth, and finally, the individual's nature is an ongoing *interaction* between the person and the particular environment. Taken together, these eight aspects help us define and understand personality; they are the subject of this book.

Personality and Science

Modern personality psychologists are scientific in the sense that they attempt to use methods of scientific inference (using systematically gathered evidence) to test theories. Although a person might be able to learn a great deal about personality by reading a Tolstoy novel or seeing a Shakespearean play, such insights are not scientific until they have been tested in a systematic way. As we will show, scientific methods have yielded insights into personality that are not available to a keen novelist or philosopher.

It is said that former president Ronald Reagan and his wife, Nancy, used astrology to help them judge other people. Why shouldn't you rely on such stargazers in assessing personality? Or, why not go to the nearest carnival and have your personality read from the lines in the palms of your hands? Perhaps you should turn to physiognomy—the art of face reading—to evaluate others. Should you make personality inferences about people who have large foreheads? No, such approaches do not work. All of these techniques are generally invalid; they are wrong or vague as often as they are right. However, through an understanding of personality psychology—classic theories and modern research—meaningful answers about personality *are* available.

Some scientists believe that rigorous study of personality must become mathematical and involve numbers—for instance, statistics such as correlations. A correlation coefficient is a mathematical index of the degree of agreement (or association) between two measures. For example, height and weight are positively correlated: in most (but not all) cases, the taller a person is, the more the person weighs. Extroversion and shyness are negatively (inversely) correlated: knowing that a person scores high on a test of extroversion lets

Figure 1.1

Correlation between Dating and Introversion. These data show a negative (inverse) correlation between introversion and dating: the more introverted, the fewer dates, generally speaking. Note, however, that Candy is quite introverted but still gets an average number of dates. Such statistics are used to evaluate the validity of both the measure and the construct of introversion.

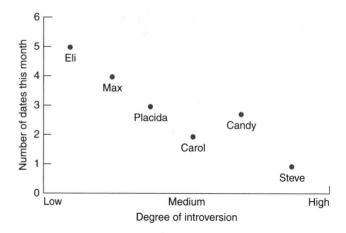

us predict that the person will not often act in a shy manner. In the example shown in Figure 1.1, there is a negative correlation between a person's degree of introversion and the number of dates the person went on last month. Such statistics help us quantify relationships.

Correlations tell us about associations, but not about causal relationships. For example, if we learn that fat people tend to be jolly, that positive correlation does not tell us why the relationship exists. Is there some underlying predisposition that makes certain people tend to eat a lot and also be happy? Does plentiful food and extra weight make a person feel happier? Do happy people not worry about their looks and so gain weight? Do fat people hide an inner loneliness by pretending to be jolly? Do other people assume that fat people are jolly and therefore approach them in a kidding way, thereby making them more jolly? What are the causal relationships? The scientific study of personality helps us untangle these webs of associations. We explain the methods of the scientific study of personality throughout later chapters.

Although statistics such as correlations can indeed be extremely helpful, they are only tools to be used to help uncover the truth. Personality psychology does not always have to be mathematical to be scientific. In this book, we present various sorts of systematic analyses in addition to correlational analyses, including case studies (intensive focus on an individual), cross-cultural comparisons, and research into biological structures. By piecing together insights from these and other sources, we can gain a deep and valid understanding of personality.

Is a person outgoing or even domineering? Preoccupied with sexual attraction and sexual fulfillment? Does he or she have very good or very poor work habits? Insecurities that seem to arise from childhood experiences? High goals but doubts about ability to achieve them? Personality psychology provides the tools to begin to understand why people are the way they are.

Where Do Personality Theories Come From?

Many personality theories have arisen from the careful observations and deep introspection of insightful thinkers. For example, Sigmund Freud spent many hours analyzing his own dreams, which revealed to him the extent of the conflicts and urges hidden within. He had first noticed the power of repressed sexual urges in his patients, and he developed this idea into a comprehensive theory of the human psyche. Working from his assumptions about the struggle with sexual urges, Freud elaborated his theory to account for the many problems he saw in his medical practice and then to broader conflicts in society. The analysis develops from fundamental postulates about the nature of the mind. This is mostly a **deductive approach** to personality, in that the conclusions follow logically from the premises or assumptions. In deduction, we use our knowledge of basic psychological "laws" or principles in order to understand each particular person.

Second, some personality theories arise directly out of systematic empirical research. For example, we might be interested in knowing which basic dimensions or traits (such as extroversion) are essential to understanding personality. By collecting many trait-relevant observations on many people, we can get a sense of which traits are fundamental and which are less important, vague, or redundant. We can gather lots of systematic data from many people and continuously revise our conclusions as new data are gathered. This is an **inductive approach** to personality because concepts are developed based on what carefully collected observations reveal. Induction works from the data up to the theory.

A third source of personality theories involves analogies and concepts borrowed from related disciplines. For example, much progress is currently being made on understanding the structure and function of the human brain. Three types of brain scans are being used. Magnetic resonance imaging (MRI) scans use magnetic fields, and computerized tomography (CT) scans use X-rays, to obtain detailed pictures of the living brain. Positron emission tomography (PET) scans can even show ongoing brain activity by tracing where radioactive glucose is being channeled as people think and respond. These techniques are often applied to people with abnormal personalities—such as schizophrenics and those with brain damage—to search for reasons for their disorders. Certain models of personality become implausible if they are inconsistent with what we know about the structure and function of the brain. On the other hand, pictures of the brain can suggest new ways to think about its psychological organization.

Similarly, anthropologists have provided basic information both about human evolution and about differences between cultures. Some things about humans, such as our social nature, exist across time and space; people tend to live together in groups—family groups and cultural groups. On the other hand, some things, such as the degree of emphasis on individuality, tend to vary dra-

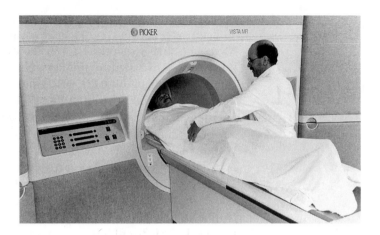

As we learn more about brain structure and function through modern technologies such as magnetic resonance imaging (MRI), we achieve a better understanding of the biological contributions to personality.

matically across cultures. For example, Americans tend to celebrate individual achievement and individual freedoms, but Japanese value harmony and the avoidance of personal distinction. Any successful approach to personality must take into account such anthropological facts.

In actual practice, almost all personality theories involve some elements of all these approaches. All theories develop in part by deduction, in part by induction, and in part by analogy. Occasionally, an interesting misunderstanding arises from a failure to recognize this fact. For example, we show in Chapter 3 that a basic tenet of Freudian theory is that little boys are motivated to "get rid" of their fathers and "marry" their mothers. The resolution of this conflict is said to have a direct effect on adult personality. Interesting predictions about personality can be deduced from this tenet or assumption. What is fascinating is that often young parents who have taken a course in personality psychology are amazed to see their four-year-old son march into their bedroom and attempt to climb into bed and order the father out!

The parents may respond, "My gosh, Freud was right!" The boy's behavior is taken as proof of a deduction from Freudian theory. What the parents fail to recognize is that Freud used such observations in constructing his theory in the first place, so it is not surprising that they will be observed by others. (Freud, like most personality theorists, was an expert observer.)

This line of thinking leads us to an important point: Various personality theories will predict and can explain many of the same behaviors. It is thus difficult to prove an approach entirely "wrong." In well-established physical sciences such as physics, a theoretical framework or paradigm, such as Einstein's relativity theory, can be devised that radically overthrows previous understandings, and a new generation of scientists moves rapidly to embrace and elaborate on the new theory (Kuhn, 1962). Personality psychology, however, does not have one overarching framework that is generally accepted. This means that competing explanations for personality phenomena must be examined, but it also means that personality psychology is characterized by an intellectually stimulating set of rival approaches. In addition, some theories are more applicable to certain domains than to others. For these reasons, we will show the strengths and weaknesses of various approaches in understanding personality. A sound theory will be comprehensive (explain various phenomena), parsimonious (explain things concisely), falsifiable (able to be tested for correctness), and productive (lead to new ideas, new predictions, and new research) (Campbell, 1988).

Preview of the Perspectives

Everyone has heard of Sigmund Freud's theories, and you may have heard that Freud says that in dreams the following objects may be symbolic of a penis: hammers, rifles, daggers, umbrellas, neckties (long objects peculiar to men), snakes, and many other objects. They are all phallic symbols. You might also have heard that the vagina may be dreamt of as a path through the brush, or as a garden, as in a dream in which a young woman asks a gardener if some branches could be transplanted to her garden. Taken out of context, such assertions may seem senseless, yet Freud has greatly influenced twentieth-century thought. We will attempt to show why Freudian theory has had such a tremendous impact.

Many other personality theorists and researchers are quite well known, but the best and most modern understanding of personality comes from a synthesis of psychological research on such matters as the nature of the self, psychobiology, learning theories, trait theories, existential approaches, and social psychology. As a taste of what lies ahead, here is an introduction to the concepts and the psychologists we will be investigating. Major features of the perspectives to be covered are presented in Table 1.1 on page 8.

Overview of the Eight Perspectives

In Chapter 3 we examine the psychoanalytic aspects of personality, with a focus on the unconscious. Interestingly, study of the unconscious has once again become a significant area of ongoing research in psychology. In Chapter 4, we focus on the ego or "self" aspects of personality, tracing notions of the self from Alfred Adler's work on inferiority complexes right up to modern theorizing about multiple selves.

Just as people come in different sizes, shapes, and colors, so too do people differ somewhat in their biological systems. Chapter 5 studies the biological aspects of personality, a topic often overlooked in personality texts. An individual's characteristic emotional and motivational nature is generally known as temperament. Such matters have attracted the attention of leading scientists since the time of Charles Darwin.

Table 1.1 **The Eight Basic Aspects of Personality**

Perspective	Key Strength
Psychoanalytic	Attention to unconscious influences; importance of sexual drives even in nonsexual spheres
Ego	Emphasis on the self as it struggles to cope with emotions and drives on the inside and the demands of others on the outside
Biological	Focuses on tendencies and limits imposed by biological inheritance; can be easily combined with most other approaches
Behaviorist	Can force a more scientific analysis of the learning experiences that shape personality
Cognitive	Captures active nature of human thought; uses modern knowledge from cognitive psychology
Trait	Good individual assessment techniques
Humanistic	Appreciates the spiritual nature of a person; emphasizes struggles for self-fulfillment and dignity
Interactionist	Understands that we are different selves in different situations

In Chapter 6, behaviorist and learning aspects of personality are considered. Starting with the work of radical behaviorist B. F. Skinner, we examine the extent to which personality can be "found" in the external environment. Chapter 7 analyzes the cognitive aspects of personality, with a focus on people's consistencies in perceiving and interpreting the world around them. In Chapter 8, trait and skill aspects of personality are the focus. Earlier in this century, the Harvard psychologist Gordon Allport almost single-handedly developed intriguing trait approaches that have dominated this area ever since, although there has been a recent resurgence of scientific interest in trait approaches.

Humanistic and existential aspects of personality, which focus on freedom and self-fulfillment, are the subject of Chapter 9. Starting with the influential work of Carl Rogers, we examine what seems to make humans uniquely human. In Chapter 10, person–situation interactionist aspects, the most modern personality approach, are explained.

Are Personality Aspects Really Separable?

Is this the best way to divide the field of personality? Some researchers might quibble with this classification scheme because all brilliant personality theorists necessarily include more than one aspect of personality in their writings. For example, Freud had many biological notions in his theories, and he certainly appreciated the major role played by socialization forces. Similarly, B. F. Skinner, the ultimate behaviorist, well understood the tremendous influence of other people in our lives, despite his research focus on the conditioning of laboratory animals. Our goal in this book is not to place sophisticated theories into narrow pigeonholes, but rather to provide an in-depth examination of the different sorts of significant insights into the nature of personality that have been developed during the past century.

Which personality perspective is right? Are people governed by traits or hormones or unconscious motives or nobility of spirit? This is a different question from "Which personality *theory* is right?" or "Which *hypothesis* is true?" Theories and hypotheses are testable and, by their nature, can be proven wrong. That is, they are falsifiable. We will examine many such theories and hypotheses later in this book and show which aspects are wrong or doubtful. But the question here is "Which personality *perspective* is correct?" This question is easy to answer: All eight are right in that they all provide some important psychological insight into what it means to be a person. In other words, we can benefit from learning about the strengths (and the weaknesses) of all eight perspectives.

This answer is not an evasion or dodge. Human nature is tremendously complex and needs to be examined from multiple perspectives. In fact, it is a meek strategy to rely too much on one approach and ignore the valuable insights provided by other perspectives and scientific research. It is important to remember that each of these perspectives adds richness to our understanding of personality. On the other hand, it is inappropriate to perpetuate notions that are not supported by evidence.

A Brief History of Personality Psychology

A number of scientific and philosophical forces that converged early in the twentieth century made possible the birth of personality psychology. Sigmund Freud, very conscious of these new beginnings, deliberately published one of his major books, *The Interpretation of Dreams*, in the year 1900 (rather than in 1899). By the 1930s, modern personality theory was taking shape. So, personality psychology is little more than a half-century old. But its roots go back through human history. The time line in Figure 1.2 on page 10 shows the approximate sequence of important milestones in the history of personality psychology, and their relationship in time to important world events.

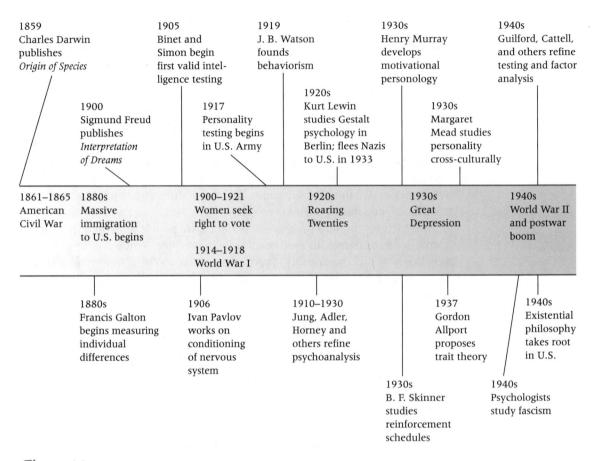

1859
Charles Darwin
publishes
Origin of Species

1905
Binet and
Simon begin
first valid intel-
ligence testing

1919
J. B. Watson
founds
behaviorism

1930s
Henry Murray
develops
motivational
personology

1940s
Guilford, Cattell,
and others refine
testing and factor
analysis

1900
Sigmund Freud
publishes
*Interpretation
of Dreams*

1917
Personality
testing begins
in U.S. Army

1920s
Kurt Lewin
studies Gestalt
psychology in
Berlin; flees Nazis
to U.S. in 1933

1930s
Margaret
Mead studies
personality
cross-culturally

1861–1865
American
Civil War

1880s
Massive
immigration
to U.S. begins

1900–1921
Women seek
right to vote

1914–1918
World War I

1920s
Roaring
Twenties

1930s
Great
Depression

1940s
World War II
and postwar
boom

1880s
Francis Galton
begins measuring
individual
differences

1906
Ivan Pavlov
works on
conditioning
of nervous
system

1910–1930
Jung, Adler,
Horney and
others refine
psychoanalysis

1937
Gordon
Allport
proposes
trait theory

1940s
Existential
philosophy
takes root
in U.S.

1930s
B. F. Skinner
studies
reinforcement
schedules

1940s
Psychologists
study fascism

Figure 1.2

Time Line of the History of Personality Psychology. The major developments in
the field of personality psychology can be seen here in historical relation to one
another and in relation to their broader societal and cultural contexts.

Theater and Self-Presentation

Some of the roots of personality psychology can be traced to the theater.
Theophrastus, a pupil of Aristotle, is one of the earliest known creators of
character sketches—brief descriptions of a type of person that can be recognized across time and place—such as someone who is cheap or tidy or lazy or
boorish (Allport, 1961). Ancient Greek and Roman actors wore masks to show
that they were playing characters, different from themselves. This indicated a
fascination with the true (unmasked) nature of the individual. By Shakespeare's time, the masks were mostly gone, but there was a tremendous de-

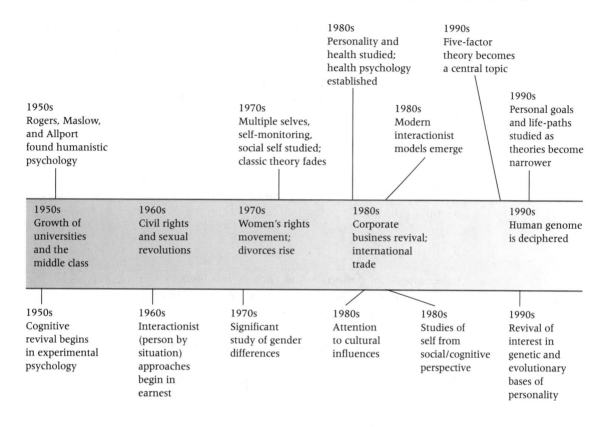

1980s
Personality and
health studied;
health psychology
established

1990s
Five-factor
theory becomes
a central topic

1990s
Personal goals
and life-paths
studied as
theories become
narrower

1950s
Rogers, Maslow,
and Allport
found humanistic
psychology

1970s
Multiple selves,
self-monitoring,
social self studied;
classic theory fades

1980s
Modern
interactionist
models emerge

1950s
Growth of
universities
and the
middle class

1960s
Civil rights
and sexual
revolutions

1970s
Women's rights
movement;
divorces rise

1980s
Corporate
business revival;
international
trade

1990s
Human genome
is deciphered

1950s
Cognitive
revival begins
in experimental
psychology

1960s
Interactionist
(person by
situation)
approaches
begin in
earnest

1970s
Significant
study of gender
differences

1980s
Attention
to cultural
influences

1980s
Studies of
self from
social/cognitive
perspective

1990s
Revival of
interest in
genetic and
evolutionary
bases of
personality

light with the roles people played. In *As You Like It,* Shakespeare observed that "All the world's a stage, and all the men and women merely players." By this time it was clear that the role of jealous king or spurned lover could be occupied (played) in similar ways by different people. Everyone recognizes and understands the basic characters.

Is there really something fixed beneath the surface of the parts people play in their lives? In the twentieth century, theater took another imaginative step as playwrights such as Pirandello toyed with the idea that characters could step outside the action of their plays. For example, a player could move totally off the stage (or out of the movie set) and comment on the drama. Suddenly, the character seems to have a reality of its own. At the same time, social philosophers began considering the idea of a relative self—that is, there is no underlying self and outward-facing mask, but rather the "true" self is comprised merely of masks (Hare & Blumberg, 1988; G. Mead, 1968). In other words, these twentieth-century musings challenged the idea that there is any core self or personality to be discovered.

All these theatrical notions have subsequently been addressed in personality psychology, especially in understanding the importance of the social situation. They have also influenced existential and humanistic psychologists who have speculated about what it means to be a human being. But where theater gives momentary insight, personality psychology seeks lasting and universal scientific principles.

Religion

Other aspects of personality psychology can be traced to religious ideas. The Western Judeo-Christian tradition asserts that humankind was created in God's image and from the beginning has faced temptation and moral struggle. People fulfill a divine purpose and struggle for good and against evil. In this tradition, people's nature is primarily spiritual—a spirit inhabits the body while it is on earth. These conceptions discourage and even preclude a scientific analysis of personality because they regard people not as part of nature but rather as part of the divine order.

At the same time, Eastern philosophies and religions emphasize self-awareness and spiritual self-fulfillment, through such techniques as meditation. There is also much attention directed at altered states of consciousness (such as trances). Here too, there is little room for objectivity. These Eastern concerns with consciousness, self-fulfillment, and the human spirit came to play an important role in certain aspects of modern personality theory. This influence is most clearly seen in the work of humanistic and existential psychologists such as Abraham Maslow, but Eastern thought has also influenced such seminal personality psychologists as C. G. Jung. Most university research in personality today is, however, much more in the arena of modern, positivistic science and less concerned with spiritual matters.

Religious influences on Western conceptions of human nature began eroding during the Renaissance, especially during the seventeenth century. In the writings of Descartes, Spinoza, and Leibnitz and their followers in the 1600s, we see debates about the mind and the body, emotion and motivation, and perception and consciousness. The nature of the human spirit was not taken for granted but was analyzed and observed. This concern continued to develop for the next two centuries. In modern personality theory, these influences show up as concerns with the integration and unity of the individual personality. They are also seen in attempts to integrate biological and psychological knowledge—the mind and the body.

Evolutionary Biology

The most direct influences on modern personality psychology can be traced to developments in the biological sciences during the nineteenth century. Why are some animals such as tigers aggressive loners, whereas others such as chimps are social and cooperative? What characteristics do humans share with other animals? The greatest development in biological thinking in the nineteenth century was the theory of evolution. Charles Darwin, following on the ideas of others, argued that individual characteristics that evolved were those that enabled the organism to pass on genes to offspring. Individuals who were not well-adapted to the demands of their environment would not survive to reproduce. So, for example, a strong sex drive had adaptive value—those without it would be less likely to reproduce. Similarly, a certain amount of aggressiveness and a certain type of social cooperativeness might prove adaptive. Animals that could dominate others for food and mates, and animals that could cooperate with others to secure their safety, would survive and pass on their genes. This focus on function—that is, the utility of behavior—has remained an important aspect of our thinking about personality.

The key contribution of Darwinian evolutionary theory to personality psychology, however, was the way in which it freed thinking from assumptions of divine control. If we think that a divine force is in total control of human activity, then there is little reason to look for other influences on the individual. Once it became clear that people are subject to the laws of nature, then scientists began to study human behavior systematically. For better and for worse, evolutionary notions have had a major influence on the twentieth-century study of personality.

One little-mentioned corollary of the Darwinian doctrine is that other animals, especially other primates, should have at least some elements of personality. This may come as no surprise to pet owners, who often describe the personalities of their dogs, cats, and horses. But personality psychologists have conducted very little research on animal personality. Obviously, we

Even though pets can't take personality tests, their owners can describe their "personalities"—the ways in which they behave as individuals rather than as simply dogs or cats.

cannot ask animals to introspect about their inner minds, but it may be the case that research on animal personality will help us think in new ways about assessing and conceptualizing human personality. This is a topic for future generations of psychologists.

Testing

Attention! The purpose of this examination is to see how well you can remember, think, and carry out what you are told to do. We are not looking for crazy people. The aim is to help find out what you are best fitted to do in the Army.

So began the instructions for a test that was administered to over one million young American men, as the United States entered the First World War in 1917 (Yerkes, 1921). Americans had a job to do and thought they could do it better if they measured people just as they measured machinery. This practical, "can-do" approach of American psychology brought a distinctive perspective to the study of individual differences.

Much psychological research on personality has been supported by wartime strategies for combat or peacetime efforts for the national defense. Even today the U.S. armed forces employ hundreds of psychologists to conduct research and testing on uniformed personnel. The general aim continues to be placing soldiers and sailors into suitable slots in a well-oiled military "machine."

In 1917, the Army was mostly concerned with weeding out so-called imbeciles, but they also looked for tendencies of applicants to collapse under stress. For example, one inventory asked recruits, "Do you feel like jumping off when you are on high places?" (Woodworth, 1919). It is this type of questionnaire that contributed to the development of modern personality tests.

The army tests were developed under the influence of psychologists Lewis Terman of Stanford and Robert Yerkes of Harvard, who were primarily interested in intelligence testing. This was the first mass use of mental tests. The psychologists hailed the great success of their testing. They imagined many future uses for the tests, such as the mass screening of school students to find those who would become the future elite of society. Unfortunately, this testing also set the stage for the use of biased tests to discriminate unfairly against those groups least favored by the test-givers. For example, the "smartest" immigrants were found to be those from northern Europe (whose culture was most in tune with the American tests). And those with darker skin, who were already the victims of rampant educational and social discrimination, were certified as inferior by the tests.

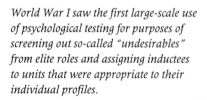

World War I saw the first large-scale use of psychological testing for purposes of screening out so-called "undesirables" from elite roles and assigning inductees to units that were appropriate to their individual profiles.

Intelligence and creative abilities are often separated from personality in the belief that they are more like "skills" such as physical strength than they are like "traits" such as extroversion. However, to the extent that intellectual abilities are central to an individual's psychological make-up, they should be considered part of personality. On practical grounds, the vast information available on intelligence cannot be fully integrated into our analysis of personality. We do, however, include certain relevant pieces in this book.

Knowledge of testing and measurement, applied to personality by such psychometricians as J. P. Guilford (Guilford, 1940), soon combined with insights emerging from clinical (therapeutic) work and with approaches evolving in experimental psychology to form the basis of modern personality theory and research.

Modern Theory

Modern personality theory began to take formal shape in the 1930s. It was heavily influenced by the work of three men—Gordon Allport, Kurt Lewin, and Henry Murray. Allport, who was broadly trained in philosophy and the classics, devoted his attention to the uniqueness and dignity of the individual. Allport defined personality as "the dynamic organization within the individual of those psychophysical systems that determine his unique adjustment to his environment" (1937, p. 48). Building on the work of psychologist–philosopher William James, he rejected the idea of trying to break down personality into basic components (such as sensation, or innate drives) and instead looked for the underlying organization of each person's uniqueness.

Kurt Lewin came out of the Gestalt tradition in Europe. The Gestalt psychologists emphasized the integrative and active nature of perception and thought, suggesting that the whole may be greater than the sum of its parts. For example, the Gestalt pioneer Wolfgang Kohler gives the example of trying to memorize a list of pairs of nouns, such as lake–sugar, boot–plate, and girl–kangaroo. Kohler notes that these words are not normally associated with each other, but the pairings may be easily learned. The Gestalt explanation is as follows: "When I read those words I can imagine, as a series of strange pictures, how a lump of sugar dissolves in a lake, how a boot rests on a plate, how a girl feeds a kangaroo. If this happens during the reading of the series, I experience in imagination a number of well-organized, though quite unusual, wholes" (Kohler, 1947, p. 265). This emphasis on the whole picture that a person imagines when encountering a situation had a tremendous influence on Lewin, and subsequently on personality and social psychology.

Lewin's approach, like Allport's, was dynamic, as he looked for systems that underlie observable behavior. Lewin drew attention to "the momentary condition of the individual and the structure of the psychological situation" (1935, p. 41). In other words, Lewin emphasized that the forces affecting a person change from time to time and from situation to situation. Modern personality theories have adopted these emphases on understanding the current state of a person in a particular situation.

The third main sculptor of modern personality theory was Henry Murray. Murray spent most of his career at the Harvard Psychological Clinic, where he could attempt to integrate clinical issues (problems of real patients) with theory and assessment issues. Importantly, Murray believed in a comprehensive orientation, including longitudinal research—studying the same people over time. He took a broad approach to personality, defining it as the "branch of psychology which principally concerns itself with the study of human lives and the factors which influence their course, [and] which investigates individual differences" (1938, p. 4).

His emphasis on studying the richness of the life of each person led Murray to prefer the term "personology" to the term "personality"; modern psychologists working in the Murray tradition often call themselves "personologists." Murray, too, emphasized the integrated, dynamic nature of the individual as a complex organism responding to a specific environment. Murray also stressed the importance of needs and motivations, an emphasis that has proved quite influential.

In short, Allport, Lewin, Murray, and their associates set the stage for modern personality theory by emphasizing that the whole human being should be the focus of study, not parts of the being and not collections of organisms. Each person at each moment in each situation is a unique collection of related psychological forces that together determine the individual's responses. In other words, a successful approach cannot ignore the integrity of the individual or the various forces—conscious and unconscious, biological and social—operating at a given moment. This is the modern view of personality.

Lurking in opposition to these developing ideas were the new learning theories of Clark Hull and his associates at Yale, and the behaviorist theories of B. F. Skinner and his associates at Harvard. This opposition eventually led to a stimulating tension, which helped refine modern notions of human nature.

Also influential in the 1930s—though probably not as influential on personality psychology as it should have been—was the startling work of anthropologist Margaret Mead. In her book *Sex and Temperament in Three Primitive Societies,* Mead showed that masculinity was not necessarily associated with aggressiveness and femininity was not necessarily associated with cooperativeness. Rather, personality was heavily influenced by culture. According to Mead,

> *We have now considered in detail the approved personalities of each sex among . . . primitive peoples. We found the Arapesh—both men and women—displaying a personality that, out of our historically limited preoccupations, we would call maternal in its parental aspects, and feminine in its sexual aspects. We found men, as well as women, trained to be cooperative, unaggressive, responsive to the needs and demands of others. We found no idea that sex was a powerful driving force for men or for women. In marked contrast to these attitudes, we found among the Mundugumor that both men and women developed as ruthless, aggressive, positively sexed individuals, with maternal cherishing aspects of personality at a minimum. (1935, p. 190)*

Mead's work unequivocally demonstrated that personality should not be studied in only one culture or one context. She also shattered many myths about the nature of man as compared to the nature of woman, as well as ideas of innate and unchangeable sexual aggressiveness. Unfortunately, Mead's lesson was generally ignored by personality researchers. American psychology has often overlooked the importance of culture in shaping people's lives (Betancourt & Lopez, 1993). In this book we have tried to be especially sensitive to cultural issues; it is good science to be so.

Some Basic Issues: The Unconscious, the Self, Uniqueness, Gender, Situations, Culture

Certain issues in the study of personality psychology appear and reappear at different times and in different theories; they are fundamental to understanding personality. Several are introduced in the sections that follow.

What Is the Importance of the Unconscious?

You may have noticed that some male friends or relatives are attracted to and marry women who are similar to their own mothers. Of course, most men do not consciously set out to find wives who are like their mothers. At times, though, we seem to be influenced by internal forces of which we are unaware or we may feel inner urges or feelings that we do not understand. On the other hand, it is generally believed that people are responsible for their own actions. Except for the insane, we expect that people know what they are doing and why they are doing it; they act consciously. So we face the dilemma of conscious versus unconscious determinants of behavior. Personality psychology struggles to understand how and to what extent unconscious forces play a role in human behavior.

What Is the Self?

Carl Jung said that the "meeting of two personalities is like the contact of two chemical substances; if there is any reaction, both are transformed" (1933, p. 57). Should we think of the self as a complex chemical substance or (as Jung also sometimes said) as a spirit? How important are social influences on the self? Is the self really more like Carl Rogers's notion of a set of perceptions about the characteristics of "me," which attempts to fulfill its human potential? Is the sense of self merely an inconsequential epiphenomenon or secondary perception arising from other forces (such as biological drives) that really matter? What is the core of who we are? All these questions are legitimate issues in personality psychology.

Does Each Individual Require a Unique Approach?

To what extent can we apply general methods to all people? Or is it possible, even necesssary, to use a unique approach to the special qualities of each individual? Science, by its nature, searches for universal laws. It is therefore often **nomothetic,** which means that it seeks to formulate laws (from the Greek *nomos,* which means "law," and *thetic,* to "lay down"). However, Gordon Allport strongly argued that a key aspect of the study of personality must focus on the individual and thus be **idiographic**—involved with the study of individual cases (from *idio,* Greek for "private, personal, distinct"). Certainly it makes sense to use intensive biographical analysis to understand a person, but each person's biography is different. So how can we generalize? This dilemma remains a significant challenge. Many years ago, Allport complained that most introductory psychology textbooks threw in (half-heartedly) a chapter on personality, usually at the tail end, that ignored or failed to capture the vital, dynamic individuality of each human being. Researchers were so concerned with being scientific that they ignored the most interesting (but complex) aspects of personality. This problem is still with us today.

Are There Differences between Men and Women?

What are the differences between men and women, and where do they come from? The most basic sex differences are of course the anatomical ones, and they are clearly determined by our genes, before we are born. But what are we to make of the various psychological differences between men and women that appear in our society? Why do men often seem more aggressive, dominant, antisocial, and better in mathematical and spatial tasks? Why are women generally more socially connected, more prone to depression, and more nurturant? Who has the greater sex drive and who controls sexual encounters and why? Such fascinating issues are basic to the study of personality and have been addressed by almost all personality theorists. Although we offer no simple answers to these questions, we do offer a sophisticated and reasoned consideration of the relevant issues.

The Person versus the Situation

Since the very beginnings of modern personality theory earlier in this century, it has been well recognized that there are inconsistencies in every individual's behavior (Woodworth, 1934). An individual who acts extroverted one day may act introverted the next day in a different situation. Furthermore, it has been established since the 1920s that some individuals are much more self-consistent than others (Hartshorne & May, 1928). For example, some children almost always behave honestly but others vary quite a bit in their responses.

If extroverted people can act like introverts, or if honest people can behave dishonestly, what sense does it make to talk about personality? And how do we take into account the fact that everyone is influenced, at least in part, by the situation? These matters have been addressed in a number of ways that are considered throughout this book.

To What Extent Is Personality Culturally Determined?

The poet Walt Whitman wrote, "It is native personality, and that alone, that endows a man to stand before presidents or generals, or in any distinguished collection, with *aplomb*—and *not* culture, or any knowledge or intellect whatever" (1871, *Democratic Vistas*). This statement summarizes the position that personality is innate—that we are born with a certain temperament and character, and that is the way we will always be.

Of course, there is also good reason to believe that children are affected by the environments and cultures in which they grow up. As we will see, although the nature–nurture relationship is tremendously complex, many answers are now available. We do not have to equivocate and assert that personality is partly innate and partly culturally determined. Instead, we will ascertain which parts of personality are relatively fixed and which are more changeable.

Is Personality a Useful Concept?

Is personality a useful scientific concept for understanding human behavior, or is it merely an illusion, a misunderstanding of causality? Most of us have probably received cards from close friends with flattering messages such as this:

> *It's not your name or background*
> *Or great things that you've done.*
> *It's not your help that makes you*
> *The best friend that I've found.*
> *It's not your smarts I count on,*
> *Though you're nice and honest, too.*
> *It's what you are that makes you*
> *A very special friend.*

Such verses assume that there is some inner essence that makes us who we are. Unfortunately, such notions of "personhood" are vague and misleading. For example, lovers are often shocked to discover that their partner, whose essence they knew so well, actually had a criminal side, or an adulterous side, or an aggressive side. Further, efforts to capture this inner core generally prove scientifically fruitless. People are complex creatures, and it is important to avoid simplistic illusions or wishful thinking about a personality.

Does this mean that the scientific study of personality should be abandoned? Absolutely not. As we will show, the multiple scientific techniques used to study and understand personality are among the most sophisticated to be found in any science.

In addition to these basic issues of personality psychology, there are many topical questions of interest in modern personality research. Most current researchers are not constructing new grand theories of personality, but rather are working to answer applied questions such as the role played by personality in physical health and sickness, and in marriage and divorce. Is there a disease-prone and a self-healing personality? Do certain personalities make good lovers or good marriage partners? The answers to such questions, addressed later in this book, turn out to be quite complex.

Personality in Context

During the 1930s and 1940s, American psychologists were investigating the Authoritarian personality, an excessively masculine, cold, and domineering personality that tended to become a fascist and to persecute members of the out-group. At the same time, fascist (Nazi) German psychologists were investigating the Anti-Type—people who were likely to be weak, liberal, artsy, and effeminate (Brown, 1965). What Americans called rigidity, the Germans called stability. What the Germans called eccentricity, Americans called individuality. What the Germans called perversion, the Americans called esthetic sensitivity. Without doubt, the Nazis were fantastically destructive murderers while the Americans of that era were striving to promote freedom and security. Still, it is interesting to see the ways in which observations about personality could be strongly influenced by the cultural contexts in which they occurred.

Today, most personality research has a distinct flavor of Western culture in general and mainstream American culture in particular. The unique viewpoints of Asian, Latin, African, and Native American cultures are too often overlooked. For example, in American society, individuals who want to "do things their own way" and who challenge the conventional expectations of their companies or the government usually would be positively viewed as assertive and independent (and possibly even heroic). But in Japanese society the same behavior would be viewed as rude, uncooperative, selfish, and antisocial. In other words, our explanations of human behavior are dependent on our cultures. Some amount of bias is inevitable.

In this book, we try to pay attention to the cultural context of personality theory and research, often by focusing on the theorists' own lives as an illustration. It is important not to allow critiques of ideas to become ad hominem arguments; that is, we must evaluate the quality of theory and research on its own terms, rather than in terms of the theorist who proposed it. Just because many of Sigmund Freud's patients were middle-class, Jewish, European women at the turn of the past century does not mean that his insights are not applicable to others. Nevertheless, explanations are more likely to be valid if they take into account the contexts in which the theories arise.

Finally, let us do a little demonstration. Suppose we tell you that people with the following characteristics are likely to develop significant personality problems in later life:

These people often have feelings of loneliness and sometimes question their self-worth. They wish they were more popular. They regularly have sexual thoughts and sexual dreams about certain special others. They wish that they had better bodies. They are sometimes unsure about who they are and why they are alive.

Figure 1.3

The Zodiac Signs, and "Prophetic" Message, of a Horoscope. Are people who believe in astrology more likely to accept generalized personality descriptions of themselves than are skeptics? One study confirmed that astrology believers are indeed especially susceptible to the Barnum effect, but almost everyone finds personal meaning in vague generalities to some degree (Glick, Gottesman, & Jolton, 1989).

With your recent maturation, the time is right for you to develop the special relationship that you have been seeking.

In fact, this is phony information. But such a description would characterize many college students. That is, many college students would feel that this description applies to them as individuals (and that therefore they are prone to personality problems) even though the profile is ridiculously general, as in the example in Figure 1.3. This tendency to believe vague generalities about one's personality is sometimes termed the **Barnum effect** (first shown by Ulrich, Stachnik, & Stainton, 1963; Snyder et al., 1977). This demonstration illustrates the care that is required to ensure that personality theories and assessments are specific and have been scientifically validated. Personality is a fascinating field but it is one that is subject to abuse and distortion if the utmost care is not taken by those who evaluate theories.

Before we can delve deeply into personality, we need to have some idea of how personality can be studied and assessed. This is the subject of the next chapter.

Summary and Conclusion

Personality psychology asks the question, "What does it mean to be a person?" In other words, "How are we unique as individuals? What is the nature of the self?"

Personality psychology answers these questions in terms of systematic observations about how and why individuals behave as they do, with a focus on the thoughts, feelings, and behaviors of real people. Personality psychology can be defined as the scientific study of the psychological forces that make people uniquely themselves. To be comprehensive, we can say that personality has eight key aspects, which together help us understand the very complex nature of the individual. In this book, we examine each of these perspectives in detail, with an emphasis on drawing the best insights from each.

Personality psychologists attempt to use methods of scientific inference to test theories. Techniques range from the most formal mathematical assessment of traits and abilities to the careful, rich examination of a single individual's thoughts, feelings, and behaviors. Why does a certain eighteen-year-old high school senior seem consumed by intrusive thoughts and sexual fantasies? Is it hormones? repressed sexual drives? the influence of the surroundings? past experiences and conditioning? an existential crisis? combinations of these and other personal influences? A thorough understanding of personality involves a firm grasp of the meaning, validity, and implications of these various perspectives.

Personality theories arise from various sources. They come from careful observation and from deep introspection; from systematic measurement and from statistical analyses; from biological brain scans and from studies of mental illness; from anthropology and sociology and economics and philosophy. Theorists apply these sundry insights to a psychological understanding of the individual.

Some of the roots of personality psychology can be traced back to the theater. Other aspects derive from religion, and from Eastern and Western philosophical traditions. Darwinian evolutionary biology had a profound influence on personality psychology, an influence that is currently enjoying a resurgence. Breakthroughs in personality testing and intelligence testing helped shape both the theories and the methods of modern personality psychology, although the significant effects of culture on test scores were often ignored.

Modern personality theory began to take formal shape in the 1930s, thanks to the pioneering work of three men—Gordon Allport, Kurt Lewin, and Henry Murray. Allport defined personality as "the dynamic organization within the individual of those psychophysical systems that determine his unique adjustment to his environment." Lewin's approach was also dynamic, as he looked for systems that underlie observable behavior. Lewin drew attention to "the momentary condition of the individual and the structure of the psychological situation." Murray believed in a comprehensive orientation that included longitudinal research—studying the same people over time. He took a very broad approach to personality, defining it as the "branch of psychology which principally concerns itself with the study of human lives and the factors which influence their course, [and] which investigates individual differences." Contemporaneously, Margaret Mead demonstrated that personality was heavily influenced by culture, but her work was not fully appreciated at the time.

Certain basic issues in the study of personality appear and reappear at different times and in different theories. These include

What is the importance of the unconscious?

What is the self?

To what extent can our approaches be nomothetic (concerned with universal laws) as opposed to idiographic (studying individual cases)?

What are the differences between men and women, and where do they come from?

Which affects behavior more—the person or the situation?

To what extent is personality culturally determined?

Is personality a useful scientific concept or merely a convenient illusion?

In sum, personality psychology addresses some of the most interesting yet complex questions involved in understanding what it means to be a human being.

Key Theorists

Gordon Allport   Henry Murray
Kurt Lewin

Key Concepts

personality psychology   Darwinian evolutionary theory
deductive versus inductive approach   nomothetic science versus idiographic
   to personality   science
eight perspectives on personality   Barnum effect

Suggested Readings

Allport, G. W. (1968). *The person in psychology: Selected essays.* Boston: Beacon Press.

Benjamin, L. T., Jr. (Ed.). (1988). *A history of psychology: Original sources and contemporary research.* New York: McGraw-Hill.

Craik, K., Hogan, R., & Wolfe, R. N. (Eds.). (1993). *Fifty years of personality psychology.* New York: Plenum Press.

Gadlin, H., & Ingle, G. (1975). Through the one-way mirror: The limits of experimental self-reflection. *American Psychologist, 30,* 1003–1009.

Loevinger, J. (1987). *Paradigms of personality.* New York: W. H. Freeman & Company.

Murphy, G. (1949). *Historical introduction to modern psychology.* (Revised ed.). New York: Harcourt, Brace.

Sahakian, W. S. (Ed.). (1968). *History of psychology: A sourcebook in systematic psychology.* Itasca, IL: F. E. Peacock Publishers.

Chapter 2

How Is Personality Studied and Assessed?

When we took our two young sons to Disneyland, they came across a 7-foot-tall pirate who looked very much like the evil Captain Hook. The pirate was mingling with the crowd, shaking hands (and hook) with passersby. Although a great admirer of pirates, our older son recognized Hook, backed away from him, and stood behind his mother. Our younger son, in dramatic contrast, marched right up to the pirate, smiled, and shook hands.

We had just stumbled on a new sort of personality test—a standardized stimulus that provokes reactions and assesses revealing individual differences. We could call it the Pirate Test for Children. We could bring other children up to the pirate and see how they respond. As personality tests go, this test is not a bad start, but it is not complete.

The Pirate Test is not very objective in yielding a test score. In an arithmetic test or a high-jump test, the results are objective scores: a percentage of correct answers or a jump height in inches. These are objective measures of ability. Some personality tests are similarly objective; they may ask the test-taker to find an embedded figure in a complex drawing or to push a button as soon as a familiar tone is heard. Clear measures emerge from such tests; in these cases, it is the percentage of embedded figures uncovered and the reaction time (to the familiar tone) in seconds. But the Pirate Test depends on observers to interpret how the child is reacting. Then again, our Pirate Test allows for an experienced observer of children to form detailed, rich impressions—that is, it allows for subjective assessment.

*S*ubjective assessment—measurement that relies on interpretation—has complementary strengths and weaknesses. The problems revolve around the fact that different observers may make different judgments, and such judgments are fallible. This challenge is not unique to psychology. In many arenas of human endeavor, the subjective judgment of an expert plays an important role. For example, consider judgments of art. Poor Vincent van Gogh and many other now-famous impressionist painters had

Observers may agree among themselves about the quality of a work of art (that is, be reliable in their judgment) but have questionable validity. Many paintings by Vincent van Gogh were considered virtually worthless in his day but now are highly valued, bringing millions of dollars when sold at auction. Observers' judgments of personality similarly may have questionable validity on certain dimensions.

trouble selling paintings a century ago. A panel of observers assembled from the mainstream existing culture or from the street would have rejected many impressionist works as not "real art." A panel of observers may disagree in their opinions; and even if they agree, their judgment may be questionable.

On the other hand, a group of experts can often see through the complexities of a rich phenomenon and gain wonderful insights. The same is true for personality psychology. Insightful clinicians, observing a child interact with Captain Hook, might notice a reaction pattern that points to a significant maladjustment or suggests a childhood trauma or perhaps indicates certain tremendous strength of adaptive personality. Many commonly used personality tests thus incorporate a subjective element. In personality assessment, we must walk the line between being so objective that our information is sterile and being so subjective that our observation is idiosyncratic and our inference is unscientific. Fortunately, there are many guidelines and techniques that promote meaningful and scientific assessment of personality. This chapter explains the valid and invalid means of measuring personality.

Measuring Personality: The Case of Personal Charisma

When asked to name leaders high in charisma, people usually name such figures as John F. Kennedy, Martin Luther King, Jr., Ronald Reagan, Mahatma Gandhi, Franklin Roosevelt, Winston Churchill, and Malcolm X. These leaders were able to attract and inspire large numbers of followers. But we meet people every day who show a kind of personal charisma—people who are attractive, influential, expressive, and who are often the center of attention. In fact, in a seminar class or other small group, there is usually considerable agreement among the members as to which one of them is the most charismatic.

How can we assess whether someone is especially expressive and likely to be an influential emotional leader in a group? How can we identify such people so that we can go on to study in more detail the notion of charisma, in terms of both the charismatic persons themselves and their

Many people attribute the success and fame of charismatic public figures such as the late President John F. Kennedy to their charm and personal appeal rather than to their policies.

social influence processes? Could we construct a simple charisma test? One simple measure of personal charisma is called the Affective Communication Test, or ACT (Friedman et al., 1980). The ACT is shown in Table 2.1. You can take this test now: rate the extent to which each statement is true of you, using a scale from –4 to +4, where –4 means "not at all true of me," and +4 means "very true of me." You will learn more about this simple test and how to score it later in this chapter.

Reliability

If you were to step on a bathroom scale (to measure your weight) every half-hour during the course of an afternoon, you would expect your weight to be about the same each time. The term **reliability** refers to the consistency of scores that are expected to be the same. A reliable scale is consistent. If the scale shows your weight changing from 150 pounds to 140 to 160 to 120 over the course of a single afternoon, you would throw out the scale as unreliable.

Of course, you might find slight differences in measured weight as the spring in the scale changes slightly due to changes in room humidity or repeated usage. Such random variations produce what is called the *error of measurement* or *error variance*—variations that are caused by irrelevant, chance fluctuations. The best scales are highly reliable; they give consistent measurement. In assessing charisma, we would expect that a person who scores as very charismatic on Monday would not score as uncharismatic on Tuesday. Reliability also implicitly contains the idea of precision. You would not be satisfied with a scale that tells you that you weigh "over 100 pounds."

Internal Consistency Reliability

The reliability of a personality test is usually determined in two ways. First, the degree of consistency is measured by seeing whether subparts or equivalent parts of a test yield the same results. For example, we might split a paper-and-pencil test in half and then figure the split-half reliability by finding the correlation between the two halves (when the test is given to a number of people). We would expect the halves of the test to be highly correlated; for example, the person who scored highest on the first half of the test should also score very high on the second half. This is termed **internal consistency reliability.** In the ACT measure of charisma, scores on the various items tend to be similar, though not identical.

Internal consistency is often measured by a statistic called Cronbach's coefficient alpha. We can think of alpha as the average of all the possible split-half correlation coefficients. Measurement becomes more consistent and stable as we take repeated relevant measures (Rosenthal & Rosnow, 1991). In statistical terms, this means that internal consistency is a function of the number of items and their degree of correlation. In constructing a personality test,

Table 2.1 The Affective Communication Test

Please Read These Instructions Carefully. Below you will find a series of statements indicating an attitude or behavior that might be true as it applies to you or might not be true of you. Your task is to read carefully each statement and circle the number between minus 4 (–4) and plus 4 (4) that best indicates your answer. The more negative your answer, the more you believe the statement is false as it applies to you. The more positive your answer, the more you believe the statement is true of you.

Example:

*I feel very happy when I see pretty flowers.   Not at all true of me   –4   –3   –2   –1   0   1   2   3   4   Very true of me

Circling 2 would indicate that you feel somewhat happy when you see flowers but not as much as if you had circled number 4. If you had circled –4, this would mean that the opposite is true—that you feel very unhappy when you see flowers.

There are no right or wrong answers. Please circle only one number on each scale. Read each statement carefully and indicate an answer for every one.

1. *When I hear good dance music, I can hardly keep still.   Not at all true of me   –4   –3   –2   –1   0   1   2   3   4   Very true of me

2. *My laugh is soft and subdued.   Not at all true of me   –4   –3   –2   –1   0   1   2   3   4   Very true of me

3. *I can easily express emotion over the telephone.   Not at all true of me   –4   –3   –2   –1   0   1   2   3   4   Very true of me

4. *I often touch friends during conversations.   Not at all true of me   –4   –3   –2   –1   0   1   2   3   4   Very true of me

5. *I dislike being watched by a large group of people.   Not at all true of me   –4   –3   –2   –1   0   1   2   3   4   Very true of me

6. *I usually have a neutral facial expression.   Not at all true of me   –4   –3   –2   –1   0   1   2   3   4   Very true of me

7. *People tell me that I would make a good actor or actress.   Not at all true of me   –4   –3   –2   –1   0   1   2   3   4   Very true of me

8. *I like to remain unnoticed in a crowd.   Not at all true of me   –4   –3   –2   –1   0   1   2   3   4   Very true of me

9. *I am shy among strangers.   Not at all true of me   –4   –3   –2   –1   0   1   2   3   4   Very true of me

10. *I am able to give a seductive glance if I want to.   Not at all true of me   –4   –3   –2   –1   0   1   2   3   4   Very true of me

11. *I am terrible at pantomime as in games like charades.   Not at all true of me   –4   –3   –2   –1   0   1   2   3   4   Very true of me

12. *At small parties I am the center of attention.   Not at all true of me   –4   –3   –2   –1   0   1   2   3   4   Very true of me

13. *I show that I like someone by hugging or touching that person.   Not at all true of me   –4   –3   –2   –1   0   1   2   3   4   Very true of me

we want to add relevant items until the total score becomes very stable. But we don't want to add so many items that the test becomes unwieldy or boring. In tests that are to be widely employed, the coefficient of internal consistency reliability generally should be about .80.

Sometimes, the consistency issue applies to our expert observers. In the case of our new Pirate Test, we would like our observers to agree in their judgments. Usually, about twelve observers are sufficient to achieve consistency.

Test–Retest Reliability

The second measure of reliability involves the instrument's degree of consistency on different occasions. That is, people who are expressive people or conscientious people on Monday should score similarly on Thursday. In developing the ACT, researchers measured the same people twice, two months apart. This notion of temporal stability is termed **test–retest reliability.** The test–retest reliability of the ACT is about .90. Over short periods of time, ACT scores remain about the same, although there is some error of measurement. When internal consistency reliability and test–retest reliability are high, we know we are measuring something real—we have a reliable personality test.

Of course, we want to be able to take into account that people may change over time. Our biological systems mature and age, we are shaped by experiences, we gain insights into ourselves and others, and the situations we face change over time. So it makes sense that personality might change as well. This is not a problem for measuring weight—we are all too aware that our weight fluctuates as we diet or overeat. But personality by definition is assumed to be fairly stable. All this leaves us with a significant theoretical and measurement challenge: How can we have a reliable (stable) assessment of personality if personality may change?

There are two sorts of sophisticated answers to this challenge. First, as Gordon Allport repeatedly emphasized, personality consists of **patterns** that dynamically direct activity. Although a person's particular activities and daily responses may change, the basic underlying patterns remain relatively stable. In fact, the temporal (time) dimension should be included in many studies of personality; that is, we should ascertain the individual's patterns of response over time (Larsen, 1989). Consistent patterns often emerge. For example, if a person cycles between being manic and being depressive, this is not a reliability problem if we consider the personality to be manic-depressive. If we did not examine patterns over time, however, we might conclude (erroneously) that our measurement is unreliable—first the person seemed manic and then depressive.

The second answer to the challenge of personality change is to allow that personality may change over the long term (or after a major trauma), and to expect personality stability only over shorter periods of perhaps several years. For example, it would be useful if we could reliably measure extroversion at age sixteen if identifying that trait helped us understand the person's behavior in college and young adulthood. If the person then became introverted after many years, that would not necessarily be a problem for the reliability of our concepts. In fact it might be an interesting phenomenon in its own right: why do some extroverts become more introverted? Studying and measuring personality always involves these sorts of trade-offs. Measuring conscious biological systems (people) is not like measuring physical quantities like height and weight. People grow and change, and even their basic patterns of responding may change.

Construct Validity

Suppose we went to a shopping mall and stood on a scale every hour all afternoon and kept getting the same, reliable result; the scale, one of those electronic devices with a computer voice, keeps announcing "11, 11, 11." That seems like a funny weight. It turns out that the scale is specially designed for shoe stores and it is really using pressure to measure the length of our feet (and intoning our shoe size, very reliably). Is the test measuring what it is supposed to be measuring? What is it measuring? This is the issue of validity.

The most important (and complex) aspect of validity is **construct validity.** Construct validity refers to the extent to which a test truly measures a theoretical construct. For example, is the ACT really measuring personal charisma, or is it perhaps measuring friendliness or nurturance?

Construct validity is ascertained by seeing if the assessments predict behaviors and reactions implied (theoretically) by the construct. Charismatic people should do more than score high on a paper-and-pencil measure. They should engage in certain charismatic activities, and they should show a certain pattern of responses on other measures. For example, they should be more extroverted than introverted. Construct validation is an ongoing process and involves showing that (1) the assessment is related to what it should theoretically be related to—this is called **convergent validation;** and (2) the assessment is not related to what it should not be related to—this is called **discriminant validation** (Campbell & Fiske, 1959). If the ACT is related to extroversion scales (as it should be), then that is evidence for convergent validity. If the ACT were related to intelligence (as it should not be), then that would be evidence that it is lacking in discriminant validity.

Ultimately, construct validation is a process closely tied to theory development. Only a theory can tell us what our personality construct should and should not relate to. Theory development in the social sciences is notoriously complex. Theories are a function of many assumptions and many hard-to-measure entities. Paradoxically, the theory informs the assessment and the assessment in turn informs the theory. We begin with certain ideas about personality, and as we measure personality, we refine our theories. This is why assessment is a recurring theme in any course on personality. For example, the ACT originally set out to measure nonverbal expressiveness, but as more was learned, it became clear that the ACT was a good, quick measure of personal charisma. For example, the number one Toyota salesperson in the United States scored very high on the ACT.

What if we created a brief new paper-and-pencil intelligence test that correlated well with other paper-and-pencil intelligence tests, but we never bothered to see whether scores were related to real-world problem-solving ability? To demonstrate our test's validity, we must also show that our test relates to the outcome criteria in the expected ways, using different assessment methods. This is sometimes termed **criterion-related validation**—whether our measure predicts to outcome criteria. For example, the ACT predicts who is likely to be a leader, just as it should. Because proper test validation involves assessing various traits and utilizing multiple assessment methods, the validation approach is termed a multitrait-multimethod perspective (Campbell & Fiske, 1959).

Content Validity

Content validity refers to whether a test is measuring the domain that it is supposed to be measuring. For example, a test might seem to be measuring creative ability but might in fact be measuring only artistic ability and ignoring musical ability, writing ability, and other aspects of creative ability. In gathering items for the ACT, we collected a wide range of characteristics that seemed relevant to having a highly expressive style. Unreliable items and ambiguous items were discarded, but the final scale includes items about nonverbal expressions (such as touching and laughing and facial expression), about acting, about social relations (such as behavior at parties), and about interpersonal expressive communication (such as giving a seductive glance). The ACT tries to capture many of the content dimensions of personal charisma.

Item Selection

Which items are best for a personality test? Obviously, items should be clear, relevant, and relatively simple, if at all possible. Beyond that, the choice depends a lot on assumptions about the nature of personality; assessment should not proceed in the absence of theory. The mathematical assumptions underlying the construction of reliable and valid personality tests can become quite complicated. There are psychologists who spend their entire careers working on the best ways to design and score assessments. For example, we have already noted that lengthening an assessment generally improves its reliability and validity (up to a certain point), but at added expense. Although efforts are made to select the best items and reject poor items, defining *best* in this context is not so simple.

One desirable quality of a test item is that it should discriminate among test takers; an item is useless if everyone answers it the same way. So generally speaking, each item in an assessment should divide the group of test-takers into roughly two groups. Also relevant, however, is that all the items should be intercorrelated (or related to one another); each item is measuring some aspect of the overall construct. This item intercorrelation in turn affects the discriminability issue—too high an intercorrelation merely provides redundant information. The total scores on the assessment should also have the proper distribution. That is, we need to be able assess a full range of people. The ACT, for example, should measure the few who are extremely charismatic, the few who are extremely uncharismatic, and the many who are in between.

One particular mathematical approach to choosing the best items has undergone a lot of development in recent years. It is termed **Item Response Theory** (IRT). Using item response mathematical techniques, we can examine the probability of a positive response on a particular item, given the person's overall position on the underlying trait being measured by the test (as estimated by the other answers). Some items might perform differently for men than for women (that is, be diagnostic only for one gender) and thus would be considered biased items. A description of the mathematics of IRT can be found in current technical books and articles on personality assessment (Flannery, Reise, & Widaman, 1995).

Response Sets

In scoring the ACT, items 2, 5, 6, 8, 9, and 11 (Table 2.1) are worded in the reverse direction. Agreeing with these items indicates a lack of expressiveness. Reverse wording is done to combat an **acquiescence response set.** Some people simply are more likely than others to agree with anything you ask them. Response sets are biases, unrelated to the personality characteristic being measured. So, in addressing the acquiescence response set, it is important to include items that are worded in the reverse direction. Before scoring the ACT, you must reverse the responses to these items.

An especially difficult challenge is posed by a **social desirability response set.** Many people want to present themselves in a favorable light or respond so as to please the experimenter or test administrator. Few people will agree truthfully with a statement like "I have thought about molesting young children." On the other hand, someone who wanted to pretend to be mentally ill might untruthfully agree with such a statement. One way to try to deal with social desirability response sets is to present items of equal desirability and ask the test-taker to choose between the two.

Similarly, sometimes people give purely random answers to a multiple-choice personality test. Perhaps they cannot read very well, or they are trying to subvert a study (being conducted by a researcher they dislike), or they are tired of filling out forms as part of a psychology class experiment. Some tests therefore have lie scales, which include items like "I have walked on the moon (yes/no)." Such items help pick out the liars (but may mess up when testing that rare astronaut).

Table 2.2   **Norms for the ACT Scale**

Overall mean	71.3
Overall median	71.2
Overall mode	68.0
Minimum score obtained	25.0
Maximum score obtained	116.0
Standard deviation	15.7
Mean for females	72.7
Mean for males	69.5

Note: Based on a tested population of 600 college students.

Even a cleverly designed personality assessment is subject to various sources of distortion or bias. You could easily distort your score by lying on the ACT. It is therefore valuable for the personality psychologist to employ multiple means of assessment, as we describe later in this chapter. On the other hand, it is important to note that assessments can have some bias and still be of value. Most established personality assessments have at least a fair to good degree of validity; they yield worthwhile information on most people in most circumstances.

The norms of the ACT are shown in Table 2.2. To compute your ACT score, first add 5 points to each item (to eliminate negative numbers). Then, reverse the scores for the six reversed items (items 2, 5, 6, 8, 9, and 11), so that a 1 becomes a 9, a 2 becomes an 8, and so on. Finally add all the item scores.

Ethnic Bias

When our children were reacting to Captain Hook at Disneyland, another child was having a very different reaction. Evidently from Asia, this puzzled little boy did not seem to know who or what Captain Hook was all about.

Our Pirate Personality Test might have been inappropriate for this little boy because it makes certain assumptions about the knowledge and background of the "test-taker." Like many tests, this test is culturally biased and should therefore be used only with a certain subset of the population.

Although all tests rely on a set of assumptions and thus might be called biased, the tests are not necessarily bad or worthless. Rather, they must be properly used and interpreted to be valid. A man who took multiple wives, beat his children, and regularly sacrificed animals in religious rites would be evaluated quite differently today than he would have been in earlier times (when such behaviors were common). Personality assessment has meaning only in context. We should become sensitive to the context of all our assessments.

As noted, one of the most common types of test bias is **ethnic bias.** All too often, tests fail to take into account the relevant culture or subculture of the person being tested; theories and measures developed in one culture are improperly applied to another culture. For example, well-socialized Asian Americans are often raised to behave with cooperation, humility, and modesty, whereas equally well-socialized Italian American children are often expected to be assertive, outgoing, and expressive. Of course, it is true that both subcultures usually produce well-adjusted, successful adults. It would be an assessment mistake to label the average Asian American child as "excessively shy," or to label the average Italian American child as "especially aggressive." On the other hand, it might prove helpful to compare an Asian American child who seems painfully shy with other Asian Americans; and it might prove similarly informative to compare an Italian American child who is experiencing difficulties with friends with other children raised in the same subculture.

Sometimes, bias causes a cultural strength to be perceived as a weakness. For example, Hispanic American children have sometimes been viewed as lacking in achievement motivation (viewed as a deficit), when in fact they have been raised to be more cooperative with their peers (which is often a strength).

It can be difficult to notice ethnic prejudice in our own theories and assessments, so let us consider an example from the 1800s. For much of the nineteenth century, criminal personality was seen as an innate characteristic, fixed at birth (Gould, 1981). Crime was considered to be the result not of an abusive childhood, peer pressure, lack of opportunity, lack of education, or social stress; rather it was the result of having a criminal nature. Not surprisingly, people who were not part of the dominant mainstream culture were especially likely to be so labeled. Such blind prejudices have a long and sordid history in American culture, in which African Americans have often been labeled as having an innate criminal nature. Ironically, during the decades of American slavery, the slaves were seen by their masters as obviously having a docile, slave-like personality (except when they tried to escape; then they were seen as innately criminal).

It is difficult to emphasize how subtle and yet how ingrained in our society are such biases. Personality psychology too often studies samples of convenience—one's patients, one's students, one's neighbors, one's children—and too rarely makes a systematic attempt to ascertain whether conclusions apply to other peoples, in other places, in other times.

Gender Bias

Let us say we are developing a new test of extroversion, and preliminary results with our scale show that women score higher than men. What do we do? Do we throw out those items on which women score higher, thus "equalizing" the scores? We might do this if we had a strong theoretical reason to assume that men and women are equally extroverted. Usually, however, we have no such theoretical reason; we merely have prejudices. We adjust the test scores to fit our prejudices. A second common type of test bias is gender bias.

Consider a problem often diagnosed in women: a self-defeating personality (Tavris, 1992). Many popular theories and associated assessments attempt to document and explain why many American women are unhappy, frustrated, and over-trusting, and are often stuck in miserable marriages and dead-end jobs. Tests can demonstrate that these women are masochistic, codependent, love too much, want too much, are addicted to men, or are simply basically depressive. Less frequently is the focus turned to the environment—toward abusive husbands, job discrimination, or lack of equal educational opportunity.

Consider also gender-related expectations for a healthy personality. If a woman scores as highly nurturant toward children, highly cooperative toward others, horrified by violence, fearful of mice, very concerned with her looks, and enchanted by crocheting, baking, and decorating, this woman will usually be scored as mentally healthy. But what if a man showed the exact same pattern? We examine these troubling issues of gender bias as they arise throughout this book.

Even well-designed personality tests are a tool, and like other tools they may be properly used or blatantly misused. For example, although tests may be dangerous when they carelessly assert dramatic personality differences among ethnic groups, they may be helpful in examining personality differences *within* ethnic groups (say, among Asian Americans). Furthermore, testing may uncover interesting group differences that should be followed up by other research techniques. Thus we should not ban tests because they might be biased, just as we should not ban tools because they may be misused. Rather, we should learn the limits of our assessments. These matters are considered further in the section on the ethics of personality testing, later in this chapter.

One of the great triumphs of personality testing of the past century has been the development of many different types of personality tests. When properly used, all of these tests have something to contribute to our understanding of the complexity of what it means to be human. In the remainder of this chapter, we describe the various types of personality tests, in a format that allows you actually to begin to assess personality.

Varieties of Personality Measures

There are both theoretical reasons and methodological reasons for having different types of personality tests. On theoretical grounds, it is apparent that many sorts of tests are more or less appropriate for measuring the aspect of personality under consideration. For example, it does not make sense to ask people to report about their unconscious motivations; by definition, such motivations cannot be consciously grasped and reported.

On methodological grounds, it is important to have various ways of measuring personality because each suffers from inherent biases. For example, interviews can probe more deeply and reactively into a person's inner thoughts and feelings than can a standardized questionnaire. On the other hand, observations of behavior or the analysis of a person's expressive style are often best at capturing what a person actually does. The weaknesses in one assessment technique can be compensated for by other techniques, thus helping us achieve a more complete understanding of personality. Table 2.3 lists the major types of personality measures, along with examples of each type.

Table 2.3 **Types of Personality Measures**

Type of Test	Examples
Self-report tests	Minnesota Multiphasic Personality Inventory (MMPI); Affective Communication Test (ACT); Millon Clinical Multiaxial Inventory; NEO-PI; Personality Research Form (PRF); Myers-Briggs Type Indicator (MBTI)
Q-sort tests	Self-concept; self-esteem; family; therapeutic; generativity
Ratings and judgments by others	Ratings by parents, teachers, friends, spouse; judgments by psychologists
Biological measures	Reaction time; skin conductance; electroencephalogram (EEG); positron emission tomography (PET) scan, magnetic resonance imagery (MRI), functional MRI (fMRI); hormonal levels; chromosomal analysis
Behavioral observations	Experience sampling; judgments by videotape coders
Interviews	Type A structured interview; Kinsey sexual interview; clinical (psychiatric) intake interview
Expressive behavior	Speech rate; gaze patterns; posture; gesture; gait; interpersonal distance
Document analysis	Psychobiography; dream diaries
Projective tests	Draw-A-Person; Rorschach Inkblot; Thematic Apperception Test (TAT)
Demographics and lifestyle	Age; cultural group; sexual orientation; political affiliation

Self-Report Tests

The most common personality tests are, like the ACT measure of charisma, dependent on the test-takers' self-reports. Such tests are easy and inexpensive to administer, and are often objective, but their validity must be carefully and continuously evaluated.

One comprehensive, self-report personality test is the well-known Minnesota Multiphasic Personality Inventory (MMPI). Responding to about five hundred statements, the test-taker answers either "true," "false," or "cannot say." The MMPI was created using criterion-related item selection. That is, the selected items distinguished between a target group such as depressed people and a normal control group. It was thus focused on assessing psychopathology (mental illness). The inventory was revised in 1989 (to the MMPI-2) in an attempt to eliminate outdated terms and to create norms from a sample that better represents the population of the United States (Butcher, 1990).

Enhancing the individual scale scores, MMPIs are often evaluated using a picture or profile that graphs the *pattern* of scale scores. For example, some people score very high on the three MMPI scales called hypochondriasis (complains of physical symptoms), depression (feels depressed), and hysteria (turns psychological problems into physical problems); these people are especially interesting to researchers in behavioral medicine because this triad often describes patients who report being in chronic pain. High scorers on these three scales may also be more likely to overuse medical facilities and to benefit from psychological treatment that accompanies their medical treatment.

In this tradition of using personality tests to help therapists design treatments, the recent Millon Clinical Multiaxial Inventory, based on Theodore Millon's notions of psychopathology, is a thorough attempt to assess personality disorders (Craig, 1993; Millon, 1997). For example, it helps in diagnosing clinical syndromes, such as alcohol dependency, and personality patterns, such as the so-called passive-aggressive, in which people hide their aggressiveness through a phony pleasantness (talking sweetly to the spouse but refusing sexual relations). Scales such as the Millon are less useful in telling us about the personality of normal (nondisturbed) populations of well-functioning individuals.

There are several excellent, modern personality inventories that attempt to measure basic dimensions of personality in normal adults. One of these, the NEO-PI, is built around the idea of five basic dimensions of personality (Costa & McCrae, 1992a, 1992b). This approach to measuring personality relies heavily on the statistical technique termed *factor analysis*. Factor analysis starts with the correlations among a number of simple scales and then reduces this information to a few basic dimensions. For example, notions about being outgoing, active, warm, talkative, energetic, sociable, and so on are captured in the factor called Extroversion. This data-based approach to measuring personality was pioneered by J. P. Guilford, L. Thurstone, and R. B. Cattell. Primarily descriptive, the factors must then be explained by a theory. The five basic dimensions of personality—Conscientiousness, Extroversion, Agreeableness, Neuroticism, and Openness—are considered in detail in Chapter 8.

A complementary approach to self-report scales is taken by the Personality Research Form (PRF) (Jackson & Messick, 1967). The PRF starts out with an attempt to measure the basic needs and motivations proposed by Henry Murray (1938). The test is thus driven by theory but was developed using correlational techniques. Another self-report assessment based directly on personality theory is the Meyers-Briggs Type Indicator, or MBTI (Hammer, 1996), which was built on Carl Jung's Type Theory. (This instrument also is discussed in Chapter 8.) Personality assessment always struggles with this tension between inductive approaches that begin with lots of data, and deductive approaches that begin with a compelling theory. As we will see, both approaches have proved helpful.

Q-Sort Tests

An interesting method for collecting self-reports that is more active than questionnaires is the **Q-sort.** In the Q-sort, a person is given a stack of cards naming various characteristics and asked to sort them into piles on a dimension such as least characteristic to most characteristic of oneself. A card might say "Is basically anxious" or "Is thoughtful." By telling the test-taker how many piles to make and how many cards to put in each pile, the examiner can ensure that the self-reports form a desired statistical distribution. (If a normal curve is approximated, then this is called a *forced normal distribution.*) Note that the test-takers make comparisons among their own characteristics but do not compare themselves to other people.

A peculiar advantage of the Q-sort is that the items (characteristics) being sorted can be held constant while the context can be changed. For example, after sorting (describing) himself, a man might be asked to use the same Q-sort cards to describe his wife, or the way he was as a child, or the way he ideally would like to be. Comparisons among the Q-sorts might be quite revealing about the person's approach to the characteristics under study (Ozer, 1993).

Ratings and Judgments by Others

In 1921, Lewis Terman began a study of over 1,500 bright young boys and girls in California schools. Terman, who developed the Stanford-Binet intelligence test, was interested in seeing how very bright children grew up. Would they turn out to be odd, unsociable nerds? high achievers? persuasive leaders? To explore these matters, Terman undertook a life-long study of these children—

examining not only their high intelligence, but also their personality and social skills (Terman, 1921).

Reliable and valid self-report personality tests had not yet been developed. Fortunately, Terman had a brilliant idea, an idea that should be followed more often in personality research today. Terman collected various sorts of other information about these children. For example, during the 1921–22 school year, Terman had parents and teachers rate the youngsters (who were about eleven years old) on a number of dimensions, including the following:

> prudence/forethought
>
> freedom from vanity
>
> conscientiousness
>
> truthfulness

Together, these ratings clearly formed an excellent scale of conscientiousness/social dependability. It is very reasonable to expect that parents and teachers can discern whether an eleven-year-old child is conscientious and socially dependable. It turns out that these ratings *are* reliable; for example, the coefficient alpha for these four ratings is .76. It also turns out that these ratings are valid; they predict well to many other behaviors that we would expect of such children. Most interesting, however, is that these conscientiousness/ dependability ratings (from 1922) turn out to be a good predictor of longevity across the life-span! Children rated as more conscientious live significantly longer than those rated as low on this scale (Friedman et al., 1993). The effect is comparable in degree to well-known biological markers of health such as cholesterol level. Obviously, something important about the individual is being measured by these parent and teacher ratings that are derived from their answers to questionnaires like the one shown in Figure 2.1. In short, the judgments of knowledgeable others can sometimes be an exceedingly effective way to assess personality.

The use of ratings implies that others can make valid judgments of one's personality. Can they? There is indeed much evidence that this is true, including recent systematic studies of the personality assessments that others— friends, acquaintances, and even strangers—can make (Funder & Dobroth, 1987; Funder & Colvin, 1991; Funder & Sneed, 1993; Kenny, Horner, Kashy, & Chu, 1992). For example, judgments of teachers' overall nonverbal style, made by viewing them on tape for segments of less than thirty seconds (observing "thin slices of behavior"), were able to tell something about how the teachers would be evaluated by others (Ambady & Rosenthal, 1993). In other words, our initial impressions of another on certain dimensions like extroversion can sometimes be quite accurate.

Traits such as extroversion are comparatively easy to judge (even by strangers) because they involve relations with others; these activities are readily observable. Other aspects of personality such as hidden internal conflicts

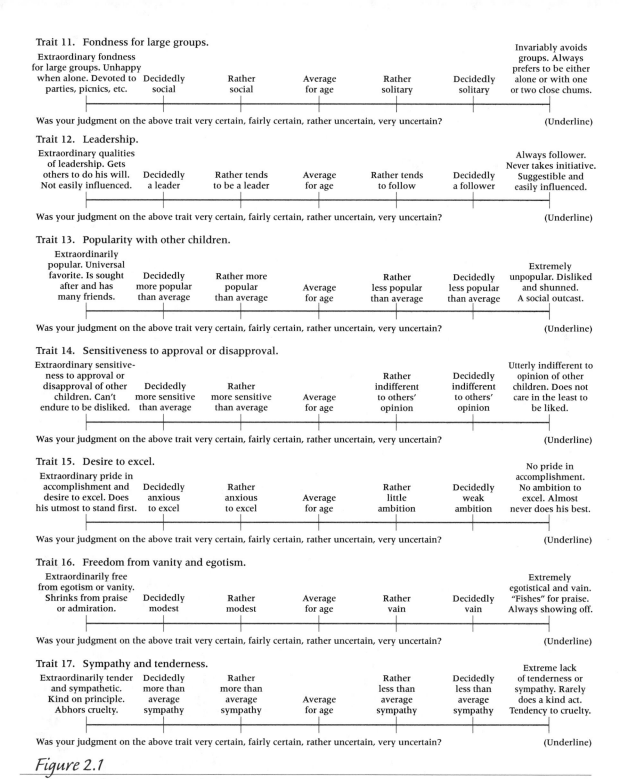

Trait 11. Fondness for large groups.

Extraordinary fondness for large groups. Unhappy when alone. Devoted to parties, picnics, etc. | Decidedly social | Rather social | Average for age | Rather solitary | Decidedly solitary | Invariably avoids groups. Always prefers to be either alone or with one or two close chums.

Was your judgment on the above trait very certain, fairly certain, rather uncertain, very uncertain? (Underline)

Trait 12. Leadership.

Extraordinary qualities of leadership. Gets others to do his will. Not easily influenced. | Decidedly a leader | Rather tends to be a leader | Average for age | Rather tends to follow | Decidedly a follower | Always follower. Never takes initiative. Suggestible and easily influenced.

Was your judgment on the above trait very certain, fairly certain, rather uncertain, very uncertain? (Underline)

Trait 13. Popularity with other children.

Extraordinarily popular. Universal favorite. Is sought after and has many friends. | Decidedly more popular than average | Rather more popular than average | Average for age | Rather less popular than average | Decidedly less popular than average | Extremely unpopular. Disliked and shunned. A social outcast.

Was your judgment on the above trait very certain, fairly certain, rather uncertain, very uncertain? (Underline)

Trait 14. Sensitiveness to approval or disapproval.

Extraordinary sensitiveness to approval or disapproval of other children. Can't endure to be disliked. | Decidedly more sensitive than average | Rather more sensitive than average | Average for age | Rather indifferent to others' opinion | Decidedly indifferent to others' opinion | Utterly indifferent to opinion of other children. Does not care in the least to be liked.

Was your judgment on the above trait very certain, fairly certain, rather uncertain, very uncertain? (Underline)

Trait 15. Desire to excel.

Extraordinary pride in accomplishment and desire to excel. Does his utmost to stand first. | Decidedly anxious to excel | Rather anxious to excel | Average for age | Rather little ambition | Decidedly weak ambition | No pride in accomplishment. No ambition to excel. Almost never does his best.

Was your judgment on the above trait very certain, fairly certain, rather uncertain, very uncertain? (Underline)

Trait 16. Freedom from vanity and egotism.

Extraordinarily free from egotism or vanity. Shrinks from praise or admiration. | Decidedly modest | Rather modest | Average for age | Rather vain | Decidedly vain | Extremely egotistical and vain. "Fishes" for praise. Always showing off.

Was your judgment on the above trait very certain, fairly certain, rather uncertain, very uncertain? (Underline)

Trait 17. Sympathy and tenderness.

Extraordinarily tender and sympathetic. Kind on principle. Abhors cruelty. | Decidedly more than average sympathy | Rather more than average sympathy | Average for age | Rather less than average sympathy | Decidedly less than average sympathy | Extreme lack of tenderness or sympathy. Rarely does a kind act. Tendency to cruelty.

Was your judgment on the above trait very certain, fairly certain, rather uncertain, very uncertain? (Underline)

Figure 2.1

A Sample of Questions from Terman's Longitudinal Study. Through questionnaires such as these, Terman obtained information from the parents and teachers of the children he was studying. These childhood ratings have been shown to be predictive of adult personality.

are of course more difficult to observe, although even these sometimes "leak out" through nonverbal cues like hand gestures. Expressive cues are further considered later in this chapter.

Biological Measures

In the early 1800s, the writings of Franz Joseph Gall led thousands of people to attempt to assess personality by feeling the shapes of and bumps on people's skulls. This practice was called *phrenology* (DeGiustino, 1975). The idea was that different psychological characteristics are represented in the brain (a reasonable idea) and that highly developed abilities or deficits show up in skull distortions. As more and more was learned learned about brain function, of course, this inference about skull shape was shown to be ridiculous. The brain's response depends on its networks of nerve cells, not on the peculiarities of the skull. Even so, the basic idea of phrenology has influenced subsequent thinking about biological assessment of personality.

Modern biological assessments of personality are based on the assumption that the nervous system (including the brain's network of neurons) is the key. So, assessments may try to measure nervous-system–related behaviors such as reaction time or skin conductance (sweating), but such attempts have often been disappointing. More exciting are current attempts that focus on the nervous system by aiming directly at the brain—measuring evoked potential on electroencephalograms (EEGs) and tracing glucose metabolism (using positron emission tomography, or PET). The output of a PET scan is shown in Figure 2.2.

The brain is composed of various interrelated subsystems. As they become better understood, psychological assessment of the future will likely address the

Figure 2.2

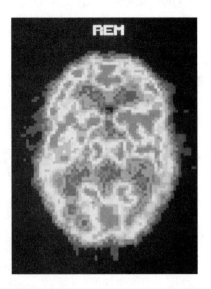

PET Scan of a Normal Brain during REM (Rapid Eye Movement) Sleep. PET images of the brain record the activity level of brain areas while the person performs a specific task. Researchers get useful information both about usual patterns of an individual's brain activity and about how that pattern is changed by various brain disorders. In this image, the lightest color represents the brain areas with the highest level of metabolic activity.

functioning of each of these subsystems (Matarazzo, 1992). For example, the use of evoked potentials—brain waves measured by EEG—to study attitudes is just beginning (Cacioppo et al., 1993). Some day, perhaps in the foreseeable future, we may be able to gauge at least some aspects of people's general reaction patterns or tendencies by monitoring their brain wave functioning.

Positron emission tomography (PET) scanning is a fairly new but very promising technique that can show brain activity by recording the brain's use of radioactive glucose. (Cells use glucose to make energy.) We can watch brain activity while people think or cope. It is possible that systematic individual differences in thought processes can eventually be revealed by this technique (Posner, Petersen, Fox, & Raichle, 1988). However, so little is currently known about brain function that little is likely to be learned about personality in the near future.

Hormone levels are another promising biological measure. Certain aspects of the bases of personality are undoubtedly tied to hormones. For example, people deficient in the thyroid hormone thyroxin may act sluggishly or become depressed. Perhaps the clearest example of hormone effects are the sex hormones such as testosterone and the estrogens. These hormones certainly influence and change the personality of adolescents at puberty. However, even in rats there is no simple correspondence between hormones and behavior. For example, the sexual activity of castrated rats is partly affected by their previous experiences and the eliciting stimuli around them (Whalen, Geary, & Johnson, 1990), as well as by their hormone level. It is an oversimplification to say that testosterone causes sexual activity, even in rats. The relationships in humans are far more complex. Although it is important to avoid jumping to silly, simplistic conclusions about hormones and personality, it is true that gross deficiencies or excesses of certain hormones, which can be detected through blood assays, can have a profound effect on personality.

In the cases of certain diseases, biological assessment may again provide valuable information about personality—in this case, an abnormal personality. For example, mania or lethargy caused by a tumor on the thyroid gland may be detected by a thyroid function test. Mild brain poisoning (such as by mercury or lead poisoning) can be detected by blood screenings. Schizophrenia-like symptoms can be a result of various sorts of poisons. Or, measurement of brain chemicals like serotonin may be able to shed light on depressive personalities. Antidepressant medications like the psychiatric drug Prozac can produce remarkable changes in personality. In addition, certain major genetic diseases such as Down syndrome, which has effects on intelligence and personality, can be easily spotted in a chromosome analysis. These biological matters are considered in more detail in Chapter 5.

Sometimes, self-report questionnaires are based on biologically derived theories of personality, as well as on empirically observed interrelations of traits. An example of such an approach is the Eysenck Personality Questionnaire (EPQ). (We explain biological influences on personality in Chapter 5.)

For instance, the EPQ contains a Neuroticism dimension, which measures emotional stability. Neuroticism makes sense as a basic dimension of personality both in terms of nervous system reactions and self-report patterns of traits. The best personality assessments (and the most helpful theories) of the future will likely have even closer ties to the biological underpinnings of personality (Strelau & Eysenck, 1987).

Behavioral Observations

Francis Galton, the nineteenth-century British scientist, pioneered many approaches to understanding individual differences, including techniques of behavioral observation. In his anthropometric laboratory, Galton collected all sorts of physical measurements of people, and he then began studying their reactions in controlled situations (Galton, 1907). For example, Galton's whistle elicited subjects' reactions to high pitches and his instruments measured the strength of their grasps. He suggested using a pressure gauge hidden under people's chairs to measure their degree of "inclination," and he used his sextant to measure unobtrusively the dimensions of "bounteous" women.

Brilliant as he was, Galton was also clearly influenced by the prevailing attitudes of his time and social class; for example, he spoke in racist terms about "the highest Caucasian" and "the lowest savage." Many outstanding personality researchers during the past century were similarly blinded by the racist prejudices that pervaded their intellectual environments.

In the modern study of personality, behavioral observation can be as simple as counting people's experiences (such as how many times they stutter or scratch themselves, or how many drinks they take). Or it may become quite complex, as researchers attempt to understand the individual's interactions with others. (Videotapes may be employed here.)

The existence of electronic pagers has allowed more complete sampling of behavior. The experimenter decides the time intervals to be sampled and sends an electronic page. When the participant's beeper goes off, he or she calls the experimenter or makes a diary notation about current activity, or perhaps even thought processes (Stone,

Sir Francis Galton (1822–1911) was an English scientist who was focused on measuring individual differences on many variables, using ingenious instruments.

Kessler, & Haythornthwaite, 1991). This is sometimes termed the experience sampling method of assessment. (It is amazing how many college students are caught daydreaming about sexual activity.)

Use of behavioral observation assumes that present behavior is a reliable and valid predictor of future behavior. When an adequate sample of present behavior is collected, this assumption generally does prove true.

Interviews

A seemingly obvious way to find out about someone's personality is to conduct an interview. The classic interview in psychology is the psychotherapeutic interview, in which the client (patient) talks about important or troubling parts of his or her life. In psychoanalysis, the patient does indeed often lie on a couch.

The validity of an assessment interview is difficult to ascertain. Certainly there are many reasons why some people may be unwilling or unable to talk about their deepest thoughts, feelings, and motivations. One way the validity of a psychotherapeutic interview can be judged is by the results of the therapy. Presumably, an interview diagnosis that results in a clearly effective treatment is more likely to be correct than a diagnosis that results in a failed treatment. Many other factors of course enter in. Still, interviews often prove quite valuable assessment tools.

In the 1940s and 1950s, Alfred Kinsey (Kinsey, Pomeroy, & Martin, 1948) used interviews to probe human sexuality. By building a sense of trust with those he interviewed, Kinsey was able to elicit disclosures that those people would never have committed to paper. Kinsey also knew how to ask leading questions and how to pursue a line of questioning doggedly until sensitive information was revealed. Interviews can be quite loose and subjective, but a skilled interviewer may uncover startling information not available by any other means. For example, many of Kinsey's participants eventually told him about their hidden homosexual experiences, their sexual relations with animals, and their extramarital affairs.

In recent years, assessment interviews have tended to become more systematic or structured. Rather than follow the interviewee's meanderings, the interviewer follows a definite plan. In this way, it is hoped that similar types of information can be elicited from each interviewee and the assessment can become more valid. One of the best-studied structured interviews is the one used to assess the Type A behavior pattern.

In the 1950s, two cardiologists proposed that certain people—characterized by a tense, competitive style—are especially likely to develop coronary heart disease. They termed these people (mostly men) "Type A." There are now a few standardized interviews that have proven quite reliable in assessing Type A personality. By the way, the most recent health data suggests that people assessed as especially competitive and hostile are indeed more likely to experience cardiovascular disease, although the precise causal links are still unknown.

In the Type A structured interview, the interviewer asks a series of challenging questions (Chesney & Rosenman, 1985). Many of these questions concern competitive situations with others: "What do you do when you are stuck on the highway behind a slow driver?" Interestingly, Type A is diagnosed based on both the verbal and the nonverbal responses to such questions. A driver who answers angrily with rapid words, loud voice, and clenched teeth, "I would cuss out the slow-poke," would probably be viewed as Type A. One of the most Type A men we ever interviewed was asked whether he played games in order to win. He shouted back, "I play to kill!"

Assessing the Type A pattern also raises the issue of Types versus Traits, a longstanding puzzle in personality theory. A typology is a categorical scheme in which people are in either one group or another. For example, being male or female is a Type. Everyone is either one or the other, with very rare exceptions. However, what about masculinity—having psychological characteristics (like aggressiveness) typically ascribed to males? This is not a Type but a Trait because people (both males and females) can be more or less masculine. Trait approaches are much more common than Type approaches in personality research today.

Type A, which arose from medical research, was originally intended as Type: you either have it or you don't, just as you either have tuberculosis or you don't. Some argue that it should indeed remain a Type (Strube, 1989) because there are some discontinuities involved. In recent years, though, Type A has been conceived more in terms of an aggressive competitiveness or hostility—a trait on which everyone can be ranked. Note that our measurement techniques have implications for our theories, *and* our theories have implications for our measurement techniques.

In general, interviews have the significant disadvantage of being subject to bias by the behaviors of the interviewer. An interviewer who expects a client (or a patient or an applicant or a student) to be "troubled" can often draw out those expected behaviors from the interviewee. Further, as with self-report questionnaires, the interviewer can best retrieve information that the interviewee knows and is willing to reveal. On the other hand, as noted, a good interviewer can probe dynamically for facts and feelings that are difficult to find any other way.

Expressive Behavior

In the case of the Type A structured interview, personality assessment is based partly on the verbal responses but partly on the nonverbal vocal responses such as the loudness and rate of speech. Nonverbal cues of expressive style are in fact an interesting way of assessing personality, even by themselves. The modern study of expressive style and personality got a big push in the 1930s from the work of Gordon Allport and P. E. Vernon (1933).

Some people have extraordinary expressive skills, which allow them to portray different characters successfully; they can adopt widely varying emotions, demeanors, postures, and styles.

Often, the way people do things is more informative than what they do. Some people talk loudly, some softly; some smile a lot and are very expressive, but some look angry or depressed. We can often recognize a phone caller by the way she says "Hello," and we can often recognize our friends by their gaits as they move across campus. Expression, particularly emotional expression, seems closely tied to dynamic, motivational aspects of personality. Expressive style and personality are considered further in Chapter 8. (Note that observation of expressive style, though considered a part of "behavioral observation," has its own distinct flavor.)

Expressive style is an excellent way to assess personal charisma—more valid, but also more demanding of the examiner than a self-report questionnaire like the ACT. For example, charismatic people show fewer nervous, body-focused type gestures, and they tend to have more fluent, inspiring speech. In fact, they tend to attract the attention and interest of strangers. For assessing such aspects of personality, expressive style is clearly one of the best techniques.

Like other measures, expressive style is often biased by cultural factors. For example, people from the American South tend to speak more slowly, in a southern drawl. It would be a mistake to equate this slow speech with the speech of a New Yorker who spoke slowly; for the New Yorker the unusual (slow) speech is probably revealing of personality, but for the southerner the slow speech is reflective of regional culture. Or, consider differences in gaze—people's patterns of looking. White Americans in a conversation tend to look at their partners while listening but look away while speaking; African Americans do relatively more looking while talking and relatively less looking while listening (LaFrance & Mayo, 1976). If these cultural norms are not taken into account, then errors in personality assessment will occur. For example, a white person might assess a black person as less cooperative than he really is.

Some nontraditional assessors like fortune-tellers probably often rely on expressive style in making their judgments. For example, imagine that an overweight young woman gingerly approaches a fortune teller and asks him about her future in a soft, squeaky voice, filled with nervous laughter, while standing in a submissive body position. The fortune teller replies, "You probably have trouble meeting men due to your shyness. . . ." And so on. Of course the fortune teller, who makes a somewhat valid but vague assessment, is reading neither her mind nor her palm; rather, he is reading her expressive style.

Document Analysis and Life Stories

It is perhaps not surprising that diaries and other such personal records can be a rich source of information about personality, but such resources are rarely employed in personality psychology. Gordon Allport regarded letters and diaries as an excellent source of information for the study of personality change (since they continue across time) and contended that they would be a good test of the value of a personality theory. He wrote that "psychologists are on safe ground so long as they talk in abstractions about personality-in-general" but that the true test comes when the psychologist tries to explain the life of a single, real person. In 1965, Allport published *Letters from Jenny*, a collection of about three hundred letters written by Jenny Gove Masterson over a decade late in her life, along with his "explanation" of Jenny, in which he applied personality theory to the letters.

Jenny led a self-defeating and pessimistic life. Trying to explain Jenny from her correspondence proved a difficult challenge for Allport. For example, in one of her letters, Jenny writes, "I often feel that I am the loneliest woman in the world" (October 13, 1935). Are we to take such comments at face value, or do we see them as shaped by a variety of forces? Because we have only the letters, it is difficult to know how to proceed. Given such difficulties, it is not surprising that few personality psychologists have since attempted such an effort. Yet document analysis is one of the few ways to achieve a comprehensive understanding of an individual across time. (The experience sampling method of behavioral observation is another.)

Document analysis can also be focused on more narrow questions. In an interesting archival analysis of Galton's intelligence, Lewis Terman, using mostly letters, claimed that Galton must have had an IQ of at least 200 (Terman, 1917). For example, before he was five years old, Galton wrote a letter boasting that he could read any English book, had substantial knowledge of Latin, knew his multiplication tables, and could read a little French. He knew the *Iliad* and *Odyssey* by age six, and read Shakespeare for pleasure by age seven. He was also described by those who knew him as an honorable, affectionate, and altruistic child. By comparing Galton's accomplishments to those of children twice his age, Terman was able to estimate and document Galton's genius.

Diaries can provide especially useful data about the personalities of those who lived in other times and places. Figure 2.3 shows a page of the diary kept by Anne Frank during the Nazi holocaust. One of the most interesting conclu-

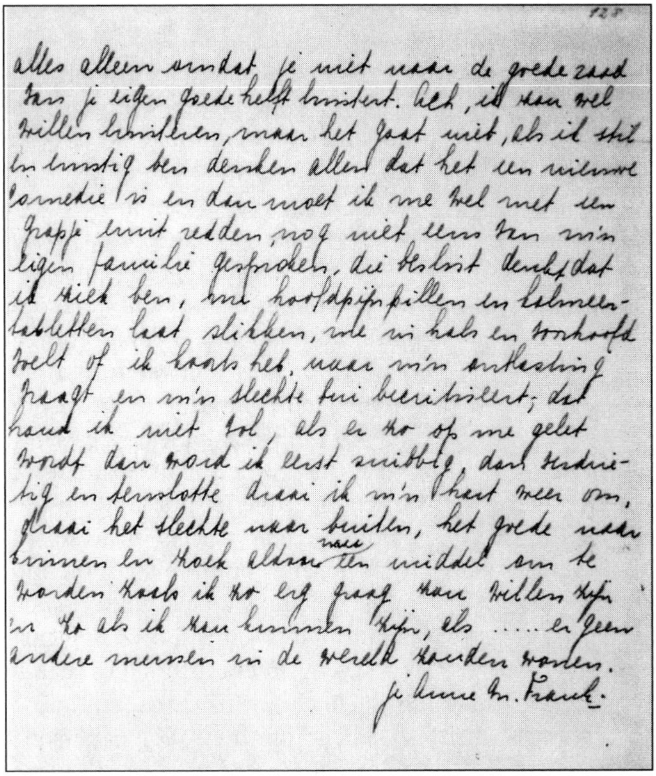
128

alles alleen omdat je niet naar de goede raad
van je eigen goede helft luistert. Ach, ik zou wel
willen luisteren, maar het gaat niet, als ik stil
en ernstig ben denken allen dat het een nieuwe
comedie is en dan moet ik me wel met een
grapje eruit redden, nog niet eens van m'n
eigen familie gesproken, die beslist denkt dat
ik ziek ben, me hoofdpijnpillen en kalmeer-
tabletten laat slikken, me in hals en voorhoofd
voelt of ik koorts heb, naar m'n ontlasting
vraagt en m'n slechte bui bekritiseert; dat
houd ik niet vol, als er zo op me gelet
wordt dan word ik eerst snibbig, dan verdrie-
tig en tenslotte draai ik m'n hart weer om,
draai het slechte naar buiten, het goede naar
binnen en zoek steeds naar een middel om te
worden zoals ik zo erg graag zou willen zijn
en zo als ik zou kunnen zijn, als ..... er geen
andere mensen in de wereld zouden wonen.
je Anne M. Frank.

Figure 2.3

A Page from Anne Frank's Diary. Document analysis allows us to gain insight into the personality of an individual through his or her writings, especially autobiographical writings such as diaries and letters. Here, we have a page from the diary of Anne Frank, who lived in hiding with her family in Amsterdam during the 1940s in an ultimately unsuccessful attempt to avoid being killed by the Nazis. This entry, written in Dutch, was the last one Anne wrote. Discovered a few days later, she was sent to a concentration camp, where she died.

sions we can draw from an analysis of that document is that, even in one of the most horrific and terrifying environments imaginable, Anne was still strongly focused on many of the normal concerns of the preadolescent and adolescent—her physical appearance, her independence from her parents, her developing identity, and her sexuality.

Many insightful biographers rely on the paper trail left by important figures in history. Of course, there are reasons why documents such as love letters or employment applications or autobiographies may not be completely honest disclosures of thoughts and feelings, but the pattern of such documents may nevertheless prove revealing. Document analysis is especially useful when the goal is to understand the psychological richness of a particular individual's life. These successes are usually psychobiographical studies of complex individuals about whom we have abundant information from other sources. For example, exceptional insights come from Erik Erikson's works on *Young Man Luther* (a study of Martin Luther) and *Gandhi's Truth* (a study of Mahatma Gandhi). Personal writings are very helpful when our assessments can be confirmed by other sources of information.

Projective Tests

When a child has gone through a traumatic experience such as sexual abuse, a gory traffic accident, or a battlefield (as in a civil war or a violent cult), psychologists and psychiatrists are often called in to assess the effects on the child's long-term functioning. A commonly used assessment technique in these situations is to ask the child to draw a picture or a series of pictures.

The use of pictures as part of psychological assessment dates back to the 1920s. The idea is that the child (or adult) may be willing to put into a picture certain things that are too uncomfortable to discuss. Or, it is thought that pictures may sometimes reveal things that are even outside consciousness, such as unconscious motivations. If a child draws a picture of a father with a tremendously large penis, or without facial features, or surrounded by snakes, the drawing may indicate a psychological problem.

Draw-a-person assessment techniques are subjective. (Attempts to make them objective by finding firm links between particular features of pictures and particular aspects of personality have been unsuccessful.) Their utility thus depends on the skill of the interpreter, who is usually a therapist. But as noted, pictures do allow for potentially rich insights into the "artist." An example of this test is shown in Figure 2.4.

Assessment techniques that attempt to study personality through use of a relatively unstructured stimulus, task, or situation are termed **projective tests** because they allow a person to "project" his or her own inner motivations onto the assessor's test. In addition to drawing a picture, projective tests include telling a story, completing a sentence, or doing word associations.

Projective tests seemed especially valuable to proponents of psychoanalytic theories because the theories are based on unconscious motivations and projective tests attempt to capture such motivations. (Psychoanalytic theory is explained in detail in Chapter 3.)

In the early part of this century, a Swiss psychiatrist named Hermann Rorschach began showing inkblots to his patients and asking for descriptions. The Rorschach has since become one of the most widely used projective tests. An example of the type of inkblot used for the test is shown in Figure 2.5. Like other projective tests, the Rorschach presents vague and ambiguous stimuli

Figure 2.4

A Child's Response to the Draw-A-Person Test. Projective tests allow the individual to determine the content of the response. This picture was drawn by a nine-year-old child, in response to the request, "Draw a person." Some psychologists believe that we can gain insight into the child's personality by analyzing the characteristics of the picture he or she draws.

Figure 2.5

A Rorschach-Type Inkblot. The Rorschach test asks the examinee to describe each of a series of inkblot images. The actual inkblots used in the Rorschach test are not permitted to be reproduced here, but this inkblot is similar in character to the originals.

and notes a person's responses (Exner, 1986). As a person views and responds to a series of ten inkblots, the Rorschach examiner records what is said and later notes whether the person is looking at the whole inkblot or parts, "seeing" an object in motion, reacting to shading, and so on. The examiner may then follow up with questions such as "Where in this picture was it that you said you saw a bouncing ball?"

Because people are often unaware of factors motivating their behavior, exploring such motivations is no easy matter but essential if behavior is to be understood. Projective tests, by using vague tasks or stimuli and then gauging the participant's emotional or motivational response, attempt to get at deep personal styles in viewing the world. Our Pirate Test for Children has some projective aspects, as pirates may evoke dramatic responses in kids; and there is no obviously correct way to respond. For example, a child who lets out a lusty pirate scream when he meets Captain Hook, and who often marches around at home with a sword and bandanna of his own, might be correctly assumed to have an aggressive aspect to his personality.

The Rorschach shares a significant problem with all projective tests, namely scoring. The examiner's personal interpretations might give us some interesting insights to follow up, but there would be no reliability. That is, different examiners or even the same examiner at different times might come up with a different interpretation (score). This problem might be addressed by training scorers in a standardized scoring system; for example, people who see a grayish scene in most inkblots might be labeled as depressed. Unfortunately, most research using the Rorschach has not found it to be highly valid, but still of useful potential, especially for gaining clinical insights (Exner, 1986; Peterson, 1978).

In projective testing, the person is told that there is no correct answer and indeed there is no correct answer. One of the most commonly used projective tests is the Thematic Apperception Test, or TAT (Bellak, 1993). In administering the TAT, the assessor simply tells the participant to make up a story about a picture that will be presented, including a prediction on what will happen next. The assessor then holds up the first picture (which may be of a young boy contemplating a violin). Sometimes the assessor writes down the story; sometimes the participants write down the stories themselves. The TAT thus attempts to see how a person places order on a vague stimulus. For example, if the participant decides that the boy is distressed because he has just dropped the violin down the stairs and is afraid his father will beat him, the assessor may begin to look for clues of latent aggression.

It is important to note that projective tests, like all personality tests, make assumptions about the nature of personality and about behavior. Projective tests assume that there are deep, basic motivational patterns and that these patterns show up in how we respond to perceptual stimuli. Tests like the TAT were seen as especially valuable by Henry Murray because Murray's theory of personality was based on the idea of unconscious needs struggling to be realized (Smith, 1992).

Demographics and Lifestyle

It is not that unusual to hear someone say, "I can't stand a Capricorn, but I'm really attracted to an Aries." The speaker is relying on astrology—using celestial bodies and the signs of the zodiac (an imaginary belt of the heavens)—for clues about personality. Astrology began well over 2,500 years ago, when many ancient peoples believed their fate was written in the stars. Today astrology usually charts the positions of the sun, moon, and planets at the time of a person's birth in an attempt to predict the person's characteristics and fate.

It is not impossible that celestial happenings influence human behavior; for example, the moon affects the tides, solar radiation affects magnetic fields on earth, and the earth's position affects the weather. But astrology has relied mostly on superstition and faith rather than on any rigorous scientific analysis. It has no known scientific validity. The stubborn popularity of astrology reminds us of the willingness of many people to accept almost any explanation of personality.

Nevertheless, in attempting to understand an individual, it is generally helpful to ascertain various sorts of demographic, if not astrological, information—age, cultural place of birth, religion, family size, and so on. All such information relevant to population statistics helps provide a framework for better understanding the individual. The assessment of a twenty-year-old should generally be different in its conduct and interpretation than the assessment of an eighty-year-old. But by itself demographic information can be misleading, as in the case of twin brothers who share all the statistical characteristics but have completely different personalities.

To gain a good understanding of an individual, we need to know the person's cultural milieu and cultural identity. This is especially true if the culture is outside the mainstream. Many silly attempts have been made to assess personality in African Americans without any attempt to understand African American culture. For example, the Black Panthers, who emerged from the civil rights movements of the 1960s, were often seen by the dominant culture as troubled and aggressive rebels, even though the Panthers were rarely violent and were heavily involved in social programs benefiting their communities. Similarly, gays (homosexuals and lesbians) in America are increasingly influenced by gay culture, especially in large cities like San Francisco, Los Angeles, and New York. A gay individual's unusual (nonmainstream) pattern of behavior might erroneously be attributed to personality if the relevant culture were not taken into account.

These demographic and cultural groupings are not psychological, and so do not fit smoothly into most personality theories. On the other hand, personality psychologists too often overlook such societal influences. For example, the fact that there were so many communists in Russia in the 1920s, and so

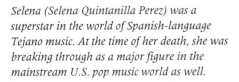

Selena (Selena Quintanilla Perez) was a superstar in the world of Spanish-language Tejano music. At the time of her death, she was breaking through as a major figure in the mainstream U.S. pop music world as well.

Without an understanding of the cultural and ethnic factors that influence a person, we cannot distinguish the behaviors and attitudes that derive from the person's individual personality from those that are a product of his or her culture.

many hippies in California in the 1960s, and so many divorces in the United States in the 1970s are best explained in terms of social and societal factors rather than through notions that the individuals involved had communist personalities, or rebellious personalities, or divorce-prone personalities.

Is There One Best Method of Assessment?

Which personality assessments are best? The answer depends in part on the person, the assessor, and the purpose of the assessment. For example, if we are interested in seeing which aspects of personality predict coronary heart disease, then we should strive to refine and utilize assessment techniques that do indeed accurately and usefully predict heart disease. If we are interested in unconscious motives behind aggression, we should use projective tests or behavioral observations rather than self-report personality tests. And so on. Most important is that we retain a strong focus on continuously evaluating validity.

Furthermore, it is important to remember that the validities of almost all personality assessment techniques are threatened by the overgeneralization phenomenon of the Barnum effect, the tendency of individuals and clinicians to readily accept vague personality descriptions as though they were valid and specific (Cash, Mikulka, & Brown, 1989; Prince & Guastello, 1990). Valuable assessment shows what is special or different about the person being assessed.

How Not to Test Personality

It is amazing to see how much time and money some people spend attempting to assess personality in ways that are marginally valid at best. Many are simply frauds or fantasies. We briefly discuss some of them here.

As noted, one of the oldest and silliest methods is astrology, learning about your personality from the stars. Many newspapers still print astrological charts, proffering vague advice such as "Your fortune is near." They are about as valuable as fortune cookies, except they do not taste as good.

Another set of invalid methods involves physical body measurements. As mentioned earlier, one of these—phrenology (also called cranioscopy)—depends on the incorrect nineteenth century theory that your head shape is a clue to your brain and your brain shape is a clue to your personality. When first proposed, this idea was not totally laughable because little was known about the workings of the brain. It is interesting, however, that similar invalid and obsolete methods persist to this day.

Then there are the assessment methods used in carnivals, private parlors, or bogus religions. Traditionally these have included palm-reading and numerology, but today they may extend to pseudo-high-tech nonsense such as hair analysis or computer-interpreted voice analysis.

More problematic are assessment techniques that involve aspects of expressive style; they are problematic because expressive style (especially emotional style) *can* be a valid indicator of personality. One of these dubious techniques is graphology, or handwriting analysis. Handwriting analyses are often sold to businesses as a means of screening potential employees. Although there is no decent evidence to justify the detailed assessments offered by graphologists, it is probably the case that some information is revealed by a person's handwriting (see Figure 2.6). For example, male handwriting is probably often distinguishable from female writing; old, infirm handwriting is distinguishable from younger, healthy writing; and perhaps a few other dimensions are usually discernable. But such information is even more obvious in an interview! It is a long way from such mundane observations to absurd pronouncements like, "The way she crosses her *t*'s indicates that she will not persevere in her work."

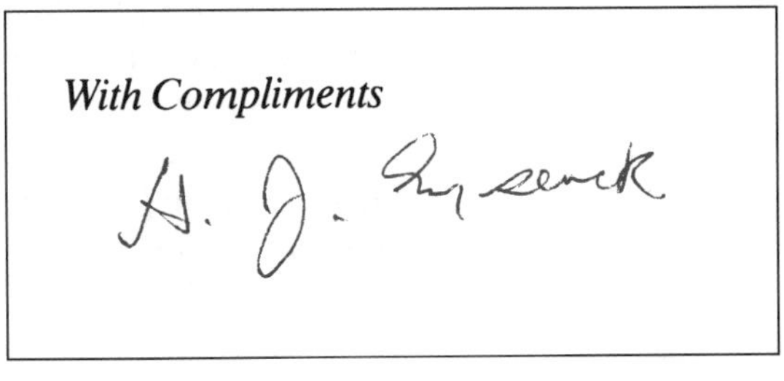

Figure 2.6

The Signature of Hans Eysenck. Do you think you can tell from this signature whether the writer is an introvert or an extrovert? (Used by permission.)

With Compliments

It is not the case that graphology could not in principle tell us something about personality. Rather we should ask ourselves, What is the theory underlying graphology? Is this consistent with what we know about human biology and human behavior? What are the reliability studies? What are the validity studies? Has the evidence been confirmed by independent scientific work? In other words, have all the usual standards been applied? In the case of handwriting analysis, they have not. One of the prime advantages of the in-depth study of personality is that it leaves us better prepared to make such determinations throughout our lives.

The Ethics of Personality Testing

The first psychological tests of any substantial validity are just a century old. Alfred Binet pioneered valid intelligence testing in Paris at the end of the nineteenth century. His goal was a noble one: his tests could be used to find students who were really quite bright but who had been mislabeled stupid as a result of problems such as hearing or language impairment. In other words, Binet aimed to help those who had been overlooked by society (Binet & Simon, 1916).

The same sorts of arguments for testing apply to people with other psychological or relationship problems. In order to help people with problems, an accurate diagnosis of their problems and their strengths is useful. Thus, fair and valid testing can be beneficial to everyone. There is always a danger that test results will be wrong due to various limitations. Inaccurate testing will be a major problem if testing is being done to identify people who are less "worthy." In this case, an error or bias is especially tragic.

Unfortunately, just as the first intelligence tests were quickly corrupted to search for "morons" and "idiots," psychological assessment is sometimes used today for purposes of discrimination and persecution. For example, tests might be legitimately designed to screen job applicants. But such a test easily could be biased (intentionally or unintentionally) against those from traditionally less-employed groups. It is as if medical diagnosis were being used, not to help in successful medical treatment, but rather to decide who should be shunned as "diseased."

In his book *The Mismeasure of Man,* paleontologist Steven Jay Gould (1981, 1996) describes the sorry saga of scientific racism. Focusing on intelligence, Gould tells how even the most eminent scientists were blinded by their prejudices while believing they were engaged in purely scientific assessment. For example, in the mid-nineteenth century, the respected physician Paul Broca used skull size (craniometry) to "prove" that men are smarter than women and Caucasians are smarter than Africans. Broca, like many well-intentioned scientists who followed him in the twentieth century, was probably not conscious of the distortions in his data. He was simply biased by his powerful preexisting beliefs. Undoubtedly, such biases also afflict modern personality testing, but without the benefit of hindsight, they are difficult to uncover.

Because of the abuses of assessments, some have argued that testing should be outlawed. This is an extreme reaction. It is sort of like saying that we should outlaw science because scientific developments have led to the creation of terrible weapons. Or that we should outlaw surgery because many people die on the operating table. The real problem is that some personality tests are poorly constructed, improperly used, and wrongly employed. The solution is to ensure that educated people are well versed in understanding the valid uses and the severe limits of personality tests.

The issue is not a trivial one. The assertions of the psychiatric community are likely to be believed by an uninformed lay public. Therefore, students of personality have a responsibility to evaluate continuously the validity and the conclusiveness of their findings, and the societal implications of their conclusions.

Summary and Conclusion

Personality tests involve standardized encounters that provoke and assess revealing individual differences in reactions. Objective tests have correct answers that are easily measured and defined, but they may miss more subtle aspects of personality. Subjective tests rely on interpretations by observers or test-givers, but they may result in disagreements about interpretations. The best assessment relies on multiple measures to paint a picture of the individual.

Personality tests should be reliable. Reliability refers to the consistency of scores; people should receive similar scores on the same test on different occasions because personality is assumed to be relatively stable. Good assessments take into account that basic patterns remain stable, even though day-to-day responses may seem to change. (Personality may change, however, in the long run or in response to traumatic events.) Internal consistency reliability examines the subparts of a personality test. Test–retest reliability compares the scores on different occasions, usually several weeks apart.

Is a test measuring what it is supposed to be measuring? What is it measuring? These are issues of validity. The most important aspect of validity is construct validity. Construct validity is ascertained by seeing if the assessment predicts behaviors and reactions implied (theoretically) by the construct. Is an assessment related to the things to which it is supposed to be related? If so, it has convergent validity. On the other hand, the assessment should be distinguishable; that is, it should not be related to theoretically irrelevant constructs. This is termed discriminant validity. Content validity refers to whether a test is measuring the domain that it is supposed to be measuring.

One desirable quality of a test item is that it should differentiate among test-takers. Items should also be intercorrelated (i.e., related to one another) because each item is measuring some aspect of the overall construct. Finally, the items should produce a useful distribution so that the test is able to assess a full range of individuals.

Response sets are biases, unrelated to the personality characteristic being measured. People with an acquiescence response set are more likely than others to agree with anything you ask them. An especially difficult challenge is posed by a social desirability response set. That is, many people are likely to want to present themselves in a favorable light or to try to please the experimenter or test administrator. Although all tests rely to some degree on a set of assumptions and thus might be called biased, the tests are not necessarily bad or worthless. Rather, they must be properly constructed, used, and interpreted to be valid.

One of the most common types of test bias is ethnic bias. Tests often fail to take into account the relevant culture or subculture of the person being tested, and theories and measures developed in one culture are improperly applied to another culture. For example, Hispanic American children have sometimes been viewed as lacking in achievement motivation when in fact they have intentionally been raised to be more cooperative with their peers. Personality psychology too often studies samples of convenience—patients, students, neighbors—and too infrequently makes a systematic attempt to ascertain whether conclusions apply to other people, in other places, at other times.

Gender bias is also a prevalent type of test bias. Tests may demonstrate "problems" with women without turning the focus to the environment—toward husbands, job discrimination, or lack of equal educational opportunity.

One of the great triumphs of personality testing of the past century is that many different types of valid personality tests have been developed. The most common and easy-to-administer personality tests depend on the test-takers' self-reports; among these are the MMPI, the Personality Research Form, the Millon, and the NEO-PI. A more active self-report than questionnaires is the Q-sort technique. In the Q-sort, a person sorts a stack of cards naming various characteristics into piles on a dimension such as "least characteristic" to "most characteristic" of him- or herself. A peculiar advantage of the Q-sort is that the items (characteristics) being sorted can be held constant while the context is changed.

Many important personality assessments do not rely on self-report. The use of ratings by others shows that friends, acquaintances, and even strangers can make valid judgments of personality. Modern biological assessments of personality are based on the assumption that the nervous system is key. Exciting current assessment attempts in this area focus on the brain, measuring evoked potential on electroencephalograms (EEGs), and glucose metabolism (using positron emission tomography, or PET). Behavioral observation such as counting people's experiences or behaviors is another technique that has proved valuable. An experimenter who calls or pages the person to make a diary notation about current activity or thought processes is employing the experience sampling method of assessment.

The classic interview in psychology is the psychotherapeutic interview, in which the client talks about important or troubling parts of his or her life. In recent years, assessment interviews have tended to become more systematic or structured. Rather than follow the interviewee's meanderings, the interviewer follows a definite plan. In the case of the Type A structured interview, personality assessment is based partly on the verbal responses and partly on the nonverbal vocal responses, such as the volume and rate of speech. Nonverbal cues of expressive style are in fact an interesting and underutilized way of assessing personality. For example, expressive style is an excellent way to assess personal charisma. In contrast, letters and diaries (which contain no nonverbal cues) can be a fine source of information for the study of personality change becuase they provide data from multiple points in time.

Projective tests such as the Rorschach present an unstructured stimulus and allow a person to "project" his or her own inner motivations onto the assessor's test. They include drawing a picture, telling a story, completing a sentence, or doing word associations. The main drawback of projective tests is the problem of scoring. The examiner's personal interpretations may give us some interesting insights to follow up, but there is no reliability. That is, different examiners or even the same examiner at a later time might come up with a different interpretation. This problem can be partially addressed by training scorers in a standardized scoring scheme.

Finally, if we are to gain an accurate understanding of an individual, we need to know the person's cultural milieu and cultural identity. This is especially true if the culture is outside the mainstream. For example, silly attempts have been made to assess personality in African Americans without sufficient attempt to understand African American culture.

Personality testing can be and has been incorrectly employed. Because of the abuses of assessments, some have argued that testing should be banned. But the real problem is that some personality tests are poorly constructed, improperly used, or wrongly employed, for political ends or other agendas. The solution is for people to achieve a good understanding of the valid uses and the severe limits of personality tests, in the context of personality theories.

Key Concepts

objective assessment versus subjective
  assessment

reliability

construct validity

response set

bias

self-report tests

Q-sort tests

ratings and judgments by others

biological measures

behavioral observations

experience sampling method of assessment

psychotherapeutic interview

structured interview

expressive behavior

document analysis

projective tests

demographics and lifestyle information

Suggested Readings

Aiken, L. R. (1996). *Personality assessment: Methods and practices* (2nd ed.). Seattle, WA: Hogrefe & Huber Publishers.

Campbell, D. T. (1960). Recommendations for the APA test standards regarding construct, trait, and discriminant validity. *American Psychologist, 15*, 546–553.

Fiske, D. W. (1971). *Measuring the concepts of personality.* Chicago: Aldine.

Gould, S. J. (1981/1996). *The mismeasure of man* (2nd ed.). New York: W. W. Norton. (Originally published 1981.)

Pervin, L. A. (Ed.). (1990). *Handbook of personality: Theory and research.* New York: Guilford Press.

Psychoanalytic Aspects of Personality

In 1882, Dr. Sigmund Freud fell in love with a slender young woman named Martha Bernays. Unfortunately for Freud, he had neither the money nor the social status for an immediate marriage, and his sexual urges could not be soon gratified. Consistent with the times and their Austrian-Jewish culture, Freud and Martha, then in their twenties, would not engage in premarital sexual relations. They had to wait four long years until marriage, during which time Freud, a very perceptive young scientist, thought deeply and often about the pressures that his sexual longings had on other aspects of his life. Ten years later, in the 1890s, Freud began developing his psychosexual theories of the human psyche.

Freud's mother was the third wife of his father, Jacob Freud, who was twenty years her elder. She was quite attractive, and the young Freud, as well as others, adored her. Freud later recalled the impression it made when he, as a young child, once saw his mother nude. He incorporated love and thwarted-love relations into the foundations of his theories.

When Freud was two and a half years old, family complications arose: his mother gave birth to his sister, raising his wonder about human reproduction and provoking deep concerns of sibling rivalry in the highly intelligent little Sigmund. Further complicating the picture was the fact that Freud's two adult stepbrothers (from his father's previous marriage) lived nearby and seemed quite attached to his young mother. Why did his half-brother flirt with his mother? In later years, Freud well remembered the tangle of erotic relationships of his childhood (Gay, 1988; Jones, 1953).

The young Sigmund Freud with his adored mother, Amalie.

Although Freud was Jewish and his wife, Martha, was raised as an orthodox Jew, he was passionately antireligion and refused to let Martha practice much of their religion. He was quite defensive about the topic despite the fact that anti-Semitism was a significant factor in the lives of all European Jews, much as skin color is a significant factor in the lives of present-day African Americans. Trained as a physician, Freud was primarily a biologist—a biologist swept up in the writings and influences of Charles Darwin. Darwin had recently revolutionized scientific thought by proposing that people were not created by God in the Garden of Eden but rather had evolved over the eons from other life forms. People were highly intelligent animals, but animals nonetheless—biological creatures. Freud himself spent many years early in his career studying the biological evolution of fish.

Like many intellectuals of his time, Freud therefore viewed religion as an irrelevant crutch of ignorant people, something with which he would have nothing to do. It is very important to understand this aspect of Freud's work: he was primarily a biologist, a scientist, endeavoring (with all his abilities) to understand the biological structures and laws underlying psychological responses (Bernstein, 1976; S. Freud, 1966; Gay, 1988; Jones, 1953).

*T*his discussion of the early life of Sigmund Freud has hinted that childhood experiences, repressed erotic feelings, and unconscious conflicts can affect adult behavior. This type of analysis seems perfectly reasonable to most modern-day college students, but it was actually quite rare before the beginning of the twentieth century. The naturalness of a Freudian interpretation of personality gives elegant testimony to the success and influence of many of the ideas of a Freudian, **psychoanalytic** approach to personality.

Freud visited the United States in 1909 at the invitation of G. Stanley Hall, the influential child psychologist, then president of Clark University. Freud was accompanied by Carl Jung (then in his early thirties; Freud was in his fifties). Neither man was yet well known, but their ideas about unconscious sexuality were intriguing to those Americans who read about them. They were visited at Clark by many influential psychologists, including William James, the Harvard philosopher–psychologist who was one of the founders of American psychology. Freud, though anxious before such a distinguished audience, did a fine job of presenting his ideas. This was the beginning of the significant spread of psychoanalytic ideas in North America. Freud's work is now the most heavily cited in all of psychology, and it is extensively referenced in many of the humanities as well.

Sigmund Freud is sometimes treated as a historical curiosity by laboratory-oriented modern personality researchers because some of his ideas have been disproven by modern research in biology and psychology. This attitude is a misreading of Freud's impact, and it may lead the field to overlook the insights that psychoanalytic theory can add to our understanding of personality. In this chapter we show how Freud's startling ideas are alive and highly influential even today. We also examine the limits and failures of the psychoanalytic approach.

Basic Psychoanalytic Concepts

As his young medical career began to develop, Sigmund Freud became more and more interested in neurology and psychiatry. Needing to develop clinical medical skills that could earn him money, he began paying less attention to research in biology and directed more efforts at problems plaguing patients. In 1885, Freud went to Paris to study with the famous neuropathologist J. M. Charcot.

Charcot was studying **hysteria.** Although hysteria is uncommon today, it was quite a problem a century ago. It is almost accurate to say it was a fashionable disease. Many people, especially young women, would be afflicted with various forms of paralysis for which no organic cause could be found. Sometimes, almost miraculously, they could be cured by psychological and social influences. For example, Charcot and Pierre Janet (Janet, 1907) were successfully using **hypnosis** to cure hysteria. The idea behind the therapy was that, unbeknownst to the patient, psychological forces in the mind were causing physical ailments. By unlocking the inner psychological tension, the outer body could be liberated.

The Unconscious and Therapeutic Techniques

Freud began employing hypnosis but eventually found it inadequate to treat many of his patients. So Freud, influenced by his fellow physician and physiologist Josef Breuer, began experimenting, moving from hypnosis and other forms of intense suggestion to techniques of **free association**—spontaneous, free-flowing associations of ideas and feelings; and finally he moved to dreams (Breuer & Freud, 1957). It became more and more apparent to Freud that most patients were not consciously in touch with the inner conflicts that caused their observable mental and physical problems. But dreams might provide the key to unlock their inner secrets.

Dreams have been interpreted since biblical times and even before. They were often seen as prophecies or divine revelations. But to Freud, the evolutionary biologist, dreams were a product of the individual's psyche. He saw dreams as pieces of and hints about the **unconscious**—that portion of the mind inaccessible to usual, conscious thought (Freud, 1913).

Freud called dreams the "royal road" to understanding the unconscious. Let us say that you repeatedly dream that you are chasing your boss up the stairs. You run faster and faster and become more and more frustrated but never reach the peak. Freud interpreted such activity as representing sexual intercourse, but intercourse that is never consummated. Why might one have such a dream? Because it might be too threatening, psychologically speaking, to admit to such thoughts. It would be threatening to one's marriage and to one's self-concept and to one's sense of morality to admit to such lustful urges. The urge is therefore turned into a nonthreatening symbol—running up flights of stairs.

In dreams, almost any phallus-like object—from a clarinet to an umbrella—could represent a penis, that is, be a phallic symbol. And any enclosed space such as a private, walled courtyard, or a fur pocket, or a box could represent female genitalia. However, Freud, a great cigar smoker, is said to have commented that sometimes a cigar is just a cigar. (By the way, Freud's smoking was his ultimate undoing; he died of cancer of the mouth and jaw in 1939.)

Sigmund Freud's study in Vienna. His patients would recline on the couch and let their free associations flow.

But what about people who do indeed dream about having sexual intercourse with their boss or their coworker? Why isn't their sexual motivation hidden? Among Freud's patients, their problem was often some inner conflict or tension. This was especially true in the straight-laced Victorian society of a century ago, in which sexual matters were scandalous. Explicit lustful dreams were rarely encountered in patients; and if they were, they were interpreted as representing some other, even deeper, hidden conflict. It would be fascinating to hear what Freud would say about today's open, let-it-all-hang-out sexuality. Might he say that ours is still not really a sexually open and relaxed society?

According to psychoanalytic theory, dreams, and indeed most aspects of psychological experience, are said to have two levels of content—**manifest content** and **latent content.** The manifest content is what a person remembers and consciously considers. The latent content is the underlying hidden meaning. We might say that dreams are similar to icebergs—a little piece floats above the surface but much more is hidden underneath. This is the hallmark of the psychoanalytic approach to personality—the idea that what we see on the surface (what is manifest) is only a partial representation of the vastness that is lying underneath (what is latent). The implication of this for understanding personality is that any assessment tools or tests that rely on people's conscious replies or self-reports are necessarily incomplete; they capture only the manifest content. The unconscious can manifest itself symbolically in a dream (see Figure 3.1).

A vicious circle (or tautology) sometimes results from a psychoanalytic explanation of personality. Let us say, for example, that a young woman's severe nervous cough, squint, and partial paralysis are attributed to an unconscious conflict about her sexual abuse. In psychotherapy, the issue is gradually

Figure 3.1

The Unconscious Manifests Itself Symbolically. A dream about a tooth extraction could symbolize a fear of castration.

brought to light and thoroughly explored, its emotional energy diffused. Yet the patient still suffers from many nervous or hysterical problems. Do we therefore conclude that the psychoanalytic explanation was totally wrong? No, the psychoanalyst may search for even deeper, more hidden aspects of the problem. There is thus no logical or scientific means of evaluating the explanation. Another way of stating this problem is to say that psychoanalytic investigations *rarely have a control group;* that is, there is no comparison or standard by which to carefully evaluate the theory or the therapy. In the movie *Annie Hall,* Woody Allen's character (Alvy) tells Annie that he has been seeing a psychoanalyst "just for fifteen years." When Annie is amazed, Alvy replies that he will give it one more year and then go to Lourdes (the center of faith healing in France). The comparison of psychoanalysis to religious miracle cures is an apt one in those cases in which Freud's ideas are not subjected to the same critical scrutiny as are other psychological theories.

The Structure of the Mind

All personality theories agree that human beings, like other animals, are born with a set of instincts and motivations. Most basically, newborns will cry in response to painful stimulation and will suck milk until they are satiated. At birth, the inner motivating forces have obviously not yet been shaped by the external world. They are basic and unsocialized. Freud referred to this undifferentiated core of personality as the **id.** In German, the word was literally the "it." The id contains the basic psychic energy and motivations.

The id operates according to the demands of the **pleasure principle.** That is, the id strives solely to satisfy its desires and thereby reduce inner tension. For example, the baby is driven to suck, obtain pleasure, and relax.

However, even infants must face reality. There is a real world out there—tired mothers, dirty diapers, cold bedrooms—that soon must be responded to. The personality structure that develops to deal with the real world Freud termed the **ego,** or literally, the "I."

The ego operates according to the **reality principle:** it must solve real problems. Wishing for a breast or a cuddle does not bring it about. One must plan and act, constrained by the real world. Infants soon learn to exaggerate their crying in order to bring their mothers but not to overdo it.

Throughout life the pleasure-seeking id constantly struggles with the reality-checking ego. Individuals never outgrow the id, but most adults keep it under control. In some people, though, pleasure-seeking dominates inappropriately or too often; gratification becomes a core aspect of their adult personality. A graphic representation of the role of the id is shown in Figure 3.2.

There is still another set of problems. The young child cannot simply learn the most realistic ways of satisfying inner drives. We cannot be totally self-centered. Rather, we are forcefully shaped by our parents and the rest of society to follow moral rules. The personality structure that emerges to internalize these

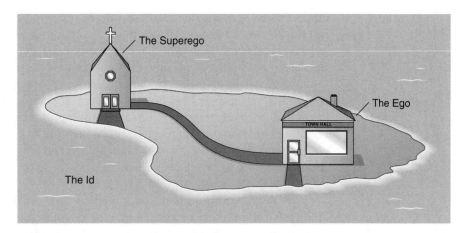

Figure 3.2

The Psychoanalytic View of the Structure of the Mind. The ego (represented here by the town hall) and the superego (represented here by the church) both have their roots and foundations in the id (represented here by the sea), just as this volcanic island arises out of, and is surrounded by, water.

societal rules is termed the **superego.** Literally, Freud thought of it as the "Over-I" because it ruled over the ego or "I." The superego is similar to a conscience, but goes further. We can think about what our conscience, our internal set of ethical guidelines, is telling us to do, but parts of the superego are unconscious. That is, we are not always aware of the internalized moral forces that press on and constrain our individual actions.

When the ego and especially the superego do not do their job properly, elements of the id may slip out and be seen. Consider the case of the anatomy professor quoted by Freud who says, "In the case of the female genital, in spite of the tempting, I mean the attempted . . . ." Freud deems the linguistic explanations of such slips inadequate and blames the error on unconscious urges (Freud, 1924). It is not simply a problem with speech; a much deeper motivation is being revealed. Such psychological errors in speaking or writing have come to be called **Freudian slips.** Temporarily forgetting your friend's name is not seen in terms of a learning theory of memory or in light of simple fatigue, but rather is seen as evidence of an unconscious conflict with this friend. Similarly, if a young woman fingers or taps her engagement ring while she talks to an attractive new acquaintance, this action is indicative of an unconscious concern regarding her fiancé.

A Freudian slip may even have occurred during the writing of this textbook, when the simple omission of the letter *n* made quite a difference in one draft. In preparing an outline of the differences between men and women, a student assistant meant to write that "it is evolutionarily important for men to have as many sexual contacts as possible, in order to perpetuate their genes." But this (female) assistant wrote, much to her embarrassment, that "it is evolutionarily important for *me* to have as many sexual contacts as possible . . . ." Needless to say, others who saw this sentence found it quite amusing.

Freud admits that slips of the tongue or pen are more common when a person is tired or distracted but argues that at such times our defenses are down and, with less resistance, unconscious impulses can more easily surface. Freud was an extremely perceptive and acute observer who was not satisfied with superficial explanations of personality. (Freud would presumably also be amused but not surprised that a leading anti-tobacco activist is named Randolph Smoak.)

We now know quite a bit about the structure and function of the human brain, but a hundred years ago, Freud and his colleagues knew very little. We now know that the brain is clearly *not* divided into id, ego, and superego compartments. But there are indeed various levels and structures in the human brain. Some are more primitive and are similar to those found in primitive animals. Other brain structures seem evolved to produce emotion and motivation. And the upper cortical layers contain complex networks of nerves that allow the higher levels of human intelligence. Freud was correct in concluding that certain parts of the mind are not subject to conscious awareness.

It is an interesting exercise to keep track of your slips and your dreams for a while. You can best remember dreams by keeping a pen and paper next to your pillow, and then lie still after awakening (with your eyes closed), trying to recall your dreams. Then write down as much as you can remember. (The process gets easier with practice.) After several weeks, search for common themes and try to relate these themes to your worries, conflicts, and friends. This exercise may or may not provoke insights, but it will provide a taste of the kinds of self-analysis that Freud worked on for many years.

Psychosexual Development

Freud saw the psychological world as a series of tensions, such as tension between selfishness and society, and inner tensions that strive for relief. Underlying these tensions, he argued, was the sexual energy, or **libido.**

In the late nineteenth century, several physicians and scientists, including Richard von Krafft-Ebing and Havelock Ellis (1913; 1899/1936), began writing books exploring human sexuality and sexual deviancy. Freud was intrigued with the wide variety of sexual experiences he read about and encountered in his own patients. Why would some people want to have sexual relations with children, with corpses, with barnyard animals, with whips and chains, with shoes, in groups, in front of observers, obsessively, and so on and so on? Freud, playing scientist rather than moralist or judge, tried to discover why sexual energy could be directed in so many ways.

Oral Stage

Infants are driven to satisfy their drives of hunger and thirst, and they turn to their mother's breast or bottle for this satisfaction, as well as for the security and pleasure that comes from nursing. Fortunately or unfortunately, at some point (usually at about age one in American society), the baby must stop sucking and be weaned. This creates a conflict between the desire to remain in a state of dependent security and the biological and psychological necessity of being weaned ("growing up"). It is one instance of the conflict between the id and the ego. Some babies easily resolve this conflict and redirect their psychosexual energy (libido) toward other challenges. But some children have difficulty with this transition, perhaps being moved to solid food before they are ready. According to psychoanalytic theory, such children remain concerned with being mothered, and taken care of, and keeping their mouths full of desired substances. In technical terms, they are said to be fixated at the **oral stage.**

As their personality develops, individuals fixated at the oral stage remain preoccupied with issues of dependency, attachment, and "intake" of interesting substances and perhaps even interesting ideas. The fixation is the framework for their development. As adults, they may derive pleasure from biting, chewing, sucking hard candy, food, or cigarettes. They analogously derive psychological pleasure from talking, being close (perhaps too close) to others, and constantly seeking knowledge.

Anal Stage

If someone today were called an anal character type, it might be seen as an insult or as some pop psychology label. This is because the context and flavor of Freud's ideas have largely been lost. Freud used an important event of early childhood as an explanation of deep patterns that underlie later personality.

All one-year-olds in American culture use diapers but almost all three-year-olds use toilets. Sometime around age two, a child has to be toilet-trained. Although most people do not remember their own toilet training, most parents remember all too well the difficulty they faced in training their children.

The two-year-old, following the urges of the id, takes pleasure in the relief—the tension reduction—of defecating. The parents, however, want to control when and where the child urinates and defecates. In other words, the parents want society's proscription against unbridled defecation represented in the child's superego.

Some children readily learn such self-control, and this becomes a healthy aspect of their personality. Others overlearn it; they take pleasure in holding in their feces in order to maintain some control over their parents. They deliver their feces only when they are good and ready. (Some children's holding back feces becomes such a significant threat to their health that they must be given laxatives.) Still other children fight the attempts to regulate their urination and

A two-year-old who takes great pleasure in feces expulsion and becomes fixated at this stage may develop a personality pattern of creativity and open expression—letting it all hang out.

defecation, trying to maintain total freedom of action. Psychoanalytic theory sees these patterns as carrying on throughout life (A. Freud, 1981; S. Freud, 1908; Fromm, 1947).

As adults, such people who remain fixated at the **anal stage** may take great satisfaction in a large bowel movement. Psychologically, people fixated at the anal stage may like bathroom humor or making messes—including messes of other people's lives. Or they may be overly concerned with neatness, parsimony, order, and organization. That is, severe toilet training may lead to a great pleasure in control over feces that (theoretically) manifests itself in adulthood in obstinacy ("I'll go when I want") and stinginess ("I'll keep it for myself"). Although this simple mechanism has not been confirmed by empirical research, and although psychoanalysis is not the best treatment for people with obsessive-compulsive disorders, the idea that such early emotional patterns and conflicts can have enormous influence on personality development has generally been accepted.

As noted, anal retentive people (who overlearned retaining their feces) may grow up to be excessively stingy. Such people are also often passive-aggressive. For example, they may not do anything overtly nasty but attack passively, such as by giving you the silent treatment. This parallels the childhood holding in of the feces—"I didn't do anything overtly wrong, Mommy; no poopy mess."

Is focusing on toilet training the best way to understand a stingy or passive-aggressive adult? If we believe that a pattern learned successfully in childhood is reapplied in assorted versions throughout one's life, then this approach often makes sense. If, however, we maintain that a fixation

Jackson Pollock (1912–1956) claimed that the inspiration for his artwork was his unconscious. He was a pioneer of unorthodox ways of using paint, often abandoning the brush to drip or pour paint directly onto his canvas.

of libido at the anal stage is a direct physiological cause of the adult behavior patterns, then we have gone well beyond what is supported by current theory and research.

In general, attempts to link adult personality directly to breast-feeding and weaning, or to age and type of toilet training, have proved unsuccessful. In extreme circumstances, a very traumatic experience in toilet training could set a pattern that persists throughout life. But for most people, their early experiences, taken in isolation, do not have simple, direct effects on later personality. Many of the clusters of characteristics are valid however. As Freud noted, and modern research confirms, being neat, stubborn, and stingy do seem to be related characteristics;, and perhaps such patterns result from a set of pressures that some parents and some aspects of society apply to certain children (Fisher & Greenberg, 1996; Lewis, 1996).

Phallic Stage

Around age four, the child enters the **phallic stage,** in which sexual energy is focused on the genitals. Children may explore their genitals and masturbate, but open masturbation is not socially acceptable. In many families, private masturbation is also forbidden by parents, who may threaten their children with dire consequences. Children also focus now on the differences between boys and girls. By age six, most children have a good sense of their gender identity. Central to this stage of Freudian theory is the **Oedipus complex.**

Oedipus Complex

In the first decade of this century, psychoanalytic ideas developed rapidly and flourished. A particularly influential case study was that of Little Hans, the subject of Freud's "Analysis of a Phobia in a Five-Year-Old Boy" (1909/1967).

Little Hans was the son of one of Freud's friends and admirers. The boy suffered from a **phobia**—an excessive or incapacitating fear. In Hans's case it was a fear of horses. (These were the days before automobiles.) He was afraid horses would bite him, to the point that he almost became afraid of going outdoors.

Different theories explain such a phobia in different ways. Freud's explanation was in terms of unconscious sexual conflict. He noted that Hans's father had a large mustache and was a large and powerful man; likewise, horses wore a muzzle across their faces and were large and powerful. Just as symbols were important in dreams, Freud viewed horses as a symbol, in Hans's mind, of his father. But why was Hans unconsciously so afraid of his father?

Freud noted that Hans, like many little boys, was very concerned with penises—his penis, his father's penis, a horse's large penis. Hans was also concerned with those people (like his sister) without penises. Hans had been threatened for playing with his penis. Freud concluded that Hans was struggling to deal with his intense love for his mother, coupled with the knowledge

Little Hans had an excessive fear of horses, which Freud viewed as Hans's displaced fear that he would be castrated by his father.

that he could not overcome his powerful father. His horse phobia resulted from this struggle. This unconscious fear is termed **castration anxiety.** Hans feared that his father would take revenge and castrate him, thus making him like his sister.

In Greek legend, Oedipus, king of Thebes, unwittingly kills his father and marries his mother. Similar legends of patricide have occurred throughout history in many cultures. Freud was very well read in classic literature and believed such legends and stories were not mere amusements; rather, they captured the fundamentals of human nature. Freud thus took the term **Oedipus complex** to describe a boy's sexual feelings for his mother and rivalries with his father. These feelings of a young boy, and his psychological defenses against threatening thoughts and feelings, are critically important because they form the basic reaction patterns that are used throughout life; that is, they form personality.

A five-year-old boy cannot kill his father and marry his mother. To resolve the unconscious tension between fear and erotic desire, a successfully developing boy turns to identification with his father. He assumes manly characteristics and tries to be like his father. In addition to diminishing the danger of castration, this identification allows the little boy to vicariously "obtain" his mother—that is, through his father.

Penis Envy

What about girls? Freud believed that little girls become quite upset when they recognize that they do not have a penis like boys and men do. This is not an unreasonable assumption in times or places where boys are granted much higher status than girls. A little girl, wondering why she is less worthy, might look to the only observable physical difference, her lack of a penis. Note also that given Freud's elevation of sexuality as *the* shaper of personality, it makes sense that little girls would be quite concerned about their lack of easily visible genitals. According to this thinking, girls develop feelings of inferiority and jealousy, a phenomenon termed **penis envy.**

Like boys, girls first develop a sexual attachment to their mothers. However, because her mother has allowed her to be born without a penis or perhaps (she thinks) has cut off her penis, the girl transfers her love to her father, in an attempt to capture a penis. Here, Freud points to the conflicting feelings of a little girl who of course loves her mother but responds to the affections and strengths of her father. This idea would not be controversial except for the sexual undercurrents that Freud attaches to these relations. (The girl's conflict is sometimes termed the Electra complex, after the maiden in Greek mythology who convinced her brother Orestes to murder her mother Clytemnestra; but Freud did not like this term.)

Just as a boy cannot marry his mother, a girl cannot marry her father. So, in normal development, a girl decides that although she cannot have a penis, she can have a baby when she grows up, thereby becoming complete. In other words, for Freud the development of a girl's personality builds on early psychosexual feelings surrounding her genital identity. It follows that a healthy adult woman should want to find a good man like her father and produce a baby.

It is not uncommon for us to know men who seem to be seeking girlfriends who are like their mothers, or who are the exact opposite of their mothers. We also know females who are seeking boyfriends like their fathers, or the opposite of their fathers. All of these motivations are directly derivable from psychoanalytic theory. Various sorts of modern-day evidence confirm that many aspects and problems of courtship and marriage revolve around issues related to the partners' parents, though not always in the ways Freud predicted. Adults may replay unresolved conflicts from their childhoods (Snyder, Wills, & Grady-Fletcher, 1991; Sullivan & Christensen, 1998).

Latency Period

It is clear to any observer that sexual drives become a significant influence at puberty. But what about the period between resolution of the Oedipus complex (around age five) and puberty (around age eleven)? Freud did not note any important psychosexual developments during this time, and so he called it a **latency period.** During this period, because it is usually not possible for sexual urges to be directly expressed, sexual energies are channeled into such activities as going to school and making friends.

The fact that Freudian theory has little to say about the grade school years reveals a significant weakness of the whole approach. These years are the time when a child learns to make friends, to become a leader or follower, to cooperate with teachers and other authorities, and to develop study and work habits. Such matters are not easily explained in terms of unconscious motivations and sexual drives. To understand such matters, we need to understand more about the self-concept and about traits and abilities, issues that are considered in later chapters of this book.

By the way, although Freud did not know it, it turns out that this is by no means a dormant period of biological development. In the years before puberty (between ages six and eleven), the adrenal glands are maturing, and there is a growth spurt coupled with changes in adrenal-stimulated hormones. It is not unusual for there to be sexual attraction in the fourth grade, well before the individuals reach sexual maturity (McClintock & Herdt, 1996).

Genital Stage

If a person makes it through the many challenges of early childhood with enough sexual energy still available (that is, without strong fixations), then there will supposedly be a fairly well-adjusted life, dominated by the **genital stage.** In other words, Freud thought that if a person was not trapped or hung up along the way, then adolescence marks the beginning of an adult life of normal sexual relations, marriage, and child-rearing.

Freud was correct in proposing that deviant experiences in childhood can produce personal idiosyncrasies or personality problems in adulthood. Indeed, this assumption is the basis of much modern-day psychotherapy, in which the early environment is seen as setting the pattern for later life (Horowitz, 1998). It seems, however, that Freud was off track in assuming that it is childhood sexual urges that suddenly spring to life in adolescence. It is now clear that striking hormonal changes occur at puberty, and the adolescent struggles to become independent. Many conflicts occur at puberty, but they do not seem closely tied to the psychosexual development of infants and toddlers. Further, it is now much clearer that there are many issues of adult sexuality and adult behavior that must be considered on their own terms, rather than in the context of one overarching psychoanalytic psychosexual model.

In the genital stage, attention is supposed to turn away from masturbation and toward heterosexual relations. Any deviation (for example, remaining single, remaining childless, homosexuality, other sexual behaviors) is considered a flaw, unnatural. In this regard, Freud was clearly wrong. Cultural and biological research indicates that varying mating patterns, masturbation, homosexuality, and a wide variety of sexual activities are found in psychologically healthy, productive, well-adjusted people. One may have religious, moral, practical, or cultural reasons for discouraging various forms of adult sexuality, but there is no scientific or biological reason for such prejudice (Kaplan, 1983; Masters & Johnson, 1966). Freud made this mistake, and many other well-intentioned people make the same mistake today.

Freud was a physician and his theories arose from treating patients. By definition, his patients had problems or else they would not have been seeking his specialized care. Thus Freudian theory is based on a medical model of pathology, therapy, and cure. This is an odd way to construct a general psychological theory; as you might suspect, it is apt to overemphasize pathology. Indeed, this is a significant criticism of Freudian theory: it tends to focus on the deviance and the problems in human development and therefore tends to view too many behaviors and reactions as sick or inappropriate or conflict-based. There are many other important motivations and experiences that shape human personality, which are considered in later chapters of this book.

Male versus Female

With his focus on sexuality as a key force in human nature, it is not surprising that Freud's theories quite often dealt with the penis. In theorizing about women, it seemed logical to examine the implications of the absence of a penis.

Freud noted the significance of minimizing the importance of a girl's clitoris. Even in today's vastly more open societies, girls are often not taught the name for their clitoris and are rarely taught to examine it or stimulate it. A self-focus on the clitoris might diminish the importance of men to women's sexual experience, and indeed, today it is generally the most feminist women who emphasize clitoral education. Seen in this light, it is understandable that Freud would propose that the mature sexual development of a girl involves shifting pleasure-seeking to the vagina. Freud therefore postulated a "vaginal orgasm," which is psychologically and biologically superior to a "clitoral orgasm." A vaginal orgasm supposedly results from "natural" stimulation by a penis, whereas a clitoral orgasm could result from artificial stimulation.

Modern research on human sexual response by Masters and Johnson (1966) and others has not confirmed such different types of orgasms. An orgasm is an orgasm. Freud's male-centered and societally influenced speculations, as developed by his followers, have led to much distress for women, as many women have been treated by therapists for not having the "correct" vaginal orgasm. This is another example of Freud having good ideas but poor data. It makes sense (then and now) to view a mature person as one who can achieve sexual satisfaction in a deep relationship with a partner. But it does not make sense biologically to postulate that the female orgasm is different whether it results from penile-vaginal stimulation or from some direct stimulation of the clitoris. (In fact, penile stimulation of the vagina does stimulate the clitoris.)

Freud, like many others of the late-nineteenth-century Western culture, viewed men as inherently superior to women. His theories thus focused on male behavior as the norm and female behavior as a deviation.

One of Freud's arguments was that women have an unconscious desire for suffering (and receive unconscious pleasure from suffering). Freud had observed many women trapped in uncomfortable or abusive relations with men, and yet they stayed in such relations and explained to him why they preferred such relations. Freud had uncovered the extreme limits to which people will go in order to rationalize their life situation. Freud's female patients were trapped in such relations because women of the time had few opportunities for social or educational or economic attainment on their own. Freud saw such women as masochistic. Today, in an age of tremendous social changes, such women are more likely to be viewed as brainwashed, or self-defeating, or as victimized. Viewing women as victims, however, was virtually impossible for men of Freud's time because all the institutions of society—religious, political, educational, judicial, familial—saw women as subservient and subordinate to men.

In this area as in many others, Freud had achieved a basic insight whose implications were distorted by those who came later. Boys and girls do indeed show different patterns of development. As women's rights have come to be recognized, the value and importance of the "female" tendencies are increasingly appreciated. Most psychologists today, including feminist psychologists, agree that there are vast differences in the psychosocial tendencies of men and women. (These are explored in Chapter 11.) But the implications of these differences are now reversed. Women's emotionality and family orientation are now seen as healthy nurturance and cooperativeness, whereas men's toughness and independence are seen as aggressiveness and lack of relatedness.

Defense Mechanisms

The ego, governed by the reality principle, tries to deal realistically with the environment. However, sometimes we must distort reality to protect the ego against the painful or threatening impulses arising from the id. The processes that distort reality to protect the ego are called **defense mechanisms.** Some of the most interesting and influential insights from Freud's psychoanalytic approach concern defense mechanisms.

Repression

Not long ago, a retired man went on trial for murdering an eight-year-old girl. Surprisingly, the murder had taken place twenty-one years earlier. Why was the man accused only now? The new evidence was the sudden testimony of the man's twenty-nine-year-old daughter. She reported that an old memory suddenly flashed into her consciousness after more than two decades. She now recalled that when she was eight, she saw her father molest and then bludgeon to death her young classmate. According to Freud, **repression** is the ego defense mechanism that pushes threatening thoughts back into the unconscious.

Could such an important memory be repressed for twenty-one years? Can we believe that it is accurately remembered when it bursts into consciousness decades later? Could each of us be harboring such hidden memories?

George Franklin, Sr., was tried and convicted of murder on the basis of his adult daughter's testimony that she had just remembered watching him molest and kill her playmate twenty years earlier. Was this a true memory, long repressed because of the daughter's fear and horror, that rose to consciousness? (The verdict was later overturned.)

Interesting evidence along these lines is provided by what has come to be called **posttraumatic stress** (posttraumatic stress disorder or posttraumatic stress syndrome). After the Vietnam War, it was noticed that many thousands of U.S. veterans began experiencing nightmares, anxiety, sleep difficulties, and failed marriages (Jaycox & Foa, 1998). The only clue to their troubles was that some of the veterans reported daytime flashbacks to combat experiences, which they persistently tried to avoid thinking about. It seemed, as Freud postulated, that the conscious mind could not face overwhelmingly stressful and grisly memories, in this case of burned, maimed bodies and butchered children. Self-disclosure groups with other veterans and psychotherapy focused on discussing the traumatic event have often proved helpful as treatment (as Freud suggested). Note that if the veteran knows that his problems are the result of combat experience, then the defense is not repression because it is not unconscious. However, in many cases, people who have faced early traumas overcome the initial shock and seem to go on with their lives, but the hidden memories pursue and plague them. Such cases seem to validate the existence of repression.

In line with Freud's concern with repressed sexuality, another area in which repression is often discussed in today's practice of psychology is incest. Freudian theory maintains that sexual assault by one's father or mother would be so psychologically distressing that it might very well be repressed. Freud himself, however, believed that most such parent–child sexual activity was imagined rather than real (Masson, 1984). (Some feminists accuse Freud of succumbing to his sexist orientation in denying the common assaults on little girls.) These matters currently draw a lot of attention in courtrooms (Loftus & Ketcham, 1991; Crews, 1996). Grown children may sue their parents for alleged abuse that occurred many years before. Interestingly, a general population study in St. Louis found that people most likely to be suffering from post-traumatic stress disorder were men who were combat veterans and women who were the victims of physical assault (Helzer, Robins, & McEvoy, 1987).

If there is no objective evidence of abuse other than the child's formerly repressed memory, a very unfortunate legal situation results. The alleged victim, who may now be a twenty-two-year-old woman with anxiety disorders, accuses her father or her uncle or a neighbor of incest or molestation or perhaps other crimes. The defendant, presumed innocent under the law, who is perhaps a fifty-five-year-old married man, is forced to defend himself against scandalous activities that allegedly took place many years before.

By the way, in the case described of the father accused of murder that his young daughter had supposedly witnessed and repressed, he was indeed convicted of murder and sent to prison. He was, however, later released after a federal appeals court overturned the conviction. Although his daughter remains convinced of his guilt, no one knows for sure except the man himself. (These issues are considered further in this chapter's Self-Understanding box.)

To further complicate matters, well-meaning psychotherapists can sometimes plant the idea of abuse in the client's memory. For example, if a college-age women seeks therapy because she is depressed, has nightmares, and cannot relate well to men, the therapist might say, "Were you ever sexually abused as child? Such abuse, even at an early age, can produce symptoms like yours." This comment might get the client thinking that she might have been abused. She may then search her memory for evidence or clues. In the current social climate, in which many women trace their problems to early sexual abuse, the woman may convince herself that she was indeed molested. Modern research on memory clearly demonstrates that false memories can sometimes be "implanted," just as preferences for certain styles of clothing or certain political beliefs can be induced through subtle social influence. We can come to believe stories and recall experiences that in reality never happened to us (Appelbaum, Uyehara, & Elin, 1997; Loftus & Ketcham, 1991).

On the other side of the coin is the unavoidable question of the prevalence of child molestation, incest, and other forms of abuse (Herman, 1992; Koss & Harvey, 1991). When Freud began exploring the childhoods of his patients, he found that a surprising number of them seemed to be struggling with sexual conflicts, traceable to childhood molestation. This was quite shocking in the prudish times in which Freud lived, but Freud persisted with this line of exploration. Indeed, the attention he drew to the influence of sexuality on personality is one of Freud's major and lasting contributions. However, as we have noted, Freud either could not or did not want to believe that so much sexual abuse of children was occurring. So, in Freudian theory, most sexual conflict is thought to be imagined; children become fearful that their father will harm their genitals but, he contended, the danger is only in their imaginations. Modern population surveys do indicate, however, that many more people (especially women) are molested than is commonly thought.

Thus, many current issues of guilt and innocence, abuse and justice, depend on an understanding of the phenomenon that Freud termed repression. Unfortunately, there are as yet no simple answers. There is no litmus test we can use to decide if a thought that suddenly appears is a genuine long-repressed memory or a false inference resulting from suggestion or other influence processes. Only a careful analysis of the evidence in each particular case, coupled with an intelligent, state-of-the-art understanding of how the mind works, can rightfully be employed. Here is a clear example of how the study of personality psychology can prove very important for people's daily lives.

Repression has remained a key concept in many areas of psychology. In addition to its importance to understanding mental health, it seems relevant to our relations with others and to our general physical health (Emmons, 1992; Blatt, Cornell, & Eshkol, 1993).

Reaction Formation

Televangelists—religious evangelists who preach on television—can reach millions of viewers with their expressions of holiness and their urgings of people to follow religious gospel. It must be an interesting experience to talk passionately about deeply personal religious feelings in front of such a large public. What motivates such televangelists? In most cases it seems that these preachers have a sincere, overwhelming desire to help other people achieve spiritual rewards. Psychoanalytic theory, however, suggests a very different sort of explanation.

Jim Bakker was an extremely popular televangelist who seemed to epitomize righteousness and convinced millions of viewers to send him money to do the Lord's work. It eventually turned out that Bakker was engaging in a number of unethical, illegal, and immoral activities. When caught, he collapsed in tears and was eventually

Jim Bakker was an outspoken television minister who headed a multimillion-dollar religious empire and preached moral rectitude. He resigned after it was revealed that he was committing adultery with a church secretary and using ministry money to buy the woman's silence. Convicted of fraud and conspiracy in taking ministry funds for his personal use, Bakker was sentenced to a prison term and a large fine.

sent to prison. Jimmy Swaggart was another well-known televangelist of recent years who ranted and railed against sexual immorality. He resigned from his church after being photographed with a New Orleans prostitute. He too tearfully confessed and his ministry collapsed. Later in California, he was cited for three traffic violations while riding with a woman who reported being—guess what—a prostitute.

According to psychoanalytic theory, the base, inner drives of such people (the id forces) are pushing them to engage in behaviors—various sexual acts, greed, deception—that are incompatible with their religious beliefs. Their sense of self is thus severely threatened, and the self (the ego) distorts these unconscious urges and turns them into their opposites. So, instead of acting out their sexual desires, such people may instead preach vehemently against sexual "sins."

Reaction formation is the process of pushing away threatening impulses by overemphasizing the opposite in one's thoughts and actions. Reaction formation is a controversial notion because it suggests that many apparently "moral" people are really struggling desperately with their own immorality. Are some ministers acting pious because they really feel devilish and unholy? Are people who proudly refuse to serve alcohol in their homes really motivated by their own inner desires to let go and get drunk? Are gay-bashers in fact unconsciously threatened about their own possible latent homosexual impulses?

Reaction formation is a fascinating idea that has rarely been systematically evaluated by modern personality research. Occasionally, when it is studied, support does indeed emerge. For example, one study of self-identified heterosexuals compared homophobic men (those who had very negative feelings toward homosexuals) to nonhomophobic men in terms of how aroused they became when viewing very erotic videos of heterosexual and homosexual couples. Only the homophobic men showed an increase in penile erection when viewing the male homosexual stimuli (Adams, Wright, & Lohr, 1996).

Denial

When a tragedy has occurred, it is the job of certain police officers or other public servants to visit homes in their city and inform the parents that, for instance, their child has been killed in an accident or homicide. Sometimes, the response of the parent is simple: "No, that can't be. I'm on my way now to meet my child at the grocery store." The parent absolutely denies the terrible fact. Similarly, a teenage girl in the advanced stages of an unwanted pregnancy may deny, to herself and to others, that she is pregnant at all, despite all the evidence to the contrary.

Research on response to physical pain and injury reveals a similar phenomenon. For example, one workman slipped and put a screwdriver through his hand. He didn't feel any pain until he looked down at what he had done and saw the blood; then the truth gradually began to "sink in." Soldiers injured in battle or even football players injured on the field often do not feel the pain of their injury until many hours later. The mind has a means of keeping its own sensations out of conscious awareness.

Denial, simply refusing to acknowledge anxiety-provoking stimuli, is not usually seen in adults except in such conditions of severe stress or pain. However, people will sometimes distort some aspects of a situation, say, telling their friends that a terrible fight with their spouse was really just a lover's quarrel. In such instances, they lie to themselves. Like repression, denial is a mechanism that has been subject to some active attention by researchers studying stress, coping, and health (Fernandez & Turk, 1995), considered in Chapter 12.

Projection

Projection is a defense mechanism in which anxiety-arousing impulses are externalized by placing them, or projecting them, onto others. A person's inner threats are attributed to those around them.

Consider an extremist conservative politician on the rampage against people involved in premarital sex, children born out of wedlock, homosexuals, and sex education teachers in the schools, claiming, "Those subversive pinkos are wrecking our moral fabric!" Is this politician a noble and moral prophet bringing a better life to all, or a disturbed personality, hung up on sexuality and afraid of the surging id forces within? Freud was willing to apply his theories to major issues in society, such as the causes of prejudice and war.

In some ways, the true motivations of our extremist politicians (or anyone) cannot be scientifically proven. This is one of the weaknesses of this aspect of Freudian theory, and of psychoanalytic theory in general. For example, the traditional Freudian sources of "proof," namely further disclosures during psychotherapy and improvement in psychological functioning after disclosure or therapy, can easily be the result of other factors. And if the patterns continue after psychotherapy, it may be claimed that the unconscious urges are even more deeply hidden; this finding is unprovable. On the other hand, if a conservative politician shows certain behaviors, then a psychosexual dysfunction seems more likely. In the extreme, if we find that a married conservative politician who is always talking about family values turns out to have a long-time secret lover, then we may rightly wonder if that politician was struggling with his libido using reaction formation (doing the opposite of one's urges) and projection (placing one's urges onto others). This would be confirmed if the politician showed other signs of instability. Other examples are more subtle.

Consider the case of a female community activist who attends school board meetings to ensure that children are not taught about sexuality and birth control in the public schools. Because she is also strongly against abortion, she argues that sexuality and contraception are a matter for the family to discuss at home (or in church). If this is really her motivation, then this woman should be able to provide the relevant information to her children; she should be very comfortable with and knowledgeable about such matters as the erection of the penis, the lubrication of the vagina, orgasms, and so on, and sexual problems such as premature ejaculation, vaginismus, and sexually transmitted diseases like AIDS and chlamydia. This could be ascertained in private adult discussion. If the woman can intelligently discuss such matters, perhaps in the context of her religious beliefs, then a Freudian interpretation does not seem applicable. If, however, the woman turns bright red, becomes extremely hostile, or brings up irrelevant matters when basic facts about human sexuality are discussed, then a Freudian would be confident about the motivation for the woman's conservative behaviors.

An analogous kind of analysis could be applied to a liberal politician or activist who seemed especially concerned with ideas of free love or the public expression of erotic art. Freud's perspective would allow an observer to ascertain whether this is a rational and logical set of beliefs, or an irrational adaptation to uncontrolled, instinctual sexual forces. Discussion and research on defensive projection has remained a fascinating topic throughout this century, with at least some support found for Freud's views (Allport, 1954; Newman, Duff, & Baumeister, 1997; Vaillant, 1986).

Displacement

Remember that in the case of Little Hans, the boy was afraid that a horse would step on him, but in actuality he feared that his big, strong father would castrate him. This is an example of **displacement.** Displacement is the shifting of the target of one's unconscious fears or desires.

A classic example of displacement is the case of a man who, when he is humiliated by his boss, goes home and beats his children and kicks the dog. Such an example is an interesting one because there are other theoretically interesting alternative explanations. Displacing the anger to the dog implies that the unacceptable feelings of wanting to kill one's boss are released, more acceptably, on the poor canine. This is a **hydraulic displacement model** that is typical of Freudian explanations. Pressure builds up like steam in a boiler and must be released. Other, non-Freudian explanations would focus more on the situation that releases the aggressive action, or on previous learning history, or on the man's aggressiveness, or on his sense of self and sense of purpose. The explanation is important because there are different implications for preventing the aggression (Neubauer, 1994; Melburg & Tedeschi, 1989). According to the hydraulic displacement explanation, some release valve must be found for the bottled-up aggressive impulses triggered by frustration and humiliation.

Freud analyzed the Italian artist Michelangelo (1475–1564) from archival materials. Freud determined that Michelangelo was a repressed homosexual dominated by his mother, who sublimated his sexual energies into great creativity as a sculptor, painter, architect, and poet. This is Michelangelo's statue of the biblical giant-slayer David.

Sublimation

Sublimation is the transforming of dangerous urges into positive, socially acceptable motivations (Loewald, 1988). For example, anal retentive impulses based on the holding back of feces might have led to a desire to control and order the lives of everyone at home and at work. Through sublimation, these drives might be transformed to a desire to organize children's activities or to clean up the local riverfront.

Artistic endeavors are often attributed to sublimation. In a psychohistorical analysis of Leonardo da Vinci, Freud (1947) argued that his genius arose from his sublimation of sexual energies into a passion for scientific creativity and discovery. Of course, innate talent was also necessary; not everyone with sublimated sexual energies can become a Leonardo. Freud did a similar analysis of Michelangelo.

Freud viewed society as a means to turn sexual energy away from sexual ends and toward societal goals. According to this view, society fears nothing more than that sexual urges may return to their original goal—sexual fulfillment. It can be argued that modern society provides an ongoing test of Freud's theory. Since Freud's prudish time, a sexual revolution and a dramatic sexual liberation have occurred. As people become more and more sexually liberated, psychoanalysis predicts that art, creativity, and even civilization itself will suffer and eventually disintegrate.

Regression

In **regression** we return to earlier, safer stages of our lives. This defense mechanism is most easily seen in children. A recently weaned child may try to return to the bottle or breast. A threatened child beginning school may begin acting like a toddler. In particular, there may be regression to the stage at which there was previously a fixation.

In adults, regression is difficult to document. Classic examples include an anxious adult who begins whimpering like a child, looking for maternal care.

Or a distraught man may try to curl up to his wife's breast, or a stressed woman may climb into her husband's lap. The regression defense reminds us that psychoanalytic theory is a stage theory: psychosexual development proceeds along fixed, well-delineated steps.

Rationalization

Rationalization is a mechanism involving post hoc ("after the fact") logical explanations for behaviors that were actually driven by internal unconscious motives. Psychoanalysis well recognizes that the explanations we give for our behavior are not necessarily even remotely related to the true causes. Rather than admit that we moved across the country to be near a sexy lover, we may explain (not only to others, but to ourselves) that we were looking for better job opportunities or new challenges. The dangers of rationalization (leading to illogical behavior) have also been emphasized by many other approaches to personality; however, if the defense is not seen as a protection against threatening urges from the unconscious, then it is not a psychoanalytic defense mechanism.

In general, the idea of defense mechanisms has not received a lot of direct scientific study in modern, mainstream personality psychology. But some interesting empirical study of psychoanalytic defense mechanisms has been conducted in recent years on a sample of middle-aged and older men who have been followed for many years, since junior high school (Vaillant et al., 1986). Descriptions of how these men responded to challenges in their lives were converted into a defense mechanism framework. Most basically, this work suggests that defensive style is an enduring aspect of personality. The maturity of the defenses was also found to be associated with independently measured indexes of the men's psychological maturity—better overall mental health.

Cross-Cultural Issues

Freud explored the unconscious in exquisite detail, but he was relatively unconcerned with possible cultural variations. Although he was very interested in applying psychoanalysis to understanding culture, he believed the same basic psychodynamic forces underlay all cultures, in particular, the dynamics surrounding the Oedipus complex. In his book *Totem and Taboo,* Freud (1952) traced the origin of civilization to the time when brothers came together and murdered the primal father of the tribe, co-opting his power and his wives. Freud thought that this would leave traces in all civilizations in the form of cultural taboos, such as the taboo against incest. Similarly, religion was seen as arising from psychodynamic forces; he did not consider that religion may have created certain psychodynamic forces.

Freud also engaged in psychobiography; in fact, Freud and his colleagues founded this field of inquiry. When he turned his attention to Leonardo da Vinci, Freud analyzed him from archival materials as a repressed homosexual who was dominated by his mother and who sublimated his sexual energies. And again, Freud proceeded to assume that the phenomena he had uncovered were universal. The psychoanalytic principles derived in nineteenth-century Austria could be directly applied to understanding the life of a man in fifteenth-century Italy. In this climate, cultural anthropologists of the first half of the twentieth century became intrigued with the idea that variations in child-rearing practices across cultures would produce systematic variations in personality—that is, that each society produces a basic personality type (Linton, 1945). For example, if the society allowed a much greater degree of sexual play among children (than Freud's strict Victorian Europe), the children should grow up with systematically different personalities.

It is known that Germans have stricter child-punishing habits than Americans. Can we therefore infer that the outcome is an inherently rigid German personality (Rippl & Boehnke, 1995)? Analogously, are Americans innovative scientists (winning many Nobel prizes) because they are raised in a more liberal, child-centered society and grow up with an independent personality? Do Japanese schools, with their emphasis on uniformity, produce adults with a personality suited to cooperative work in large impersonal conglomerates?

Although such generalization may at first appear clever, there is a serious logical error in drawing such conclusions. Why attribute such adult behaviors to a culturally induced personality when the culture itself serves as an obvious explanation? Germans drink a lot of beer, but there is no reason to postulate a German beer-drinking personality; they simply live in a culture in which drinking beer is popular. Would we say that Jews have a bagel-and-lox–prone personality? Or that Italians have a pasta-prone personality? It makes much more sense to say that people in a certain culture learn common behaviors from their families and friends. These behaviors are not a result of their personalities; if they moved to a new place with new friends, their behaviors would change. Habits are not personality. Personality should rightfully refer to individual variations within a culture.

Nevertheless, in order to test such notions of personality and culture, anthropologists turned to projective tests like the Rorschach. They reasoned that such tests (which used inkblot pictures and so were not language-specific) would be applicable (valid) in all cultures. Unfortunately, these cross-cultural studies were plagued by serious methodological flaws and false assumptions (Lindzey, 1961). Most basically, the search for basic, deep-seated personality traits that characterized a culture, using projective measures, was inherently biased. Researchers had preconceived notions of the expected cultural personality, used measures that had not been adapted for and validated in different cultures, and often did not select truly representative samples of people to study. Furthermore, if projective clinical measures of psychopathology are used in cross-cultural research, the whole foreign culture may wind up (and sometimes did wind up) labeled as pathological.

This is not to say that certain personality patterns are not more common in certain cultures; however, it does mean that such patterns have not yet been well documented. With newer research techniques that are more sensitive to the unique features of each culture, the prospects for viable cross-cultural research on personality are great (Segall, Dasen, Berry, & Poortinga, 1990).

Major Contributions and Limitations of Freudian Psychoanalysis

Before the twentieth century, before the work of Sigmund Freud, there was no personality psychology. Certainly there were explanations for individual differences. Major theologians saw human behavior as determined by divine influence, by an all-powerful God who controlled or inspired everything. More earthly theologies blamed individual frailties on the devil. Mechanical medical models saw people as influenced by internal fluids. But there was no *psychology* of human personality and behavior until Freud, following Darwin's example, asked about the reasons for—the functions of—the human mind. And there was no psychotherapy.

Freud further revolutionized psychology with his emphasis on sexuality as a prime element of personality. Ask any young man or woman with bubbling hormones whether sexuality is a significant influence on their behavior—whether they care about getting dates—and you will hear no dispute. Freud's breakthrough was to extend this idea of dynamic motivation to children—the idea of infantile sexuality—and to generalize it to a pervasive motivational force.

Freud thus stressed the importance of early childhood experiences on adult personality. This assumption has been almost completely accepted in scientific circles as well as popular culture. There are few who now doubt that neglectful or abusive treatment of young children—especially sexual abuse—can produce devastating impacts throughout their lives. Freud also argued that the essence of personality was formed by age five. This idea too has been widely accepted. The importance of the early years to later life is little challenged, although Freud's developmental approach has been extended throughout the life-span by others.

Because people are not generally aware of their inner drives and conflicts, Freud was led to explore and develop another influential contribution—the idea of the *unconscious*. The reality of Freudian slips and the potential of dream analysis are widely accepted. This in turn led to the exploration of different structures of the mind. Freud also showed that mental illness was on a continuum with physical illness and could be approached in a scientific manner. Anyone who seeks psychological counseling owes a debt to Freud. Modern brain research and cognitive psychology confirm many of Freud's observations but disconfirm his postulated structures, which were based on a primitive understanding of the brain.

Because it views behavior as a function of inner conflicts, the psychoanalytic approach is a pessimistic and deterministic view of personality. It is also oriented toward understanding pathology. (See the Famous Personalities box on pages 88 and 89.) To counteract these emphases, many theorists originally trained in psychoanalysis have moved to existential and humanistic approaches; these are explained in Chapter 9. Freud's reliance on a hydraulic model of psychic energy was also exaggerated. Modern researchers give more attention to brain structure and cognitive approaches.

Psychoanalytic approaches to personality are generally difficult to evaluate as scientific theories. They often are not disconfirmable because there is always another postulated hidden mechanism ready to explain any observations. Controlled studies are rarely employed. This is unfortunate because their absence causes many modern researchers to ignore the many insights Freud provided. Throughout this book, we try to point out the value and the weaknesses of each approach to personality. Psychoanalytic theory may be flawed but it is hardly useless.

Some modern psychoanalysts revere Freud almost as the author of a bible; psychoanalysis has some faddish, unscientific aspects, and many "adherents." Is it fair to blame Freud for his followers' quirks? When Freud set out to study personality and the unconscious, he saw his work as a temporary approximation of how the brain worked. But in some cases, psychoanalytic theory was interpreted as a theory of the physical structure of the brain, with disastrous results. **Psychosurgery**—operating on the brain in an attempt to repair personality problems—has a long and disgusting history. In the 1940s, the prefrontal lobotomy was the technique of choice. The surgeons would drill holes into the skull, insert a dull knife, and slice the brain lobes until the patient (who was under only local anesthesia) seemed totally disoriented. The purpose of the surgery was to cut the nerve connections between the higher centers of the brain and the lower "seats" of animal instincts (such as the thalamus), consistent with psychoanalytic theory. If the patient survived the operation as more than a vegetable, he or she often did indeed act less abusively and aggressively than before the surgery. Of course there are other explanations than those that involve literally cutting unconscious drives.

Freud was trained as a neurologist and a biological scientist. We could speculate that if he were alive today, he would be a neuroscientist. So, in many ways it is unfair to dismiss vast aspects of Freud's work because some of his assumptions have proved to be wrong. On the other hand, Freud liked being the center of attention and did not take kindly to criticism. His position as the founder and undisputed master of the psychoanalytic approach encouraged much of the unscientific meandering that has been launched in his name.

Freud postulated fundamental, psychoanalytically based differences between men and women, an issue we return to throughout this book. Because little girls do not pass through the Oedipus complex, Freud asserted that they do not develop a strong moral character; this radical idea has of course been thoroughly discredited. On the contrary, most women do develop a strong sense of guilt, are usually the caretakers of the weak, are empathic, and have a high concern with justice (Block, 1984; Eagley, 1987; Friedan, 1963; Hall, 1990; Tangney et al., 1996; Tangney & Fischer, 1995).

Finally, a key criticism of psychoanalysis is that Freud was relatively unconcerned with interpersonal relations or with the individual's identity and adaptation throughout life. These issues were taken up later by the neo-analysts and the ego psychoanalysts; they are considered in Chapter 4.

Famous
Personalities

Lorena Bobbitt

It was just another day in the life of Lorena Bobbitt. Her husband, John Wayne Bobbitt, came home late and made crude sexual advances toward her. This time, she denied him because he was drunk. But, despite her refusal, he overpowered her 5' 2" frame and raped her. At 4 A.M., Lorena took the kitchen carving knife to her slumbering husband's penis and dismembered him. She then put the penis, with ice, into a zip-lock bag and held it as she drove around the city. Finally, she discarded it from the window of her car and continued driving, toward the house of a friend.

Lorena was a twenty-four-year-old manicurist who, until that night, appeared to live an average and uneventful life.

What could have triggered her to commit such an aggressive act? According to Lorena's later accounts, John had abused her emotionally, physically, and sexually throughout their marriage. She was sometimes beaten, forced to have anal intercourse, and even coerced into having an abortion. Another complaint was that he never, ever waited for her to come to orgasm. But if this had

been going on for four years, what was different about this particular night?

Lorena said that after she was assaulted that evening, she began to have flashbacks about all the other times her husband had terrorized her. She said that she then lost her grip on reality and was not in control at the time she attacked her husband. Twenty-six-year-old John denied abusing his wife, although he did admit to having extramarital affairs. Was Lorena simply getting revenge for his unfaithfulness and making sure that he would never be able to cheat on her again? What might Freud have to say about all of this if he were alive?

According to psychoanalytic theory, there was more going on here than meets the eye: Lorena's behavior was likely attributable to unconscious motives influenced by her internal sexual conflicts. Lorena was not necessarily a total victim because, the Freudians argue, many women have an unconscious desire for suffering (as evidenced by the many battered women who stay in abusive relationships). A more likely explanation is that the

Modern Developments from Experimental Psychology

For many years, mainstream experimental psychology ignored or even actively ridiculed the ideas that were fundamental to a Freudian approach. Particularly during the decades when **behaviorism** dominated the entire realm of experimental psychology (from the 1920s through the 1950s), any consideration of the role of unconscious influences was strictly excluded. Behaviorist approaches explicitly limited allowable data to those actions that were externally observable, and limited allowable theories to those that related observable aspects of an organism's environment to observable aspects of that organ-

problem was Lorena's inability to control her id, which was seeking to relieve her libidinal tensions.

In simple terms, Lorena was suffering from penis envy, which most girls suffer but few act on directly. If Lorena had been able to give birth to her baby, this may have been avoided. Giving birth is one of the ways in which the ego tries to satisfy the female desire for feelings of strength and self-worth that men have by virtue of their male anatomy. Instead, she was compelled by her husband to abort her child, and perhaps therefore she was still seeking to recapture the penis that was denied her at birth. These feelings of desire help to explain why she carefully preserved the organ in a zip-lock bag with ice—it was valuable to her.

What is highly unusual in this case is that Lorena actually acted directly on her concerns about her man's penis. According to Freudian theory, such conflicts are unconscious and so usually show up in other ways.

Lorena claimed that she "just wanted him to disappear," and it is interesting that her way of removing him from her life was to remove his penis, causing him to be, in a Freudian view, a worthless and inferior man. The vengeful blow also indirectly enabled her to obtain a penis of her own.

Lorena was tried but acquitted because her impulses were believed to be irresistible. The jury found that she couldn't have prevented herself from doing this act. So in a sense, modern society accepts the idea of overpowering unconscious motivation. Freud might have said that Lorena's ego and superego both failed to control her inner drives, and her id won in its battle for what it wanted most. In fact, Freudian theory has been the subject of many hot disputes about legal theory. In the eyes of the law, if we are sometimes controlled by our ids, how can we be held responsible for our actions?

The Bobbitt case is a good example on which to launch a discussion of the strengths and weaknesses of Freud's theories. On the one hand, it is virtually impossible ever to uncover Lorena's true motivations in a straightforward scientific manner. On the other hand, the tremendous fascination with this case around the world hints that something very basic to human behavior—some deep dark secret—has been tapped, just as the doctor from Vienna would have predicted.

ism's behavior. This approach left no legitimate place for the consideration of unconscious processes or unconscious motivation and emotion, nor for the exploration of the contents of people's dreams and memories (which by their very nature preclude direct observation). In fact, the behaviorists even excluded consideration of those ideas, memories, and processes that subjects were consciously aware of, viewing conscious and unconscious aspects of "the mind" as equally unfitting material for scientific study.

Note that the psychoanalytic movement, outside mainstream psychology, has always had its own professional journals and scientific societies. But this work often proceeded down its own path, divorced from most academic departments of psychology. For example, psychoanalytic work rarely appears in mainstream psychology journals like the *Journal of Personality and Social Psychology.*

In more recent decades, though, as behaviorism ceded its position to alternative approaches to studying human behavior, many of Freud's ideas resurfaced in more mainstream (nonpsychoanalytic) psychology, though somewhat transformed. For instance, Freud's ideas were tremendously influential in shaping humanistic approaches to personality; these matters are considered in detail in Chapter 9. Freud's impact has also resurfaced in modern cognitive psychology (Cohen & Schooler, 1997).

As human cognition developed into a strong and rigorous area of study, researchers from within this domain came upon their own need to consider unconscious processes. Despite the fact that the methodologies, approaches, and goals of cognitive psychology are vastly different from those of psychoanalysis, the cognitivists have found themselves looking at many of the same aspects of human behavior that interested Freud. This interest in unconscious processes was not novel within experimental psychology; it was rather a rediscovery of a domain that had been off-limits for years, but that had been of interest before being banished by behaviorism. In the very early years of psychology's development, even the most rigorous experimentalists saw the need to posit internal processes that occurred outside the scope of awareness. For example, Hermann von Helmholz, a nineteenth-century pioneer in the study of human perception, claimed that visual perception required unconscious inferences to be made (1866/1925).

Consider the following example of unconscious sensation. Most people do not fall out of bed each night. Yet in a state of deep sleep, you wouldn't know if someone slipped into your room, looked at you, and walked out. We keep ourselves in bed, but we are unaware of surrounding events. Further, in the morning, we do not remember the times that we almost fell out of bed but caught ourselves in time. This simple example suggests that some sensory systems are constantly at work, even when we are not aware of them. On the other hand, someone hospitalized in a coma or on drugs may indeed fall out of bed; hospital beds have guard rails to prevent such accidents. Thus there must be different types of being unaware or "unconscious." Modern research has followed up on many of Freud's ideas about unconscious processes, although not always in the ways he expected.

Unconscious Emotion and Motivation

Is there any evidence that part of the mind, full of emotional forces, exists outside consciousness? The idea of unconscious motivation is clearly supported by research on emotion, which indicates that emotional-motivational states such as anger can exist independently of thought. Some of this research relies on brain studies that reveal distinct neurological systems (Panksepp, 1991). In other words, through the course of evolution, nerve circuits have developed in the human brain that are relatively independent of higher cortical functions involving thinking. These circuits can fire even if not triggered by a higher level (cortical) thought.

Other research on certain emotions reveals that they are innate, universal, neuronally tied to facial expressions, and able to be induced independently of thought (cognition). All of this research is consistent with the Freudian notion that we can experience internal arousal that we do not cognitively understand or appreciate. Freud could not have known the precise biological structures that comprise the brain, but many of his guesses were on the mark (Izard, 1992).

Hypermnesia

When sitting and talking with a childhood friend, we described an experience we enjoyed together long ago—making ice cream sundaes. Suddenly, our friend's memories came flooding back, as she recalled various related experiences that she had not remembered in thirty years. **Hypermnesia** (literally, "excess memory") refers to a situation in which a later attempt to remember something yields information that was not reportable on an earlier attempt to remember. A central phenomenon in the psychoanalytic literature, hypermnesia also has its counterpart in the modern-day cognitive research psychology literature (e.g., Madigan & O'Hara, 1992).

In general, human memory tends to fade over time; as the original event becomes more distant, less is remembered about it. Thus, the characteristic finding in memory experiments is that people show the best memory for an event when they are questioned immediately following its occurrence, and that their memory declines (at first rapidly, and then more slowly) as time passes. A traditional explanation from stimulus–response psychology ("learning theory") is that the memory or association extinguishes or disappears over time; it is eroded away. That, however, is not the whole story of human remembering. Many factors other than the simple passage of time have now been shown to be important determinants of what can be reported.

In psychoanalysis, free association is used as a key method of uncovering memories that are initially not accessible to the patient's consciousness. After years in analysis, people often do report previously "forgotten" (unreported) material: traumatic events from their childhoods or evil wishes and terrifying thoughts from their pasts. These recovered memories are viewed within psychoanalysis as the fruit of the joint efforts of patient and therapist to overcome the defense mechanisms that initially succeeded in keeping the memories repressed. There are two basic questions that a skeptic (or a modern-day cognitive psychologist) would ask: First, are these memories veridical; that is, did these past events, wishes, and thoughts that the patient now reports really occur? Second, did these memories just now rise to consciousness, having earlier been inaccessible, or is it rather that the analyst and the analytic environment help to evoke the report of the memories? (See the box on page 93.)

In psychoanalysis, the difficult task of verifying childhood memories is usually not even attempted. But, from the perspective of understanding human memory, it is a critically important issue. In everyday life, people often report vivid memories that turn out to be inaccurate in light of objective factual information. For example, an eyewitness to a crime is certain she recognizes a suspect, who later turns out to have been out of the country; a student reports a vivid memory of being in Spanish class when he heard about the explosion of the *Challenger* shuttle, but his transcript shows that he didn't take Spanish that year; and so on (Harsch & Neisser, 1989).

There are many sources of inaccuracy and distortion in memory, all of which can independently influence both what is initially encoded from an experience and what is later retrieved from memory about it. A subjective feeling of certainty is not always correlated with the real accuracy of what is remembered. Psychoanalytic technique is presented as a method of uncovering the repressed memories that are interfering with good psychological health, but if the material that comes out of the therapy is not accurate (in the sense of at least being what the person originally experienced, if not what objectively occurred), then this whole line of argument crumbles. Serious scientific exploration of this issue is only just beginning (Conway, 1996; Pezdek & Banks, 1996). The matter is still poorly understood.

The second critical question—whether the information is newly remembered versus newly reported—is one that has been explored in the memory experiment. One robust finding is that different methods of probing a subject's memory for an event yield different amounts of information recalled (Baddeley, 1990). For example, suppose two groups of subjects study a word list. Subjects in one group are then given blank sheets of paper and asked to write down as many words from the list as they can remember (a procedure known as **free recall**). The other group is given pairs of words and asked which word from each pair appeared on the list (a procedure called *forced-choice recognition*). Not

Self-Understanding

Repressed Memories of Sexual Abuse?

In 1993, Joseph Cardinal Bernardin of Chicago was publicly scandalized when he was accused by a man named Steven Cook of sexually molesting Cook seventeen years earlier. The Catholic priest heatedly denied the charges, but Cook claimed to have remembered the molestation after reportedly being treated by a hypnotherapist. Later, after further psychological and legal investigation, Cook recanted and admitted he was mistaken to accuse the cardinal. He had misremembered. In many such cases, it may be that the therapist, wittingly or unwittingly, is the source of the "memories."

About the same time, television comedian Roseanne Barr was in the news claiming that she had been sexually molested by her father; her parents vigorously denied the charges. Similar cases have appeared involving thousands of people (usually women). A woman who is currently having psychological or sexual problems seeks psychotherapy. During therapy, the problems are traced to childhood sexual abuse, the memory of which has been repressed. Should these accusations be believed? Are the memories accurate? How can one evaluate one's old "memories"?

There is no simple answer to this question because two established phenomena are in conflict. Ironically, both of these phenomena were a focus of Freud's work. First, it is known that memories can indeed be separated from painful feelings in the mind. A traumatic experience can produce emotional distress such as sleeplessness, nightmares, anxieties, while the conscious mind refuses to think about the horrific image. Second, it is known that people are suggestible; they can distort their memories and can be influenced by their therapists. Often, memory cannot be trusted.

Complex childhood memories are generally not eidetic—they are not like photographs. A child who was repeatedly molested between the ages of three and five would, as an adult, have memories that were influenced by all the subsequent events in her life. Thus we should be suspicious when a distressed adult suddenly begins blaming all her problems on her early childhood, without confirming evidence. Clear memories of such an ongoing molestation are unlikely to reappear suddenly out of the deepest unconscious. An innocent person, even a cardinal, could be smeared. On the other hand, an alarming number of children are indeed molested.

A memory of a single, shocking scene, however, may indeed be repressed in a form that can be almost wholly retrieved. Someone, child or adult, witnessing a bloody murder, or a mutilation, or even an extremely embarrassing social misstep, might carry that memory for many years.

The late Joseph Cardinal Bernardin was accused of sexual abuse in a "recovered memory" case. The accuser later withdrew his accusations, disclaiming the memories.

surprisingly, subjects' reports are more accurate in the forced-choice condition; it is easier to correctly select the studied word from a presented pair than it is to generate it without any external cues. Does this mean that the strength or accuracy of the underlying memories differed between the groups? Given that the groups were not differentiated until the time of testing, it can only be the method of testing that causes the apparent difference in memory. The availability or accessibility of a memory can be increased by providing appropriate cues, hints, and probes (Tulving, 1968). In the psychoanalytic setting, directed questioning by the therapist or talking about events related to the previously unavailable memory may allow or prompt its retrieval. In this way, cognitive psychology has validated this aspect of psychoanalytic remembering.

Especially relevant to skepticism about the power of psychoanalytic technique is another finding in human memory—that the likelihood of reporting a memory varies not only with the availability or strength of the memory itself, but also with the rewards and penalties of accurate and inaccurate report. These influences have been extensively studied under the concept of what is called **signal detection theory** (Swets, 1996; Commons, Nevin, & Davison, 1991). Consider again controlled studies of word-list learning. We can probe memory by presenting words to a subject one at a time; for each word, the subject must say yes if it was on the list and no if it was not. Words that actually were on the list can either be hits (subject says yes on correctly detecting a studied word) or misses (subject incorrectly says no to a studied word). Words that were not on the list can either be correct rejections (subject says no to a nonstudied word) or false alarms (subject incorrectly says yes to a nonstudied word). A subject's apparent level of memory in this task turns out to be sensitive to the reward and penalty structure of the task. If subjects are highly rewarded for hits, with small penalties for misses and false alarms, and small rewards for correct rejections, they will say yes to more items. If the false-alarm penalty is high (relative to the consequences of the other three possible outcomes), they will say no to more items. When there is any uncertainty about remembering an item, subjects will "guess" in accordance with the payoff matrix: more false alarms accompany a higher level of hits, and more correct rejections are accompanied by more misses.

What are the implications for psychoanalysis? Patients in psychotherapy who are trying to retrieve significant memories can be viewed as being in this signal detection situation. For each thought that comes to mind, they have to decide (not necessarily consciously) whether or not to report it. The psychoanalytic situation can be seen as one with a high reward for hits (both the patient and the therapist can see "progress"), with little penalty for false alarms (false memories can be just as good "material" for therapy as true ones), big penalty for misses (the true memories are not explored), and little reward for correct rejections. Under these circumstances, patients are likely to be less critical in distinguishing memory from confabulation. The errors in reported memory that result are a significant weakness of psychoanalysis.

Can hypnosis help? Should police interrogators use hypnotists to help elicit long-repressed memories of criminal molestation? Early in his development of psychoanalysis, Freud and his colleague Josef Breuer used hypnosis—intensive suggestion by the therapist—to attempt to access hidden memories in their patients. In modern experimental psychology research, this would be termed *hypnotic hypermnesia* (Kihlstrom, 1998). Lab experiments demonstrate that hypnotic hypermnesia does sometimes appear—hypnosis is sometimes effective—but it is not any more effective than other memory-enhancing effects such as using relevant cues to elicit the memory. In fact, hypnosis seems somewhat less effective (Kihlstrom & Barnhardt, 1993); in other words, experimental research supports the superiority of free association and related exploratory and cueing processes over hypnosis. Freud was correct in abandoning hypnosis early in the development of psychoanalysis.

Infantile Amnesia

According to Freud, most human motivation arises from desires in early childhood that are unacceptable in adult society, such as a boy's desire for intimate relations with his mother. We have seen that adult neuroses are viewed as the result of repressed internal conflicts. In support of this idea, Freud insightfully noted that most adults cannot remember much from their early years, although they can remember quite a bit from their elementary school years—a phenomenon termed **infantile amnesia.** This observation that adults do not remember much of what happened to them before age three or four has been confirmed in a number of studies (Pillemer & White, 1989). Yet young children certainly do a tremendous amount of learning during these years, and they seem to have good memories at the time. A three-year-old can do a remarkable job of describing last week's visit to the zoo. Are these memories later repressed?

As with much of Freud's work, the phenomenon is accepted but the explanation has changed. One problem with Freud's idea is that his theory explains only why threatening early memories are forgotten, but practically all early memories are forgotten, not merely the traumatic ones. So recent attention has been focused more on the cognitive structure of memory. Perhaps young children have a brain that is too immature and disorganized for long-term memory. But research indicates that even young children have at least some well-organized memories that are similar to those of adults (Nelson, 1993). Instead, it may be the case that young children have not yet developed the ability to think about their own history nor the ability to share their memories with others in conventional ways. For example, older children may talk about how lucky they were to go on a favorite vacation and thus practice (rehearse) the memory and incorporate it into an idea of how they think about themselves (Nelson, 1993). Then the event is much easier to remember. However, this explanation of infantile amnesia has not been proven or even much explored. Note also that it is linked to the idea of forming an identity, which is precisely what Freud asserted. All in all, the reasons why we forget our earliest and most important years are still largely a mystery. Yet here again, Freud was asking a significant question.

Subliminal Perception

Want to improve your self-esteem, lose weight and develop a sexy body, perform better in sports, without wasting time or effort? Want to learn these things while you sleep? Millions of dollars are spent by consumers each year on so-called subliminal audiotapes that promise miraculously to affect your unconscious motivations (while you sleep, read, or watch TV). Do these techniques work? Can they possibly have any scientific validity?

These subliminal perception techniques may sound plausible to lay people who have heard a little Freudian theory. Most people believe that things go on in their minds outside their conscious awareness, so it seems sensible to try to alter these unconscious forces. Are subliminal tapes the way to do this?

Gustav Fechner, the founder of the field of psychophysics, believed that the human perceptual apparatus was constituted in such a way that very weak stimuli could indeed be perceived and processed without conscious awareness of any stimulus having even occurred—that is, that **subliminal perception** could and did occur. Subsequent research confirms that we are sometimes not consciously aware of stimuli that are nevertheless being processed by some parts of our brains (Reder & Gordon, 1997). But this phenomenon is quite different from what the hawkers of subliminal learning tapes would like us to believe.

There are two serious flaws in the subliminal learning technique. The first and most substantial problem is that many of the tapes contain messages that simply cannot be perceived by humans. The messages are too soft or too fast or otherwise imperceptible. Experiments have indicated that they cannot be distinguished from random noise. In fact, some of these expensive tapes contain only random noise! If the messages cannot make their way into our brains, they certainly cannot have any influence on us (Moore & Merikle, 1991).

The second flaw with subliminal learning concerns the strength or power of such influence. Let's assume that some of these messages are actually heard. For example, let's say a motivational audiotape was audible, and all day long it softly played the reminder, "You will stick to your diet. You will stick to your diet." Most people on a weight-loss diet really are trying to stick to their diets in the first place, but they find it very difficult to do so. Why should a boring audiotape succeed when many other, more powerful sources of motivation (like comments from a lover) fail? In brief, the audiotape will not succeed.

People also sometimes worry that advertisers are influencing them through subconscious messages embedded in movies, TV shows, or records.

Can a Machiavellian movie producer convince you to vote for his candidate for president by inserting into his movie a frame of the smiling candidate? Here again, if it's not perceptible, it's not effective. And if it is perceptible, its influence is probably minimal. Ironically, people worry less about the barrage of explicit, conscious advertising that really *is* influencing them! People also worry little about movies or television docudramas that distort history in a conscious attempt to manipulate the audience. In reality, these are the more dangerous threats.

Note that so-called subliminal audiotapes are different from other sorts of subtle influence. For example, let us say that we turn past an ad for Calvin's blue jeans while reading the morning paper; and the TV in the next room is airing a Calvin's commercial; and we drive past a billboard with a Calvin's ad on the way to school. We may not consciously pay any attention to these ads. If asked whether we saw a Calvin's ad, we might say, "Not that I recall." But such ads may indeed have a cumulative effect on us. Note though that this type of subtle influence is far from subliminal. The ad, the commercial, the billboard are certainly there to see if we choose to look at them.

Subliminal perception should be distinguished from phenomena involving the direction of attention. It is well established that our awareness is affected by where we direct our attention, both internally and externally. For example, people with anxiety disorders often attend excessively to their bodily sensations (such as pains or spasms), looking for signs that they are ill. They then feel greater pain. Such anxious people may also search the external environment for threats. For example, one study employed a dichotic listening task in which people wear earphones and are asked to repeat (attend to) the words presented in one ear (Mathews & MacLeod, 1986). In the other, unattended ear, the researchers presented threat words like "emergency." It was found that people with anxiety disorders (but not normal control subjects) had problems with the prescribed ongoing task when the threat words were presented, even though they did not report hearing the threat words. Note that in such cases, the threatening stimuli are out of conscious awareness because one's attention has been directed elsewhere, but the threatening stimuli are not inaccessible to consciousness. That is, if they switched attention to the other ear, the participants would clearly hear the threatening words.

Memory

The direct study of human memory provides many a good example of how cognitive descriptions intersect with psychoanalytic ones. The verbal learning approach—learning word lists—generated thousands of published experiments about how subjects' later memory for the studied words is affected by the ways in which the materials are presented. That research focused primarily on the importance of such variables as the rate at which the list was presented, the number of words on the list, how long each word was, the relationship among the words on the list, how many other lists were studied before or after that list, how much time elapsed between studying a list and being tested on it, and the ways in which word memory was tested.

Two phenomena repeatedly noticed in this research are relevant to a cognitive reinterpretation of Freudian ideas. First, what is remembered about an event is not identical to the event itself, but rather is a personalized, interpreted, internalized representation of that event. Two people who are exposed to what is overtly the same event will not necessarily have identical memories of that event. Instead, every person experiences every event from a unique, individual perspective that depends on that person's needs, goals, assumptions, and other experiences, both at the moment the event is experienced as well as before the event occurred. Even for an event as seemingly trivial and unambiguous as the presentation of an ordinary, familiar word, variability in individual experience still occurs. Individual subjects will differ in the particular items they remember correctly and in the errors they make on items that are not remembered correctly.

The more complex the original information is, the more variability there will be in what is remembered. A complex story engenders more varied recollections than does a simple word list. In other words, memory is an integration or blend of information about the actual event and a person's expectations and beliefs (Bartlett, 1932; Owens, Bower, & Black, 1979). Such findings verify Freud's notions that extraneous factors distort memories, but the emphasis in modern research is more on the complex structures of the mind and less on defenses against unwanted thoughts.

Second, even this individualized memory is not one single, crystallized entity that must be either present or absent in the person who experienced the event, but rather it is a complex, multifaceted, constantly changing representation. What is reported about the event (even whether anything at all is reported) varies tremendously with the circumstances under which that memory is probed. Empirical findings repeatedly indicate that memories that can be shown by various means to "be there" might not be reported by a subject who is questioned at a different time or by a different method. In modern jargon, a memory might be available but not always accessible. For example, we have noted that retrieval cues—something associated with the memory—are tremendously helpful to recall.

These findings are relevant to a Freudian view because they exemplify a methodologically rigorous approach to aspects of consciousness and the unconscious that are central to Freud's work. In psychoanalysis, the therapist will encourage repeated attempts to remember important early memories, to remember the context of the events (such as the house where they occurred), the people who were involved, and the feelings that were present. All of these strategies are consistent with what modern research shows is helpful in re-membering (e.g., Williams & Hollan, 1982). Most people going through such therapy report achieving a clearer understanding of important influences in their lives that they had never considered before. All of this is consistent with Freud's basic point that a great deal of what constitutes personality lies be-neath the surface of conscious awareness.

Although the cognitive psychology literature uses somewhat different terminology, many other of Freud's notions about the existence and impor-tance of the unconscious are mirrored in modern cognitive approaches. For example, experiments have been able to demonstrate remembering without awareness. We typically think of memory as **explicit memory**—we can recall or recognize something. But there is also **implicit memory**—we might change how we think or behave as a result of some experience that we do not consciously recall (Schacter, 1987). Normal people can "forget" (that is, can fail to show evidence of any explicit memory for) a prior experience like solv-ing a puzzle or learning a new motor skill, but at the same time they show in their skill at actually performing the task that they have practiced it before. In other words, the person being studied cannot consciously remember some event that the experimenter knows has occurred because it happened within the setting of the experiment, and that the subject was clearly conscious of at the time it occurred. But at a later time, although the subject cannot con-sciously remember having had that experience, he or she still performs the task better than a novice presented the task for the first time. This dissociation between explicit and implicit memory demonstrates that experiences that are not consciously remembered can still influence our behavior.

This phenomenon of implicit memory is usually now interpreted within a strictly cognitive (non-Freudian) perspective. The cognitivists tend to see it as evidence that the representational code in which skills tend to be encoded in the brain is not necessarily compatible with verbal reporting. The represen-tation of the skill itself can be present in memory (in a procedural format not available to consciousness), even in the absence of conscious memory for the event during which the skill was acquired. In cognitive terminology, **proce-dural memory** (memory for how to do a task) is separate from **declarative memory** (memory for facts about a task or event), and either may exist with-out the other (Schacter, 1987). If you have ever found yourself saying "I used to know how to do that" (about playing a game, tying a knot, riding a unicy-cle, playing a musical instrument), you have implicitly expressed that your de-clarative knowledge about some experiences has survived, despite the fading of the relevant procedural knowledge. Conversely, if you have ever found yourself saying about some skill-based activity, "I can't tell you how I do it, but I can show you," you are claiming that some skill is represented in your mem-ory in a format that is not compatible with overt verbal description.

Amnesia

Related interesting cognitive research on the entire phenomenon of memory without awareness has focused not on ordinary people but on patients with a form of amnesia in which no new conscious memories can be successfully re- trieved even minutes after an experience has occurred. You could have a long conversation with such a person, then leave the room and return five minutes later—and the amnesic will claim never to have seen you before! What is fas- cinating about these patients, though, is that they can learn new skills. For example, one such "anterograde amnesic" patient was given repeated practice over many days in solving a complex maze. Over time, his skill at tracing out the correct path through the maze improved, just as it would in a person with normal memory. What is interesting is that even as he became extremely pro- ficient in performing the task, he claimed each day that he had never before so much as seen the maze (Milner, 1962). His performance clearly showed the influence of experiences for which he had no reportable memory.

Memory research on such amnesic patients focuses on exposing them to many categories of experiences (such as learning new motor skills, hearing new songs, seeing new events, meeting new people, exploring new physical envi- ronments, reading new facts, and the like), and looking for principles that dif- ferentiate the kinds of experiences that can be reported as "remembered" from the kinds of experiences that influence performance even though they are not "remembered." In this research, one prominent finding has been that the abil- ity to report experiences as consciously remembered does not coincide with the extent to which those "forgotten" experiences influence behavior (Warrington & Weiskrantz, 1978; Graf, Mandler, & Squire, 1984). That is, there is strong ev- idence for a dissociation between the conscious memories of amnesic patients and those events that have actually influenced them. To the extent that this finding is applicable beyond the clinical population, it implies that many expe- riences that influence our ongoing psychological lives are not readily available to consciousness, just as Freud suggested.

One other major goal in pursuing research on amnesia has been a better understanding of normal memory. If detailed examination of many memory- impaired people shows that certain clusters of memory capacities tend to be lost together, it is likely that the capacities within each cluster depend on some un- derlying shared basic process (Kihlstrom & Glisky, 1998). In other words, this modern research assumes (and finds evidence for) the idea that there are dif- ferent systems operating independently in the brain, outside conscious aware- ness, and with occasional communication between systems. This is precisely a core notion of Freud's view.

Despite this additional evidence within cognitive psychology that many important psychological events occur outside our conscious awareness, Freud's views of the unconscious differ from the more modern cognitive views in important ways. Freud not only proposed that unconscious processes play a dominant role in human psychological functioning; he also believed that the unconscious contains what is most important about people's lives, and he thought that what is in the unconscious tends to remain there through an active process of repression. As noted, Freud thought that repressed beliefs, feelings, and desires show up as errors in speaking (or writing) that distort what the person consciously intended to say. A perspective from experimental psycholinguistics (the study of the psychology of language) explains the same errors without mentioning psychodynamic mechanisms. Some examples are shown in Table 3.1 on page 102.

Further, Freud viewed the unconscious as the repository for the libido—the most threatening, most sexually charged, most socially unacceptable, most irrational drives. Cognitive psychologists view the unconscious much more benignly as a collection of information (memories, concepts, processes) currently outside the limited scope of conscious awareness, either because it is irrelevant, because it is too weakly represented to be called forth, or because it is by its nature represented in a manner incompatible with conscious awareness. For example:

- You might not consciously be aware of your memories of your first teenage date as you currently go about dating or hoping to date. Is this because those memories are not relevant to your current focus of attention or because there is some unresolved sexual urge?

- You might not be readily able to recall the names of all the second grade teachers in your elementary school on request, although you knew them all when you were in second grade. Is this because those memories are too weakly represented to be easily accessed without proper cueing or because you were sexually molested at about that time?

- You can't explain why you intensely dislike the taste of olives, or how you even identify the taste of olives. Is this because this kind of process can never be brought into consciousness or because of some repressed feelings about testicles?

In the cognitive view of the unconscious, there is no active process of protection from the potentially painful and harmful contents of the unconscious (Kihlstrom, 1987). There is no widely accepted cognitive parallel to Freud's notion of the dynamic unconscious. It remains to be seen whether Freud was overgeneralizing and overinterpreting his observations about unconscious processes and memory, or whether modern cognitive psychologists are overlooking a phenomenon of great importance.

Table 3.1   **Reinterpreting Slips of the Tongue (and Pen)**

What Was Said or Written	Psychoanalytic Interpretation	Psycholinguistic Explanation
Gentlemen, I take notice that a full quorum of members is present and herewith declare the sitting closed.	The speaker consciously intended to open the meeting, but unconsciously wished for it not to proceed. (*This is Freud's own interpretation of this example.*)	The terms *open* and *closed* are closely associated semantically; the unintended word *closed* was highly activated by the intention to say *open*.
I have a snore neck . . .	The problem of the sore neck is unconsciously believed by the speaker to somehow be related to sleeping.	*Sore* is changed to *snore* due to phonological anticipation: the *n* sound that will be uttered in *neck* is moved to the preceding word *sore*. Error made more likely because it forms a real word.
I'm allergic to lasses . . . glasses.	Speaker reveals his fear and distaste toward females or has an unconscious association between a pair of round eyeglasses and female breasts.	Consonant cluster *gl* is reduced. May be caused by perseveration of the initial sound of the previous stressed syllable (*LER* in *allergic*).
I worry about testes all week . . .	The student is unconsciously worried about his sexual identity. He may fear infertility or be worried that he got his girlfriend pregnant.	*Tests* and *testes* are almost identically spelled, differing only by the presence of an *e* (which is often silent in that position).
Magellan was the first man to circumcise the globe.	The student has severe castration anxiety.	In searching for the correct word in his mental lexicon, the student is seeking an uncommon verb that begins with the prefix *circum-*. When he finds one, he utters it.
[The industrial revolution brought] a mechanical raper that could do the work of ten men in half the time.	The student views rape as a common avenue by which male sexuality is expressed.	In writing an unfamiliar word for an unfamiliar concept, the cognitive effort required makes error more likely. In this situation, the letter *e* is accidentally dropped (from *reaper*). The resulting error forms a legitimate word, making it less likely that the writer will notice the error.

Note: Examples are taken from Hansen (1983), Freud (1974), Jaeger (1992), and Dell (1995).

Evaluating the Perspectives

Advantages and Limits of the Psychoanalytic Approach

- **Quick Analogy**

  Humans as a bundle of sexual and aggressive drives contained by civilization.

- **Advantages**

  Emphasizes the effects of patterns established early in life on personality development.

  Attempts to understand unconscious forces.

  Considers basic motivational drives of sex and aggression.

  Considers defense mechanisms as an essential aspect of personality.

  Assumes multiple levels are operating in the brain.

- **Limits**

  Pessimistic overemphasis on early experiences and destructive inner urges.

  Relatively unconcerned with interpersonal relations or with the individual's identity and adaptation throughout life.

  Difficult to test empirically.

  Many ideas about structure have been discredited by more modern research on the brain.

  Assumes any deviation from heterosexual relations is pathological.

  Focuses on male behavior as the norm and female behavior as a deviation.

- **View of Free Will**

  Behavior is determined by inner drives and conflicts.

- **Common Assessment Techniques**

  Psychotherapy, free association, dream analysis.

- **Implications for Therapy**

  Because personality problems are the result of deep inner conflicts, real change must come through long-term, insight-oriented psychotherapy, in which you explore your inner self through hypnosis, free association, or dream analysis, guided by your highly paid psychotherapist. Traditional psychoanalytic psychotherapy can last years, but newer shorter-term, insight-oriented psychotherapies try to create a therapeutic alliance between practitioner and client in which the client is guided toward meaningful insights.

Summary and Conclusion

Although Sigmund Freud is sometimes treated as a historical curiosity by laboratory-oriented modern personality researchers, a misreading of Freud's impact may lead one to overlook the numerous insights that psychoanalytic theory can add to our understanding of personality. Many of Freud's startling ideas have been disproven or superseded by modern research in biology and psychology, but many others are alive and highly influential even today. This chapter points out the significant intellectual contributions but also notes the limits and failures of the psychoanalytic approach.

Early in his career, Freud began to develop his theories of the importance of the unconscious, initially using hypnosis to tap this area of the mind but soon moving on to free association and dream analysis. Freud believed that dreams and other thoughts are made up of images that are readily accessible to recall (or manifest) but that these images are often symbolic of unconscious issues and tensions (that is, they have latent meaning).

As Freud listened to the dreams and problems of his patients—and as he remembered his own childhood—he developed the theories of the structure of the psyche and of psychosexual development for which he is well known today. According to Freudian theory, individuals have a core being, called the *id,* which is the most primitive part of the psyche and which is motivated to obtain pleasure. At the next level is the *ego,* whose goal is to find practical ways to satisfy the needs of the id. Finally, the *superego,* which is similar in concept to the conscience but includes an unconscious aspect, internalizes societal norms and guides our goal-seeking behaviors toward socially acceptable pursuits.

Freud's psychosexual theory of development proposed that individuals encounter stages in their developmental trajectories in which certain goals are most important. He further posited that if the conflict associated with a particular stage were not resolved, the individual would become *fixated* at that stage. The first stage (oral stage) is a period during which drives to satisfy hunger and thirst are of paramount importance; individuals who become fixated here are overly concerned with issues of dependency and consumption. The second stage (anal stage) deals with the relief of defecating and issues of doing so at socially appropriate times; individuals fixated at this stage may be passive-aggressive or excessively neat or sloppy. During the third stage (phallic stage) the focus is on the genitals, and it is during this time that boys are postulated to face an Oedipus complex (whereas girls experience an Electra complex), resolved through identification with a parent. The fourth stage is relatively longer than the first three stages and is termed the latency stage because sexual energies are not visible but are channeled into more academic and friendship pursuits. The successful resolution of the last stage (the genital stage) is indicated by a healthy adult heterosexual relationship, loving marriage, and the rearing of a family. The idea that the patterns of resolution of such childhood conflicts can greatly influence adult personality has generally been accepted, but many of the specific predictions have not been strongly supported or have been proven to be too closely tied to Freud's times, culture, and biases.

Freud also developed complex but influential theories of the defense mechanisms—the mind's attempts to distort reality to make life more palatable and less threatening. One key defense mechanism is *repression,* or the ability to relegate painful memories to the unconscious. Post-traumatic stress disorders and repressed memories of sexual abuse, issues often seen in today's headlines, are direct applications of this idea of repression. Another of Freud's defense mechanisms is called *reaction formation.* In reaction formation, if a person has urges that go against his or her own fundamental beliefs, these urges may be transformed into their opposite form and that opposing urge may then be acted upon. A related mechanism is that of *sublimation,* the transformation of dangerous urges into altruistic or otherwise useful and socially desirable motivations. *Denial,* another defense mechanism, is the inability (or refusal) of the mind to acknowledge some undesirable reality; in cases in which the truth cannot be completely denied, portions of it may be distorted. *Projection* occurs when anxiety-provoking impulses are attributed to someone else, rather than being claimed by the individual who generated them. *Displacement* occurs when threatening feelings are attributed to something or someone other than their true cause; the new target is generally more manageable and less threatening than the original target. In *regression,* individuals "go back in time" to a safer and happier period in their lives, to escape present threats. Although regression may be seen in early childhood, it is difficult to substantiate in adults. Finally, and perhaps most common, is the defense mechanism of *rationalization*—assigning logical explanations to behaviors and events that were originally motivated by unconscious motives.

Although Freudian theory is sometimes denounced as primitive, it should be remembered that Freud's ideas were bold and innovative, fostering many important later developments in theory and research. In addition to the extensive current psychoanalytic theory and practice that grew directly out of the work of Freud, Freudian theory can be used as a basis to begin exploring many current topics in psychology. For example, hypermnesia, the phenomenon in which a later attempt to remember something yields information that was not reportable on an earlier attempt to remember, has taken a central place in modern cognitive psychology research, as the remembering of supposedly early memories involving child abuse is studied. Likewise, infantile amnesia, the phenomenon that people generally do not remember things from infancy and very early childhood, is of great interest to those studying child development and language. Studies of subliminal perception and of implicit memory, also popular today, are derived from Freudian ideas about the unconscious, even though the modern research techniques and theories are based on much new knowledge. Finally, although Freud's preoccupation with human sexuality and the id are nowadays viewed as an overemphasis, it remains to be seen whether Freud overinterpreted his observations or whether modern psychologists are missing phenomena of great consequence.

Key Theorists

Sigmund Freud

Key Concepts

unconscious
manifest content versus latent content
structure of the psyche—id, ego, superego
pleasure principle versus reality principle
psychosexual theory of development
libido
Oedipus conflict
castration anxiety
penis envy

defense mechanisms
hydraulic displacement model
hypermnesia
infantile amnesia
subliminal perception
explicit memory versus implicit memory
procedural memory versus declarative
   memory

Suggested Readings

Cohen, J. D., & Schooler, J. W. (Eds.). (1997). *Scientific approaches to consciousness.* Mahwah, NJ: Lawrence Erlbaum.

Freud, S. (1917/1924). *A general introduction to psychoanalysis.* J. Riviere (Trans.). New York: Washington Square Press. Original work published 1917.

Freud, S. (1963). *Three case histories: The "Wolf Man," the "Rat Man," and the psychotic Doctor Schreber.* (P. Reiff, Ed.). New York: Macmillan.

Gay, P. (1988). *Freud: A life for our time.* New York: Norton.

Masson, J. (1984). *The assault on truth: Freud's suppression of the seduction theory.* New York: Farrar, Strauss, & Giroux.

Chapter 4

Neo-Analytic and Ego Aspects of Personality: Identity

Consider Michael, a college student who struggles to relate to his peers—struggling so much that he is sometimes labeled as having an inferiority complex. That is, he is overly concerned with how his self-image compares to the status of others; he is always trying to outdo others, but still feels inferior. Could it be that his pattern of responding originated in unresolved conflicts in Michael's childhood?

The term "complex" was coined by C. G. Jung to refer to repressed drives that affect later behavior (as in Freud's Oedipus complex). But the word was soon applied by psychoanalyst Alfred Adler to refer to a child's struggle to repress and thereby overcome feelings of being small and powerless.

For example, a young boy might feel himself to be inferior in everything from athletic ability (compared to his older brother) to penis size (compared to his father), and an intrapsychic struggle to cope with these matters would inevitably ensue. Adler called this complex the "inferiority complex," the same term that is now in common usage.

What is significant about Adler's notion is that it explicitly involves comparisons and rivalries with other people. For Adler, social interest is a primary source of motivation. The internal drives emphasized by Freud are complemented by external pressures, especially those arising from relationships.

Sara, Michael's nineteen-year-old college classmate who is studying to be a doctor, sometimes cannot sleep nights, kept awake by worries about her career choice. She does well in her premed studies, but she is the first in her family to head toward medicine. Indeed, many of her relatives did not attend college at all. In addition, she has left her high school friends behind, and sometimes she is not sure about who she is and what she should do. She resents the sexist comments made by her male classmates about "ugly women doctors." We would understand if she were said to be having an "identity crisis."

In puberty and young adulthood, the individual faces sexual maturity (and the ability to act on sexual urges), a break with the continuity of childhood, and a great concern with how he or she is seen by others. The psychoanalyst Erik Erikson (1950) described these psychosocial events as a stage of development of the teenage years, which often shows itself in such well-known teenage phenomena as cliques and puppy love. If this stage of life is successfully negotiated, the teenager can go on to the next stage—mature adulthood—capable of true intimacy. Note that these stages of personality development are occurring well past the point at which Freud thought that personality was formed.

Although Sigmund Freud believed that people are dominated by their instincts (id), major thinkers working in the Freudian tradition soon recognized and argued for the importance of the feelings of self (ego) that arise throughout life from our interactions and conflicts with others. These psychologists and psychiatrists are much more concerned with the individual's sense of self (ego) as the central core of personality. Note that the term "ego" as used by these individuals is not quite the same as the Freudian ego. Here, the idea of the ego is broader, defining the core individuality of the person. Because these theorists start from psychoanalysis but expand it in new directions, this approach is often called **neo-analytic** (that is, the "new analysis"). Furthermore, in the latter half of the twentieth century, these ego approaches allowed the development of theories of the self that ever more completely discard Freudian notions of the id but still emphasize motivations and social interactions. All these approaches are less biological, more social, and thus more optimistic than Freud's approach. They are the subject of this chapter.

Carl G. Jung and Selfhood

History abounds with stories in which the crown prince or successor has a bitter falling out with the king or the chairman of the board. Take, for example, the biblical account of Absalom's treason against his father, King David. Even if you are not familiar with the story, you can probably correctly guess many of its components. You might guess that King David was a wise and good ruler who tried to do what was right. You might also guess that Absalom was a spoiled and greedy son who became so enchanted with the idea of having power and riches that he was willing to betray his own father in order to obtain these things for himself. (You would be correct on both counts.)

Why is it that themes like this spring so easily to mind? Why is such a scenario so easy to imagine? Carl Jung believed that we are preprogrammed to see and accept certain truths not only because of our own past experiences but also because of the cumulative past experiences of our ancestors. This belief provided an important foundation for his theory of personality.

The story of David and Absalom has repeated itself over and over again through the centuries. But not all of the stories are so extreme. The next time you are flipping through the channels on television, look at the line-up on many of the talk shows: Children feuding with parents and stepparents, employees sniping in bitter antagonism against their bosses, and "followers" denouncing their gurus and stepping out to become leaders and champions of their own causes. This pattern was also true of Freud and Jung, with Carl Jung (Freud's "crown prince") providing the key initial break with Freudian orthodoxy.

Background to Jung's Approach

Jung's Childhood

Carl Gustav Jung was born in July 1875, in Kesswil, Switzerland. He grew up in a religious home; his father, the Reverend Paul Jung, was a country minister, and his mother, Emilie, was a minister's daughter. Jung's theories of personality were unique, and their roots can be traced to thoughts and experiences from his childhood. In particular, two themes became prominent in Jung's childhood beliefs, themes that would later become the basis for his theory of personality.

The first was his belief that he was, in fact, two different personalities: he was both (1) the child that he outwardly appeared to be and (2) a wise and cultured gentleman of the previous century. Jung was an introverted and withdrawn child who spent much time alone, in solitary play and contemplation. He would often sit on a large stone in his garden and focus alternately on two ideas: that he was a boy sitting on a stone and that he was a stone being sat upon by a boy. His ability to take the perspective of the rock gave him the idea that he might actually have more than one form of being. This notion seemed to solidify when the father of a friend chastised him for a misdeed. As he was being scolded, he suddenly felt indignant that this man should be treating *him* in such a way. *He* was an important and distinguished person who should be respected and admired. At the same time, he was aware that he was also a naughty child, presently being reprimanded by an adult. It was thus that Jung fully realized his dual personality.

The second, and closely related, theme from Jung's childhood was that the visions and dreams he often experienced were not unimportant coincidences, but instead were valuable communications of information from the realm of the paranormal. This idea would later form the basis for his concept of the collective unconscious. Around the age of ten, Jung carved for himself a small wooden mannequin, carefully dressed it in homemade attire, and hid it, along with a small painted stone, in the attic of his house. Thinking of this mannequin and stone hidden away secretly together was pleasurable for Jung and somehow had the ability to calm him when he became distressed. He would also write coded messages on little scrolls of paper, to be tucked away with the mannequin—a sort of furtive library for its pleasure (Jung, 1961a).

Beginnings of Jung's Theory

It wasn't until years later, while doing research for a book, that Jung read about "soul stones" (located near Arlesheim) and some of the ancient monumental statue-gods. As he read, he easily formed a mental picture of the stones and statues because they were very similar to his painted stone and mannequin of childhood. He had never before seen pictures of these objects, nor had he read about them (he checked his father's library to be sure), yet he had created them for himself as a young child. These occurrences indicated to him that there were certain psychic elements that are passed from generation to generation through an unconscious channel.

Jung studied medicine at the University of Basel, and it was here that he became interested in psychiatry (to the dismay of some of his professors). He graduated in 1900, the same year that Freud's *Interpretation of Dreams* was published. Jung read this book and in 1906 began a correspondence with Freud. The two quickly became mutual admirers, and by April 1907, it was clear that Freud had chosen Jung as his protégé to carry on the psychoanalytic tradition.

But although things went smoothly for a time, Jung believed that the goals and motivations of individuals were just as important in determining their life courses as were their sexual urges. He had come to believe in the existence of universal archetypes (emotional symbols), which he recognized over and over in his conversations with patients. While Freud believed that personality was largely fixed by middle childhood, Jung preferred to look at personality in terms of its goals and future orientation. Eventually, the rift between these two pillars of psychological thought grew to the extent that a parting of ways seemed the only answer. They went their separate directions in 1913, after which Jung withdrew to the privacy of his home for a period of solitude and introspection that lasted for several years. During this time, he searched himself deeply, getting to know the individual components of his psyche. When this period ended, he was more firm than ever in his belief that the basic tenets of his theory were universally valid. To distinguish his theory from that of Freudian psychoanalytic theory, he called it *analytic psychology*.

Jung's Analytic Psychology

According to Jungian theory, the mind or psyche is divided into three parts: (1) the conscious ego, (2) the personal unconscious, and (3) the collective unconscious. Jung's **ego** is quite similar in scope and meaning to Freud's. It is the aspect of personality that is conscious, and it embodies the sense of self. (Jung believed that this personal identity, or ego, developed around age four.)

The Personal Unconscious

Jung's second component of the mind, the **personal unconscious,** contains thoughts and feelings that are not currently part of conscious awareness. Thoughts from the personal unconscious can be accessed, however. The personal unconscious contains both thoughts and urges that are simply unimportant at present and those that have been actively repressed because of their ego-threatening nature. For example, when you are in psychology class you are not thinking about last night's date (we hope). That information has not been repressed; it's just not relevant at the moment. The person sitting next to you might harbor deep resentment and animosity toward a sibling because of extensive past rivalries and yet belong to a family in which love for family is of paramount importance. This individual might repress these resentments because they threaten her ability to view herself as a "good" person. Both of these thoughts and urges are considered to be part of the personal unconscious by Jung. (Note that the thoughts about last night's date would likely be termed "preconscious" by Freud.)

Jung also saw the personal unconscious as containing both past (retrospective) and future (prospective) material. This grew from the observation that many of his patients experienced dreams that were related to future issues and events. It is not that they "see" the future, but rather they sense things that are likely to happen. Finally, he believed that the personal unconscious serves to *compensate* (balance) conscious attitudes and ideas. That is, if a person's conscious views are very one-sided, the personal unconscious may accentuate the opposing viewpoint through dreams or other means, in an attempt to restore some sort of equilibrium (Jung, 1961c, 1990).

The Collective Unconscious

The third component of the psyche was termed the **collective unconscious** by Jung. Perhaps the most controversial, it comprises a deeper level of unconsciousness and is made up of powerful emotional symbols called **archetypes.** These images are common to all people and have been formed from the beginning of time (that is, they are "transpersonal" rather than personal or individual). These archetypes are derived from the emotional reactions of our ancestors to continually repeating events, such as the rising and setting of the sun, the changing of the seasons, and repeating interpersonal relationships such as mother–child. The presence of such archetypes or emotional patterns predisposes us to react in predictable ways to common, recurring stimuli. Jung described many different archetypes, including the hero, the wise old man, the trickster, and the shadow, all of which clearly appear in popular movies such as the *Star Wars* trilogy (with the wise old Obi-Wan Kenobi, the demonic Darth Vader, the hero Luke, and so on). The following are descriptions of some of his best-known archetypes (see also Table 4.1).

Animus and Anima.   Two important archetypes are the **animus** (the male element of a woman) and the **anima** (the female element of a man). The animus archetype implies that each woman has a masculine side and a corre-

Table 4.1   **Jung's Archetypes and Modern Symbols**

Archetype	Examples
Magician (or Trickster)	sorcerer, wizard, clairvoyant
Child-God	elf, leprechaun
Mother	wise grandmother, virgin Mary
Hero	king, savior, champion
Demon	Satan, anti-Christ, vampire
Shadow	"the dark side," evil twin
Persona	mask, social facade, actor

sponding innate knowledge of what it means to be male; the anima archetype implies that a feminine side and therefore a knowledge of what it means to be female resides in every man.

Persona and Shadow.   These two opposing archetypes represent the differences between our outward appearances and our inner selves. The **persona** archetype (Latin for "mask") represents the socially acceptable front that we present to others. Although each persona, when viewed outwardly, is idiosyncratic, the archetype itself is an idealized picture of what people should be; it is modified by each individual's unique efforts to achieve this goal. In contrast, the **shadow** archetype is the dark and unacceptable side of personality—the shameful desires and motives that we would rather not admit. These negative impulses lead to socially unacceptable thoughts and actions, much as the unchecked desires of Freud's id might instigate outrageous behavior.

Mother.   The **mother** archetype generally embodies generativity and fertility. It may be evoked by an actual mother-figure (for instance, one's own mother or grandmother) or a figurative one (for example, the church). Additionally, the mother archetype may be either good or evil, or perhaps both, much as real mothers have the potential to be.

Hero and Demon.   The **hero** archetype describes a strong and good force that does battle with the enemy in order to rescue another from harm. The opposite of the hero is the **demon,** which embodies cruelty and evil. In our example of David and Absalom, King David would represent the hero, whereas his ungrateful son would be the demon.

Jung's beliefs about the collective unconscious and its archetypes, although intriguing, should not be accepted without thoughtful skepticism. Modern scientific psychology doubts the existence of the collective unconscious, at least in the sense of memories in the brain that resulted from the experiences of our ancestors. However, a more complex version of Jung's idea probably does have some validity.

Throughout time people seem to struggle with the same issues over and over. For example, for thousands of years war has been waged in the name of God, and even today this continues. Modern examples include the ongoing feuds between Catholics and Protestants in Ireland and between the Muslims and Christians in Bosnia, but these are by no means rare and isolated examples. Another issue that every generation wrestles with is gender differences: What are the differences and how important are they? (See Chapter 11 for a fuller treatment of gender issues.) Our Western society has progressed far from the days early in the twentieth century when women could not attend college, could not vote, and were considered to be the property of their husbands. But

Carl Jung's (1875–1961) analytic psychology was less sexually focused, more historically oriented, and more attuned to the spiritual and supernatural than Freud's psychoanalytic psychology.

despite this greater equality, society is still interested in *differences*. The recent best-seller *Men Are from Mars, Women Are from Venus* (Gray, 1992) focuses on the differences in men's and women's ways of communicating.

Why do we continue to be interested in topics like gender differences and finding the "true God" or the "right religion"? Perhaps because, on some level, Jung was right. It seems that we as people share certain interests, certain passions, in a way that borders on instinct. These sorts of questionings and strivings are part of what it means to be human. Some of the more modern theories try to be more "objective" in their data, at the expense of ignoring these deep and fundamental questions. To avoid that mistake, we try in this book to show the strengths *and* weaknesses of the various approaches to personality.

Complexes

For Jung, a **complex** is a group of emotionally charged feelings, thoughts, and ideas that are all related to a particular theme (for instance, Sara's identity or Michael's inferiority). The strength of any given complex is determined by its libido, or "value." Note that Jung's definition of libido differs from Freud's in that it describes a general psychic energy that is not necessarily sexual in nature.

Jung substantiated his claims of the existence of complexes with his word-association test. He presented his clients with a list of words (see Table 4.2), arranged in what he believed was an optimal ordering scheme, and the clients were to respond to each word with the word that most quickly occurred to them. Jung and his colleagues would measure the amount of time it took a client to respond (delays indicating an abnormality or conflict of some kind), rate of respiration, galvanic skin response, and memory on retest. In this way he identified certain words that produced emotional arousal, and with prodding, these words could often be used to uncover the nature of the complex. Interestingly, similar (but more sophisticated) methods are used today in cognitive psychology. Jung believed that personality is made up of opposing forces that continually pull against one another, thus establishing (in

Table 4.2   **Some Stimulus Words for Jung's
Word-Association Test**

head	blue	frog	to wash
green	lamp	to part	cow
water	to sin	hunger	friend
to sing	bread	white	happiness
death	rich	child	lie
ship	to prick	pencil	narrow
to pay	pity	sad	brother
window	yellow	plum	to fear
friendly	mountain	to marry	stork

Note: Jung was the first to use word associations to explore personality. Do your associations to some of these words point to patterns of inner conflicts or obsessions?

Source: From Jung, C. G. (1909). *The collected works of C. G. Jung* (p. 440). Princeton, NJ: Princeton University Press.

the healthy person) some measure of equilibrium. He eventually concluded, however, that the word-association test by itself was not able to discriminate properly between feelings related to imagined stimuli and feelings related to actual occurrences, and he abandoned the method.

Functions and Attitudes

Jung posited four *functions* of the mind: (1) sensing ("Is something there?"); (2) thinking ("What is it that is there?"); (3) feeling ("What is it worth?"); and (4) intuiting ("Where did it come from and where is it going?"). Thinking and feeling were termed rational by Jung because they involve judgment and reasoning. In contrast, sensing and intuition he called irrational because conscious reasoning is virtually absent from these processes. Although all of these functions exist in every individual, one of them normally dominates.

In addition to these four functions, Jung described two major *attitudes:* extroversion and introversion. These terms are in wide use today but are generally understood as being opposite poles of the same dimension, rather than two separate and opposing constructs as Jung thought of them. And, analogously to functions, extroversion and introversion both exist in every individual, but one is usually dominant. Extroverts direct their libido (psychic energy) toward things in the external world, whereas introverts are more inwardly focused. The combination of these two attitudes with the four functions yields eight possible personality types. Take, for example, a person whose dominant function is feeling and whose dominant attitude is extroversion; the "feeling" tendencies of the person would be directed outward. This is to say that, in general, the person would make friends readily, would tend to be loud, and would be easily swayed by the emotional feelings of others. If, however, the predominant attitude was introversion, the "feeling" tendencies of the person would be channeled into introspection and a preoccupation with inner experiences that might be interpreted as cold indifference and, ironically, a *lack of feeling* by observers. Thus, you can see that any dominant function may take on a very different flavor when paired with one or the other of the two attitudes, yielding eight very different categories or types of personalities. This typology forms the basis for one well-known personality inventory—the Myers-Briggs Type Indicator.

Most significantly, it was Jung who challenged Freud and broke the new conceptual ground about motivation and the ego, allowing other approaches to flourish. It should also be noted that Jung's willingness to concern himself with more mystical and spiritual aspects of personality had an important influence on existential-humanistic approaches; these are considered in Chapter 9. Like Freud, Jung was one of the intellectual giants of the early twentieth century, sweeping away medieval cobwebs of ideas that had been passed down for generations, and opening up new ways of thinking about what it means to be a person. However, Jung was more a philosopher than a scientist.

Alfred Adler, the Inferiority Complex, and the Importance of Society

A few years ago, the U.S. Attorney General, commenting on the importance of being an advocate for children's rights, stated that "working with dropouts at 12 or 13 is too late—they have already formed inferiority complexes" (*Newsweek*, 1993). As noted earlier, Carl Jung coined the idea of complexes, but the *inferiority* complex is Alfred Adler's contribution.

Born in Vienna in February 1870, Alfred Adler was Jewish by birth but seemed to feel no strong ties with his heritage. As a child, Adler was frail and, in fact, came close to death on several occasions. He suffered from rickets, which often forced him to play the role of observer to his siblings' games. During his fifth year he contracted such a severe case of pneumonia that the family doctor gave up hope of his recovery (fortunately, his parents sought a second opinion). He was run over in the street, not once, but twice—the trauma being extensive enough to cause him to lose consciousness (Orgler, 1963). These flirtations with death and the knowledge of his own fragility left him feeling powerless and fearful. He determined to become a physician in order to learn to defeat death.

Adler studied medicine at the University of Vienna (although Freud lectured at the university while Adler was there, the two did not meet then), graduated in 1895, and started his own practice soon thereafter. He was married two years later to Raissa Epstein; two of their four children later went on to become psychologists.

Adler's Differences with Freudian Theory

In 1902, Adler was one of those invited to attend some small, casual seminars with Freud. Although his views were somewhat different from those of the Freudian psychoanalysts, he remained a member of the group for a number of years. But by 1911, the disagreements between Freud and Adler had become heated and emotionally intense; Adler resigned from his position as president of the Vienna Psychoanalytic Society (as the group had come to be called) and ended all contact with it. The debates with the domineering Freud and other members of the group had, however, helped Adler to think through his own emerging theory of personality. He soon started his own society, called the Society for Free Psychoanalysis (later changed to the Society for Individual Psychology).

One of the central ways in which Adler's views differed from those of Freud was the emphasis each placed on the origin of motivation. For Freud, the prime motivators were pleasure (remember that the id operates on the so-called pleasure principle) and sexuality. For Adler, human motivations were much more complex.

Adler's Individual Psychology

Adler called his theory **Individual Psychology** because he firmly believed in the unique motivations of individuals and the importance of each person's perceived niche in society. Like Jung, he firmly proclaimed the importance of the teleological aspects, or goal-directedness, of human nature. Another major, and related, difference in their philosophies was that Adler, much more concerned than Freud with social conditions, saw the need to take preventive measures to avoid disturbances in personality.

Striving for Superiority

For Adler (1930), a central core of personality is the striving for superiority. When people have an overwhelming sense of helplessness or experience some event that leaves them powerless,

Alfred Adler (1870–1937). Many of Adler's theoretical constructs (inferiority complex, organ inferiority, masculine protest) echo his personal experiences as a sickly child.

Famous
Personalities

Hugh Grant's Ego

It was 1:30 Tuesday morning. A man was driving home from a late dinner in Los Angeles. Cruising in his white BMW down Sunset Strip, he saw a woman walking. He stopped and gave her $45, she got in the car, and they parked along a side street. While they were in the back seat, a police car pulled up; the officer investigated and immediately arrested the pair. It would have been a typical night in LA, except that the man in the mug shot was actor Hugh Grant.

A celebrity at that moment, Grant had starred in a string of very successful movies–*Nine Months, Sirens,* and *Four Weddings and a Funeral.* Not only was his acting career peaking in both England and the United States, but his personal life was about to climax as well: he was engaged to his girlfriend of many years, Estée Lauder spokeswoman Elizabeth Hurley. Why, then, would this thirty-four-year-old with the leading-man looks and the supermodel fiancée risk his newfound image by employing a prostitute?

For Grant, Stella Thompson (alias "Divine Brown") was reportedly the image of his sexual fantasies. She was dark, sensual, and illegal. A fantasy, she may have symbolized something that Grant, growing up, felt he could not have. As a youth raised by a mother who was an English schoolteacher, and later going on to Oxford for his degree, Grant was probably restricted and guided by socially conservative values. Grant admitted that he had grown up desiring something he could not have, or rather someone, or a type of someone. This was superbly illustrated by his recollection that he'd always had crushes on cheerleaders, with Catholic cheerleaders being his most favorite.

Psychoanalysts might remark that Grant grew up with an inner conflict between his id, which desires forbidden fantasies, and his superego, which (usually) restrained him from this archetype of forbidden fruit. His ego was unable to negotiate a complete compromise for the id (despite Elizabeth Hurley) because there is no way to have these forbidden girls in a socially and morally acceptable manner. But as Grant achieved more and more success, id, already in the pattern of getting everything, came to exert greater influence. Further, Grant had not had any behavior-related problems recently, and so perhaps his superego was off guard; society's restraints were not salient to him. But it was his ego that failed him. Many successful Hollywood actors develop ego problems. Rather than working through challenges toward maturity and wisdom, they wallow in the false and superficial adulation of an adoring public that sees their image but not their true selves.

Driving down Sunset Boulevard, Hugh was tempted by that old desire to have what was morally and socially unacceptable—that off-limits yet sexually appealing woman. He had the money, he was great, he was loved by everyone, so why not? With a well-developed ego testing reality and telling him that this indulgence was irrational, untrue to his fiancée, illegal, dangerous, and "nuts," he would have kept on driving.

Psychoanalytic theory would argue that this whole fiasco was traceable to one of Grant's early id desires that was repressed by the superego. But the neo-analysts focus more on his ego—his sense of who he was and what he should be doing. Grant had everything and was used to getting what he wanted. Why stop?

they are likely to feel inferior. If these feelings become pervasive, an **inferiority complex** may develop. An inferiority complex takes normal feelings of incompetence and exaggerates them, making the individual feel as if it is impossible to achieve goals and therefore hopeless to try. Take the case of David, who has never done very well in school. He's not a terrible student, but beside the honor-roll records and academic accomplishments of his two siblings, his record looks paltry. Over time, he has developed an inferiority complex—an uncomfortable sense of being dull, yes even inferior to his brother and sister.

An individual struggling to overcome such a complex might fabricate a **superiority complex** as a way of maintaining a sense of self-worth, and in fact this is what David has done. If you were to meet him for the first time, you wouldn't guess that there was an "inferior" bone in his body. He appears to have a very high opinion of himself—always bragging and quick to argue that his solution to a problem is the right one. If you look a bit deeper, though, you see that this exaggerated arrogance is really an overcompensation for what David believes he lacks; he has developed a superiority complex as a way of counteracting the inferiority he feels. He is trying to convince others and himself that he is valuable after all. Unfortunately for David, superiority complexes are usually perceived as obnoxious by others, and he is therefore likely to be treated with reserve or even distaste when he exhibits his overbearing attitude. This rejection in turn might increase his inner feelings of worthlessness, leading to even more aggressive compensation—and a maddening spiral has begun. (See the Famous Personalities box on page 118.)

The Evolution of Adler's Theory

Adler's theory underwent a series of changes as his thoughts about human motivations changed. The first concept he described was that of **organ inferiority**—the idea that everyone is born with some physical weakness. It is at this "weak link," says Adler, that incapacity or disease is most likely to take root, and so the body attempts to make up for the deficiency in another area. (Note that this idea is somewhat similar to the homeostasis theory that is discussed in Chapter 12.) He contended that these infirmities (and perhaps more important, individual *reactions* to them) were important motivators of people's life choices.

A short time later, Adler added the concept of the **aggression drive** to his model. He believed that drives could be either directly effective or reversed into an opposite drive (similar to a Freudian defense mechanism). Aggression was particularly important to Adler because he believed it was a reaction to perceived helplessness or inferiority—a lashing out against the inability to achieve or master something.

Adler's next step was what he termed the **masculine protest.** He did not mean, however, that only boys experienced this phenomenon. During that period in history, it was culturally and socially appropriate to use the words *femininity* and *masculinity* as metaphors for inferiority and superiority. Adler believed that all children, by virtue of their relatively powerless and dependent position in the social order, were markedly feminine and that both boys and girls experience this masculine protest, in an effort to become independent from and eventually equal with the adults and people of power in their little worlds. Masculine protest is an individual's attempt to be competent and independent—autonomous, rather than merely an outgrowth of one's parents. Sometimes, striving for superiority can be healthy, if it involves a positive assertiveness.

This search for autonomy and for a sense of control and efficacy was later incorporated into the theories of many, many other personality psychologists. For example, Robert White (1959) brought the ideas of effectance motivation and competence into the mainstream of psychoanalytic thought. He felt that these had come from his own experiences and desires for competence and dignified assurance as a younger person—motivations that White thought Freudian philosophy overlooked.

A related aspect or concept important to Adler was termed **perfection striving.** His belief was that people who are not neurotically bound to an inferiority complex spend their lives trying to meet their **fictional goals.** (This is sometimes termed "fictional finalism.") These goals vary from person to person, reflecting what each person sees as perfection and requiring the elimination of their perceived flaws. The belief in the reality of such fictional goals is sometimes called an "as if" philosophy. Each of us has fictional goals. For example, one of Cleo's fictional goals is to have a "perfect career." She envisions herself sailing through school with good grades, completing a prestigious internship, and being invited to join an international company with a pleasant working environment, enviable pay, and a chance to travel. Of course, she will also be very successful and efficient in her job, pleasing all of her superiors and amazing them with her great talent. In reality, Cleo is not "sailing" through school; she is working very hard to maintain her high GPA. It remains to be seen whether she will get a prestigious internship or just a run-of-the-mill job, and whether she will climb the corporate ladder or be a bench player. But having these fictional goals gives her focus and motivation, and envisioning her sparkling future is its own small reward. If she set her sights lower, it is likely that she would never achieve any of these dreams. But instead she is aiming high, and although she will doubtless encounter some disappointments, she will probably make many of her wishes come true.

Adler was very concerned with individuals' perceptions of social responsibility and their social understanding. Building on Freud's attention to love and work, Adler identified three fundamental social issues that he believed everyone must address: (1) occupational tasks—choosing and pursuing a career that makes one feel worthwhile; (2) societal tasks—creating friendships and social networks; and (3) love tasks—finding a suitable life-partner. He also believed that the three were intertwined; that is, experiences in any one arena would have influences on the other two.

The Role of Birth Order

By focusing on social structure and making astute observations (both of others and of his own childhood), Adler came to believe in the importance of birth order in determining personality characteristics. *First-born children* live for a time as the favored child because they are "only children." They later must learn to deal with the fact that they are not the sole focus and that parental attention must be shared with the other sibling(s). This rather rude awakening may create the tendency for independence and striving to regain status, or the first-born may become a socially oriented pseudo-parent, helping to nurture siblings and others. *Second-born children* are born into a situation of rivalry and competition. Adler himself felt a great sense of rivalry with his older brother, and his inability to compete on a physical level because of his ill health led to subsequent feelings of inferiority. Although this may be useful in that it pushes the second child toward greater achievements, repeated failures have the potential to be quite damaging to the self-esteem. *Last-born children* are usually more pampered than any of the others. They will remain forever the "baby of the family." Adler believed that the overabundance of sibling role models might lead this child to feel overly pressured to succeed in all areas, and the likely inability to do so might result in a lazy and defeatist attitude.

These ideas about birth order and personality (which actually derived in part from the earlier work of Francis Galton) have generated a tremendous amount of research; among the many findings, first-borns are indeed more likely to go to college and to achieve success as scientists (Simonton, 1994). But later-borns may be more likely to be creative, rebellious, revolutionary, or avant-garde. The book *Born to Rebel* (Sulloway, 1996) proposes that revolutions in science, religion, politics, and social movements are very disproportionately driven by later-borns. On the basis of a broad review of the biographies of 6,000 people prominent in Western history, Sulloway concludes that while first-borns show a pattern of high achievement, they are overwhelmingly less likely to propose or support revolutionary viewpoints than later-borns.

Sulloway points to the dynamics of the family—in which first-born children seem to adopt different survival strategies than their later-born siblings—to explain this effect of birth order on the propensity to foment dissent and accept radical ideas. Charles Darwin himself is a classic example of a later-born revolutionary: the data on which Darwin based his theory of evolution in 1837 were broadly available to scientists of his era, but it took the rebelliousness of a later-born to recognize that the data required a heretical rethinking of the accepted doctrine of divine design. Note that, for Sulloway's approach as well as Adler's, it is not the birth order position per se that is important, but rather the motivations it creates. Adler thus paved the way for many future motivational psychologists.

Adler's Personality Typology

Adler created a typology of personality using the Greek idea of four humors (or bodily fluids), one of which would be dominant in any individual. A predominance of blood was believed to result in a cheerful (sanguine) temperament; yellow bile was indicative of an irritable (choleric) temperament; black bile resulted in a brooding (melancholic) temperament; and phlegm resulted in a lethargic (phlegmatic) temperament. To this basic pattern, Adler added his ideas about varying levels of social interest as well as a consideration of activity level. As Table 4.3 shows, he renamed the four components of his typology: (1) Ruling-Dominant (aggressive and domineering); (2) Getting-Leaning (takes from others; somewhat passive); (3) Avoiding (conquers problems by running away); and (4) Socially Useful (meets problems realistically; is cooperative and caring). As with most grand theories, it has proved very difficult to establish a simple, empirical validation of this typology.

Some of Adler's conceptions concerning the great importance of social situations were further developed by Harry Stack Sullivan, who is considered in Chapter 10 (on interactionist approaches to personality). Adler also paved the way for thinkers like Erich Fromm, who accepted both the basic, biologically driven side of personality and the severe societal restraints on personality, but who also tried to reconcile these forces with ideas of creativity, love, and freedom. Fromm and these ideas are considered further in Chapter 9 (on humanistic and existential aspects of personality). Perhaps Adler's greatest gift to personality psychology was his insistence on the positive and goal-oriented nature of humanity. He leaves us with a picture of people striving to overcome their weaknesses and to function productively—in other words, people contributing to society.

Table 4.3   **A Comparison of Adler's Typology with Classical Greek Typology**

Greek Humors	Greek Types	Social Interest	Activity	Adler's Types
Yellow bile	Choleric	Low	High	Ruling-Dominant
Phlegm	Phlegmatic	Low	Low	Getting-Leaning
Black bile	Melancholic	Very low	Low	Avoiding
Blood	Sanguine	High	High	Socially Useful

Karen Horney, Culture, and Feminism

When the bright, ambitious girl named Karen Danielson was growing up in Hamburg, Germany, at the end of the nineteenth century, she faced many personal and social challenges. Her father, a sea captain, had lost his first wife after having four children. He remarried the attractive and sophisticated Clotilde, who was eighteen years his junior. They had a son, and four years later, a daughter—Karen. Karen thus grew up in a world of stepsiblings who never fully accepted the new family additions (Horney, 1980; Quinn, 1987).

Her father, fifty years old when she was born, was a stern and very religious man. He based his beliefs about the inferiority of women on his interpretations of the Bible, and he ruled his family with a firm hand. Although he was more openly affectionate with Karen's brother Berndt, he nonetheless did care for Karen. He sometimes brought her gifts from far-off lands and even allowed her to accompany him on several trips aboard the ship. Thus Karen grew up with conflicting feelings toward her father: she admired him, yet she felt less loved by him than she would have liked. She and her mother were quite close, however.

Although Karen was not unattractive, she believed that she was homely, and early on she determined that if she could not be pretty, at least she could be intelligent. She loved school and became an excellent student. By the time she was twelve, she had decided to become a physician, a choice that did not please her father. But with Karen, Berndt, and Clotilde all urging him, he finally agreed to provide the tuition money for Karen to attend a premedical school.

In society at large, relations between the sexes were in turmoil at this time. Women were clamoring for more rights and educational opportunities. Karen was one of the first women to be allowed to attend advanced high school (the German gymnasium). Medical schools were also just opening their doors to women. In 1906, Karen began her medical training in Freiburg, Germany. It was during this time that she met Oskar Horney (pronounced *Horn-eye*), and the two quickly developed a strong friendship. They married in 1909, and by 1910, their first child was on the way. This was a stressful year of many changes for Karen. She was newly married and pregnant. She was undergoing psychoanalysis with Karl Abraham, a disciple of Freud, to ready herself for the practice of psychiatry. And, to top it all off, her mother died shortly before Karen's own child was born.

Karen and Oskar had three children in all, and each of the daughters later remembered that their mother was somewhat detached from them during childhood. Although part of this was no doubt intentional, an effort to foster independence (something both Karen and Oskar firmly believed in), there was also a lack of warmth and interest in her style of child-rearing. This is particu-

Karen Horney (1885–1952) modified Freudian psychoanalysis to show the social and cultural influences on personality, rejecting Freud's emphasis on innate sexuality and the penis. Her feminist perspective countered the patriarchal Freudian view.

larly interesting in light of Karen's own feelings of neglect during childhood and her later theories of the role of parental indifference in fostering neuroses.

In the early 1920s, Karen and her husband began to drift apart. Then, tragedy struck. In 1923, Oskar's financial investments went sour, and with inflation running rampant, his salary was no longer enough to keep the family from bankruptcy. In addition, he suffered a severe case of meningitis, which left him weak and frail. It was also during this year that Karen lost her beloved brother Berndt to a lung infection. Both Karen and her husband sank into depression, and by 1926, it was clear that their marriage would not survive. Karen and the three daughters moved to a place of their own that very year, but Karen and Oskar's divorce was not final until 1939.

Karen Horney's ideas were in some ways similar to Adler's. Horney believed, as did Adler, that one of the most important discoveries a child makes is that of his or her own helplessness and that it is the ensuing struggle to gain individuality and control that molds much of the self. She believed strongly in the importance of self-realization and growth for each individual. And she was much more focused on the social world and social motivations than were the Freudians (who focused almost exclusively on sexual drives). In 1932, Karen emigrated from Berlin to the United States. This tremendous cultural change further opened her eyes to the influences of society on the individual's development.

Rejection of Penis Envy

Freud's analysis of women was built around the concept of penis envy. Horney rejected the notion that women felt their genitals were inferior, yet her careful observation revealed that women often *did* feel inferior to men. Freud, making the same observation, explained it in terms of an anatomy-based cause—lack of a penis. Horney, however, argued that women's feelings of inferiority stemmed from the ways they are raised in society and from an overemphasis on securing the love of a man. She believed that if women were raised in environments in which "masculinity" was defined as strong, brave, competent, and free, and "femininity" as inferior, delicate, weak, and submissive, then women would of course come to see themselves as subordinate and to therefore desire "masculine" things as a way to gain power. But she did not agree with Freud that it was a penis that women wanted; rather, they wanted the autonomy and control that they associated with maleness. She also postulated that men are unconsciously envious of some feminine qualities, such as the ability to bear children.

Basic Anxiety

Because children are powerless—unable simply to go out into the world and claim their rightful place—they must repress any feelings of hostility and anger toward the powerful adults in their worlds and instead strive to please these adults as a means of getting their needs met. Horney thus replaced Freud's biological emphasis with the idea of basic anxiety. **Basic anxiety** is a child's fear of being alone, helpless, and insecure. It arises from problems in the child's relations with his or her parents, such as lack of warmth, stability, respect, or involvement. Eventually, Horney believed, the basic anxiety could be directed at virtually everyone, in which case the internal turmoil would be focused outward, on the world in general. Thus, although Horney accepted Freud's basic psychoanalytic notion that people are driven by unconscious, irrational motives that develop in childhood, she saw these motives as arising from social conflicts within the family and larger conflicts within the society (Horney, 1968, 1987, 1991).

In reaction to basic anxiety, individuals were hypothesized to settle into one primary mode of adapting to the world. Those who believe that they can get along best by being compliant adopt the **"passive style";** those who believe in fighting to get by adopt the **"aggressive style";** and those who feel that it's best not to engage emotionally at all adopt the **"withdrawn style."** These ideas are of much more than simple historical interest; they form a widely accepted framework for understanding good child-rearing. Much of the modern-day concern with providing warm, respectful family environments for children derives from such neo-analytic theorizing about the role of society in taming biological instincts.

The Self

Neo-analysts focused on identity and sense of self. In analyzing neurotics, Horney described different aspects of self. First, there is the **Real Self,** the inner core of personality that we perceive about ourselves, including our potential for self-realization; this core is damaged by parental neglect and indifference. This parental neglect can produce the **Despised Self,** consisting of perceptions of inferiority and shortcomings, often based on others' negative evaluations of us and our resulting feelings of helplessness. Perhaps most important, Horney identified the **Ideal Self**—what one views as perfection and hopes to achieve, as molded by perceived inadequacies. In describing the Ideal Self, Horney referred to what she called the "tyranny of the should," which is the litany of things we should have done differently, and with which we torment ourselves. The Ideal Self is a composite of all of these "shoulds." For Horney, the goal of psychoanalysis was not to help someone achieve his or her Ideal Self, but rather to enable the person to accept his or her Real Self. Someone who is alienated from his or her Real Self becomes neurotic and develops an interpersonal coping strategy to "solve" the conflict.

Neurotic Coping Strategies

Horney then proposed a series of strategies used by neurotics to cope with other people. The first of these approaches she referred to as "Moving Toward" people—that is, always attempting to make others happy, to gain love, and to secure the approval and affection of others. Horney believed that individuals employing this coping strategy are overidentifying with a Despised Self and are therefore seeing themselves as unworthy of love. Their actions to gain love are attempts, on the one hand, to disguise what they believe to be true of themselves and, on the other, to make others believe that they are worthy of affection. For example, women raised by alcoholic parents may have learned to obtain self-esteem by conforming to exploitive demands; as adults, these women may seek out exploitive men and devote themselves to attempting to make the men happy and thereby win their approval (Lyon & Greenberg, 1991). In popular jargon, this disturbed pattern of relationships is sometimes referred to as codependency.

Horney called the second approach "Moving Against" people—that is, striving for power, recognition, and the admiration of others. Horney believed that these individuals, instead of overidentifying with the Despised Self, are overidentifying with the Ideal Self. They have come to believe that all the things that they wished they were are true, and their strivings for recognition and power are an effort to reaffirm for themselves the truth of this illusion.

A third approach was called "Moving Away" from people—that is, the withdrawal of any emotional investment from interpersonal relationships, in an effort to avoid being hurt in those relationships. Horney believed that these individuals want to overcome the Despised Self, and yet they feel incapable of ever becoming the Ideal Self. They see themselves, in their present state, as unworthy of the love and attention of others, and yet they feel unable to achieve anything greater. Thus, to avoid the unpleasant contrast—the gap—between these two aspects of self, they hide behind independence and solitude.

Horney's Impact on Psychoanalytic Thinking

In sum, Karen Horney helped move psychoanalytic thinking about personality away from purely biological, anatomical, and individualistic emphases. While she accepted the significance of unconscious motives developed in childhood, Horney emphasized the importance of a warm, stable family, as well as the impact of the larger society and culture. Furthermore, just as Horney struggled with society's obstacles to women's achievement in her own life, she rejected the idea that women's nature makes them inherently weak and submissive. She saw the influences of the family and the culture on each person, and she insisted that people could strive to overcome their unconscious demons. She emphasized the distress of the "tyranny of the shoulds"—the neurotic internal demands for perfection. She wrote that psychoanalysis is not the only way to resolve inner conflicts—that "life itself" is a very effective therapist (Horney, 1945).

Despite Horney's efforts, psychoanalysis remained heavily male-centered and paternalistic. As feminist Germaine Greer (1971) quipped, "Freud is the father of psychoanalysis. It had no mother."

Other Bridges from Freud to More Modern Conceptions

Anna Freud

Anna Freud was born in December 1895 to Sigmund and Martha Freud—parents who had previously decided that they would have no more children. In childhood and adolescence, she was shy and quiet but quite attached to her father. When she was in her early twenties, she underwent psychoanalysis (including by her father) and subsequently became a part of the Vienna Psychoanalytic Society.

In 1922, she presented her first paper to the society, and in 1923, she entered the practice of psychoanalysis, with no formal credentials in psychology or medicine. This was also the year that her father's cancer of the jaw was diagnosed. The ensuing surgeries brought about a host of complications and perhaps helped to fuel her own passionate work to extend her father's theories.

In contrast with her father, Sigmund, who attempted to uncover childhood from the adult patient's perspective, Anna Freud worked directly with child patients. She adapted psychoanalytic techniques to the special needs of children, as necessitated by their different verbal skills and attention spans. For the next half-century, Anna Freud followed in her father's footsteps, applying psychoanalytic theory to children and teens. Although she never strayed far from traditional psychoanalytic thought, she nonetheless began to build the

Anna Freud (1895–1982) is shown here at age seventeen with her father, Sigmund, during a family vacation in 1913. Her work focused on applying psychoanalytic approaches to children and teenagers.

bridge that later neo-Freudians would cross, by lending credibility to the direct study of the ego. She brought the ego more clearly into focus with her emphasis on the influence of the social environment, yet she maintained the ego's links to the id and superego. She also moved psychoanalytic thinking slightly away from determinism; that is, although she certainly did not renounce the importance of the id forces or the superego constraints, she endowed the human ego with a bit of proactive, independent functioning that later theorists were able to expand on (A. Freud, 1942).

Heinz Hartmann

Heinz Hartmann has sometimes been called the father of ego psychology. Like Anna Freud, Hartmann worked within a classical Freudian framework, while expanding and strengthening Freud's conception of the ego. Hartmann did not believe the ego was under the control of the id, but he also did not see it as completely autonomous. Rather, he believed that the id and ego worked in a compensatory fashion, each regulating the other. Because Hartmann accepted the idea that the "job" of the ego was to help a person function within the world, he had to modify the traditional Freudian concept of the individual as a purely tension-reduction and pleasure-seeking organism. Instead, he saw that the ego was often able to direct a person to do things that in the long run were self-preserving but in the short term were unpleasant. The ego not only defended against libidinous urges, but also functioned independently to cope with society's demands (Hartmann, 1958).

Object Relations Theories: A Conceptual Link between Self-Identity and Social Identity

Overall, as psychoanalytic approaches to personality continued to develop, it became clearer and clearer that attention should be expanded away from the individual's inner psyche and toward relations with other people. In other words, the essence of who we are cannot be understood without understanding our relations with significant others. These approaches are sometimes called **object relations** theories. They focus on the objects of psychic drives not as instinctual targets, but rather as important entities in their own right. That is, the child learns about self and others primarily through interactions with other people.

It is sometimes difficult to distinguish among object relations psychologists, ego psychologists, and neo-analytic psychologists; it is rare that a theorist limits his or her theorizing strictly to one area. However, one thing that object relations theorists have in common is their focus on the importance of relations with other individuals in defining personality. (See the Self-Understanding box on page 130.)

Margaret Mahler

It was Margaret Mahler's work with emotionally disturbed children that led her to develop her theory of *symbiosis*. She observed that children who today might be called autistic seemed unable to form emotional ties with other human beings (notably their mothers), and in this way they shut themselves off from the world. **Symbiotic psychotic** children, on the other hand, formed emotional ties that were so strong that the child was unable to form a sense of self—that is, he or she had no autonomous being. Mahler believed that forming ties with the mother was of utmost importance to psychological health and that children who formed normal ties with their mothers were *normal symbiotic* children. They developed empathy and a sense of being a separate but loving person. Like Anna Freud and Heinz Hartmann, Mahler placed increasing importance on the individual's potential for mastery of his or her world, and on the creation of a healthy ego. But most especially, Mahler (1979) added the importance of effective mothering skills for the development of an emotionally healthy child.

Melanie Klein

The Vienna-born British psychiatrist Melanie Klein (1882–1960) also worked closely with children and focused on how children came to think about and represent others (in their own minds). She might be seen as the first significant child psychoanalyst. Klein was willing to be patient so as to observe young children at length during their free play. Her approaches, however,

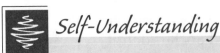 *Self-Understanding*

Ego Assessment

Ego approaches to personality focus on the conscious self—who we think we are—as a central aspect of the individual. For insight into ego assessment, we present three different exercises; each exemplifies a different ego psychology approach to this issue.

I. **What Do Your "Fictional Goals" Reveal?**
   1. What are the three main goals (your strivings for self-improvement) in your life right now?
   2. What do these fictional goals tell you about yourself?
   3. What do they tell you about your perceived weaknesses, or perhaps even weaknesses that you haven't admitted to yourself?
   4. How might these fictional goals help to shape your life in the future?
   5. Will changing your goals do anything to change your identity?

II. **An Exercise to Think Critically about Ego Approaches**
   This exercise requires a partner who knows you. First, in private, each of you write five short (one-sentence) self-descriptions. These descriptions may be general or specific; the important thing is that they attempt to capture the essence of **who you are.** Now, take a moment to think about your partner, and then each of you write five short (one-sentence) descriptions of the other person. When you have done this, compare lists.

   How well did your partner describe you? How well did you describe your partner? If there are inconsistencies (and most pairs will have some), do these say anything about the differences between your social and personal self? Do you define yourself in terms of social roles? in terms of goals? Does knowing how others see you cause you to redefine yourself in any way?

III. **Dream Analysis**
   We all dream every night, although many of us forget our dreams. Keep a notebook and a pencil next to your bed, and keep a dim night-light on. When you wake up during a dream at night or early in the morning, keep your eyes closed for a moment and focus on remembering your dream. Then open your eyes and quickly write what you remember. (You should get better at recalling details over the course of a couple of weeks.)

   Look over your dreams for recurring themes or motivations. Then compare these to goals and themes and motivations in your daily life. For example, is there anger or conflict in your dreams that corresponds to some ongoing anger or conflict in your daily life? a concern with failure? a focus on love? Are any of Jung's archetypes represented?

   If you do this, say, every December for several years, you can look for changes in your motivations and identity.

were heavily influenced by experience doing therapy, in which relations with others are generally of utmost importance. Her ideas were also shaped by the emerging notions of social interaction and self-identity—the idea of a social self—that form the basis of modern social psychology.

Klein was a developer of "play therapy," in common use today. For example, children grieving over the death of a parent or an assault on their bodies might today be treated at a grieving center, where they work out their unconscious feelings and conflicts while playing with toys or crafts, much as an adult might do through dream analysis or free association. Would you recommend such treatment to the child of a friend or to a child in your family who is facing grief? Answering such questions is facilitated when we understand the origins of and theories underlying such treatments.

Taking Freud's ideas in new directions, Klein (1975) examined such early patterns as the infant's reaction to the removal of the mother's breast after nursing. The breast is the infant's first source of satisfaction, and when it is removed, the infant in some sense blames the mother. This conflict is resolved when the infant comes to understand that the mother's love is not simply her breast. There is a differentiation. This early development of the understanding of other people sets the pattern for future relations with others.

Heinz Kohut

Heinz Kohut (1971) was also instrumental in creating new notions of the self. A psychoanalyst, Kohut argued that a key problem for many anxious people is the fear of the loss of an important love object (most often the parent). He worked with patients who had a *narcissistic personality disorder*, meaning that they felt powerless and dependent yet projected bravado and self-aggrandizement. He believed that the problems of these patients stemmed from a lack of acceptance on the part of their parents, which resulted in an inability on the part of the patients to fully accept themselves. He found that by playing the part of the therapist–parent he could often reverse this process and enable his patients to develop a healthy self-concept.

As an example, let's look at Philip, a twenty-four-year-old who is seeking treatment for his very low self-esteem. His self-concept is so completely wrapped up in what others think of him that he can barely make decisions on his own; he constantly worries about what people are going to think. At the same time, this insecurity makes him feel entitled to special attention. His therapist, using Kohut's framework, has determined that Philip experienced a traumatic event involving one of his parents (probably his mother) before he was old enough to have fully made the distinction between "mom" and "self." As part of Philip's treatment the therapist will utilize *idealizing transference;* that is, Philip will come to see the therapist as the parental love-object. The therapist qua parent can then help Philip develop an internal system for maintaining self-esteem, rather than depending on others for that esteem. In this approach, a flavor of the humanistic personality psychology of Carl Rogers is evident (see Chapter 9). Indeed Kohut was a bridge between Freudian psychoanalysis and the more optimistic and ego-based approaches of many humanistic psychologists.

The Contribution of Object Relations Approaches

Object relations approaches, with their attention to the child's perception of the environment, also foreshadowed the cognitive approaches to personality, which are dealt with in detail in Chapter 7. Further, they led to various forms of cognitive psychotherapy in which certain psychological disorders are attributed to a poorly structured ego. Each of these object-relations theorists, following in the footsteps of Sigmund Freud, attempted to describe the structure of both the healthy and the unhealthy human psyche, and to explain the ways in which developmental outcomes are reached. These theorists, however, began the shift toward viewing the ego as a much more *independent* entity than had Freud, and they brought to the forefront the importance of human individualization and mastery.

In brief, it is important to recognize that a series of brilliant thinkers took Freudian theory (which had shattered previous ideas about human nature) and developed it so that it could deal with emerging insights into what it means to have a social self—an identity in a social world. Many of these neo-analytic ideas—of inferiority complexes, of psychic archetypes, of strivings for mastery, of sibling rivalries, of basic anxieties and the importance of mother–infant relations, of the differentiation of identity, and many more—permeate our modern notions of child-rearing, families, and human nature. These ideas are now found in literature, in politics, in the arts, and in education. A wise student of personality will recognize these now-common assumptions in everyday life and will have some idea of their origins and history.

It is interesting to note that important elements of neo-analytic ego theories grew out of the strong Jewish cultural and intellectual tradition that was flourishing in late nineteenth-century Europe; many were based on the study of the ancient commentaries known as the Talmud. Talmudic analyses were very concerned with the nature of humans and the promotion of human morality. In fact, it can be argued that many of the neo-analytic theorists are moralists as much as psychologists. This Talmudic tradition also emphasizes the importance of discussion, subtlety, and various points of view as each human struggles to be a just person in a demanding society. It is not surprising that the neo-analytic theories are relatively unconcerned with biology and fixed personality structures but are very concerned with the nature of the self that emerges when basic instincts clash with the varying expectations of society.

Erik Erikson, Life Span Identity, and Identity Crises

Just as Adler expanded psychoanalytic theorizing to include social influence, and Horney altered its conceptions of women, Erik Erikson moved psychoanalytic thought beyond childhood. For Erikson, adulthood was not simply a reaction to childhood experiences, but rather a *continuing* developmental process that was influenced by its own previous stages.

Erikson's Life Path

Born in Frankfurt, Germany, in 1902, young Erik was unsure of his life's direction as he grew to maturity. Erik's stepfather (who he thought was his father) was Jewish. (His Scandinavian birth father abandoned Erik's mother before Erik was born.) Erik's blond hair and blue eyes made him feel different from the rest of the family. At school he was called a Jew by his classmates, yet at the temple he was referred to as a "goy" (non-Jew). Not surprisingly, he felt as if he didn't belong anywhere.

His stepfather, Theodor Homburger, was a physician, and as Erik grew up, it became clear that the kindly man hoped that Erik would follow in his footsteps. Erik, however, wanted to make his own way in life—to be different. He went to art school and became a wandering artist, but he still wasn't completely happy. He enjoyed his art and the freedom from social responsibility that it afforded him, yet he yearned to devote himself to something truly meaningful. There seemed to be no occupation that could fill both of these conflicting needs.

As time went on, Erik learned self-discipline and joined the faculty of a school in Vienna. Erik became fascinated with child development, and it was during this time that he met Anna Freud and the rest of the Vienna circle. Erik greatly respected Sigmund and Anna Freud and saw psychoanalysis as a field that might allow him to be productive without having to go through all the traditional steps to success (that is, without going to medical school). He underwent psychoanalytic training with Anna Freud, and with only this and a Montessori diploma, he managed to become one of the most influential psychologists of this century.

During the Nazis' rise to power in Germany in 1933, Erik and his wife emigrated to Boston. When he became an American citizen, he thought carefully about who he was and who he wanted to be. He changed his name from Erik Homberger (Homberger was his stepfather's name) to Erik H. Erikson. It is interesting that he chose to reiterate his first name with his last—perhaps hinting at what he had found his own "identity" to be. For a while he worked with Henry Murray, who was also concerned with personality changes across

Table 4.4   **Erik Erikson's Stage Theory**

Ego Crisis	Freud's Stage	Ego Skill Gained	Age
Trust versus Mistrust	Oral	Hope	Infancy
Autonomy versus Shame and Doubt	Anal	Will	Early childhood
Initiative versus Guilt	Phallic	Purpose	Early to mid-childhood
Industry versus Inferiority	Latency	Competence	Mid- to late childhood
Identity versus Role Confusion	Genital	Loyalty	Teenage years
Intimacy versus Isolation	none	Love	Early adulthood
Generativity versus Stagnation	none	Caring	Middle adulthood
Ego Integrity versus Despair	none	Wisdom	Late adulthood

the life span (Murray's work is described in detail in Chapter 10). Erikson then developed his own theory about personality development from a life span perspective. An outline of his stage theory of personality development is shown in Table 4.4.

Identity Formation and Ego Crises

According to Freud, identity was fixed in childhood—formed by age five or six. Erikson renounced this notion, arguing that identity formation is a life-long process. In part, Erikson was rejecting European notions that personality is fixed and life is determined; instead, he adopted the more American philosophical view that individuals could and did undergo significant change. This view also implies that the individual must take some personal responsibility for his or her life.

According to Erikson, personality (actually, Erikson focused on *identity*) develops through a series of eight stages as life unfolds (Erikson, 1963, 1978). The outcome of each stage (that is, the resultant personality) is dependent to some degree on the outcome of the previous stage, and successful negotiation of each of the ego crises is essential for optimal growth. He used as his basis Freud's stages of psychosexual development, and indeed his first five stages reflect ego crises that are tied to Freud's stages.

The child's first ego crisis occurs in infancy, when the child must come to believe that the environment can be trusted to satisfy his or her needs.

Trust versus Mistrust

The first ego crisis Erikson termed Trust versus Mistrust. During this stage (at about the same time period as Freud's oral stage), the infant is struggling to achieve successful nursing, peaceful warmth, and comfortable excretion. If the environment provided by the mother satisfies the infant's needs, the child develops a sense of trust and hope. However, disruptions at this stage can produce feelings of mistrust and abandonment. An infant whose mother does not respond reliably to its hungry cries or who is rarely held is likely to experience feelings of insecurity and suspicion of the environment—the world cannot be trusted. If this ego crisis is never resolved, the individual may have difficulties establishing trust with others throughout life, always convinced that other people are trying to take advantage of him or her in business dealings, or that friends cannot be confided in.

Autonomy versus Shame and Doubt

The second ego crisis Erikson called Autonomy versus Shame and Doubt. During this time (corresponding approximately with Freud's anal stage), the young child is learning that he or she has control over his or her own body. Parents should ideally guide the child, teaching him or her to control impulses, but not in an overly harsh manner. Successful negotiation of this stage results in a child who knows the difference between right and wrong, and is willing and able to choose "right" most of the time. Overly controlling and punitive parenting results in feelings of "I'm always bad . . . I don't know how to be successful" on the part of the child.

Initiative versus Guilt

Erikson called the third stage (which corresponds with Freud's phallic stage) Initiative versus Guilt. The child enters this stage knowing that he or she is an independent and autonomous person, but not much else. It is during this period that the child learns how to plan and carry out actions, as well as how to get along with peers. Unsuccessful negotiation of this stage results in a child who may be able to envision possibilities but is too fearful to pursue them. If such feelings are not resolved, an individual emerges in later years who cannot take initiative or make decisions, whose self-confidence is low, and who has little will to achieve.

Industry versus Inferiority

The fourth stage was termed Industry versus Inferiority (similar to Freud's latency stage). At this time, the child learns to derive pleasure and satisfaction from the completion of tasks—academic tasks in particular. Successful completion of this stage yields a child who can solve problems and who takes pride in accomplishments. This is a child who is competent. On the other hand, a child who does not master this stage feels inferior, as if he or she were incapable of reaching positive solutions and unable to achieve what peers are accomplishing.

Identity versus Role Confusion

The fifth ego crisis (corresponding roughly to Freud's genital stage) is the most famous and influential of Erikson's stages: Identity versus Role Confusion. At this stage the adolescent experiments with different roles, while trying to integrate identities from previous stages. For instance, the child is both son (or daughter), student, friend, and possibly sibling. How do these fit together into a cohesive whole? To complicate matters, at the same time adolescents are trying to figure out who they are and who they want to become, society is beginning to allow them more freedom in the areas of friendships and careers. Successful completion of this stage results in a person who has a clear and multifaceted sense of self—one who has managed to integrate many roles into

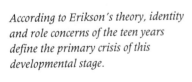

According to Erikson's theory, identity and role concerns of the teen years define the primary crisis of this developmental stage.

Jennifer Capriati made her debut as a tennis prodigy at age thirteen but took a leave from the professional circuit at age seventeen as a result of her inability to cope with the stress of competing as an adult when she was a young teenager. Following this, the Women's Tennis Association ruled that no girl could play in a major tournament before age sixteen, an implicit acknowledgment of the importance of psychological development, not merely athletic skill, in determining who can be a professional player.

a single "identity" that is his or her own. Erikson traced the self-consciousness and embarrassment of the teenage years to an identity confusion—an uncertainty about one's abilities, associations, and future goals. He termed this confusion an **identity crisis.** A failure to successfully work through this ego crisis results in an individual with a perpetual identity crisis—someone who is not sure who she or he is, and who is still struggling to find out.

Intimacy versus Isolation

The sixth stage (it is here that Freud's stages end and Erikson breaks totally new ground) was called Intimacy versus Isolation. During this time period, young adults are learning to interact on a deeper level with others. They are

Kurt Cobain, who was lead guitarist and singer of the grunge rock band Nirvana, was addicted to drugs and killed himself in April 1994. Cobain had had a troubled youth and could be said to have failed to successfully navigate Erikson's stage of Identity versus Role Confusion.

allowing others to get to know this newfound "self" in an intimate way. The goal in this stage is for the individual to find companionship with similar others, specifically to develop a love relationship with a partner. The inability to create strong social ties without losing oneself in the process results in isolation and loneliness instead of love and fulfillment. Such a person may be unable to form intimate relationships at all, either becoming a "loner" or striking up plenty of superficial relationships.

For example, Ann seems popular and some of her classmates are envious of her apparent social ease. She always has a date and is usually surrounded by people. Despite this, she feels lonely inside. Nobody knows the real Ann, and she can't seem to get close enough to anyone to let them see what she's like on the inside; she's afraid nobody will like her true self. In contrast, Jill lives her life in a much quieter way. She's not disliked, but neither is she terribly popular. She has quite a few acquaintances (people to whom she says, "Hi, how's everything going?" when she sees them in the hallway), but only two close girlfriends. Her friendships with these two, however, are deep and satisfying. In addition, she is dating someone that she cares for; they have been going out for nearly a year, and she feels close to him, almost as if they have known each other all their lives. Although to the casual observer Jill might appear to be more isolated than Ann, she has actually dealt much more effectively with the Intimacy versus Isolation ego crisis than has Ann.

Generativity versus Stagnation

Erikson called his seventh stage Generativity versus Stagnation. It is at this stage that the individual comes to value a giving of self to others. This often takes the form of bearing and raising children, but it is also reflected in other activities such as community service. The idea is to give something back to the world, to do something to ensure the success of future generations. You probably know people who, having achieved many of their material goals, have set new goals for themselves—goals that embody helping others. For example, some successful artists and celebrities donate time and money to charitable causes or become spokespersons for organizations they see as important. Your own parents probably made financial sacrifices in order to give you opportunities to attend college, take music or dance lessons, or participate in sports. The inability to take this generative perspective results in a feeling that life is worthless and boring. This individual may be achieving worldly goals, but underneath the overt success, life seems meaningless.

Ego Integrity versus Despair

The eighth and final stage of ego development Erikson called Ego Integrity versus Despair. In this stage, old age, the individual derives wisdom from life experiences and can look back on life and see meaning, order, and integrity. Reflections are pleasant, and present pursuits are in keeping with the integrated life goals the person has pursued for years. Psychosocial failure at this stage means a sense of despair: I have not accomplished what I would have liked to in life, and it is now too late to do anything about it.

Resolving the Ego Crises

It is important to remember that Erikson emphasized a *balanced* outcome as optimal for each of these eight ego crises; this characteristic of his theory is often oversimplified and misunderstood. At the first stage, the goal is for the child to develop trust, yet it would not be good for the child to be totally gullible and naive. An overemphasis on trust might lead to just as many problems as an overemphasis on mistrust. Instead, the individual at this stage must learn the ability to trust, and should perhaps have trust as a first inclination, but should nonetheless maintain the ability to be skeptical and self-preserving when necessary. The same is true for each of the stages. At each stage one of the two features should prevail, but true maturity includes rather than excludes the other pole.

Erikson (1969) not only expanded the focus of personality throughout the life span, but he also emphasized the importance of society. He studied culture, history, and anthropology, and he profiled such famous men as Martin Luther and Mahatma Gandhi. These personality profiles provide deeper historical looks at important figures, as well as elegant examples of Erikson's theories in action. His life span approach, combining as it did both positive and negative potentials, is more realistic for looking at ordinary human growth (as opposed to focusing only on human problems). Neo-analytic ego psychologists like Erikson have retained the more meaningful aspects of psychoanalytic theory while creating new solutions for its more difficult areas. Always, their eyes are on the goal of understanding what it means to be an individual. This is not an easy task. As poet Alan Watts put it, "Trying to define yourself is like trying to bite your own teeth" (Life Magazine, 4/21/61).

When we talked to him in the 1970s, Erikson seemed to be living out his own theories. He was wise and mature, but still reading, writing, and learning. He died in 1994 at the age of ninety-one.

Erik Erikson is himself a good example of the positive resolution of the final stage of ego development. In old age, he exemplified wisdom and integration.

Some Modern Approaches to Identity

The modern ego psychologists are usually not much concerned about tracing adult motivations back to childhood traumas. Their view is expresssed by Holden Caulfield (J. D. Salinger's adolescent antihero in *Catcher in the Rye*, 1951): "The first thing you'll probably want to know is where I was born, and what my lousy childhood was like, and how my parents were occupied and all before they had me, and all that David Copperfield kind of crap, but I don't feel like going into it" (p. 22). Instead, modern ego psychologists focus on the present: Who are we today? What defines us? What influences us? What do we hope to become? And, how do our aims for the future help us to create our present identities? As noted in Chapter 1, twentieth-century writings in drama and philosophy have toyed with the notion of multiple selves.

Personal and Social Identity

One contempoary researcher who is very interested in the psychology of identity is Jonathan Cheek. Instead of attempting to determine whether identity is more accurately conceptualized as an internal and personal construct (as a traditional ego psychologist might argue) or an external, socially defined construct (a pure social psychologist's view), he posits that some people might best be defined by the personal view and others by the social view (Briggs & Cheek, 1988; Cheek, 1989). That is, for some individuals, the most important part of "self" might be who they are in relation to others: "I am a good father" or "I am popular and have lots of friends." For other individuals, however, the social roles may be less important, and "self" is best described with introspection: "I am someone who believes in making a kinder world" or "I am very creative."

Cheek has developed a scale that measures both personal and social identity. Cheek and his colleagues present individuals with a list of entries such as "my thoughts and ideas" or "my attractiveness to other people" and ask participants to rate each item's importance to their sense of self. The goal is to better understand what people are like inside; that is, what is their internal scheme for organizing their various social and personal roles. Eventually, as with the ego psychologists, the goal is to be able to explain what a person's self-concept is, how it develops, and how it changes.

Self-Monitoring

Another approach to understanding the extent to which a person has a more social or more personal identity is Mark Snyder's concept of self-monitoring. Self-monitoring involves self-observation and self-control guided by situational cues to the social appropriateness of behavior. Someone who is high on self-monitoring is willing and able to engage in self-presentation—doing what is socially expected. The former president (and former actor) Ronald Reagan was very willing and able to present himself; in fact, he was known as the Great Communicator. But low self-monitors are often not aware of social expectations or are unwilling or unable to act according to social expectations, and they may be more inward-looking and reflective. That is, there tends to be a *dispositional orientation* in low self-monitors, but a *situational orientation* in high self-monitors.

Snyder (1987) and other modern theorists are thus turning to a functionalist approach for explaining personality. That is, what is the function or purpose of certain behavior? They see (1) what people want, (2) why they want it, and (3) how they try to get it, as important for defining who people are. Mark Snyder has spent much of his research career looking at the environments people choose to put themselves in. This is important because our environments help to determine our behaviors, and even our thoughts, thus shaping our identities. In order to say something about what kind of a person you are, Snyder would want to see what kinds of people you spend your time with, what kinds of hobbies you enjoy, and so on. Because these are choices over which you have much control, they say a lot about who you are and how you view yourself. For example, who will volunteer to help AIDS patients (Omoto & Snyder, 1995)? A motivation to help that fulfills a need of one's personality is one key predictor. This type of analysis is a modern update of neo-analytic concerns with social motivation and social identity, but without the underlying Freudian assumptions. On the other hand, these modern approaches are much more modest in the scope of what they can explain.

The Role of Goals and Life Tasks

A related way that modern researchers are helping to define identity functionally is by asking people what their personal goals are—what they find important. For instance, Brian Little (1993) uses the phrase "personal projects" to refer to goals or activities that people are currently working on. There are big projects, like "becoming a physician," and little projects, like "not biting my fingernails." These personal projects are specific tasks that motivate people on a daily basis. Robert Emmons (1992) describes more abstract goals as "personal strivings" (for instance, "impress my friends") that may be satisfied by a number of different behaviors. For example, you could probably impress your friends by getting all A's, by dating someone attractive, by driving a fancy car, or by being a good conversationalist. Therefore, personal strivings are overarching goals that subsume, and make functionally equivalent, lots of smaller goals and behaviors.

Psychologist Nancy Cantor (1994), a leading modern-day identity theorist, focuses on what she calls "life tasks." These are age-determined issues on which people are currently concentrating. Cantor gets down to the nuts and bolts: What do college students think about their dating relationships? What do they say about them? What do they do about them? For example, following their past ego development, some individuals seek to build a union with a special other and some do the opposite: work to maintain their independence. Some people reveal their innermost secrets, whereas others want to keep some things (such as a diary) completely theirs alone.

Cantor is working in the framework established by Erik Erikson, in that an individual's tasks are defined to a large extent by the stage of life. For example, a three-year-old is unlikely to have "finishing high school" as a goal, but this is an important and normal life task for a sixteen-year-old. Similarly, young adults should ideally learn who they are—they should have identity as a goal—before attempting to form close and lasting bonds with partners, as in marriage. However, where grand theorists such as Adler and Erikson coupled in-depth study of certain individuals with wide-ranging theoretical observations about social conditions, modern personality researchers are much more likely to collect systematic, comprehensive data on a group of people sampled from the relevant population. So, for example, in Erikson's sixth stage, which begins around age twenty-one, the individual must begin to search out true intimacy and love or else face a self-centered isolation. Modern theorists seek to discover, in specific terms, with comprehensive data, precisely how this is (or is not) accomplished.

Cantor, like most modern researchers in personality, also heavily emphasizes the importance of situational influences on the individual. Approaches that explicitly consider both the individual and the social situation—so-called interactionist approaches—are taken up in more detail in Chapter 10.

The Search for a Meaningful Life

Roy Baumeister is another contemporary researcher who is trying to more fully explain what we mean by "self." But he believes that much of human preoccupation with "finding oneself" is really a disguised search for a meaningful life. We all have a need to belong—a desire for interpersonal attachments (Baumeister & Leary, 1995). He points out that life is constantly changing (our communities, our goals, our jobs, our friends), and yet the meaning we would like to attribute to life is a constant (our values). Therefore, to Baumeister, self (or meaning) might best be defined by our abilities (1) to find purpose, (2) to make a difference, (3) to justify actions, and (4) to feel self-esteem. This view of identity is more philosophical in nature than those of some of the other modern theorists we have noted. But it shares with them the concepts of identity creation and the functional importance of the ego. These modern theorists, without exception, argue that individuals continue to grow psychologically after childhood and that looking at people's goals and their strategies for achieving them provides valuable insights into their identities. (See the Evaluating the Perspectives box.)

Evaluating the Perspectives

Advantages and Limits of the Ego (Neo-Analytic) Approach

- ### Quick Analogy
  Humans as conscious actors and strivers.

- ### Advantages
  Emphasizes the self as it struggles to cope with emotions and drives on the inside and the demands of others on the outside.

  Emphasizes the importance of the positive and goal-oriented nature of humanity.

  Acknowledges the impact of other individuals, society, and culture on personality.

  Attempts to explain the structure of the healthy and unhealthy psyche.

  Assumes development continues throughout the life cycle.

- ### Limits
  Relatively unconcerned with biology and fixed personality structures.

  Very difficult to test empirically.

  Sometimes a hodgepodge of different ideas from different traditions.

  Sometimes relies on abstract or vague concepts.

- ### View of Free Will
  Though personality is largely determined by unconscious forces, individuals do have the ability to overcome these.

- ### Common Assessment Techniques
  Varies from free association to situational and autobiographical study with an emphasis on self-concept.

- ### Implications for Therapy
  As with psychoanalytic therapy, insight into inner motivations is key, but because the ego is central, there is less concern with unconscious motivation. So, for example, you could work with a therapist to understand your constant bragging to friends or your fear of getting close to a lover in terms of early fears of abandonment, insecurity, mistrust, and feelings of inferiority. You may come to see your faulty patterns of relations with peers as derived from poor patterns of relations with your parents or siblings or early teachers.

Summary and Conclusion

Although Sigmund Freud placed the ego between the struggles that pitted the id against the superego, he was more fascinated with the drives and the struggle and less concerned with the ego. Many of Freud's successors took up the cause of the ego, as they recognized that it was an important and independent force of the psyche, and not just a response to the id. The notion of the conscious "self"—who we think we are—remains a major element of modern conceptions of personality.

Carl Jung was interested in the deepest universal aspects of personality and expanded ideas of the unconscious to include emotionally charged images and quasi-instincts that seem characteristic of all generations. In particular, he was interested in beliefs that we all share and in how our many similarities develop. He developed conceptions of the collective unconscious and archetypes; and although these ideas are not accepted by contemporary personality theorists in their simple and literal sense, Jung's brilliant creativity in this area has opened doors for subsequent theorists, and this portion of his theory may in time be accepted in some more complex form. Another Jungian contribution—the concept of complexes (emotionally charged thoughts and feelings on a particular theme)—has been well-accepted by the psychological community. Indeed, the term has made its way into our everyday language. Finally, Jung described personality as being comprised of competing forces, pulling against one another to reach equilibrium, best illustrated by the dimensions of extroversion and introversion—a tendency toward outward focus and a tendency toward inward focus. These terms are also widely used today, although they are usually conceptualized as opposite poles of the same dimension.

Alfred Adler focused attention on the social world and its impact on ego or identity formation. We owe to him our current conceptions of the inferiority complex (exaggerated feelings of personal incompetence) and the corresponding superiority complex (ego-protective feelings of grandeur). Adler's is an individual psychology that focuses on the uniqueness of individuals and the importance of how they perceive themselves. He believed that many personality problems could be avoided by using detailed knowledge about individuals to construct more healthy social environments. Adler also developed a personality typology based loosely on ancient Greek notions of the bodily humors, but he is perhaps best known as someone who firmly believed in the positive, goal-oriented nature of humankind.

Karen Horney changed the way that psychoanalytic theory viewed women, putting aside Freudian beliefs about penis envy and replacing them with theories, based on her own observations, for the reasons why women often did feel inferior to men. She emphasized the social influences on women—their relative lack of opportunities—as determinants of these inferiority feelings. She also modified Freudian biological determinism with her concept of basic anxiety (the child's sense of helplessness and insecurity). Thus, she moved psychoanalytic thought away from its predominately deterministic view and toward a more inclusive and interactive interpretation.

Erik Erikson demonstrated that important developmental steps mark the individual's route through life. The first stages of his developmental theory of personality look similar to a neo-analytic version of Freud's psychosexual stages, but Erikson did not stop there. Instead of viewing adulthood primarily as a reaction to childhood experiences, he saw it as a continuing developmental process, with its own issues and conflicts. At each stage a certain ego crisis must be resolved, and successful resolution of each crisis enables healthy development at later stages, throughout life.

Modern personality approaches to identity are not so apt to offer sweeping generalizations about large classes of people. Just as the neo-analytic theorists revised Freudian theory to take into account the effects of society, of culture, of gender differences, and of development across the life span, modern identity theorists further focus on the unique personal and situational demands facing each individual in the ongoing struggle to maintain a sense of self—of who we are. Modern identity theorists often take a functional approach to personality; that is, they look at motivated behaviors and goals in order to understand the self that underlies them. Some researchers believe that day-to-day goals have the most impact on personality, whereas others believe that our far-reaching, abstract goals are more significant. Some place more importance on the ways individuals plan to reach their goals than on the goals themselves. But all of these researchers agree that it is useful to look at these building blocks of identity (goals, motives, strivings, desires) to understand more fully the person beneath.

The questions of Where is the ego? and What constitutes an identity? will not be easily answered. We must agree first on what the definition of *identity* will be. Will it be global in nature, encompassing aspects of the individual as he or she relates to the world? Or will it be more internal, personal, and introspective? In either case, it is of the utmost importance that the self-directedness of the individual is not lost, for it is the ability of psychology to see and study this proactive nature that the neo-analysts have worked so hard to create.

 *Key Theorists*

Carl Jung	Karen Horney
Alfred Adler	Erik Erikson

Key Concepts

personal unconscious versus collective
   unconscious
archetypes
Jung's four functions of the mind
extroversion versus introversion
individual psychology
inferiority complex
superiority complex
organ inferiority
aggression drive

Adler's personality typology
basic anxiety
object relations theories
symbiotic psychotic versus normal
   symbiotic
Erikson's stages of identity formation
identity crisis
self-monitoring
self-presentation

Suggested Readings

Adler, A. (1959). *The practice and theory of individual psychology.* Totowa, NJ: Littlefield
   Adams.

Bottome, P. (1957). *Alfred Adler: A portrait from life.* New York: Vanguard.

Brome, V. (1981). *Jung: Man and myth.* New York: Atheneum Books.

Coles, R. (1970). *Erik Erikson: The growth of his work.* Boston: Little, Brown.

Erikson, E. (1963). *Childhood and society.* New York: Norton.

Horney, K. (1950). *Neurosis and human growth.* New York: Norton.

Horney, K. (1980). *The adolescent diaries of Karen Horney.* New York: Basic Books.

Jung, C. (1961). *Memories, dreams, reflections* (Aniela Jaffe, Ed.). New York: Pantheon.

Jung, C. (1968). *Analytical psychology: Its theory and practice.* New York: Pantheon.

Quinn, S. (1987). *A mind of her own: The life of Karen Horney.* New York: Simon & Schuster.

Snyder, M. (1987). *Public appearances, private realities: The psychology of self-monitoring.* New
   York: Freeman.

Young-Bruehl, E. (1988). *Anna Freud: A biography.* New York: Summit.

Chapter 5

Biological Aspects of Personality

Ask almost any parents why their children behave differently from each other and they will tell you that the kids were born that way. Mothers (and fathers) often insist that their children come into this world with their own personalities and ways of doing things—that is, with minds of their own.

American child psychology, however, has tended to focus on the environmental influences on personality. Families are bombarded with advice on how to raise a productive, contented, well-adjusted member of society. Books about child care have generated great interest, as North American parents strive to take an active role in helping their children grow up.

Professionals emphasize the importance of a loving environment in which children are praised for their accomplishments.

This emphasis on the environment is due in part to Americans' long-held cultural belief in opportunities for self-improvement. We do not accept the view that a person's place in life is fixed at birth. We like to believe that almost any child, with enough motivation and the proper upbringing, can go on to achieve almost anything he or she desires. These beliefs go back to the Enlightenment and its philosophical musings about the potential for glorious accomplishments by free men, which influenced the thinking of the American Revolution against the British in 1776. For example, the seventeenth-century English philosopher John Locke wrote that the human mind is a blank slate—*tabula rasa*—at birth (1690/1964). With the right upbringing, anyone could become a person of distinction.

*T*here is no doubt that the American dream of self-fulfillment through proper rearing and hard work does indeed come true in many cases. There is also no doubt, however, that biological factors affect a person's characteristic responses. A person is *not* born a blank slate that is then written on by the environment; rather, people start with certain inherent predispositions and abilities. Instead of arguing about the relative effects of heredity versus effects of the environment, it is more productive to try to understand the effects of human biology on human personality. With a careful analysis, we can avoid understating, or overstating, or misstating, the impacts of heredity.

Direct Genetic Effects

In the middle of the nineteenth century, Charles Darwin turned the life sciences upside down by arguing that people are not special creatures of divine creation but rather evolved directly from more primitive species. We are not made in God's image, but are cousins of chimps and apes. This idea was so radical that Darwin spent much effort arguing such points as that human bones, nerves, and muscles are similar to those of other primates. Such close anatomical relations, although "obvious" to us today, were not appreciated or accepted at the time.

Natural Selection and Functionalism

Darwin (1859) points out that each person is different from every other person. Some of these differentiating characteristics help the individual to survive—that is, to reproduce and pass on his or her genes to offspring. The process by which certain adaptive individual characteristics emerge over generations is known as **natural selection.** For example, in a dangerous environment full of predators, those individuals who are large or tough or fast or smart or able to organize defenses are most likely to survive. In a Darwinian analysis, attention is thus drawn to the *function* of a characteristic (such as speed or intelligence) in survival.

But which characteristic is the most important? In the predatory environment, was it the size or the speed or the intelligence of the individual, or organizational abilities, or camouflage techniques that made the difference to survival? Or perhaps it was something else altogether. This is a major difficulty with developing the details of a Darwinian approach: it is hard to know what the precise selection pressures were that shaped human evolution over millions of years. This problem plagues the modern application of Darwin's ideas—sometimes called *evolutionary personality theory* (Buss, 1990; Simpson & Kenrick, 1997). Still, it is clear that many of our individual tendencies are "in our bones" or, more accurately, in our genes.

Angelman Syndrome

Consider this example. Can you imagine an excessively happy child, one who is always filled with glee and good humor? In fact, such a condition is one of the signs of a rare genetic disorder called *Angelman syndrome.* Such children are usually also especially attractive and friendly. Sound good? Unfortunately, they also suffer mental retardation, sleep very little, and walk with a jerky movement, sort of like a puppet.

Angelman syndrome is a biological disorder caused by a defect on chromosome 15 (Zori et al., 1992). Human cells have twenty-three pairs of chromosomes, with half of each pair contributed by each parent. The chromosomes contain the genes, which control the body's manufacture of proteins. Genes affect development in many ways, including structural development—how our brains and bodies grow—and physiological development—how our hormones and general metabolism function.

Extreme cases like Angelman syndrome demonstrate that genetic factors set before birth can dramatically influence later personality. Although we know that genes *can* dramatically influence personality in unusual cases, the question remains as to *the extent* to which genes affect personality in normal development, and *which* aspects they shape (DiLalla, 1998).

■ ■ ■

It is easy to assume that a strong sex drive has survival value; individuals with no interest in sexual relations are usually unlikely to pass their genes on to offspring. Yet people vary markedly in their sex drives (libidos). It is also probably safe to assume that love and fear and anger have a genetic basis. They are universal and eternal. Unfortunately, this knowledge does not help us much in explaining the variations from person to person. To do that, we have to find stable individual differences in biological responsiveness. The remainder of this chapter explores such differences.

Genetic Effects through Temperament

Ivan Pavlov, the Russian physiologist who discovered classical conditioning in the salivation responses of dogs, was also very interested in differences in individuals' nervous systems (Pavlov, 1927). His investigations focused on an animal's orientation responses to new stimuli. Pavlov knew that the organism must respond appropriately for the organism to orient adaptively to the environment. For example, the organism must have the correct sensitivity to detect food or danger, but an overreaction to stimuli would leave the organism overwhelmed or unable to discriminate appropriately. We need to respond when danger is near but not to respond as if everything is a danger.

At birth, certain temperamental and sensitivity differences among babies are apparent. The term **temperament** is used to refer to stable individual differences in emotional reactivity. For example, some babies are cuddly, quiet, and may sleep soundly much of the day. Others are exceptionally active, or cry a lot, or respond poorly to cuddling, and drive their parents to exasperation.

Longitudinal developmental studies begun in the 1920s suggest that at least some of this reactivity remains stable over time as the children mature. On a physiological level, people exhibit different nervous system responses to unpleasant stimuli (like immersion of their elbows in ice water), and these individual response patterns likewise remain stable over time (Kagan & Moss, 1962; Kagan, Snidman, & Arcus, 1995; see also Conley, 1984; Goldsmith, 1989). (See the Self-Understanding box.)

Differences in temperament are visible in the way children of the same age react to strangers. Some children try to avoid interacting with new people, whereas others seek out such opportunities.

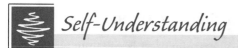

Self-Understanding

What Is Your Biological Temperament?

Although the best ways to assess biological aspects of personality will eventually incorporate direct biological assessments (such as measurement of hormone release, heart rate reactivity, and PET scans of the brain), we can often get a sense of our temperaments by looking for certain themes that we see in ourselves, or that others see in us.

I. Introversion–Extroversion
    a. Do you prefer being in crowds and at parties or more by yourself?
    b. Do you hate public speaking? Does it give you a pounding heart?
    c. Do you seek out roller coasters, parachute jumps, exotic travel?

II. Emotionality
    a. Were you a fearful child?
    b. Are you easily aroused to anger (hot-tempered)?
    c. Do you have mood swings, from very high to very low?

III. Activity
    a. As a child, were you always in motion?
    b. Are you more passive? restful? lethargic?
    c. Do you hate to sit around?

IV. Impulsiveness/Aggression
    a. As a child, were you more of a bully or more of a peacemaker?
    b. Do you win conviviality awards or cold-shoulder awards?
    c. Do you tend to make and follow plans, or do you rush off in new directions?

V. Other Drives
    a. Do you have a very high sex drive?
    b. Do you have a large appetite for food and/or drink?
    c. Do you resemble one of your parents in a drive or ability that has always seemed to be natural and special rather than trained or learned (such as artistic or musical talent, athletic ability, high intelligence, impulsiveness)?
    d. Do you have a deficit in some biological ability that has led you to over-develop a compensating ability?

Remember that biological factors combine with the other aspects of personality in complex ways to produce adult patterns of behavior.

Activity, Emotionality, Sociability, Impulsivity

Temperament is easy to see in other animals. It is certainly well known that many animals such as dogs and roosters can be bred to be more fierce and aggressive or more gentle and cooperative. In the human domain, children's counselors and psychologists are often surprised to notice that so-called problem children, youngsters who are especially aggressive or hyperactive, sometimes come from very stable, warm families; their parents complain (often correctly) that the kids were born that way. So, as the limits of simple environmental explanations become apparent, there has been increasing attention to theories and research on temperament.

Although there are differing accounts and models of temperament, most agree on the following four basic aspects of temperament (Buss & Plomin, 1984; Rothbart, 1981; Thomas, Chess, & Korn, 1982). First, there is an *activity* dimension. Some children are almost always in vigorous motion while others are more passive. Second, there is an *emotionality* dimension. Some children are easily aroused to anger or fear or other emotions, whereas other children are more calm and stable. Third, there is a dimension of *sociability*. Sociable children approach and enjoy others. Fourth, there is an *aggressive/impulsive* dimension, which characterizes the extent to which children are aggressive and cold rather than conscientious and friendly.

However, do not assume that science is unanimous on temperament. Decisions about scientific models and dimensions of temperament are usually based on data that come from having parents or other adults observe, count, and code certain behaviors in their children. For example, parents might record how many times a child cries in a given day. Or the children's reactions to meeting strangers might be systematically observed. Depending on the behavior recorded, the coding criteria, the task used, the coders, the situation, the subculture, and similar factors, somewhat different results will emerge.

Eysenck's Model

The best way to clear up these discrepancies about basic temperaments would be to find the actual biological substrates of these observable patterns of emotional reactivity. That is, it would be helpful to track the nervous system and hormonal changes that accompany stable patterns of reactivity. Perhaps several patterns of physiological responsiveness could be identified. This is a tremendously difficult problem, given our current state of knowledge. Some of the most interesting evidence for the effects of biological temperament on personality comes from British psychologist Hans Eysenck, particularly in the area of introversion–extroversion. Introverts are generally quiet, reserved, and thoughtful. Extroverts are active, sociable, and outgoing. The introversion–extroversion dimension thus combines elements of the activity dimension and the sociability dimension of temperament. Although notions of introversion–

extroversion appear in many personality theories, Eysenck ties the dimension directly to the central nervous system. His is a biologically based personality theory.

The basic idea is that extroverts have a relatively low level of brain arousal, and so they seek stimulation. They want to get things "juiced up." Introverts, on the other hand, are thought to have a higher level of central nervous system arousal, and so they tend to shy away from stimulating social environments. In particular, Eysenck points to the part of the brain known as the ascending reticular activating system (Eysenck, 1967). There is as yet, however, no solid empirical evidence that this brain system is directly related to personality. The argument has also been extended by Eysenck and others to a neuroticism–emotionality dimension, with the point being that stable people are said to have a well-modulated nervous system, whereas neurotic people have a very reactive nervous system, which promotes emotional instability. The validity of this intriguing model also is unknown (Gale, 1983).

There are many problems in trying to test a nervous system–based theory of temperament, which Eysenck himself acknowledged (Eysenck, 1990). First, it is difficult to define and measure nervous "arousal"; there is no impartial gauge like a thermometer and no single response like a fever. Second, many problems arise from the fact that the human body is a system that attempts to maintain equilibrium; responses rise and fall, varying in baseline, intensity, and duration.

Some individuals are more likely than others to seek out exciting (and potentially dangerous) activities. Possibly, they are seeking arousal from the environment to compensate for their lower levels of internal biological activation.

There is, however, assorted evidence that extroverts do indeed differ physiologically from introverts, though not in any simple way (Stelmack, 1990; Stelmack & Pivik, 1996). Some of this corroboration comes from studies using electrodermal measures—monitoring the electrical activity of the skin with electrodes. (This method is also used in so-called lie detector tests: sweaty hands are better conductors of electricity.) There is also some evidence that, as predicted, introverts are slower to habituate to (get used to) sensory stimuli such as unusual tones that are played (Crider & Lunn, 1971). Stimulation bothers them. In colloquial terms, it "gets on their nerves."

Some electroencephalography (EEG) studies also lend support to Eysenck's nervous system model. (EEG uses electrodes attached outside the skull to measure electrical brain-wave activity.) For example, at a very simple level, extroverts generally show less EEG arousal than introverts. Although this preliminary approach is definitely promising, it is likely that a more complex model of brain arousal and temperament will need to be developed, one that does not rely on only one aspect of nervous arousal (Eysenck, 1990; Gale, 1983).

Sensation Seeking, Emotions

A related nervous system approach to personality focuses directly on **sensation seeking** (Zuckerman, 1983). Think about people who are always on the lookout for a new challenge or a new high. Sensation seekers have a consistent tendency to seek out highly stimulating activities, such as sky-diving, and they are also attracted to the unknown. Sensation seekers, however, have no consistent preference as to whether they enjoy being around others. Thus they are not simply extroverts. But this theory similarly proposes that sensation seekers may have a low level of natural (internal biological) activation and so seek arousal from the environment. Consistent with Pavlov's original notions, sensation seekers seem to have a strong, nervous system–based, orienting response. They seem biologically primed to seek out and engage their environments. Unfortunately, such natural inclinations cannot be well understood until psychologists learn a lot more about the workings of the brain and the nerves.

The human brain has two distinct halves—a left brain and a right brain. One promising method of addressing biological differences in personality focuses on individual differences in hemispheric activity; that is, relative differences in activation between the right and left cerebral hemispheres in the brain (Davidson & Fox, 1989).

Although the two hemispheres communicate extensively with each other, each has its own structures and functions. There is reason to believe that the left anterior hemisphere plays a key role in positive emotion, but activation of the right anterior hemisphere seem to be key in negative emotion (Glick, 1985). This specialization of functions of different brain areas should not be confused with the once-popular pseudoscience of phrenology (see Figure 5.1).

Figure 5.1

A Phrenological Diagram of the Brain, from Gall. Attempts to relate personality to the brain have a long history, much of it in approaches that were later discredited. This diagram shows the locations in the brain where Gall, a phrenology theorist, believed that personality traits were located. Phrenologists observed the shape, size, and irregularities of people's external skulls and related these to psychological characteristics.

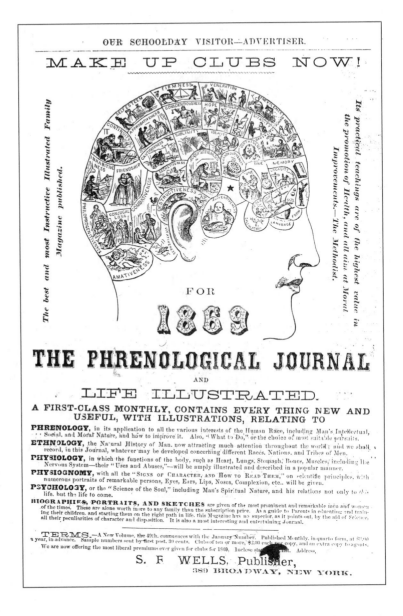

Alpha brain waves, known to be inversely related to brain activation, can be measured with EEGs. How is all this relevant to personality? The idea is that relatively greater activation of the right hemisphere is associated with greater reactions of fear and distress to a stressful situation; that is, individuals who have a relatively more active right hemisphere are more likely to overreact to a negative stimulus. Although evidence that is based on such EEG studies is necessarily weak, such approaches may yield important insights as active, "on-line" brain scanning techniques become more available for research (Haier, 1998).

If certain aspects of personality are indeed based on biologically induced temperament, then we should expect to see such differences in all cultures. Indeed, the introversion–extroversion dimension does seem to appear worldwide (Eysenck, 1990). Also of interest, recent studies of brain development and brain activity reveal that the brain reaches its maximum number of synaptic connections and its greatest metabolic activity around age three or four, thus supporting the psychoanalytic observation that the basis of personality is formed by around this age. The brain can, however, alter its organization to some extent later in life (Thompson, 1993).

Twins as a Source of Data

We should also be able to detect systematic biological differences by studying twins. Twin research is indeed now one of the most active areas of research in the study of the biological aspects of personality. Many intriguing studies have compared identical twins to fraternal twins. Identical twins share the same genetic make-up, but fraternal twins (who develop from separate fertilized eggs) have a comparable genetic overlap to ordinary brothers and sisters. On certain key dimensions—emotional stability and extroversion—identical twins are indeed more similar than fraternal twins (Heath et al., 1989; Rose et al., 1988; see also Loehlin, 1992). Does this prove a biological basis? Not necessarily, because identical twins may be treated more similarly than fraternal twins. (Identical twins look more alike, and their parents may dress them alike, and so on.) Or, identical twins may consciously try to act more similarly than fraternal twins. For these reasons, it is much more informative to compare twins who have been adopted and raised apart from each other.

Sir Francis Galton

In the latter half of the nineteenth century, the British scientist Sir Francis Galton began the study of genetic influences on personality (Galton, 1869). He was inspired by the work of his cousin Charles Darwin. Galton drew family trees of blood

Parents may draw attention to the similarity of identical twins by dressing them in the same clothing, by providing matching hairstyles, and by treating them identically. If identical twins are treated more similarly to each other than fraternal twins are, then we cannot conclude that greater similarity in personality among the identical twins is of purely genetic origin.

relatives of famous and eminent people. Sure enough, he found that eminence seemed to run in families. For example, a son might succeed his father as a professor at a university chair (professorship). Galton also noticed that among the lower classes in nineteenth century Britain, hardly anyone achieved eminence.

Although one of the most brilliant men of his time, in retrospect Galton was what we could today call a benign racist. He endeavored to be scientific but he began from the supposition that upper-class Englishmen were a superior population. It is hardly surprising that the son of a wealthy, well-educated professor would be more likely to achieve prominence in a hierarchical society than would the son of poor, illiterate parents. To his credit (given the tenor of the times), Galton recognized this possibility, and he suggested that adopted children be studied, including adoptive twins. So it was Galton who began the study of adoptive twins. But Galton did not worry that too much would come of such studies; he was convinced of his own natural superiority (and that of his relatives and friends).

It is curious that one seemingly obvious flaw in Galton's line of thinking did not jump out and destroy it—namely the case of women. Female children of eminent British professors did not follow their fathers into professorships. Women were generally not even allowed access to the best schools. (In the United States, women could not graduate from top colleges like Yale or Princeton until the 1970s.) The same lack of access and resources of course applied to the lower classes—men as well as women—in Galton's Britain.

Interestingly, Galton also began the eugenics ("good birth" or "good genes") movement. He argued that eminent families should have lots of children, thus improving human blood lines. Unfortunately, this seemingly well-intentioned line of thinking contributed to the scientifically "justified" worldwide racism (even genocide) that has tainted the twentieth century. We return to this issue later in this chapter. Biological theories of personality seem inextricably tied to social and political outcomes.

Minnesota Twin Study

Consider now the case of Jack and Oskar. Jack and Oskar are identical twins who were separated in infancy but brought together as adults. Oskar was raised in Germany by his Catholic maternal grandmother; Jack was raised outside Europe by his Jewish father. It turns out that these twin brothers share many traits and habits. They are both absent-minded, like spicy foods, and most important for our purposes, have a domineering, angry sort of temperament.

As identical twins, Jack and Oskar have the same genes (that is, are *monozygotic*—coming from the same zygote or fertilized egg). Given their disparate upbringings, their similarities must somehow be due to their genetic endowments. No one has a problem with this argument in terms of Jack's and Oskar's striking physical resemblance. But direct genetic control of personality is less easy to swallow.

The case of identical twins separated at birth provides a potentially rich source of information about the roles of genetic and environmental factors in determining personality. These twins didn't even know of one another's existence until they met as adults and discovered striking parallels. Both had become fire captains, wore similar mustaches and glasses, and had many of the same personality traits.

These identical twins and others, raised apart from each other, have been gathered in an ongoing study at the University of Minnesota (Bouchard et al., 1990). Such studies have found impressive similarities in personality between people who have the same genetic make-up. These similarities are less than those of identical twins raised together, thus showing the influence of the environmental upbringing. But the similarities of

Famous Personalities

Music and the Jackson Family

At the 1995 MTV Video Music Awards, Michael Jackson received three awards for his *Scream* video. Also receiving three awards was Michael's sister Janet. Not only did the two artists work together, but Janet signed a multimillion dollar recording contract, putting her alongside her brother at the top of the music industry. According to industry managers and agents, Janet reached the top because of that rare and genuine talent it takes to achieve long-term success. Innovative dance skills, creative choreography, music that is constantly evolving, and lyrics that continue to express exactly what the audience is feeling are the talents that both Michael and Janet Jackson have demonstrated in abundance.

The public has not been surprised at Janet's achievements, in part because she is related to the megastar Michael; it must run in the family. Janet's success is accepted as only natural because she shares a biological musical propensity with Michael. Indeed, there are many other examples

of musical talent running in families. But if the super-musician genes that the two stars got from their parents are the reason for their success, what about their sister Rebbie, who is least known to the public?

Though Rebbie is the oldest of the Jackson children, she keeps a low profile. Not pursuing a career in the music industry, as the rest of her siblings continue to do, Rebbie wished only to devote her life to a religious cause. Her brothers were all part of the musical group The Jackson Five, and her two sisters, Latoya and Janet, also have careers in the music business. If the music gene was passed so obviously to Katherine and Joseph Jackson's offspring, then why isn't Rebbie a musical talent?

Although each person's genetic make-up is unique (except for identical twins), perhaps genetic predisposition isn't the only key factor determining the outcome of a person's musical development. Indeed, another factor often used to explain this success is early environment. So what identical twins are greater than those of fraternal twins, who have overlapping but not identical genetic make-ups (Pedersen, Plomin, McClearn, & Friberg, 1988; see also McCartney, Harris, & Bernieri, 1990).

The controversy arises as to *why* identical twins have such similar personalities. Is there a gene for being stingy and a gene for being optimistic? Probably not. But, as noted above, there may very well be patterns of genes that affect our temperaments and our behavioral predispositions—for example, that make us more aggressive or more sensitive and cautious. When these innate tendencies encounter similar environmental pressures, they may often result in similar patterns of behavior—that is, similar personalities (Waller et al., 1990). For example, a cautious, unaggressive boy, with a body that is sensitive to pain and stimulation, may be unlikely to become a football tackle. This is not to say there is a gene for "sports interest," but there likely is a genetic influence on relevant responsiveness. The distinction is important because it implies that given the right circumstances, the cautious, sensitive, unaggressive boy might very well become a star football tackle.

type of environment were the Jackson siblings raised in, and how was it different for Rebbie?

After the fifth son was born, the boys in the Jackson family were all encouraged by their parents to develop their musical abilities. Latoya and Janet were born among the boys and grew up seeing this exceptional emphasis on musical development from their parents. This probably influenced them to pursue their own careers in music. Because the innate abilities of each of these children encountered similar environmental pressures, they became musically oriented people. But Rebbie, being the oldest and a female sibling, did not grow up with that parental pressure to perform; she was already a teenager by the time The Jackson Five began jamming. Because her parents were urging this musical development primarily in their sons, Rebbie did not feel the need to divert her attentions from other interests. Any biological predisposition Rebbie may have had in this regard was not activated into development, and thus did not emerge. This illustration thus stresses that although certain abilities and predispositions have a genetic component, personality development is rooted in an interaction of genetics and appropriate environmental stimulation.

When two members of the same family are strikingly successful in the same domain, it is likely that both hereditary similarities and a common home environment are responsible. Michael and Janet Jackson are shown here after she presented him with a Grammy Living Legend Award.

There is an ongoing search for a gene that might underlie certain aggressive personalities. Following Galton's example, researchers have been constructing family trees of a group of aggressive men in the Netherlands (Morell, 1993). It is thought that a genetic defect prevents manufacture of an enzyme that breaks down certain **neurotransmitters**—the chemicals nerves use to communicate. When faced with environmental challenge, these men are primed to "go off"—to overreact because their nervous systems are not being properly regulated. Note that if such a link does become firmly established, the gene itself does not directly cause the aggression. Rather, the gene affects an enzyme, which predisposes the body to react in certain ways; the actual reactions are then determined by the environment and by other aspects of the person.

There is much controversy about how much of personality is genetically determined. Children of the same parents who are raised in the same family share both some biological endowment and much environmental influence; yet their personalities are often strikingly different (Saudino, 1977). To some extent, children in the same family have different experiences and are treated differently, but it is difficult to know precisely how and why (Dunn & Plomin, 1990; Baker & Daniels, 1990). Significantly, in moving from childhood to adulthood, the environmental effects on personality become more evident. There is an inverse correlation between personality similarity and age for both monozygotic and dizygotic twins: as twins get older, their personalities become more different (McCartney et al., 1990).

In the case of studies of identical twins raised apart, many complex questions arise. Were they placed into similar types of homes by adoption agencies? Did they learn about each other, perhaps through hearing about their twin? Do they try to act similarly upon being brought together, knowing they are twins? Perhaps most important, was the process of their similar personality development much more complex than a simple genetic model would assume?

So again, how much of personality is genetically determined? No simple answers are expected to be forthcoming in the near future. In fact, the question itself is too simplistic to be helpful in understanding individual differences. Biological predispositions interact with the eliciting circumstances of the environment. However, it is important to become familiar with this topic, as it has many implications for society.

Schizophrenia

It is easy to overgeneralize the importance of genetics to personality. Consider the case of schizophrenia. Schizophrenia is a devastating condition in which a person loses touch with reality. For example, such people may have delusions, become paranoid, and generally talk or behave very strangely. There has been an intensive search for biological causes of this disorder. Many studies have indicated that schizophrenia tends to run in families (Schiffman & Walker, 1998). That is, if one has a schizophrenic parent, the odds of schizophrenia rise dramatically. They rise even further if one has a fraternal twin with this condition. If one has a schizophrenic identical twin, the odds approach 50-50 of developing this strange syndrome of distorted reality and odd emotional reactions. A correlation exists even if the twins are raised in different families (Gottesman, 1991).

Inferences from Twins

Because of these correlations, some have concluded that schizophrenia is a genetic disease. This is an imprecise deduction at best, as many of the identical twins of schizophrenics never develop the condition. (In comparison, the identical twin of someone with blue eyes always has blue eyes.) If schizophrenia is simply a direct result of defective genes, then the identical twins of schizophrenics should likewise have the condition. Furthermore, a careful analysis of the brains of identical twins cast doubt on this assertion of direct genetic causation. In this study, fifteen sets of identical twins were studied; in each set, one twin had schizophrenia and the other was normal. As identical twins, the members of each pair had identical genetic make-up. However, using brain MRI scans and related techniques, scientists were able to show clear differences in their brain structure. The afflicted twin usually had larger fluid-filled ventricles, suggesting that some brain tissue was missing. The schizophrenic twins also had some signs of brain atrophy or developmental failure (Suddath et al., 1990). Because identical genes would give identical instructions to the body for brain development, something else—some other factor—must be contributing to the schizophrenic brain development (or lack thereof).

Faced with this puzzle, researchers now say that there is a "genetic predisposition" to schizophrenia. That is, certain genes make schizophrenia more likely, but they are not the sole, direct cause. If you think about it, this explanation is something of an intellectual cop-out. What it really means is, "Genes play some role but we really don't know how the process works."

The same is true of many other genetic influences on personality. For example, the probability of a match—called concordance—of manic-depressive illness is very high. If an individual swings regularly from wildly enthusiastic energy (a raving maniac) to hopelessly dark depression, then the identical twin is also very likely to suffer this disorder. The concordance is high (Suinn, 1995). Yet it is also well established that depression is a complex phenomenon, heavily influenced by the environment. It would be a serious mistake to think of it as solely biologically determined. We should always remember to consider the influence of biological factors on personality in a broad context. This necessitates sophisticated thinking about biology and personality.

Homosexuality

People who are sexually attracted to members of their own gender have existed throughout history; even the Bible describes homosexual practice. It has also existed in all societies around the world. In addition to engaging in non-normative sexual practices, gay men and lesbians sometimes exhibit expressive behaviors that appear to indicate a homosexual orientation. Homosexuality or heterosexuality is clearly an important aspect of personality, one that a personality theory should be able to explain.

Freud, in a now-discredited analysis, regarded homosexuality as an illness, resulting from a disruption of normal psychosexual development. According to Freud, a normal child passes through psychosexual stages until his sexual urges can finally be directed, in a mature way, at an appropriate love object of the opposite gender. Most children pass through a stage in this process with a love of their own genitals—a self-focused, narcissistic love. But some children retain a focus on their own genitals as a love object: some little boys do not grow to identify with their fathers but instead try to please their fathers and eventually look to find lovers with genitals like their own. That is, they become homosexuals. This argument, though unsupported by research, did have a major impact on the practice of psychiatry. Not until 1974 did the American Psychiatric Association evaluate the scientific invalidity of the Freudian explanation and remove homosexuality from its handbook of men-

Although homosexuality appears to have a biological basis, gays—like all people—are heavily influenced by their cultures and upbringings. This is beautifully illustrated by this wedding picture of two lesbians who chose to wear traditional wedding gowns during their commitment ceremony.

tal illnesses, much to the relief of the thousands of well-functioning homosexuals. In fact, much of the distress felt by homosexuals can be traced to society's severe reactions against them (Herschberger, 1998).

Many homosexuals report being attracted to members of their own gender even before having any sexual experiences. Most face societal persecution or discrimination; there is little reason to think that gay people actively choose to have these feelings and attractions. Because homosexual just seems to be the way some people are, interest has been drawn to possible biological bases. But because of the great societal stigma attached to homosexuality, research on homosexuality is sparse, contradictory, or uninformative. Some recent research suggests that a homosexual predisposition is at least partly (but only partly) genetically determined (Bailey & Pillard 1991; Buhrich, Bailey, & Martin, 1991). Homosexuality tends to run in families and is more common among monozygotic (identical) twins than among fraternal (dizygotic) twins. There is also some evidence that part of the brain's anterior hypothalamus, known to be related to sexual behavior, is significantly smaller in gay men (LeVay, 1991). None of these factors alone proves that homosexuality has a genetic origin. But, taken in concert with the fact that homosexuality seems universal across time and culture, these findings are strongly suggestive of at least some biological origin for the tendency toward homosexuality.

On the other hand, the fact that the associations between genetic heritage and homosexuality are nowhere near perfect suggests that environmental factors often play an important role in this aspect of personality. As we have seen with other biological predispositions, biological sexual orientation probably grows or matures certain ways in certain contexts. It is also possible that some instances of homosexuality have nothing to do with genetics and are instead the result of conditioning or other experiences. Some homosexuals, especially those who reach puberty early, may be surrounded by friends of the same sex (most eleven-year-old boys have only other boys as close friends); and so these boys may have their first sexual fantasies or early experiences with same-sex others (Storms, 1981). Such pleasurable experiences may then be sought in the future. This is a possible but unproven environmental basis for some homosexuality. As we argue repeatedly in this book, the different perspectives on personality are not mutually exclusive; on the contrary, we need various approaches in order to understand fully the diversity of human behavior. This may not be satisfying to those who seek a simple, definitive explanation of complex behavior patterns, but it is a reflection of the state of our current understanding.

Exotic Becomes Erotic

Another approach that attempts to combine biology and socialization into explaining some cases of homosexuality or bisexuality is what Daryl Bem (1996) calls "Exotic becomes erotic." Simply stated, Bem proposes that inborn temperament influences young children to engage in gender-congruent (socially expected) behavior or not. For example, a little girl who likes to play quietly in a nurturing way will have girls as friends. But if she tends to prefer lots of rough and tumble ("tomboy") activities, then she will have many boys as friends. In this latter case, boys will seem common and ordinary. What happens at adolescence? As the hormones of puberty hit, so do strong feelings and physiological arousal. Although most girls apply this arousal to exotic figures like music stars and movie actors and then even to those unfamiliar boys at her school, the tomboy already has lots of boys as friends and so she may see certain girls as exotic, and then as erotic. The opposite is true of certain boys: some of those who grow up with many female friends might become intrigued with boys. Although this theory has not yet been well tested, it does illustrate that there are various possible complex pathways to sexual attraction.

Kin Selection

How can homosexuality have been selected through evolution, given that homosexuals usually have few if any children of their own? That is, why didn't tendencies toward homosexuality disappear long ago, since there does not seem to be much survival value inherent in this tendency? The answer probably lies somewhere in the fact that the subtleties and mechanisms of evolution are not fully understood. One possibility involves what is called **kin selection** (Burnstein, Crandall, & Kitayama, 1994). If the nieces and nephews of homosexuals are especially likely to survive, then the genetic tendency toward homosexuality will also survive (because nieces and nephews share some genetic make-up with their homosexual aunt or uncle). Such analyses shift attention away from the individual's survival and toward analysis of the whole population—that is, population genetics.

Hormones and Experience

It may also be the case that any biological bases of homosexuality may result from early hormonal experiences. For example, medical conditions or drugs in the mother may affect the child in the uterus or in early infancy; these may not be genetic (Persky, 1987). Indeed, many biological bases of personality result from early experiences rather than from genes. The growth of the brain and the rest of the nervous system—a biological factor—is strongly influenced not only by genes but also by the environment.

It might also be the case that a genetic tendency toward homosexuality has some unknown survival advantage in people who do not become gay. For example, perhaps the straight sisters of gay men are especially likely to have lots of children. The important point here is that biological influences on personality and behavior are rarely simple, and any simple conclusions are almost certainly erroneous.

Finally, in gaining a sophisticated understanding of the biological bases of personality, it is important to note that unique results emerge when certain biological aspects of personality are combined with certain environments. These results cannot be predicted by either the biology or the environment alone. For example, in a hard-driving autocratic family in which the father uses lots of punishment to raise his two sons, the inherently aggressive, outgoing son might grow up hard-driving and autocratic like his father, whereas the sensitive, emotional son might grow up kind and charitable, vowing never to behave like his cruel, loudmouthed father. If, however, the same two sons were raised by a very nurturant, democratic father, the results might almost reverse; the sensitive son might grow up more assertive while the aggressive son might channel his energies into helping others. In other words, there is an interaction effect. In mathematical terms, personality is a multiplicative function of the two influences, rather than an additive function. This means that we cannot simply average together the biological influences and the environmental influences to predict personality; rather, we often must often analyze the uniqueness that results when the two combine.

Mediated Effects of Biology

Effects through Environmental Toxins and Physical Illness

Vincent van Gogh, the brilliant impressionist painter, was long thought to be such an intense genius that he drove himself mad. Indeed, van Gogh often behaved oddly and even cut off his own ear (and then painted a self-portrait). He committed suicide in 1890. It now appears that van Gogh may have suffered, not from a personality dysfunction, but from Meniere's disease, an inner-ear disorder that can produce disabling dizziness, nausea, and auditory disturbances (Arenberg, 1990). Illness can cause dramatic effects on our patterns of reactions.

Vincent van Gogh (shown here in self-portrait) cut off part of his own ear with a razor after a quarrel with Paul Gauguin and committed suicide shortly thereafter. His bizarre behavior may have been the result of the psychological effects of organic disease.

Poisoning

In *Alice in Wonderland,* Alice encounters the Mad Hatter. The phrase "mad as a hatter" has been in common use for over a century. It arose because hat makers in fact suffered brain damage as they worked with mercury in making felt hats. It is now well documented that dramatic changes in personality can result from poisoning and from illnesses such as strokes.

Today, mercury is commonly used in industry and agriculture and sometimes shows up in fish that lived in polluted waters. People who eat such contaminated fish soon start behaving quite strangely. In short, ingestion of mercury is occasionally known to produce marked changes in personality, even today (Fagala & Wigg, 1992). Because mercury is a component of dental amalgams (cavity fillings), there has been much speculation in recent years about possible subtle effects on physical and mental health. There is, however, no evidence that people are being inadvertently poisoned by their dentists.

Although mercury poisoning is relatively rare, heavy metal poisoning is widespread. Today a significant number of children suffer gradual brain damage traceable to lead poisoning. Many hundreds of thousands of children are exposed to potentially toxic levels of lead from old paint or plumbing fixtures, leaded gasoline, and other environmental sources. (The root *plumb* in the word plumbing in fact comes from the Latin word for "lead"; lead poisoning is sometimes termed "plumbism.") Lead poisons the child's developing nervous system, impairing cognitive function and producing deviant (often antisocial) behavior (Needleman & Bellinger, 1991).

Many other metals likely affect personality, though to an unknown degree. People who mine manganese sometimes become compulsive fighters and later develop Parkinson's disease. Manganese also seems to affect some Pacific islanders, whose volcanic soil is rich in this and other metals.

Brain Disease

A stable personality depends on a healthy, well-functioning brain. Diseases or toxins that affect brain function often affect personality (Grunberg, Klein, & Brown, 1998). Besides metals, there is a long list of toxic substances known to affect personality. In many cases of brain disorders, it is not known whether the problem is triggered by toxins, microbes, or the body's own failings. Alzheimer's disease is a devastating ailment of the brain's cerebral cortex. Although it usually strikes only the elderly, its cause is unknown. The early psychological manifestations of Alzheimer's are often quirks of behavior and some memory loss. As the disease progresses, alterations in personality are dramatic; the patients seem to lose their personalities altogether. These effects are often the most difficult to bear for the (grown) children of elderly Alzheimer's patients. It is tragic to watch a parent lose his or her personality and become a stranger.

The pain we experience in facing such changes demonstrates the great degree to which we do indeed love people for their personalities.

Strokes, which damage parts of the brain, also can have dramatic effects on personality. Often, a kind person who has a stroke becomes aggressive and uncooperative; sometimes the reverse occurs. It depends in part on which region of the brain is damaged. Many other medical conditions (such as temporal lobe epilepsy) and various surgical procedures also can produce biologically based changes in personality, but these are rarely studied by personality psychologists. For example, many people complain to doctors that their spouses' personalities became somehow "different" after they underwent coronary bypass surgery, but this phenomenon is not fully understood. One possibility is that the life-support and anesthesia procedures used in the operating room may damage small areas of the brain. It is interesting to speculate that a wide range of diseases may have poorly understood or subtle effects on personality. Just as diseases such as Alzheimer's and poisons such as lead were not understood for many years, there are undoubtedly many conditions and toxins that today affect personality, though they are unknown to us.

Our understanding of such biological influences on personality has major implications for our beliefs about law and justice. One extreme position is that most criminal or evil acts are committed by people who couldn't help themselves; they are either compelled, or not restrained, by some disorder in their nervous system. Interestingly, although this position is often identified with a very liberal or left-wing political orientation, it is actually quite similar to the position that some people simply have "bad genes." This latter argument is usually made by conservative, right-wing politicians. Thus, ironically, both extreme political positions are often comfortable with the idea of biological determinism of personality.

The more difficult, complex position is the one that acknowledges that biological factors influence personality but still recognizes the individual's capacity to challenge and sometimes overcome these biological tendencies. In fact, we usually attribute the mantle of true heroism only to those noble people among us—such as Helen Keller or Vincent van Gogh or poet Sylvia Plath—who can overcome the frailties inherent in their "nature."

Effects from Legal and Illegal drugs

Many chemical effects are not accidental. Widely prescribed drugs such as tranquilizers (like Valium), sleeping pills (like Halcion), and various antidepressants are known to have short-term and sometimes long-term effects on personality. Long-lasting, dramatic alterations in personality are thought to be quite rare, but they can occur with a single dose of a drug such as cocaine or LSD. The fact that dramatic changes occur at all should make us wonder about more widespread, subtle effects (Alessandri et al., 1995; McMahon & Richards, 1996).

Consider the case of chronic cocaine users. Cocaine tends to produce symptoms of paranoia. Users may become hypersensitive—to light, to noise, to other people. They may worry, become obsessed with details, and feel they are being persecuted. Cocaine addicts may become nervous and depressed. There is evidence that cocaine prevents the reabsorption of the neurotransmitter dopamine. (Dopamine is a chemical that certain neurons use to communicate with each other.) When dopamine concentrations rise after a cocaine hit, the initial effect is an emotional high; but brain activity is disrupted as dopamine levels later crash. It is likely that some people have natural or disease-caused defects or weaknesses in their dopamine systems. These individuals might be prone to paranoid personalities. They may also be especially susceptible to cocaine addiction. Similarly, it has long been noticed that people with Parkinson's disease seem to be stoic; since Parkinson's disease involves a defect in the dopamine system, it may be the case that this defect produces this aspect of personality. Unfortunately, this whole field of neurotransmitter abnormality and personality is still in its infancy (Menza et al., 1990).

When legal (prescription) drugs are tested for their safety and efficacy, there is rarely if ever much comprehensive, in-depth tracking of effects on personality. We may hear about the murderer who blames her criminal behavior on her sleeping pills, but there is no regular monitoring of whether various medications increase the likelihood of divorce or child abuse or sociability. Given the vast numbers of people who consume potent legal and illegal drugs, it is surprising that so little is known.

Because drugs and poisons can have such major and dramatic influences on personality, a basic field of study called "personality toxicology" is in order. There should be experts who focus on the major and minor effects of environmental substances and toxins on human personality. Unfortunately, the study of personality is usually seen to be so far removed from the study of biochemistry that there is little intersection of the fields. (The reverse is also true: Could you imagine a biochemistry course having a major section on personality?) Some psychiatrists do indeed study the role of drugs and other toxic substances in causing and treating psychiatric disturbance—the field is called *psychopharmacology*—but this work has little to do with the mainstream study of personality.

Finally, it should be noted that the existence of many environmentally based biological influences on personality is another reason to be cautious about assuming hereditary causes of personality. That is, many correlations between biological functioning and personality undoubtedly will be found that derive from a common environmental cause, not from heredity. For example, if the children of felt hat makers have a manic personality like their fathers', it is not their genes that are at fault, but rather the mercury that is coming into the home. Just because a disease runs in families does not mean it is genetic. Similarly, but less obviously, if high-strung people who are prone to heart attacks are found to have very reactive nervous systems, the link is not necessarily ascribable to their inherited constitutions.

Effects from Creation of Environments

We earlier pointed out that chronically active, crying infants can drive their parents into states of frustration and exasperation; the infant then lives in this frustrated, exasperated environment. An intriguing way that biology can affect personality is by affecting the environments in which we find ourselves. That is, certain of our biological influences may cause us to wind up in certain situations, and these situations may then influence our personalities (Scarr & McCartney, 1990).

Consider the case of a person who experiences a series of stressful life events such as loss of a loved one, a move, a new job, new friends (Plomin & Neiderhiser, 1992). Such stressful events are usually considered to be random intrusions of an unpredictable environment. In fact, there are stress scales that measure the amount of stress or challenge in a person's life.

But sometimes these events may not be totally outside the influence of the individual. In fact, genetic or other biological characteristics may influence the likelihood that we will experience certain events. For example, people with an innate tendency toward being more aggressive might be more likely to experience divorce. Extroverts, seeking stimulation, might be more likely to experience job changes and other moves. And so on. Certain characteristics of the individual lead to certain experiences which in turn influence individual responding (Saudino et al., 1997). Similarly, people who are very active, strong, and athletic may seek out certain environments where sports are common and available; these environments then in turn may shape a "sports personality" (Scarr & McCartney, 1990).

Sensitive, active infants and children may create disorganization, anxiety, or sleeplessness in their parents' lives. The children then experience a very different family life than if they were calm, cooperative children. They are now active children in a challenging environment.

Biological influences on the creation of environments can also function in even more subtle and complex ways. For example, consider the case of blindness. Various biological conditions lead children to be born blind or to lose their sight early in life. The lack of sight would naturally be expected to produce certain common personality characteristics. For example, blind children with a creative bent are obviously more likely to be drawn to activities that use nonvisual senses, such as hearing (music) or touch (sculpture). Blindness is easily identified. But imagine that two people are born to perceive the world in special but similar ways. Perhaps they have an excellent sense of smell or vision, or perhaps they have exceptional hand–eye coordination, or perhaps their minds tend to work in terms of images rather than in terms of words (sort of like the difference between road symbols and road signs). In such cases, the biological predisposition will lead to an attraction to certain environments or activities which will in turn sometimes have systematic influences on personality. (See Chipuer et al., 1993, for the case of genetics, personality, and adults' perceptions. See also Plomin & Nesselroade, 1990.) For example, it might be the case that children with fine artistic vision select a whole host of activities that helps shape their "artistic personality." Such processes are little studied.

Do Looks Reveal Personality?

In his play *Julius Caesar*, Shakespeare wrote, "Cassius has a lean and hungry look" (Act I, Scene 2). If Cassius were fatter, he presumably would be less dangerous. Do looks really reveal personality? Systematic study of this topic began with the work of the German psychiatrist Ernst Kretschmer (1934). Observing his patients, Kretschmer speculated about the association between physique and mental disorders. For example, he thought that schizophrenics were more likely to be slender people. W. H. Sheldon elaborated on this idea and applied it to normal people (Sheldon & Stevens, 1942). Sheldon measured people's proportions and their personalities and developed a theory of body types, or *somatotypes*.

Somatotypes

Sheldon's **somatotypology** differentiates between three body types: (1) **mesomorphs,** muscular, large-boned athletes; (2) **ectomorphs,** slender, bookworm types; and (3) **endomorphs,** roly-poly, and supposedly good-natured, types.

Although Sheldon's work attracted a lot of attention, it was not supported by most research. We cannot gather important information about someone's personality by measuring his belly size. The idea was undoubtedly too simplistic. Sheldon's work is thus sometimes noted in psychology books today as a historical curiosity. But could such an approach to body types have contained a kernel of truth? Could there be a physiological basis for the possible relations between physical characteristics and personality?

Beyond Somatotypes

There are several possibilities. First, it could be the case that a certain type of physiology affects both personality and physical shape. For example, perhaps a nervous system that makes one shy and introverted is also a nervous system that keeps one thin. This might be because of a high metabolism or a hunger mechanism that is easily satiated. Such relations have not yet been identified.

Many people who suffer from the eating disorders of anorexia and bulimia severely endanger their health and even their lives.

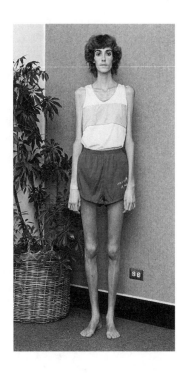

Social influences may also be involved. For example, consider the case of anorexia, a condition in which an otherwise healthy person eats less and less and becomes thinner and thinner (Mussell & Mitchell, 1998). The anorexic may even die of complications of the weight loss, as happened with singer Karen Carpenter. Anorexics are usually very sensitive young women who are shy and have a low self-esteem; they are often hassled by their families and feel out of control. In such cases, physical characteristics (being excessively thin) are a good marker for personality (shy, introverted, sensitive). Unfortunately, the precise relations among personality, physiology, and conditions such as anorexia have not been studied thoroughly enough to allow documentation of any underlying physiological explanations.

Furthermore, it could be the case that dramatically changing one's physical characteristics—say, by gaining a lot of weight or by becoming a serious body builder—might also change one's usual physiological reaction patterns. It is known that changing one's physical condition does indeed influence such bodily conditions as resting heartbeat, heartbeat change in response to challenge, cholesterol level, blood pressure, lung capacity and function, and similar physiological characteristics, any or all of which might indeed affect psychological responses. Personality may thus be affected. Although the impact of such changes on personality has not yet been studied in detail, it is a potentially fruitful topic for future research. (The relationship between emotional expression and personality is taken up in Chapter 8 in our discussion of traits.) In sum, it is conceivable that there are direct physiological ties between personality and body shape, but these have not been much studied by modern research.

It is undeniably the case that our physical characteristics can influence the reactions of others (Heatherton & Hebl, 1998). For example, if people such as teachers approach children who are thin and "intellectual-looking" with the belief that these children are likely to be good students, then they may make their own expectations come true. For this to be a significant influence on personality, people must share stereotypes about the personalities associated with physical characteristics, and indeed they do (Tucker, 1983). This line of thought is the subject of the next section.

Effects from Reactions of Others

The greatest environmental influence on psychological development is the reactions of the people around us. One's sense of identity depends to a large extent on how we are treated; if our parents and teachers and friends like us and expect great things from us, we are likely to form positive self-images. Unfortunately, the reverse is also true; undesirable physical characteristics can lead to unpleasant reactions, and consequently, to negative self-images.

Think about people's reactions to those of us who are either very short or tall. We tend to "look up to" tall people, but "look down on" short people. Tall may be exalted, lofty, and prominent, but short may be low, debased, and squat. For women, there are further restrictions because women are not expected to be taller than men. Of course these reactions are stereotypes, but they are so common and so strong that they often have an indelible effect on short or tall people. This effect is in addition to the effects caused by creation of environments—the places and activities that tall and short people may seek out. For example, not all short guys are precluded from excelling in high school sports, but their peers may also expect them to be less physically successful. These expectations can in turn affect personality.

One young girl suffering from throat cancer found her personality changing as surgical operations distorted her looks. Her classmates began to avoid her, and she could not remain her friendly former self. Many victims of serious burns or physical stigmas likewise suffer from low self-esteem and shyness. These are biological influences on personality, but they arise from strictly social mechanisms—the expectations and reactions of others.

Physical Attractiveness Stereotype

Research in social psychology has documented that many people expect physically attractive others to do good and to be good (Dion, 1972, 1973; Hatfield & Sprecher, 1986). This physical attractiveness stereotype has been summarized as our tendency to believe that "What is beautiful is good." Adults have higher expectations for attractive children, and most of us think that attractive people are more successful and more likely to succeed. What is the likely effect on personality? Not surprisingly, physically attractive people tend to be happier, although they may suffer more if they lose their attractiveness as they age. Here again, personality is partially a result of biology (physical attractiveness), but it is not a direct effect of genes; rather it operates through reactions of others.

Similar processes apply to children who have a skin color, eye shape, or other ethnic sign that is different from the majority. There are positive expectations for children with the culturally "desirable" characteristics, and often negative expectations for children with "undesirable" features. As we have seen, such negative expectations may be compounded and reinforced by biased testing of such children. The long-term results on personality are hard to assess, but they undoubtedly are substantial.

What happens when we put all these sorts of biological influences together? Well, we should find many arenas in which biological aspects of personality have a profound effect on social life. For example, consider the case of divorce. There is evidence that concordance for divorce is significantly higher in monozygotic twins than in dizygotic twins (McGue & Lykken, 1992). That is, if you have a twin with identical genes and you are divorced, then your twin is more likely to get divorced than if he or she is a fraternal twin. Does this mean that divorce is genetically determined? Such an assertion is ridiculous; the likelihood of divorce varies dramatically as a function of upbringing, religion, income, culture, time period, and other environmental factors. However, identical twins may indeed share temperaments, abilities, sex drives, reactions from others (to their beauty, height, etc.), self-created marriage environments, health, and so on, involving the various factors we have discussed in this chapter. The result is an apparently "genetically" correlated likelihood of divorce.

We said it is ridiculous to assert that divorce is genetically determined; many environmental factors obviously have a big impact on divorce. But the history of the twentieth century shows us that many very smart people are willing to make many silly and dangerous assumptions about the genetic basis of personality. There is something very captivating about reducing the complex influences on personality to a simple (though invalid) explanation of genetic causation.

Personality and Public Policy

Darwin proposed that species evolve because those individuals who cannot compete well in the environments in which they live tend to be less successful in growing up and producing offspring. For example, animals that can outrun or fend off predators are more likely to have offspring than their slower or more defenseless comrades. This notion, termed "survival of the fittest," is one of the most misunderstood and misused concepts in all of science.

Social Darwinism and Eugenics

This unfortunate expression—survival of the fittest—has sometimes been changed from a biological principle to a moral imperative and interpreted to mean that weak creatures *should not* survive. In fact, it has been used as a license to kill.

In America, importation of slaves from Africa began well before the time of Darwin. Asians, Native Americans, and other groups were similarly considered inherently inferior, well before Darwinian theory. For example, it was believed that Negroes were by nature incapable of learning to read, so it was just as well that they were picking cotton. Just to be on the safe side, it was also illegal to try to teach a plantation slave to read.

Pseudoscience

What evolutionary theory did, however, was to provide a pseudoscientific justification for the oppression that was occurring in any case. Many leaders, including many intellectuals and scientists, were quick, at the end of the nineteenth century, to adopt views of "genetic inferiority" for those thought inherently inferior. The worst distortion appeared in what came to be known as **Social Darwinism** (Hofstadter, 1959). Applying evolutionary theory in a crude way to societies, Social Darwinism argued that not only individuals but societies and cultures naturally competed in a survival of the fittest. It followed therefore that it was biologically and morally just (and even imperative) that white people invade, conquer, and dominate other societies. After all, the whites saw themselves as more "fit."

In various ways, such ideas, which amounted merely to prejudice against culturally different others, greatly affected American governmental policy. For example, American immigration laws passed in the early 1920s strictly limited immigration from "inferior" or "unfit" places such as eastern and southern Europe and Asia. (And not surprisingly given American history, Africans were considered the most unfit.) Sad to say, psychologists and other scientists of the time played an important role in providing flimsy justifications for the discrimination. Psychologists were involved in creating biased tests that "proved" that the undesirable cultures were indeed intellectually and morally subordinate (Gould, 1996; see also Chapter 2).

Many psychologists, like many other intelligent people, were caught up in the bigoted ideas of their time, and they allowed their thinking and research to be distorted. Many wrote of the importance of preserving or purifying the gene pool of the elite. This eugenics movement advocated such steps as the forced sterilization of the poor. (If you or any of your friends have ever been poor, the idea of some government official taking a knife to your reproductive organs probably does not sound like such a good idea.) It is important for personality psychologists of today to be aware of this history, so that the chances of making similar mistakes can be diminished.

Sociobiology

On the more scientific side, Darwin's theory can, if carefully applied, lead to interesting insights about the bases of personality. The scientific study of the influence of evolutionary biology on individual responses regarding social matters involves the field called **sociobiology.** Sociobiologists study the reasons for (the functions of) the evolution of animal behaviors. For example, various colors, scents, calls, or dances have been shown to have evolved as part of species' mating rituals or territorial defense or social organization. During mating season, males of various species (from deer to tropical fish) engage in ritualized duels for the most desirable mates.

It is also clear that some species have evolved to be monogamous (at least for each breeding season), whereas in other species, a dominant male has access to most of the females for mating. Although such patterns sometimes break down in unusual circumstances, it is generally safe to say that many such patterns are "in the nature" of the particular species. These analyses work best with animals like ants, fish, spiders, bees, and many birds, since much of these animals' behaviors are governed by instincts or fixed patterns of responding (Wilson, 1975).

Much more complex are attempts to apply these sorts of analyses to large-brained animals like humans. Here sociobiologists often must walk the fine line separating themselves from the ideas of Social Darwinism and eugenics. The display of bright plumage is an integral part of the mating ritual of peacocks. People also wear fancy clothes to attract mates, but it is obviously a mistake to assume that the same simple courtship mechanisms are applicable.

Most commonly, sociobiological-type analyses are applied to human aggression, human courtship, and human family relations, since aggression, mating, and raising of the young are a prime focus of evolutionary biologists studying organisms like insects, fish, or birds. For example, in all human societies, a close bond, or **attachment,** develops shortly after birth between the infant and the caretaker (usually the mother). This is also true in nonhuman primates (and indeed in many mammals), and it certainly appears to have a biological basis. Using this evolutionary approach, John Bowlby and Mary Ainsworth explain how the infant clings, gurgles, smiles, and so on to attract the mother, while the mother in turn nurtures the infant (Ainsworth, 1979; Ainsworth & Bowlby, 1991; Bowlby, 1969). This strong attachment system helps ensure the survival of the infant, and thus helps ensure the passing on of the mother's genes. There is an evolutionary function that explains why babies are so cute.

Cinderella

Consider now the case of Cinderella, who was abused by her cruel stepmother. Cinderella and untold numbers of other children have been mistreated by their stepmother or stepfather. There is indeed some evidence that stepchildren are treated worse than one's genetic children, and that this difference cannot be easily explained by social factors like poverty level. Sociobiologists suggest that the Cinderella phenomenon results from natural selection, in which parents have evolved to give preference and protection to their biological children (Daly & Wilson, 1988a, 1988b).

Such analyses can be provocative and intellectually stimulating when they help us to think about innate tendencies on which human cultures have been built. For example, to what extent do societal taboos against incest and societal patterns of homicide and aggression have their roots in ancient pressures for survival (Daly & Wilson, 1988)? Perhaps families have an innate predisposition to defend themselves and their territories. However, such evolutionary analyses can be foolish or dangerous when they ignore the tremendous influences of human learning and human culture on human behavior. It is certainly the case that aggression varies markedly as a function of cultural times and places. For example, even if relations with stepchildren are more likely to be conflict-prone due to evolutionary pressures (which is a reasonable hypothesis but not scientific fact), this does not mean that loving, wonderful relations with stepchildren do not occur. Many adoptive parents would give up their own lives for their adopted children. The speculations of sociobiologists can be twisted by politicians for their own ends.

As we have seen, human personality does indeed have a significant biological basis, but the specific patterns of a given person's behavior are overwhelmingly influenced by upbringing and environment. It is a difficult task to try to capture fully and scientifically the vastly diverse forces that shape personality (Petrinovich, 1995).

Culture, Nazis, and "Superior Races"

Many millions of people have been murdered in part because of a misunderstanding and misuse of the notion of biological influences on personality. In Europe early in the twentieth century, misunderstanding of differences among people was carried to its most awful extreme. Adolf Hitler and a small band of ruthless fascists took over a German society that was willing to believe in a genetically superior "master race."

There is of course good evidence that people from different cultures differ systematically from each other, but there is little evidence that these differences are genetically based. When immigrants come to the United States from Asia or Africa or Europe or wherever, their children for the most part become capitalistic, freedom-loving Americans, fond of baseball and football, Mickey Mouse, automobiles and open roads, American music, and so on. That is, the children of immigrants soon come to behave more like Americans than like the cultures of their parents and grandparents. People in China behave differently from people in New York or Nairobi because of their culture.

Yet biological determinism of personality has its allure. Even educated people are attracted to the idea that "other" people are inherently inferior and therefore less deserving of freedom, success, and even life. In the case of Hitler and the Nazis, the inferior, subhumans were Jews, Gypsies, homosexuals, and those with physical or mental handicaps. Many physicians helped lead the way to mass murder (Lifton, 1986). In the United States, those labeled innately inferior by the dominant society have traditionally been people of colored (nonwhite) skin and homosexuals. Although this subject is a complex one, it is important for students of personality to be knowledgeable about the common societal errors and biases about the nature of personality.

The Human Genome: Racist Eugenics of the Future?

Biologists are currently hard at work on the human genome project, an effort to identify each of the tens of thousands of genes in our chromosomes. The immediate goal is to develop treatments for inherited diseases such as muscular dystrophy. However, it is likely that genes (or patterns of genes) that influence people's propensities to be aggressive or depressed or intelligent or shy and so on will eventually be discovered. Should these genes be altered to make a "better" human being?

A subtle kind of genetic racism often creeps into the thinking of even talented researchers in this area. The argument goes as follows: Modern medicine is keeping alive people who otherwise would have died. Therefore, "survival of the fittest" is defunct, and the human genetic pool is deteriorating. Therefore, if we are to evolve, we must engage in genetic engineering to fix and preserve the healthy gene pool. By the way, who should be in charge of these efforts? Why, the geneticists of course.

The racist errors made by this argument are more subtle but just as menacing as those made by the Social Darwinians. There is no evidence that the human gene pool is deteriorating. In fact it is hard even to define what such a statement might mean. Certainly, physical characteristics of humans are improving rather than declining: people are taller, stronger, and longer-lived than ever before. In terms of mental or artistic abilities, it would be a dangerous lie even to hint that we have any idea about the genetic bases of such accomplishments. Musical genius or artistic genius or scientific genius often arises in "unexpected" places—in descendants of serfs or slaves or laborers. Furthermore, we know very little about the human characteristics that have been selected for over the millennia; anyone who claims to know the precise selection pressures operating throughout evolutionary history either is a fool or has some political agenda in mind.

Going beyond these racist errors, the question still remains as to whether we should tinker with our genes to make a "better" person. Wouldn't it be nice if no one were genetically predisposed to be a criminal? Why not eliminate school-yard bullies? How about even weeding out those people who are a stubborn pain in the neck? Answering these questions intelligently requires a good knowledge about what it means to be person—in other words, a good knowledge of personality psychology.

If you or your relatives have some genetic disease or defect that makes life especially difficult, you would probably be very happy if science could repair the problem. But what about defects in your personality? We all have them. Would you like some scientist to "fix" you? How would you feel if your best friend or lover suddenly decided to undergo such repair work? For example, perhaps your lover thinks he or she is too sweet and sentimental and wants to be altered to become more sensible and pragmatic. Or maybe your child's teacher or doctor recommends "fixing" your child's unruly behavior.

Evaluating the Perspectives

Advantages and Limits of the Biological Approach

- ### *Quick Analogy*
  Humans as genes, brains, and hormones.

- ### *Advantages*
  Emphasizes the tendencies and limits imposed by genetics, physical health, and bodily endowment on personality.

  Acknowledges the effects of biological influences on the reactions of others and the environments that individuals choose.

  Can be combined with other approaches.

- ### *Limits*
  Tends to minimize human potential for growth and change.

  Serious danger of misuse by politicians who oversimplify its findings.

  Uses biological concepts, which may not be most appropriate for psychological phenomena.

  Difficult to capture consciousness.

- ### *View of Free Will*
  Behavior is determined by biological tendencies.

- ### *Common Assessment Techniques*
  Neuroscience, heritability studies, physiological measures.

- ### *Implications for Therapy*
  Since behavior is seen as resulting from evolved biological structures, genes, hormones, chemical imbalances, and environmental interactions with these structures, therapy is focused on biological interventions: psychotropic drugs like Prozac or Valium for mental "illness," hormones for conditions such as PMS irritability, plastic surgery (or liposuction) for physical abnormalities, and antihistamines or cleaner environments for allergy- and toxin-related conditions. General health-promoting activities like exercise may prove helpful (such as in treating anxiety and depression). Eventually, gene therapies may be commonplace, with the attendant moral dangers.

Summary and Conclusion

Do relatively unchangeable biological characteristics such as genetic inheritance, the neuroendocrine system, bodily endowment, and physical health affect personality? Undoubtedly at times they do, and such influences should be carefully studied by the serious student of personality. Gordon Allport wrote decades ago that although psychology is the safest approach to follow in constructing the science of personality, "Some day the 'biological model' may catch up" (1961, p. 73). Today, biology has indeed provided many insights into what it means to be a person. For the most part, these insights concern the outer parameters or limits of human responding.

Americans like to believe that almost any child who has enough motivation and the proper upbringing can go on to achieve almost anything he or she desires. Success does indeed come from hard work and proper "rearing" in many cases, but there is also no doubt that biological factors affect a person's characteristic responses. A person is not born a blank slate that is then written on by the environment; people start with certain inherent predispositions and abilities.

Charles Darwin turned the life sciences upside down by arguing that people are not special creatures of divine creation but rather evolved directly from more primitive species. In a Darwinian analysis, attention is drawn to the *function* of a characteristic (such as speed or intelligence) in survival. A prime difficulty of a Darwinian approach is that it is hard to know precisely which selection pressures worked to shape human evolution over millions of years. This problem plagues the modern application of Darwin's ideas—the field of evolutionary personality theory.

Ivan Pavlov proposed that the organism must have the correct sensitivity to detect food or danger, but an overreaction to stimuli would leave the organism overwhelmed or unable to discriminate appropriately. The term *temperament* is used to refer to stable individual differences in emotional reactivity. Four dimensions of temperament are usually isolated: (1) an activity dimension, (2) an emotionality dimension, (3) a sociability dimension, and (4) an aggressive/impulsive dimension.

The introversion–extroversion factor combines elements of the activity dimension and the sociability dimension of temperament. The basic idea of Hans Eysenck is that extroverts have a relatively low level of brain arousal, and so they seek stimulation. Introverts, on the other hand, are thought to have a higher level of central nervous system arousal and so tend to shy away from stimulating social environments. There are many problems in trying to test a nervous system–based theory of temperament, which Eysenck himself acknowledged.

Another promising method of addressing biological differences in personality focuses on individual differences in hemispheric activity—that is, relative differences in activation between the right and left cerebral hemispheres. The idea is that relatively greater activation of the right hemisphere is associated with greater reactions of fear and distress to a stressful situation; in other words, individuals who have a relatively more active right hemisphere are more likely to overreact to a negative stimulus.

Many studies of twins have found impressive similarities in personality between people who have the same genetic make-up. The similarities of identical twins are greater than those of fraternal twins. But the similarity of twins raised apart is less than that of twins raised together, evidence of the influence of the environmental upbringing. Further, when innate tendencies encounter similar environmental pressures, they may often result in similar patterns of behavior—that is, similar personalities. There is thus much controversy about how much of personality is genetically determined. Interestingly, siblings raised by the same parents often have personalities that are strikingly different. In moving from childhood to adulthood, the important environmental effects on personality become evident. There is an inverse correlation between personality similarity and age for both monozygotic and dizygotic twins; as twins get older, their personalities become more different.

It is now well documented that dramatic changes in personality can result from poisoning and from certain illnesses, such as strokes. A stable personality depends on a healthy, well-functioning brain. It follows that diseases or toxins that affect brain function often affect personality. And the list of toxic substances and illnesses known to affect personality is a long one. Because drugs and poisons can have such major and dramatic influences on personality, there should be a basic field of study called "personality toxicology."

Our understanding of biological influences on personality has major implications for our beliefs about law and justice. One extreme position is that most criminal or evil acts are committed by people who couldn't help themselves—they have some disorder in their nervous system. Interestingly, although this position is often identified with a very liberal or left-wing political orientation, it is actually quite similar to the right-wing position that some people simply have "bad genes."

An intriguing way that biology can affect personality is by affecting the environments in which we find (or put) ourselves. That is, certain biological influences may cause us to wind up in certain situations, and these situations may then influence our personalities. For example, extroverts, seeking stimulation, might be more likely to experience job changes and other moves. Certain characteristics of the individual lead to certain experiences which in turn influence individual responding.

Many victims of serious burns or physical stigmas suffer from a changed personality. These are biological influences on personality but they are attributable to strictly social mechanisms—the expectations and reactions of others.

"Survival of the fittest" is one of the most misunderstood and misused concepts in all of science. This unfortunate expression has sometimes been changed from a biological principle to a moral mandate and interpreted to mean that weak creatures *should not* survive. In fact, it has been used as a license to kill. Applying evolutionary theory in a crude way to societies, Social Darwinism argued that societies and cultures naturally competed for survival of the fittest. It followed therefore that it was biologically and morally just (and even imperative) that white people invade, conquer, and dominate other societies. The eugenics movement advocated such steps as the forced sterilization of the poor. It is important for personality psychologists of today to be aware of this history, so as to avoid making similar mistakes.

There is a certain lure of biological determinism of personality. Even educated people are attracted to the idea that "other" people are inherently inferior and therefore less deserving of freedom, success, and even life. In the case of Hitler and the Nazis, the inferior, subhumans were Jews, Gypsies, homosexuals, and those with physical or mental handicaps. In the United States, those labeled innately inferior by the dominant society have traditionally been people of colored (nonwhite) skin, Asians, and homosexuals. Going beyond these racist errors, the question still remains as to whether we should tinker with our genes to make a "better" person.

Unfortunately, it is very easy for people to accept stereotypes and to rationalize the inequities in the status quo. Until very recently, most men (and most women) "knew" that men were better suited by their nature to run governments, to manage property, to become scientists and artists, and to run businesses. It was thought to be women's nature—as the weaker sex—to stay home, manage households, and nurture children. Thus it was perfectly logical that women were not allowed to attend the best colleges, vote or hold office, own property, and so on. Allowing women to do so was seen as "going against nature."

Today's unfounded prejudices are of course more difficult for us to see (after all, they are prejudices). Should we be suspicious of those political leaders who play up the importance of genetic determinism and ignore the many other important aspects of personality? Given the sad history of misguided searches for "genetic purity," we must be on guard.

Key Theorists

Charles Darwin   Hans Eysenck
Ivan Pavlov   Francis Galton

Key Concepts

evolutionary personality theory   kin selection
natural selection   somatotypology
four basic aspects of temperament   survival of the fittest
introversion–extroversion dimension   Social Darwinism
   of temperament   sociobiology
nervous system arousal   attachment
sensation seeking   human genome project
neurotransmitters   biological determinism
eugenics

Suggested Readings

Buss, A. H., & Plomin, R. (1984). *Temperament: Early developing personality traits.* Hillsdale, NJ: Erlbaum.

Buss, D. M. (1991). Evolutionary personality psychology. *Annual Review of Psychology, 42,* 459–492.

Daly, M., & Wilson, M. (1988). *Homicide.* New York: A. DeGruyter.

Dunn, J., & Plomin, R. (1990). *Separate lives: Why siblings are so different.* New York: Basic Books.

Eibl-Eibesfelt, I. (1972). Similarities and differences between cultures in expressive movements. In R. Hinde (Ed.), *Non-verbal communication.* Cambridge, MA: Cambridge University Press.

Ekman, P. (1973). Cross-cultural studies of facial expression. In P. Ekman (Ed.), *Darwin and facial expression.* New York: Academic Press.

Eysenck, H. J. (1967). *The biological basis of personality.* Springfield, IL: Charles C. Thomas.

Zuckerman, M. (1979). *Sensation seeking: Beyond the optimal level of arousal.* Hillsdale, NJ: Erlbaum.

Chapter 6

Behaviorist and Learning Aspects of Personality

A few years ago, a friend of ours came into a small fortune as the result of a successful business venture. Feeling happy, generous, and curious, he took a short taxicab ride and paid the $5 fare with a $100 bill. Carefully watching the unfolding expressions on the cabdriver's face, our friend said, "Keep the change," and went on his way.

This cab driver had never received such a lavish tip and was unlikely to receive another for a long time, if ever. Yet we can predict that this cab driver will look for customers who resemble our friend, try to behave as he did when traveling with our friend, and in general drive his cab in the hopes of another such tip; and he may do so for a long time to come. In other words, the cab driver is now acting in a consistent and relatively predictable manner thanks to receiving a significant reward from a patron. In a sense, this behavior is now part of his personality.

A large, unpredictable reward such as the cab driver's tip is called a **partial reinforcement** by behaviorist psychologists. Partial reinforcement has been studied in laboratory rats and many other animals. Experimental results show that a significant reward that comes rarely (i.e., is partial) is more powerful in shaping behavior than a reinforcement that is continuous. People will continue their activities for that occasional but highly rewarding birdie golf shot, slot machine jackpot, sexual liaison, A+ grade from a professor, or $100 tip. This chapter explains how certain reward structures in our environments can produce consistencies in an individual's behaviors.

*B*ehaviorist approaches strike at the very heart of most other personality approaches, which rely on ideas of internal traits, tendencies, defenses, and motivations. Behaviorists reject such concepts; they see people as controlled absolutely by their environments. Much controversy has necessarily resulted. Poet W. H. Auden (1970) wrote,

> *Of course, Behaviorism "works." So does torture. Give me a no-nonsense, down-to-earth behaviorist, a few drugs, and simple electrical appliances, and in six months I will have him reciting the Athanasian Creed in public.*

As you will see, Auden's description is not an accurate one, but the controversial issues behaviorism raises about the nature of human beings are very real. This chapter considers the strengths and weaknesses of behaviorist and learning approaches to personality.

The Classical Conditioning of Personality

One of the philosophic bases for the learning approach to personality was laid down by the English philosopher John Locke (1632–1704). Locke viewed an infant as a blank slate—*tabula rasa*—on whom the experiences of life would write their tale. This assumption does not preclude certain other approaches to personality, but it definitely elevates the great influence of the situation. However, as all psychology students know, it was the brilliant Russian physiologist Ivan Petrovitch Pavlov (1849–1936) who laid the foundation for modern learning approaches.

Conditioning a Response to a Stimulus

Studying digestion in dogs, Pavlov discovered the important principle called **classical conditioning.** He presented food (the unconditioned stimulus), which caused salivation in dogs (the unconditioned or automatic response), to a hungry dog, at the same time pairing it with something that normally did not cause salivation, such as a bell (a neutral stimulus). Pavlov found that if he paired the food presentation and bell a number of times, eventually merely the sound of the bell elicited salivation. That is, the conditioned stimulus (the bell) came to elicit a conditioned response (salivation). Similarly, people can be conditioned to salivate in response to the sound of a food chime on a ranch. Normally, of course, bells have nothing to do with salivation. But dogs and people can learn (that is, be conditioned to) an automatic association.

Pavlov also noted that the conditioned response would occur in response to stimuli that were *similar* to the conditioned stimulus, indicating that there was **generalization** of the conditioning. However the conditioned response would not occur for *all* possible similar stimuli, indicating that the animal also could learn to tell the difference between different stimuli; this is termed **discrimination.** Thus, if the food followed a bell of only one tone and did not follow the ringing of a bell of other tones, the dog would discriminate this one tone, and the conditioned response would occur only in response to that particular relevant tone. Analogously, a young boy who is stung by bees and bitten by mosquitoes might become fearful of (be conditioned to react to) the buzzing of all insects (generalization). Or, on the other hand, if he sees that the flies and gnats buzzing around him do not cause any problems, he may learn to discriminate the buzzing of stinging insects from that of other flying insects.

Ringing the dinner bell can cause humans to salivate, a classically conditioned reaction virtually identical to what Pavlov observed in his laboratory dogs.

Reaction Patterns as a Result of Conditioning

Many reaction patterns are explainable by classical conditioning. Neutral stimuli associated with positive, enjoyable occurrences become "likes"; but events or consequences associated with negative responses become "dislikes" (or worse). For example, a college student might learn to associate drinking at parties with having a pleasant, sociable time with friends. On the other hand, a woman date-raped at a fraternity house party might develop a "personality" that fears college social events that involve alcohol.

Pavlov's constructs thus often provide a basis for explaining emotional aspects of personality. For example, why do some people have extreme fear reactions (phobias) to certain things while other persons do not? Many people are herpetaphobic and have extreme emotional reactions even to still pictures of snakes. This might be conditioned if a grandmother took her five-year-old granddaughter to the zoo and exhibited great anxiety in the child's presence when they approached the "snake house." This conditioning explanation of a phobia is very different from a biological explanation that relies on an innate fear of snakes, or a psychoanalytic explanation that sees snakes as symbolic of a threatening penis, or a neo-analytic explanation in which fear of snakes is part of our collective unconscious.

Extinction Processes

What happens if pairing of the conditioned and unconditioned stimulus stops? Then, **extinction** may occur. That is, the conditioned response becomes less frequent—the association weakens—over time until it disappears. In other words, "personality" (pattern of response) changes. A rape victim who developed a fearful personality (afraid of going to parties, out on dates, or even going to shopping malls) could undergo a dramatic personality change for the better if she repeatedly experienced these events in the calm presence of a supportive friend. Unfortunately, people who have learned to fear certain things will often *avoid* them, thus not allowing their fear to extinguish.

Conditioning and Neurotic Behavior

But how does behaviorism explain a complex personality dimension like neuroticism? Pavlov in fact was able to condition a response similar to neurotic behavior in a dog. First, he associated food presentation with a circle but not with an ellipse. Then, he gradually increased the roundness of the ellipse so it approximated the circle. When the dog could no longer discriminate the circle from the ellipse, it began to exhibit neurotic behaviors (Pavlov, 1927). This hints that neuroticism may be a conditioned response, fostered by an environment that requires the individual to discriminate between events under conditions in which that judgment is almost impossible (Wolpe & Plaud, 1997). For example, some children find it impossible to predict the reactions of their unstable parents. If children are never sure whether to expect praise or punishment, they may feel frustrated, anxious, and depressed.

Pavlov was the son of a Russian Orthodox priest and intended to become a priest himself. However, as a young man, he read with fascination the recently published theories of Charles Darwin and turned to a career in science (Windholz, 1991). His studies of the function and control of salivation were firmly rooted in Darwin's ideas.

Complexities in Application of Conditioning Principles

Modern research suggests that classical conditioning is not as simple as Pavlov had hoped. For example, he assumed that conditioning principles were general rules that applied uniformly to all animals, but it is now known that different organisms are more easily conditioned to respond in certain ways to certain stimuli (Garcia & Koelling, 1966). Hungry dogs can be conditioned to salivate with a bell that is paired with the sight and smell of meat, but each species and even each individual has certain tendencies that facilitate or impair certain learning. For example, humans rely more on visual cues than smells, and different people have different perceptual and aesthetic inclinations. Yet classical conditioning remains a powerful explanation of response patterns, especially when there is a strong natural pairing of stimulus and automatic response. However, much more of our learned patterns of responses comes by experiencing or anticipating the consequences (effects) of our actions. This is the focus of behaviorist approaches to personality. (See the Famous Personalities box on page 188.)

The Origins of Behaviorist Approaches: Watson's Behaviorism

Around the turn of the century, not only Freud but also many experimental philosopher–psychologists, such as Wilhelm Wundt, were studying psychology using subjective analyses of the human mind. That is, people were being asked to introspect about their thoughts, or to free associate to reveal unconscious processes. This approach was fraught with methodological difficulties. There was no way of validating or verifying the data and conclusions. How could we know if what people reported thinking was really a good representation of their psyche?

*Famous
Personalities*

John Travolta: Reinforcement of Stardom?

Like flashes in the dark, celebrities come and go. As overnight success stories whose careers are launched by the fuel of public appeal, these rockets become teen idols, figures of adolescent crushes, and objects of adult envy. With their stardom shining bright in the public eye, these sudden success stories often fizzle out just as quickly.

Until 1994, film star John Travolta's career fit just that pattern. First hitting the spotlight in the 1970s, Travolta's career skyrocketed with his performances in the blockbuster movies *Saturday Night Fever* and *Grease*. During that period, Travolta was considered by many to be the biggest box-office property around. After a brief period of stardom, though, Travolta was eclipsed. Still in his twenties, he became a "former movie star," accepting a few roles in mediocre movies and then turning down roles that were offered to him.

What makes Travolta's story different from the usual path of the has-been is that he made a successful comeback. Twenty years after the roles that initially brought him stardom, and after more than a decade of near-invisibility, he surprised the public with his on-screen reappearance in Quentin Tarantino's award-winning pop-culture film *Pulp Fiction*. Soon after came another successful film role in *Get Shorty*, and his career again took off.

Can these phenomena exemplified by Travolta's career (sudden stardom, rapid eclipse, later reemergence to stardom) be understood by a behaviorist interpretation? One way to describe Travolta's early upward trajectory is that his behavior (in this case, his role selection and his acting) was shaped through positive reinforcement (in the form of money, the "perks" of stardom, respect from his colleagues, and public admiration). In operant conditioning terms, the more closely his behavior resembled that of the ideal star, the more he was rewarded. The contingencies of Travolta's environment conditioned him to become a star.

Then what happened? Perhaps one or two poor choices of roles (or possibly just unlucky choices in a fickle industry) led to the extinction of those behaviors that had propelled him to success. Perhaps, after not being reinforced for engaging in his "star" behavior—that is, after his failure in several movies—Travolta slid into a downward spiral of the extinction of his "star" behavior. Having not been reinforced for several movies he did take on, he may have been reluctant to accept new roles. As he became less visible, he was less likely to be offered new roles, and the ones he was offered would have been less desirable. The downward path may have become a spiral of negative reinforcement: by not taking on any new roles, he could avoid reexperiencing the scorn and bad reviews that his recent roles had brought.

And how to account for his comeback through behaviorist principles? Perhaps Travolta's experiences out of the limelight (his more recent reinforcement history) had brought about a change in his responses to seeking or accepting a movie role. Perhaps the actions of the director of his comeback movie were more successful in evoking Travolta's long-dormant behavior patterns from his days of stardom. Once these appropriate responses had been restimulated and reinforced, they became more likely to reappear in subsequent situations—the movies following *Pulp Fiction*.

The Rejection of Introspection

In response to the perceived limitations of introspectionism, **behaviorism,** the key learning approach in psychology, was founded by John B. Watson. Watson wanted to develop a rigorous science and thus completely rejected introspection. According to Watson, thoughts and feelings elicited through introspection are unobservable and unscientific.

Watson was born in Greenville, South Carolina, in 1878. His experiences led him to start graduate study in philosophy at the University of Chicago, but he soon switched to psychology and also studied neurology, physiology, and animal research. Interestingly, while doing his dissertation, Watson noticed that he had a dislike of using human subjects; he much preferred using animals. Watson believed that he could learn the same things by using animals that others claimed to learn by studying humans.

Watson was a professor at Johns Hopkins University from 1908 to 1919. His basic theories about studying observable behavior and disregarding introspection were laid out in 1914 in his book *Behavior*, and he and Rosalie Rayner wrote an important book about behaviorism in 1919 called *Psychology from the Standpoint of a Behaviorist*. In a sweeping critique, they condemned both introspectionists, who were studying consciousness, and psychoanalysts, who concentrated on the unconscious.

Applying Conditioning Principles to Humans

Watson demonstrated the manner in which emotional responses are conditioned when he applied Pavlov's theory, developed through the study of animals, to the conditioning of little Albert, an eleven-month-old boy (Watson & Rayner, 1920). They conditioned fear of a rat by making a loud, scary noise (hitting a hammer against a steel bar—a noise that had severely frightened little Albert during pretesting) to startle the infant when the rat was presented, or when he reached for the rat with interest. Soon the mere sight of the rat made him cry.

Generalization was also demonstrated as little Albert's conditioned fear generalized to other furry objects, including a rabbit, a dog, and a fur coat. Poor Albert even feared a Santa Claus mask. This study thus suggested that an emotional response that was conditioned to one stimulus could result in later emotional reaction to a variety of events/stimuli. It also demonstrated that any neutral stimulus might end up eliciting an emotion. Watson believed that this was how most of personality was formed. Confident that Freud's notions of the sexual basis of personality were ridiculous, he teased Freudians by maintaining that Albert's fear of fur would be interpreted by a psychoanalyst in terms of an early experience with pubic hair.

Jones (1924) used Watson and Rayner's approach to countercondition the fear of rat, rabbit fur, feather, and the like, in a little boy called Peter. He brought Peter to play with three others while a fear-inducing rabbit was present, gradually extinguishing the fear by slowly bringing the rabbit closer and closer to the child while keeping him happy. This was one of the first documented cases of the use of what has come to be called **systematic desensitization.** Peter was desensitized to the rabbit; thus this aspect of his personality changed. This deconditioning of phobias by treatment using systematic desensitization techniques is now a common and successful form of therapy. It suggests that even highly emotional aspects of personality can disappear (be extinguished) over time.

Another early application of conditioning principles was to the treatment of bedwetting (Mowrer & Mowrer, 1928). An electrical device—a loud bell—awakens the child when the slightest wetness is detected. Such a treatment is effective for many children. Soon, the child learns to respond to the sensations before becoming wet. This approach contradicts the Freudian explanation of bedwetting as the result of a personality disorder resulting from being fixated at a stage of psychosexual development. The focus is on conditioning from the outside rather than on psychic distress on the inside.

In 1919, Watson divorced his wife and married his student assistant. This scandalous act in the environment of the time (undoubtedly linked to poor

When people suffer from phobias, they often can be successfully treated by desensitization training, which applies the principle of extinction. The fear response is "deconditioned" by pairing the experience of being calm and anxiety-free with successively closer approaches to the fear-inducing situation. Here, a group of fearful fliers approaches an airplane to learn about how the plane operates—part of a fear-reduction program that relies on a combination of behavioral and cognitive methods. Almost all the participants will be ready to take an actual flight as the climax of the course.

moral conditioning in childhood) resulted in great social pressures, and he had to leave Johns Hopkins University. This disruption produced a major change of career for Watson. He applied his learning theories to the marketplace and became a successful consultant to business. He published another book, *Behaviorism*, in 1924, but his career as an experimental psychologist pretty much ended when he left the university. Watson died in 1958.

In modern research, the effects of classical conditioning on personality provide an interesting way to think about the *initiation* of many habits and addictions, but patterns of behavior are maintained when they are rewarded. For example, smoking, drinking, and gambling may initially elicit an unconditioned positive response (of positive arousal, euphoria, excitement), but the persistence of the behaviors in the long run may be better explained as a consequence of the rewards they provide.

Watson took seriously the idea that a child was a blank slate. He boasted, "Give me a dozen healthy infants, and my own specific world to bring them up in and I'll guarantee to take any one at random and train him" to be anything, from a doctor or lawyer to a beggar or thief, regardless of his talents, color, inclinations, or whatever (1924). In other words, Watson is proclaiming much more than a specific theory about personality; he is espousing a world view in which the *environment* is key to understanding a person. Accordingly, if children are raised properly, they will behave properly, because their personalities are a function of the environment. This perspective is in marked contrast to the perspectives described in other chapters of this book. It was Watson's assumptions that laid the basis for the work of B. F. Skinner.

The Radical Behaviorism of B. F. Skinner

Burrhus Frederick Skinner (his friends called him Fred) was born in 1904 in Susquehanna, Pennsylvania. His lawyer father and his mother followed a stringent morality. According to Skinner, they lived in a stable, loving home. His parents and grandparents taught him to respect the Puritan work ethic, virtues, and morals.

As a child, Skinner constructed machines (scooters, rafts, seesaws, slingshots, blow guns, steam cannons) and invented contraptions (among others, a flotation system to separate ripe from green berries), and these childhood interests may have been reflected later in his building and using laboratory equipment and machines (Hall, 1967). From his early years, he was also very interested in animals and their behavior; for example, he watched the trained pigeons at the fair.

Skinner would later say that he could trace his adult behaviors to his childhood reinforcements, not to "personality development" as described by personality theorists such as Freud and Jung. Skinner emphasized that who he was, his personality, was clearly the result of his reinforcement history as a child—the rewards and punishments he experienced. His life and personality were determined and controlled by environmental events.

When Skinner was studying literature at Hamilton College, a small liberal arts college, he sent some stories to the poet Robert Frost, who recommended he continue to write. After graduation he did spend a year trying to write but determined that he didn't have anything significant to say. (We might wonder why Robert Frost's positive reinforcement did not encourage him to keep trying. Was it the limited positive reinforcement he received? Did his behavior extinguish without further rewards?) He then spent six months in Greenwich Village during which time he read Pavlov's *Conditioned Reflexes* and some works by and about Watson. He was also influenced by the pioneering experimental psychologist Edward Thorndike, whose Law of Effect argued that the consequences of a behavior (that is, the effect) will either strengthen or weaken that behavior. Learning initially comes about through trial and error. We learn to do those actions that bring us rewards or help us avoid pain.

Skinner decided to do graduate work in psychology at Harvard after determining that one needs to understand behavior (as a psychologist does), not just describe it (as a writer does). During graduate school he concluded that the environment controls behavior: environmental events, particularly the *consequences of behavior*, are responsible for most behavior. That being the case, Skinner reasoned, one must uncover the environmental conditions surrounding any behavior in order to understand the behavior. Skinner endeavored to explain behavior without having to refer to physiology or internal personality constructs. He took his Ph.D. in psychology from Harvard in 1931.

Operant Conditioning

After Harvard, Skinner went to Minnesota, and then to Indiana for a short time, and finally returned to Harvard in 1948. He became sort of an animal trainer using his newly developed principles called **operant conditioning.** In operant conditioning, behavior is changed by its consequences. That is, Skinner manipulated the environment in such a way that he was able to train animals (rats, pigeons) to do things (such as playing badminton) that were far from their native behaviors. He did this by gradually shaping successive approximations to the desired behavior. Trained seals do not jump through hoops because of their personality but rather because they have been rewarded with fish for performing the behaviors desired by their trainers.

Skinner's theory of operant conditioning emphasized the study of overt, observable behavior, environmental conditions, and the process by which environmental events and circumstances determine behavior. Thus, the theory places its emphasis on the function of behavior (what it does) rather than the structure of personality. It is also a *deterministic* theory, in which there is no free will.

Operant Theory as an Alternative Description of Personality

According to Skinner, the term "personality" is meaningless. There is no place for internal components of personality, psychical structures (id, ego, super-ego), traits, self-actualization, needs, or instincts. The thing we know as personality is merely a group of responses to the environment. To Pavlov's ideas, Skinner added and developed the important notion that responses produced by the organism have environmental consequences; if the responses are rewarded, then they are more likely to appear again. Skinner argued that most behavior of a person or other organism is of this type and that it is these operant behaviors, taken together, that we call personality.

In a clever manner, Skinner analyzed the behavior of a superstitious individual, without relying on any internal aspects of personality. How can we understand a person who wears lucky shoes to important exams, eats only peanut butter sandwiches before job interviews, and always wears a silver bracelet when going to a party to look for a date? Skinner would explain that if a person has experiences in which a behavior (like wearing one's shiny black shoes) coincides with getting an A on exams, especially on a few random occasions, the person continues that behavior because the reinforcement strengthens the performance of the behavior even though there is no causal connection. There is no need to propose a "superstitious personality."

Skinner found that any one animal's learning and behavior did *not* look like the average animal's behavior, emphasizing the individuality of environmental conditions and responses. He therefore stressed that we must apply the principles of learning to each organism individually. Thus, his was an idiographic (rather than nomothetic) approach. He did, however, look for general laws of learning that would apply equally to all organisms, human and nonhuman, underscoring a common process.

Of course, Skinner did not consider himself a personality psychologist. On the contrary, notions of internal, nonobservable psychological characteristics were anathema to him. He relied heavily on animal research, whereas other personality theorists studied the development of human personality as a uniquely human process.

Because Skinner believed that the laws of behavior acquisition are virtually identical across all organisms, he chose to test his theories on rats and pigeons—which can be used more conveniently than humans as research subjects.

Skinner believed that the universal laws of behavior acquisition, resulting in what we know as personality, operate in the same manner in human and animal, maybe just more simply in nonhuman animals.

Noam Chomsky, the linguist and political commentator, was one of many who detested the view of humanity propounded by Skinner:

> *Suppose that humans happen to be so constructed that they desire the opportunity for freely undertaken productive work. Suppose that they want to be free from the meddling of technocrats and commissars, bankers and tycoons, mad bombers who engage in psychological tests of will with peasants defending their homes, behavioral scientists who can't tell a pigeon from a poet, or anyone else who tries to wish freedom and dignity out of existence or beat them into oblivion.* (1973, p. 345)

Is it true that Skinner couldn't "tell a pigeon from a poet"? As we have noted, Skinner studied literature and loved to write. He did, however, view the consistencies in behavior of his laboratory pigeons and his Harvard colleagues as similar in principle. In person (especially in his later years), Skinner, contrary to reputation, generally acted as a polite and friendly gentleman.

Controlling the Reinforcement

Because Skinner, like Watson, believed that a child (like a pigeon) was a function of the environment, he set out to design the best ways to raise children and even to structure whole communities. His inquiries led to the invention of what is sometimes called the **Skinner box** (although Skinner himself did not call it this and did not like others to use this designation). In this enclosure, the animal (or child) was segregated from all irrelevant environmental influences, except those under the control of the experimenter. For animals, the box contained either a lever (to be pressed by the rat) or a key (to be pecked by a pigeon). This lever or key, when pecked or pressed, triggered release of a food pellet (providing positive reinforcement) or stopped the administration of an aversive stimulus like a shock (providing negative reinforcement). The reinforcement rate could be carefully calibrated and controlled electronically and the rate of pressing/pecking was registered electronically. This allowed accurate measurement of the response rate while the reinforcement rate and schedule were controlled. Partial reinforcement schedules, in which the reward was delivered intermittently, were generally found to be most effective at shaping behavior patterns. These techniques were later applied to the design of teaching machines and self-paced teaching regimens, in which students receive rewards as they master skills. As applied to a young child, this might be a sort of fancy playpen that provides structured feedback about how the world works. As applied to a corporation employee, it might be a salary bonus schedule tied to certain productivity or profit increases (Skinner, 1938).

Skinner's Behaviorist Utopia: *Walden Two*

But Skinner, like Freud and other influential theorists, also had a broad vision for the design of society. In his novel *Walden Two*, Skinner (1948) describes a utopian community that is behaviorally engineered, based on principles of operant conditioning. A benevolent government rewards (reinforces) positive, socially appropriate behavior. Walden Two is problem-free because only positive reinforcement is used; people always behave reliably and responsibly, and they are invariably very competent. There is no issue of freedom because Skinner believes free will is only an illusion.

In a sardonic move, Skinner carefully selected the title for his novel from the work of the nineteenth-century essayist Henry David Thoreau. Thoreau had lived alone for two years in a cabin at Walden Pond in Massachusetts; the experience had been the inspiration for his classic *Walden*. Thoreau was an individualist who called for self-reliance and rejection of authority. The individual was seen as the source of freedom. In Skinner's Walden Two, there is no freedom, only perceived freedom, as the community engineers everyone's behavior.

Time magazine called *Walden Two* a "depressingly serious prescription for communal regimentation, as though the author had read Aldous Huxley's *Brave New World* and missed the point" (*Time*, 2/22/54). Skinner of course had not missed the point. He well knew about fears that the government would take over control over self-destiny, but he himself did not fear this. Indeed, he did not worry at all because he believed that all behavior is determined anyway. Rather, he believed that a desirable utopian community could be designed by controlling the environment rather than leaving it unstructured.

Skinner formalized these ideas in his 1971 book *Beyond Freedom and Dignity*, a nonfiction treatise advocating a society like Walden Two. He proposed a behaviorally engineered society, using environmental control to shape human behavior—a technology of behavior in which environmental conditions are manipulated to shape human actions. Although Freud believed that horrible human problems could be

In the years immediately following the publication of Skinner's Walden Two, *several small communities were founded on behaviorist principles. Here, a community member works at Twin Oaks Community (in Louisa, Virginia), which began as a Walden Two society in the 1960s but has evolved away from behaviorism.*

traced to id forces and the death instinct, and although many biological psychologists believe that there is an evolved aggressive drive, Skinner believed that most such problems—including war and crime—are just human behaviors that can be shaped through learning. If society could reinforce better behaviors, they would supersede the maladaptive ones. Skinner's (1974) ideas stand in precise opposition to visions of individual freedom and self-fulfillment, discussed in detail in Chapter 9.

Skinner was willing to apply some of his principles to his own life. For example, he arose at the same time early each morning and sat at the same writing table to establish the habit of daily productive writing. As he became older, he was less and less willing to interrupt this structure. College students who seek advice about improving their grades are often advised to adopt just such a regimen—to arrange their study materials in a quiet place and go there every single day at the same time. This conditioning can produce a "productive personality." Of course, many students reject such advice, seeking to be more spontaneous, intuitive, and "free."

What about maladaptive behaviors? According to Skinner, psychopathology is learned in the same manner as all other behaviors: the adaptive or maladaptive personality (that is, behavior) is learned by reinforcement. People have either not learned the appropriate response and have a behavioral deficit, or they have learned the wrong response. Also, some individuals may have been punished for adaptive behaviors. Thus the treatment for "mental illness" is to set up environmental contingencies that reward desirable behavior. This approach has been operationalized to some extent in schools and group homes for children with cognitive and emotional disabilities. Interestingly, Skinner agrees with Karl Marx and Erich Fromm that an incoherent, oppressive society leads to the many problems of individuals in modern life; but for Skinner it is behavior, not consciousness or psychic stability, that is fragmented by disorganized reinforcers (Skinner, 1974). To Skinner, a neurotic is someone who has been reinforced for overly emotional behavior.

Applying Behaviorism: Personality Change and Individual Differences

An example of current research in line with this Skinnerian approach is a Japanese study that examined thirty-six men who exhibited the unhealthy, stress-prone Type A personality (see Chapter 12 for more information on this syndrome). The study demonstrated the role of operant conditioning in the alteration of these assumed "personality characteristics" by training these men with operant self-control procedures, such as rewarding more constructive behaviors, so that all the subjects were able to *learn* to reduce their Type A behaviors. The focus was not at all on the internal personality or hostility, but rather on their externally observable behavior (Nakano, 1990). If personality

A Skinnerian approach to altering behavior is to set up environmental contingencies that reward desirable behavior. This approach has been successfully adopted in many "special" schools and treatment centers for children and adults with emotional and cognitive disabilities. In this day-treatment center for mentally disabled adults, there is a "token economy" where appropriate behavior is rewarded with tokens that can be exchanged for treats and privileges— the tokens thus serve as secondary reinforcers. Here, a staff member is helping a client (on the left) select a reward to buy with his tokens in the center's store.

is merely learned behavior, as this school of thought contends, it can then presumably be unlearned using the same conditioning processes by which it was first learned. (See the Self-Understanding box on page 198.)

Skinner did not deny that there are genetic differences among organisms. Instead, he said that the role of biological factors was to define the organism's range of responses and the organism's ability to have its behavior strengthened by environmental events. He emphasized that the environment is of primary importance even in hereditary characteristics because the environment selects behaviors that encourage procreation and survival; that is, in a relatively constant environment, the environment will "select" individuals who have the most adaptive behaviors to survive and reproduce. But ascribing any behavior to "instinct" is a mistake because it again ignores the role of environmental circumstances.

Internal Processes and Behaviorist Theory

Skinner acknowledged that we have emotions, thoughts, and internal processes, but he dismissed these as irrelevant in the explanation and understanding of behavior. Thoughts and emotions do occur, according to Skinner, but they do not cause behavior. Thoughts, emotions, and other internal "stuff" are, as are all characteristics of the organism, *caused by* environmental events. In any case, we cannot operationalize internal processes or measure their magnitude. So rather than ask if someone feels tired or how tired they are, look to the environment—when they last slept, how much they slept, and so on. These environmental events are the factors that can be measured and studied scientifically. Thus, contrary to what many personality theorists have emphasized, personality is not something that is specially or uniquely human. Because personality is merely a group of behaviors that have been well supported by the environment, any organism could potentially have a "personality" as Skinner's theory defines it. (Certainly many pet owners would attest to the fact that their pets do indeed have very distinct "personalities.")

 *Self-Understanding*

Ben Franklin's Habit Chart

Although behaviorist theories of learning and reinforcement were developed in the twentieth century, key elements of the approach have been understood by some people for many centuries. (Throughout this textbook, we show how the eight aspects of personality embody basic approaches to understanding the complexities of human nature.) One of the keenest insights into behaviorist principles was given by Benjamin Franklin (rpt. 1906) in his autobiography more than two hundred years ago. Rather than paying for a New Age course in self-improvement, you might try Franklin's method for yourself.

In an effort to improve the moral quality of his life, Franklin made a list of thirteen virtues that he thought desirable. For example, he wanted more temperance (not overeating or drinking), frugality, industry ("be always employed in something useful"), and humility. He saw that the virtues were composed of specific behaviors, which together comprised habits. To change his habits, Ben constructed a calendar book, with rows of the virtues and columns of the days of the week (see chart). At the end of each day, he would put a black mark on his chart if he had violated the virtue that day. Aiming to create a clean slate, he had the reinforcement of seeing the number of black marks decrease. In this way, Franklin gradually minimized his bad habits.

Franklin, with great insight, went even further. At the beginning, he focused on one virtue at a time, so that he would not be distracted or discouraged by attempting too much at once. Second, he arranged or ordered the virtues in a way that each one would facilitate the learning of the next one. (For example, once he was no longer dull with too much food or drink, he could more easily move on to tackle the next set of habits.) Third, he gradually increased the reinforcement intervals: over time, he returned to his notebook less and less often, although he always kept it with him.

Interestingly, Franklin also recognized some of the limits of the behaviorist approach. He wrote little encouraging mottoes and sayings and poems in his notebook (a quote from Cicero here, a Bible verse from the Proverbs there), to

External Causation versus
Free Will or Free Choice

Like Freud, Skinner was a **radical determinist,** which means he believed that all human behavior is caused. Both believed that there is absolutely no evidence that people have "free choice" in their behavior. For Freud this determinism was biological, whereas for Skinner it was environmental. Accord-

	Sunday	Monday	Tuesday	Wednesday	Thursday	Friday	Saturday
Temperance							
Silence							
Order							
Resolution							
Frugality							
Industry							
Sincerity							
Justice							
Moderation							
Cleanliness							
Tranquility							
Chastity							
Humility							

Benjamin Franklin's Habit Chart. Almost two centuries before behaviorism was formalized, Franklin had a sophisticated and insightful approach to modifying his own behavior using a form of negative reinforcement (a decrease in the black marks that signified violations of the virtues to which he aspired).

inspire and motivate him further. Although he was not religious in the orthodox sense, he well understood and reflected on the importance of the religious underpinnings of what he was attempting. He thus integrated what today would be called a cognitive and motivational approach to behavioral change.

In the end, Ben Franklin said that although he could not achieve perfection, the endeavor made him a better and happier man than he otherwise would have been.

B. F. Skinner is shown here with a "teaching machine" he devised to administer controlled reinforcement to a human learner. It was used to help teach an undergraduate course at Harvard in the 1950s, establishing the "programmed instruction" approach to teaching.

ing to Skinner, considering internal causes just confuses our study, diverting important attention from the real causes of behavior—the organism's reinforcement history. He was concerned that a focus on internal explanations for behavior entails the risk of eventually neglecting the key influence of the environmental events. Skinner died of leukemia in 1990 at age eighty-six.

Other Learning Approaches to Personality

In the 1930s and 1940s, a number of experimental psychologists became dissatisfied with the notion that behavior is totally a function of the events in the environment. They believed it was also important to take into account internal characteristics of the organism, such as how hungry or tired it was. But they still wanted to maintain a totally objective (often rat-based) approach. One of the most influential of these theorists was Clark Hull.

The Role of Internal Drives: Clark Hull

Hull was born in New York and later studied at the University of Michigan. He studied math, physics, and chemistry, intending to become an engineer, but he contracted polio and had to recast his plans. He turned to psychology, encountered the views of Watson and Pavlov, and soon became an influential professor at Yale. In 1943, he wrote *Principles of Behavior*. Hull's emphasis was on experimentation, an organized theory of learning, and the nature of **habits,** which were, according to Hull, simply associations between a stimulus and a response.

For Hull, the organism (usually a white rat) makes responses that lead to a goal that alleviates a drive. These responses in themselves become stimuli for further responses and *intervene* between the stimulus (e.g., hunger) and response (e.g., eating). So, for example, the rat must learn to make a variety of moves to get through the maze before it can reach the food and reduce its hunger drive. As applied to humans, this explains how a goal such as becoming rich can be learned, even though it is quite distant from an innate drive such as hunger. We learn that money and success can lead to drive reduction (such as allowing us access to good food). But it all comes back to basic innate or primary drives—hunger, thirst, sex, and the avoidance of pain.

What is important for understanding Hullian learning approaches to personality is that Hull turned attention to the internal state of the organism during learning, although he still emphasized the reinforcements provided by the environment. This allowed later development of more complex learning-based approaches than would result from a strict focus on stimulus and response.

Social Learning Theory: Dollard and Miller

A very productive and influential group of investigators from various backgrounds coalesced at Yale in the 1930s and were heavily influenced by Hull. One of these was Neal Miller, who received his Ph.D. at Yale in 1935. Interestingly, Miller did postdoctoral work at the Vienna Institute of Psychoanalysis, where he was exposed to Freud's ideas at the height of their European influence. Miller later also became an expert physiological psychologist. Putting all these background pieces together, Neal Miller worked in a research paradigm of environmental reinforcements in laboratory rats, like a good experimental behaviorist; however, he continued Hull's focus on internal drives, both in terms of physiology (such as brain mechanisms) and motivation. Furthermore, he tried to understand the deeper issues of the psyche that Freud and others had raised. He stayed at Yale until 1966, when he went to Rockefeller University and became a leader in the new field of health psychology, working on such topics as biofeedback and the voluntary control of processes like heart rate. He was the president of the American Psychological Association in 1951.

At Yale, Miller met John Dollard, who had received his Ph.D. in sociology at the University of Chicago. Chicago, at the time, was the center of the sociological and anthropological approach to social psychology, which emphasized the social or relative nature of the self. Dollard had also studied psychoanalysis in Berlin. So, when Dollard and Miller met and started collaborating, they together represented almost all the important traditions relevant to the study of personality—the psychoanalytic and ego aspects, the social and anthropological aspects, and the biological and cognitive aspects, all in the overall context of a learning and behaviorist framework. It is fascinating to see what emerged from this blend of fundamental ideas—an approach to personality called **social learning theory.**

Simply put, social learning theory proposes that our likelihoods of responding in certain ways—termed habits—are built up in terms of a hierarchy of secondary, or *acquired*, drives. For example, suppose you are mugged and beaten up while walking down a dark alley. Not only would you probably learn to avoid such situations (remembering the pain), but you would feel anxiety in similar situations. This learned anxiety is now an acquired drive that can motivate new behavior. You could be reinforced (and thus learn new aspects to your personality) when this drive is reduced, such as always walking at night with a confident friend. You might even learn to enjoy sipping wine with funny people when the sun begins to set (if this reduced your anxiety). Note that the funny people will not protect you from being mugged in the dark alley; rather, a hierarchy of responses has been built up from the learning and reducing of new drives.

In other words, for Miller and Dollard (1941) there is a learned hierarchy of likelihoods that a person will produce particular responses in particular situations. They call this a **habit hierarchy.** In essence, the individual's experiences result in learning the likelihood that a specific response in a particular situation results in reward. Using this information, the individual ranks the probability of responses in the habit hierarchy. Social learning theories see this personal ranking as responsible for individual differences that we often term personal style or personality. Furthermore, many of the important reinforcers are social in nature, coming from people in the social environment.

The concept of secondary drives attempts to describe how the (adult) human personality, in all of its complexity, can be conditioned from the infant stage, at which the child is just a bundle of undifferentiated physiological drives and responses. The concept of secondary drive explains traditional personality constructs, like the trait of extroversion, as learned secondary drives. For example, if the active orientation toward others (which characterizes an extrovert) brings milk from the mother or a clean diaper from the father, a drive toward these behaviors will be learned. And so on, as the child develops. Such notions are useful in understanding why some cultures (like Japan, which promotes group cohesion) have more shy people than other cultures (like the United States and Israel, which reward individual activity and assertiveness). Children are socialized—they learn drives and behaviors—through social rewards.

How far can this theory be extended? Does it work? An aspect of this notion of secondary drives as derived from the primary drive of feeding was applied to the concept of attachment to the mother and examined by Harry Harlow's famous studies of rhesus monkeys (Harlow, 1986; Harlow & Mears, 1979). Infant monkeys were separated from their mothers, and some of the infants were fed by feeding bottles attached to a bare wire cylinder. Harlow demonstrated that infant monkeys did not develop a secondary drive of attachment to these wire surrogate mothers; they preferred soft, terry cloth–covered surrogate mothers (even nonfeeding ones). In other words, attachment did not derive from its association with nourishment. Although this finding did not totally negate the concept of attachment as a secondary drive, it did suggest that contact comfort itself has a primary drive status in these infants. Not only did such studies suggest that the developing child needs more than to have primary needs like hunger satisfied, but they also showed the difficulty of simply accounting for the social needs and tendencies.

As noted, both Dollard and Miller had studied psychoanalysis, were impressed with its many insights, and were eager to combine them with experimental findings. But although Freud had psychoanalyzed a neurotic man obsessed with images of rats (whom he called Rattenmann, or "man of the rats"), of course Freud had never psychoanalyzed a rat. Dollard and Miller (1950) agreed that Freud had identified crucial periods in the child's personality development, but they changed the explanations to ones involving learning, through rewards and punishments. For example, they named critical times during development (feeding, cleanliness training, early sex training) when the reinforcement contingencies provided by the parents are particularly relevant. If a hungry child is not fed, she may develop anxiety or passivity rather than sociability and love. If a child is punished for messes and toilet accidents, she may learn to avoid her parents to reduce anxiety. If a child is beaten for masturbation, he may learn to associate anxiety with all aspects of sexuality. Such reinterpretations and refinements to psychoanalytic notions, made by Dollard and Miller and many other psychologists during the 1930s, 1940s, and 1950s, have come to play a dominant role in American approaches to child socialization.

What about the mental illnesses and repressed conflicts that Freud wrote so much about? Extending Hull's concepts of drives, learning, and secondary drives, Dollard and Miller attempted to explain the development of internal conflicts that result in behaviors (symptoms) of neurosis and disorders such as obsessive-compulsive behavior. For example, children have sexual drives but sometimes may be punished for acting on them. If the punishment results in the conditioning of a fear response to this drive, the primary and secondary drives may conflict. This is termed an **approach–avoidance conflict.** The individual is both drawn to and away from the sexual object, resulting in anxiety and neurotic behavior. There can likewise be an **approach–approach conflict,** in which a person (or rat) is drawn to two equally attractive choices, and an **avoidance–avoidance conflict,** in which the individual is repulsed by two equally undesirable choices. This can make a rat run back and forth in a maze, not knowing which drive to reduce first—a neurotic rat!

Another important example of the work of the so-called Yale Group is their idea that aggression is always the result of blocking, or frustrating, an individual's efforts to attain a goal. This theory was propounded in the influential book *Frustration and Aggression* (1939). Here again we have an important psychological concept—aggression—that figures prominently in both psychoanalytic and biological approaches to personality. But it is now analyzed in terms of drives, habits, and learning (including social learning), thus taking into account the complex, multidimensional nature of aggression.

For example, it is interesting that a frustration coming from the environment may lead to aggression against a different target. If your boss blocks you from achieving your promotion, you may come home and yell at your family. In some ways, this idea is similar to Freud's *displacement* defense mechanism, in which an aggressive impulse is channeled elsewhere. The frustration–aggression hypothesis, like the Freudian notion of a death instinct and like the evolutionary proposition of an evolved domineering aggression, also allows for a biological tendency to aggress. However, Dollard and Miller's approach ties these notions more closely to the environment and the ways one has learned to satisfy basic drives (an idea derived from Hull). Aggression can be learned; it can also be unlearned or prevented. And aggression clearly varies from situation to situation, from family to family, and from culture to culture. In other words, the social learning approach endeavors to integrate key ideas from other theories, but all within a learning framework. These ideas are important because they led to modern cognitive-social learning and interactionist approaches to personality.

Patterns of Child-Rearing and Personality: Robert Sears

Another member of the Yale Group, Robert R. Sears, performed a series of studies designed to examine the efficacy of Dollard and Miller's (and Hull's) theoretical explanations for personality. Specifically, Sears wanted to examine psychoanalytic constructs in terms of the real, observable behavior of parents and children. He described personality as "potentialities for action" that included motivation, expectations, habit structure, the nature of the instigators to behavior, and the environmental events produced by that behavior. For example, Sears studied the child-rearing antecedents of dependency and aggressiveness in children (Sears, Maccoby, & Levin, 1957). Childhood personality was measured by teachers' ratings, behavioral observation, and doll play. Child-rearing practices were obtained by maternal report (a major methodological problem because mothers' reports may be distorted). Still, Sears found that the amount that the parent reported punishing the child for dependency was rather highly related to both dependency and aggression in the child.

Overall, the study found that although many child-rearing practices were weakly or not at all related to personality characteristics in children, Dollard and Miller's theory that many Freudian disorders and neuroses resulted from parenting practices of punishments—that punished children for undesirable behavior—was somewhat supported by the data. In other words, this empirical approach took the conflicts described by Freud and endeavored to test them through study of parental responses. Freud never conducted such tests, but they grow naturally out of a learning approach to personality.

Why does it matter that Dollard and Miller (and other colleagues such as O. Hobart Mowrer and Leonard Doob) were working at Yale in the 1940s, where they were heavily influenced by Hull, who in turn had been influenced by the 1920s work of Watson? We are endeavoring to show that there is no simple answer to what it means to be a person. There is no single and comprehensive theory that has been established and universally adopted throughout personality psychology. Rather, there are complex systems of ideas and insights that derive from various intellectual traditions and historical movements of ideas. By tracing these developments and presenting them as eight fundamental perspectives on personality (Chapters 3 through 10 of this book), we can achieve a rich, multifaceted appreciation of personality that goes well beyond the simple assumptions of a layperson.

Evaluation

The emphasis of the behaviorist and learning approaches is on using completely controlled scientific experiments. In terms of research, this emphasis has led to a focus on laboratory pigeons and rats. In terms of concepts, this approach has led to an unwillingness to make inferences about the "mind" or the "spirit." Turning first away from introspectionism, some in this field (like Skinner) eventually refused to concede any kind of internal structures, cognitions, motives, or traits whatsoever. Further, behaviorism admits no internal motivation to self-fulfillment or self-actualization, and no true heroism; there is only history of reinforcement.

Behaviorist and learning approaches to personality have forced the field of personality to be much more experimental in its research and rigorous in its concepts than it would otherwise have been. Notions of conditioning, reward, and extinction now pervade psychology, including personality and clinical psychology. Moreover, this approach provides an empirically well-supported explanation of why behavior is not as consistent across situations as many other personality theories might imply. The situation itself must be considered an aspect of personality (see Chapter 10).

On the other hand, because radical behaviorists are unwilling to recognize any sorts of internal structures of the mind, they tend to be less able to profit from the many advances being made in cognitive psychology and the other brain sciences. Until the day he died, Skinner was relentless in his attack on cognitive psychology, even though cognitive psychologists are usually very strict in their experimental designs and scientific methods (see Chapter 7). Similarly, behaviorists are often unwilling to benefit from the many developments in trait approaches to personality (see Chapter 8).

Perhaps more important, behaviorists refuse to concern themselves with "unscientific" notions like freedom, dignity, and self-fulfillment. Such things are seen as *epiphenomena*—that is, secondary phenomena that are derived from "real" phenomena of experience. For example, Skinner repeatedly asserts that though people may sometimes feel "free," they are in actuality always controlled by the contingencies of the environment. For Skinner, people feel free when they do not recognize that they are being controlled. Education and religion are said to be two means through which the control of behavior is disguised or concealed (Skinner, 1974). Many psychologists view this perspective as a terribly demeaning and insulting view of what it means to be a person. A person is qualitatively different from a laboratory rat. Writer Arthur Koestler (1967) charged that behaviorism "has substituted for the erstwhile anthropomorphic view of the rat, a ratomorphic view of man." Such matters are taken up in the next four chapters of this book.

There is some unfortunate truth to the claim that psychology has studied the white rat and the white sophomore to the exclusion of a broader view. (Tom Cheney © 1993 from the New Yorker Collection. All rights reserved.)

"Oh, not bad. The light comes on, I press the bar, they write me a check. How about you?"

Evaluating the Perspectives

Advantages and Limits of the Behaviorist and Learning Approach

■ *Quick Analogy*

Humans as intelligent rats learning life mazes.

■ *Advantages*

Forces attention to the environmental influences on behavioral consistencies.

Demands rigorous empirical study (usually laboratory).

Stresses the importance of applying the principles of conditioning to each organism individually.

Looks for general laws that apply to all organisms.

■ *Limits*

Extreme behaviorism may ignore insights and advances from cognitive and social psychology.

May tend to dehumanize unique human potentials through comparisons to rats and pigeons.

Tends to refuse any notion of enduring dispositions within individuals.

Tends to view humans as objects to be trained.

■ *View of Free Will*

Behavior is determined by environmental contingencies.

■ *Common Assessment Technique*

Experimental analysis of animal learning.

■ *Implications for Therapy*

Since personality is conditioned and learned, therapy is based on teaching desirable habits and behaviors, and on extinguishing undesirable ones. Disruptive or aggressive children may be rewarded when they act cooperatively or quietly. Fears of elevators or airplanes are treated through systematic desensitization, in which relaxation is slowly and progressively paired with the fear-provoking stimuli until the fear is extinguished. In aversion therapy to treat stubborn bad habits such as alcoholism, the therapist may prescribe a drug (e.g., Antabuse) that produces nausea when alcohol is consumed.

Summary and Conclusion

Most approaches to personality start with complex patterns of human behavior and try to break them down into simpler, understandable components; instead of breaking down, behaviorist and learning approaches start with simple stimuli and responses of lower animals and try to build up an understanding of human complexity.

Following up on the classical conditioning work of Ivan Pavlov, John B. Watson, the early twentieth-century behaviorist, rejected introspectionism and psychoanalysis, and instead demonstrated how little Albert's emotional "personality" could be trained by hitting a hammer against a steel bar to severely frighten the infant in the presence of a conditioned stimulus. Principles of learning, generalization, and extinction were also applied to children, as the learning approach explored how "personality" is located in the environment, not in the depths of the psyche.

According to B. F. Skinner, personality is a repertoire of behavior learned from an organized set of environmental contingencies. (Many of the important terms and principles of behaviorism are listed in Table 6.1.) That is, personality is the group of commonly performed responses that a person has learned. Because it is environmentally determined, behavior is therefore very situation specific.

Skinner's approach emphasized the function of behavior, and it is a deterministic theory, in which there is no free will. He stressed that we must apply the principles of learning to each organism individually. In his novel *Walden Two*, Skinner describes a utopian community that is behaviorally engineered, based on principles of operant conditioning; a benevolent government rewards positive, socially appropriate behavior, and all is well.

According to Skinner, the motivations that Freud called the drives of the id are better understood as biological reinforcers of the environment; and the part of the psyche that Freud called the superego (conscience) is better understood as the contingencies that society creates and imposes to control the selfish (individualistic) nature of the individual. For Skinner, personality traits such as extroversion are just groups of behaviors that have been reinforced. Behaviorist approaches forced personality theorists to become more empirically minded, and many untestable Freudian assumptions were discarded.

Dollard and Miller developed a complex and wide-ranging approach to understanding the relation between learning and personality, based on drives, behaviors, and reinforcements. They said that in order to learn, one must "want something, notice something, do something, and get something" (1941, p. 2). Thus they allowed for internal motivations, both biological and cognitive, and for reinforcements, both personal and social. According to Dollard and Miller, the connection between stimulus and response is called a habit;

Table 6.1   **Some Terms and Concepts from a Behaviorist and Learning Approach**

Term or Concept	Definition or Example
principle of reinforcement	Frequency of behavior depends on its consequences—that is, the types of outcomes following behavior. The response is made contingent on a sought-after outcome.
reinforcement	An event that strengthens a behavior and increases the likelihood of repeating the behavior in the future.
negative reinforcement	An aversive event that ends if we perform a behavior, making us more likely to repeat the behavior in the future. For example, an individual with an obsessive-compulsive personality (such as Lady MacBeth) continually washes her hands because it reduces the likelihood that she will see blood on them.
punishment	An event that decreases the likelihood of performing a behavior in the future by following the response with unpleasant consequence. Although punishment does reduce the probability of undesired behaviors, the effect of punishment is temporary and is not very effective in permanently eliminating undesirable behavior. Skinner emphasized the importance of the use of hidden reinforcements rather than punishment in the successful shaping and control of behavior.
primary reinforcement (for Dollard and Miller)	An event (such as eating food) that reduces a primary drive (such as hunger).
secondary reinforcement	A conditioned (learned) reinforcer; that is, a neutral stimulus that is paired with a primary reinforcer, eventually becoming a reinforcer by itself. Maternal love supposedly is not in itself a primary reinforcer because, according to these theories, it does not reduce a drive; but the infant learns to associate Mom with important primary reinforcers—say, food. Some secondary reinforcements (such as mother, money, love, and praise) will be associated with a variety of primary reinforcers and so may become generalized reinforcers.
reinforcement schedules	The frequency and the interval of reinforcement. A schedule may be based on time (animal is reinforced every ten minutes—"fixed interval") or responses (animal is reinforced every ten pecks—"fixed ratio"). Or, these schedules may be variable, that is, with irregularly spaced reinforcement ("variable interval"—reinforced at varying times; or "variable ratio"—reinforced after varying numbers of responses). In the real world, responses are seldom reinforced each time, or even at regular intervals. Variable reinforcement increases resistance of the behavior to extinction. For example, a superstitious or obnoxious behavior might be only occasionally reinforced but may be extremely difficult to eliminate.

(continued)

Table 6.1 **Continued**

Term or Concept	Definition or Example
extinction	The process by which the frequency of the organism's producing a response gradually decreases as the behavior is no longer followed by the reinforcement.
generalization	The tendency for similar stimuli to evoke the same response. This may help explain the seemingly general nature of personality—a person behaves similarly in similar situations. According to Skinner, this is because the response is generalized to comparable situations, not because of a stable, internal personality characteristic. For example, the individual who is rewarded on a variable schedule for doing his job may behave in a "conscientious," hard-working manner in all similar "work" situations. From the observer's standpoint, this behavior, which has generalized to similar situations, looks like a stable, lasting "personality trait."
Thorndike's Law of Effect (1905)	When a response follows a stimulus and results in satisfaction for the organism, the connection between stimulus and response is strengthened; however, if the response results in discomfort or pain, the connection is weakened. This principle was the precursor of notions of operant conditioning.
shaping	The process in which undifferentiated operant behaviors are gradually changed (shaped) into a desired behavior pattern by the reinforcement of successive approximations, so that the behavior gets closer and closer to the target behavior. Using this technique, Skinner could teach animals complex "human-type" behaviors. For example, trainers can shape hoop-jumping seals, dancing bears, or table tennis–playing pigeons.
Skinnerian reinterpretation of Freud's "reality principle"	Reality-oriented behaviors come about because people are reinforced for socially appropriate actions and for waiting for satisfaction.

therefore, what we call personality is primarily made up of habits, and the relations among various habits. Secondary drives are learned—acquired by association with the satisfaction of primary drives. Abstract constructs such as happiness and status are considered to be based on learned drives. The rich man who is continually driven to accumulate wealth (which a trait psychologist might label as greed) has developed (learned) a behavior pattern as a result of money being paired with strongly reinforcing primary drive reduction (food, sex). Dollard and Miller and their colleagues worked to combine the insights of psychoanalysis and sociology with the laboratory experiments of the behaviorists. This in turn led to social and cognitive learning theories that are common in the study of personality and psychopathology today.

In other words, Dollard and Miller (1941, 1950) tried to understand the development of the variety and complexity of personality in terms of conditioning and learning, broadly construed. Their theory crossed the biological and psychodynamic issues with conditioning processes. Dollard and Miller recognized that psychoanalytic theory provided helpful observations of human behavior, and so they decided to try to understand these observations in more objective terms. As did Skinner, they saw personality as the result of the accumulation of conditioned behaviors, but unlike Skinner, they saw value in "internal" constructs (like drives and motivations) and higher mental processes. Importantly, they recognized that human behavior was embedded in a culture.

The behaviorist and learning approaches to personality, with their emphasis on the environment, drew significant attention to the situational specificity of behavior. In other words, we should not expect that a person will behave the same way in every situation. These insights are now incorporated into the most modern conceptions of what it means to be a person.

Key Theorists

Ivan Pavlov
John B. Watson
B. F. Skinner

Clark Hull
John Dollard and Neal Miller
Robert Sears

Key Concepts

partial reinforcement
classical conditioning
generalization
discrimination
extinction
behaviorism
systematic desensitization
Thorndike's Law of Effect

operant conditioning
shaping
radical determinism
social learning theory
secondary drives
habit hierarchy
frustration–aggression hypothesis

Suggested Readings

Catania, C., & Harnad, S. (Eds.) (1988). *The selection of behavior: The operant behaviorism of B. F. Skinner: Comments and consequences.* New York: Cambridge University Press.

Pavlov, I. P. (1927). *Conditioned reflexes.* Oxford, England: Oxford University Press.

Skinner, B. F. (1938). *The behavior of organisms.* New York: Appleton-Century-Crofts.

Skinner, B. F. (1948). *Walden Two.* New York: Macmillan.

Skinner, B. F. (1971). *Beyond freedom and dignity.* New York: Knopf.

Chapter 7

Cognitive Aspects
of Personality

More than two thousand years
ago, the Chinese philosopher
Mencius (Meng-tsu) wrote, "The
superior man will not manifest
either narrow-mindedness or the
want of self-respect" (1898). Most
people today would likewise prefer
to think of themselves as broad-
minded and having a positive self-
image. But what does it mean to
have a broad mind or a narrow
mind? Are there distinctive ways
that individuals perceive and think
about the world?

Some people are dreamers
and some are realists. Some are
optimists and some are pessimists.
Some see the glass as half empty,
while others looking at the same
glass see it as half full. Some people

looking at a burning bush see destruction, others see the opportunity of newly cleared land, others see divine inspiration, and still others see air pollution.

How can we understand these variations in response? Why do children react differently to certain movies than do adults? Why do many African Americans react differently to some criminal prosecutions than do many Euro-Americans? Why do some people face up to life's hardships while others crumble or retreat? One key approach is to understand the cognitive structures or concepts that people have, and the perceptual processes they employ—what they attend to, what they comprehend, and how they conceptualize.

Why should we expect to see theorizing about personality that gives cognition a central role? One explanation is that we must understand how people receive and process information about our environments in order to understand *any* complex aspect of human functioning, including personality. Many of the processes required for dealing with information about our external environment and our internal environment (our own feelings, thoughts, and sensations) remain the same regardless of the specific content—we need to attend to information, comprehend and interpret it, and place it within the framework of all the other knowledge and information we have (Norem, 1988).

The ways in which people view the world vary greatly, and from the cognitive perspective, this variability is an important source of individuality. Here, the French painter René Magritte (1898–1967) shares some of his "personality."

People think about and try to understand the world around them. This fact is so important that all personality theories attempt to take it into account. But cognitive approaches to personality view human perception and human cognition as the core of what it means to be a person. The way that people interpret their environments is seen as central to their humanness, and the ways in which people differ from one another in how they do this is seen as central to their individuality. This chapter examines the cognitive aspects of personality. We begin with basic ideas about cognition and perception, and then move on to more complex notions of cognitive styles and expectancies. But first, let's look at a brief history of the cognitive approach to personality.

Roots of Cognitive Approaches

Although philosophers have long been concerned with the nature of the human mind, it was not until Charles Darwin's theory of evolution liberated thinking about human nature that cognitive psychology could begin in earnest. That is, only after the human mind came to be seen as a biological organism rather than a fixed creation from the divine being could scientists begin to explore how thinking changed as a child developed, was influenced by different circumstances, and was shaped by culture. In addition, the effects of each person's differing abilities could be compared. (It is interesting to note that the explanation we have just given is a cognitive one; that is, scientists were unable to behave as psychological experimenters until they were able to *think* a certain way.)

Roots in Gestalt Psychology

Gestalt psychology was a movement that began in Germany just before the beginning of the twentieth century. It became very influential in Germany in the 1920s, and it was brought to America in the 1930s as many of its foremost advocates fled fascism. The central tenets of Gestalt theory are threefold: (1) human beings seek meaning in their environments; (2) we organize the sensations we receive from the world around us into meaningful perceptions; and (3) complex stimuli are not reducible to the sum of their parts.

The German word **gestalt** means pattern or configuration. The view from Gestalt theory is that the configuration of a complex stimulus is its essence (Kohler, 1947). From this perspective, component elements of a stimulus or experience cannot be added up to recreate the original. The essence of the original resides in its complex relationships and overall configuration, which are lost when subparts are analyzed separately. For example, the "triangle" in Figure 7.1 is not actually drawn on the page, but it is constructed by the viewer. When we are observing a triangle, it is more than three straight lines, and when we are looking at a triangular relationship among lovers, it is more than three separate relationships.

Figure 7.1

A Typical Gestalt Perceptual Figure. Gestalt theories claim that perception involves a search for meaning and that this meaning can be an emergent property that is not found within any single element. Here, the triangle that most people perceive "emerges" from the juxtaposition of incomplete circles; it exists in the mind of the perceiver, but not in the picture itself.

Although Gestalt theory was primarily applied to the areas of perception and problem solving, several aspects were put to use in the developing discipline of personality as well. For example, researchers studied the perceptual idea in vision that even though a large object that is far away and a small object that is nearby both cast similar-sized images on the retina, we come to take distance into account. Some people do this better than others—perhaps the extroverts, who are more focused on the outer world. But it was not until the work of Kurt Lewin that the Gestalt approach strongly influenced personality psychology.

Kurt Lewin's Field Theory

Kurt Lewin came directly out of the Gestalt tradition, but unlike most Gestalt theorists, he focused his efforts in the areas of personality and social psychology rather than perception and problem solving. Lewin published his **field theory** in 1935. His notion of "field" can be seen either as a field in the mathematical sense of vector forces or as a playing field (a field of life). It focuses on the **life space**—all the internal and external forces that act on an individual—and the structural relationships between the person and the environment. For example, a person's family life might be one region of the life space, and his religion another. For some people, the spaces are cleanly and clearly divided, with boundaries that keep issues and emotions from each region fully independent. Other people have more openness in the boundaries, so the different regions of life exert more influence on one another.

Lewin's definition of personality focused on the momentary condition of the individual—the idea of **contemporaneous causation.** Because Lewin attended so closely to what was going on in a person's mind at any moment, his orientation can be considered a cognitive position, although its simultaneous attention to the situation also makes it an interactionist position. (The interactionist position is covered in detail in Chapter 10.) As we have seen, the various approaches to personality can sometimes overlap more than one of the basic aspects.

Field Dependence as a Personality Variable

As an example of an early but influential cognitive-perceptual approach to personality that grew directly out of Gestalt psychology, let us consider the phenomenon called field dependence. All individuals have distinctive, enduring, cognitive styles of dealing with their everyday cognitive tasks of perception, problem solving, and decision making (Bertini, Pizzamiglio, & Wapner, 1986; Scott & Bruce, 1995; Porter & Suedfeld, 1981). People differ on a myriad of dimensions, such as whether they are color reactors or form reactors (that is, when objects vary in both color and form, which dimension is seen as most important); generally attentive or inattentive; analyzers (who concentrate on separate parts of things) or synthesizers (who concentrate on patterns); evaluative or nonevaluative; people who see the world in complex, sophisticated terms and those who see it in simpler terms; and so on. These differences explain why one person shows up at a garden party wearing a Hawaiian sport shirt with polyester plaid pants and white buck shoes, while another comes dressed all in black cotton with a touch of white trim.

One such cognitive style variable that has been well explored is **field dependence.** People who are rated as highly field dependent are very influenced in their problem solving by salient but irrelevant aspects of the context (or field) in which the problem occurs. Other people are field independent.

A common demonstration of field dependency comes from a task that requires a subject to adjust a bar so that it is fully vertical. One version of this task is shown in Figure 7.2. On some trials, the bar is within a rectangular frame that is slightly offset from the vertical. People who tend to align the bar with the surrounding frame (and thus do not make the bar fully vertical) are said to be field dependent on the rod-and-frame task. That is, their perception of the position of the rod is influenced by the context or field in which it occurs. This orientation is shown on the left panel of the figure. People who align the bar vertically despite the tilted frame (see the right panel of the figure) are termed field independent; that is, they escape the influence of the field in their problem solving.

In an alternate version of the task, a person sits in a special chair with controls for adjusting the tilt; the subject is then asked to position the chair so that it is fully upright, while seated in a specially constructed room that has a tilted floor. In this case, the field-independent individual is able to ignore the visual cues about which way is up—cues that are misleading in this situation— and instead is guided by internally generated cues about body positioning. The field-dependent person is so influenced by the irrelevant cues from the tilted room that he or she ends up aligned with the tilted room rather than aligned

Figure 7.2

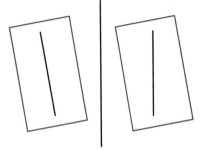

The Rod-and-Frame Test. The test for field independence measures how well a person ignores the irrelevant context of a problem. The field-dependent individual (left panel) is led astray by focusing on the context and aligns the rod with the frame. The field-independent individual (right panel) can ignore the misleading frame and find the true vertical, which is the goal.

with true vertical. In these simple situations, there is a benefit to being field independent—it gets you the correct response—but over the broad range of situations people normally confront, neither extreme is universally preferable. Most people fall near the center of this continuum, with a mix of field-dependent and field-independent characteristics.

The field-independent style is more analytical and allows for more complex levels of restructuring in problem solving. These individuals are more influenced in their behavior by internalized aspects of the problem-solving situation. The field-dependent person, on the other hand, has a greater sensitivity to the context of a problem and tends to be more holistic and intuitive in problem solving. Field-dependent people also show greater sensitivity to their social and interpersonal contexts.

Field dependence was first explored as a personality variable in the 1940s by Herman Witkin (1949) and Solomon Asch (1952). In the ensuing half-century, this variable has inspired thousands of studies. Field dependence is useful as a description of individual differences in personality because it is reliably measurable across many different instruments; moreover it tends to be consistent in an individual over time (even from childhood to adulthood). A person's standing along the field-dependence continuum is associated with many aspects of behavior, especially interpersonal behavior. Some of the differences that have been demonstrated are listed in Table 7.1.

Table 7.1 **Characteristics Associated with Field Independence**

Domain	Characteristics
children's play preferences	Field-independent children are more likely to favor solitary play over social play.
socialization patterns	Field-independent people are more likely to have been socialized with an emphasis on autonomy over conformity.
career choices	Field-independent people are more likely to be in technological rather than humanitarian occupations.
preferred interpersonal distance for conversation	Field-independent people are more likely to sit farther away from a conversational partner.
level of eye contact	Field-independent people make less frequent and less prolonged eye contact with a conversational partner.

When field independence is examined over groups (rather than over isolated individuals), there is a modest but consistent gender difference, with females tending more toward field dependence than males. This is certainly consistent with many aspects of gender difference in personality and cognition, such as greater social sensitivity and more contextually bound moral reasoning. Later in this book we point out that these differences could also be explained in terms of traits, but field dependence relies on perception—a cognitive process—as the basis for the explanation.

When field dependence is examined in a cross-cultural context, differences also emerge. Witkin provided evidence that societies could be characterized in terms of the predominant cognitive style of their members (e.g., Witkin & Berry, 1975). Witkin claimed that people in hunter–gatherer societies tended to be more field independent than people in predominantly agrarian societies. He attributed the difference to the adaptive value of each style for the differing demands on the individuals in each group: Hunter-gatherers need to be more analytical in order to find game and to keep track of their locations so that they can find their way home again. Farmers tend to have more elaborate systems of social interaction, and conformity to group norms and interpersonal sensitivity would be of primary importance in that environment.

Cognitive and Perceptual Mechanisms

Anyone who has attended school knows that children differ markedly in how they think about and react to problems, and that these reactions change with age. That is, we can gain insights into the cognitive aspects of personality by examining mechanisms of expecting, attending, and information processing.

Schema Theory

Jean Piaget was born in Switzerland in 1896. Like Freud, Piaget was first interested in biology (he studied mollusks), and then studied for a while with Carl Jung. However, he soon turned to a focus on intellectual development (including the development of his own children) and went on to have a major impact on cognitive conceptions of the development of personality. Piaget proposed a cognitive-structure explanation of how children develop concepts about the world around them.

According to Piaget (1952), children progress through a series of cognitive stages as they mature. At each stage, the content of their knowledge and the nature of their reasoning become more sophisticated. New cognitive structures, called **schemas,** build on the structures (schemas) acquired earlier. For example, we now know that human newborns have an innate preference to listen to human speech (more than to other sounds) and to focus their eyes on human faces (more than on other visual stimuli). As babies encounter human speech and human faces, they build on this groundwork to develop complex cognitive structures—patterns of understanding the world. A nine-year-old child viewing a sexual scene on a TV soap opera actually "sees" or understands something different than does either a two-year-old or a mature adult.

The schema that is activated in a given situation is a major determinant of a person's expectations, inferences, and actions in that situation (Abelson, 1981). Such schemas exist at many levels, and schemas at different levels can simultaneously be active in influencing our behavior. Suppose, for example, a person (Pat) is going out on a first date with a new acquaintance (Chris), planning to have dinner and then see a movie. As Pat sits down at their table in the restaurant, many schemas are simultaneously relevant in guiding Pat's behavior. One of these might be a schema for the event of eating in a restaurant. (Sometimes a schema for a familiar event is called a "**script**" because, like the script of a play, it specifies the roles and actions of all the participants along with the props and the setting.) Pat knows, among other things, what the waiter is likely to say and how to respond appropriately. We usually do not think about these schemas or scripts unless they break down, as might be the case when we travel to a different country.

Another relevant schema for Pat might be the script for a first date, which influences Pat's expectations of what to do, as well as what to expect that Chris will do. Pat will be using the specific conversational and linguistic schemas that govern the ways of talking to people who are in particular social categories (such as friend), or who have particular roles to play in an interaction (such as date). If Chris responds with a "business associate script," that may very well be the end of that relationship. In other words, personality can be viewed as a series of cognitive scripts.

Piaget's foundation (and subsequent research on schemas and scripts) is so important because it suggests, first, that our ways of understanding unfold in a fairly logical order and, second, that new cognitions build on older cognitions (Rumelhart, 1980). According to this view, a good teacher cannot directly teach or reinforce, but rather must guide learners to their own discoveries. This is a distinctive view of human nature.

Categorization

A related, powerful feature of human cognition is our tendency to organize our experience by assigning the events, objects, and people we encounter into categories. **Categorization** is omnipresent and occurs automatically (that is, without our effort or conscious intention). What does this mean?

The actual physical stimuli that are encountered by our sensory organs are extraordinarily complex. The visual scene in front of you right now, for example, contains millions of bits of information, even if it were to be described only in terms of the visual characteristics of each tiny sector of the visual field (such as a computer could understand). This is the information that reaches your eye, but it is not what you "see." What you experience instead are the identifiable, familiar objects that are present—things like this page, your own hand, a pen, a door. It is impossible for people *not* to categorize. We experience the world through our interpretations (Bruner, Goodnow, & Austin, 1956).

In human perception, automatic categorization of very complex scenes often occurs even when the simple characteristics of the stimulus are too brief or too weak to reach our conscious awareness. One striking example involves our ability to detect information about the emotional states of other people from briefly displayed facial expressions. Without necessarily being aware that we detected a particular facial muscle twitch or a flared nostril or dilated pupil, sometimes even without our having conscious or reportable knowledge of what such a signal might mean, we recognize the emotions associated with those brief stimuli (DePaulo & Friedman, 1997; Rosenthal, 1979). We perceive anger or interest or disgust, without consciously analyzing the signals that conveyed that information.

Consider now what happens when you enter a classroom you have never been in before. Normally, you will perceive objects such as chairs, windows, an instructor's desk, and other classroom paraphernalia. Of course, you have never seen these particular chairs or windows before, but by an automatic and effortless process you categorize them. And although there may be some unique features to these objects, you make the assumption that they have most features in common with already familiar instances of the category, for both physical and functional characteristics. But there are individual differences: the set of categories a person uses depends heavily on both the expectations that are aroused by the current environment and on his or her relevant prior experience.

This same powerful, automatic process of categorization, though,

In many situations, people normally begin their consideration of an object by assigning it to a category. For most of us, male or female is the first categorization we make when we encounter a new person. Many people find that their normal modes of interaction are very disrupted when one of the most salient characteristics, gender, is indeterminate.

can have negative effects, as it is just a tiny step from a useful category to a harmful stereotype. The same informational efficiency that provides us with useful expectations and interpretations can lead us to premature judgments (prejudice). The existence (and persistence) of negative social stereotypes about social, religious, ethnic, or racial groups can be explained by the confluence of several cognitive factors that play a pervasive role in our processing of information. The primary factor is the one discussed above—the power of categories to guide people's interpretations and expectations (Taylor & Crocker, 1981). Once a category exists for us, when we encounter something or someone who matches a few features of that category, we "fill in the blanks" with the rest of the information that applies to the category (Srull & Wyer, 1989). From a strictly cognitive perspective, the stereotypes associated with categories of people are no different in terms of their representation and use than, say, categories of houses or flowers. Some people are quick to categorize other objects and other people. This is part of the reason why white Americans and black Americans often tend to have different views of judicial proceedings in which ethnic group or color is an issue; their differing experiences have led them to different schemas and categories in processing the same information.

Another, related characteristic of human cognition also encourages the use of stereotypes: people are much more likely to notice information that supports their expectations than information that is contradictory to their expectations. Thus, as we look at a new person who is a member of some group or category, under most conditions we are more likely to notice those characteristics that fit the stereotype than characteristics that do not. When we believe it, we see it (Hamilton & Sherman, 1994).

Control of Attention

How do we "see" (and hear and smell and feel and taste) persons and objects and events in ways that are meaningful to us? Often it is through the control of attention. Because humans do such a remarkable job of extracting meaning from what William James (1890) called a "blooming, buzzing confusion," most of us are not aware of the sophisticated mechanisms by which we continuously control our attention and interpret our surroundings. Here, however, is an exercise you can do right now to demonstrate this capacity to yourself.

Continue to read this paragraph, and while you are reading, also listen to the background noises in your environment, feel the contact of your clothing with your skin, feel this book touching your hand, smell the scent in the air around you, taste the taste inside your mouth, and attend to the visual scene beyond the edges of this page in your peripheral vision.

Of course, paying attention to all those things at once is difficult, and also interferes with your ability to concentrate on what you are reading. What is interesting about this exercise, though, is that all the sensory information that allowed you to hear, smell, feel, taste, and see the previously unattended aspects of your internal and external environment is always present, always impinging on your sensory systems. Fortunately for our sanity, we aren't constantly noticing and attending to it all. On the other hand, we are constantly doing *some* monitoring of our environments in all modalities; for example, if there were even a faint smell of smoke, you would probably notice it (Triesman, 1964). People pick up on a few key features of their current environments and filter these in light of their current goals. This combination of internal and external information sources is the primary determinant of the allocation of attention among the different signals in the internal and external environment. Our attention is allocated not only to the tasks of operating on the environment around us, but also to the control of some of our internal mental processes as well.

Individual Differences in Attention: ADHD

One striking way in which individuals differ is in the extent to which their attention is under their intentional control. People who have atypical attentional processes are often diagnosed as having ADHD—**attention-deficit/ hyperactivity disorder.** According to the Diagnostic and Statistical Manual of Mental Disorders (American Psychiatric Association, 1994), the term ADHD is used for people with or without the hyperactivity component; that distinction is made by a subcategorization. Attentional behavior in these individuals differs in several ways from that of most other people (Barkley & Edwards, 1998). Paradoxically, attention is not uniformly worse in all respects in people with ADD/ADHD; instead, it is different in ways that make it simultaneously better and worse. People with ADD are often capable of very intense concentration on a task that engages their interest—with deeper or longer-lasting concentration than people who are otherwise comparable (in age, education, intelligence). For example, a school-aged boy with ADD may concentrate for long periods of time on a computer game, continuing to be engaged in the task long after his age mates have grown bored and moved on to something else. During this period, the child may appear to be utterly oblivious to his surroundings and completely focused on his game—an ideal demonstration of paying attention to a task. Conversely, though, people with ADD often fail to shift their attention appropriately to important aspects of their environments. They might fail to notice that the other students have put away their books, not be aware that their companions have left the video arcade, not pick up on social cues from others that their behavior is inappropriate. This variability across people in how their attentional processes operate is directly relevant to personality because of its significant influence on how a person interacts with social environments. It is relevant also because it influences how that person is perceived by others—as alert versus inattentive, as "with it" versus "out of it," as responsive versus standoffish.

Many children are now treated with the stimulant Ritalin to improve their classroom performance (and control their classroom behavior). The treatment is controversial, however, because the nature of attentional variation is not well understood (Barkley & Edwards, 1998). Some argue that we are merely drugging children to deal with the deficiencies of the school environment. They ask, "Whose attention disorder is being treated?" Is it the child's problem, or is it the case that the educators are not attending to the right priorities in their schools? This is a good example of how understanding cognitive aspects of personality can have important societal implications.

Humans as Scientists: George Kelly's Personal Construct Theory

Each of us tries to figure out how our worlds work; can we therefore think of ourselves as good or poor scientists, actively trying to make sense of the world around us? This is the basic thrust of George Kelly's influential perspective on personality, that each of us tries to understand the world and that we do so in ways that are different. Because its focus is on people's active endeavors to construe or understand the world and construct their own versions of reality, this approach is (sensibly) called constructivism, or **personal construct theory.**

Kelly's (1955) fundamental postulate is that "a person's processes are psychologically channeled by the ways in which he anticipates events" (p. 46). According to this approach, people change as they reorganize their construct system. Kelly's theorizing was especially focused on the domain of interpersonal relationships. What guides a person's behavior is his or her interpretation of the surrounding environment and the resultant expectations about it.

Individuals as Amateur Personality Theorists

Kelly explicitly used the model of the scientific method to describe general human behavior. Kelly claimed that "every man is, in his own particular way, a scientist" (1955, p. 5). Like the scientist who specifies a hypothesis and then conducts an experiment to see if the hypothesis accurately predicts the outcome, individuals make up their own "theories," and then use their personal experiences as the "data" that support (or invalidate) the theory.

According to George Kelly, we are each a personality theorist.

One key feature of Kelly's theory clearly differentiates it from many other approaches to personality. For example, trait approaches to personality (discussed in Chapter 8) posit a specific set of traits as being central to explaining human personality. Kelly (1963) had a radically different idea: We each have our own system of constructs that we use to understand and predict behavior (both our own and others'). That is, Kelly argues that each person is more or less a personality theorist, with a personal system of explanations of human behavior!

The Role Construct Repertory Test

Kelly devised a unique assessment instrument that was designed to evoke one's personal construct system. Rather than asking people to rate or rank a set of traits or dimensions of personality that the test creator thinks are important, the goal of this instrument is to allow the person's own understanding of personality to emerge through the process of making comparisons. This well-known instrument is called the **Role Construct Repertory Test,** or Rep test. (You can take a similar test yourself in the Self-Understanding box.) The examiner first elicits the names of twenty to thirty people who fit specific roles in the person's life (such as father, previous boyfriend/girlfriend, disliked teacher). Then, the examiner puts together triads (groups of three) of these figures and the examinee is asked to identify how two of them differ from the third. The dimension that differentiates among the group is the construct generated by the subject. For example, suppose a person is given the triad of her sister

Cognitive Personality Assessment
Using a Role Construct Approach

Based on the Work of George Kelly

From taking this brief test, you can get a sense of how a role construct approach works. If you are interested in exploring your own constructs further, you can add more roles to the list in section I, and more triads to the list in section II.

I. For each of the roles described, write the name of a specific person who has that role in your life.

_____ 1. Your mother or father
_____ 2. Your best friend
_____ 3. Your sister nearest in age (or female most like a sister)
_____ 4. Your brother nearest in age (or male most like a brother)
_____ 5. Your spouse (or boyfriend/girlfriend)
_____ 6. A teacher you liked
_____ 7. A teacher you disliked
_____ 8. Your boss
_____ 9. A successful person you know
_____ 10. An unsuccessful person you know

II. Consider each group of three listed in the first column below (the numbers refer to the people named in section I). Think of a way in which two of them are similar to each other and different from the other one. Write the numbers of the two who are similar and a term that describes how they are similar (their shared characteristic). Then, write the number of the one who is different and a term that describes how he or she differs.

Group	Which two are similar?	Shared characteristic	Who is different?	Different characteristic
1, 4 5	_____	_____	_____	_____
2, 3, 9	_____	_____	_____	_____
4, 6, 10	_____	_____	_____	_____
2, 4, 7	_____	_____	_____	_____
6, 8, 9	_____	_____	_____	_____
1, 7, 8	_____	_____	_____	_____
4, 7, 9	_____	_____	_____	_____
5, 8, 10	_____	_____	_____	_____
1, 3, 8	_____	_____	_____	_____
3, 5, 6	_____	_____	_____	_____

III. Look over the list of contrasting pairs of terms you generated. Your list is a reflection of your personal constructs—how you think about people.

Annette, her boss Geraldine, and a disliked teacher Mr. Sorensen, and is asked to say how one of them differs from the other two. If the subject says that her sister and her boss are both nervous but her disliked teacher is calm, a construct of *nervous–calm* is generated. This procedure is repeated a few dozen times with different triads, resulting in a set of constructs that is taken to be a reflection of the hierarchy of constructs (dimensions) that the examinee believes are important in understanding and predicting behavior. Each person's constructs are a unique expression of that individual's own view of which characteristics of people are important.

Kelly's major work was published in 1955, a decade before cognitive psychology was established as a field of study within psychology. Nonetheless, Kelly's work helped pave the way for more modern social cognition approaches such as attribution approaches and social learning theories (see the following sections). These theories, like Kelly's, try to explain the ways in which the individual perceives the social world and anticipates events, and view these processes as central to understanding human behavior. But it is important to remember that each person's explanations function in an interpersonal, cultural, and historical context. That is, the explanations can change depending on the particular persons, histories, and situations involved (Hermans, Kempen, & van Loon, 1992).

George Kelly's work remains influential, with his approach to personality reflected in an ongoing journal exploring that theoretical approach: *The International Journal of Personal Construct Psychology*.

Social Intelligence

Obviously, people differ widely in their cognitive abilities, but does such information help us better understand their personalities? Many of the concepts we have been discussing coalesce in the idea of social intelligence (Cantor & Kihlstrom, 1987). The idea is fundamentally quite simple: just as individuals vary in their knowledge and skills relevant to many aspects of their lives (for example, in mathematical ability, in musical aptitude, in reasoning skills, and so on), they also differ in their level of mastery of the particular cluster of knowledge and skills that are relevant to interpersonal situations—their **social intelligence.**

This approach claims that people vary in their abilities to understand and influence other people. Success in interpersonal interaction is easy for some people and difficult for others. Some are diplomats while others are boors. The construct of social intelligence tries to capture the ways in which individuals differ from one another in their interpersonal skills.

A similar idea about the existence of such a cluster of abilities has also arisen from a very different source. Howard Gardner, a prominent educational psychologist interested in educational implications of individual differences, devised a theory of "multiple intelligences" that has become influential in the field of education (Gardner, 1983). This theory claims that all human beings have at least seven different intelligences—seven different ways of knowing about the world—and that people differ from one another in their relative strengths in each domain. Gardner's seven intelligences include knowing the world through language, logical-mathematical analysis, spatial representation, musical thinking, bodily-kinesthetic intelligence (control of one's body as a gymnast might have), and understanding of the self and others. Under Gardner's approach, each person is characterized by a profile of intelligences rather than by a single, global measure of intelligence (such as an IQ). Gardner rejects traditional intelligence measures as too narrow. He claims that they usually reflect people's differential abilities in one or two of the ways of knowing, but pick up almost no information about their abilities in the other spheres. Both social intelligence researchers and multiple intelligence researchers argue that individual differences in people's abilities in the social-interpersonal domain should be viewed as a sort of intelligence—that these abilities form internally coherent clusters and are measurable within an individual-differences framework in the same way as any other aspect of cognitive skill. In other words, if you have the cognitive skills and attentional control to be empathic, sensitive, influential, popular, inspiring, compassionate, exciting, humorous, charming, and so on, then you are socially intelligent. Note that this conception involves cognitive skills, which presumably can be learned and cultivated to some degree. In this scheme, aspects of personality can be changed through skill training.

Explanatory Style as a Personality Variable

As the cognitive approach to personality has continued to evolve, increased attention has been devoted to the cognitive styles (or characteristic perceptual modes) that people use to try to understand their environments. **Explanatory style** refers to a set of cognitive personality variables that captures a person's habitual means of interpreting events in his or her life. There are a number of different approaches to this central idea of explanatory style.

Optimism and Pessimism

One version of this approach sets up optimism and pessimism as the extreme poles of explanatory style. People with an optimistic explanatory style tend to interpret events in their lives with an optimistic perspective, even perceiving neutral events as positive and seeing potential or eventual positive outcomes in negative events. Those with a pessimistic style, on the other hand, tend to focus on the negative potential in a situation. For example, if a student with an optimistic explanatory style receives an uncharacteristically poor grade on an exam, she might consider that to be useful feedback, informing her that she needs to change her study or note-taking techniques. Once she makes those changes, she confidently expects a better outcome on the next exam.

If the same student's explanatory style were closer to the pessimistic pole, she might view the poor grade as a sign of her own lack of ability; this is a stable attribution to an internal cause. Or she might blame factors that are out of her control, such as an overly tough professor; this is a stable attribution to an external cause. In either case, her expectations for her future performance would be lower, and she may even become depressed (Peterson & Barrett, 1987; Peterson & Seligman, 1987).

In general, having an optimistic explanatory style is associated with better outcomes. In one study, students with an optimistic explanatory style (as measured by a standardized instrument) were more likely than their more pessimistic peers to believe that effort, improved study habits, and greater self-discipline could make a difference in their grades. And the optimists were more likely to do well (Peterson & Barrett, 1987). In another study, the work of low-achieving students was measurably improved by an intervention that was focused on overcoming their pessimistic interpretation of their performance (Noel, Forsyth, & Kelley, 1987).

Note, however, that excessive optimism may be detrimental to success in situations in which optimism leads a person to overlook or downplay potential problems. For example, it is not helpful for an optimistic dieter to think that ice cream does not really have a lot of calories and fat. Excessive optimism may even be considered maladaptive. A person who is always upbeat and positive, even in times of sadness or crisis, is considered "abnormal."

Attributional Model of Learned Helplessness

What happens when an individual learns that he or she cannot control any of the things that are important? Martin Seligman (1975) uses the term **learned helplessness** to describe a situation in which repeated exposure to unavoidable punishment leads an organism to accept later punishment even when it is avoidable. In a classic series of experiments, unpleasant electric shocks were administered repeatedly to dogs who could not escape. When the restraints were removed, the dogs could easily have avoided continued shocks, but they tended to stay in place and suffer further punishment. In the initial series of shocks, they had learned that they were helpless to control the punishment, and so they gave up trying to escape or avoid it (Overmier & Seligman, 1967).

Analogous experiments with people show the same result: once an individual learns that he or she is not in control, the motivation to seek control may be shut down, even when control later becomes possible. During the initial phase, the control truly is external. But with sufficient experience under external control, the participant no longer attempts internal, self-directed con-

Famous Personalities

Presidents and Achievement

Do you feel confident and able to meet your goals? Could you be president? Albert Bandura describes self-efficacy as an individual's belief that he or she can successfully perform a particular action. Self-efficacy beliefs are domain-specific. That is, you have different beliefs in your self-efficacy to perform different tasks. So whereas you might have poor belief in your self-efficacy in mathematics, you might have high self-efficacy about your writing ability. According to Bandura (1982), self-efficacy beliefs have important effects on—in fact are the most important motivators of—an individual's achievement. People are much more likely to engage in activities that they believe they can successfully accomplish than to undertake a task that they do not believe they are competent to achieve.

Self-efficacy decisions are based on four different kinds of experiences. First, previous successful experiences with the task demonstrate the ability to perform the task competently. Second, seeing others successfully perform certain tasks increases the perception that they are "do-able." Third, the verbal persuasion of others encourages us by telling us that we are capable of succeeding at a particular activity. Finally, our levels of physiological arousal give information as to whether or not we can cope in a particular situation. These factors together culminate in the individual's perception of ability to accomplish a task or goal—his or her self-efficacy for that situation.

Relatedly, attribution theorists like Bernard Weiner emphasize that one's achievement derives from one's manner of interpreting success and failure. There are three properties of perceived causality for events in one's life: (1) situations are perceived as being either internally caused (caused by some factor of the individual) or externally caused (due to situational issues); (2) events are seen as the result of either controllable factors or uncontrollable factors; and (3) the causes of occurrences are perceived as being either stable (lasting across time) or changing (Weiner, 1985). Weiner hypothesizes that one's usual style of explaining causes of success and failure is responsible for the expectancy of success and therefore for one's achievement-oriented behaviors. According to this theory, high achievers tend to perceive the causes of their success as internal, controllable, and stable. These ideas seem to hold true across cultures (Betancourt & Weiner, 1982; Schuster, Forsterling, & Weiner, 1989).

A clear example of the importance of the response to failure in determining ultimate achievement can be seen by looking at the history of Bill Clinton's 1992 presidential campaign. When he lost the New Hampshire Democratic primary race, many political pundits considered his chance at the nomination to be doomed. But Clinton styled himself the Comeback Kid and attributed his poor showing to the scandals that had recently plagued

trol. Depression, stress, and apathy are commonly the consequences. This line of thought is currently used in studying and treating depression, in conjunction with the idea that depressive people have a depressive schema in which they generate more and more depressive thoughts (Abramson, Metalsky, & Alloy, 1989; Beck & Freeman, 1989). (See the Famous Personalities box.)

his campaign—an external attribution. Of course, there are many factors that determined his ultimate success in that campaign, but Clinton's success expectancy and his attribution of failure to an external cause put him in a strong position with respect to how he ran his campaign. He had previously engineered the same remarkable reversal when he lost and later regained the governorship of Arkansas. Furthermore, he had spent almost all of his adult life either preparing for elected office, or running for office, or holding elected office (previous success and lots of encouragement).

Psychologist Carol Dweck and her associates take a different approach to understanding the relation between cognitions about task performance and success. She has found that children tend to show one of two behavior patterns in achievement situations: a maladaptive "helpless" response or an adaptive "mastery-oriented" response. Helpless behavior involves avoidance and poor performance in the face of challenges or obstacles. Children who show mastery behaviors, on the other hand, do well when activities are demanding and continue to strive and succeed when they encounter difficulties (Diener & Dweck, 1980; Elliott & Dweck, 1988). These individual differences in trying and persisting at difficult tasks were found even among children of similar abilities.

Children who are helpless tend to attribute their failure to internal characteristics and inadequacies such as low intelligence, poor memory, or poor problem-solving capacity. These attributions accompany low expectations for future successes. Such children also show accompanying emotional reactions like anxiety or boredom. Helpless children's performance tends to sink into a slow decline, and interestingly, helpless children often interpret successful performance as deficient in some manner. Children who are mastery-oriented, however, act very differently in the face of difficulty. These children tend not to view the difficulty as a failure but instead, like Bill Clinton, look at obstacles as interesting challenges to be faced and surmounted. They increase their effort and concentration, and they exhibit optimistic and positive emotions. (Many have called Bill Clinton the ultimate optimist.)

Some individuals have goals that permit them to see achievement situations as opportunities to learn, expand their abilities, and become more competent. Whereas Weiner thinks individual differences in attributions for success and failure cause high and low achievement behavior, Dweck counters that the patterns of goal-making that an individual uses are ultimately responsible for the type of attributions made about performance. If we don't worry about performance and evaluation but instead focus on the paths to our goals, we are much more likely to achieve them (and perhaps even become president).

Fortunately, there is evidence that teaching children to challenge their pessimistic thoughts can "immunize" them against depression (Seligman et al., 1995). That is, a cognitive intervention—teaching people to change their thought processes—can affect subsequent behavior. Note again that personality is seen here as a kind of cognitive skill.

The consequences of these personality differences sometimes can be seen in terms of differential memory. For example, when memory is examined for information that came from an emotionally threatening source, people with a repressive coping style show reduced memory for information from that threatening source, whereas people with a more information-seeking coping style manage to remember and use the information. Other experiments show that people with dispositional pessimism may have a generalized expectancy that bad things will happen to them, and they remember bad things and even reinterpret good things as not so good (Carver & Scheier, 1981; Scheier & Carver, 1985). As we saw in Chapter 3 on psychoanalytic approaches, certain aspects of cognitive approaches can be seen as modern realizations of directions that Sigmund Freud first proposed.

Interestingly, purely cognitive, explanatory attempts at psychotherapy sometimes run up against unconscious processes. If you try too hard to think in certain way, you may wind up thinking in the opposite way—the antidote becomes the poison (Wegner, 1994). For example, if you are on a diet and try very hard not to think about ice cream and other delicious fatty foods, you may very well set in motion a set of unconscious thought processes focused on just those treats, and ready to spring into eating action as soon as you let down your guard.

Julian Rotter's Locus of Control Approach

The cognitive approach can be combined with social learning theories (introduced in Chapter 6) to produce a quite sophisticated view of personality. For example, it seems as if a personality theory should be able to take into account that people work to attain their goals both because of the consequences (rewards) and because of their thoughts and perceptions about the outcome and its likelihood. People plan and make choices before they act. Julian Rotter (rhymes with "voter") was a social learning theorist whose work considered just such matters. Rotter was an important bridge between traditional social learning theories and the most modern ideas that have come to be called social-cognitive theory (Rotter, Chance, & Phares, 1972).

According to Rotter, our final choice of behavior depends both on how strongly we expect that our performance will have a positive result (**outcome**

expectancy) and how much we value the expected reinforcement (**reinforcement value**). Rotter's theory focuses on why an individual performs a behavior and which behavior he or she actually performs in a specific situation.

Generalized versus Specific Expectancies

In any environment, people have a variety of possibly relevant behaviors in their repertoire. Some of these are more likely to occur in a particular situation than others. Rotter calls this likelihood that a particular behavior will occur in a specific situation its "**behavior potential.**" A particular behavior, like laughing loudly, may have a high behavior potential in some situations (during a hilarious movie) and low behavior potential in other situations (during a final exam).

There are *specific* expectancies that a particular reward will follow a behavior in a particular situation and *generalized* expectancies that are related to a group of situations. For example, a person might have the generalized expectation of enjoying parties, but the additional specific expectancy of not enjoying his father's office Christmas party. Using these constructs, we might think of the more stable, situationally consistent personality characteristics that we ascribe to people as being the result of their generalized expectancies (which result in similar behaviors in a variety of similar situations). Those behaviors that people engage in that are often labeled as being contrary to their personality may arise from their specific expectancies about a particular situation (resulting in a different behavior than is usual for them). Since, as outside observers, we rarely have access to the internal information that directs the actor in specific situations (which contributes to his specific expectancies and thereby affects his behavior in that situation), his behavior—in this case, avoiding the holiday party—appears to us to be inconsistent with his personality.

When do generalized expectancies influence our behavior more than specific expectancies, and vice versa? Rotter says that we tend to weigh generalized expectancies more heavily in new situations and use specific expectancies when the situation becomes more familiar (and we better know what to expect).

The Role of Reinforcements

Rotter also proposes that an individual will prefer some reinforcements more than others and this will affect the likelihood of occurrence of behaviors associated with different reinforcements. The greater the subjective value of the reinforcement, the more likely a person is to perform a behavior associated with that valued reinforcement. The value of any reinforcement is considered in relation to the values of other available reinforcers. According to Rotter, the reinforcer that will have the highest value is the reinforcement that we expect will lead to other things we value (such as money, prestige, and so on). These secondary reinforcers are of value because of their association with the satisfaction of important psychological needs.

Rotter describes six psychological needs that develop out of biological needs: recognition–status (need to achieve, be seen as competent, have positive social standing); dominance (need to control others, have power and influence); independence (need to make decisions for oneself); protection–dependency (need to have others give one security and help one achieve goals); love and affection (need to be liked and cared for by others); physical comfort (need to avoid pain, seek pleasure, enjoy physical security and a sense of well-being).

The Psychological Situation

Behavior potential, outcome expectancy, and reinforcement potential all come together to form what Rotter terms **"the psychological situation."** Rotter (1982) notes that the power of the situation in behavior is frequently downplayed; what is really important, he contends, is not necessarily the objective situation (as behaviorists might suggest) but the *psychological situation.* The psychological situation represents the individual's unique combination of potential behaviors and their value to him or her. It is in the psychological situation that a person's expectations and values interact with the situational constraints to exert a powerful influence on behavior.

Locus of Control

The best-known feature of Rotter's theory is the concept of external versus internal control of reinforcement, or **locus of control.** There is either the generalized expectancy that the individual's own actions lead to desired outcomes—an **internal locus of control.** Or, there is the belief that things outside of the individual, such as chance or powerful others, determine whether desired outcomes occur—an **external locus of control.** Rotter developed a scale of Internal-External Locus of Control, which measures an individual's beliefs about the determinants of his or her behavior.

Unlike the strict behaviorists described in Chapter 6, Rotter does believe that individuals have enduring dispositions, despite the important role of the situation in determining behavior. In his original conception, Rotter saw locus of control as a stable individual difference variable with two dimensions (internal and external), influencing a variety of behaviors in a number of different contexts. More recently, locus of control (LOC) has been found to have three somewhat orthogonal (independent) dimensions—internality, luck or chance, powerful others (Levenson, 1981). That is, external people not only believe that events are beyond their control, but they do so either in terms of chance or powerful others.

Internal-LOC individuals are more likely to be achievement-oriented because they see that their own behavior can result in positive effects, and they are more likely to be high achievers as well (Findley & Cooper, 1983). External-LOC people tend to be less independent and also are more likely to be depressed and stressed, just as Rotter predicted (Benassi, Sweeney, & Dufour, 1988; Rotter, 1954).

Albert Bandura's Social-Cognitive Learning Theory

Before the first time you ever drove a car, you had already learned many things about how you should and should not drive. Much of that knowledge was gained while you were a passenger, before you ever stepped into a Driver Ed class. It came from observational learning processes—watching another person perform the task. This fundamental aspect of human behavior is the focus of Albert Bandura, a social cognitive theorist whose major work addresses the nature of observational learning as well as the manner in which the inner person and the demands of a situation combine to determine a person's actions.

Bandura was greatly influenced in his training by his exposure to the work of learning theorist Clark Hull. Unlike classical behaviorists, who insisted that learning mechanisms be restricted to explaining the relationships between observable variables, Hull believed that there was a place in learning theory for unobservable variables (intervening or internal variables) that mediate the relationship between stimulus and response.

The Self-System

Bandura gives an important role in personality to what he calls the "**self-system**"—the set of cognitive processes by which a person perceives, evaluates, and regulates his or her own behavior so that it is appropriate to the environment and effective in achieving the individual's goals (Bandura, 1978). Thus the individual is affected not only by external processes of reinforcement provided by the environment, but behavior is also determined by expectations, anticipated reinforcement, thoughts, plans, and goals—that is, by the internal processes of the "self." The active, cognitive nature of the individual *during* learning is critical: rather than just responding to direct reinforcement after the fact by altering behavior in the future, the person can think about and anticipate the effects of the environment. The individual can anticipate the possible consequences of his or her own actions and thereby choose an action based on the anticipated response of the environment and others in it. While classical, behaviorist learning theory assumes that a person's behavior changes over time in reaction to the direct effects of reinforcement (and punishment) on the stimulus/response link, Bandura's theory claims that the effects of prior reinforcement are internalized and that behavior actually changes because of changes in the person's knowledge and expectations. Knowing that a particular behavior (by the self or another) in a particular situation was reinforced in the past allows the individual to *anticipate* that she will be reinforced for that behavior in the same (or similar) situations in the future. This approach thus draws on the strengths of both the learning and cognitive approaches to personality.

Observational Learning

One of Bandura's (1973) key contributions was his explanation of how new behaviors can be acquired in the absence of reinforcement. Bandura noted that people learn so many complex responses that it is impossible for each learned response to result simply from the operation of reinforcement; so he expanded the scope of learning theory beyond what was included in the traditional behaviorist approach. He theorized mechanisms by which people can learn simply by watching others perform a behavior—learning without performing the behavior themselves and without being directly rewarded or punished for the behavior. This is called **observational learning** or **vicarious learning** (vicarious because it is gained second-hand by watching the experience of another). It is also referred to as *modeling,* meaning that a person forms him- or herself in the image of another.

In Bandura's view, people do not mindlessly copy the behavior of others, however, but rather they decide consciously whether or not to perform a behavior that was learned by observation. Thus, there is a clear distinction between the acquisition of a behavior (adding it to the individual's repertoire of behaviors) and the later overt performance of that behavior. The individual can learn, or acquire, a vast number of behaviors through observational learning, but whether the individual actually ever performs any particular behavior depends on a variety of factors, discussed below.

Learning of Aggressive Behavior

Bandura and his colleagues conducted a series of studies, now quite well known, on the observational learning of aggressive behavior by children. In these studies, children watched a film that showed an adult behaving aggressively toward an inflated plastic clown doll—punching, hitting, kicking, and hammering on the Bobo doll. Children who saw the aggressive behavior were more likely to behave aggressively when they were later allowed to play with the doll themselves. Further, when the children saw the adult rewarded for the aggression, the children were more likely to behave aggressively themselves than were children in the control condition, in which the adult was neither rewarded nor punished. Conversely, the children who saw the adult punished were less likely to behave aggressively than the control children. But seeing the aggressive behavior rewarded was not necessary to induce increased aggression. Children who saw unrewarded aggression were later more aggressive than children who saw the same adult model display neutral behavior (also unrewarded). The observational learning did not require observation of the reward; just seeing the aggressive behavior itself was enough to "teach" it to the children.

Outcome Expectancy

Many subsequent experiments have demonstrated that people learn a variety of novel responses merely by watching others perform them. This is a concern as people watch ever larger quantities of ever more violent movies and televi-

Many children watch hours of television each day, seeing repeated acts of violence. Does such visual exposure to violence produce more aggression in children, or do more aggressive children have a greater preference for violent shows?

sion shows. Bandura claimed that individuals can put together information from multiple, separate observations so that new patterns of behavior can be developed that are somewhat different from any that have actually been observed.

Note, however, that all television viewers do not become homicidal maniacs. In Bandura's view, the most significant influence on whether an observer will reproduce an observed behavior is the expected consequences of the behavior—its **outcome expectancy:** individuals are more likely to imitate behavior that they believe leads to positive outcomes. Outcome expectancy is based not only on observed consequences of reinforcement or punishment, but also on anticipated consequences (Bandura & Walters, 1963).

Whose Behavior Is Modeled?

In addition to outcome expectancy, other factors also influence the likelihood that another person's behavior will be modeled. These include characteristics of the model: age, gender, similarity to the observer, status, competence, and power. Characteristics of the behavior are also important in determining modeling; for instance, simple behavior is more likely to be modeled than complex behavior. Further, some categories of behaviors are more *salient*, and this salience may result in that behavior being observed and reproduced more often. In addition, a behavior that is admired or desired is more likely to be modeled.

The likelihood of modeling is also influenced by some attributes of the observer (the potential imitator): people with low self-esteem, people who are more dependent, and people who have had their imitative behavior reinforced more in the past are more likely to imitate. And, by necessity, observers' ability to imitate a model is limited by their cognitive and physical development; that is, successful modeling requires the ability to correctly perceive, encode, and reproduce the behavior. Of course, children's skills in these tasks improve with age, allowing the older child to model behavior that is beyond the modeling capability of the younger child.

Observational learning provides a mechanism for the acquisition of behavior that is so dangerous that one might not live to learn to perform it if it had to be acquired by shaping. For example, the circus tightrope walker would probably be dead (or at least maimed) long before learning to shape his behavior into an acceptable performance by successive approximation, without prior observational learning. (The same is true of driving, fencing, or crossing the street). Relatedly, some behavior, like operating a control tower or raising a baby, is so complex that learning would take an excessive amount of time were it to be acquired solely through direct reinforcement. In domains such as these, the rudiments can and must be acquired by observational learning.

Another insight of this approach is the acceptance that complex behavior can change very rapidly—perhaps as when someone undergoes an epiphany

Observational learning and modeling, according to Bandura, are likely to occur when the behavior and the model are admired.

or a conversion. As any parent can attest, children can, with very limited exposure, learn behaviors that adults consider undesirable.

Social-cognitive observational learning can also provide at least a partial explanation of the often-strong behavioral resemblance between parent and child: According to Bandura, observational learning allows the child not only to acquire specific behavioral sequences from the parent, but also to internalize broader patterns of behavior and emotional response—resulting in a child who seems to resemble the parent in personality. This explanation in terms of observational learning is quite different from other mechanisms that lead to parent–child similarity (such as the biological, cultural, and psychoanalytic explanations we discuss in other chapters).

Comparison with Reinforcement-Oriented Learning Theory

In contrast to Skinner's and other conditioning theories (see Chapter 6) that are completely dependent on the construct of reinforcement, Bandura's cognitive social learning theory accounts for the learning of novel behaviors in the absence of any observable reinforcement. It allows for the learning of behavior for which neither model nor observer is rewarded—a common occurrence that behaviorist theory cannot easily explain. Observational learning also explains how a person learns to inhibit socially unacceptable behaviors without first having to produce them inappropriately. In addition, observational learning offers reasons why an individual will disinhibit a normally inhibited or suppressed behavior, and subsequently produce an unacceptable behavior, as a result of exposure to a model that performs the behavior. This explains group violence and mob behavior (like looting)—behavior in which people engage when they see others performing the behavior, but that they would never think of performing alone.

Unlike behaviorist theorists, whose research relies primarily on animals, Bandura uses the model of cognitive theorists and performs rigorous empirical study of his constructs with human subjects. In fact, observational learning can explain the acquisition of personality characteristics and behaviors that are uniquely human and not well accounted for by traditional learning theories—moral behavior, delay of gratification, self-critical behavior, and achievement orientation.

Processes Underlying Bandura's Observational Learning

According to Bandura, the observation of models and the repetition of the models' behavior are not just matters of simple imitation; observational learning also involves active cognitive processes with four components: attention, retention, motor reproduction, and motivation. *Attention* is mainly influenced by the characteristics of the model and the situation. *Retention* is influenced by the cognitive ability of the observer and his or her capacity to encode the behavior (by the use of images or verbal representation). *Motor reproduction* is influenced by characteristics of the observer, such as the ability to turn the mental representation into physical action and the ability to mentally rehearse the behavior. *Motivation* most influences the actual performance of the behavior that has been observed.

That is, even when a person has observed and acquired a behavior, it will be performed when it leads to valued outcomes and not performed if it is expected to lead to negative outcomes. For example, television programs model many illegal activities that we are not likely to imitate because to do so would put us at risk of punishment by law enforcement. Thus the motivational component is highly influenced by both the expected (imagined) and the observed consequences of the behavior. Although social-cognitive learning theory has been criticized for oversimplifying the cognitive processes involved in learning, the basic structure proposed is consistent with widely accepted cognitive principles of attention and memory.

Acknowledgment of the concept of self-reinforcement—that we think about the potential consequences of our actions—leads to the construct of **self-regulation.** That is, Bandura recognizes that the individual's internal processes of goals, planning, and self-reinforcement result in the self-regulation of behavior. Self-punishment can range from feelings of self-disgust or shame to actually withholding a desired object from oneself (say, not watching a favorite sit-com). In addition, the concept of self-regulation suggests the operation of internal standards of behavior against which we measure our own success or failure. Bandura believes that these internal standards may be internalized originally through observational learning (especially from parents, teachers, and other important models) but eventually may reflect past behavior acting as a standard against which future behavior is judged.

Self-Efficacy

Bandura (1997) adds one more important cognitive element to the formula: the personality characteristic of **self-efficacy.** Self-efficacy is an expectancy—a belief (expectation) about how competently one will be able to enact a behavior in a particular situation. Positive self-efficacy is the belief that one will be able to successfully perform the behavior. Without a feeling of self-efficacy (which is a very situationally specific belief), the person is much less likely to even try to perform a behavior. According to Bandura, self-efficacy determines whether we try to act at all, how long we persist in the face of difficulty or failure, and how success or failure at a task affects our future behavior. The concept of self-efficacy differs from the concept of locus of control in that self-efficacy is a belief about our own ability to successfully perform a certain behavior, whereas locus of control is a belief about the likelihood that performing a certain behavior affects the ultimate outcome.

Our self-efficacy beliefs are the result of four types of information: (1) our experiences trying to perform the target behavior or similar behavior (our past successes and failures); (2) watching others perform that or similar behaviors (vicarious experience); (3) verbal persuasion (people talking to us, encouraging or discouraging performance); and (4) how we feel about the behavior (emotional reactions). Of these, the most important source of information is our own performance experiences. The next most important is vicarious experience, followed by verbal persuasion and then emotion. We use these four sources of information to determine whether we think we can competently perform a behavior. This is an important personality characteristic because it is an essential cognitive determinant of our actions.

Bandura has most recently pursued the construct of self-efficacy in the health domain. Self-efficacy has been found to be related to physiological aspects of health: people who do not feel self-efficacious experience stress along with its concomitant health and immune system implications. Self-efficacy is also related to the individual's potential production of healthy behaviors: people who do not believe that they can effectively perform a health-promoting behavior are much less likely to try (Bandura, 1992).

Although self-efficacy is an internal characteristic that influences behavior and reactions in relatively constant and predictable ways, self-efficacy is also situationally determined. To expand the example above, an individual has specific self-efficacy beliefs about his or her ability to perform specific health behaviors. Mary may believe that she can successfully exercise on a daily basis to reduce her weight, but she may be certain that she cannot resist her craving for ice cream; Bandura would say Mary has high self-efficacy in the exercise domain but low self-efficacy about her eating habits. On the other hand, Bandura also suggests that one might have "higher order," or less specific, self-efficacy beliefs in a broader, more general domain. For example, a student may have a general belief that he can achieve academic success, even though he may simultaneously have very low self-efficacy about his ability to perform well in a particular history class.

Humans as Computers

With the rapid spread of computers, it is not surprising that the newest cognitive approach to personality views people primarily as information processors. This perspective implies that the human personality is analogous to a sophisticated computer program that processes information from the environment in a manner similar to that of humans. Computers manipulate information as their central function—all they are is information processors. Perhaps that is all that people are as well?

Can the linking of on–off switches be made to represent consistencies in human behavior? Can human personality be captured fully in a machine-based information processing system? If we were successful in creating a human-like program using the capabilities of a computer, that would support the idea that humans can be understood (to a significant degree) as information-processing devices.

Is it reasonable to think we can build a computer that has a "personality"? Could we simulate a generic person, or even a specific person—a Martin Luther King, Jr., or an Adolph Hitler? What will this effort tell us about what it means to be a person?

There are many computer programs that use artificial intelligence (AI) to simulate human functions. By and large, these programs perform a variety of cognitive tasks but do not attempt to create a full "personality." There are many reasons why this is so. For example, consider the relative usefulness of an AI device that can serve as an individual tutor to a student in a training class on how to troubleshoot electronic equipment versus a device that can act as "class clown" in the same course.

To the extent that most AI programs exhibit any "personality" characteristics, these seem to be a consequence of features programmed in with the explicit purpose of aiding the program's function rather than making it seem more human. For example, a computerized training program can be viewed as being "patient" when it doesn't get "frustrated" at having to explain the same homework problem seven times, and as "conscientious" because it doesn't "goof off" or get sidetracked onto unrelated topics. (These are common failings of human tutors.) But, of course, the program is neither patient nor conscientious—the program is merely a set of instructions to carry out behaviors which people can associate with those human personality traits.

Human characteristics are commonly ascribed to computers. We tend to anthropomorphize complex machines: "The computer thinks I wanted to reformat the whole document," or "The program is trying to print the letter," or "The statistics package is mixing up my dependent and independent variables." We attribute goals, beliefs, and mental states to machines because of how *we* process information. As we have seen, when we observe ourselves or others in action, we make such attributions, and we tend to carry that process over to our understanding of other complex entities—often inappropriately. But that does not mean we truly think of them or treat them as fellow humans.

Shortly after World War II, when primitive computers were first under development, the British mathematician Alan Turing proposed a standard test by which to judge whether a computer could adequately simulate a human. The **Turing Test** sets up a situation in which a human judge interacts (via computer keyboard or teletype) with two hidden others. One of the hidden others is a person; the other is a computer program. The judge asks questions of each party and, on the basis of the answers typed back by each one, attempts to determine which is the person and which is the machine (Crockett, 1994) . If the judge cannot accurately distinguish between the person and the machine, the computer "passes" the Turing Test. So far, no computer has robustly passed the test; that is, no computer program can adequately simulate a human well enough to fool a human judge, even when the interaction is limited to written language.

A very interesting contrast to this phenomenon is that in many areas computers can greatly exceed human performance. This is the case not only in arithmetic calculations, at which machine superiority is clearly expected, but also in domains that require extensive knowledge and reasoning. In chess, for example, expert computer programs can beat chess grand masters—even the highest-ranked human chess player in the world. If a machine can be programmed to play world-class chess, why can't it appear convincingly human in conversation? One answer is that you don't need a human personality to play excellent chess, but you surely need one to seem human.

Evaluating the Perspectives

Advantages and Limits of the Cognitive Approach to Personality

- **Quick Analogy**

  Humans as scientists and information processors.

- **Advantages**

  Seeks to explain personality through study of the uniquely human processes of cognition.

  Captures active nature of human thought.

  Differences in cognitive skills are viewed as central to individuality.

  Studies perception, cognition, and attribution through empirical experimentation.

- **Limits**

  Often ignores the unconscious and emotional aspects of personality.

  Some theories (social learning theory) can tend to oversimplify complex thought processes.

  May underemphasize situational influences on behavior.

- **View of Free Will**

  Free will through active human thought processes.

- **Common Assessment Techniques**

  Decision tasks, biographical analysis, attributional analyses, study of cognitive development, observation.

- **Implications for Therapy**

  Uses understanding of perception, cognition, and attribution to change thought processes. For example, to treat marital problems, each partner might be shown the workloads and viewpoints of the other, might role-play the other's role, might receive training in listening carefully to his or her partner, and also might be shown examples of couples engaging in cooperative interactions. Cognitive-behavioral therapy promotes self-efficacy by giving the client successful experiences with the task, showing that similar others can successfully perform the task, using verbal encouragement, and conditioning control of excess physiological arousal. Self-help support groups (such as for coping with serious illness) often use this approach.

Summary and Conclusion

All the cognitive approaches to personality described in this chapter have in common the view that the essence of personality is to be found in the way people think—that is, in how we understand the events in our world, how we understand the nature and actions of other people, how we learn from our social environments, and how we control and understand our own behaviors.

In many cases, the cognitively oriented theories of personality were outgrowths of prior theories that were more directly cognitive. Kurt Lewin took the Gestalt approach, which had previously been applied chiefly to perception and problem solving, and developed it into his field theory of personality. Another outgrowth of Gestalt psychology was the development of the concept of field dependence as a personality variable. People who are more field dependent are more influenced by the surrounding context in their perception and problem solving; that is, the "field" in which the object or problem appears is viewed as an integral part of it. This sensitivity to context leads a field-dependent person to respond more holistically and intuitively, in contrast to the more analytical and abstract responses of the field-independent person. Field dependence is reliably measurable across many different instruments, tends to be consistent in an individual over time, and predicts many aspects of behavior, especially interpersonal behavior.

Cognitive and perceptual mechanisms of expecting, attending, and information processing are a central part of our understanding of human behavior, and they have been applied to the study of personality by many of the more cognitive approaches. Schemas are the cognitive structures that organize our knowledge and expectations about our environments. Schemas exist on many levels of complexity, and many can simultaneously be part of our understanding and expectations of a single event or entity. Complex schemas (also called scripts) guide our behavior in social situations. Our personality, according to this view, is seen as the series of scripts that direct and circumscribe our behavior.

Categorization processes are central to human cognition (and underlie our ability to evoke appropriate schemas). Our perceptual processes take in highly complex ensembles of information consisting of millions of bits of information, but what we experience is filtered through our categorization processes into a small number of identifiable and familiar objects and entities (words, individual people, household objects, and so on). It is impossible for people *not* to categorize—we experience the world through our interpretations. Our categorization processes pick up on a few features of some entity and automatically invoke a category. This is informationally efficient, allowing us to assign categories without in-depth analysis, but it leads us to miss details that may not match the usual ones for the category. To the extent that individuals have had different experiences, they may have developed somewhat different categories, and thus the same event or object may be interpreted quite differently by different people.

George Kelly developed the personal construct theory, whose fundamental postulate is that "a person's processes are psychologically channeled by the ways in which he anticipates events." Kelly's theorizing was especially focused on the domain of interpersonal relationships. Kelly proposed that we each have a unique system of constructs that we use to understand and predict behavior (both our own and that of others). Kelly's Role Construct Repertory Test results in a set of constructs that reflects the hierarchy of dimensions that the examinee believes are important in understanding and predicting behavior.

Social intelligence theory proposes that people vary in the abilities pertinent to understanding and influencing other people. Success in interpersonal interaction is easy for some people and difficult for others. The level of mastery of the particular cluster of knowledge and skills relevant to interpersonal situations is called social intelligence.

Explanatory style refers to a set of cognitive personality variables that captures a person's habitual means of interpreting events in his or her life. There are a number of different approaches to this central idea of explanatory style. One version has poles of optimism and pessimism as the extremes of explanatory style. People with an optimistic explanatory style generally interpret events in their lives with an optimistic perspective, whereas those with a pessimistic style tend to focus on the negative potential in a situation. People whose explanatory style is closer to the pessimistic pole may be more prone to depression. Conversely, having an optimistic explanatory style is associated with better outcomes. Another approach to explanatory style is the attributional model of learned helplessness. The term "learned helplessness" describes what happens when an individual learns that he or she cannot control any of the things that are important: repeated exposure to unavoidable punishment leads an organism to accept later punishment even when it *is* avoidable. Depression, stress, and apathy are commonly the consequences. There is evidence, though, that cognitive intervention—teaching people to change their thought processes—can affect subsequent behavior. Overcoming learned helplessness assumes that personality is seen as a kind of cognitive skill.

Rotter's social-cognitive theory claims that people choose their behaviors on the basis of the likelihood of the behavior in that specific situation (its behavior potential), an expected result (its outcome expectancy), and how much we value that outcome (its reinforcement value). These factors constitute the "psychological situation," which ultimately determines behavior. The best known feature of Rotter's theory is the concept of external versus internal control of reinforcement, or locus of control. Either individuals hold the generalized expectancy that their own actions lead to desired outcomes—an internal locus of control; or they believe that things outside the individual, such as chance or powerful others, determine whether desired outcomes occur—an external locus of control. Internal-LOC individuals are more likely to be achievement-oriented and high achievers, whereas external-LOC people tend to be less independent and also are more likely to be depressed and stressed.

Bandura's social-cognitive learning theory can be seen as an application and refinement of the classical learning theory that dominated psychology for much of the twentieth century. Bandura drew attention to observational learning (vicarious learning), which was poorly explained in classical behaviorism. He showed that learning by observation did not require any overt reinforcement. In Bandura's theory, the individual's internal processes of goals, planning, and self-reinforcement result in the self-regulation of behavior. Bandura adds one more important cognitive element to the formula: the personality characteristic of self-efficacy, a belief (expectation) about how competently one will be able to enact a behavior in a particular situation.

All of these cognitive approaches to personality share the view that human perception and human cognition are at the core of what it means to be a person. The way that people interpret their environments is seen as central to their humanness, and the ways in which people differ from one another in how they do this are seen as central to their individuality.

Key Theorists

Kurt Lewin
Jean Piaget
George Kelly

Julian Rotter
Albert Bandura

Key Concepts

Gestalt psychology
field theory
life space
contemporaneous causation
cognitive style
schemas and scripts
categorization
personal construct theory
Role Construct Repertory Test
social intelligence

multiple intelligences
explanatory style
learned helplessness
behavior potential
internal versus external locus of control
self-system
observational learning
self-regulation
self-efficacy
Turing Test

Suggested Readings

Bandura, A. (1977). *Social learning theory.* Englewood Cliffs, NJ: Prentice-Hall.

Bandura, A. (1997). *Self-efficacy: The exercise of control.* New York: W. H. Freeman.

Cantor, N., & Kihlstrom, J. F. (1987). *Personality and social intelligence.* Englewood Cliffs, NJ: Prentice-Hall.

Ellis, A., & Harper, R. A. (1975). *A new guide to rational living.* Hollywood, CA: Wilshire Books.

Hastorf, A. H., & Cantril, H. (1954). They saw a game: A case study. *Journal of Abnormal and Social Psychology, 49,* 129–134.

Mischel, W. (1973). Toward a cognitive social learning reconceptualization of personality. *Psychological Review, 80,* 252–283.

Rotter, J. B. (1966). Generalized expectancies for internal vs. external control of reinforcement. *Psychological Monographs, 80* (No. 609).

Seligman, M. E. P. (1991). *Learned optimism.* New York: A. A. Knopf.

Chapter 8

Trait and Skill Aspects of Personality

Starting in May 1978, an unknown person began sending letter bombs to scientists around the country. More than a dozen such bombs over seventeen years led to the critical injury of twenty-three innocent people, and three deaths. The FBI, analyzing construction of the explosive devices, determined that they were made by the same person, years before the media started receiving letters from the "Unabomber." More surprising is that the FBI used the pattern of the bombings to construct a psychological profile of the bomber. According to published reports, the FBI profiled the bomber as an obsessive-compulsive male in his late thirties

249

or early forties, educated, who likes to make lists, dresses neatly, is a quiet neighbor, and probably has poor relations with women. Remember that the FBI did not know this person—rather, they assembled a psychological profile that the person would likely fit.

Such criminal profiles are often uncannily accurate. In many cases, it seems as if details of an individual's personality can be inferred from certain distinctive patterns of behavior. (In the case of the Unabomber, the FBI was only partly correct.) What is interesting to us about such cases is that they rely quite heavily on a trait approach to personality. That is, they assume that much about an individual's consistent reaction patterns can be predicted from knowing his or her core personality traits. A **trait** approach to personality uses a basic, limited set of adjectives or adjective dimensions to describe and scale individuals.

*H*ow many traits are there? This question turns out to be the pivotal one in the trait approach to personality. The English language contains thousands of words that can be used to describe personal qualities (Allport & Odbert, 1936). *Aberrant, abeyant, abhorrent, able, abominable, . . . zany, zingy, zombied, zoned-out.* In fact, Gordon Allport counted about eighteen thousand adjectives. Does this mean that there are thousands of personality traits? If so, it would be very difficult to study personality. For a trait approach to succeed, it should use a relatively small number of traits to account well for a person's consistencies. The approach would be even easier if the same traits could be applied differentially to all people—that is, if everyone could be rated on every such trait. But this is not absolutely necessary; perhaps a subset of traits could be used for each person. Furthermore, we need not be limited to simple adjective descriptions of personal qualities; people also seem to differ in terms of their motivations and abilities.

Trait approaches to personality are certainly common in the popular culture. We think nothing of describing an acquaintance as extroverted or conscientious or selfish. We understand what it means to say that a bomber is quiet and reserved yet obsessive-compulsive and shy around women. Can such traits be reliably measured, and do they validly summarize and predict reactions? Can the FBI accurately anticipate a criminal's personality? It turns out that the successful trait psychologist must be a detective who is every bit as astute and observant as Sherlock Holmes. This chapter explains the trait and skill aspects of personality.

The History of Trait Approaches

Ancient Conceptions

The idea of using traits to describe people dates back thousands of years. The biblical book of Genesis, for example, tells us that Noah was a just man who walked with God. Descriptions of such righteous men were often illustrated with narratives of their righteous deeds, but the trait itself was assumed to be a stable characteristic. Many of the names given to newborns in our society derive from biblical characters, perhaps in the hope that they will grow up to share the distinguishing and honorable characteristics of their namesakes.

The first systematic approach to analyzing traits arose in ancient Greece. Hippocrates described human temperament in terms of the so-called bodily humors—sanguine (blood); melancholic (black bile); choleric (yellow bile); and phlegmatic (phlegm). The dominance of a humor—the prevalence of one of the four fluids—supposedly determined typical reaction patterns. The sanguine was hopeful and cheerful, the melancholic was sad and depressive, the choleric was angry and irascible, and the phlegmatic was slow and apathetic. Intriguingly, although the idea was biologically groundless, the humoral approach did an excellent job of describing basic reaction patterns. It was not until the seventeenth-century renaissance in biology that humoral notions began to be discarded.

In addition to temperaments, character descriptions also began in classic Greece. As we noted in Chapter 1, Theophrastus, a pupil of Aristotle, is one of the earliest known creators of character sketches. The sketches are brief descriptions of a type of person that can be recognized across time and place—such as the buffoon or the temptress or the miser or the boor (Allport, 1961). Theophrastus's famous "Penurious Man," described over two thousand years ago, divides up the dinner check at a restaurant according to what each person ate. He searches out bargains and is stingy with his guests. He would move all the furniture in the house to find a penny. And so on. Such a person is still easy to recognize. In the twentieth century, the vaudeville and television comedian Jack Benny made a very successful career out of portraying just such a "cheapskate." Trait approaches to personality attempt to capture such notions of personality reliably and validly, through systematic, scientific means.

In the nineteenth century, Charles Darwin liberated conceptions about the sources and causes of human variation. Demons and spirits were replaced by mutation and natural selection, and individual differences became a prime topic for scientific study. Consistencies could be sought in psychobiological characteristics of the person. As Freud began to probe the unconscious, human motivation and differences in individual development moved to center stage.

In addition, Francis Galton's (1907) extensive attempts to measure human abilities spurred intelligence testing and the assessment of other aptitudes. The final necessary ingredient was the development of modern statistical techniques, which provided the quantitative foundation for the study of traits to begin in earnest.

Jung's Extroversion and Introversion

Carl Jung, though a psychoanalyst, set in motion an influential stream of work on traits when he began to employ the terms **extroversion** and **introversion** in a theory of personality (Jung, 1921/1967). Jung's use of these terms was somewhat different than most current uses. For Jung, extroversion refers to an orientation toward things outside oneself, whereas introversion refers to a tendency to turn inward and explore one's feelings and experiences. Thus, for Jung, a person could have tendencies toward both introversion and extroversion, but one would be dominant. It was not until Hans Eysenck's work in the early 1950s that the terms took on their current meaning, discussed below. (Some theorists prefer the spelling "extraversion" and others use "extroversion"; to avoid confusion we will stick with the more common extroversion.)

The Myers-Briggs Type Indicator is a widely used instrument that attempts to measure introversion and extroversion as Jung defined them. In addition to global introversion–extroversion, there are subclassifications: The Sensation–Intuition scale indicates whether a person is more prone to realism or imagination. The Thinking–Feeling scale indicates whether a person is more logical and objective, or more personal and subjective. There is also a Judgment–Perception scale, which indicates one's orientation toward evaluating or perceiving things. Some people are more structured and judgmental while others are more flexible and perceptive.

This Myers-Briggs scheme has often been successfully used by vocational counselors (Bayne, 1995). Thus, for example, some people direct their attention inward (i.e., are introverted) and rely on feelings and intuition in evaluating new situations. Such people might make good clinical psychologists. How about an extrovert who is realistic, thinking, and judging? Such a person might make a good military officer. What is interesting about this pioneering approach is that it systematically classifies individuals according to a psychologically rich yet understandable set of categories.

In general, subsequent research has validated the importance of the introversion–extroversion division, but the usefulness of further dividing people into subtypes along the lines of Jung's theory has not been scientifically demonstrated as a general approach to personality. Empirically speaking, Jung's divisions are not the best ones. Rather, schemes such as the Big Five dimensions of personality (see below) are clearer and more helpful (McCrae & Costa, 1989;

Myers, 1962; Carlson, 1980; Myers & McCaulley, 1985). Jung set the stage by drawing attention to the observation that some people are oriented to look inward, others outward, and that this dichotomy is a stable individual difference. Subsequent empirical research refined and developed these ideas.

The Use of Statistics: R. B. Cattell

As the psychoanalytically based theorists like Jung were proposing theories of the basic tendencies motivating personality, more quantitatively oriented psychologists such as C. Spearman, J. P. Guilford, and L. L. Thurstone began developing and using statistical approaches to try to simplify and objectify the structure of personality. Some of the major steps along this path were taken by R. B. Cattell, starting in the 1940s.

Remember that Allport had found thousands of personality adjectives in the English language, but he concluded that his list must be reduced by eliminating terms that were clearly synonymous. Cattell went much further with this lexical (language-based) approach. The traits listed by Allport were further grouped, rated, and then factor analyzed by Cattell. That is, Cattell, like Allport, assumed that language has evolved to capture the important aspects of personality. So, he started with a list, derived from Allport's, that seemed to contain all the nonsynonymous adjectives that refer to personality. People were then rated on these characteristics, and the ratings were combined through statistical techniques, primarily factor analysis. Cattell repeated this basic process in many ways and on various data sets throughout the years.

Factor analysis is a statistical technique. Like other statistics, it helps us rework or reduce information we already have in order to make it more understandable. For example, a list of numbers (scores) can be summarized in terms of two numbers—a mean (average) and a measure of variation (such as the standard deviation). These are statistical summaries. Similarly, the relation of two variables—that is, pairs of scores—can be summarized in terms of correlation coefficients (such as r). Factor analysis goes one step further—it is a way of summarizing correlation coefficients. That is, if we know the correlations (associations) among a number of variables, factor analysis can help us summarize these relations in terms of a small number of dimensions. By taking into account the overlap (that is, shared variance), factor analysis mathematically consolidates information. Variables that are correlated with each other but not with other variables form a dimension or factor. Factor analysis thus can help us reduce or even eliminate the redundant information in a list of personality descriptors.

Cattell was born in 1905. He did his graduate work with Charles Spearman, the English psychologist and statistician who is famous for his pioneering work on assessing intelligence, including the development of the idea of a general factor of intelligence termed *g*. Cattell, like most psychologists of his day, also received training and experience in clinical psychology. He moved from England to the United States in 1937, permanently, to work with E. L. Thorndike. Thorndike, like Spearman, was very interested in the measurement details of assessing intelligence so it is not surprising that Cattell's approach to personality is reminiscent of factor analytic approaches to intelligence. Cattell gathered lots of personality ratings and then analyzed them in various clever ways.

Q-data is the name that Cattell gave to data that are gathered from self-reports and questionnaires (Questionnaire data). But recognizing that people often do not have a good understanding of their own personalities, Cattell argued that two other kinds of information should also be collected. **T-data** are data collected by placing a person into some controlled test situation and noting or rating responses; these data are observational (Test data). **L-data** consist of information gathered about a person's life, such as from school records (Life data). Obviously, a valid personality trait should show up in the course of life; for instance, we would expect more club presidents to be extroverts than introverts. In other words, Cattell endeavored to see if the same trait could be captured in different ways. This approach to construct validation has been used frequently since then in assessing the validity of personality traits.

Cattell was well-versed in personality theory and carefully relied on theory to select the variables to consider in his analyses. He well knew that in factor analysis as in many other spheres of life, "garbage in" yields "garbage out." In other words, if we have poor information to start with, then even the most sophisticated attempt to summarize or analyze the data will yield useless results. He was theoretically sophisticated in generating the raw data, yet his approach to personality from that point on was unequivocally statistical.

Based on his factor analytic findings, Cattell (1966) proposed that there are sixteen basic personality traits. Cattell labeled the factors with letters of the alphabet to be sure that they were an objective result of the statistical method, not biased by preconceived notions. In simple terms of dichotomies, these sixteen are as follows:

> outgoing–reserved
>
> more–less intelligent
>
> stable–emotional
>
> assertive–humble
>
> happy-go-lucky–sober
>
> conscientious–expedient
>
> venturesome–shy

tender-minded–tough-minded

suspicious–trusting

imaginative–practical

shrewd–forthright

apprehensive–placid

experimenting–conservative

self-sufficient–group-tied

controlled–casual

tense–relaxed

These are typically assessed using the Sixteen Personality Factors Question-naire (16PF).

Like most other trait psychologists, Cattell thus argued that there are strata, or layers, of traits; certain tendencies are more fundamental and serve as the source for other traits. He also showed the necessity of testing trait schemes in applied settings—in clinical work, in business organizations, in schools, and so on—and then using the findings to understand the traits better. This process—going from theory to assessment to applied work, and then back to theory and assessment—has become the standard process for all modern trait approaches to personality.

In sum, Cattell and his colleagues propelled trait approaches to be ori-ented much more empirically and statistically. He emphasized the value of carefully collecting key information about a person from questionnaires, from testing situations, and from life paths, and then objectively combining that in-formation using sophisticated quantitative tools.

In the late 1930s, and continuing through the 1940s and 1950s, Cattell's quantitative approaches, as well as the then-popular behaviorist and psycho-analytic approaches, exerted a significant influence on Gordon Allport. Allport saw serious problems with all three! Yet it was Allport who had a tremendous influence (probably the greatest influence) on trait psychology.

Gordon Allport's Trait Psychology

Variability and Consistency

Anyone who has observed people knows that the same person may behave differently in different situations. The same person may also behave differently at different times, with different people, and at different ages. Thus a simplistic notion of stable traits is obviously inadequate—even the most cheerful and friendly person will at times be angry and aggressive.

This variability was well recognized by Gordon Allport, who argued that although behavior is variable, there is also a constant portion for each person. In other words, some invariant aspect of behavior accompanies the changing parts. It is this constant portion that is captured by the modern conception of traits.

The notion of traits assumes that personality is rooted very much within the person. Remember from Chapter 1 that Allport defined personality as the "dynamic organization within the individual of those psychophysical systems that determine his characteristic behavior and thought" (1961, p. 28). According to this view, each person has unique, key qualities. In recent years, some influential approaches to personality have expanded the focus on the individual to incorporate aspects of the situation as well. These so-called interactionist approaches simultaneously study the person-by-situation interactions. They are considered in detail in Chapter 10.

Gordon Allport was born in Indiana in 1897. He spent a long career at Harvard University and died in 1967. His father was a doctor, his mother a teacher, and his older brother Floyd also became a distinguished psychologist. An excellent and well-educated student throughout his life, Allport was renowned for his scholarly knowledge and abilities. He was one of those scholars who picked interesting topics to study and then brought to bear a wide assortment of relevant evidence and original thinking.

At the age of twenty-two, Allport visited Europe and wrote to Sigmund Freud asking for a meeting. Allport reports that Freud opened their meeting with an expectant stare. After all, Freud was a master clinician, and people generally came to him seeking advice. Not knowing what to say, Allport reported an incident he had seen on the tram: a clean little boy seemed to have a severe phobia about dirt or getting dirty. Allport himself was rather fastidious and well-starched. Freud looked at him and asked, "And was that little boy you?" (Allport, 1968).

Allport was shocked that Freud would seek to see a deeper meaning in such a simple remark. Recalling this meeting later, Allport reported that it taught him to look more at surface-level, manifest aspects of personality before probing deeply into the unconscious. Freud emphasized instinctual drives but Allport emphasized traits. Of course, a Freudian might speculate that Freud was right on the mark in his question to Allport and that is why Allport was so shocked and bothered. A psychoanalyst would see Allport's later explanation ("rationalization") as merely a defense mechanism. To the contrary, Allport saw himself as a man of great common sense and rationality. It is interesting to note how a down-to-earth, scholarly boy from the American Midwest would develop a scholarly, meticulous, and common-sense theory of personality.

How meticulous and rational was Allport? We have seen that he pored over the entire English language to gather a data base of adjectives for thinking about traits. Allport's fascination with words evidently began at a young age. He reports that when he was ten years old, one of his jealous schoolmates pointed at him and said, "Aw, that guy swallowed a dictionary" (Allport, 1968, p. 378). His personality remained stable—as a professor he reported reading *Psychological Abstracts* from cover to cover (Allport, 1968). Similarly, he examined dozens of definitions of personality before constructing his own. His definition is so carefully worded that it has been quoted in many, many books. The idea of personality as the dynamic organization within the individual of those psychophysical systems that determine his characteristic behavior and thought is the essential trait perspective. It sees personality as an organization within the individual.

Allport held a lifelong concern with studying prejudice, with the hope that it could be reduced. Like Kurt Lewin, Allport believed that theories would be helpful in practice, and that theories in turn should be informed (and enriched) by practice. Allport studied American prejudice against Negroes (as they were then called) and Jews at a time when it was not fashionable to do so. He was one of the first American intellectuals to recognize the truth about the Nazi genocide, and his book *The Nature of Prejudice* (1954) remains remarkably modern even though it was written nearly a half-century ago.

Allport was well aware of cultural influences on personality. In fact, he helped found Harvard's Department of Social Relations, which grouped the areas of personality and social psychology with sociology and anthropology. (This department was dissolved in 1972, as many psychologists shunned such a broad perspective on human behavior.) In all of these matters—doing applied work in sensitive areas, examining cultural variations, questioning approaches that were too deep or too shallow—Allport was well ahead of most of his contemporaries and indeed ahead of many modern personality researchers.

Allport integrated the ideas of hundreds of philosophers and scholars, from classical times onward, into his writings. One perspective that particularly bothered him, however, was the behaviorist work of B. F. Skinner. Allport could not stomach any attempts to reduce the complexity and nobility of each human being. Allport thus heartily encouraged the development of humanistic psychology (see Chapter 9), fearing humans would be degraded if their behavior were explained in terms of the conditioning of rats and pigeons.

Allport also thought that factor analysis could not possibly depict in full the life of an individual (Allport, 1961, p. 329). Thus he was no fan of Cattell. Because a factor is no more than a statistical composite, it could not possibly do justice to an individual. Taking bits of information from studying lots of people could not disclose what is revealed by intensive study of a single individual. Furthermore, Allport pointed out that factor analysis produces a cluster (a factor) but does not name the factor; naming the factor falls to the factor analyst, and there is often reason to doubt whether the name truly captures the essence of the factor. In this way, the factor analyst may be misled by his or her own statistics.

Yet Allport obviously could not deal with thousands of personality traits. How did he reduce and structure the mass of individual thoughts, feelings, and actions? He believed that regularities arise (1) because the individual views many situations and stimuli in the same way, and (2) because many of the individual's behaviors are similar in their meaning—that is, they are **functionally equivalent.** In his words, a trait is an internal structure that "renders many stimuli functionally equivalent" and can "guide equivalent forms of adaptive and expressive behavior" (1961, p. 347).

For example, a so-called superpatriot (Allport made up the name "McCarley") might view communists, college professors, peace organizations, Jews, the United Nations, antisegregationists, and so on as objects to be despised and scorned; they are seen as equivalent by this extremist. Such a person might in turn give hate-filled speeches or join a lynch mob; these are equivalent behaviors. These consistencies are what form the basis for Allport's conception of personality. He analyzed these consistencies in terms of common traits and personal dispositions.

Common Traits

Because people have a common biological heritage, and because people within a culture have a common cultural heritage, it makes sense to assume that people have in common many organizing structures (traits). Allport termed these **common traits.** Common traits are traits that people in a population share; they are basic dimensions.

For example, in American society, some people constantly push to get ahead of others and to dominate their environment. Other people develop a comfortable style of going along with the flow of things (including yielding to or ignoring the pushy people). Allport thought people could usefully be compared on such dimensions, but he did not believe that such an analysis provides a very deep understanding of personality.

What about the motivation driving a person to keep everything clean and well ordered (sort of like Allport himself)? Allport accepts the Freudian idea that such motivation could have its origins in the childhood socialization of instinctual tendencies. However, in adulthood these motives or strivings take on a life of their own. Allport said that this means that many motives are **functionally autonomous**—they have become independent of their origins in childhood. Thus it would not make sense to try to trace them back to early childhood (except perhaps in cases of serious psychopathology). The childhood experiences may be the root or origin of the adult tendencies, but they do not continue to influence these tendencies. It would be useful to understand that a desire for neatness and order dominates a person's approach to life, but it is not necessary to unearth where these tendencies originated.

Allport sometimes used the term **proprium** to refer to the core of personality. (Proprium simply means one's own or one's self.) By this he meant that there are layers within the human psyche, including an irreducible core that defines who we are. In this sense, Allport's view was close to Freud's. Both theorists felt that there are central forces underlying our everyday diverse behaviors. Presumably this core has a biological counterpart (as both Freud and Allport explicitly expected); but as noted in Chapter 5 on the biological aspects of personality, such biological structures have not been fully identified, at least not yet. In any case, Allport thought these core motivations were much more rational and positive than the Freudian approach described them.

Personal Dispositions

We learn to recognize thousands of different people by their faces. No two people look exactly alike (except for some cases of identical twins). So it should not be surprising that no two personalities are exactly alike. To fully understand individuals, we need to use methods that take into account each person's uniqueness. Such methods are termed **idiographic.** Useful idiographic methods include document analyses (such as of diaries), interviews, behavioral observations, and flexible self-reports such as Q-sorts. Using these methods, different people can be described differently, rather than in terms of the same few dimensions.

Allport conceived personal dispositions in terms of a person's goals, motives, or styles; he called it a "nuclear" quality. A Michael Jackson or a Madonna or a Bill Clinton has a style that is quite distinctive. Or, consider the complex personality of an artist like Picasso, whose unique personality is revealed through his expressive style. This is a complex personality that can be and has been studied in depth, but not in terms of common traits. Thus, for Allport, a **personal disposition** is a trait—a generalized neuropsychic structure—that is peculiar to the individual (Allport, 1961, p. 373).

Personal dispositions that exert an overwhelming influence on behavior are termed **cardinal dispositions** (or ruling passions of a life). Allport gives examples such as Albert Schweitzer's reverence for life, realized in his total devotion to missionary doctoring, or the Marquis de Sade's sexual cruelty, realized in his consuming sexual passions. For the bomber described at the beginning of this chapter, the cardinal disposition might be a compulsion toward control over a certain self-appearance or worldview, coupled with an immense frustration and insecurity that led to the painstakingly planned violence. Usually, however, personality is organized around several **central dispositions.** For example, central dispositions are qualities that a professor would mention in writing a letter of recommendation for a student.

The idea that each individual has some organization of personality that is unique is very troubling to some quantitatively oriented psychologists. If each person is unique, we cannot validly assess each person on the same dimensions, and, so the argument goes, we cannot uncover basic laws of personality.

Plus, what a headache the study of personality will be if we cannot administer the same personality tests to everyone, but must tailor them to the individual!

Allport's response to such criticisms is quite insightful. He does not dismiss nomothetic searches for common traits (seeking general laws for all persons) as futile. He says only that such efforts are incomplete. From a biological perspective, Allport has a good point: Modern biology recognizes the unique variations of each individual. The artistic vision of Picasso can probably not be placed in the same framework as the vision of most people. And from a psychological perspective, no two people share the same upbringing and experiences. Allport thus sees great value in the in-depth psychological study of the individual.

It is an empirical question as to whether Allport is correct about the need for an idiographic approach—the need to assume personal dispositions. Perhaps Allport is wrong; perhaps evidence will eventually demonstrate that everyone can be fully described in terms of a set of common traits. But don't underestimate the dangers of *assuming* that personal dispositions can be ignored. Researchers who rely only on common traits may assume that a single test can be used in all cultures or subcultures. This assumption has, in the past, repeatedly been proven wrong, as exemplars of the dominant culture (European white males) have been used as the standard by which to evaluate others. Interestingly, an early personality textbook by Ross Stagner (1937) that gave significant emphasis to the social and cultural aspects of personality has been mostly ignored until very recently. Allport did not make such ethnocentric mistakes.

An approach to personality that is too ready to discard idiographic approaches may also be an approach that misses important unique information about women, about the elderly, and about people from different religions, cultures, and ethnic groups. Finally, a strictly nomothetic approach may be too imprecise, just as it makes little sense to try to describe Einstein's intelligence in terms of a general intelligence factor *g* that can be measured in all people. With these caveats from Allport in mind, we now turn our attention to the most successful modern efforts to establish a useful nomothetic scheme—the factor analytic search for common traits.

A Contemporary Trait Approach: The Big Five

One of the most remarkable but controversial developments in the trait approach to personality has been the emergence of a high degree of agreement about an adequate dimension scheme—one based on five dimensions. Starting in the 1960s but accelerating in the 1980s and 1990s, a vast body of research has converged on the idea that most common trait approaches to personality can be captured by five dimensions. Listed below, they have come to be called the **Big Five:**

Extroversion (also called Surgency): Extroverted people tend to be energetic, enthusiastic, dominant, sociable, and talkative. Introverted people tend to be shy, retiring, submissive, and quiet.

Agreeableness: Agreeable people are friendly, cooperative, trusting, and warm. People low on this dimension are cold, quarrelsome, and unkind.

Conscientiousness (also called Lack of Impulsivity): Conscientious people are generally cautious, dependable, organized, and responsible. Impulsive people tend to be careless, disorderly, and undependable. Early research in personality called this dimension Will.

Neuroticism (also called Emotional Instability): Neurotic people tend to be nervous, high-strung, tense, and worrying. Emotionally stable people are calm and contented.

Openness (also called Culture): Open people generally appear imaginative, witty, original, and artistic. People low on this dimension are shallow, plain, or simple.

How Was the Big Five Model Developed?

This model has resulted from extensive analyses of the adjectives used to describe personality and from equally extensive factor analyses of various personality tests and scales (McCrae & Costa, 1985; Goldberg, 1990; John, 1990; Norman, 1963). Note that the Big Five approach to personality is mostly research-driven, rather than theory-based. It is an inductive approach to personality, which means that the theory emerges from the data.

Are the Big Five traits really there? That is, can these traits be confirmed in some way other than through analyses of language-based ratings? Dimensions that emerge from a factor analysis or other clustering techniques do not necessarily represent real entities. If we mathematically cluster a number of masculine and feminine characteristics (such as dominant, aggressive, tough, tender, nurturing, feminine), we find evidence for two dimensions—male-like and female-like. These are of course "real" categories. That is, we can find biological counterparts to the clusters—men and women. If we cluster personality characteristics, can analogous biological characteristics be found? Allport points out that at one time, the atom—the smallest component of an element—was merely a hypothetical construct. But the development of new theories and new measuring instruments then proved the atom's existence, its

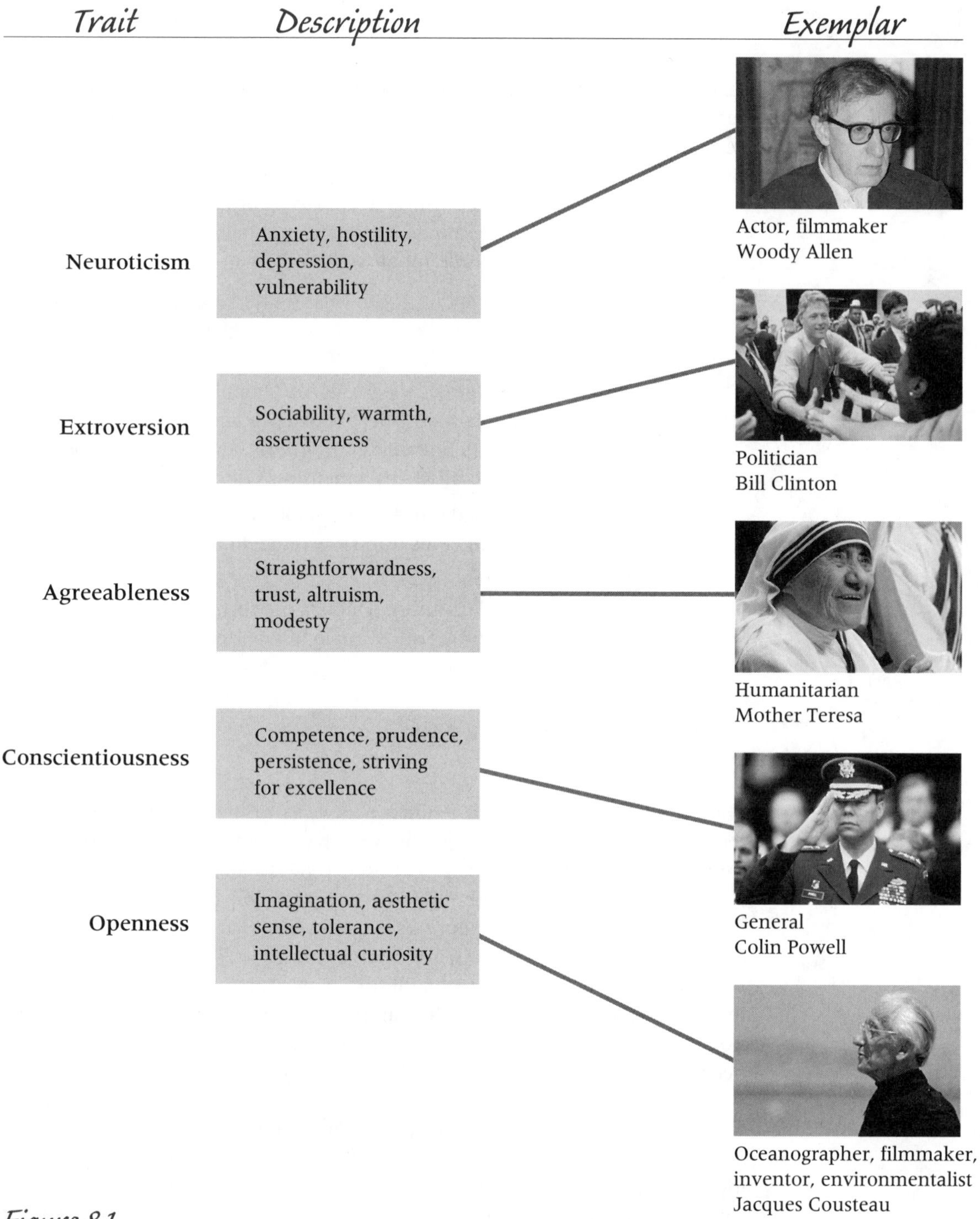

Trait	Description	Exemplar

Neuroticism — Anxiety, hostility, depression, vulnerability

Actor, filmmaker
Woody Allen

Extroversion — Sociability, warmth, assertiveness

Politician
Bill Clinton

Agreeableness — Straightforwardness, trust, altruism, modesty

Humanitarian
Mother Teresa

Conscientiousness — Competence, prudence, persistence, striving for excellence

General
Colin Powell

Openness — Imagination, aesthetic sense, tolerance, intellectual curiosity

Oceanographer, filmmaker, inventor, environmentalist
Jacques Cousteau

Figure 8.1

The Big Five Dimensions of Personality as Conceived by the NEO-PI and Similar Measures. Every person can be described in terms of all five of the Big Five dimensions; however, certain individuals are characterized by extremely high values on one of the dimensions—for example, the well-known public figures pictured.

"reality." There can be hypothetical constructs that represent something that is really there, even if we are not yet sure exactly what that "something" is. Many researchers believe that some biologically based origins of the Big Five will eventually be found.

On the other hand, the Big Five dimensions derive mostly from lexical approaches to traits. That is, people (either naive raters or professional psychologists) have described and tested and categorized others, and these ratings have been reduced to five dimensions. The problem with this is that the raters may be wrong. Raters can be wrong in two ways. First, they can see things that are not really there. It may be that people are prone to see other people in terms of five dimensions. This type of biasing tendency is sometimes called **implicit personality theory.** It means that there are consistencies (and biases) in how we see things, particularly other people's personalities. We may erroneously tend to see certain traits as going together. Just as stereotypes bias our perceptions of an out-group, implicit personality theories may bias our perceptions of others. If this is the case, then factor analyses may be capturing the implicit personality theories rather than the basic dimensions of personality.

Second, raters can be wrong by missing (not seeing) things that are really there. Even the best scientists viewed our world as three-dimensional until Einstein showed mathematically that time is a fourth dimension, continuous with the other three. Everyone thought we lived in a three-dimensional world, but everyone was wrong. Analogously, perhaps observers of personality are wrong, missing a key aspect of others' patterns of responding.

How can these issues be resolved? There is now good reason to believe that at least some basic trait dimensions really do exist; perhaps three, perhaps sixteen, but most probably five or so dimensions. Research using behavioral genetic and other biological approaches confirms that it makes sense to say there is biological evidence for a small number of dimensions, although somewhat greater or lesser numbers of basic dimensions are not precluded by these analyses (Loehlin, 1992). For example, regardless of whether extroversion will eventually be understood in terms of a responsivity of the nervous system or a genetically programmed orientation or a developed pattern of behavior or even as a compound product of several other elements, there seems little doubt that there is great value in seeing the construct as representing something that is probably real in a biological sense.

Cross-cultural research further confirms the utility of five or so dimensions, as does research in populations of young and old, educated and uneducated (McCrae & John, 1992). If the Big Five dimensions were the result of some sort of biasing stereotypes, then they would not replicate in other cultures. But, so far at least, the scheme seems to work quite well throughout the world.

However, cross-cultural research also yields some warnings about uncritical usage of the Big Five dimensions of personality. Although many cultures recognize that people vary along such dimensions, cultures differ markedly in how much they value each trait. A good example concerns pressures toward competition versus cooperation—striving independently for success versus helping others. Comparisons between Mexicans and Americans, and between Mexican Americans and European Americans, have shown some fascinating differences. Americans (and Euro-Americans) are expected to compete, to dominate, to win. Mexican (and Mexican American) culture, on the other hand, prizes trust, cooperation, and helping one's peers. These preferential differences can have important implications, such as in the classroom. Should we continue the traditional American practice of encouraging competition in the classroom, in which students compete for the highest grades? Or, should we strive to develop more cooperative learning environments, in which children must help one another to learn? Such issues remind us that individual differences in traits do not develop or have their effects outside a specific cultural context; culture is always relevant (Kagan & Madsen, 1972; Aronson, 1978). Cultural influences are further considered in Chapter 13.

Do the Big Five factors have useful applications? Extroverts, with their enjoyment of others, boldness, energy, ambition, and, yes, big mouths, tend to be politicians or other high visibility leaders. People scoring high on Conscientiousness seem to do well at work, especially in corporate settings. Their persistence, responsibility, and strong sense of purpose help them accomplish goals and secure their bosses' admiration (Barrick & Mount, 1991). People high on Agreeableness are likely to be altruistic, involved in helping others (Graziano & Eisenberg, 1997). Neurotics, who may be anxious, tense, and fretful, can move in one of two main directions—either channeling their worrying into a kind of compulsive success or else letting their anxiety lead them into recklessness. You probably know both kinds of people. Finally, people high on Openness tend to be creative and to value aesthetic and intellectual pursuits, and because they seek a wide range of experience, they may be artists or writers (McCrae & Costa, 1997). Of course, since people are thought to vary on all five dimensions, these illustrations only serve as useful examples.

More Than Five? Fewer Than Five?

In the view of Allport and others, certainly more than five trait dimensions are needed to characterize each individual—that is, when an idiographic approach is taken. The Big Five are meant to be used in nomothetic analyses—that is, when the same dimensions are applied across individuals. But are five dimensions enough for summarizing common traits? This question cannot yet be answered. The reason again is that there is no compelling and comprehensive theory that explains why five dimensions are sufficient to capture what we need to know when comparing and contrasting individuals.

What might such a theory look like? It might be derived from new knowledge of brain biology; for example, perhaps five distinct types of biological responding might be identified. Or, it might be derived from a functional analysis of evolutionary pressures on survival; for example, perhaps five sorts of skills—such as bonding with others, or finding resources—may be key to what it means to be a human being. Relatedly, however, it may have been most useful (in an evolutionary sense) for people to be able to ascertain these five dimensions in others. It can be argued that we need to know who will cooperate with us (i.e., be Agreeable), who is going to be a successful leader (i.e., be Extroverted), and who is going to be dependable (i.e., Conscientious) (Buss, 1995a). Therefore, people may have evolved an ability to detect and understand these individual differences in others.

Despite progress in understanding the Big Five, Cattell has continued to assert that sixteen general personality factors are essential. In fact, the most current advances in Cattell's factor approach to personality assume the necessity of sixteen traits and go on from there. Cattell seems impatient with psychologists who do not accept his scheme, frustrated that psychologists do not, he says, want to remember sixteen things at the same time (Cattell, 1990). Cattell himself also turned his attention to motives and interests. He believes that a psychometric approach should be used to analyze instinctive drives—sex, fear, assertion, self-protection—and attachments such as love of home, or spouse, or job. Importantly, Cattell also urges analysis of changes over time. For example, does getting married tend to change the conscientiousness factor of personality in systematic ways, making one more conscientious? How is this transformation best represented mathematically? By turning his attention beyond fixed traits located within the individual, and toward everyday motives, interests, and behaviors, Cattell and other personality researchers are now pointing to the complexity of human personality and to the necessity of considering the broader context of personality. Chapter 10 covers this in more detail.

Interestingly, even proponents of the Big Five approach to personality generally find it expedient to turn to additional trait descriptions to describe personality fully. (They do this even when talking about common traits.) Sometimes these are called subfactors or facets, but they all involve a further elaboration of the Big Five model. For example, anxiety and depression are closely related aspects of Neuroticism, but clinicians treating anxiety disorders and depressive disorders find the distinction to be a very significant one. In fact, different psychotropic drugs may be prescribed to treat the two conditions—for example, Valium for anxiety and Prozac for depression. The fact that these drugs act in different ways in the brain suggests that Neuroticism may prove to be too broad a factor. But if anxiety and depression turn out to be two variants of what can go wrong with the same underlying neurological system, then the superordinate category Neuroticism may prove correct after all.

Could there be fewer than five basic dimensions of personality? It might be that two or three of the Big Five trait dimensions are a core part of the organism, with the other two or three merely derivatives. That is, perhaps biological factors predispose a person to behave in one of three basic types of ways, but that these can be clearly subdivided. For example, the basic extroverted individual could then be further categorized in terms of activity level, sociability, and excitability. This is the position of Hans Eysenck.

Eysenck's Big Three

In discussing the biological aspects of personality in Chapter 5, we noted the nervous system–based theory of Hans Eysenck. According to this approach, people whose nervous systems need extra stimulation become extroverts; but those sensitive to external stimulation become introverts. Relying on this bio-

*Famous
Personalities*

Madonna: What's Her Trait?

Sensuous, sexy, eccentric, frank, proud, creative. Men find her erotic yet many women have admired her unique style as a strong female figure. "Who's that girl?" It's Madonna.

This entertainment artist receives media attention for just about everything she does. With her records, videos, movies, marriage, divorce, motherhood, and flames (both male and female), she has been on the cover of almost every magazine, from *Time* to *Penthouse*. As a feminist she emphasizes the importance of being attractive, sensual, energetic, ambitious, aggressive, and humorous. Although known for controversial videos which explicitly display messages about sex, race, and religion, her concerts are just as controversial: her choreography has included rubbing her female endowments and masturbating. Taking an active role in political issues such as the rights of homosexuals and support for AIDS research, this opinionated woman openly criticized Catholicism as disgusting and hypocritical. Is there one dimen-

sion or a few traits that could accurately capture her personality?

Interpreting Madonna's personality using the trait and skill approach, Jung might have said that she is an introvert because of the importance to her of dealing with feelings, intuitions, and experiences. On the other hand, she is also realistic and thinking, aggressively standing up for her own discontents and being unashamed to speak her mind in a variety of controversial arenas. So, Jung might have seen her as having extroverted tendencies as well.

Modern trait psychologists, using the Big Five personality dimensions, would describe Madonna as extroverted because of her frequent displays of energy and the active enthusiasm that fuels her dominant, social, and talkative characteristics. Indeed, it takes stamina to tour the world performing theatrical concerts, staging dance routines, releasing hit albums, starting a record label, and on and on. Her imagination, aesthetic sense, logical approach, Eysenck believed that fewer than five basic dimensions are the basis of personality. Rather, he sees all other traits as deriving from three biological systems (although as we have seen, the underlying biological systems are still not well delineated or understood). (See the Famous Personalities box.)

Whereas Cattell believes that personality theory should be the criterion for selecting the variables—that is, the data—to be used in factor analyses, Eysenck (1994; Eysenck & Eysenck, 1985) goes further and believes that other evidence should also guide the selection of the factors. That is, factor analyses alone should not guide our structuring of the basic dimensions. For example, there is evidence that people's tendencies on at least three characteristics—anxiety level, friendliness, and openness to new experiences—generally remain stable throughout adult life (Costa & McCrae, 1987a). If you are calm and outgoing at age twenty-five, you will probably not be crotchety and nervous and dogmatic at age sixty-five.

and curiosity would also qualify her as high on Openness, but Extroversion and Openness do not fully capture her personality. Although she strives for excellence, her vanity and her willingness to throw caution to the wind show her as low on Conscientiousness.

Perhaps we should look to Eysenck's work. He also would likely label Madonna as an extrovert, based on the insensitivity of her nervous system. Because Madonna surrounds herself with people and engages in activities that promote stimulation and draw attention, she reveals that her nervous system inherently is not very sensitive and is seeking the arousal her body needs.

Could we say her personal dispositions are centered about exploration and expression of sexuality? Featured in *Penthouse*, Madonna harbors no inhibitions or insecurities about who she is as a female. When dressed, she's been noted for wearing conical shaped brassieres, pink girdles, men's pin-striped suits, and boxers. Her videos also usually feature a masculine figure whom she lusts for, or who lusts for her. Because this nuclear quality influences much of her behavior, it can be seen as a cardinal disposition. But that simple summary does not seem to do her justice. It appears that a richer analysis of motives is in order.

Perhaps she fears being left alone and therefore situates herself so that she is always surrounded by people—motivated by strong needs for sex, for power, for affiliation. In *Truth or Dare*, a documentary of her Blond Ambition concert tour, we see Madonna forming personal relationships with her huge cast of performers, technicians, and staff. She acts as a big sister, a domineering mother, a preacher, an authoritative leader, and a lover. She comments, "Power is a great aphrodisiac." In every situation she is the center of attention and her word is treated as law. She is off the scale on Murray's notion of exhibition—a need to perform and be the center of attention. So, not surprisingly, Madonna's expressive style is the key to her personality. Her loud and frank speech, her sexual dance moves, and her unmasked facial expressions reveal central insights to her character.

Eysenck was born in Germany in 1916 and fled to England in 1934, where he was long an important voice in psychology. He died in 1997. The first dimension of personality according to Eysenck is extroversion. It includes Cattell's factors of outgoingness and assertiveness. The second is neuroticism; this dimension includes Cattell's factors of emotional instability and apprehensiveness. The third factor is psychoticism—a tendency toward psychopathology, involving impulsivity and cruelty. Psychoticism includes Cattell's factors of tough-mindedness and shrewdness. In terms of the Big Five, Eysenck's psychoticism involves low Agreeableness and low Conscientiousness; his extroversion and neuroticism dimensions are similar to those of the Big Five. Eysenck does not directly account for the Openness factor, and indeed, Openness is the least defined and most murky Big Five factor, both theoretically and statistically.

Eysenck's approach is one of the few to endeavor to take into account both the biological bases of personality (what Allport termed its "psychophysical" aspects) and the evidence arising from rigorous empirical and statistical analyses of traits. Interestingly, Eysenck's parents were actors and he himself became an extremely passionate and outspoken psychologist and intellectual, often at the center of intellectual controversy. Thus it is not surprising for Eysenck to ask such intriguing questions as whether extroversion runs in families.

Consensus in Personality Judgments

Is "love at first sight" merely a lustful attraction, or can we really tell something instantly? What happens when we first see a stranger? Can we make reliable and valid initial judgments about personality? Or are we usually misled by stereotypes? These questions bear directly on the validity of a trait approach to personality.

If observers can make accurate judgments about others' personalities—that is, judgments that are confirmed by other testing—then the trait approach has validity. Most basically, observers can usually tell whether a stranger is male or female; this gives us a lot of important information about how that person will behave on many dimensions. We can also sometimes judge age, ethnic group, and perhaps ill health; here again we are gathering important information. But what about judging aspects of personality like extroversion or neuroticism?

Suppose we have strangers rate a group of people on a number of trait dimensions. We then factor analyze the ratings, and the factor analysis shows five basic dimensions (the Big Five). How can we be sure that the consistency does not result from cognitive representations in the minds of the raters? Perhaps raters "see" certain traits as naturally occurring together. Perhaps factor analysis detects something about the minds of the raters rather than something about the personalities of those being rated.

Analogously, if the ratings that are used in factor analyses of traits are self-ratings, then a similar problem of inference arises. That is, let us say that a group of people rate themselves on a number of traits, and factor analysis of their self-ratings shows that they can be summarized in terms of five dimensions. The question that arises is whether we have uncovered people's ideas about how their traits can be grouped—that is, their self-images—rather than objective dimensions of their personalities.

Suppose, however, that we have the subjects' peers—friends of the people—rate them on a number of trait dimensions, and this factor analysis also shows five dimensions (the Big Five). Suppose further that the friends' ratings agree with the self ratings and are more accurate than the strangers' ratings. This would start to indicate valid judgment of personality rather than stereotyped judgments. Just these sorts of studies have been conducted (Funder & Colvin, 1988, 1991; Norman & Goldberg, 1966; Watson, 1989).

Zero Acquaintance

When we observe someone with whom we have never interacted—such as a new classmate in a new class—we are in a state that has been termed **zero acquaintance.** Interesting findings have emerged concerning the zero acquaintance state (Kenny et al., 1992). First, observers do indeed tend to agree in their judgments—there is consensus at zero acquaintance. In other words, consensus among observers is one additional piece of information about personality traits; this is evidence for the reliability of personality. But are observers depending on some stereotype, thus making invalid, inaccurate (though similar) judgments? And which traits are most reliably judged? The studies of personality judgments by strangers and by friends have shown that the friends' judgments agree more with each other and agree more with the target persons' self-ratings than do the judgments made by strangers.

If you had been a student of personality at Harvard in the 1950s, you probably would have rated this man as Conscientious. A cardinal disposition of Gordon Allport was his meticulous and wide-ranging approach to the study of personality.

Another clever solution to this problem is to use self-ratings, and peer ratings, and even add spouse ratings. (People's spouses presumably know a lot about their personalities.) When this is done, the same Big Five dimensions emerge (McCrae & Costa 1987). In total, these corroborations are good evidence that the Big Five scheme is valid and is not some kind of artifact. Furthermore, the Big Five factors can be recovered from (found in) Q-sort assessments of personality (see Chapter 2), as well as in assessments using other traditional self-report measures such as the Myers-Briggs scale and the MMPI (McCrae & Costa, 1989). Finally, these ratings can be used successfully to predict future behavior.

 *Self-Understanding*

Human Nature, Five Factors, and the Personality of Personality Psychologists

The historian of science Thomas Kuhn (1962) popularized the idea of paradigms and paradigm shifts in understanding how scientific theories develop and change. The basic idea is that scientific thinking grows and changes, not by a slow, incremental accumulation of knowledge, but by sudden shifts in the way we view the world. For example, the view of physics proposed by Newton was instantly outmoded by the relativity theories of Einstein. The view of health as determined by bodily humors proposed by the ancients, Aristotle and Galen, was replaced by the modern conceptions of anatomy and physiology discovered during the Renaissance. Interestingly, it is often not the case that existing theories are discarded by their proponents in light of new evidence. Rather, a new generation of scientists comes along and enthusiastically adopts the new perspective. It seems to take a fresh mind to reject the conventional wisdom and embrace the new paradigms that discoveries bring. Unfortunately, sometimes new paradigms are wrong, and it is foolish to adopt them.

Similar but smaller paradigm shifts seem to occur in psychology. Throughout this book, we emphasize that personality psychology can be used to examine the basis of human nature—what does it mean to be a person? Different psychologists are comfortable with different assumptions and perspectives. These disagreements occur even among personality psychologists who generally accept the value of a trait approach. Currently, major controversies continue to swirl around the validity and utility of a five-factor approach.

Paul Costa, Jr., R. R. McCrae, and Lewis Goldberg, for example, are vociferous proponents of the five-factor model. Jack Block doubts the wisdom of this approach. And Hans Eysenck insisted that a three-factor model is much superior (Block, 1995a, 1995b; Costa & McCrae, 1995a, 1995b; Eysenck, 1992; Goldberg & Saucier, 1995). How can we decide?

One of Block's (and Eysenck's) major objections to the five-factor approach is that it is grounded in the statistical technique of factor analysis. Simply

Interestingly, observers have particularly high agreement about and accuracy in judgments of Extroversion and of Conscientiousness (Funder & Sneed, 1993; Funder & Colvin, 1991; Watson, 1989). In other words, observers can judge whether people are sociable, talkative, neat, and organized; this finding makes sense since these dimensions are important to social relations. How do they do so? It seems as if certain cues are best suited for inferring certain aspects of personality. These cues are not always available in all situations. For example, it is easy to tell if a party guest is talkative, but it may be difficult to tell whether a party guest is organized. So, observers with insufficient information and exposure may make errors, but observers with relevant information across

put, factor analysis reduces or restates the data (usually correlations) that are fed into it. If the data points fed in are not adequate to capture fully the nature of personality, then no amount of analysis or reduction will come up with the "basics." Relatedly, the five-factor approach is usually heavily dependent on language, which may have its own artificial structures, although the five-factor model has been replicated in other languages and some claim it represents a "human universal" (McCrae & Costa, 1997b). Also relevant is the point that there is no strong a priori theoretical reason why there should be five (not three, four, sixteen, or whatever) basic factors. (It's not as if someone has discovered the corresponding five basic parts of the brain.)

The other main area of disagreement about the five-factor model involves how well it explains existing data. Does it capture and simplify what we already know about personality? Part of the answer is statistical—in the jargon, this comes out as "unexplained variance." Part of it is conceptual—does it help us in a subtle yet comprehensive manner to be more insightful? In short, can we describe personality well with five factors, or is there a lot of "stuff" left unexplained? Here, much of the argument has the flavor of a discussion about whether the glass is half empty or half full. Is the five-factor model an elegant edifice or an ugly obstruction?

For this paradigm shift to general acceptance of the five-factor approach to personality to occur, the bottom line is really fairly simple: The approach must be able to fully (sufficiently) account for personality in an economical and efficient (parsimonious) way, and it must lead to new research that provides a broader and deeper understanding of personality. Many researchers argue that the five-factor approach is doing just this, but doubters remain unconvinced. We will have to wait and see whether future generations of personality psychologists will feel most comfortable with this approach, believing that it accounts for the most data, fits best with other knowledge, and does so in the most parsimonious and elegant fashion. In the meantime, you might want to explore the advantages and limits of the Big Five in your own studies of the personalities of yourself and others.

situations are more successful. All in all, these studies are finding encouraging evidence for the idea of several stable dimensions of personality—although not necessarily precisely five factors. (See this chapter's Self-Understanding box on pages 270–271 for further discussion of this question.) But discovering the details of the trait picture is a matter for future study.

Limits

There is always some danger that we will not be careful in how we use the idea of traits. We might underestimate the role of other aspects of personality and the role of the social situation. We might overlook personal dispositions or the fact that basic dimensions do a better job in describing some persons than others. Note also that trait conceptions generally lie in direct contradiction to behaviorist and social learning approaches, which emphasize the environmental causes of patterns of behavior (Costa & McCrae, 1994). Still, when we follow the lead of Gordon Allport (1968) and apply the empirical approach to understanding the person as a whole (as a Gestalt), we can indeed succeed. If we view traits as a critical but complex aspect of personality, we do achieve a significantly better understanding of what it means to be a person.

Do professional profilers of criminals at the FBI do even better? One study compared professional profilers to other detectives, psychologists, and college students (Pinizzotto & Finkel, 1990). When presented with actual materials from a sex crime case, the professional profilers were indeed more accurate and comprehensive, but the experienced police detectives and the psychologists also did quite well. Only the college students did poorly. At the least, this and related studies suggest that experience in studying personality and motivation can lead to some documentable improvements and successes, but the optimal way to proceed is as yet unknown.

Types

Sometimes it seems possible to divide people into certain categories or classes. For example, it is easy to distinguish men from women, or preadolescents from sexually mature adults. In discussions of personality, these categories or classes are often termed **types.** The notion of types was first raised in Chapter 2, when we discussed assessment of people thought to be prone to heart disease—the idea of Type A versus Type B. When discussing psychoanalysis, we mentioned the Freudian idea of an anal character type, who is stingy. In our discussions of the biological aspects of personality, Sheldon's theory of body types (somatotypes) was considered (in Chapter 5).

The idea of types is that there are discrete classes of people. Boundaries between classes are usually not so clear-cut, however, when we are dealing with psychological characteristics. Some categories such as extroversion and introversion are broad, but no one is completely introverted or completely extroverted. Rather, it is a matter of degree. Theories of personality that include types are usually just the first step on the way to a more complete understanding of traits. Nevertheless, type theories may be useful in providing an ideal or model personality to which real people can be compared (Allport, 1961). Or, there may indeed be certain ways in which people are categorically different and do not fall along a continuum. Rather than make blanket assertions about type theories at this time, it is prudent simply to examine each such theory as it is proposed.

Motives

Closely related to, but distinct from, traits are motives. Motives are internal psychobiological forces that help induce particular behavior patterns. The concept of motives captures the idea that there are forces within the human organism pushing for expression—needs for food, for play, for pleasure, and so on. In some sense motives are more basic than traits because motives can be seen as underlying traits.

Motives involve a goal. Consider the case of explaining why Linda goes to lots of parties with her friends. A trait explanation might find she is very high on agreeableness and extroversion—she is friendly, cooperative, and warm. This might be a good summary, useful in predicting other aspects of Linda's life. But what if we explain Linda's party-going in terms of a fear of being left alone, or a high sex drive, or a desire for happiness, or a need to be around people? These latter explanations are motivational. Needs, drives, and emotions are all related to motives. The concept of a motive has the advantage of taking into account the emotional dynamism of a person. At the same time, it has the significant danger of being imprecise.

Henry Murray, a founder of the motive-based study of personality, used the term **need** to refer to a readiness to respond in a certain way under given conditions (Murray, 1962). Basic needs include a need for achievement, for affiliation, for dominance, and for exhibition. Murray's sophisticated approach is heavily dependent on the social situation and so we consider it in Chapter 10, in our focus on person-by-situation interactionist approaches to personality.

Some of the most modern approaches to personality use the concept of "motives" to understand personality but are more modest in their scope. For example, we might analyze a specific set of goals or "life tasks" such as doing well in school (Cantor et al., 1987). Many college students see this as a key motivation in their lives. But note that this life task is not a vast and complex trait like extroversion. Rather, it helps us understand specific behaviors and consistencies in college-related situations.

Similarly, Emmons (1986) uses the idea of what he calls "personal strivings," which are types of goals that people try to achieve in their daily behavior. Like all motives, these strivings energize as well as help channel our behaviors. For a college student, a personal striving might be to become emotionally and financially independent. This goal, however, might conflict with a striving to woo a mate and get married. People who experience ambivalence and conflict in their strivings may behave erratically or show signs of distress. Relatedly, people who have many avoidance strivings, such as not to be a bore, not to be passive, not to be fat, and so on, tend to be neurotic and unhappy; it may therefore be better to have many positive goals (Elliot, Sheldon, & Church, 1997). As noted in Chapter 4, these matters are often tied to issues of ego identity.

Need for Achievement: n Ach

In America, where people's identities are closely tied to their success, it is not surprising that there has been tremendous interest in the **need for achievement.** This is sometimes abbreviated as "n Ach."

One of our colleagues, an accomplished professor, has an almost unbelievably strong desire to achieve more and more, especially in comparison to other professors. He writes many books and articles, gives many invited talks, and works hard to make his accomplishments known to others. Interestingly, this need to achieve so dominates his life that he seems quite immature on other dimensions, despite his impressive credentials.

People with a high need for achievement are persistent and even driven to succeed on tasks that society sets out for them. They may obtain a string of college degrees or a shelf of awards. They tend to rise to the top in business, especially if quantity is more important than quality, or if shrewdness or persistence can lead to triumph. For example, they may be first-rate stockbrokers or salesmen (McClelland, 1961). However, they may be less successful once skills of diplomacy or cooperation become more important to the job.

In the motivational approach to traits, this achievement motivation is usefully contrasted with two other basic needs that have also attracted significant research attention: the need for affiliation and the need for power.

Need for Affiliation: n Aff

Early in the twentieth century, one of the founders of modern psychology, William McDougall (1908), wrote about a "gregarious" instinct, which causes people to want to come together in groups. McDougall then developed the notion of a "sentiment," which is an instinct that is socialized to be attached to an object. The instinct to seek out other people might become the motivation to have lots of friends. This idea of a motivation to affiliate set in motion a century of research. For example, Henry Murray proposed both a need for affiliation and a need to reject. But it has been the **need for affiliation** (n Aff)—the need to draw near to and win the affection of others—that has attracted the most attention.

People with a high need for affiliation want to come together and spend time with other people. It is an intriguing motive because it prompts people both to have friends and to please their friends (so as to maintain the friendship). Such people may be extroverted, agreeable, and conscientious: they are extroverted because they seek the stimulation of other people; they are agreeable because they want to act friendly; and they are conscientious because they are dependable. Such a motivational approach thus cuts across a five-factor trait approach (Winter, 1993). With a need, the goal determines the behavior. For example, in this case the goal is to have friends, and the goal can be realized through certain traits, such as agreeableness. On the other hand, a lone bomber might be the result of an unaffiliative person, unwilling or unable to reach out and have friends and a lover; conflict over a desire to express one's ideas but having no intimate listeners might lead to a violent striking out.

Need for Power: n Power

Murray also identified a need for dominance (n Dominance), which has come to be termed a **need for power**—n Power. People with a high power motivation naturally seek positions and offices that allow or invite them to assert control over others. We all know some people like this: they like to usurp the leadership of small groups, accumulate possessions, and control territory, although they may be quarrelsome and somewhat insecure. Of course many politicians are high on power motivation, although some are more motivated by achievement; that is, some want to gain credit and status and success (achievement) rather than money and influence (power) (Winter, 1992). An interesting study of the inaugural speeches of American presidents indicated that those scoring high on the need for power were more likely to make important decisions that led to their being viewed as great presidents (Winter, 1987).

By understanding his stupendous need for power (n Power), one can capture the essence of the personality of emperor Napoleon Bonaparte.

Measuring Motivation

Individual differences in motivations can be assessed by observing behavior across time and situations. This is, however, a difficult and time-consuming process. Is there an easier way to measure motivations? Standardized self-report tests like the Personality Research Form (Jackson & Messick, 1967) can sometimes do a good job at assessing needs by forced response to short standardized items. Personal goals can sometimes be assessed by asking people to write about those things that are the focus of their daily efforts.

However, if people are mostly unaware of the needs that are motivating their behaviors, then a more subtle approach may sometimes be necessary. Motivational psychologists like John Atkinson (1958), David McClelland (1984), and David Winter (1973) have therefore attempted to use more projective measures—such as Murray's Thematic Apperception Test, or TAT—to measure motivation. For example, a person might be presented with an ambiguous scene in which an attractive man is seen to be pushing ahead of an attractive woman while entering a hotel lobby doorway. If the person explains the scene as an attempt by the man to meet his client and complete a sale he has been pursuing, then this would be classified as indicating high achievement motivation. Because of the difficulty and ambiguity of projective testing, such motivational approaches to personality have received somewhat less attention in recent years, but they still hold high promise.

Need for Exhibition

Another key motive involves the need for emotional communication, which Henry Murray termed **need for exhibition.** People high on this need want to show themselves before others and amuse, entertain, excite, or even shock others. They are colorful, spellbinding, noticeable, dramatic, and showy. This is usually studied through a focus on their expressive style (Friedman, Prince, Riggio, & DiMatteo, 1980).

Mickey Mouse and Donald Duck are not only known but also liked around the world. What makes a cartoon character successful? Walt Disney should know. Disney said that showing individual personality in a cartoon is the key to success.

Expressive Style

How can a cartoon character have a personality? Of course it cannot have a real, biologically based personality. But a successful cartoonist, or a successful novelist for that matter, can use intuition to capture distinctive styles of behaving. What is especially interesting about a cartoon character is that much of this information is communicated through expressive style—elements such as vocal characteristics, facial expressions, and body gestures and movements. After just a few minutes of watching Donald Duck in action (and listening to his quackish speech), we know what kind of character he is. A detailed tracking of his behavior, or a personality test like the 16PF, is not necessary.

As Gordon Allport and other personality psychologists have long known, we can similarly gather important information about an individual's personality by observing expressive style. In 1933, Allport and Vernon published a book called *Studies in Expressive Movement.* This was one of the first major works on personality and expressive style. A consummate observer, Allport was not blind to the limits of simple approaches to expressive movement. He did not expect that an individual would always show the same expressive movements. Rather, he felt that there was some underlying consistency in a person's style, and that this would reveal itself in characteristic ways in certain situations. For example, an extrovert would not necessarily gesture expansively when she was feeling nervous. Even so, subsequent research suggests that a noteworthy degree of consistency characterizes an individual's gesturing, body incline, and voice cues, even across interactions with different people (Levesque & Kenny, 1993).

Emotional Expressiveness

How or why is expressive style related to personality? There is evidence that it is the emotional aspect of expressive behavior (which Allport usually called temperament) that is the key to understanding its ties to certain personality traits (Buck, 1984; Friedman, 1991; Friedman, DiMatteo, & Taranta, 1980; Friedman, Riggio, & Segall, 1980). That is, an individual likely has typical ways of expressing or inhibiting feelings like anger or joy. As we saw in Chapter 5 on biological aspects of personality, some of this seems to be innate: there are consistencies in inhibited and uninhibited expressive styles that have been first seen in babies and then documented in longitudinal research spanning many years (Kagan et al., 1988).

Perhaps the most significant individual dimension of style is overall expressiveness. People vary in the intensity, expansiveness, animation, and dynamism of their nonverbal (and verbal) behaviors (e.g., Friedman et al., 1980; Gallaher, 1992; Halberstadt, 1991; Manstead, 1991). This expressiveness can be measured and defined as the ease with which people's emotions can be read from their expressive behaviors, even when they are not trying deliberately to communicate their feelings to others. Such people are often uninhibited and charismatic (Friedman et al., 1980, 1988).

Expressive people are often perceived as more attractive than unexpressive people (DePaulo et al., 1992; Friedman et al., 1988; Larrance & Zuckerman, 1981; Riggio, 1986; Sabatelli & Rubin, 1986). That is, expressiveness makes one seem more attractive. In fact, studies of personal charisma that look at both fixed attractiveness (in photographs) and expressiveness suggest that expressiveness is at least as important as physical attractiveness—and perhaps even more so—in accounting for favorable first impressions (Friedman et al., 1988). Many charismatic and captivating actors would be judged plain and unappealing from photographs; conversely, a positive perception of a striking beauty can be obliterated by the first few minutes of a conversation. Expressiveness also seems to run in families (Halberstadt, 1991).

Extroversion is the trait that is mostly readily seen in expressive style. That is, extroversion is somehow "behaviorally visible." People who score as extroverted on personality tests look animated when they are observed by others, both friends and strangers (Albright, Kenny, & Malloy, 1988; Borkenau & Liebler, 1993; Cunningham, 1977; Funder & Sneed, 1993; Kenny et al., 1992; Riggio & Friedman, 1986; Scherer, 1978, 1982). In fact, not much information is needed by observers in order to make accurate judgments of extroversion (see cartoon). The judgments are not perfect, but they are reasonable, given the limited information that is available. Other traits of social importance such as affiliation, exhibition, dominance, nurturance, and playfulness also seem to be

Some personality traits are associated with characteristics that can be picked up by casual observation. Posture and gestures are cues as to whether a person is more extroverted (like the person on the left) or more introverted (like the person on the right).

closely tied to nonverbal expressive cues. Expressive people are more extroverted, dominant, impulsive, playful, and popular. In contrast, more individually oriented characteristics, such as motivations toward achievement, autonomy, order, understanding, and so forth, may be less evident nonverbally (Gifford, 1994).

Dominance, Leadership, Influence

Another of the aspects of personality that is linked to expressive style is dominance, although this characteristic often involves social variables as well as personality. Dominant people (like kings on thrones or judges on benches) sit higher, stand taller, talk louder. They are likely to invade the space of others, as when they put their feet up on their desk or your desk. Dominant people also have more expansive gestures, walk at the front of the line or parade, and sit in the first row or at the head table. During interactions, they can interrupt more, control time (as you wait in their waiting room), and can stare at you more if they want, but can also look less if they so choose (Ardrey, 1966; Exline, 1972; Exline, Ellyson, & Long, 1975; Goffman, 1967; Henley, 1977; Mehrabian, 1969; Sommer, 1969, 1971). Even among children, those who lower their brows and thrust their chins forward are more likely to win competitions and keep disputed toys than those whose faces appear less dominant (Camras, 1982; Zivin, 1982).

Expressive people grab attention (Sullins, 1989), and they may inspire or activate the expressive behavior of other people, whose own feelings then become clearer. In addition, nonverbally expressive people are more likely to distinguish or individuate themselves. That is, you know who they are and they are likely to differentiate themselves in ways that lead to a relatively strong impact on others (Whitney, Sagrestano, & Maslach, 1994).

The most successful communicators are able to read the cues of others and, in return, are spontaneously able to express the appropriate emotions; that is, they are nonverbally sensitive, nonverbally expressive, nonverbally self-controlled, and motivated to perform for their "audiences." Former president Ronald Reagan was an outstanding example of such a communicator. His personality was such that most people liked him as a person, even if they strongly opposed his politics. (Not surprisingly, Reagan had been successful as a professional movie actor.)

Expressiveness and Health

It is interesting that researchers of the so-called coronary-prone personality (Rosenman, 1978) also study and attend to many of the same nonverbal characteristics (such as emphatic movements and fluency of vocal cues) that are relevant to extroversion and expressiveness. A charismatic expressiveness, involving fluid, outward-focused gestures, is a sign of health, whereas nonverbal cues of an impatient hostility (for example, explosive, accelerating speech and clenched fists) are signs of an unhealthy personality. Unexpressiveness by itself is not necessarily an indicator of an unhealthy personality if the lack of expressiveness results from a calm, content, yet reserved orientation. Rather, the unexpressiveness is unhealthy when it is a sign of alienation, depression, or repressed anxiety (Friedman, 1991; Friedman & Booth-Kewley, 1987a, 1987b; Friedman, Hall, & Harris, 1985; Hall, Friedman, & Harris, 1986; Pennebaker, 1990).

There is some indication that outwardly stoic people are internally reactive (physiologically), whereas outwardly expressive people are more inwardly calm (e.g., Buck, 1979). Characteristic preferred modes of emotional responding are likely biologically determined by birth or soon thereafter, but expressive responses are heavily socialized during childhood, both in general and for specific social situations, with implications for health. As a simple example, take an inherently unexpressive child and place him in a family who expects the child to become an aggressive salesperson. Or take an inherently expressive child and place her in a setting where the expectations are that she will be a "good girl"—reserved and obedient. For both childen, the effects on adjustment, coping, and health are likely to be striking (see Chapter 12).

Further evidence that expressive style is tapping some basic element of personality, just as Allport suspected, is supplied by studies in which people try to control or to increase their expressiveness. Although expressive people generally are talented at enacting emotions, they are less successful than unexpressive people at deliberately appearing neutral—they still appear emotional (Friedman et al., 1980). Even when it is important to hold back their expressions so as not to embarrass others, expressive people may have trouble squelching their emotional expressions (Friedman & Miller-Herringer, 1991). Interestingly, expressive people who are deliberately trying to act unexpressive do not seem as unexpressive as unexpressive people who are acting naturally (DePaulo et al., 1992). Note that being emotionally passionate in public might lead to social problems in Japan or Britain, but may lead to social success in America, Italy, and Israel. This again indicates the importance of the interaction of personality traits and the situation, which we take up in Chapter 10.

Trait research that focuses on expressive style is often termed the study of "nonverbal social skill," or more simply, "social skill" (Riggio, 1986, 1992; Rosenthal, 1979). The study of nonverbal skills in personality is different from the usual focus on traits in at least three ways (Friedman, 1979). First, the concept of nonverbal skills shifts attention toward emotion. That is, aspects of personality like empathy, sympathy, and anger communication come to the fore.

Singer/actress Madonna. Whether theorizing in terms of traits, dimensions, motives, needs, types, personal strivings, or expressive style, personality psychologists seek a systematic description of what makes each person unique. Individuals who represent extreme points on the aspects being measured can illustrate a theory—or challenge it (see the Famous Personalities box on pages 266–267).

Second, there is a shift away from the usual focus on internal traits and motives and toward observable abilities. For example, instead of studying extroversion per se, the focus might be on facial, bodily, and vocal expressiveness. Third, there is a shift toward the ongoing process of social interaction. That is, there is more concern with personality in the context of communication with others.

Skills

Thomas Jefferson declared that all men are created equal, but not that they are created identical. He found it intolerable that a person could become king just because his father was king before him, or that immense wealth and privilege should pass unconditionally from generation to generation. Arguing for democracy, Jefferson sought a society in which the most talented and qualified men would rise to the most important jobs. (As a product of his historical context, though, he did not view women, however talented and qualified they might be, as candidates for public positions.) People differ markedly in ability and character. For example, Jefferson himself was an immensely talented architect, author, statesman, diplomat, and inventor. For Jefferson and for most of us, our talents are an integral part our personalities—of who we are.

Intelligence

One of the best-studied abilities is intelligence. Some aspects of intelligence are captured in the Big Five dimension called Openness. However, many people who are witty, sophisticated, and cultured (that is, high on Openness or Culture) would not necessarily score high on a traditional test of intelligence.

Traditional tests of intelligence measure aspects of reasoning ability such as vocabulary use, mathematical skills, and sometimes performance skills like memory, reaction time, spatial reasoning (puzzles and mazes), and so on. These abilities are very stable and tend to be interrelated. Although high intelligence of this sort is necessary for success in certain tasks and careers (say, rocket scientist or college professor), it is not very relevant to career success in most endeavors (such as acting, sales, politics, sports, manufacturing) or to many forms of interpersonal success (such as success in marriage). Traditional intelligence tests do not measure other talents or aspects of intelligence that involve relations with other people.

A different sort of theory argues that there are three traditional types of intelligence: linguistic (language) ability, logical-mathematical (quantitative) ability, and spatial ability. But there are also at least three important nontraditional types of intelligence. These are musical ability, bodily-kinesthetic intelligence (control of one's body as a gymnast or surgeon might have), and personal intelligence, which involves the emotional and nonverbal abilities discussed above (Gardner, 1983).

Social-Emotional Intelligence

Going even further, we could try to combine notions of nontraditional types of intelligence with notions of nonverbal social skills. This leads to the idea of what is sometimes termed "social intelligence" or "emotional intelligence." That is, people not only have characteristic ways of responding to others, and they not only have certain motivations in responding to others, but individuals also have specific social and emotional abilities in dealing with other people. For example, some people are empathic while others are clueless, and some people are charming while others are boorish (Rosenthal, 1979).

Psychologist Daniel Goleman (1995) claims that emotional intelligence has five components: being self-aware; controlling anger and anxieties; being persistent and optimistic in the face of setbacks; being empathic; and interacting smoothly with others. As we will see in the next chapter, these are the same skills that lie at the root of self-fulfilled, self-actualized individuals.

Given that much of the trait approach to personality uses statistical techniques originally developed for the study of intelligence, it is somewhat odd that a skill or ability approach has rarely been taken in the study of personality. Intelligence is the ability to *do* certain things but personality has generally been conceived as *being* rather than *doing* something. However, although the study of intelligence is legitimately part of the study of personality, the area is so complex as to deserve a textbook of its own. Therefore, the intelligence aspects of personality will not be considered in greater detail in this book. Nevertheless, we believe that it is important to retain a focus on styles, motives, and skills when we employ a trait approach to thinking about personality.

Evaluating the Perspectives

Advantages and Limits of the Trait and Skill Approach

- **Quick Analogy**

  Humans as clusters of temperaments, traits, and skills.

- **Advantages**

  Simplifies personality to a small number of basic dimensions.

  Looks for a deeper consistency underlying surface variations in behavior.

  Good individual assessment techniques.

  Allows for comparisons to be made between individuals.

  Uses both lab and field studies, theoretical and applied.

- **Limits**

  May reach too far in trying to capture the individual in a few ways.

  May label people on the basis of test scores.

  Sometimes underestimates variability across situations.

  May be biased by implicit personality theories.

  Difficult to determine the number of reliable personality dimensions.

  May underestimate the influence of unconscious motives and early experience.

- **View of Free Will**

  Allows for free will at the margins, after predispositions and motives exert their influence.

- **Common Assessment Techniques**

  Factor analysis, self-reports, testing of styles and skills, document analysis, behavioral observation, interviews.

- **Implications for Therapy**

  If much of personality is structured around a small number of key dispositions, motives, or traits, then we can change our goals, skills, and orientations but probably not our basic dispositional "natures." So, for example, if you are introverted, conscientious, and hard-working but lonely, it is not sensible to try to become a glad-handing class president or the life of the party; but you might set a series of limited goals aimed at making a few close friends who share your intensity and conscientiousness. You might also pay attention to improving your conversational skills.

Summary and Conclusion

The trait and skill approaches to personality search for a small number of core dimensions that can usefully summarize a person's consistent patterns of responding. The number of such dimensions is still in dispute. Cattell's factor approach to personality sees the necessity of sixteen traits. Eysenck believes that theory should also guide the selection of the factors, and he sees all traits as deriving from three biological systems. His three factors are extroversion, neuroticism, and psychoticism. But many if not most researchers now agree that five dimensions do a satisfactory job in most circumstances—the so-called Big Five of Extroversion, Agreeableness, Conscientiousness, Neuroticism, and Openness.

From roots in ancient Greek notions of temperaments and characters, the trait approach bloomed in the 1930s, fed by Jung's notions of inward and outward orientations, the statistical analyses of quantitative psychologists, and Gordon Allport's extensive theorizing about capturing the fullness of each individual's life. Modern approaches have adopted Allport's notion that traits are the invariant aspects of a person that accompany the changing parts. In other words, there are core tendencies that give a life its uniqueness and consistency, even though personalities undergo variations across time and situation.

Common traits are traits that people in a population share, and personal dispositions are traits (generalized neuropsychic structures) that are peculiar to the individual. Motives are internal psychobiological forces that induce behavior or push for expression; motives always involve a goal, such as food, friends, or power. For Allport (as opposed to Freud), motives are functionally autonomous; that is, have become independent of their origins in childhood. Recent research on expressive style suggests that there is a noteworthy degree of consistency in an individual's gesturing, body incline, and voice cues, even across interactions with different people, and that the emotional facet of expressive behavior is a key aspect of personality. For example, people vary systematically in the intensity, expansiveness, animation, and dynamism of their nonverbal and verbal styles. Such expressive style approaches may view personality in terms of social and intellectual skills.

Most trait psychologists assume that there are biological bases to these consistencies, and so they are quite interested in the proliferation of knowledge about the biological bases of personality, which is examined in Chapter 5. Most trait psychologists are also willing to accept that there are cognitive and psychodynamic influences on traits. Yet a trait approach, like any other single approach to personality, has proved inadequate to capture fully what it means to be a person. In particular, trait approaches need to be complemented by approaches that recognize the noble, spiritual aspects of human beings and that consider the situational demands on behavior. The humanistic and existential aspects are considered in Chapter 9, and the person–situation interactionist aspects are considered in Chapter 10.

Key Theorists

Carl Jung
R. B. Cattell
Gordon Allport

Hans Eysenck
Paul Costa Jr. and Robert McCrae
Henry Murray

Key Concepts

Myers-Briggs Type Indicator
factor analysis
functionally equivalent
common traits
functionally autonomous
proprium
cardinal dispositions
personal dispositions

central dispositions
Big Five approach
implicit personality theory
types
motives
needs
expressive style

Suggested Readings

Allport, G. W. (1961). *Pattern and growth in personality.* New York: Holt, Rinehart and Winston.

Allport, G. W. (1966). Traits revisited. *American Psychologist, 21,* 1–10.

Eysenck, H. J., & Rachman, S. (1965). *The causes and cures of neurosis.* San Diego, CA: Robert R. Knapp.

Guilford, J. P. (1959). *Personality.* New York: McGraw-Hill.

John, O. P. (1990). The "Big Five" factor taxonomy: Dimensions of personality in the natural language and in questionnaires. In L. A. Pervin (Ed.), *Handbook of personality: Theory and research.* New York: Guilford.

Jung, C. G. (1924). *Psychological types.* New York: Harcourt Brace.

Loevinger, J. (1987). *Paradigms of personality.* New York: W. H. Freeman. (See pages 93–120, The psychometric approach: Traits.)

McCrae, R. R., & Costa, P. T., Jr. (1990). *Personality in adulthood.* New York: Guilford Press.

Mischel, W. (1968). *Personality and assessment.* New York: Wiley.

Nyborg, H. (Ed.) (1997) *The scientific study of human nature: Tribute to Hans J. Eysenck at eighty.* New York: Elsevier Science.

Smith, C. P., Atkinson, J. W., McClelland, D. C., & Veroff, J. (Eds.) (1992). *Motivation and personality: handbook of thematic content analysis.* Cambridge, England: Cambridge University Press.

Chapter 9

Humanistic and Existential Aspects of Personality

Mohandas Gandhi, called the Mahatma or "Great Soul," led a life defined by commitment to principle. He had the personal strength to become one of the most influential leaders ever, pioneering nonviolent political resistance and winning political freedom for India. Anatoly (now Natan) Sharansky was falsely convicted of treason in Moscow; his only "crime" was being a civil rights activist trying to emigrate to Israel. Facing more and more pressure and long-term imprisonment, he became more and more resolute, eventually winning his freedom and freedom for others. Martin Luther King, Jr., faced down police dogs, fire hoses, and a long-entrenched racist society in the United States in winning dramatic civil rights reforms. How are we to understand such personalities, such modern-day heroes, who represent what is spiritual and noble about human beings?

What is the nature of the human spirit? Why are we here? Why are we born and why must we die? What is love? How do we measure human success? At certain times these questions become burning issues in the lives of many ordinary people. Most adolescents agonize over their true identity, their purpose, and their future. Many middle-aged adults face an existential midlife crisis. Many of the elderly contemplate the value and meaning of their lives. Issues of love, responsibility, anxiety, and self-fulfillment permeate these thoughts.

These questions and quandries are uniquely human. Dogs do not ponder the meaning of their existence. Yet even young children ask about death, and why people suffer, and what is right and wrong. Any full psychological understanding of what it means to be a person should provide a psychological perspective for addressing individual differences in approaching these age-old questions. These questions are the focus of the work of humanistic and existential approaches to personality.

Filmmaker Woody Allen captures the existential crises that can dominate a person's life; in his films, Allen usually plays characters obsessed with the existential issues of death, love, and the meaning of life. For example, consider his Academy Award–winning movie *Annie Hall*. When—in a crisis of love—the Woody Allen character breaks up with his girlfriend, Annie Hall, they must divide up all the belongings from their shared apartment. Annie reminds him that all the books on death and dying are his. He is obsessed with death. But he is also obsessed with the meaning of life. He bombards Annie with discussions of philosophy, culture, Nazi death camps, illness, aging, the meaning of love, and other central issues of human existence, all in a chronic search for life's meaning. He is appalled by people who continue on their merry way in life, wallowing in self-deception and oblivious to real human suffering. This is symbolized by his visit to "tinsel-town" Hollywood at Christmastime, portrayed as the height of superficiality, where even the snow is fake.

Not only in films but in real life, people who are struggling for a sense of value and direction in their lives are often overwhelmed with anxiety; they become neurotic and otherwise psychologically impaired. On the other hand, people who are totally self-absorbed and lead egocentric or hedonistic lives often wind up even more distressed than the neurotics. This chapter explains how existential and humanistic perspectives on personality point the way toward resolution of basic human conflicts about value and meaning, issues that are often ignored by other approaches to personality.

Existentialism

In the most simple terms, **existentialism** is an area of philosophy concerned with the meaning of human existence. Existentialists sometimes speak of **being-in-the-world.** This idea comes from Martin Heidegger (1962), an early twentieth-century German philosopher. It addresses a thorny philosophical problem that challenges psychological science. A traditional positivist view of the world focuses on the laws that govern the behavior of objects in the world. For example, rats who are reinforced with food pellets for turning left in a maze soon become left-turning rats. This is regular, lawful behavior. But would this law exist if there were no people to think about it? To answer this question, other, nonpositivist philosophers have focused on the subjective nature of existence, arguing that nothing would exist if people were not here to see it.

Alternatives to Positivism

According to this view, the world changes as people's ideas about it change. In other words, the idea of a world is a distinctly human construction. The problem with this subjective approach is that there are indeed objective laws that do an excellent job of describing the world. Positivist science works—it makes valid predictions. Both the positivist, objective viewpoint and the nonpositivist, subjective viewpoint are substantially but not completely correct. Each makes an important point. Existentialists, therefore, address these matters by referring to "beings-in-the world." Simply put, the self cannot exist without a world and the world cannot exist without a person (a being) to perceive it.

This existential philosophical orientation is especially important for personality psychology. A physical scientist such as an astronomer can usually safely ignore these issues, at least up to a point. When tracking comets or analyzing radio waves, the scientist's conception of human existence is irrelevant. (However, when issues of cosmology arise, such as the origin of the universe, even an astronomer must consider philosophy.) But for a personality psychologist, existential puzzles have direct and constant implications. People are active, conscious beings, always thinking. Is true love a product of the mind of the lover, or is it an ephemeral and unimportant product of some neurophysical state? Probably it is simply neither. Existential theories suggest that attempts to focus exclusively on self-concepts and cognitive structures, or exclusively on environmental contingencies, must ultimately fail. Instead, we also must examine people striving to make sense of their worlds. We must examine human beings in their worlds (Hoeller, 1990).

The existential examination is not tuned to uncovering logical inconsistencies or rationalizations. For example, take the cases of religion, belief in magic or the afterlife, and anxiety about death. The existential approach does not consider *why* we think this way, but *that* we think this way. Similarly, questions about choosing to be ethical and moral, and guilt about being immoral, are seen as essential aspects of being human, rather than as incidental by-products of the biological nature of human beings (Vandenberg, 1991). Ethical and spiritual matters are neither to be ignored nor explained away.

The Phenomenological View

Aspects of existential approaches are sometimes termed **phenomenological.** This means that people's perceptions or subjective realities are considered to be valid data for investigation. Two people can perceive the same situation very differently, and this difference—this phenomenological discrepancy—is often a focus of attention in existential approaches to personality. In a dispute between a husband and a wife, for example, a phenomenological approach would attend to the needs and perceptions of the participants rather than to their psychological history or the rewards and contingencies of the situation. However, because the situation influences the perceptions, it would by no means be ignored.

Because existentialism argues that it is an oversimplification to view people as controlled by fixed physical laws, the approach is nondeterministic. That is, people cannot be correctly viewed as cogs in some vast machine. This approach therefore encourages theories that consider issues of individual initiative, creativity, and self-fulfillment. These are especially the matters of concern for humanistic psychologists. Humanistic approaches to personality psychology focus on the active, positive aspects of human growth and achievement.

Humanism

Humanism is a philosophical movement that emphasizes the personal worth of the individual and the centrality of human values. A humanistic approach to personality likewise attends to matters of ethics and personal worth. Many approaches to personality, being deterministic, emphasize the degree to which our behavior is controlled by unconscious forces or prior experiences. For example, we have seen that the psychoanalyst sees humans as driven by the primitive instincts of the id, and we have seen that the behaviorist sees people as conditioned by the contingencies of the environment.

Giving a Role to the Human Spirit

Humanistic approaches, however, resting on the more complex philosophical foundation of existentialism, are more free to give credit to the human spirit. Abraham Maslow thus called humanistic psychology the "third force" (the first two forces being behaviorism and psychoanalysis).

Humanistic approaches emphasize the creative, spontaneous, and active nature of human beings. They usually are optimistic, as when they focus on the noble human capacity to overcome hardship and despair. Sometimes, however, these approaches turn pessimistic, as when they contemplate the futility of one person's actions. Nevertheless, these approaches are willing to take on the spiritual and philosophic aspects of human nature (Rychlak, 1997). (See Self-Understanding.)

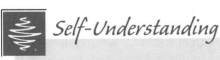

Self-Understanding

Are You Creative?

One modern researcher working in the humanistic tradition is Chicago psychologist Mihaly Csikszentmihalyi, who is known for his work on self-actualized people. Recently, Csikszentmihalyi (1996) outlined some of the characteristics of highly creative people. Of interest is his finding that creative people often have traits that are seemingly contradictory. These antithetical traits seem to produce a "dialectical tension" that may play a role in creativity. (*Dialectic* refers to the process by which two contradictory forces or tendencies lead to a resolution or synthesis, in this case creative production.) What exactly does this mean?

Creative individuals are usually very smart, but they may be naive at the same time. For example, Albert Einstein needed his wife's help to manage his financial affairs. Or, they may be wise but childish, as Wolfgang Amadeus Mozart was reported to be. Furthermore, they may value playfulness; yet creative accomplishment, such as in the arts, usually requires incredible discipline. They take risks when necessary for creative achievement.

Creative people usually have very high levels of energy. As Freud suggested, this is often sexual energy, and they may have huge sexual appetites. On the other hand, they can usually focus this energy and so may in fact avoid sexual involvements. Similarly, creative people can seem quite extroverted and be the life of the party, but they often consider themselves introverted and even shy. They can be simultaneously humble and deeply proud of their significant accomplishments.

According to Csikszentmihalyi, creative people tend to have both masculine and feminine characteristics. Creative men are often sensitive and nurturing, and creative women are often assertive and dominant. They can suffer because of their extreme sensitivity, but they can also achieve the peak experiences of self-actualization.

Note that this sort of analysis is uniquely humanistic and existential in flavor. It is not an explanation in terms of hormones and brain structures, conditioning and reinforcement schedules, or instincts and socialization. Rather, it often involves a phenomenological examination of matters that are uniquely human, and it is comfortable with notions of creativity, freedom, and self-fulfillment.

Relations with Other People Define Our Humanness

Building on existentialism, the humanistic approach stresses the "being" in human beings. That is, it emphasizes the special active and aware quality of human beings. Life develops as people create worlds for themselves. This view also often moves from humans "being" to humans "becoming"; that is, the healthy personality exhibits an active movement toward self-fulfillment. In addition, the humanistic approach adopts the existential idea that our existence comes especially from our relations with other human beings (Buber, 1937). An important focus is on direct, mutual relations, which philosopher Martin Buber called the **I-Thou dialogue.** In this dialogue, each human confirms the other person as being of unique value. This is distinguished from a utilitarian relationship (called the **I-It monologue**), in which a person uses others but does not value them for themselves. Although Buber proffered this argument in a religious context, many humanistic psychologists focus on spiritual matters without religious content, or even while being pointedly antireligion and antibureaucracy.

The Human Potential Movement

The so-called **human potential movement,** which began in the 1960s, is one example of the existential-humanistic approach to personality. Through small group meetings, self-disclosure, and introspection, people are encouraged to realize their inner potentials. In the 1960s and 1970s, the "human potential" milieu was more often than not a hippie commune in the woods, where encounter

Many forms of group interaction were developed as part of the human potential movement. Although the heyday of such groups is past, many of the ideas and approaches they espoused have become integrated into the mainstream.

groups, body massage, meditation, consciousness-raising, organic health foods, and communing with nature were heavily employed. Currently, although these practices still remain, the impact of these ideas can also be seen in more mainstream society. For example, protecting humans' relations with an unsullied, unpolluted natural ecosphere is now a major political force worldwide. In the area of business, promoting the individual worker's self-development and concern with the feelings and ideas of small groups of workers are now major issues in industrial psychology and corporate culture. And in psychotherapy, concern with unconscious conflicts has often been replaced with techniques to facilitate personal growth. The implications of humanistic approaches for healthy personality development are being felt throughout society.

Love as a Central Focus of Life: Erich Fromm

Most parents say that love is the most important thing that they can give to their children. Most adults say that love is the most fulfilling aspect of their lives. Yet many approaches to personality pay little heed to love, or else they dismiss it as an unimportant by-product of the true determinants of personality. On the contrary, existential and humanistic approaches often focus directly on love.

Loving as an Art

The well-known humanistic psychoanalyst Erich Fromm maintained that love is an art (Fromm, 1956). Love is not a state that people stumble into, nor is love some nebulous epiphenomenon that has no real meaning. Love requires knowledge, effort, and experience. The capacity to love must be developed with humility and discipline. According to Fromm, love is the answer to the unavoidable question—the problem of human existence. Love alone enables us to overcome our isolation from others but still maintain our individual integrity. But Fromm maintains that love cannot exist apart from a mature, productive personality.

Fromm is concerned that in modern society, we are alienated from ourselves, from others, and from nature. We are often unaware of our longing for transcendence and unity. We try to cover this inner alienation by "having fun." When we are immature, the world is seen as one big breast, and we are the sucklers. To overcome this existential alienation of modern society, Fromm suggests that we must master the discipline to be patient, to concentrate, and to live actively in the present, overcoming our narcissism. Paradoxically, as humans have gained more and more freedom through the ages, we have felt more and more anxious and alone. If we do not fight this loneliness and isolation by working in a loving way to help others, then we may choose the opposite extreme: we may escape from the burden of freedom by giving it up, such as to a dictator or other authoritarian force.

Fromm and his followers are willing to tackle some of the basic philosophical and religious issues in Western and Eastern thought; and to do so in terms of the psychological idea of a fully realized and fully developed personality. The mystical aspects of Judaism, Islam, and Christianity have long emphasized the importance of deep prayer and spirituality; and Eastern philosophies have long pointed out the psychological advantages of meditation, sensation, and playful thought. For example, Zen Buddhism emphasizes that life's mysteries can be successfully addressed through intuition and active consciousness of one's life. Fromm and his colleagues replace philosophical, meditative, and religious musings with systematic accounts based on understanding of human personality psychology.

Fromm would undoubtedly be distressed with a society that has replaced communal activities with solitary television viewing; with a society that has relinquished cultural traditions to standardized Big Mac hamburgers; and with a society that has traded charitable concerns about helping others for self-indulgent trips to visit Mickey Mouse. He would predict that individuals in such a society would be alienated, unloving, and unfulfilled, and further, that they would be susceptible to the appeals of a totalitarian government.

Dialectical Humanism: Transcending Conflict

Like many twentieth-century intellectuals, Fromm was influenced by the Marxist preoccupation with the exploitation of workers, as well as by Freud's theories of unconscious motivation. Born into an orthodox Jewish family in 1900, Fromm (like many influential European-born psychologists) was heavily shaped by the Talmud, the collection of ancient Jewish commentaries on and interpretations of the Hebrew Bible. Although Fromm was trained in psychoanalysis in Berlin, he soon discarded many of its tenets and began to emphasize the effects of social and societal factors on personality. Fromm's approach, sometimes called **dialectical humanism,** tries to reconcile both the biologically driven and the societally pressured sides of human beings with the belief that people can rise above, or **transcend,** these forces and become spontaneous, creative, and loving. Fromm died at the age of eighty, in 1980.

As Fromm well knew, the struggle between concepts of free will and determinism is a long-standing one. In the twelfth century, the influential religious philosopher Maimonides wrote, "Do not think that character is determined at birth. . . . Any person can become as righteous as Moses or as wicked as Jereboam. We ourselves decide whether to make ourselves learned or ignorant, compassionate or cruel, generous or miserly" (Mishnah Torah, Hilchot Teshuva, 5.1). People were not to blame their failings on others or on evil spirits. Although God was considered all-knowing, it would not make sense to ask people to live righteous lives if they had no free will. This dilemma was sharpened when Freud gave a scientific explanation for evil spirits—namely, the inner drives of the id. A Freudian view of personality is a pessimistic, deterministic one.

Consistent with the existential assumptions of beings-in-the-world and free will, Erich Fromm traces human behavior to neither inner drives nor societal pressures but rather to a conscious person with certain needs existing within a network of societal demands. Fromm noted various character types or personal orientations; he utilized such dimensions as activity, love, and relatedness. The most mature personality is one that transcends the ordinary demands of life and creates an active positive identity involving productive, respectful love of others. Such people achieve a productive orientation as they aim to enrich the world through their own creative endeavors and humanitarian ethics.

Is There Evidence Supporting Fromm's Approach?

Evidence for Fromm's ideas necessarily comes from analysis of cultures or subcultures rather than from a contextless analysis of an individual. How do the personalities of people in selfish, individualistic, opportunistic societies differ from the personalities of people in loving, respectful, spiritual communities? On a more local level, what are the personalities of people raised to love, help, and have faith in others, as opposed to people raised to disregard ethics and exploit others?

Although these complex matters have not yet been rigorously studied by personality psychologists, some trends do support Fromm's ideas: for example, the rate of major psychological depression in Western countries has risen steadily during the past fifty years (Cross-National Collaborative Group, 1992). In addition, as Fromm predicted, an alienated, noncommunal American society is increasingly afflicted with violence, divorce, and unrest. Observation of the alienation and destruction present in many modern cultures suggests that existential ideas about the importance of an active love deserve serious attention.

Responsibility: Carl Rogers

A key postulate of existential approaches is that each person is responsible for his or her own life and maturity. This idea is best exemplified in the work of the influential humanistic psychologist Carl Rogers. Rogers believed that people have an inherent tendency toward growth and maturation. But this maturation is not inevitable. Rather, people can gain self-understanding in a supportive psychosocial environment. People are potentially free to exercise control over their own selves; they are not merely driven and shaped. But, people must strive to take on this responsibility for themselves. Responsibility, like love, is a term often heard in humanistic analyses of personality but rarely heard elsewhere.

Rogers's Background

Carl Rogers, born in 1902, was raised in a strict religious atmosphere with close family ties. His upbringing was so sternly ruled by ethical demands that he reports feeling slightly wicked when he had his first bottle of soda pop. He spent his teenage years on his family's farm learning principles of scientific agriculture. Rogers attributed his success in part to the independence, scientific approach, and observational skills he developed during this period.

After graduating from the University of Wisconsin, Rogers attended the Union Theological Seminary in New York to prepare for the ministry but gradually moved into child and clinical psychology. It is interesting to note that many humanistic ideas (from Rogers, Fromm, and others) are derived from religious or quasi-religious sources. In contrast to those psychologists who learned about personality from the perspective of evolutionary biology or neurological impairment or animal behavior or information processing, humanistic psychologists often have had a life-long concern with religion and matters of the human spirit. Rogers died in San Diego in 1987, after surgery for a broken hip; to the end he was active at his Center for the Study of the Person.

Growth, Inner Control, and the Experiencing Person

A linchpin of Rogers's perspective is that people tend to develop in a positive direction; that is, unless thwarted, they fulfill their potential. This idea can be traced back to the eighteenth-century French political philosopher Jean Jacques Rousseau, who believed in the natural goodness of human beings. Rousseau argued that schools should encourage self-expression rather than disciplining "improper" behavior. A similar position is taken by humanistic psychologists. According to Rogers, a psychologically healthy person is one who has a broad self-concept that can understand and accept many feelings and experiences. Inner self-control is healthier than forced, external control.

In addition, Rogers takes a phenomenological approach: important issues must be defined by the individual. The focus of humanistic psychology is on what he called the **experiencing person**. Of special concern are discrepancies between what a person thinks of himself and the total range of things he experiences. Inabilities to accept aspects of oneself are stumbling blocks on the path to personal growth.

Rogerian Therapy

Rogers had a tremendous influence on the practice of psychotherapy. In Rogerian therapy, the therapist tends to be supportive and nondirective. The therapist is empathic and gives unconditional positive regard. During his years in child guidance and clinical psychology, Rogers came to understand that it is the client and not the therapist who best understands where the problems are and in what directions therapy should proceed. Consistent with the existential viewpoint, Rogers viewed a person as a process—a changing constellation of potentialities, not a fixed quantity of traits. In the supportive psychological atmosphere of client-oriented Rogerian therapy, a person learns to drop his or her masks and become more open and self-trusting.

For constructive personality change to occur during psychotherapy, Rogers includes the following two necessary conditions: First, the therapist demonstrates unconditional positive regard for the client. And second, the therapist experiences an empathic understanding of the client's internal frame of reference and communicates this experience to the client (Rogers, 1951). In other words, a genuine integrated therapist can sense the client's tensions and incongruent feelings, reflect them back to the client, and thereby assist the client to become more mature and self-integrated. These ideas have guided the training of countless therapists. Note, however, that Rogers is willing to be rigorous in his approach; for example, he suggests that the empathy of each therapist might be evaluated by independent judges. He welcomed systematic testing of his ideas. In fact, Rogers was among the first to conduct demanding evaluations of psychotherapy.

Becoming One's Self

From a Rogerian perspective, it is of the utmost importance that we come to terms with our own nature. Although we all have ideas of what we *should be like,* Rogers says that a person should "become one's self." A healthy personality can trust his or her own experience and accept the fact that other people are different. Existential anxiety and inner conflict often arise, according to Rogers, when we put up a facade and try to conform to the expectations of others. For example, toward the end of successful therapy, one of Rogers' clients writes,

From Carl Rogers's perspective, the role of the therapist is to be empathic and supportive, and to reflect back the client's own tensions and conflicts.

Famous Personalities

Existential Prince

Finding success on the silver screen with the movie *Purple Rain*, and in the music industry with numerous albums (fifteen in as many years), Prince had become a public star of the highest magnitude. This success, eventually backed by a $100 million contract (equivalent to Michael Jackson's mega-contract) was considered a great achievement for any entertainer. Why then, within months of signing that contract, would the thirty-four-year-old musician decide to retire from the business?

Announcing that he was diverting his attention from studio recording to pursue alternative media, Prince was obviously not retiring in the old-fashioned sense of "rest and relaxation," but instead was redirecting his creative energies toward new horizons. What tempting direction, though, could cause someone to walk away from an astonishingly successful career and a $100 million contract? A resultant Prince album was a self-titled collaboration with supporting artists, The New Power Generation. This album features tunes that one reviewer described as sounding like experiments, revealing Prince in a transitional stage.

In Prince's opening song on the album, he claims to be the one and only, revealing that he has a strong sense of personal worth and value. The claims that Prince makes about himself show that he has also come to realize the opposing forces that make up who he is, and that he has accepted these aspects. Existential theorists might say that Prince gave up the $100 million lifestyle because he experienced an existential midlife crisis. This means that his attitude changed from submitting to societal norms and values (pursuing the contract and prolonging his "success") to being guided by the unrestricted, conscious being he has come to realize within himself. Because character is not existentially determined at birth, Prince is seen as having free will and as having taken sole responsibility for his own growth. To signify the new man, he changed his name to "the Artist formerly known as Prince." Later, he changed his "name" yet again—to an unpronounceable symbol.

Continuing in this existential explanation of Prince's new direction in life, Prince is viewed as focusing on his inner, personal growth potential and achievement. This desire to self-actualize is considered an inherent tendency of all humans, though not all humans will recognize that they are the determiners of the boundaries of their potential. Revealing Prince's search for self-actualization, his songs express the central theme that the artist has been torn between heaven and hell—a concern for spiritual fulfillment, which is a key component in existentialism.

As Prince searches to integrate various (and sometimes warring) psychic forces within himself (such as righteousness and sinfulness) and become whole, he is existentially aware of his being and is taking active measures to guide it. Experimenting and exploring with different styles of music, creating a conglomerate of soul, jazz, rap, funk, rock, and pop, Prince's dance rhythms and groove ballads not only form new insights in the music-making world, but also allow Prince to test his capabilities and capacities.

Spiritually fulfilled, comfortable with himself and others, Prince seemed to grow in a self-realizing, self-actualizing direction. This is reflected in the personal characteristics often attributed to existential fulfillment: love, creativity, realism, and productivity, sometimes tinged with anxiety. With knowledge and acceptance of himself, Prince was freed from the goals of attaining and fulfilling a music contract. Once free, he attempted to take full charge of his own life.

"I've always felt I had to do things because they were expected of me or, more important, to make people like me. The hell with it! I think from now on I'm going to just be me" (Rogers, 1961, p. 170). (See Famous Personalities.)

Take the case of a feisty schoolyard bully or a pushy, disgruntled coworker. How do we react to such a person? Should we reciprocate aggression toward such a person? Should we place blame on hidden dysfunctional aspects of this annoying person's personality? Rogers tells us that such behavior would be inherently destructive to ourselves. Instead, a healthy person should be optimistic and understanding toward obnoxious colleagues, searching for their humanity. Sometimes this orientation will result in a dramatic shift in the bully's behavior; but even if it does not, the important thing (for Rogers) is that we have maintained our own humanity.

What about our own feelings? Should we try to deny our feelings of anger toward an obnoxious coworker? On the contrary, Rogers urged experiencing or getting in touch with our feelings, but then using our ethical standards to take responsibility and not to let our angry feelings lead to aggressive behaviors. A fully functioning person leads a spiritually enriching, exciting, and courageous life.

One assessment technique that is well-suited to a Rogerian perspective is the Q-sort (see Chapter 2). For example, a person might sort self-descriptions of a real self and an ideal self before psychotherapy and then again after psychotherapy; the therapist could evaluate whether the therapy has led to a greater integration of personality (Rogers & Dymond, 1954).

Implications of Humanism for World Peace

You may have noticed that this perspective has implications for international relations, and indeed Rogers and other humanistic psychologists are quite concerned not only with personal peace but with world peace. For example, late in life Rogers began to tackle religious strife in Northern Ireland. In simple terms, the basic issue is whether acquiring the toughest war machine is the best path to world peace or whether the use of military force ultimately backfires by sowing the seeds of further destructiveness, despair, and aggression. In real-world situations, the considerations and the policy details are of course much more complex. Yet arguments about international relations and policy often depend on assumptions about human personality.

Rogers, a humanistic psychologist, viewed responsibility in a positive, self-liberating, and self-enhancing light. But some of his existential counterparts were not so sanguine and optimistic. For example, the twentieth-century French writer Jean Paul Sartre (1956) also argued that the individual should find meaning for his or her own life—meaning would not be provided by some external world. But although Sartre like Rogers stressed responsibility, it was as a counterweight to existential anxiety and despair, not as a launchpad for maturity.

Anxiety and Dread

Computers do not become anxious, and information-processing approaches to understanding people mostly ignore matters like anxiety. Ironically, when placed in a high-tech environment, surrounded by computers, many people feel anxious. Think about how you feel on a day when every phone call you make is answered by a computer-generated electronic voice, the bank is closed and you have to use the automatic teller machine, the gasoline station has a credit-card controlled self-service pump, and your professor grades your multiple-choice exam using e-mail. Does anyone know you're alive? Many people under this electronic onslaught feel depersonalized, anxious, and even a sense of dread, as their spiritual lives—their spirits—are ignored. This sense of alienation from modern society was foreseen by the nineteenth-century Danish philosopher Søren Kirkegaard, who emphasized the importance of human faith, and the nineteenth-century German philosopher Friedrich Nietzsche, who showed the importance of passion and creativity.

Anxiety, Threat, and Powerlessness: Rollo May

Existential psychologists are willing to consider anxiety, dread, and even despair as core elements of human existence—of what it means to be a human being. Anxiety has been a particular focus of the existential psychologist Rollo May, who sees anxiety as triggered by a threat to one's core values of existence. A sense of powerlessness is often key. For example, a young woman's anxiety could be engendered by her being ignored by her parents, or alienated from her religion, or treated as an object by her peers. Or, perhaps, she is a victim of rape or abuse. To combat the alienation, she may turn to drug abuse or sexual promiscuity or to a violent cult. In Western societies, psycho-

The Scream, *by Edvard Munch. A Norwegian artist and a founder of modern expressionism, Munch revealed a tormented sensibility in his art, suggesting a modern alienation and despair.*

tropic drugs like Valium are among the most widely prescribed medications, with hundreds of millions of pills swallowed every year. And alcohol is even more widely used and abused, often to ward off anxiety.

Rollo May's sense of deep inner reflection intensified when, as a young tuberculosis sufferer, he was forced to spend several years in a sanitarium. In institutions, feelings of depersonalization and isolation can be especially intense. Later, as a therapist, May saw many patients searching for meaning in their lives, an observation that refined his interest in isolation and anxiety. It is also interesting to note that May, like the other founders of existential-humanistic approaches to personality, received both divinity training and psychoanalytic training (including study with Fromm).

Rollo May (1969, 1977) bridges the gap between existential and humanistic approaches to personality. Although he focuses on the anxiety that must accompany any attempt to live life to its fullest, May sees the human journey as a noble and dignifying one. In this sense, his view is consistent with much religious philosophy about the inherent worth of humankind: There must be struggle for there to be dignity.

Personal Choice: Victor Frankl

Similarly, existential-humanistic theorists like Victor Frankl (1962) emphasize the benefits of personal choice. If people choose to grow and develop, the challenge of the unknown produces anxiety; but this anxiety can lead to triumph and self-fulfillment. Frankl was imprisoned in a Nazi concentration camp. He survived psychologically by choosing to find meaning in the suffering, and by adopting the responsibility to control the little bit of his life that was left to him. He did not passively accept and comply with the horrors that surrounded him.

Although Frankl's parents and pregnant wife were killed in the camps, he went on to become one of the most influential existential psychologists, reaching out to those weighed down with despair or emptiness. He called his approach *logotherapy*—the search for the meaning of existence. True to his theory of personal mastery, Frankl died in Vienna in 1997 at the ripe old age of 92.

An existential struggle can lead to a triumph of the human spirit. Our modern-day heroes are those who can resist the pressures of an authoritarian society run wild. This shows that in many ways the existential and humanistic perspectives are opposite sides of the same coin.

One area in which such existential-humanistic approaches have had a tremendous effect is among people facing life-threatening illnesses. Small groups of similarly affected people now commonly come together for weekly intimate discussions. Such groups initially sprang up among people with cancer but today have spread to almost every serious medical problem (Kelly, 1979; Gottlieb, 1998). In these groups, people typically disclose their fears and anxieties about bearing pain and facing death, consistent with the existential em-

Existential-humanistic approaches have fostered the proliferation of support groups for people facing serious illness. There is some evidence that participation in such groups eases adaptation and fosters recovery.

phasis on actively facing such challenges. Participants also assist one another in both tangible (e.g., informational) and spiritual ways. Typically, the results of such experiences are the affirming of human feelings of trust and companionship, and a sense of inner triumph. These positive outcomes are right in line with existential-humanistic predictions. Such intimate self-disclosure and bonding may even be life-prolonging (Pennebaker, 1990). Yet rarely is the existential-humanistic source of this orientation explicitly acknowledged. This is an example of how our assumptions about personality subtly pervade many areas of our daily lives, whether we are aware of them or not.

Is There Free Will?

A number of years ago, we saw a debate between B. F. Skinner and Rollo May. The arguments focused around whether people have free will or whether their actions are predetermined, but the discussion ranged freely to other fundamental life questions as well. After about ninety minutes, it became clearer and clearer to many in the audience that both May and Skinner were correct. Each had highly developed ideas and deep insight into what it means to be a person. But because of their different perspectives and different interests, they never dealt with precisely the same matters. It was impossible to prove one or the other wrong through any simple psychological arguments or studies. That is why this textbook repeatedly argues that a full understanding of personality requires a willingness to study and understand eight basic but differing approaches.

Self-Actualization

Do people value wisdom, creativity, insight, and communion, or do they prefer food, drink, and sex? Humanistic psychologists cannot deny the importance of basic urges; after all, humans are also animals. But people are also

Figure 9.1

"How many psychologists does it take to change a light bulb? Just one, but the light bulb has to want to change!" This joke reflects the view of humanistic psychologists—that people have free will and can will themselves to grow and change for the better.

more than animals. Many theorists in this area therefore speak of three aspects of human nature—the biological, the social, and the self-fulfilling or personal (Frankl, 1960; Maddi, 1970). Being deprived of companionship or being deprived of meaning for one's life can be just as terrifying, and deadly, as being deprived of food.

Early Ideas about Self-Actualization in Jung's Work

Self-actualization is the innate process by which a person tends to grow spiritually and realize his or her potential. Few people become highly self-actualized but many go far along this path. Interestingly, the idea of self-actualization was first propounded by Carl Jung, who began his career working closely with Sigmund Freud. Unlike humanistic psychologists, Jung strongly believed in the unconscious forces of the id, but he counterbalanced this orientation with the belief in a human tendency to integrate the various psychic forces and thereby become a "whole" person. For Jung, unconscious, selfish drives were undeniable, but they could be explored, understood, and integrated with the more spiritual aspects of human beings. In this way, through self-exploration, a person could live in harmony with nature and with all of humanity, the community with which each person shares deep biological ties.

Is it surprising that Jung, trained in psychoanalysis, propounds many humanistic notions? Not if we recall that Jung was well read and extremely knowledgeable about Eastern religions and about psychological anthropology. These literatures exalt the universal importance of nature, spiritual matters, symbols, and balance or spiritual integration. Jung took these disparate conceptualizations and developed an optimistic, even mystical, approach. He was well aware of the dangers of alienation. Although Jung believed in unconscious motivation, he also believed in **teleology**—the idea that there is a grand design or purpose to one's life (Jung, 1933). Thus Jung's ideas about what it means to be a person cannot be neatly categorized. For Jung, quasi-religious, spiritual integrations are a key part of human nature, but Jung well-appreciated the instinctual inner demons that can torment us. As in Freud's approach, struggle is constant.

Peak Experiences: Abraham Maslow

Consider now the other extreme, a self-actualization approach that is so positive that it sees people's spirits as not only without demons but in fact almost godly. This is the approach of Abraham Maslow, who is famous for his work on **peak experiences.**

At certain times in our lives, everything seems to fall into place. This special moment might occur while listening to a moving piece of music, creating an ingenious solution to a nagging problem, experiencing a tremendously sensual or artistic moment, or the like. At such times, people seem to transcend the self and be at one with the world. They are completely self-fulfilled. Are not such positive, meaningful experiences a significant aspect of personality? Maslow thought so and investigated these so-called peak experiences. The idea originated in the late nineteenth-century work of William James, who wrote of "mystical experiences"—indescribable, fleeting, and truth-illuminating spiritual happenings. In more recent years, such phenomena have been studied by researchers like Mihaly Csikszentmihalyi (1990, 1996), who writes about the "flow" that comes with total involvement in an activity.

Abraham Maslow was born in New York in 1908 to Russian-Jewish immigrants. He died in California in 1970. A very bright child, Maslow endured a terrible relationship with a strict mother who often engaged in bizarre behaviors. He described himself in his early years as shy, bookish, and neurotic. Yet Maslow did not remain neurotic or become self-hating. Rather, he fully realized his potential, becoming a leading humanistic psychologist who inspired much positive societal change.

Interestingly, Maslow was initially trained in behaviorism. He did his graduate work with Harry Harlow, the well-known, behaviorist-oriented primatologist. But as a professor at Brooklyn College in the 1930s and 1940s, Maslow was exposed to the flood of brilliant intellectuals fleeing to New York from the Nazis, including Erich Fromm, Alfred Adler, and Karen Horney. His intimate knowledge of behaviorism facilitated Maslow's serious and repeated attacks on behaviorism and its ignoring of creativity, play, wonder, and love.

Peak experiences are common to people who are fully self-actualized. The insights these epiphanies provide help to maintain the mature personality. Such people are spiri-

Abraham Maslow put self-actualization at the top of the hierarchy of human needs. He focused on understanding the self-actualized person as a way to better understand what it means to be human.

tually fulfilled—comfortable with themselves and others, loving and creative, realistic and productive. Examples include Albert Einstein, Thomas Jefferson, Eleanor Roosevelt, and of course Maslow himself. (See Table 9.1 for examples of individuals Maslow pointed to as models of self-actualization.) Interestingly, although many theories of personality are derived from studies of hysterics or neurotics or other unhealthy people, Maslow examined ideal, healthy lives. The orientation is thus optimistic and spiritual, and, like Rogers, Maslow stresses the positive potentialities inherent in all human beings. Many personality theories were built on the study of patients who were psychologically disturbed; Maslow turned the tables to study those people with the greatest mental health.

Such self-actualized people have a realistic knowledge of themselves and accept themselves. (Unactualized people may occasionally have a peak experience but are more likely to be frightened than enlightened by it.) They are independent, spontaneous, and playful. They tend to have a philosophical sense

Table 9.1 **Examples of Maslow's Self-Actualized Historical Figures**

Self-Actualized Person	Self-Actualizing Accomplishment
Albert Einstein	Applied his creative genius to rethink fundamental assumptions of time and space.
Eleanor Roosevelt	Showed concern for all humankind and worked to help improve human lives.
William James	As a founder of psychology, he brought a creative new perspective.
Baruch Spinoza	Defied the religious orthodoxy of his time to propound ideas considered heretical.
Abraham Lincoln	He fought for a moral idea of freedom, at great personal cost.
Thomas Jefferson	He was an architect and philosopher of a new form of government built on democratic principles.
Pablo Casals	Became what many considered to be the greatest cellist of the twentieth century.
George Washington Carver	Showed great creativity and achievement in the face of hardship and discrimination.

of humor; you will not find them cracking ethnic jokes or engaging in crass sexual innuendos. They can establish deep, intimate relationships with other people, and they generally have a love of humankind. They are nonconformist but highly ethical. And, they have had peak experiences.

A sexual orgasm is not a peak experience, but it may lead to a peak experience if it opens the way to a deep spiritual love for another. In this regard, humanistic psychology is again quite close to many religious teachings, which see sexuality as a divine gift to be used for positive ends. During a peak experience, time may seem to stop and the immediate environment may recede.

Some have argued that the study of peak experiences and other spiritual aspects of personality goes well beyond the traditional existential-humanistic framework and so should be considered a separate perspective on personality. However, the aspects of this framework that truly go beyond, into a different realm—matters of cosmic awareness, for example—fall outside the subject matter of personality psychology.

Peak experiences are not necessarily other-worldly or sacred. Rather they may be found in friendship, in family, in work—in the pattern of ordinary life. In this and other aspects of his theorizing, Maslow reflects the influence of the Eastern philosophies and religions, in which he was well read. Spiritual growth and awareness are grounded in the full appreciation of the everyday world.

Mohandas Gandhi

The Reverend Martin Luther King, Jr.

Natan Sharansky

How are we to understand spirituality, nobility, and courage?

The Internal Push for Self-Actualization

For Maslow, as well as for Rogers and Jung, there is a natural tendency or pressure toward self-actualization. That is, the push for development comes from inside the growing organism rather than from outside, in the external environment. Such theories are sometimes termed **organismic** because they assume a natural unfolding or life course of each organism (Goldstein, 1963). For example, the influential neuropsychiatrist Kurt Goldstein emphasized the natural unity and coherence of the lives of most individuals.

Note, however, that the motivation to grow and self-actualize is different from the drives to satisfy hunger, thirst, or libido and thus relieve tension, in that it is not strictly necessary for survival. Rogers emphasized a mature harmony of the self-concept, whereas Maslow focused on growth toward a higher plane. Whether this organismic unfolding is genetically determined or is more complexly influenced is not clearly specified. Rather, an evolved tendency for growth is simply assumed. Here we see the influence of Charles Darwin on humanistic approaches that are quite distant from modern biological thinking, where we might take his impact for granted.

There is another way that Darwin's influence is felt in existential-humanistic psychology. In the nineteenth century, most scientists focused on each species as a whole collective. It took the genius of Darwin to note the uniqueness of each individual and the importance of each individual's characteristics (Mayr, 1991). (Individual variation forms the basis for natural selection.) Humanistic psychologists are similarly focused on the uniqueness of each individual, appreciating the natural—inherent—value of each variation.

Maslow's Hierarchy of Needs

Maslow divided organismic needs into two categories. First, he identified several categories of deficiency needs—"D-needs" (or "D-motives")—which are necessary for survival. The *physiological needs* are the basic biological necessities such as food, water, sex, and shelter. The so-called *safety needs* involve the necessity of a generally predictable world, one that makes some sense. *Belonging and love needs* involve psychologically intimate relations with other people. And *esteem needs* involve respect for oneself and for others. All of these D-needs motivate us through deficits—we need something to fill a drive or void.

Maslow argued that the correct social conditions are needed to encourage *self-actualization*. That is, he thought people cannot reach the "being" level ("B-level," with "B-values" or "B-motives") if they are preoccupied with satisfying their more basic needs. We cannot usually fulfill our complete human potential and search for truth and beauty if we lack food, safety, love, and esteem.

Maslow (1987) arranged all of these needs into a hierarchy, as shown in Figure 9.2 on page 308. As in psychoanalytic theory, the lower, biologically

Figure 9.2

Maslow's Hierarchy of Needs. In Maslow's view, the highest form of need is the need for self-actualization. In this hierarchical model, the individual's lower needs must be largely satisfied before higher needs can become important.

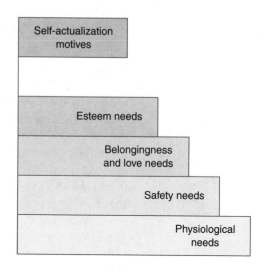

based drives are shared with most animals. But in a departure from psychoanalytic theory, the higher, uniquely human needs are seen as also biologically based but transcendent. Like Jung, Maslow said that the highest evolved state is to be at peace with oneself, a peculiarly and preciously human quality. Ironically, this assumption is contradicted by modern evolutionary thought. Although most modern biologists admit that humans are more intelligent on most dimensions than other animals, biologists do not believe that humans are "superior" in an evolutionary sense. In other words, humans are not thought to be at the top of the evolutionary tree, merely on one of its branches. (Humans are not the fastest animals or the strongest, not the best-hearing or the most monogamous, not the most peaceful, and on and on.)

Although research does suggest that people who generally reach a mature state of personality—people like Mahatma Gandhi—are more likely to act in self-actualized ways, there are also some cases in which people coming from very difficult circumstances and struggling with extraordinary challenges do become self-actualized. It thus seems that Maslow was incorrect in assuming a hierarchy of needs in a literal sense. For example, consider a poor, single mother concerned with issues of beauty and with an artistic bent—she loves to visit art museums and to sketch. Such a person may achieve many elements of self-actualization despite facing many unfilled survival needs. Note also, however, that it was Maslow and the humanistic psychologists who were most willing to emphasize the importance of issues like beauty in the first place.

Maslow and his associates turned the study of personality away from psychopathology and toward the study of the most well-adjusted, self-actualized people. This emphasis has also had a more general impact in our approach to physical as well as mental health. Traditional medicine has focused on curing disease. However, the impact of humanistic psychology has led to ever-greater attention being devoted to issues such as wellness—why some people stay especially healthy. These issues of personality and health are considered in detail in Chapter 12, in which we look at stress, adjustment, and health.

Measuring Self-Actualization

What evidence is there for Maslow's humanistic conceptualization of self-fulfillment? Are self-actualized people physically and mentally healthier? Maslow himself used any assessment techniques that he could—interviews, observations, self-report questionnaires, projective tests, biographical study, and others. This broad approach is necessitated in part by the subjects themselves. Self-actualized people tend to be independent, resist social pressures, are freedom-loving, and have a high need for privacy. Further, their personalities are complex. Thus they may be difficult to find, assess, and evaluate.

The problem with this loose assessment approach is also a problem with the whole theoretical approach—namely, that it provides insight and perspective but few scientifically verifiable conclusions. One scale that attempts to be more rigorous in its assessment of self-actualization is called the Personal Orientation Inventory, or POI (Shostrom, 1974). A self-report questionnaire, this inventory asks people to classify themselves on a number of dimensions such as whether they can develop intimate relations with other people, whether they are spontaneous and uninhibited, and so on for the various characteristics of self-actualization. It also assesses whether the person lives optimistically and realistically in the present, as opposed to worrying excessively about the past or the future.

Research using this inventory does seem able to identify self-actualizers, at least in the sense of finding people whose life orientations and behaviors are in line with what Maslow would expect. This is not surprising, however, since these matters are what the questionnaire asks about in the first place. More sophisticated, comprehensive research on such topics tends not to be done; personality theorists who adhere to Maslow's ideas generally feel uncomfortable translating lofty humanistic notions into cut-and-dried questionnaires. The research that has been done using the POI finds that the scale has various validity and reliability weaknesses but does capture at least some aspects of a healthy personality (Burwick & Knapp, 1991; Campbell et al., 1989; Weiss, 1991; Whitson & Olczak, 1991). In other words, self-actualization has not been tightly defined and assessed in an operational sense; it does seem to be a component of mental health, but we do not yet know exactly what it is or how to best measure it.

Yet Maslow's conceptions have had an impact on more narrow aspects of personality, such as assessments of mental health. Most clinicians will attempt, for example, to see if their clients have that spontaneous, playful, creative quality about them. This can be especially important in cases of adoption or child custody. Furthermore, the most rigorously developed modern tests of personality are sure to assess these aspects of personality, even if it is not called self-actualization.

In the best existentialist tradition, Maslow pointed out that science does not exist outside the humans who create it. Thus science is never value-free. This viewpoint is increasingly recognized throughout the fields of science, as scientists question whether they should build nuclear bombs or chemical weapons or genetically altered embryos. In personality psychology, the issue is especially important because personality psychologists claim to have scientific evidence about human nature—about what it means to be human. Maslow was rightly concerned that a pessimistic view of humans as a collection of base biological drives or as environmentally controlled robots would soon become a self-fulfilling prophecy, as the spiritual and noble aspects of people were increasingly discounted.

In the last years of his life, Maslow became more philosophical in his thinking and more realistic in his insights: he recognized the weaknesses inherent in each person and the conflicts inherent in society. For example, Maslow wrote in his journal about his self-actualized friends, "all at the top & yet all limited . . . the top are far from perfect" (1965, p. 328). Lamenting that so many intellectuals are self-centered and unable to work together—he called them prima donnas—Maslow devised a scheme by which each "king of the hill" would control his own empire. (Most universities in fact function just this way.) In other words, Maslow strived to believe the best about the potentialities of human beings, but, like Jung and many others, ultimately had to admit that the darker, weaker side of people could never be eliminated.

Further Evaluation of Existential-Humanistic Approaches

Existential and humanistic approaches to personality are in some ways reminiscent of psychoanalytic approaches: they derive from complex and dynamic inner motivations. This is in contrast to theories that look for structures within the individual or for structures in the environmental reinforcers. However, existential and humanistic theories allow for free will and for true creativity, heroism, and self-fulfillment. Existential approaches are necessarily idiographic approaches; they consider each individual experience unique.

Existential philosophers place responsibility for personality squarely on the shoulders of the individual. How will I deal with love, with ethics, with anxiety, with freedom, with death? Will I allow alienation to sink me into the deepest despair, or will I use my free will to triumph and self-actualize? Inherent in existential dilemmas are the possibilities for the triumph of the human spirit.

Humanistic approaches, based on existentialism but rejecting its pessimism, are the most optimistic approaches to personality, viewing human beings and spiritual matters in a positive light. The humanistic orientation of Abraham Maslow, with its emphasis on studying self-fulfilled, fully mature individuals, brought much-needed attention in personality psychology to these positive and spiritual aspects of human beings. Nevertheless, the inconsistencies and ambiguities in Maslow's writings make his contribution less of a true theory and more of an influential approach or orientation.

The humanistic approach to personality is conducive to the cross-cultural study of personality and the study of ethnic groups, a need we emphasize in this textbook. Many of the existential and humanistic psychologists were terribly shocked—both personally and intellectually—by the fascism of the 1930s and 1940s. For example, Fromm repeatedly warns of the dire consequences of trying to run from the existential anxiety produced by modern freedoms. Humanistic theorists are willing to explore alternative views—such as Eastern views or religious views—of what it means to be human.

One area in which humanistic approaches to personality have had a large practical and continuing impact on general society is in the area of personal retreats. Today we do not think it odd if a hard-working adult (or even a small group of coworkers) goes away for a retreat. This "get-away" differs markedly from a traditional vacation of sports or sightseeing. During a personal retreat, we might hide away in a scenic location, try to get in touch with our feelings, renew our love for our partner, work on our art or music or creativity, exercise, and perhaps meditate or pray. Such activities derive from the humanistic assumption that each individual has a unique inner potential that will unfold if properly nurtured.

Humanistic personality psychology differs from other approaches not only in its subject matter and its philosophy, but also in its ideology. Humanistic theories explicitly condemn reductionistic psychology that strives to "reduce" human beings to drives or neurons or conditioned reflexes. Although this orientation has implications for the conduct of science (such as strict protection of the rights of human subjects), it is also in part a set of personal preferences about the nature of humanity. Humanistic psychologists are explicitly concerned with human dignity and growth. Some people find this approach ennobling, but others find it irritating. (We might even consider one's orientation on such matters to be a personality variable.)

Rogers, Maslow, and other humanistic psychologists were particularly irked by B. F. Skinner's views of personality. It was not just that Skinner claimed to be studying human psychology by observing pigeons and laboratory rats. What was particularly irksome was that Skinner boldly spelled out the parameters of a utopian society (in his book *Walden Two*). Skinner, purporting to move beyond freedom and dignity, proposed setting up the contingencies of the environment so that humans would learn to behave responsibly. This was anathema to Rogers and Maslow, whose approaches are forged on just such notions of freedom, dignity, and individual responsibility.

Evaluating the Perspectives

Advantages and Limits of the Humanistic-Existential Approach

■ **Quick Analogy**

Humans as free, sentient beings seeking spiritual fulfillment.

■ **Advantages**

Emphasizes courageous struggle for self-fulfillment and dignity.

Appreciates the spiritual nature of a person.

Often based on the study of healthy, well-adjusted individuals.

Considers each individual's experience unique.

■ **Limits**

May avoid quantification and scientific method needed for science of personality.

Sometimes insufficiently concerned with reason or logic.

Theories are sometimes ambiguous or inconsistent.

■ **View of Free Will**

Free will is essential to being human.

■ **Common Assessment Techniques**

Interview, self-exploration, art, literature, biographical analysis of creativity and special achievement, self-report tests, observation.

■ **Implications for Therapy**

Encourages self-knowledge through experiences (including spiritual experiences) appropriate to the individual. Values retreats (get-aways), self-disclosure, communal trust. May encourage creativity and self-expression through art, writing, dance, or travel. Rogers's client-centered therapy offers a genuine, empathic therapist who offers unconditional positive regard. Encourages realization of your own goals through supportive reflections (by friends or therapist) of your own advances. Encourages devotion and service to combat anxiety and alienation.

Summary and Conclusion

What is the nature of the human spirit? What is love? How do we measure human success? Any full psychological understanding of what it means to be a person should provide a relevant psychological perspective for addressing these age-old questions. Existential-humanistic approaches to personality tackle these issues head on.

Existentialism is an area of philosophy concerned with the meaning of human existence. Existentialists speak of beings-in-the-world; simply put, the self cannot exist without a world and the world cannot exist without a person (a being) to perceive it. People are active, conscious beings, always thinking. Similarly, questions about choosing to be ethical and moral, and about feeling guilt and anxiety, are seen as essential aspects of being human, rather than as incidental by-products of the biological nature of human beings.

Aspects of existential approaches are sometimes termed phenomenological, in that people's perceptions or subjective realities are considered to be valid data for investigation. The existential approach is also nondeterministic because it argues against viewing people as controlled by fixed physical laws.

Humanism is a philosophical movement that emphasizes values and the personal worth of the individual; a humanistic approach to personality likewise attends to matters of ethics and personal worth. Abraham Maslow called humanistic psychology the "third force" in psychology, with only humanistic approaches emphasizing the creative, spontaneous, and active nature of human beings. Life develops as people create worlds for themselves. This view moves from humans "being" to humans "becoming"; that is, there is an active movement toward self-fulfillment in the healthy personality. The human potential movement, which began in the 1960s, is one example of the existential-humanistic approach to personality, but the implications of humanistic approaches for healthy personality development are being felt throughout society.

The humanistic psychoanalyst Erich Fromm maintained that love is an art—not something that one stumbles into, and not some nebulous epiphenomenon that has no real meaning. Love requires knowledge, effort, and experience. Fromm's concern was that in modern society, we are alienated from ourselves, from others, and from nature. We try to cover this inner alienation by "having fun." If we do not fight loneliness by working in a loving way to help others, then we may escape from the burden of freedom by giving up our freedom, such as to a dictator. For Fromm, the most mature personality is one that transcends the ordinary demands of life and creates an active positive identity involving productive, respectful love of others. As Fromm predicted, an alienated, noncommunal American society is increasingly afflicted with violence, divorce, and civil strife.

The influential humanistic psychologist Carl Rogers likewise believed that people have an inherent tendency toward growth and maturation. But the maturation is not inevitable. Rather, people can gain self-understanding in a supportive psychosocial environment if they take responsibility. According to Rogers, a psychologically healthy person is one who has a broad self-concept that can understand and accept many feelings and experiences. Inner control is healthier than imposed control. Of special concern are discrepancies between what a person thinks of himself and the total range of his experiences. Inabilities to accept aspects of oneself are impediments on the path to personal growth. Rogers says that a person should "become one's self."

Some existential perspectives are not so sanguine and optimistic, focusing instead on the anxiety and dread that the freedom to create one's own meaning brings. This sense of alienation from modern society was foreseen by two nineteenth-century philosophers: Søren Kirkegaard, who emphasized the importance of human faith, and Friedrich Nietzsche, who showed the importance of passion and creativity. In this tradition, Rollo May bridges the gap between existential and humanistic approaches to personality with a focus on the anxiety that must accompany any attempt to live life to its fullest. Such existential-humanistic approaches have had a tremendous impact among people facing life-threatening illness.

Self-actualization is the innate process by which one tends to grow spiritually and realize one's potential. Although few people become completely self-fulfilled, Abraham Maslow thought positive and peak experiences to be a significant aspect of personality. During a peak experience time may seem to stop and the immediate environment may recede. According to Maslow, self-actualized people have a realistic knowledge of themselves and accept themselves, and are independent and spontaneous. Such aspects of humanistic psychology are quite close to many Western and Eastern religious teachings. Maslow helped divert the study of personality away from psychopathology and toward the study of the most well-adjusted, self-actualized people. And in the best existentialist tradition, Maslow pointed out that science does not exist outside of the humans who create it. Thus science is never value-free. Existential and humanistic theories allow for true creativity and heroism.

Existential-humanistic approaches, which are necessarily idiographic approaches, consider individual experience unique. This approach to personality is also conducive to the cross-cultural study of personality and to the study of ethnic groups. Its proponents vehemently denounce reductionistic psychology that strives to "reduce" human beings to drives or neurons or conditioned reflexes. On the other hand, critics have accused humanistic approaches to personality of being insufficiently concerned with logic and reason; indeed, the intellectual forefather of humanistic psychology, Jean-Jacques Rousseau was also condemned for proclaiming the value of feelings over reason.

Key Theorists

Erich Fromm   Victor Frankl
Carl Rogers   Abraham Maslow
Rollo May

Key Concepts

existentialism   Rogerian therapy
being-in-the-world   self-actualization
phenomenological   teleology
nondeterministic   peak experiences
humanism   organismic
I-Thou dialogue versus I-It monologue   hierarchy of needs
human potential movement   deficiency needs
dialectical humanism   Personal Orientation Inventory
the experiencing person   dialectical tension

Suggested Readings

Csikszentmihalyi, M., & Larson, R. (1984). *Being adolescent: Conflict and growth in the teenage years.* New York: Basic Books.

Frankl, V. E. (1984). *Man's search for meaning.* (Rev. and updated.) New York: Washington Square Press.

Fromm, E. (1941). *Escape from freedom.* New York: Farrar & Rinehart.

Lowrey, R. (1973). *A. H. Maslow: An intellectual portrait.* Monterey, CA: Brooks-Cole.

Maslow, A. H. (1970). *Motivation and personality.* New York: Harper & Row.

May, R. (1969). *Love and will.* New York: Norton

Rogers, C. R. (1951). *Client-centered therapy: Its current practice, implications, and theory.* Boston: Houghton Mifflin.

Rogers, C. R. (1961). *On becoming a person: A therapist's view of psychotherapy.* Boston: Houghton Mifflin.

Rogers, C. R., & Stevens, B. (1967). *Person to person: The problem of being human.* New York: Simon & Schuster.

Wexler, D. A., & Rice, L. N. (1974). *Innovations in client-centered therapy.* New York: Wiley.

Chapter 10

Person–Situation Interactionist Aspects of Personality

In 1927, a number of school children were placed (by researchers) into a situation in which they had the opportunity to copy correct answers to an examination from an answer key. The researchers wanted to measure the students' degrees of honesty—to see if they would cheat! As we might expect, some of the students cheated, but others did not. They were then given the opportunity to "find" money that had been planted in a puzzle box by researchers. Some students kept (stole) the money, but others did not. What was the personality of the cheaters and thieves? One interesting result of this research was that students who appeared honest on some tasks appeared dishonest on

317

others (Hartshorne & May, 1928). A "cheating personality" could not be found.

Is this result so surprising? On the one hand, most people consider themselves quite different from "crooks," whom they believe should be locked away. (And when caught, they might insist, "I am not a crook!") On the other hand, many people consider themselves to be basically honest but know that they may not do the perfectly honest thing in all situations. They may pocket incorrect change, or get help with their homework, or exaggerate their tax deductions. There are few people who are always honest or always dishonest.

Studies like the 1927 cheaters study, which observe behavior in order to measure personality, have the advantage of relying on tangible, meaningful data. But a problem arises from the fact that people are inconsistent. Perhaps we must agree with the character in William Shakespeare's *The Winter's Tale* who proclaimed, "Though I am not naturally honest, I am so sometimes by chance" (spoken by Autolycus, Act 4, Scene 4.)

Such inconsistencies led researchers in the 1930s to wonder about the general importance of personality, and these concerns were picked up again by researchers in the 1960s (Mischel, 1968). How can we talk about personality if people change their behavior from situation to situation? Tackling these matters head on, psychologists have been able to make sophisticated progress in understanding how personality interacts with the social situation.

The founders of modern personality psychology grappled with these same problems. For Kurt Lewin (1935), behavior was clearly a function of both personal characteristics and the immediate social situation. In fact, he summed it up in the equation $B = f(P,E)$—behavior is a function of the person *and* the environment. Gordon Allport (1961) addressed the dilemma and concluded that part of each behavior pattern represents an unvarying, underlying predisposition, but that the propensity to act is realized in different ways in different situations. (This was discussed in Chapter 8 on trait and skill aspects.) And for Henry Murray (1938), needs motivated the individual from the inside *and* an environmental "press" (such as family conflict) affected the individual from the outside.

Thus the idea that personality and the situation interact to affect behavior is an old one. People express their personality in different ways in different situations. What is new about person–situation interactionist approaches to personality is that they attempt explicitly to consider the social situation. This chapter traces the roots of the interactionist approach to personality and explains some of its most modern realizations. It helps us understand who is a crook.

Harry Stack Sullivan: Interpersonal Psychiatry

Imagine a baby boy whose needs for love and tenderness are not being met by his mother. His mother behaves erratically, is unhappy with her life, and is often absent. His father, frustrated and unemotional, withdraws into himself. Further imagine that the boy is a Catholic growing up in a prejudiced Protestant farming community. Finally, add in the pressures of homosexual feelings stirring within a boy growing up in an aggressively heterosexual world. This describes the early life of the influential psychiatrist Harry Stack Sullivan (Chapman, 1976; Pearce, 1985; Perry, 1982). Although Sullivan proposed his theories in the 1940s, his ideas are very relevant to the personality theories of the 1990s.

Perhaps the easiest way to understand a key contribution of Sullivan to personality theory is to consider his idea of "chumship." Think about the influences—the social situations—of a ten-year-old boy like Harry. (Sullivan focused on boys but analogous issues occur for girls.) The preadolescent is putting some distance between himself and his parents, but earnestly seeking acceptance by his peers. Significant psychosocial threats to well-being are loneliness, isolation, and rejection. Note that all of these threats are inherently *social:* it makes no sense to speak about rejection unless some group is doing the rejecting. For Sullivan, it is of the utmost importance

According to Sullivan's idea of chumship, a preadolescent's pals serve as a social mirror for forming his or her identity. Just as we look in a real mirror to adjust our clothing, we look in a mirror of friends for feedback about our values and our personal strengths and weaknesses. This notion is derived from the sociological idea of a social self.

to understand the feelings of anxiety that arise when interpersonal rejection occurs. He thus locates healthy or unhealthy psychological development in the reactions of one's peers.

Interpersonal Psychiatry Contrasted with Psychoanalytic Theory

Like many influential personality theorists, Sullivan was conversant with psychoanalytic thought. Others trained in psychoanalysis, such as Karen Horney and Erich Fromm, had begun turning away from Freud's focus on internal drives and struggles and had begun emphasizing instead the social environment. Horney and the object relations theorists (see Chapter 4) were very concerned with the anxiety created in a child by unstable parenting. But the major shift in this field came from Harry Stack Sullivan. For Sullivan, personality is inextricably tied to social situations; personality is "the relatively enduring pattern of recurrent interpersonal situations" that characterizes a person's life (Sullivan, 1953, p. 111). Sullivan's approach is thus sometimes known as the **interpersonal theory of psychiatry.** It focuses on the recurring social situations that we face. It constituted a major break from psychoanalytic and ego traditions. Note that it is midway between the inner emphasis of the psychoanalysts and the outer emphasis of the behaviorists.

Sullivan's approach, like that of Kurt Lewin, is closely tied to social psychology. Sullivan (who, like Lewin, developed his main ideas in the 1930s) was heavily influenced by the so-called Chicago School of sociology and philosophy, particularly by George Herbert Mead (1968) and Edward Sapir. (Remember that it was called the Chicago School because its scholars were based at the University of Chicago.)

Mead is best known for his intriguing writings about the social self. The **social self** is the idea that who we are and how we think of ourselves arises from our interactions with those around us. While Freudians were focusing on the child's struggle with internal Oedipal conflicts, Mead was looking at the child's ongoing social interactions with significant others. If a four-year-old says, "I'm a very smart and handsome little boy," where does this self-concept come from? For Mead, the source was clearly the child's understanding of his interactions and discussions with his parents.

Personality as a Pattern of Interpersonal Interactions

Edward Sapir, the other key influence on Sullivan, was an anthropologist, best known for his work on language and culture. By studying diverse societies, Sapir (1956) saw that behavior was heavily influenced by culture. Harry Stack Sullivan integrated the work of Mead and of Sapir and concluded that enduring patterns of human relationships—shaped by family and society—form the essence of personality. In this sense, Sullivan's work is similar to that of Erik Erikson (discussed in Chapter 4). Sullivan, like Erikson, believed that to understand personality, we must look to recurring patterns of social relations in a real societal context. A ten-year-old farm boy who cannot develop interaction patterns of mutuality and reciprocity with a chum may be at high risk for a life of loneliness and possibly despair.

Sullivan was born in upstate New York in 1892. Sullivan's early education and his medical training were undistinguished. His first professional work was in a series of mental hospitals, and there is some indication that Sullivan himself struggled mightily to maintain his emotional equilibrium. (It often seems that "it takes one to know one." Theorists rely heavily on their own personal insights in their theorizing.) But his career blossomed as his intriguing personality and his unorthodox ideas gained greater and greater acceptance. Although he had much in common with Horney, Sullivan's approach is not neo-Freudian (Pearce, 1985). For Sullivan, personality is not built around the unconscious impulses of the id, nor is it fixed in early childhood. Rather, it constantly changes as a function of relations with others. Ironically but perhaps not surprisingly, Sullivan died alone after attending a meeting in Paris in 1949.

To a personality psychologist like Sullivan who believes in the idea of a social self, we actually become "different" people in different social situations! That is, in each social situation, we imagine how others think of us and respond accordingly. Sometimes people move to a new town to make a "fresh start"— they try to present a new image to new friends, new neighbors, new coworkers. This can be successful if they are careful not to fall back into recreating old patterns. Or, a college student may behave very differently when he or she returns home on vacation and interacts with old high school friends; the high school friends have different expectations than the new college friends, and the student responds appropriately. The situation affects (elicits) the personality. This idea can be extended to all social situations. Personality emerges as a combination of individual inclinations and the social situation. In fact, Sullivan termed the idea that a person has a single, fixed personality the **illusion of individuality.** In a sense, we may have as many personalities as we have interpersonal situations.

This student is very serious and conscientious in this situation, where she is attending a course lecture. To what extent can we use this information about her to predict her behavior in other situations?

Since personality is primarily a function of social expectations, Sullivan blames society (not internal neuroses) for most of the individual's problems. Society is seen as stifling the creative growth needs of the individual. Anxiety comes from without, not from within. In this regard, Sullivan has much in common with the humanistic and existential psychologists. So, for example, Sullivan promoted the idea that it is more often harmful than helpful to lock away the mentally "ill" in mental "sanitariums." And indeed, social policy gradually changed and many mental hospitals closed. Here is an example of how personality theory can sometimes have dramatic effects on social policy. Sullivan was often successful as a psychiatrist by having himself and his staff become like "chums" to his patients. He overcame many of his own problems and he believed that healthy, positive interpersonal relations could help other people overcome their problems.

Thus, for Sullivan, the focus of personality study should be on the interpersonal situation, not on the person. With this emphasis on the social situation, Sullivan and others who well understood social psychology helped lay the groundwork for modern interactionist approaches. But perhaps the most influential precursor of the modern movement was Henry A. Murray.

Motivation and Goals: Henry Murray

In 1933, Henry Murray read a scary story to children at his daughter's birthday party, and he found that they projected their fear onto others—they saw pictured men as more insidious and threatening. During World War II, Murray had to give up his lectern and put his theories and methods to patriotic work—the U.S. Army had him screen men who would be trained as spies and sent on dangerous missions. Murray's (1948) team used interviews and projective tests but also created challenging, stressful situations for the select recruits to react to. For example, who would climb to a dangerous height, and why? Murray thus combined his deep knowledge of human motivation with his sensitivity to social and situational demands to create a view of personality that has stimulated much work and many students. By the way, spy and counterspy agencies like the CIA and FBI now routinely conduct psychological screening on their potential employees.

Henry Murray defined personality as the "branch of psychology which principally concerns itself with the study of human lives and the factors which influence their course, [and] which investigates individual differences" (1938, p. 4). Since Murray viewed personality as the study of human lives across time, he necessarily watched and analyzed the interactions of individuals and the situations they encountered throughout their lives. Murray took the unconscious motivations from Freud, Jung, and Adler, the environmental pressures from Lewin, and the sophisticated trait concept from Allport and synthesized them into a comprehensive approach to personality. Murray thus can be considered a primary founder of the interactionist approach to personality.

Henry Murray was born in New York and became a physician doing biochemical research (with a Ph.D. from Cambridge University) before turning to psychology after visiting Carl Jung in Zurich. Murray was psychoanalyzed first by Jung and then by Franz Alexander, a leader in psychosomatic medicine. He reports that these giants led him to experience the great power of unconscious motivation. Murray became director of the Harvard Psychological Clinic (treating people with psychological problems) but decided that he could learn more by studying healthy people. He blended psychoanalytic and neo-analytic ideas into a basis for empirical research. He was one of the first to do so.

The Personological System

Due to his emphasis on studying the richness of the life of each person, Murray preferred the term "personology" to the term "personality"; even today, psychologists working in the Murray tradition often call themselves "personologists." Furthermore, Murray was influenced by the twentieth-century philosopher Alfred North Whitehead to focus on the "process" of personality rather than to rely on static concepts such as enduring structures in the mind. Systems—dynamic influences with feedback—are key. Thus he referred to his theory as a **personological system.**

Murray emphasized the integrated, dynamic nature of the individual as a complex organism responding to a specific environment. Therefore, on the one hand, Murray stressed the importance of needs and motivations, an emphasis that has proved quite influential. (See Table 10.1 on page 324 for some of the needs identified by Murray.) On the other hand, Murray also emphasized the **environmental press**—the push of the situation. These are directional forces on a person that arise from other people or events in the environment. For example, seeing one's friends getting good grades in school might be a press spurring one's own efforts to excel. Take the case of whether a student will cheat: we might find that a high need to achieve in school might combine with a situation in which a lot can be gained by cheating, at low risk or cost; in this situation, cheating would be the result.

Thus, unlike behaviorists like Skinner, Murray accepted (and studied) unconscious fantasies and instinctual drives. Unlike trait theorists like Allport, who stressed internal structure and self-consistency, Murray emphasized social roles and situational determinants. He was a humanist who assumed and applauded creativity, but he allowed that some of this energy arose in unconscious urges. But most important, he looked at the *combination* of internal motivations and external demands.

Table 10.1   **Examples of Murray's Needs**

Need	Description
Affiliation	Need to be near and enjoyably reciprocate with another.
Autonomy	Need to be free and independent of others.
Dominance	Need to control or influence others.
Exhibition	Need to be seen and heard, to entertain and entice.
Harm-avoidance	Need to avoid injury, take precautions.
Nurturance	Need to help, console, comfort, nurse the weak.
Order	Need for organization and neatness.
Play	Need for enjoyment and fun.
Sex	Need to form an erotic relationship.
Succorance	Need to be nursed, loved, controlled.
Understanding	Need to speculate, analyze, generalize.

Note: Needs are internal (but can be provoked by the environmental press), and they necessitate taking action in the social environment. The approach is thus interactionist. Examples of environmental press range from simple exigencies of life, such as getting out of the rain and getting enough to eat, to more complex sociopsychological demands, such as dealing with rejection or competition.

Source: Based on Murray, 1938.

Thema

For Murray, typical combinations of needs and presses were termed **thema.** He measured them with his Thematic Apperception Test, or TAT. Remember that the TAT is a projective test, in which a person is presented with a series of ambiguous pictures (for example, two women who could be mother and daughter) and composes a story. It is an "apperception" test because the person reports not what he or she sees ("perception") but rather a narrative or imaginary interpretation. One's own needs are found in (projected upon) the ambiguous stimulus, just as Murray's daughter's friends projected their own fears onto pictures of "threatening" men. Themes of identity are thus then derived. For example, if the TAT-taker says that one of the two women in the cue picture is probably a loving, giving, saintly person who has been jilted by two insensitive boyfriends, then we may have a clue that such conflict is an organizing theme or pattern in her own life. The thema is an interaction between her need to be spiritually close to others and the environmental press of the men she dates, who want her to have sex without love.

What do you think might be happening in this picture? In Murray's Thematic Apperception Test (TAT), a person is asked to provide a narrative or imaginary interpretation of an ambiguous photograph. The response is interpreted as a reflection of an important thema for that person.

Although there is still ongoing controversy about the validity of the TAT as a measure of personality, it seems to be the case that it is a valuable tool when it is not used alone but in conjunction with other means of discovering themes that govern an individual's identity. Murray's explicit statement of this interaction between needs and presses provided the cornerstone for interactionist approaches to personality.

The Narrative Approach: Murray's Influence

A modern example of Murray's emphases in thinking about personality is the work of psychologist Dan P. McAdams, who endeavors to study the full life context of the "whole person." He does this (as Murray urged) by studying motivations through biographies—that is, life stories. The idea is that the story of one's life becomes one's identity. This approach is sometimes termed the **narrative approach** to personality. For example, McAdams (1991) studies the intimacy motive—the need to share oneself with others in intimate ways. How can we do this in a broad context? Let us consider the hypothetical case of Susan.

First of all, Susan developed a trusting nature thanks to positive, stable interactions during infancy and childhood (she was very close to her loving mother). In later childhood and adolescence, Susan was drawn to reading stories and joining groups associated with love, cooperation, and communion (Girl Scouts, her youth group, and the church choir). As a college student, Susan was idealistic, very concerned with issues of justice. Now, later in life, Susan creates a self-identity of altruistic helper (teacher, doctor, child psychologist)—she is a pediatrician. Her patients and their parents love her as a sincere and dedicated physician, and Susan loves sharing what is innermost in others. In later years, Susan may become a "generative" senior (as Erik Erikson put it), making a positive contribution to future generations by offering mentoring guidance and acting as an intimate confidante.

At each stage of life, internal inclinations lead us to seek out and respond to certain situations, which in turn help to further shape our inclinations and identity. In one study of these issues, generative, award-winning school teachers were interviewed for several hours about their lives—their important memories—and these accounts were then later coded by trained scorers. As predicted by McAdams, themes of love, caring, and community were especially likely to appear in the self-reported identities of these generative teachers (Mansfield & McAdams, 1996).

Other Influences on Murray's Approach

Murray was influenced significantly by the field theories of social psychologist Kurt Lewin. Lewin, well known for his proposition that behavior is a function of the person and the environment, believed this, however, in the sense of **contemporaneous causation.** That is, behavior is caused *at that moment* as a function of a variety of influences. Some of these influences may be residues of past behavior or previous events, but Lewin (1947) and the other field theorists did not see earlier events such as a childhood conflict or repressed drives as directly causing adult behavior. For example, in explaining why a man might pick up money that wasn't rightfully his, Lewin might accept that the man did not have a very strong moral upbringing, but the emphasis of the explanation would be on the temptations of the moment and the absence of situational inhibitions. Murray's concept of needs, however, left him more closely tied to the dynamic motivational ideas of the neo-analysts like Jung, who saw unconscious motivation as a prime element of personality; to this, Murray added the weight of the environmental press and the organic quality of behavior across time.

Also influencing Murray and the move to a more interactionist approach were the behaviorists such as B. F. Skinner. As we have seen, for Skinner, personality exists in the environment, not in the individual—in a sense, we are whatever is reinforced. According to Skinner, similar situations evoked similar responses. These concepts paved the way for interactionists, making it natural to pay more attention to the effects of the situation. Murray's view was of course very, very different from Skinner's, but Murray (who knew Skinner at Harvard) did indeed incorporate significant situational influences into his theory. Finally, Murray and his students were influenced by the humanistic notions of internal motivations toward creativity and self-fulfillment.

In short, from the 1930s to the 1950s, a number of different theorists grappled with ways to move beyond the internal, person-based notions of personality, and they endeavored to integrate the influence of the situation and the interaction between the person and the situation. Harry Stack Sullivan turned completely to the recurring social situation; for Sullivan, personality does not exist outside of social relations. For Henry Murray, the individual brings needs and motivations to recurring social situations. Together, the ideas of these insightful theorists and their colleagues laid the basis for modern interactionist approaches to what it means to be a person.

Modern Interactionist Approaches Begin

In 1968, echoing the breakthroughs of the 1930s, psychologist Walter Mischel again stirred up significant interest in interactionist approaches by arguing that a person's behavior varies so much from situation to situation that it simply did not make sense to think in terms of broad personality traits.

Mischel's Critique

Although it was by then well accepted that situations influence behavior, Mischel (1968) looked at the *size* of the relations between a person's behavior across situations, and their variability. He claimed that no matter what the trait or topic, you could not validly predict what an individual was going to do based on a previous measure of that person's traits. For example, one person might be fearful and anxious when speaking in front of a group, another person has that same reaction when on top of a mountain, and a third person feels that way when going out on an intimate date; no general trait of fear and anxiety could account for these variations. So, should we give up trying to understand or assess personality and instead look at the situations that affect behavior?

Many of Mischel's arguments rested on the size of the relations between personality and behavior, and between behaviors across situations. That is, how well could we predict people's behavior knowing something about their traits, and just how consistent is personality-based behavior across situations?

Mischel relied on the correlation coefficient *r*. As we have seen, this statistic tells us how well one variable predicts, or is correlated with, another variable. With perfect positive correlation, the coefficient equals 1.0. (This would mean, for example, that knowing a woman was extroverted, we could always correctly predict extroverted behavior from her.) But Mischel claimed that most such correlations involving traits were less than 0.30, or slightly higher. Therefore, it did not make much sense to talk about personality traits; rather, there were more productive ways to think about these issues.

Two problems weaken this analysis. First, it assumes a fixed, simple model of personality in which traits lead directly to behavior. Second, what does it mean to say that most correlations of personality with behavior are "only" 0.30?

As we have repeatedly shown in this book, there is no reason to expect that traits or other aspects of personality will be perfect, straightforward predictors of behavior. Personality is complicated, and behavior is partly dependent on the situation. We have seen that personality (say, as viewed by the neo-analysts) sometimes involves opposites; for instance, feelings of inferiority may cause an individual to act superior. If a man with an Adlerian inferiority

Self-Understanding

Some of the People Some of the Time

Although there is ample evidence that people behave differently in different situations and at different times, and although people may change as they grow and age, perhaps we should not be too rigid and demanding in our search for personality. That is, perhaps we should try to build these variations into our personality theories—trying to take them into account.

One way to do this is to classify people as to how consistent they are on a given trait (Bem & Allen, 1974). For example, we can ask people if they are consistently friendly or consistently honest. Some honest people, like clergy, might indeed be more consistently honest across situations, for a variety of reasons. In fact, there is evidence that consistency varies across people; traits do a lot better at predicting behavior for people who are consistent on that trait.

We might also examine the stability of one's identity. Someone whose identity is still evolving, such as a teenager or a person from an unstable home, might behave inconsistently compared to someone whose identity is much more solidified. Similarly, someone facing significant challenges to self-identity, such as those brought on by a divorce or a major move or a job loss, might behave inconsistently during the period of flux but might later behave much more consistently.

Finally, we might analyze people in terms of their life paths or life courses. A variation in behavior that might seem puzzling in isolation might make sense when the person's whole life history is understood. A rebel leader might seem warm and nurturant to his allies but amazingly hostile and devious to his oppressors, but only during the time of the conflict.

See for yourself, either by talking to a close friend or by studying the biography of a famous person. You could examine the extent to which your target person intends to be consistent on a set of behaviors (as someone devoted to a heartfelt cause might), or, on the other hand, feels the necessity to be expedient (as a politician might). You could then examine the extent to which his or her behavior is more variable at times of flux and identity change, as during career changes. Finally, you could examine the extent to which inconsistencies are more understandable in light of the person's long-term mission or ideology.

complex tries to compensate (cope) by acting superior, or if a man defending his psyche against strong libidinal urges instead behaves in a puritanical, straitlaced manner, his behavior might seem unpredictable, but only until we better understand the underlying personality dynamics. (See Self-Understanding.)

Furthermore, we have seen that variability was well recognized by trait psychologist Gordon Allport, who argued that although behavior is variable, there is also a constant portion for each person. In other words, some invariant aspect of behavior always accompanies the changing parts. Allport believed that regularities arise because (1) the individual views many situations and stimuli in the same way and (2) many of the individual's behaviors are similar in their meaning—that is, they are *functionally equivalent*. A racist may do different things in different situations, but the behaviors may all derive from his racist personality structure. Even the biological perspective on personality (Chapter 5) does not assume an invariant link between dispositions and behaviors; rather, each biological inclination develops and is realized in a particular environment.

The second limitation on Mischel's analysis is the assumption that a correlation between personality and behavior (that arises in personality studies) of "only" $r = 0.30$ or 0.40 is small. In a statistical sense, such a correlation is small *if* we expect to be able to predict perfectly. But in real life, an effect this large is often considered very important and meaningful. For example, the effects of dietary intake of cholesterol on mortality risk, or the effects of airbags on the automobile death rate, or the effects of greenhouse gases on global warming are all smaller than this. Yet no one would dismiss them as irrelevant. From this perspective, personality traits actually do quite well in predicting behavior. Furthermore, if we take into account that some traits are useful for understanding only some people or some situations, we can do even better.

The argument that personality is not a valuable concept because it is not highly correlated with behavior across situations has the implicit assumption that it is more important to understand situations than people. If traits do not well predict behavior, then focus on situations. However, if we examine the influence of the situation on behavior, we find that situations are no better predictors. Most studies in social psychology (which manipulate situations) also have an effect size in the range of $r = .30$ or so (Funder & Ozer, 1983). It is true that a shy person may sometimes be quite sociable, even rowdy, at a party, but it is also true that a person's behavior at one party is not a perfect predictor of that person's behavior at other parties! Still Mischel's work served a highly useful purpose in drawing further attention to the interaction of the person and the situation, which was one of his primary goals all along.

Mischel's Theory

Mischel was born in Vienna in 1930, came to the United States when young, and lived in New York. He was an undergraduate at City College of New York, went to graduate school in clinical psychology at Ohio State University, and worked with psychologists who took both a cognitive and learning approach to personality. While a professor at Stanford University he was also influenced by the social learning theories of Albert Bandura.

If you are offered a piece of chocolate cake at a birthday party, do you gobble it down and hope for seconds, or do you push it aside so that you will later be able to fit into your sexy clothes? Mischel's early work dealt primarily with cognitive and situational (that is, social learning) factors that influence behaviors like the delay of gratification in children. **Delay of gratification** is a specific aspect of self-control that occurs when an individual chooses to forgo an immediate reinforcer to wait for a later, better reinforcer. Mischel has studied the variables that influence the individual's ability to delay gratification: modeling (that is, seeing another person delay), the visibility of the desired object (out of sight helps keep it out of mind), and cognitive strategies like thinking about other things (distraction).

More recently Mischel has examined individual differences in the meanings people give to stimuli and reinforcements—he calls these personal meanings **strategies,** or styles. Mischel suggests that these "cognitive personality characteristics" are learned during experiences with situations and their rewards. Thus, despite Mischel's apparent emphasis on the situation (which grows out of cognitive psychology and learning theories), he also lends some credence to internal person characteristics that look suspiciously like personality. In other words, the approach to personality has been improved by evaluating the strengths and weaknesses of previous approaches.

In particular, Mischel has discussed four personality variables: **competencies**—the person's abilities and knowledge; **encoding strategies**—the schemas and mechanisms one uses to process and encode information; **expectancies,** including outcome expectancies for our own behavior, and self-efficacy expectancies; and **plans.** His studies demonstrate that personality is not merely an internal condition that pushes the individual toward behavior regardless of the situation, nor is the individual simply at the mercy of environmental events. Instead, an individual's actions, like delay of gratification, are the result of both environmental constraints (such as the visibility of and experience with the desired object) and internal, cognitive characteristics of the individual (such as self-regulatory strategies). All in all, this work supports the basic tenet that the person and his or her behavior and the environment are continuously interacting with and influencing one another. We have personality, but it is in flux.

In short, in much research using this social-cognitive personality approach, Mischel and colleagues (e.g., Mischel & Shoda, 1995) find that part of the "consistency" of personality seems to be due to similarity of the perceived features of situations—that is, people identify situation–behavior relationships that become **behavioral signatures** of their personalities (Shoda, Mischel, & Wright, 1994). These signatures are idiographic (individual) (Lord, 1982). In a sense, one might say that personality is in fact the interaction, or intersection, of the cognitive "person" characteristics and the environment (Krahe, 1990).

Similarly, personality is sometimes viewed as a "transaction" that occurs when a person's unique personal strategies and styles interact with the particular styles of others (Thorne, 1987). These are more modern conceptions of the social nature of personality that Harry Stack Sullivan so cleverly argued. They are now common in modern approaches to personality (Ozer, 1986).

Implicit Personality Theory

If there really is limited validity in how well traits themselves can be used directly to describe people and predict their behavior, then why do we rely on them so often? That is, why do people in their daily lives seem to assume that traits are not only real but really important, making such observations as "She's very extroverted," "He's so shy," "She's quite conscientious," and so on? According to one explanation, traits are in the observer's mind. This approach derives from the cognitive perspective on personality.

Attributions

Attribution theories in the field of social psychology have examined the ways we draw inferences about other people's behavior. They often find that we have biases and make errors when judging others (Jones & Nisbett, 1987). For example, we are likely to explain some observed behavior of our friend as a quirk of his personality, while the friend may see the same behavior as situationally determined. We may see our friend Sam as selfish or fearful because he refuses to donate blood during a blood drive, but Sam may know that he was exposed to hepatitis and so is not an acceptable donor and besides, his parents frown on this behavior. In other words, we as observers are focused on Sam's particular behavior and draw an inference about his personality, but Sam sees different forces pressuring him to behave as he does. Because we do not see those forces, we overexplain—incorrectly—in terms of personality.

Relatedly, people are willing to fall back on stereotypes to help simplify how they see the world. So, if the grocery clerk at our supermarket wears loud clothing, has a scar on his face, and doesn't speak English very well, we might come to some conclusions about his personality (what kind of person he is) even though we know next to nothing about him. This stereotyping may come all the more easily if we see the person in only a few situations.

So, for example, you may always see your professor in formal settings—the lecture hall or the office—and therefore you might assume that your professor is rather rigid and serious. However, if you could see your professor on a vacation in Hawaii, or flirting at a party, or dancing at a nightclub, you might make a very different inference. We often overgeneralize about someone's personality, but this does not mean that we could not come to a better inference if we undertook a more comprehensive assessment.

Connected to this analysis is the idea that people tend to overestimate just how consistent their behaviors are. If we think we are honest, then we tend to ignore, forget, or rationalize any of our behaviors that might be seen as dishonest. We often desire to have a consistent self-image. We may then convince others that we have this stable trait.

Validity

Recent research suggests that although biases do sometimes cause us to overascribe to personality and sometimes overemphasize its importance, there is good reason to believe that some aspects of these inferences about personality are quite valid (Funder, 1987; Funder, Kolar, & Blackman, 1995). Systematic study indicates that although we sometimes make biased or distorted inferences, in general there is good evidence for validity. For example, different judges of a personality (such as if your parents, your friends, and your classmates judge your personality) tend to agree, and knowing the target in the same context enhanced but was not necessary for interjudge agreement; so cross-situational consistency is common. Furthermore, personality judgments by your acquaintances show better interjudge agreement (and agreement with your own judgments of your personality) than do judgments by strangers. In short, observers agree in their judgments of personality, and this interjudge agreement seems to arise, at least in part, from mutual accuracy.

The Power of Situations

One reason that personality is sometimes a weak predictor of behavior is that the power of the situation is sometimes so strong that it overrides our inclinations. To take an extreme example, if a fire breaks out in a theater and the crowd panics and rushes toward the exits, it is not surprising that a calm, rational person caught in the crowd will act excitedly and irrationally.

Or consider college students of the late 1960s, caught up in antiwar protests and the hippie revolution against the establishment. Even some of the most conscientious and law-abiding young people used illegal drugs (though perhaps did not inhale), burned draft cards, engaged in illegal demonstrations, and so on. On a more massive scale, millions of otherwise decent and devout Germans cooperated with the Nazi regime, even with their murderous extermination camps and their brutal invasions. It would be foolish to try to explain such behaviors solely in terms of internal personality constructs. Sometimes the power of the situation is all but overwhelming. This analysis derives from both the behaviorist approach of B. F. Skinner (in which reinforcements determine behavior) and the phenomenological field theory approach of Kurt Lewin (in which the perceived pressures of the moment are the greatest influence on behavior).

Yet it is also an oversimplification to explain Germans' obedience to Hitler only in terms of the situation (Blass, 1991). Some people are eager to be swept up in an authoritarian movement, while others are more hesitant, and still others actively resist. Often, the power of the situation over our actions depends on the source of our identity in that situation (Milgram, 1974). For example, many individual clergy, deriving their identity from a higher morality, actively opposed the Nazis, even though most organized churches in Germany and Italy did not.

Consistency within Situations

With the emphasis of the interactionist approach on situations, a key problem is deciding how to classify situations. For example, take the case of Michael, who reports himself as being quite shy. Forced to speak in front of a group of fellow students, Michael shakes and sweats with fear, yet at home or at family gatherings, he is an active loudmouth. How will Michael behave at dinner parties? How about in his school play? How about on a date with his dream girl? Are any of these situations comparable and relevant to his shyness trait?

The "Personality" of Situations

How can we systematically classify situations? One way is to place people into a carefully controlled situation and see who behaves as expected. For example, we could create a situation that provokes aggression or one that rewards delaying gratification and then note who behaves "appropriately" (Bem & Funder, 1978). Once we identify the characteristics of people who aggress in a situation that we think is "aggressive," we can then see if these same people also behave aggressively in another situation that we also believe to be "aggressive." If the second situation does indeed elicit aggressive behavior from the same individuals, then we can deduce that it is similar to the first aggressive situation. But if the people who aggress in the second situation have different characteristics, then we conclude that the two situations are dissimilar.

Although this idea is a clever one, imagine how difficult it would be to measure all the situations we encounter. This could take forever. A simpler way would be to ask psychologists to rate or evaluate various situations, classify the situations, and then see if they elicit similar behaviors in people who score similarly in relevant personality tests. This approach appears promising but has not been much studied.

Some psychologists try to focus directly on how each individual evaluates, interprets, and reacts to the different situations he or she encounters (Magusson & Endler, 1977; Magnusson, 1990; Torestad, Magnusson, & Olah, 1990). For example, we might measure people on self-reported or physiologically assessed anxiety and then place them in different situations. In this way, we could try to tease apart the contributions to behavior of stable anxiety (personality), the situation (seen as anxiety provoking), and the interaction (only some people become anxious in certain anxiety-provoking situations).

An additional complication is the fact that no two situations are ever exactly alike; the world changes over time (Elder & Caspi, 1988). Consider a suburban American family of two parents and two children in 1955 versus in 1999. Certainly many important factors are likely to be extremely different—among others, the education and employment of the mother, the entertainment choices, the proximity of extended family, and the family's relations with other ethnic groups. Does this make it impossible to generalize about personality and situations? The two families undoubtedly share many common elements—rivalries between the children, love and attachment to the parents coupled with strivings for independence, the need for cooperative efforts for food, cleaning, transportation, and so on. Successful approaches to personality can capture recognizable patterns and regularities while also taking into account changes that occur across time. This is why ancient stories about people from Greek mythology or from the Bible can still be understood and appreciated by us today.

Thousands of years after it was first written down, the biblical story of Joseph and his brothers strikes a familiar chord. Joseph's brothers, jealous of his status as their father's favorite and resenting his beautiful coat of many colors, cast him into a pit, and then sold him into slavery. The depictions of the brothers' vengeful behavior and Joseph's willingness to rescue them years later match our contemporary views about personality and about situational influences on behavior.

Consistency Averaged across Situations

Consider a situation in which Sue, a highly extroverted woman, attends a lively party but sits by herself and hardly talks to anyone. How can this be? When personality tests fail to predict behavior in a specific situation, two faults can be argued. First is the issue of reliability. Perhaps chance factors affected the behavior in that particular situation; one sample of her behavior was not a reliable indicator of her personality. Second, there is the question of the appropriateness of that situation as being associated with the personality trait in question (Murtha, Kanfer, & Ackerman, 1996). Perhaps this party was not the right sort of occasion to elicit extroverted behavior. A way to deal with both of these issues is to gather information (observe behavior) across many situations. We could observe Sue at other parties and at other sorts of social gatherings. Her behavior could then be seen as her "average" behavior—the average across situations.

Approaches to the Big Five dimensions of personality (see Chapter 8) generally take this sort of approach. They assume that there are relatively few dimensions of personality and relatively few basic sorts of situation. They are not at all disturbed when an extroverted person does not talk at a party; they assume that the extrovert will appear sociable when her various behaviors are considered together (averaged). And in fact such approaches do provide a fairly accurate account of behavior. They might be fine, for example, in judging someone's temperamental suitability to be a salesperson.

However, such approaches would not be at all satisfying to those personality theorists who adhere to a psychoanalytic or neo-analytic tradition. Nor would such "average" explanations be satisfying to Lewin, or Allport, or Murray. These theorists would want to try to understand why Sue is sitting alone at *this* party even though internal forces are pushing her to be an extrovert.

Personal versus Social Situations

As we have seen, one of the first things a child learns is to separate the self from others. That is, one of the tasks of infancy is to learn that one's mouth is one's own, but the breast belongs to someone else (mother). By the age of two or three, the child is further learning the no-no's of public behavior—initially, these range from masturbation to picking one's nose—as well as learning the niceties of social interaction—saying please and thank you, taking turns, helping others. Some children also learn to be charming or manipulative or charismatic.

In other words, although we develop a social self, the social self is more prominent in certain people, or at certain times, or in certain situations. One of the first theories of this psychosocial differentiation involved what is called "field dependence versus field independence" (Witkin & Goodenough, 1977). As noted in our chapter on cognitive aspects of personality, field-dependent people have a harder time separating the figure from the background in a perceptual task. For example, could a person correctly judge the position of a rod, disregarding the position of the frame in which it appears? Field-independent people can judge an object, disregarding compelling background influences. Thus, in the social realm, they tend to act more independently. Field dependent people are presumably more reliant on others and so should respond in line with the demands of the social situation.

As we will see in our chapter on cultural and ethnic differences, whole cultures also vary in the degree to which they are *individualistic* or *collectivistic* (Triandis, 1989). Individualistic cultures (like the American culture) emphasize individual rights, needs, and responsibilities. The individual is the key figure against a social background. Collectivist cultures emphasize the needs and success of the group; the focus is on the group, and a figure that sticks out like a prominent nail will be hammered down.

The same issues can be approached from the neo-analytic perspective of presentation of the self. Some people are especially motivated and able to read the demands of others. They monitor their own self-presentations to make a good impression and to respond to the expectations of others. Psychologist Mark Snyder terms them high self-monitors (1974, 1987). Low self-monitors, on the other hand, are less in tune with and less concerned with the expectations of others. Their personalities may therefore be less variable as a function of the situation. Taking a slightly different tack, personality psychologist Jonathan Cheek (e.g., Cheek & Melchior, 1990) contrasts those people who are low in social identity (and so act independently and try to get ahead) with those who are low in personal identity (and so are sociable and involved with others).

Issues of shyness, self-consciousness, performance anxiety, and so on may also be relevant to this distinction (Scheier & Carver, 1988; Snyder, 1987). Some people are so tied to social roles that, almost chameleon-like, they take on the colors—the demands—of the social situation. For example, some actors seem to have almost no identity of their own—they become their current roles. On the other hand, other people are so unable to play social roles that they find social situations very uncomfortable. They may be called nerds. This could produce a consistency in personality; for example, they act conscientiously in private and continue to act conscientiously even when at a riotous party. On the other hand, if the social pressures become too overwhelming, they may act erratically; for example, a very shy and conscientious person might have such self-consciousness at a drunken party that she might act in a very unusual manner and become drunk herself.

We all probably knew a schoolmate who didn't seem to understand that he shouldn't keep his finger up his nose and, to the extent that he *did* understand, didn't seem to care what others thought of him. Some people who are little influenced by social situations may appear to have a more consistent personality. They may perceive things more independently, may be less able to read social cues, may be unmotivated to conform to social demands, and may even prefer to be unique and uninhibited. Such people have a less "social" and a more "personal" personality. A full and sophisticated understanding of personality should take such issues into account. This broad view is one of the strengths of the interactionist perspective.

Seeking and Creating Situations

Consider two high school seniors. One is a top student, kind of preppy, from a family of diplomats. The other plays three varsity sports, is very popular and earthy, from a family of farmers. Which student is more likely to apply to Princeton, and which to Indiana University? People with certain characteristics apply to and are accepted to certain colleges. People with certain characteristics are then selected and self-selected into corresponding sororities and fraternities. These houses in turn further reinforce these tendencies. We seek out situations that reinforce our self-conceptions.

In one interesting study of personality and life events, researchers followed 130 University of Illinois students for four years (Magnus et al., 1993). First, the students were administered the NEO Personality Inventory, a general measure of the Big Five factors of personality (see Chapter 8). They were then sent follow-up measures four years later, including assessments of life events (like marriage) that the students had experienced. It turned out that extroversion predisposed the students to experience positive life events, but neuroticism (tendency toward anxiety and depression) tended to predict to negative life events. Anxious people went on to experience more anxiety-provoking events. That is, personality leads us to experience certain kinds of events, which then in turn, of course, can affect personality. Of course anxious, depressed people do not always encounter bad life events, but they are more likely to.

Consider also what happens when a child who is an aggressive bully enters the schoolyard. With his arrival, the playground may soon turn into a war zone as his personality elicits and provokes certain behavior in others (Rausch, 1977).

Finally, there is evidence that consistency results in part from our own active, conscious efforts. One interesting series of studies assessed the influence of self-conceptions on the type of feedback solicited during social interactions

(Swann & Read, 1981). In one experiment, undergraduates displayed a clear preference for feedback that would confirm their self-perceived level of emotionality. Another study in this series found that the participants regarded self-confirmatory feedback (consistent with their self-images) as especially informative. In other words, people tend to regard confirming information as more compelling than disconfirming information about themselves—an instance of a more general cognitive preference for seeking out and attending to confirmatory over disconfirmatory feedback (Wason & Johnson-Laird, 1972). We may seek out friends and listen to discourse that tells us what we want to hear about ourselves. By seeking and eliciting confirming feedback from others, we may make our social environments and self-conceptions seem more stable than they really are.

Time

The existential and humanistic approach to personality (see Chapter 9) emphasizes that human beings are not fixed collections of attributes but rather we are always in the process of becoming something new. The dimension of *time* is thus increasingly seen as important in understanding personality.

Longitudinal Study

As we grow and develop, how do we change? Unfortunately, although the psychoanalysts and neo-analysts wrote about stages of personality development, changes over time have often been left out of modern scientific personality theories because they are so difficult to study. The only good way to study personality over time is to actually observe people as they age.

In other words, to really study people as they react, grow, and change in the real world, longitudinal study is necessary. Psychologist Jack Block defines **longitudinal study** as "the close, comprehensive, systematic, objective, sustained study of individuals over significant portions of the life span" (1993, p. 7). Simply put, this means following people over time.

Of course we all do this to some extent as amateurs; we watch our siblings, parents, children, spouses, and perhaps close friends over periods of many years. But doing this scientifically is much more difficult. Who can do a study that lasts many years? What about securing research funding and publishing (or face perishing)? How can we keep track of people as they move around? What if someone loses interest in participating in our study? How do we deal with changing times and changing measures? The obstacles seem insurmountable. Yet, as Block points out, "There is no alternative scientific approach that can begin to discern and disentangle the specific influential factors conjoining, interweaving, reciprocating with each other as the individual reaches out to life, is enveloped by circumstance, and forges character" (p. 7).

Following their own advice, Berkeley professors Jack Block and Jeanne Block began a longitudinal study of children in 1968 that is still going on. They collected various types of data—life data (like school information), observational data (like parents' ratings), test data (formal testing procedures), and self-report data. What have they found across three decades? One interesting finding has been that girls who became depressed by college age tended to have been shy, reserved, oversocialized, and overcontrolled at age seven. Boys who became depressed had been aggressive, unsocialized, and self-aggrandizing in their early years.

Furthermore, boys who were ego-resilient—calm, socially at ease, resourceful, insightful, not anxious—at a young age were still relatively ego-resilient two decades later. But girls' scores on this dimension in childhood were not related to their scores in adolescence. Explaining these sorts of findings is not easy, but they can be addressed by taking into account the various other sorts of data that have been collected. For example, you might anticipate that boys who were aggressive and unsocialized as children later faced a lot of strict disciplining or school failure, which would make them tend toward depression. Girls who were resilient at a young age might weaken as they reach the severe pressures of American adolescence, just as girls are subtly pressured to give up their interests in math and science. The beauty of a comprehensive longitudinal design is that such hypotheses can be tested; for example, we could compare the school records of these boys and girls.

Such an approach is sometimes called the study of personality across the life span or life path. University of Wisconsin psychologist Avshalom Caspi prefers the sociological term **life course approach.** These terms all emphasize that patterns of behavior change as a function of age, culture, social groups, life events, and so on, as well as because of internal drives, motives, abilities, and traits. In fact, these internal aspects unfold or develop in certain ways in certain contexts. Thus, they are very much interactionist. A girl with a weak ego, low self-control, and high drives toward intimacy, sexuality, and expressiveness might develop and behave very differently if she lived in a Muslim family in Saudi Arabia and went to the local girls' school, than if she lived in an agnostic family in California and went to Beverly Hills High.

Caspi and his colleagues, among others, take the idea of a life course even farther, arguing that individuals to some extent *create* their own person–situation interactions by varying how they interpret situations, by eliciting reactions from others, and by seeking out certain situations (e.g., Caspi & Bem, 1990). For example, think of all that may have happened over the years to a very aggressive young boy who grew up in your community. The aggression brings on certain events in certain situations, but it is impossible to know what behaviors will result without understanding the interactions between the person and the situation.

We knew a boy who was very smart and likable in elementary school but had an attention deficit disorder and was something of a class clown. As his teachers increasingly punished him for being disruptive, even somewhat deviant, he began looking for ways to make trouble, and he began to seek out more deviant situations and behaviors. Eventually, he dropped out of college and was arrested for pushing heroin.

Research suggests that neighborhood bullies—youngsters who torment others—actually wind up tormenting themselves by setting in motion a long-term pattern of self-defeating aggression, which creates problems for them in school and at work, in addition to their problems with peers (Huesmann, Eron, & Yarmel, 1987). An interactionist approach understands depression in much the same way: depression can lead to poor social skills and stressful situations, which can alienate others and decrease social support, thereby increasing the severity of the depression (Coyne & Whiffen, 1995).

There is one study of personality and its effects across the full life span. In 1921, the Stanford psychologist Lewis Terman began one of the most comprehensive and best-known studies in psychology. To investigate his theories of intelligence, Terman recruited 1,528 bright California boys and girls, intensively studied their psychosocial and intellectual development, and tracked them into adulthood. More than half of these participants are now dead, and we (your textbook author and colleagues) have gathered their death certificates and coded their dates and causes of death (Friedman et al., 1995). These life-span data provide a unique opportunity to address intriguing questions about the role of personality in physical health and longevity, using a **prospective design**—that is, using early measures to predict later outcomes.

Some of the most interesting findings from this project concern the role played by childhood personality. We all imagine that we can look at children and envision at least a little about their later life, but could childhood personality possibly predict premature mortality decades later? Can we validly speak of a "good little boy"? The most striking discovery in this study is that childhood conscientiousness (or "social dependability") is predictive of longevity. Children, especially boys, who were rated as prudent, conscientious, truthful, and free from vanity (four separate ratings by their parents and teachers, which we averaged) live significantly longer throughout the life span. They are about 30 percent less likely to die in any given year.

This finding that childhood personality predicts survival across the life span raises many fascinating questions concerning causal mechanisms. Why are conscientious, dependable children who live to adulthood more likely to reach old age than their less conscientious peers? Statistical analyses called *sur-*

vival analyses showed that the protective effect of conscientiousness is partly but not primarily linked to a reduction in the risk of injury: Although there is some tendency for the unconscientious boys to grow up to die a violent death, conscientiousness is also protective against early death from cardiovascular disease and cancer. An examination of unhealthy behaviors shows them also to be somewhat relevant as explanatory mechanisms. The unconscientious have less healthy habits, but a significant effect of conscientiousness still remains after controlling for such factors as drinking and smoking. What seems to be the case is that this aspect of childhood personality (unconscientiousness) sets in motion a whole string of adult actions that all lead to shortened life span. These matters are considered further in Chapter 12 on health differences. For now it is important to understand that early personality affects later personality and so can sometimes have very long-term and far-reaching effects, even on how long we will live.

Readiness

The old saying tells us that "you can't teach an old dog new tricks." This is not precisely correct, of course, since people (and dogs) can learn at any age. The adage does, however, capture two important elements of the time dimension of interactionist approaches. First, it is the case that each experience has its effects in the context of previous experiences. For example, a shy young person may be intimidated enough by a pushy salesperson to buy an unwanted item (or go on an unwanted date) the first time she is so pressured. However, the fiftieth time, she is much less likely to succumb ("Get lost, Bud!"), although she may still find the encounter unpleasant. Note that this is a characterization of the environment—it is the "fiftieth time of encountering pressure"—but the characterization only has meaning as it relates to the person experiencing the events. Thus we should not expect personality always to lead to the same behavior in the same situation. After all, people learn from and react to their experiences!

The second key point about time is that we are more affected by certain environments at certain times in our lives. Who is more affected by a very sexy peer—an eight-year-old, an eighteen-year-old, or an eighty-year old? Who can learn a new language more quickly—an immigrant couple in their early forties or their nine- and ten-year-old children? Somewhere around puberty, children lose some of their abilities to learn language. Ironically, this is often precisely the age when our junior high and middle schools begin foreign language instruction.

This leads us into the topic sometimes termed **readiness.** Konrad Lorenz, the famous ethologist (scholar of animal behavior), knew ducks and geese so well that he could induce them to trail him around, thinking he was their mother (Lorenz, 1937). During a certain critical period shortly after hatching, ducklings will "imprint" on their mother, or a clever substitute. If Lorenz walked past the nestlings at just the right time (and if their duck mother had been removed), guess who the young ducks readily adopted as their mother? Similarly, it is well established that our brains and perceptual systems need to interact with the environment to develop properly. For example, if a young animal is kept in total darkness from birth through a young age, its visual system will never develop properly, even if later experiences are normal.

There is evidence that people who face severe stress as children (such as molestation or a contentious parental divorce) are at higher risk for disorders such as depression later in life. There are many reasons why this dysfunction may occur. For example, if they grow up fearing other people, they may have less social contact and fewer sources of social support. But there is also evidence that an early biological predisposition may be created. For example, one study stressed baby rats when they were young and nursing but otherwise let them grow up normally. These rats had much higher levels of stress hormones in their blood when they were later subjected to a stressor (mild foot shock) as adults (Ladd, Owens, & Nemeroff, 1996). People with major depression as adults may be reacting so severely to stress because their nervous systems were impaired by their early experiences.

We can also imagine a more transient readiness, one that may not be biologically based. For example, after a death or divorce, there may be a period during which a person is not psychologically ready to begin a mature new relationship. Although the phenomenon is not well documented, it does seem that relationships that begin "on the rebound" are more often problematic. The effects of our personality may not be understandable unless this time-based situational variable is taken into account.

We can go even further and posit hour-to-hour fluctuations. It is known, for example, that most people are alert in late morning but have a drowsy period after lunch. But these circadian fluctuations vary somewhat from person to person. At which time would a flirtatious gesture, or an aggressive gesture, have its greatest impact on a given person? We would need to know something about both the person and the time. In short, full understanding of person–situation interaction effects should take into account the various changes that occur over both long and short periods of time.

As many personality theorists have pointed out, achieving such a full understanding demands an idiographic developmental approach. That is, the uniqueness of one individual life must be studied over time, using the insights and tools derived from nomothetic studies of many individuals.

Note that interactionist approaches accept the idea that personality has a biological basis, but they do not concede that personality unfolds in an automatic, preprogrammed sequence. Rather, just as personality cannot be understood without a focus on the individual organism, it likewise cannot be understood without a focus on the social environment.

Interactions, Emotions, and Development

Psychologists who have analyzed the interactions of people in small groups have often shown that the types of interactions that occur can be categorized along two basic, independent dimensions: (1) an *affiliation dimension* of warmth and harmony versus rejection and hostility; and (2) an *assertiveness dimension* of dominance and task-orientation versus submission and deference.

Circumplex Model

Personality researchers have found it useful to arrange these dimensions into a circle, or *circumplex model* (Bales, 1958; Freedman, Ossorio, & Coffey, 1951; Plutchik & Conte, 1997). An illustration of a circumplex approach to personality is shown in Figure 10.1.

So, for example, in your group of friends, one person may naturally become the task leader and dominate discussion, while another might strive to promote harmony among members of the group, counteracting the bad feelings instigated by a troublemaker. Someone who is nurturant might be both assertive and harmony-seeking, and so might fall in between. In other words, seeing where a person falls in terms of being cooperative and assertive in ongoing interactions, and why he or she behaves this way, is a useful and simple approach to integrating social and personality psychology.

These sorts of theoretical arrangements are still being explored to see what goes wrong in families or other social groupings (Benjamin, 1996). For example, a scale called the Inventory of Interpersonal Problems measures dis-

Figure 10.1

The Circumplex Model of Personality. This diagram depicts a circumplex (circular) approach to personality, which focuses on its interpersonal, emotional aspects.

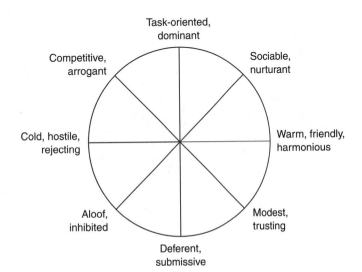

tress arising from the interpersonal problems that people experience (Horo-witz et al., 1988). A nonassertive person may find it hard to be firm or to be self-confident, and a cold, hostile person may find it hard to make friends or to show affection. In other words, these interpersonal approaches to personality concentrate on its social and emotional aspects.

Ego Development

Another interpersonal and longitudinal approach to personality focuses on what is termed **ego development** (Loevinger, 1966). Undeveloped egos are

Famous
Personalities

O. J. Simpson

For over twenty-five years, O. J. Simpson was one of the most striking figures in popular American culture. His was an image built on visibility, suc-cess, and popularity. His rise began at the Univer-sity of Southern California, when Simpson helped set a new world record in the 440-yard relay. Then, as the football team's star running back, he led the Trojans to the national championship and was named All-American. Later Simpson signed a $250,000 contract with Chevrolet and was drafted into the National Football League. After a record-breaking pro football career, Simpson, at age thirty-two, was nudged into retirement by a knee injury.

Simpson's success did not end there, how-ever. Giving smiling endorsements to R. C. Cola, Dingo boots, Tree Sweet orange juice, Schick ra-zors, and Foster Grant sunglasses, as well as yogurt stores, juice bars, and teen wear, Simpson main-tained a high public profile and steadily gained popularity. Simpson then signed on as an an-nouncer for ABC's *Monday Night Football* and as a corporate spokesman for car rental giant Hertz. Topping off his well-known, well-accepted ad campaign image, Simpson also began an acting ca-reer.

Throughout those years, Simpson portrayed the public image of a cheerful, charming "nice guy" who was always ready to give an autograph, make a joke at his own expense, or even visit ter-minally ill children. Simpson's character in the movie *Naked Gun 33¹/₃* summarized the image he projected in real life—a man who was gentle, in-nocent, and compassionate and who believed in justice and the American way. Simpson had be-come so well-known that 90 percent of American women were able to recognize him on sight, a startling statistic for a football player.

But what about O. J. Simpson's private life? If one hadn't studied personality psychology, one might assume that it too would be charmed. But evidence suggests that Simpson was, in his per-sonal sphere, a womanizer and wife-beater. It was reported that during his USC days, Simpson beat three young women whose families were paid to keep the episodes quiet. Right before his thirtieth birthday (and tenth wedding anniversary to Mar-guerite, who was carrying their third child), Simp-son began a relationship with Nicole Brown, an eighteen-year-old blond. After their marriage in 1985, Nicole was seen in public with black eyes masked with heavy make-up. In 1989, at the impulsive, self-protective, or conformist; they tend to be focused on the self and are either manipulative or blindly loyal. But highly developed egos are individualistic (broad-minded), autonomous (self-fulfilled and respectful of others), or "integrated" (Loevinger et al., 1985). (See Famous Personalities.)

This integrated stage corresponds to Maslow's portrait of the self-actualized person. Thus ego development involves a notion of maturing to higher levels. The Washington University Sentence Completion test is a projective measure of level of ego development that endeavors to reach deeper motivations than is possible with an objective, multiple-choice questionnaire. In a sentence-completion test, the subject is prompted with an emotionally loaded

Simpsons' New Year's Eve party, O. J. and Nicole began arguing and during the argument O. J. beat her—kicking her, cutting her lip, and giving her a black eye. Thus, Simpson's private life was in stark contrast to his public image. The adored celebrity, Simpson was privately an adulterer and allegedly involved in domestic violence. How could these two extremes—Mr. Nice Guy and Mr. Aggressive Macho—be part of the same personality?

These inconsistencies in personality are explained by the person–situation interactionist perspective of personality, which incorporates the influences of the social situation as an aspect of personality. For example, Harry Stack Sullivan might explain Simpson's "changes" in personality as consequences of his relations with others in different situations. Because of the social self, Simpson's varying personality manifestations are seen as an effect of the different social situations he encountered—one before his public audience, the other hidden from the public eye. Remarking on one occasion that cultivating an alternate personality for the sake of a good image was nothing shameful, Simpson was aware that this duality was a necessity of his career, and he applied it and enjoyed it.

In personal situations with women, Simpson did not have to maintain his Mr. Personality image. When with these women, he could respond to the themes of high ambition, self-centeredness, and violence that he had established earlier in his life. He had probably learned that he could get away with mistreating women because of his other successes. Indeed, even Nicole had written that he would kill her and get away with it because "he's O. J."

Given these contrasting aspects of Simpson's image, a huge controversy arose when he was charged with the brutal murders of Nicole and her friend Ron Goldman. Those who knew him through his public image found it hard to believe that such a friendly guy could commit such a violent crime. For those who were close to Nicole (and knew of their private life), it was incredible that O. J. was acquitted. However, he was found liable for the deaths in a civil trial. In this so-called trial-of-the-century defendant, personality psychologists had another example of how people may express their personalities in strikingly different ways in different situations.

phrase like "Regarding my family, . . ." and completes the sentence. A self-protective, conformist answer completion like "I think my family's the best in the neighborhood" is a sign of immaturity; but a complex, nuanced response like "I know that my parents had their weaknesses but I have come to resolve our conflicts by recognizing my own fears of sharing those weaknesses" is an indication of a mature ego.

Just as Henry Murray and Harry Stack Sullivan assumed, Jane Loevinger (1997) documents that, in the right circumstances, a psychological maturity in relating to others may develop as one ages. This maturity is characterized by an ability to be a positive leader for others—whether as a nurturant parent, a productive citizen, or a wise political or religious leader.

In the late 1940s, an impulsive man named Millard Wright was desperate to stay out of jail. A dishonest person, he was a thief all his life (*Time*, June 30, 1952). In an attempt to curb his urge to steal, Wright had a prefrontal lobotomy—a surgical operation on his brain. Alas, five years later he was arrested with a house full of stolen goods. It was reported that neither the detectives nor the neurosurgeons were any nearer to knowing what makes an incurable thief. Perhaps today they would instead make use of the sophisticated person–situation interactionist approach to personality to help poor Wright and others who want to understand and alter their behavior. Like Diogenes, who wandered through the streets of ancient Athens searching for an honest man, we are still searching, but we know better where to shine our lantern.

In short, person–situation interactionist approaches endeavor to take into account the many ways personality "is realized in," or "unfolds in," or "interacts with," the situational context. Although we have presented many of the most modern notions about personality in this chapter, it is important to recognize that they derive from and are closely tied to the other seven basic aspects of personality that we consider in this book.

Of course, to some extent, human behavior is unpredictable. In the J. D. Salinger novel *Catcher in the Rye* (1951), the narrator scorns this "psychoanalyst guy they have in there who keeps asking me if I'm going to apply myself when I go back to school in September. It's such a stupid question. I mean, how do you know what you're going to do till you do it?"

Taken together, the eight basic aspects of personality that we have discussed thus far in this book provide a sophisticated understanding of what it means to be a person. For those interested in how these perspectives can be further applied to understanding certain fascinating phenomena of individual differences, we take up four such specialties in the next four chapters of this book—male–female differences, stress and health differences, cultural and ethnic differences, and differences in love and hate.

Evaluating the Perspectives

Advantages and Limits of the Interactionist Approach

■ *Quick Analogy*

Humans as an ongoing dialogue between self and environment.

■ *Advantages*

Emphasizes interpersonal influences.

Can draw on best aspects of other approaches.

Understands that we are different selves in different situations.

Often studies personality across time.

■ *Limits*

Difficult to define situations and to study the many complexities of interactions.

Extreme positions can fail to take into account the complexity of the relationship between personality, behavior, and the situation.

May overlook biological influences.

■ *View of Free Will*

Free will exists but only to a limited degree.

■ *Common Assessment Techniques*

Observation and empirical testing of cross-situational consistency, classifying situations, self-report tests, projective tests, biographical study, longitudinal study.

■ *Implications for Therapy*

Personality can change slowly over time, as you seek out and influence situations and as the situations in turn interact with you. So, for example, if you have a strong orientation toward others and greatly like helping people, you might choose medicine if you want to further develop a biological healing orientation to life; or you might choose the clergy if you want to further develop a theological and philosophical orientation to life; or you might choose clinical or personality psychology if you like the scientific orientation and want to become more like your personality professor.

Summary and Conclusion

How can we talk about personality if people change their behavior from situation to situation? Interactionist approaches to personality explicitly attempt to consider the social situations in which people find themselves or create for themselves. Person–situation interactionist approaches to personality draw on various other perspectives and insights to create a more sensitive yet complex view of patterns of human behavior.

From the late 1930s to the mid 1950s, several converging influences forever changed our notions of personality to be more situational and interactionist. Although coming out of a psychoanalytic tradition, the work of Erik Erikson and especially Harry Stack Sullivan transformed personality psychology. For Sullivan, personality is "the relatively enduring pattern of recurrent interpersonal situations" that characterize a person's life (1953, p. 111). To a personality psychologist like Sullivan who believes in the idea of a social self, we actually become different people in different social situations. In a sense, we may have as many "personalities" as we have "interpersonal situations."

Henry Murray viewed personality as the study of human lives across time, and so he observed and analyzed the interactions of individuals and the situations they encountered during their lives. For Murray, typical combinations of needs and presses are termed thema and might be measured with his Thematic Apperception Test. As a modern proponent of Murray's approach, psychologist Dan McAdams studies the intimacy motive—the need to share oneself with others in intimate ways—in a broad context and across time.

Echoing the 1930s, the psychologist Walter Mischel in the 1960s again stirred up significant interest in interactionist approaches by arguing that a person's behavior varies so much from situation to situation that it simply did not make sense to think in terms of broad personality traits. However, there is no reason to expect that traits or other aspects of personality will be perfect, straightforward predictors of behavior. Personality is complicated, and Mischel's criticisms helped personality theorists become more sophisticated in their thinking about personality. Mischel also criticized the size of the simple relations between personality and behavior, but it turns out that situations do no better job than traits in predicting behavior. Plus, a correlation of 0.30 in this domain is actually quite important and meaningful.

Research suggests that although biases do sometimes cause us to overattribute to personality and overemphasize its importance, there is good reason, converging from multiple sources, to believe that some aspects of our inference about personality are quite valid. So, many new factors are now taken into account. Sometimes the situation is so strong that it overrides our inclinations. Sometimes we can classify situations or focus directly on how each individual evaluates, interprets, and reacts to the different situations he or she encounters. Or, the social self can be found to be more prominent in certain people, or at certain times, or in certain situations.

Some people may be less motivated to conform to social demands and may even prefer to be unique and uninhibited. Such people have a less "social" and a more "personal" personality. A full and sophisticated understanding of personality should take such motivation and preferences into account.

Sometimes personality elicits and provokes certain behavior in others, and in some cases that consistency of response results in part from our own active, conscious efforts. We may seek and elicit confirming feedback from others. And we are more affected by certain environments at certain times in our lives. But, alas, to some extent, human behavior is unpredictable.

Although an "honest" personality who is always honest or a "cheating" personality who is always dishonest has not been found, psychologists today have a much clearer understanding of the consistencies (and inconsistencies) in people's lives and the forces that maintain them. When all the relevant knowledge is taken into account, there is no reason to be disappointed or even surprised that a highly extroverted person may be sitting silently, avoiding a party; or that a highly neurotic person is sitting in a composed, poised manner, calmly comforting a child; or that there are few if any people who will always be perfectly honest. Personality psychology has provided and continues to provide important insights about the complexities of what it means to be a person.

Key Theorists

Harry Stack Sullivan
Henry Murray
Walter Mischel
Mark Snyder

Jack and Jeanne Block
Avshalom Caspi
Konrad Lorenz

Key Concepts

chumship
interpersonal theory of psychiatry
social self
illusion of individuality
personological system
needs
environmental press
thema
Thematic Apperception Test
delay of gratification
contemporaneous causation

personal strategies
behavioral signatures
implicit personality theory
"personality" of situations
attribution theories
self-monitoring
social identity versus personal identity
longitudinal study
readiness
life course approach
circumplex model

Suggested Readings

de Rivera, J. (Ed.) (1976). *Field theory as human-science: Contributions of Lewin's Berlin group.* New York: Gardner Press.

Funder, D. C. (1983). The "consistency" controversy and the accuracy of personality judgments. *Journal of Personality, 48,* 473–493.

Funder, D. C., & Ozer, D. J. (1983). Behavior as a function of the situation. *Journal of Personality and Social Psychology, 44,* 107–112.

Kenrick, D. T., & Funder, D. C. (1988). Profiting from controversy: Lessons from the person–situation debate. *American Psychologist, 43,* 23–34.

McAdams, D. P. (1988). Biography, narrative, and lives: An introduction. *Journal of Personality, 56,* 1–18.

Mischel, W. (1968). *Personality and assessment.* New York: Wiley.

Mischel, W. (1977). On the future of personality assessment. *American Psychologist, 32,* 246–254.

Mischel, W. (1990). Personality dispositions visited and revisited: A view after three decades. In L. A. Pervin (Ed.), *Handbook of personality: Theory and research.* New York: Guilford Press.

Ross, L., & Nisbett, R. E. (1991). *The person and the situation: Perspectives of social psychology.* New York: McGraw-Hill.

Male–Female Differences

John and Carol are sitting in his car after their third date. His thoughts race from one topic to another—I'm really hungry for some pizza. I wonder what Carol's breasts look like. I should wax my car tomorrow.

Carol, also sitting quietly, is studying John's face and thinking—I wonder if John is loyal and mature? Should I continue to date him this month, or should I be spending more time on my term paper? I wonder if he is tender as well as strong.

To what extent are these thoughts of John and Carol a function of their genders? What does it mean to be a man, and what does it mean to be a woman? Is gender the most important aspect of personality?

Common beliefs and stereotypes about males and females are that "Boys are adventurous," "Girls are dependent," "Men are aggressive," and "Women are nurturant." Indeed, these characteristics are commonly ascribed to individuals based primarily on their gender. Are they reasonable and accurate descriptions of personality? Is personality circumscribed by gender-linked personality traits? That is, does being male or female simply predispose or does it strictly limit an individual's personality?

In this chapter, as in all of this third section of this book, we use the tools fashioned in the earlier chapters—that is, the eight basic aspects of personality—to examine in more depth a particular applied topic of individual differences. The following questions are addressed: Are there gender-based psychological differences? What is the etiology (causal origin) of these differences? How do different personality theories explain how these differences emerge and how they are maintained? What research evidence does or does not support the reality of gender-based personality characteristics? Not only do we aim to achieve a more sophisticated understanding of these issues, but we also strive to deepen our understanding of the basics of personality psychology.

Biological differences in male and female genitalia (and the underlying chromosomes) determine one's "sex"—male or female. So traditionally, differences between men and women were studied under the rubric "sex differences." However, most psychologists now more clearly recognize that the complex ways in which people determine what is "male" and what is "female" are far more socially than biologically based, and therefore many prefer to use the term "gender differences."

Masculinity—the qualities generally associated with being a man—and femininity—the qualities generally associated with being a woman—are usually of more interest than "maleness" and "femaleness" per se because they subsume the psychological characteristics of interest (such as boldness, nurturance, and so on). As we will see, both men and women can have both masculine and feminine characteristics, in various ways and for various reasons.

Do Males and Females Differ?

In terms of physical development, there are obvious differences between men and women in average height, external genitalia, breasts, facial hair, and hair growth/baldness patterns. Moreover, there are substantial internal, physiological differences between men and women. For example, men and women have different levels of the hormones that are responsible for a variety of biological features such as fertility.

Although men tend to be physically stronger than women, baby girls and women appear to be constitutionally stronger than boys and men. Male children are more susceptible to a variety of diseases and disabilities than are females, and girls are more neurologically mature than boys at birth and through puberty ((Nicholson, 1993; Parsons, 1980). Women outlive men (see Figure 11.1).

Sigmund Freud declared, "Anatomy is destiny." Are the physical differences between males and females evidence of concomitant psychological gender differences? This is an important question because the fact that men and women differ physically and physiologically often leads to a simple biological justification for all personality differences between men and women. After all, males and females look so different, and have such different sex organs and hormones, that (it is assumed) they must think, act, and feel differently, and for primarily biological reasons. Remember that for Freud, a boy acquires his superego as he resolves the Oedipus complex and recasts the idea of marrying his mother. Girls, already lacking a penis, develop a much weaker conscience. This explanation conveniently fit in with the dominant (male) prejudices of the time, in which Freud and everyone else "knew" that women had a lesser sense of justice and reason than did men. Yet we have seen throughout this book the dangers of such simple biological explanations. For example, although groups such as Europeans, Africans, and Asians differ in appearance, it is a serious mistake simply to ascribe correspondent personality differences to biology; in fact,

Figure 11.1

Projected Life Expectancy at Birth in the United States. As overall life expectancies in the United States have increased, women's life expectancies have remained greater than men's. This female advantage holds true not only in the industrialized West but in virtually all countries, despite high levels of female mortality in childbearing in less-developed regions.
(Data are projections from U.S. Census Bureau.)

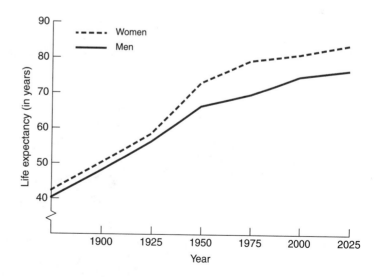

culture and social influence also play a very important part. So too with men and women: the biological differences exist in the context of and are shaped by a complex social world. It is thus challenging and interesting to explore the multiple influences on gender differences in personality.

In a casual, unscientific sense, females are often described (and describe themselves) as emotional, nurturant, submissive, communicative, sociable, poor at math and science, subjective, passive, and suggestible, with a lower sex drive than men. Men are described (and describe themselves) as more rational, independent, aggressive, dominant, objective, achievement-oriented, active, and highly sexed. In a large study conducted in 1972, male and female individuals of a variety of ages were asked to list characteristics and behaviors on which men and women differed (Broverman et al., 1972). Two interesting results stand out: first, most subjects agreed that men and women differed on over forty personality characteristics; and second, both men and women found most "masculine" characteristics to be more desirable than "feminine" characteristics. In other words, whether or not gender discrepancies in personality actually exist, many people perceive significant differences between men's and women's personalities, and these perceptions influence their attitudes about and behaviors toward others, thereby influencing personality. However, studies evaluating the reality (validity) of, and extent (size) of these perceived gender-based personality differences often have not supported the existence of many gender-specific traits. Starting with a comprehensive review of the literature on sex differences conducted in 1974 (Maccoby & Jacklin, 1974), researchers have found that, in many ways, men's and women's traits and behaviors are very similar (Hyde, 1991). That is, there is substantial overlap between the distributions of male and female traits and behaviors.

The women's movement of the 1970s signaled a major shift in women's roles in society. Although full equality in employment has not yet been achieved, we have come a long way since the days when the jobs offered in the Help Wanted ads were separated into Male and Female sections.

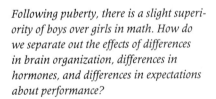

Following puberty, there is a slight superiority of boys over girls in math. How do we separate out the effects of differences in brain organization, differences in hormones, and differences in expectations about performance?

It is interesting to note that this changing perspective on gender differences began at the same time that women gained more rights in society, during the 1970s. That decade saw women being admitted for the first time to many prestigious colleges, gaining equal rights regarding property and marriage, and moving in large numbers into higher-status careers such as medicine, law, and business. As people became less likely to assume that women were inferior, they began finding less evidence of inferiority; and, at the same time, changes in understanding helped bring about these social changes. This is another illustration of the way in which our understanding of personality is partially influenced by our culture and our times, and likewise, how new insights into the nature of personality can also change our culture and our times.

There are a few areas in which reliable gender differences in psychological abilities have been found. In the cognitive domain, boys and men have better spatial abilities, on average, whereas girls and women are more verbally advanced. Girls usually start to talk at a slightly earlier age, tend to have larger vocabularies, and do better in reading through elementary school than boys. Boys do better in tasks and measures of spatial ability from grade school on, and beginning in high school, boys do better in mathematics, although these differences are small (Halpern, 1992).

There is also some evidence for gender differences in the expression of two social characteristics: aggression and communication. Boys and men are more verbally and physically aggressive than females (Eagly, 1987; Hyde, 1986a). Males commit more violent crimes. Females are better at nonverbal communication, more sensitive to nonverbal cues, and more nonverbally expressive than are males (Hall, 1990). Other commonly noted gender differences in personality and behavior, such as dependency, suggestibility, and nurturance, are more difficult to confirm (Eagly, 1995). Men are more likely to take charge in small groups, and women are more likely to be concerned about and involved with child-rearing, but there is considerable overlap, with many men being nurturant and many women being independent. On these matters, there is some evidence supporting a difference but some evidence indicating that this difference is minimal.

A Brief History of Gender Difference in Personality

Evidence from Ancient Civilizations

Archeological excavations of hunting societies that existed four to six thousand years ago have unearthed early portrayals of women—in petroglyphs, hieroglyphs, and burial statuettes—representing essentially "female" characteristics of fertility and nurturance. On the other hand, men were most often represented in prehistoric art either hunting or warring. Some of the earliest Asian religious beliefs dichotomized humanity into a female and male component, *yin* and *yang*. The yin represents the female—passive, shaded, and cold—whereas the yang portrays the male element—active, light, and hot. Leaders and priests were more likely to be male although status differences were not necessarily rigid.

As time went on, ideas about the differences between men and women were formalized into the identification of women as not only different but lesser. For example, Plato described women as weaker and inferior. Aristotle more specifically depicted women as incomplete and incompetent because of their inability to produce semen. Together with the conception of a woman as a deficient man was the view of women as possessing frail personalities—emotional, unprincipled, suggestible, and indecisive. In the Hebrew, and later the Christian Bible, men not only wielded the power but also held the higher moral authority, although women occasionally played important roles. The view of females as incomplete or imperfect males persisted for centuries, and Thomas Aquinas perpetuated this idea, providing a religious rationale for the inferiority of women.

Nineteenth-Century Views

As we have seen, under Darwin's influence, the functional school of psychology (in the late 1800s to the early 1900s) declared that behavior and thought evolve as a result of their functionality for survival. For example, proponents emphasized the issue of maternal instinct, which was defined as "an inborn

The functionalists viewed women's so-called maternal instinct as central to their lives, precluding their development of other pursuits. But pregnancy, childbirth, and lactation are central pursuits for only part of a woman's life.

emotional tendency toward nurturance that was triggered by contact with a helpless infant" (Lips & Colwill, 1978, p. 29). According to the (male) functionalists, most of a woman's energy was to be expended on pregnancy, childbirth, and lactation; as a result women had no remaining resources for developing other abilities. These theorists also explained that the maternal instinct revealed itself in other domains where women nurtured others, such as in their relationships with their spouses and close friends. These concepts were used to both explain and justify the dominant position of men and submissive position of women in the contemporary society. As we have seen throughout this book, many ideas about personality are inextricably bound up with the biases of society.

As we noted in Chapter 3 on psychoanalysis, the first modern, comprehensive theory of personality that addressed the etiology of gender differences was that of Sigmund Freud. Freud declared that the sexual dimorphism in personality (gender difference) arises from the psychological response to physical differences in the genitals. Freud's theory further promoted the conception of woman as a faulty or incomplete man. More modern psychological theories of gender development have used the various modern perspectives, looking for cultural, socialization, cognitive, and social learning explanations of gender differences in personality, in addition to recognizing physiological influences. Some recent theories postulate an interaction of biological and environmental factors that produces the traits we think of as masculine or feminine. (See the Self-Understanding box on page 358.)

Biological Influences on Gender Differences

Sex Hormones in Normal Prenatal Development

Genetic sex is determined at the moment of conception when the female's egg with its X chromosome joins with the male sperm with its X or Y chromosome, resulting in a girl (XX) or a boy (XY). Interestingly, although each embryo has

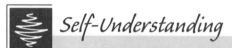

Self-Understanding

Engendering Categorical Realities
or Out of This World?

Should we even bother to study male–female differences in personality? History ("his story"?) suggests that even the most enlightened attempts to conduct research in this area generally wind up being biased by existing cultural assumptions, or they promise an ideal world of gender equality that is based more on hope than science. Perhaps we should simply study individual human beings, in all their complexity and individuality. It is not likely, however, that such a powerful set of categories can be easily eliminated from our theories or our practices; more aspects than we can imagine of our civilization and understanding are built around notions of maleness and femaleness. So, in the meantime, we must be sure to include anthropological, sociological, historical, and political studies in our attempts to understand what it means to be a person (Bohan, 1992; Morawski, 1985).

Yet in thinking about human nature, it has always been fascinating to think about what it means to be masculine and what it means to be feminine. This fascination again appeared in the public eye in 1997 with the publicity surrounding the Heaven's Gate group, which engaged in mass suicide in a mansion near San Diego. (The group intended to leave their bodies so they could rendezvous with a spaceship hiding behind an approaching comet.) Curiously, the members' bodies were found dressed in unisex clothing, with close-cropped hair. (In fact, the first news bulletins erroneously reported that all the victims were male because the women looked very unfeminine.) One of the group's tenets was rejection of sexuality. Although this is odd, it is not uncommon among religious communities (such as priests and nuns).

It was then reported that the group's leader, Marshall Applewhite, was gay but led a double life, marrying and having children. The son of a strict, authoritarian minister, Applewhite (who was a talented stage performer) had always been concerned with extremes of charm, passion, and morality. *Time* magazine reported that Applewhite was imprisoned by his own passions, and the *Washington Post* claimed that it was a crisis of sexuality that launched this strange journey (Balch, 1995; Chua-Eoan, 1997; Daniel, 1997; Fisher & Pressley, 1997). Some of the men in Heaven's Gate had had themselves surgically castrated, which is a fairly extreme way to deal with troubling sexual desires. This case thus has elements of all the personality concepts that have been applied to gender—repressed sexuality, inner conflicts, societal rejection and pressure, biological urges, social roles, social learning, and culture. Although studying masculinity and femininity can be like walking a minefield, it nevertheless seems to be an area that we cannot avoid if we wish to appreciate the full richness of personality.

the physiological structures from which both male and female genitalia can develop, at around six weeks' gestation, testes begin to develop only in embryos with XY chromosomes. The testes begin to produce sex hormones: some progesterone and estrogen (typically considered the "female" hormone) and a larger amount of androgen (typically considered the "male" hormone). The genetically male fetus then develops the internal and external male sex organs (Stockard & Johnson, 1992).

When the embryo has XX sex chromosomes, the gonad buds begin to develop into ovaries at about twelve weeks' gestational age. It appears that in the absence of testes producing large amounts of androgen, female external and internal genitalia develop. Once the gonads (testes or ovaries) develop, the genetic sex (XX or XY chromosomes) apparently has little further influence (Otten, 1985); rather, the hormones become the most critical factor.

Thus, for the male embryo, androgen initiates the development of male genitalia and may influence to some extent the organization of the brain. In addition there is some limited evidence that hormones secreted by the mother, the placenta, and the female fetus's ovaries additionally may influence female development (Otten, 1985). Thus, during this prenatal stage, physiological sex differences that will appear later in life are established by the influence of the hormones. Effects on the brain are poorly understood, but, for example, the prenatal hormones may affect the brain by influencing the manner in which the hypothalamus will regulate the pituitary gland as it controls the secretion of gonadal hormones after puberty (such as in the regulation of menstruation).

The Effects of Prenatal Sex Hormones on Gender Behavior

The fact that androgen affects the physical development of the fetus suggests that prenatal androgen exposure might also affect personality in some gender-specific manner. Two kinds of evidence support the possibility of an effect of prenatal hormones on gender behavior: (1) experimental data from animal studies, and (2) studies of humans who have experienced prenatal genetic or hormonal anomalies.

When researchers expose developing animal fetuses to androgens during early prenatal development, a typical finding is that greater amounts of androgens affect later behavior: such animals have higher levels of rough and tumble play, more aggressive behavior, and higher activity levels. This is true for both genetic males (XY) and genetic females (XX) who are so exposed (Parsons, 1980).

An analogous kind of natural experiment has occurred in humans who experience abnormal prenatal sexual development. Genetic anomalies include mutations in the number of sex chromosomes contained within the embryo's cells. In other cases, the embryo or fetus may fail to be exposed to the appropriate hormones or may be overexposed to inappropriate hormones. For example, now and then individuals are born with too many sex chromosomes, most often of the configurations XXX, XXY, or XYY. XXX people are anatomically female and fertile, whereas XXY and XYY are anatomically male (Stockard & Johnson, 1992). Despite early assumptions to the contrary, there is little evidence that the extra Y sex chromosome (in XYY) has much influence on behavior. Some researchers suggested that individuals with an extra Y chromosome experienced greater quantities of testosterone in their system and that, as a result, they were more aggressive. These individuals were identified in a prison population, however, and it was not determined properly whether or not there was an equivalent (and also unusually aggressive) proportion of XYY males in the non-incarcerated population. This lack of appropriate controls and the fact that XY males in these populations were actually responsible for a larger portion of the more violent crimes such as murder and physical and sexual assault has resulted in the conclusion that there is no greater tendency toward aggression in these XYY males (Lips & Colwill, 1978; Hargreaves & Colley, 1987).

On occasion, a child is born with a single X chromosome, an X0. This anomaly is known as Turner's syndrome. Individuals with Turner's syndrome have female external genitals but no ovaries. Because they are not exposed to androgen, they remain female but are sterile. At puberty, with no ovaries to excrete estrogen, the young women must receive hormone supplements if they are to develop secondary sexual characteristics (Nicholson, 1993; Parsons, 1980). There is some evidence that these girls engage in excessively timid and feminine behavior and may display weaker mathematical and spatial skills (Nicholson, 1993). Such findings have been used to argue that at least certain aspects of feminine behavior have a direct genetic basis.

The development of genetically female or male fetuses may be influenced by irregularities in prenatal hormonal exposure. For example, genetically female embryos may be prenatally exposed to an excess of androgen, possibly the result of defects in the adrenal gland, or because the pregnant mother takes external sources of male hormones. If the influence is more than minor, then these androgenized genetic females are born with either masculine genitals or ambiguous genitalia. In most cases, children with ambiguous genitalia undergo surgery to reconstruct normal female structures. According to parental reports, these androgenized females show more tomboy behavior and are more active than other girls. It is unclear whether these so-called masculine personality traits and behaviors (1) result from the exposure to androgen, (2) are induced by parental expectations for the behavior of daughters who were exposed to male hormones and who were born with ambiguous (or male-like) external genitalia, or (3) result from the girls' own awareness of their hormonal and physical masculinity.

Some young girls prefer the activities of their male peers rather than their female peers. Are their hormone levels and brain structures more "masculine" than those of the typical girl, or have they had different socialization experiences?

In fact, in some cases of androgenized genetic females, the external genitalia look male, and the child's "femaleness" is not detected early. These children are raised as boys and the condition not noticed until puberty when secondary sexual characteristics do not develop. At that time, because these children have experienced an extended period of sexual identification as males, they are given extra male hormones to encourage the development of male secondary sexual characteristics, and may live successful (although sterile, being genetically XX) lives as adult "males." The point is that biological bases of gender are often not as clear-cut as some would like to think.

Overall, although prenatal exposure to sex hormones does seem to influence the development of masculine/feminine behaviors to some extent, the effect of these hormones is small and is affected by the strong influence of both parental expectations and gender socialization. For example, in the 1950s and 1960s, many pregnant women took the hormone diethylstilbestrol (DES) in an attempt to prevent miscarriage. DES, like testosterone, can have a masculinizing influence, and indeed, many of the daughters of these women later developed reproductive problems. However, any behavioral effects that have been found (such as a tendency toward bisexuality) have tended to be weak (Hines & Sandberg, 1996; Meyer-Bahlburg et al., 1995). That is, the nature of the prenatal effects of sex hormones on gender-specific behavior is unclear and complex, requiring further investigation (Jacklin, Wilcox, & Maccoby, 1988).

Genetics and hormones clearly impel the physical manifestation of sex—the development of external and internal genitalia. However, the fact of, and extent of, their connection to differences in personality and behavior between the sexes remains to be demonstrated. As we have seen earlier in this book, it

When a baby is born, the parents announce either "It's a boy!" or "It's a girl!" and most parents try to dress their baby so that its sex is obvious. From the moment of birth, boys and girls are treated differently.

is an oversimplification to assume a simple genetic basis for *any* aspect of personality. Rather, biology sets the stage for the various other key influences on personality.

The Influence of Hormones during and after Puberty

The influence of biological and hormonal factors of course is not limited to the prenatal period. Starting in puberty, there are major differences in the proportions of hormones produced by men versus women, and these hormonal differences may affect personality. In addition, the cyclical versus noncyclical nature of hormonal fluctuation has been implicated in psychological gender differences, particularly for emotionality and mood.

Puberty and menstruation bring a cyclical process of hormonal release in women that has been related to changes in women's feelings and behavior at various times during the (monthly) cycle. At the start of the cycle, the pituitary gland instructs the ovaries to release a large amount of estrogen, which causes rapid growth in the lining of the uterus. Halfway through the cycle, the pituitary releases a hormone that causes ovulation. At that point the amount of estrogen drops, increases on the twentieth day, and decreases again to the end of the cycle (see Figure 11.2). Progesterone levels rise after ovulation; if the egg is fertilized, they remain high, but if it is not, they drop right before menstruation. This is the course of the female hormonal cycle most often considered relevant to personality.

Figure 11.2

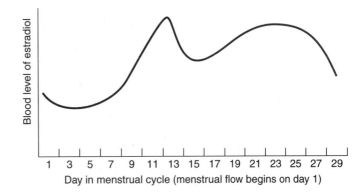

Cyclical Variation in Blood Levels of Estradiol in Females. Estradiol, a form of estrogen, shows a distinctive pattern of variation over the course of the menstrual cycle in premenopausal women.

Blood level of estradiol

Day in menstrual cycle (menstrual flow begins on day 1)

These cyclical oscillations in women's hormones are frequently said to be related to female personality characteristics including mood swings, violence, inability to make decisions, mental illness, and decreases in coordination (Moir & Jessel, 1991; Lips & Colwill, 1978; Nicholson, 1993), among others. The most persistent personality characteristic associated with female hormone cycles is emotionality, or mood swings. In fact, the concept that menstruation results in emotional instability in women is quite old, reported by the early Greek philosophers, among others. The word "hysteria" (uncontrolled outbursts of emotion) derives from the Greek word for uterus. It was thought that women's emotionality was caused by a wandering womb, and hysterectomies were performed as a cure for mental illness, even in modern times. This is a painful example of how ancient prejudices against women sometimes can make their way into modern pseudoscientific theories. A kernel of truth—hormonal fluctuations affecting mood—can be exaggerated by society into a stereotyped myth—feminine weakness and mental instability.

The assumption of psychological gender differences related to this cyclic hormonal activity has been promoted by the fact that men do not seem to experience hormonal fluctuations of this nature. At least, there are no patently visible manifestations of male hormonal cycles, as is menstruation for women. Although some studies that interviewed women about mood fluctuations during hormonal cycling have suggested that women experience more hostility, tenseness, instability, depression, and anxiety during the premenstrual period (rising estrogen) and that self-esteem and confidence are highest during ovulation (Nicholson, 1993; Stockard & Johnson, 1992; Wood-Sherif, 1980), most women do not experience all or even many of these symptoms. The majority of women report one or two at the most. In addition, the populations that have been examined in these studies have most often been clinical (unhealthy) populations, with no control group comparisons. The actual influence of hormonal cycles on personality appears to be quite small in most women. Yet such reasoning has long played a role in keeping women out of politics and denied them advancement in the military and space exploration.

Sex Differences in the Human Brain

Given the possibility that sex hormones may influence the brain, there has been much discussion, and a little study, of the question of whether significant physiological or structural differences distinguish the male from the female brain—and whether these differences imply psychological gender differences. There have been attempts, for example, to uncover the structural brain differences that result in women's better verbal ability and men's superior spatial aptitude. In most cases, verbal activities primarily involve the left hemisphere of the brain, suggesting that there might be structural or functional differences in the laterality of the brains of males and females (Witelson, 1991). The corpus callosum, the bundle of fibers that connects the two brain hemispheres, is relatively larger in women than in men. However, the mechanism by which cerebral specialization might result in a verbal advantage for women and a spatial advantage for men is unclear. Here again we see the temptation to point to simple biological differences to explain differences among people, but the true picture turns out to be very complicated and influenced by many factors. Each person differs in many ways from every other person.

Gender Differences in Personality from the Eight Perspectives

The assumptions we make about differences (or lack of differences) between men and women, and their causes, may lead to various important consequences. For example, if gender differences are seen to be primarily physiolog-

Many religions explicitly exclude women from the formal role of spiritual leader of the community (including Roman Catholicism, Islam, and Orthodox Judaism). Women are seen as inherently unsuited to the demands of providing moral and practical leadership to groups that include men.

ically and biologically determined, then they will tend to be considered permanent, unchangeable, and even morally correct. (Some religions prescribe "divinely ordained" inferior roles for women.) If these differences are seen as learned through reinforcement, they can probably be more readily changed. If they are seen as basic and large rather than as changing and overlapping, then different social roles will be assigned men and women. And so on. That is why this book has focused on understanding eight basic aspects of personality and how each affects the ways we think about what it means to be a person.

The Psychoanalytic Approach

In a sense, the psychoanalytic theory of psychological gender differences is a biological theory. It assumes that differences in a variety of traits including aggression, jealousy, passivity, rationality, and dependency arise from emotional responses to differences in the physical structure of boys and girls. If the basic mechanism by which gender-specific personality traits are attained is that of identification with the same-sex parent (which takes place at the completion of the third psychosexual stage of development at about five years of age), it is clear why Freud equated anatomy with destiny.

Remember that during the phallic stage, the boy presumably develops a strong desire for his mother, and as a result, aspires to replace his father. However, because the father is much larger and more powerful, the boy fears retribution—that is, that Dad will castrate him for desiring Mom. This castration anxiety, according to Freud, has been enhanced by (1) the importance of his penis for pleasure, (2) threats from his parents about masturbation, and (3) the fact that he has noted that girls do not have this valued appendage and therefore must have been castrated already for some devastating misdeed. To deal with this overwhelming anxiety, the boy identifies with his father, thereby taking on his father's personality traits, while additionally being able to possess his mother vicariously through his father's experience. This resolution of the Oedipus crisis results in boys incorporating "male" characteristics into their own personalities, including paternal ethics and mores, resulting in the development of the superego, or conscience.

Females, according to Freud, also begin the phallic period with mother as the strongest love object. Girls discover at this age that they do not have a penis, resulting in penis envy (which is similar to the historical notion of women as incomplete men); and girls are overwhelmed with envy, inferiority, and jealousy. To resolve this crisis, the little girl withdraws her affection from her equally inferior mother, takes on her father as a love object, and replaces her desire for a penis with the desire for a child. Thus the female incorporates the feminine personality characteristics of jealousy, envy, inferiority, nurturance, and dependence. The lack of the extreme anxiety and fear that drive the male's resolution of the Oedipal stage means that women experience a weaker repression of the crisis and, consequently, develop a weaker superego.

The Neo-Analytic Approaches

Erik Erikson provided an alternative explanation, rooted in psychoanalytic notions but shaped by society, for the development of masculine and feminine traits. It was, however, still based on the physical construction of the genitalia. Erikson's conceptualization described male traits such as being active, exploring, warring, and pragmatic, in a sense corresponding to their external, outwardly extended genitals. Little boys build phallic towers out of toy blocks. He portrayed female characteristics such as nurturance, gentleness, and peacefulness coinciding with the internal nature of female genitals. Little girls create refuges and enclosed, secure spaces. Although Erikson also saw the importance of ego factors, here too the relationship between male and female biology and personality is strong. Certainly our society is very concerned with covering up genitalia. Although erections are natural and common, when was the last time you saw an erect penis on television or in a magazine ad?

Karen Horney, in her rejection of these strict Freudian notions, suggested that penis envy was often a minor influence on personality, and in fact males envied the female ability to bear children. She turned the tables and postulated that men's efforts to control and achieve more and more in life result from feelings of inferiority due to this envy. On the other hand, some women have an unconscious fear of vaginal injury from male penetration. Horney also noted the effect of a society that defines women as inferior and severely limits their opportunities, suggesting an interaction of social forces with biological factors. Although Horney brought a new, female perspective to the psychoanalytic view, she still emphasized a strong influence of biological factors (such as the woman's ability to bear children) on personality.

Carl Jung blended the psychoanalytic theory of gender differences with the earlier Asian conceptions of yin and yang, male and female, as each being a part of the complete individual. Jung described two archetypes that represented the maleness and femaleness of humans. The anima is the female component, the feminine inner personality, as present in the unconscious of the male—the "relationship" part of the personality. The animus is the male archetype, the abstract, analytic, logical component. Jung (in contrast to Freud) generally did not attach values to male and female characteristics. Instead, Jung posited the existence of both the anima and the animus in every person and emphasized the importance of recognizing and integrating these and all other aspects of the unconscious when developing a healthy personality. This represented the first discussion of androgyny, the consolidation of both female and male traits, as the most adaptive and most healthy orientation.

The psychoanalytic and neo-analytic approaches dig deeply into the complex conflicts that affect the developing child, whose instincts repeatedly clash with the many demands of society. Many of the answers offered by Freud are clearly sexist, rooted in his historical times and influenced by generations of male political dominance. They have little direct empirical validation. On the other hand, people who have studied psychoanalytic explanations of gender differences are often willing to ruminate in depth about these complex matters. Such ruminations clearly strike a chord with the general public, as seen in the popularity of books like *Men Are from Mars, Women Are from Venus,* which focus on the ways men and women unknowingly (unconsciously) fail to communicate with each other.

Biological/Evolutionary Approaches

The evolutionary explanation for gender differences is based primarily on the argument that successful reproduction requires different sexual behaviors of women and men. According to this theory, it is evolutionarily imperative for men to have as many sexual contacts as possible in order to perpetuate their genes. Men have almost inexhaustible supplies of sperm with which to impregnate and need squander little energy or thought on propagation. Men, however, cannot be 100 percent sure that a given child is theirs. These considerations (or lack of consideration, as the case may be) result in men trying to make as many women pregnant as possible; that is, they have an inherited tendency to engage in numerous sexual contacts with multiple partners (Ehrlichman & Eichenstein, 1992).

Females, on the other hand, having limited eggs and limited child-bearing years, must be more selective in their mating practices so as not to waste eggs and pregnancies on unfit sperm. Furthermore, females must invest nine months in pregnancy and many years in child-raising. It is helpful if they choose a mate who will assist with the child-rearing (Kenrick et al., 1994).

Thus, an evolutionary interpretation provides a rationale for men being more sexually promiscuous and active than women, and for women being more nurturant and more sensitive to men's character. This line of reasoning also has been used to imply that women enjoy sex less than men (so they don't waste precious eggs on haphazard sexual contacts), although women presumably have been selected to want to become pregnant.

Most studies and surveys of American males and females have demonstrated that the average man has more sexual partners than the average woman, although of course the evolutionary psychologists knew this before they constructed their theories! Men do engage in most indicators of sexual activity—including masturbation, heterosexual and homosexual contacts, and casual sex—more often than do women at just about every age (Nicholson, 1993). However, these differences in sexual activity do not necessarily imply a biological or evolutionary explanation; many other factors such as cultural norms and expectations, social learning, and peer influences are known to have an extensive influence on sexual behavior. Because we are unsure of the precise selection pressures on our ancestors, it is very difficult to be sure that certain behaviors proved biologically adaptive.

Animal research provides strong evidence for a biological basis of maternal instinct in subhuman species. For example, when injected with the blood from rats who have recently given birth, female rats exhibit a variety of maternal behaviors such as nest-building and retrieving young. Male rats that are injected with testosterone, on the other hand, also exhibit some maternal behavior toward pups. Thus, although it seems clear that hormones can trigger maternal behavior, it is not just female hormones that account for these effects (Nicholson, 1993). Similarly, after birth, nursing causes female primates (including humans) to produce large quantities of prolactin, the hormone that causes lactation, or milk production. Prolactin has been called the "mothering hormone." However, despite this apparent hormonal influence on mothering, female monkeys are often unable to successfully care for their offspring if they have been deprived of normal opportunities to model and practice maternal behavior. In humans, the biology provides only the core of a more complex cognitive-motivational system (MacDonald, 1995). Despite the biological changes involved with motherhood, maternal "instinct" in primates has a strong learned component. Furthermore, this instinct seems to apply primarily to the nursing of newborns and does not necessarily generalize to a feminine desire to chauffeur children to their piano lessons and soccer games.

Some investigators have looked at the sex hormone testosterone as a correlate and possible direct cause of masculinity and femininity (Dabbs, 1993). The idea is that testosterone levels may be related to aggression, dominance, or achievement. As with other simple biological explanations, there is some indication that hormone levels are relevant, but many other factors must be considered to gain more than a very sketchy picture of the phenomena in question.

The Behaviorist Approach: Social Learning

According to social learning approaches, gender-typed personality charactersistics are attained through the same processes by which other behaviors are learned: reinforcement (operant learning), modeling, conditioning, generalization, vicarious learning, and other such learning processes. According to this perspective, parents, as the primary sources of modeling and reinforcement, serve as primary socializers of sex-typed traits. For example, Jenny's mom chastises her for dirtying her party dress, and compliments her for playing quietly in the corner with her dolls, encouraging passivity and compliance. Even Jenny's dress limits her activity as she must be careful to keep her legs together and not flip cartwheels (Henley, 1977). Alternatively, Peter's father wrestles with him during their play time, rides bikes and go-carts, and Peter and his dad watch the weekend football game, cheering the tackles that immobilize members of the opposing team, promoting more active, aggressive forms of interaction.

In addition, other powerful models, such as peers, teachers, and the mass media, demonstrate vicariously reinforced gender-typed behavior. Arnold Schwarzenegger provides a commanding model of the supermasculine hero, whose positive behaviors bring him extremely attractive rewards; meanwhile, the cute, feminine girls of television sitcoms employ their winsome ways and feminine wiles to accomplish their goals. Among the characteristics of models that most clearly influence children's imitation is similarity of the model to the child (Bandura, 1969). Because gender is such a salient characteristic, boys imitate the traits and behaviors they see in men, whereas girls are more likely to learn to perform like the women they see.

Learning approaches thus tend to see gender differences as both deriving from the society and changeable by society. Many modern American notions—such as the importance of providing proper role models for girls in our society—grow directly out of this social learning perspective. This is an example of why a thorough understanding of personality psychology can help us become more sophisticated in our approaches to many areas of social life and society.

The Cognitive Approach: Gender Schema Theory

Gender schema theory argues that our culture and gender-role socialization provide us with gender schemas—organized mental structures that delineate our understanding of the abilities of, appropriate behaviors of, and appropriate situations for men and women, boys and girls (Bem, 1981).

Gender schemas operate as cognitive filters or lenses through which we process gender-relevant information. For example, the schemas determine which characteristics of a situation will capture our attention, and they restrict which features of a situation we will process. They may thus affect our actions and reactions to situations. That is, these schemas affect our perceptions of others (and ourselves) and assist us in making decisions about our resulting behavior. As children, and later as adults, we use gender schemas to mentally categorize the expected characteristics of our own and the other gender. For example, when in a new doctor's office, the women working in the doctor's office are often assumed to be nurses whereas the men are presumed to be doctors. In a mixed-gender group, medical questions are more likely to be addressed to the males. When we first meet someone (or hear someone calling on the telephone), we immediately want to know if this is a male or female. This category and our corresponding assumptions about masculinity and femininity are a key influence on our resulting perceptions and interactions.

Gender schema theory also predicts that individuals who see themselves as conforming more closely to traditional gender stereotypes will use gender schemas more often to understand both their own behavior and that of others. Highly gender-typed (very masculine or feminine) individuals are more likely to organize their conceptions of themselves and others around the gender schema (Bem, 1974; Hargreaves, 1987) than are individuals who are not as gender-typed. Thus, feminine females (who see themselves as nurturant and dependent) are more likely to support political candidates whose policies promote traditional gender roles.

Gender stereotypes are more likely to be activated in certain situations such as beauty shops and automobile repair shops (Deaux & Major, 1987). Furthermore, a male car salesperson will interact differently with a nineteen-year-old college cheerleader wearing a halter top than he will with a thirty-year-old football player. The cognitive approach to personality thus draws attention to the many aspects of thinking and perceiving and interpreting that are strongly influenced by gender. (See Famous Personalities.)

Famous Personalities

Men and Cars

It has long been assumed that most men have personalities that attract them to automobiles. Most car mechanics, race drivers, car designers, and even auto dealers are men. Try to think of famous people (real or fictional) who are associated with cars. Who is on your list? Henry Ford, Ferdinand Porsche, Karl Benz, James Bond, Evel Knievel, John DeLorean, Batman, Mario Andretti, Al Unser, Richard Petty, Ralph Nader, Mr. Goodwrench, the Michelin man (made of tires), Lee Iacocca. If you are like most people, almost everyone you think of is male.

But as women increasingly earn substantial incomes and achieve career equality, the vast automobile industry is changing rapidly to pitch its appeals to women. Even its magazines are developing new tones. Whereas the typical articles and ads used to assume that men were concerned with auto styling and performance while women merely drove the kids to soccer practice and the beach, times are changing. Consider this clever opening to a story in *Motor Trend* magazine:

> *She wants trucklike security and the bold, go-any-where looks of a sport-utility, but he's looking for a seven- or eight-passenger minivan for hauling the kids and carrying weekend fun or fix-it materials.* (Keebler, 1996)

Although the paragraph refers to the man's hauling fix-it materials like plywood, he will also be hauling kids and driving on weekends; conversely the woman will be attracted by the bold looks of the vehicle. Such changes in societal expectations will have an impact on the personalities of boys and girls now growing up. Girls so inclined will not be laughed out of the field but may very well wind up as leading auto designers.

Trait Approaches to Masculinity and Femininity

Masculinity and femininity have often been considered lasting, internal personality characteristics, or traits. Although many psychologists agree that masculinity and femininity are important traits, few have actually attempted to define these characteristics. Much of the pertinent literature becomes tied up in a tautology that suggests that the traits of masculinity and femininity are composed of the characteristics exhibited by males and females respectively. The issue is further confused by the fact that culturally prescribed social roles sometimes identify different characteristics as masculine or feminine in different cultures.

Masculinity and femininity have historically been considered two opposite poles of a single trait, but there are problems with this conceptualization. The concept of masculinity and femininity as a bipolar continuum fails to explain those individuals who exhibit many masculine *and* many feminine traits or, alternatively, individuals who display few of either. Indeed, statistical analyses of bipolar measures of the masculinity/femininity (M-F) trait have often demonstrated that the traits are multidimensional (Stockard & Johnson, 1992)—a person can be both masculine and feminine. The most frequently used instruments thus now measure masculinity and femininity as separate traits.

Using the Bem Sex Role Inventory, Sandra Bem classified individuals as (1) feminine—that is, high in endorsement of feminine characteristics; (2) masculine—endorsing masculine characteristics more; (3) androgynous—high in both masculine and feminine traits; or (4) undifferentiated—low in both categories. Because individuals encounter many circumstances in life requiring a variety of appropriate responses and behaviors, Bem suggested that the androgynous person would be most functional in a number of situations, being able to nurture, to be assertive, to express appropriate emotionality, while being rational and independent when appropriate (Bem, 1974). However, the findings of empirical studies of the correlation between gender-typing and behavioral flexibility have been inconsistent. In many cases, having the "masculine" traits of independence, agency, self-esteem, and so on is healthier and more adaptive.

Aggression and Dominance

In most (but not all) animal species, males are more dominant and more physically aggressive than are females, and in those species in which females are more aggressive than males, their aggression seems to be primarily limited to protection of their young. Men are routinely considered more violent and assertive than women, little boys more pugnacious than little girls. Males, at least in our and similar societies, tend to occupy the dominant political and economic positions, and their more aggressive natures are often claimed as being at least largely responsible for this power. One of the difficulties, however, with ascribing more aggressive tendencies to one gender has to do with the many ways aggression is defined. Activities as diverse as dominating conversations and taking up weapons in war have been invoked to demonstrate the more aggressive nature of males.

The fact that most wars and violent crimes are perpetrated by men cannot be used as proof that aggression is a masculine personality trait because of the variety of alternative motives that inspire these activities, such as political strategies, history, and economic necessities. Obviously, when women are not allowed to serve as soldiers or recognized as heads of families, we do not need a psychological explanation as to why these roles are filled by men. Women's participation in violent crime and in the armed services has increased in recent years, as social and societal expectations (and laws) have changed.

Not surprisingly, an assortment of experimental and observational studies suggest that when differences in aggression are found, they tend to be in the direction of male aggressiveness, including greater verbal aggression in males than in females. Indeed, when Hyde (1986b) meta-analyzed 143 studies of gender variation in aggression, she found males more aggressive than females, with the largest effect in studies of physical aggression. In addition, Hyde found that the method of the study had an impact on the result, with naturalistic observations resulting in larger gender differences than did experimental studies. Eagly and Steffen (1986) meta-analyzed 63 studies of aggression; they also found male–female differences in aggression and reported that the effect was larger in young compared with adult samples.

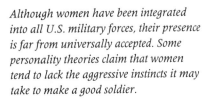

Although women have been integrated into all U.S. military forces, their presence is far from universally accepted. Some personality theories claim that women tend to lack the aggressive instincts it may take to make a good soldier.

Do men have a more dominant personality than women? If aggressive behaviors are defined as dominance, then of course the answer is yes. If, however, leadership qualities, or controlling behaviors, or behaviors that resist control are included in the description, gender differences in dominance pale (Stockard & Johnson, 1991). Because children tend to interact with members of their own gender, dominance in children has primarily been studied in these single-gender groups. In these interactions it is found that boys engage in more behaviors that are commonly thought to establish dominance, including interrupting, commanding and threatening, resisting the requests of others, and so on. Alternatively, girls take turns in conversation, make requests more politely, and agree with one another more often. These findings have also been documented in cross-cultural studies (Whiting & Edwards, 1988).

Do these differences in relationships exemplify a natural, inherent, difference in power? Here again, overly simple biological explanations are sometimes offered. A biological male-to-male link is suggested, one that causes men to stick together in hunting, building, and protecting women and children. Women, on the other hand, supposedly do not have that same biologically based leadership quality. These theories propound a biologically based dominance by males that is imperturbable. But the strict biological explanations of male dominance have failed in the face of increased female participation in leadership roles in business, universities, and politics. In addition, cross-cultural evidence reveals that male dominance in various spheres fluctuates widely. An alternative explanation of the "leadership" qualities of males is provided by Eagly's social role theory (discussed later).

Emotionality

Popular belief, expressed in song and story, often defines women as creatures of emotion, swayed by their excitable and emotional natures. These beliefs are further represented in descriptions (and expectations) of women as subjective and illogical. Men, on the other hand, are expected to be under control—rational, logical, and unemotional. How accurate are these representations? A corollary question is this: Does the actual amount of emotion experienced by males and females differ? Or do men just demonstrate or openly express emotion less often or easily than women? Or, are differences in male and female emotionality simply cultural myths that act as gender schemas, affecting our perceptions of male and female behavior?

Do girls and women cry more than men and boys? Observational studies of babies and preschool children have found that *boys* cry more often as infants, toddlers, and preschoolers. On the other hand, both self-report and observation demonstrate that older girls and women in our society probably do cry more often than older boys and men (Nicholson, 1993). During children's socialization (at least in modern, middle-class U.S. culture), crying is discour-

Do women cry more in public than men because of their hormones or their socialization? The observed differences between cultural groups in the relative levels of male and female crying imply that hormonal differences alone provide an inadequate account.

aged in little boys, whereas tears remain an acceptable means of expressing negative emotion for little girls. However, reports that some women cry more readily during certain points in the menstrual cycle suggest that hormonal levels may be partially responsible for observed sex differences in crying, again suggesting an interaction between social and physiological factors.

Fear is another emotion for which gender differences are often assumed, with women characterized as more fearful than men, but observational research has not upheld these assumptions. Preschool girls are just as adventurous and brave as boys. The tendency for girls to self-report as more fearful and boys as less fearful than observers perceive them to be suggests that all children are socialized to believe that females are more fearful, whereas boys learn early that it is not "manly" to admit to fear. Similarly, as adults, men are less likely to admit to anxiety than are women (and receive fewer prescriptions for tranquilizers, but drink more).

In terms of emotional sensitivity, girls and women are generally more influenced by the emotions of others. For example, baby girls are more likely to start crying when other infants cry. Women do better at interpreting the emotion displayed in photos and are better at expressing emotions so that they are interpretable by others. These findings suggest that women may be more attuned to both their own and others' emotional states.

Achievement Motivation

It is not uncommon for authors to point to the small numbers of women (especially famous ones) in a variety of fields ranging from economics to archeology, from physics to psychology, as a demonstration of females' reduced desire, and ability, to achieve. Are there sex differences in ambition and ability, in the desire and capability for success? A common means of measuring achievement has been by utilizing the construct of achievement motivation as defined by McClelland (McClelland et al., 1953)—the disposition to strive for success. According to performance measured by the projective Thematic Apperception Test (TAT), McClelland and colleagues concluded that women were not as motivated to achieve as men. After all, women do not run the major institutions of society—government, military, corporate, or academic. In addition, some explanations suggest that women's higher need to be accepted and liked disrupts achievement. However, by now it should be clear to you that trait theorists can overgeneralize and overinterpret their data just as much as adherents of the other perspectives can.

It has also been suggested that females get their rewards from other persons whereas males are rewarded by task performance. However, Maccoby and Jacklin's (1974) study of sex differences demonstrated that there were no gender differences in person versus task orientation; in fact, in some studies boys were more sensitive to peer presence than were girls. Another characteristic of women sometimes said to be responsible for their lack of professional success (compared with men) is their "fear of success," but empirical evidence of any such phobia has not appeared. In short, gender differences in occupational and professional success seem to derive from something other than gender differences in personality. Or, as George Eliot put it, "I'm not denyin' the women are foolish: God Almighty made 'em to match the men" (in *Adam Bede*, 1859).

Humanistic Approaches

Abraham Maslow's personality theory minimized the importance of masculine and feminine personality traits, highlighting instead the importance of self-actualization. He noted that both men and women, who had successfully become the best they could be, had a variety of traits in common including empathy and openness (often considered female qualities) and creativity and autonomy (classically male characteristics). Thus, according to Maslow, the self-actualized person has transcended the traditional conceptions of male or female personality.

Maslow noted that people vary on their feelings of dominance, which are related to self-evaluation, and he associated feelings of low dominance with feelings of inferiority, introversion, and suggestibility—characteristics our culture often identifies as feminine. In contrast to psychoanalytic and biological approaches, Maslow hypothesized that it was cultural influences such as norms, education, status, and expectations that connected women to low dominance. In a 1942 study, Maslow found that women who had strong feelings of self-worth were independent, successful, assertive, and healthy, with healthy sexual orientations.

Humanistic approaches to personality are the most willing to assume psychological equality of men and women, as each individual seeks fulfillment. They tend to expect that personality differences between men and women will become smaller as societies give more equal rights and opportunities to women.

Interactionist Approaches: Social and Interpersonal Characteristics

Careful examination reveals that many gender-relevant activities are not based solely on individual traits but rather are also heavily tied to the demands of social situations. Thus the interactionist approach to personality is often most useful in understanding these phenomena.

Helping

Although helping per se is not a personality trait, the nature of the helping situation seems to elicit a concrete manifestation of the individual's personality. Is femininity related to helping? The attribution of a greater degree of communal, nurturant, prosocial behavior to women is quite common. However, the determination of gender differences in helping may be confounded by the *nature* of the help offered, with males helping more when concrete or instrumental assistance is required and with women helping more when emotional or interpersonal support is the need. Finally, much of women's helping behavior may take place in settings that researchers do not traditionally examine, such as the home, and in occupational roles that call for helping, such as secretaries or nurses. Indeed, the research on helping finds men helping more than women, but most studies utilize contrived helping scenarios in which instrumental (task-oriented) help is most often required and that frequently include a perceived element of risk to the helper. These characteristics might be expected to bias the results of the studies toward a greater degree of male helping (Eagly, 1987). Helping situations involving friends or people with whom individuals have close or long-term relationships (in other words, the type of helping in which many women engage) have been generally ignored in research on helping.

Nurturance, Caring

Both anecdotal report and many empirical studies suggest that girls and women are more nurturant and caring than boys and men (Feingold, 1994). Although Maccoby and Jacklin were unable to find enough studies of nurturance in young children to actually determine if there are gender differences, cross-cultural studies (Whiting and Edwards, 1988) indicate that in most societies young girls nurture more than their male counterparts. There is also substantial literature suggesting that older girls and adult women nurture more than do males of corresponding ages (Stockard & Johnson, 1991). However, cross-cultural evidence of societies in which men are primary nurturers casts some doubt on the immutability of a maternal instinct in women.

Sociability

Suggestions that females are more sociable than males seem to have little or no solid empirical basis. Reviews of gender differences have not supported the existence of the following two (stereotypical) gender differences that are often mentioned: proximity seeking (girls do not appear to pursue contact with others any more than boys do) or sensitivity to social situations (Stockard & Johnson, 1991). Although female children are often described as more likely to "attach" themselves to their parents, there is no empirical evidence of differences in attachment behaviors of boys and girls (Lewis, 1987).

Nonverbal Behaviors

Women have been found to have a distinct advantage in both expressing and decoding nonverbal messages. Women are better at understanding (decoding) others' nonverbal behaviors, including facial and body cues, and at recognizing faces. Women are also better at expressing accurate, decipherable nonverbal messages, especially facial cues (Hall, 1990; Eagly, 1987).

In terms of specific social nonverbal behaviors like smiling and gazing, women smile and gaze more than men (Hall & Halberstadt, 1986). However the reasons (that is, the psychological processes) responsible for these differences are still unknown. A host of socialization pressures, different experiences, and situational demands compound any biological predispositions that may exist. There also has been some speculation, and some evidence, that men are more likely to touch members of the opposite sex than are women, perhaps to keep women "in their place" (Henley, 1977; Major, Schmidlin, & Williams, 1990). However, the issue is more complex than it may first appear (Hall, 1990; Hall & Veccia, 1990). We may touch another person for many reasons and in many ways—accidentally, instrumentally, aggressively, fearfully, sexually, to assert dominance, to express affection, to comfort, and so on—and the meaning will also depend on the preexisting relationship and the demands of the particular situation. Here as elsewhere, aspects of personality are complex but can be understood with a careful and patient analysis.

Influenceability

What about the popular belief that women are more susceptible to influence? Is there a gender difference in suggestibility such that females are more easily influenced, conform more readily, and are more easily persuaded to change their beliefs than are males? When Maccoby and Jacklin (1974) reviewed the literature, they found that whereas there were no gender differences in situations in which there was no face-to-face contact with the persuader, in personal encounters women were a little more likely to conform than were men.

Eagly and her colleagues (Eagly, 1978; Eagly & Carly, 1981) examined differences in influenceability and found small to moderate gender differences in studies of persuasion and conformity, with women conforming slightly more than men. However, these effects were confounded by the fact that male researchers tended to find women more conforming than did female researchers, suggesting a sex bias in the results. To further evaluate these findings, Becker (1986) meta-analyzed conformity and persuasion studies. She found similar small to moderate differences in the direction of more female conformity. How can we understand these differences?

Instrumentality versus Expressiveness

Instrumental behavior involves being oriented to objectives that are task-focused and separate from the interpersonal system, whereas **expressive behavior** involves the emotional well-being of one's social or family group. For the most part, women are identified as engaging in more expressive actions, whereas men are more instrumental, although both qualities are expected to exist in all individuals to some degree (Hyde & Linn, 1986). It is important to recognize that both instrumentality and expressiveness require skills and both are useful and beneficial. Being expressive does not imply being emotion-driven and incompetent, nor does instrumentality intimate an utter lack of interpersonal skills.

The social psychologist Alice Eagly has not been satisfied with traditional socialization theories and trait theories. First, she notes that the study of gender differences has focused on biology and on childhood development and socialization rather than examining what actually maintains the differences in adulthood. In addition, Eagly notes that much of the adult research has involved short-term interactions with strangers, a limited situational context that constrains the types of behaviors men and women display (Eagly, 1987). Rather than simply generalizing from these narrow instances, Eagly offers, instead, her theory describing the function of social roles as the determinants of gender differences. According to this theory, "the social behaviors that differ between the sexes are embedded in social roles—in gender roles as well as in many other roles pertaining to work and family life" (Eagly, 1987, p. 9). This is a structural and interactionist explanation of gender differences that emphasizes the fact that members of different groups, such as males and females, often also occupy different social roles that fulfill social needs. That is, men and women tend to occupy social roles (structures), including gender, occupational, and family roles, that elicit different social behaviors from the men and women who enter these roles with caring inclinations.

Eagly thus suggests that the different roles in which men and women find themselves specify behaviors. Roles more often occupied by women, such as family roles of wife and mother, and occupational roles, such as nurse, teacher, and secretary, tend to evoke communal behaviors of relationship-maintenance and caring for others. Roles in which men find themselves more often, such as the family roles of breadwinner and father, and occupational roles of doctor or manager, tend to require agentic qualities of independence and self-reliance (Eagly, 1987).

Gender roles (that is, social roles based on gender) constrain general, broad categories of behavior as individuals respond to their own and others' behavioral expectations. For example, there are strong expectations that men (in our society) will not cry in public; just about everyone agrees that this is expected, and we are aware that everyone agrees. These expectations result in men's conforming to these gender role constraints (by not crying in public), thereby producing the characteristics of the controlled, unemotional "nature" of males. The gender roles also entail beliefs and attitudes about the abilities, activities, and aspirations of members of each gender role, which additionally affect role performance. The broad influence and generality of gender roles result in the elicitation of the behaviors that the gender roles specify in a wide range of circumstances, making these behaviors look like the result of stable, internal gender characteristics or traits (Eagly, 1987).

This analysis has been applied to understanding why men are more likely to be selected for leadership positions. That is, the manner in which social roles influence the social expectations of others was demonstrated in a meta-analysis assessing the evaluations of male and female leaders (Eagly, Makhijani, & Klonsky, 1992). In this review, Eagly and her colleagues found that the evaluation of female leaders was less favorable than that of male leaders in situations calling for a stereotypically masculine leadership style, or when the leadership roles were usually male-dominated. In other words, when women behave in gender appropriate ways—such as leading in a more "communal" manner—they will be evaluated more positively by others; but when women are in masculine-dominated leadership roles, or when they lead in a gender-contradictory style, they are evaluated negatively by others.

A meta-analysis of leadership style did not find differences between males and females in interpersonal orientation versus task orientation; however, it did find that women leaders were more democratic and less directive than were male leaders (Eagly & Johnson, 1990). In short, Eagly provides an explanation for gender differences that is based on neither biology and evolution nor learning and modeling. Instead differences arise from the different social roles men and women fulfill, and to particular gender roles in particular situations.

The strong influence of social expectations and social comparison on gender-relevant behavior has been further demonstrated by social psychologist Brenda Major and her colleagues. Major's work has emphasized the fact that individuals tend to make in-group (same sex) comparisons when evaluating their behavior. These in-group comparisons are in part responsible for an individual's satisfaction with his or her social roles, even when the roles involve inferior status or compensation. Bylsma and Major (1994) found that because women base their judgments of "entitlement, performance and pay satisfaction" on same-sex, rather than opposite-sex, comparisons, women are more likely to express satisfaction with their status. This is true despite their having a clearly disadvantaged position. That is, women tend to compare themselves to other women, and as a result cross-gender inequities in status and pay are more likely to be ignored.

Cross-Cultural Studies of Gender Differences

Anthropologists and others who have studied the roles of men and women across cultures argue that those gender differences that vary among cultures are produced by the culture through socialization. Indeed, there is evidence from the study of a variety of cultures that many gender characteristics are culturally determined. A full discussion of cultural and ethnic differences in personality is presented in Chapter 13.

When Margaret Mead studied two New Guinea peoples, the Arapesh and the Mundugamor, she reported that whereas male and female Arapesh both displayed what we think of as feminine characteristics such as nurturance, among the Mundugamor both sexes seemed to be characterized by what we think of as masculine traits such as aggressiveness (Mead, 1935). Oakley (1972) described the Bamenda group, among whom women are considered the stronger individuals and are expected to do most of the heavy agricultural labor.

On the other hand, some gender differences are dependably demonstrated in a number of different cultures. For example, Whiting and Edwards (1988) studied children from thirteen different cultures, finding consistent gender differences in nurturant behavior (with girls more nurturant than boys) and "egoistic dominance," defined as trying to control the behavior of others in order to meet their own needs (with boys more egoistically dominant). Of course, socialization of certain behaviors could be consistent throughout a variety of cultures. Nevertheless, these investigators also found no dependable gender differences in several other areas, including dependency, prosocial dominance, and sociability. By now it should be clear that gender effects are not simply biological nor learned nor cultural. A sophisticated understanding requires an integration of various sorts of evidence using various relevant perspectives.

Love and Sexual Behavior

In American society, stereotypes of gender differences in love and in sexual approach and behavior abound. Men are described as dominating women in sexual relationships and as enjoying sex more than women, whereas women are said to give sex to men in exchange for getting what they (women) want in other domains. Women are stereotyped as interested in love, men as interested in sex. Unfortunately for the stereotype, these views have not always been the case. History and literature provide a multitude of opposing stereotypes of female sexuality, with women described as excessively sexual, insatiable, and therefore more likely to be vulnerable to possession by demons or the devil. In many parts of Africa, girls were (and sometimes still are) given clitoridectomies (genital mutilations) in order to interfere with sexual drives viewed as shameful. In fact, the concept of women's lack of sexuality is quite recent, stemming from the Victorian era. The fact that, despite these historical inconsistencies, the conception of men as innately more sexual than women has prevailed (with biological and evolutionary explanations routinely invoked) suggests that we should be especially wary of pseudoscience and distortion when considering these matters.

Culture provides the context in which our sexual behaviors are learned. Thus, gender differences in sexual behavior result from differential socialization for boys and girls, different models to whom they are exposed and to which they attend, and systems that reward boys and girls, women and men, differently for certain sexual behaviors. Gender differences in sexual behavior can also be classically conditioned, and likewise, socially "inappropriate" sexual behaviors may be extinguished. For example, a double standard has long existed in American society whereby married men can dally (cheat with impunity), but women who are promiscuous are seen as whores. Through these processes, boys and men learn to emphasize the physical and superficial aspects of sex, and girls and women learn to focus on the relational, love aspects of sex (Lips & Colwill, 1978). Further, cognitive processes (such as expectations and fantasies derived from mass media like movies) intercede in much sexual response and probably play an important part in gender differences in this behavior.

Many of these cultural stereotypes start with the assumption that men are dominant sexually and that women are submissive, and that men must initiate dating and sexual activity. Men are seen as having a greater sex drive, being more arousable, and being more sexually aggressive than women. Females are expected to be passive, resisting, coy, and less interested in physical arousal. However, when examined empirically, it appears that women and men are about equally sexually arousable, and many women (but few men) can have multiple orgasms. As women have gained more political power, society has grown more concerned about their sexual appetites.

Although sexual behavior is very similar for males and females before puberty, adolescence can change everything. Whereas some of the physical changes accompanying female puberty (such as menstruation) are not attended by sexual pleasure, the boy's pubertal manifestations of erections and sexual dreams do draw his attention to the gratification that his genitals can provide. Teenage boys find themselves more focused on their genitals as a

Former Surgeon General of the United States Joycelyn Elders, shown here talking about teen smoking, was hounded out of office when she publicly espoused encouraging teenagers to learn to masturbate. But for many young women, learning to masturbate to orgasm (as teenage boys almost universally do) would lead to more satisfactory sexual relationships later.

source of pleasure. In our culture and many others, boys discuss their genitals and masturbation with their peers more often than girls do (Nicholson, 1993). Girls focus their growing interest in the opposite sex more on romance and love, and they engage in less masturbation than boys. However, female interest in sexual relations may keep increasing into their twenties and thirties.

Since masturbation and sexual experience have been connected to enhanced sexual pleasure, it is not surprising that teenage boys seem to take more interest and pleasure in sexual activity than do girls. However, sex therapy research suggests that as female masturbation loses many of its taboos and is promoted more by society, the teenage differences in pleasure taken in sex will diminish.

Changes in cultural understanding of female sexuality is resulting in a closing of the gap in sexual activity between the sexes. In some subcultures, women are approaching men in the age of first sexual experience and in the number of sexual encounters, both premaritally and extramaritally. Two other aspects of sexuality for which women are now considered to be much more similar to men than previously thought are women's interest in, and arousal by, erotica, and women's fantasies and erotic thoughts. Here again, our simplistic assumptions about the nature of men and women can turn out to be wrong when they are rigorously evaluated from multiple points of view.

Unlike some animals, human sexual behavior is little influenced by hormonal levels or estrous cycles, so interest in orgasm is probably not related to reproduction. (Only about 6 percent of women are more likely to have intercourse in the middle of the menstrual cycle, when conception is likely to take place, indicating a very small effect of estrus on actual sexual behavior [Nicholson, 1993].) And, the physiological research of Masters and Johnson (1966) found that male and female sexual response is far more similar than different. Psychological influences have a much more salient effect on human sexuality than do any hormonal or physiological factors, and so cultural and learning influences come to the fore. People's approaches to love are heavily influenced by the various social and societal forces we have been discussing.

A longitudinal study of Boston-area college students provided some interesting findings on courtship. In opposition to the stereotype, the researchers found that men had more romantic notions than women and more often initiated a relationship with the hope of falling in love. Men were also more likely to "love" more than women in the relationship. When relationships ended, the demise was more likely to have resulted from the woman's misgivings than from the man's, and the men were more devastated (Rubin, 1973).

Summary and Conclusion

One of the oldest philosophical questions concerns the nature of man versus the nature of woman. Personality psychology provides its own answers to this question using psychological theories, observations, and studies. A century of research on this topic has overturned many old stereotypes and prejudices, and has refined many of the relevant issues. One of the refinements has been to understand the multiple influences on masculinity and femininity, and to therefore be less concerned with sweeping generalities about categorical differences. Although there are some striking differences between being a man and being a woman, it is also the case that there is more variation among women and among men than between men and women; the distributions significantly overlap. That is, the personalities of men and women are more similar than they are different.

Because of a combination of biological predispositions and physical differences which are then acted upon by the expectations of others and the strong socialization pressures of society, men tend to develop psychologically masculine traits, behaviors, and abilities, whereas women tend to develop feminine ones. These may then be maintained by adult social roles. In the area of cognitive abilities, men tend to do better on visual and spatial tasks; in contrast, women generally have more advanced verbal abilities. Women are more expressive and more nonverbally sensitive, and they are also more nurturant, while men are more violent and aggressive. Men are more casual in their approach to sexual relations, but women (like men) have strong sexual drives. In addition to these fairly sizable differences, men and women may develop a host of other more masculine and feminine tendencies, depending on their environments and immediate surroundings. For example, in many times and places, men have been more athletic than women, but this difference decreases rapidly when women are allowed to participate in sports and have access to the proper facilities and training. Gender is a key influence on our perceptions of another's personality; we are frustrated when we cannot tell if someone is male or female, masculine or feminine. However, our perceptions and expectations are often incorrect.

Overall, gender differences in personality are generally not innate and unchangeable, but are influenced by a combination of biological tendencies, motives and abilities, social expectations, learning and conditioning, strivings, and situational pressures. That is, gender differences are, in this regard, like other aspects of personality. By understanding the various forces that make one a person, we can understand the forces that make one masculine or feminine. With this knowledge, we become less burdened and deceived by stereotypes or false assumptions.

Key Theorists

Sandra Bem   Brenda Major
Alice Eagly   Margaret Mead

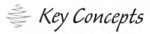

Key Concepts

functionalism   penis envy
maternal instinct   gender schema theory
genetic sex   Bem Sex Role Inventory
Turner's syndrome   androgyny
androgenized females   social roles theory
Oedipus conflict   in-group comparisons
castration anxiety

Suggested Readings

Buss, D. M. (1994). *The evolution of desire: Strategies of human mating.* New York: Basic Books.
Crichton, M. (1994). *Disclosure.* New York: Alfred A. Knopf.
Gray, J. (1992). *Men are from Mars, women are from Venus: A practical guide for improving communication and getting what you want in your relationships.* New York: HarperCollins.
Mead, M. (1935). *Sex and temperament in three primitive societies.* New York: William Morrow.
Shaver, P., & Hendrick, C. (Eds.) (1987). *Sex and gender.* Newbury Park, CA: Sage Publications.

Chapter 12

Stress, Adjustment, and Health Differences

Is it true that worriers get headaches, and repressed women get breast cancer, and Type A men get heart attacks? Are there general cancer-prone personalities and coronary-prone personalities? Are there self-healing personalities who manage to live a long and healthy life? These are some of the most fascinating yet complex questions in personality psychology.

Hard work, constant demands, and intense competition are stressful and unhealthy for some people, yet other people stay healthy and even thrive in demanding situations. These differences in responses are enhanced when there is an existing medical condition. For example, some diabetics show a dangerous increase in blood sugar when stressed, but other diabetics do not (Stabler et al., 1987). Some people seem susceptible to all types of health problems while others rarely get sick. People differ. Even when there is a life-threatening disease, people with similar medical conditions can respond in dramatically different ways to their medical treatment. There is something about certain individuals that protects their health. How is personality relevant?

In the 1940s, Franz Alexander, a leading proponent of psychosomatic medicine, described the cases of two middle-aged women with breast cancer. Two years after their mastectomies, Ginny was dying but Celia was back at her job with new responsibilities. Alexander could not find a biological explanation for the different outcomes—the case histories and tumors had been similar. So, he looked for personality differences. He found that Ginny was ostentatiously brave and repeatedly asserted that she was going to get well, but she seemed unable to face her disease or her feelings about losing her breast. Celia, on the other hand, was neither excessively optimistic nor full of despair. She admitted that losing a breast was hard and tried to find out how she could adjust (Alexander, 1950).

Are such psychological factors possibly relevant to health? A Yale study administered psychological questionnaires to fifty-two women with breast cancer and then followed them for two years (Jensen, 1987). The spread of cancer was greater among women who had a repressed personality, felt hopeless, and seemed unable to express negative emotions. As we will see, there are various reasons why this might be the case.

We have all heard about hard-working executives who drop dead while relatively young—in their forties or fifties. On the other hand, many people of prominence have led very demanding and productive lives well beyond age seventy. For example, Eleanor Roosevelt and Benjamin Franklin made major contributions to world affairs late in life. Could it be that this commitment to a better world was relevant to their health? Katherine Hepburn, Vladimir Horowitz, Pablo Casals, and many other artists have acted, played, and painted well into old age. Not only could such performers continue working late in life, but they retained that joyful enthusiasm that audiences find so appealing. Biologist Jonas Salk, pediatrician Benjamin Spock, anthropologist Margaret Mead, and many other scientists contributed important ideas at an old age. People's capacities do not necessarily decline. Personality and health researchers are providing increasing evidence that those who live to a healthy old age differ in systematic ways from those who die prematurely. The longevity of extraordinary individuals like Katherine Hepburn and

Benjamin Franklin is not in itself scientific proof. However, such personalities provide insights into the findings that emerge from scientific research.

*T*his chapter examines the relations among personality, stress, adjustment, and health. We do so with a critical eye, but also with a fascination about the many intriguing findings that have emerged in recent years. By considering personality in an applied sphere like health, we are following the advice of Kurt Lewin, Gordon Allport, Sigmund Freud, Carl Rogers, and other great theorists that the individual is best understood when studied in a real-world social context. It turns out that not only do we better understand health by studying personality, but we also come to a better understanding of personality by studying health.

Disease-Prone Personalities

Psychosomatic medicine is based on the idea that the *psyche* (mind) affects the *soma* (body). In the 1920s and 1930s, many interesting ideas about psychosomatic medicine grew out of the psychodynamic theorizing of Sigmund Freud. For example, in a classic book of the 1930s, Flanders Dunbar (1955) described a patient named Agnes, an unhappy and unattractive women of fifty plagued with a serious heart condition that her doctors labeled "cause unknown." Agnes went in and out of hospitals until, finally, she died in the hospital on her birthday. Why did she die on her birthday? As Dunbar said, Agnes had always wanted to show her resentment at being born.

Agnes had grown up in a hateful environment, with her mother constantly reminding her that Agnes was a mistake—the mother had never wanted a child. Of course, Dunbar's explanation of Agnes is a classic psychoanalytic interpretation: deep conflict with a parent leading to the symbolism of death on one's birthday. Is this understandable in terms of modern knowledge of personality and health? Can we influence *when* we will die? In fact, there is epidemiological evidence that some women are able to prolong life briefly until they have reached a symbolically meaningful occasion (Phillips, Van Vorhees, & Ruth, 1992). That is, dates of deaths are not randomly distributed.

More difficult than observing such phenomena is *explaining* them using modern scientific understanding. Why and how is personality related to health? There are a number of ways in which personality has been shown to be linked to health. These are illustrated in Figure 12.1 on page 388.

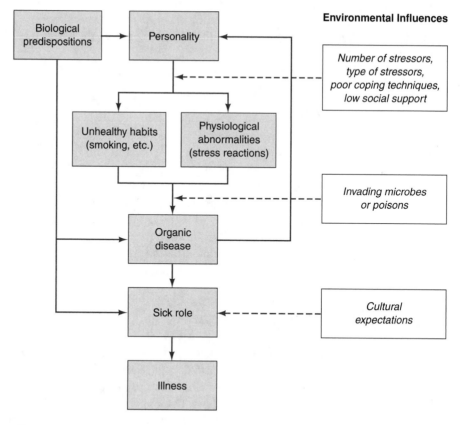

Figure 12.1

Links between Personality and Health. The relationship between personality and health is complex. Major pathways of influence are shown in this diagram.

Health Behaviors

The first major link between personality and health involves health behaviors—what people do. That is, people with certain personalities take greater risks with their health and thus die sooner. However, this connection is not as simple as it sounds.

Anyone could be hit by a car or run off the road by a truck. Sometimes such a tragedy is just bad luck. But who is more likely to wander aimlessly across a busy street—a happy, fulfilled person or a lonely, depressed, preoccupied person? Who is more likely to go out for a late-night drive alone and without wearing a seatbelt? Who is more likely to inject illegal drugs into their veins? It is

Personality can influence the likelihood of engaging in behaviors such as smoking and drinking that have negative consequences for health. Personality thus can be considered a risk factor for disease.

likely that people who are depressed, lonely, angry, or otherwise psychologically disturbed are more likely to put themselves into unhealthy situations. In other words, one very important way that personality affects health is through behaviors that lead to more or less healthy habits and environments.

It is well established that smoking cigarettes and drinking alcohol are related to a number of personality characteristics such as rebelliousness, aggressiveness, alienation, low self-esteem, and impulsivity (Conrad, Flay, & Hill, 1992; Hawkins, Catalano, & Miller, 1992; Tucker et al., 1996). Often, it is personality and social problems in childhood that lead to smoking, other drug abuse, and drinking in adolescence (Chassin et al., 1991a, 1991b; Maddahian, Newcomb, & Bentler, 1986; Webb et al., 1991). These unhealthy behaviors in turn significantly increase the risk of health problems and premature death.

Why are these particular personality characteristics associated with these unhealthy behaviors? There are two sets of reasons. First, people with problems in emotional regulation may seek the stimulating or tranquilizing effects of cigarettes, alcohol, illicit drugs, and even junk food in an attempt to change their physiologically based moods (Wood et al., 1995). For example, if your innate temperament or your early experiences lead your body often to feel sluggish, you may seek out substances such as cigarettes, or situations such as parachuting, that are stimulating. On the other hand, if you are often nervous and fidgety, you may seek out drugs that are tranquilizing.

Second, certain social factors tend to encourage unhealthy behaviors. For example, an alienated, rebellious teenager might seek out a peer group or gang that uses drugs or rides fast motorcycles (Clapper, Martin, & Clifford, 1994). These behaviors in turn lead to disease or trauma. If such an alienated teenager, in contrast, wound up in a religious peer group (even a fringe religious group), he or she might behave more like a divine angel than a Hell's Angel. Furthermore, many unhealthy behaviors that place people at high risk for medical problems are instigated by stress, which is likely to be a special problem for emotionally unstable people.

Risk taking, thrill seeking, and sensation seeking are known to be relatively stable personality characteristics. Psychologist Marvin Zuckerman (1979, 1983a, 1983b) developed a **sensation-seeking scale,** which is related, for example, to a love of travel and active sports. (The instrument has subscales of Thrill and Adventure Seeking, Experience Seeking, Disinhibition, and Boredom Susceptibility.) Is this propensity related to health? One study examined the personality correlates of drivers convicted and not convicted for offenses such as speeding or reckless driving (Furnham & Saipe, 1993). Compared with good drivers, the convicted drivers did indeed score high on sensation seeking (that is, thrill and boredom susceptibility) and high on Eysenck's psychoticism scale (one of the three main traits of Eysenck's theory).

A related approach is Frank H. Farley's **Type T theory** of psychobiological motives. Type T stands for "Thrill Seeking" (Morehouse, Farley, & Youngquist, 1990). This theory derives from Eysenck's ideas about the physiological basis for introversion and extroversion. (As we have seen, extroverts appear to have a greater need for external stimulation.) It suggests a psychobiological need for stimulation due to an internal arousal deficit. It is argued that if Type T people's needs for stimulation and risk taking can be satisfied by appropriate experiences in appropriate environments, they will be less likely to get into trouble. So, it may be a mistake to forbid thrill seekers from their heart-pounding activities. Rather, it may be better to channel these motives into activities that are safe as well as exciting.

In short, the evidence is strong that one key type of link between personality and health involves health behaviors. Certain types of people, because of their biology and socialization, are more likely to engage in risky behaviors, ranging from cigarette smoking to jumping out of airplanes. These people are prone to disease and premature mortality because of their personality-influenced behavior.

Thrill-seeking Type T personalities may be able to get the stimulation they seek from activities that do not pose serious threats to their safety. Riding a roller coaster, for example, may be a good substitute for truly dangerous pursuits that are also attractive to Type Ts.

The Sick Role

A second key reason for an association between personality and illness comes from society's idea of the **sick role.** Certain people respond to stressful life events by entering the sick role (Mechanic, 1968). The sick role comprises the set of societal expectations about how you should behave when you are not healthy—you should go see a doctor, stay home from work, be uncomfortable, act grumpy or moody, avoid strenuous activity, and so on.

Sometimes, people take on the sick role even though there is no organic (medical) condition that can account for their activities. For example, people under extreme stress or people who are not well adjusted may respond to the pressure of moving to a new job by avoiding this responsibility, losing appetite, oversleeping, being lethargic, staying away from work, and calling in "sick." These actions, or "illness behaviors," may lead to the person being defined as ill. It is not only the classic hypochondriac who is "ill" because of personality more than disease. Rather, many neurotic people retreat to the safety of the sick role when they encounter challenges in their lives. Also, note that in our society it is considerably easier and more socially acceptable for a person to seek medical care from a doctor and to adopt the sick role than it is to seek psychological help for an emotional problem.

As behaviorists like B. F. Skinner would predict, escaping from stressful situations by becoming "sick" is rewarding. You may receive sick pay, days off, sympathy from friends, care from relatives, and so on. The sick role thus exemplifies the behaviorist view that personality can be "located" in the environment.

In addition to the behaviorist explanation, cognitive factors are also quite relevant. When are we more likely to feel pain or decide that our body is not functioning correctly? Symptom perceptions are affected by factors such as a person's attention to bodily sensations and what he or she thinks about the sensations (Pennebaker, 1982; Pennebaker et al., 1977). For example, if people think prolonged fatigue is a symptom of illness, they are much more likely to define themselves as ill when they experience fatigue; others might see fatigue as a normal part of everyday life. In addition, the interpretation of a bodily sensation as a symptom of illness is affected by the person's mood and chronic emotional state. Negative moods such as depression increase the likelihood of defining symptoms as indicative of illness. In fact, it has been suggested that in many cases symptom reporting is better regarded as an indication of neuroticism (anxiety, hostility, and depression) than as a sign of organic disease (Costa & McCrae, 1987b). Many people undergo tests for organic disease (such as cardiac tests for heart disease) when their pain is, in reality, a psychophysiological reaction to stress. The pain is real but there is no underlying organic disease that any physician could find. In short, people with neurotic personalities or low self-esteem may become ill because of the social and cognitive aspects of society's sick role.

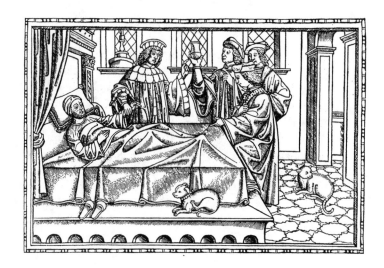

Each society in each historical period has its own well-developed set of behaviors that are associated with illness—the sick role. Regardless of the type of illness, there are certain expectations we share about how an ill person should behave.

Disease-Caused Personality Changes

The third set of reasons for associations between personality and health involves the notion that disease affects personality (rather than personality causing disease). This is sometimes termed a **somatopsychic effect** since the body affects the mind. Disease or genetic predispositions to illness can affect personality. For example, the physical weakness or oxygen deprivation resulting from a serious illness can induce depression. Or, genetic conditions can lead both to organic diseases and personality effects. For example, Down syndrome affects both personality and health (proneness to early Alzheimer's disease). In such cases the links between personality and health are real, not imagined, but health cannot be improved through psychological intervention because both are caused by the underlying third variable (such as genetic make-up or infection).

But Flanders Dunbar did not blame Agnes's illness and death on her birthday on such factors, but rather on personality-induced stress. Dunbar's point about psychosomatics was that such severe childhood stress would inevitably end up "with the outraged emotional system taking its revenge upon the body in the form of a disease which physicians will be able to recognize but not cure" (1955, p. 10). We now turn to this fourth and most fascinating type of link between personality and health.

Diathesis–Stress

Different things are stressful for different people. Some people hate having to stand up in front of an audience; others go crazy sitting at a desk all day; and still others dread travel, dogs, exams, or even sex. Interestingly, most people know these things about themselves. Sir Francis Bacon, in the year 1625, put it this way: "A man's own observation, what he finds good of and what he finds hurt of, is the best physic to preserve health."

In the late 1940s, a number of medical students at Johns Hopkins University were studied in terms of their biological and psychological characteristics. The students were categorized as either slow and solid (wary, self-reliant), rapid and facile (cool, clever), or irregular and uneven (moody, demanding). They were then followed for thirty years. During this time, about half of them developed some serious health problem. Most (77 percent) of the previously labeled "irregular and uneven" types developed a serious disorder during these thirty years, but only about a quarter of the rest suffered a major health setback. In a follow-up study on later classes of Hopkins medical students, the "irregular and uneven" temperament types were again much more likely to have disease or to have died (Betz & Thomas, 1979). They seemed constitutionally predisposed to poor health. But the environments in which they grew up were also relevant.

As we will see in Chapter 13 on cultural and ethnic differences in personality, personality has different implications in different places and different cultures. In Japan, there are well-defined social expectations concerning cooperation with the group and polite deference toward others' feelings. A Japanese individual who is loud-mouthed, aggressive, and brusque will face sanctions by the society and will likely feel distressed as a result. He may be labeled "sick" or "crazy" and may indeed become sick. In America or Italy or Israel, the opposite is common. It is the shy, reserved, and deferential individual who is likely to feel unsuccessful and isolated. Such a mismatch between a person and his or her society can be a main source of stress and an important factor in illness.

Health psychologists sometimes refer to a **diathesis–stress model** of disease. **Diathesis** is the predisposition (often hereditary) of the body to a disease or disorder. The predisposition or weakness might come from genetics or upbringing—for example, having weak back muscles. However, the illness (such as chronic back pain) would not materialize unless and until it is elicited from the environment, for example by engaging in an occupation such as farming or construction that strains the back. Or, someone who might be prone to mental illness may in fact have had a previous episode but may not have another bout of mental illness until the environmental conditions are ripe (see Figure 12.2 on page 394). This model of illness has much in common with the idea of personality interacting with the situation, which we discussed in Chapter 10. Thus, studying personality and health also helps us understand better the person–situation interactionist approach to personality.

Stress

Bernard Lown, a well-known Harvard cardiologist, has made many significant contributions to understanding heart disease and treatment. Interestingly, we believe that some of his greatest insights involve psychology—his focus on the

Figure 12.2

The Diathesis–Stress Model.
In the case of bipolar disorder
(manic-depressive illness), the
diathesis–stress model predicts
that the illness will manifest
itself in those individuals
whose genetic make-up predisposes them to bipolar disorder when they experience
highly stressful life events.
(The diagram does not reflect
actual proportions.)

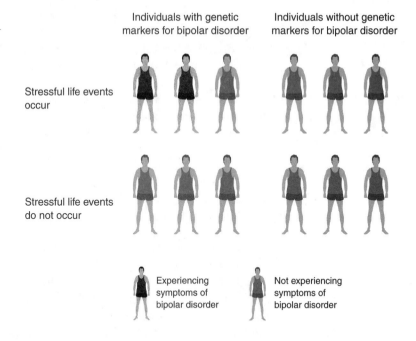

One important large-scale study of personality and health examined two
thousand men, starting in 1958. The men were all employees of the Western
Electric company in Chicago. At that time (late 1950s), some of the men scored

emotional reactions of the individual. Lown has found that the most potent
stress relates to the recall of emotionally charged experiences. Such psychological stress is uniquely individual. For example, one woman did not develop
a heart arrhythmia (technically called a ventricular premature beat, or VPB)
when told that she had advanced malignancy (cancer), but she did show a cardiac arrhythmia when she was asked to discuss her homosexual son (Lown,
1987).

It is known that stress can bring on a heart attack (Kamarck & Jennings,
1991). But why do only some people drop dead from emotional shock? Lown
proposes a three-part model to account for the variability in sudden cardiac
death after encountering stress. First, some electrical instability must already be
present in the heart muscle; this is often the result of partially blocked arteries.
(This is the medical diathesis, or predisposition.) Second, the person must be
feeling a pervasive emotional state such as depression. (This is the psychological diathesis.) Third, there must be a triggering event, such as the loss of
a job or the death of a loved one, with which the person cannot cope. In other
words, as Gordon Allport often argued, we should not expect straightforward
and direct links between personality and health. There is no simple disease-
prone personality. Personality is complicated and does not exist in a vacuum.

One important large-scale study of personality and health examined two
thousand men, starting in 1958. The men were all employees of the Western
Electric company in Chicago. At that time (late 1950s), some of the men scored

high on a measure of depression and poor social relations. That is, they responded to questionnaire items that indicated they were unhappy, sensitive to criticism, felt low self-worth, prone to disturbed sleep, unsociable, and so on. During the following twenty years, these depressed men were more likely than the other men to die of cancer. Importantly, this increased risk remained even after the researchers took into account the men's age, smoking habits, occupation, and family history of cancer. Of course, many depressed men did not develop cancer, but depression was a definite risk factor. In addition, the depressed men were also somewhat more likely to die from noncancer causes than the nondepressed men (Persky, Kempthorne-Rawson, & Shekelle, 1987). Similarly, in the Johns Hopkins Precursors Study, those physicians who seemed to have social and emotional problems were more likely to develop cancer (Shaffer et al., 1987).

Depression and Anxiety

An interesting twist on such findings was provided by a study of lung cancer in 224 men and women. Lung cancer is a relatively easy cancer for personality researchers to study because most victims are dead within a year or two. This particular study followed patients who had been diagnosed only within the past few months. As expected on the basis of biological understanding of lung cancer, most patients had died by the end of one year. As expected on the basis of psychological understanding of disease susceptibility, those patients with a reserved (as opposed to outgoing) personality were more likely to be dead. The twist was that also more likely to die were patients who had a personality that was either much more sober or much more enthusiastic than average (Stavraky et al., 1988). Just as blatant denial seems unhealthy, so too is excessive emotionality.

These studies do not necessarily allow a simple inference that personality causes cancer. In the first place, the associations are quite weak. Many people with emotional disturbances do not get cancer, and many people with cancer do not have unusual personalities. Second, personality is associated with a multitude of behavior patterns, bodily reaction patterns, and social circumstances, any of which may be routes by which cancer is more likely to take hold and progress. On the other hand, this is also true of so-called traditional risk factors. Many of us know a person in his or her sixties who eats fatty foods, smokes cigarettes, is overweight, and never exercises. Why is this person still alive? For unknown reasons, some people beat the odds. Many people who smoke cigarettes do not get lung cancer, and not everyone with lung cancer smoked (or smokes) cigarettes. In other words, for many life-threatening diseases, the risk factors are neither necessary nor sufficient causes. This unsettling state of affairs makes exact prediction impossible, but it does not make associations wrong or not worth knowing. To understand these complex patterns more clearly, we will now consider two examples. First, we examine the idea of a coronary-prone personality. Second, we investigate a longitudinal life-span study of personality and longevity.

Personality and Coronary-Proneness

A century ago, the medical educator Sir William Osler argued that there was a link between personalities always engaged in stressful activity and the development of coronary heart disease. In the 1930s, the well-known psychiatrists Karl and William Menninger (1936) maintained that heart disease is characteristic of those with repressed aggressive tendencies. But such vague propositions could not be systematically and rigorously tested until the 1950s, when two cardiologists, Meyer Friedman and Ray Rosenman (1974), proposed the idea of the **Type A Behavior Pattern.** As one source of their insight, these cardiologists noted that when their upholsterer arrived to repair the chairs in their office waiting room, he noticed that only the front edges of the cushions were worn out. Their patients literally sat on the edges of their seats.

The Type A Behavior Pattern

They proposed that Type A people, who are in a constant struggle to do more and more work in less and less time, would unleash their nervous systems in ways that would damage their hearts through excessive arousal of the sympathetic nervous system. Type As were said to be hasty, impatient, impulsive, hyperalert, potentially hostile, and very tense—a volatile package sometimes summarized as a "workaholic" personality. This idea inspired several decades of intensive research on the idea of a coronary-prone personality.

Choleric Struggle

In terms of the ancient Greek humors discussed by Hippocrates and Galen, the struggle of a Type A person is most likely to be the one of a "choleric," angry against the arbitrary controls of his or her job or life. Such a person will also have generally poor interpersonal relations. It is a bitter person who is coronary prone. But the struggle also may be the internal struggle of a "phlegmatic," apathetic and conforming on the outside but tense and distraught on the inside. Unless examined closely, such phlegmatic people may look fine until they suddenly have a heart attack.

There is now strong evidence that people who lead confrontational, competitive, and driven lives are more likely to suffer heart disease than are people with a more easy-going, laid-back lifestyle. *But it is not hard work, activity, or a challenging job that is the key problem.* Rather it is the struggle that is the problem. Many people are told to slow down, take it easy, take vacations, and even to re-

Figure 12.3

Type A Man.

(© Howard S. Friedman; drawing by Robin Jensen.)

tire from their jobs. In fact, though, there is not a shred of evidence that regular hard work increases the likelihood of heart disease in healthy people. (A different situation, of course, is a patient with an impaired heart whose doctor has advised strict limits on activity.)

Everyone likes to achieve a sense of mastery or competence. Such feelings of control are generally healthy. But people prone to cardiovascular problems (and other diseases) are especially driven to *excessive* achievement and to total mastery of their worlds. This argument was developed by David Glass, one of the first researchers to study seriously the psychological elements of coronary-proneness. In various studies, Glass showed that Type A people worked hard to succeed, refused to feel tired, and were especially likely to react with hostility when frustrated. In other words, their excessive contentiousness and competitiveness can be traced to a desire to maintain control (Glass et al., 1980). These feelings of desire for control are not necessarily bad; they are a key aspect of good health for most people. It is only when they are excessive (Figure 12.3) that there is a problem.

Giving Up

What happens when a person loses all control and "gives up"? This was the lot of many U.S. soldiers who were captured during the Korean War and imprisoned under hopeless circumstances. Soldiers called the phenomenon "give-up-itis." Such POWs were especially likely to die soon in captivity. But give-up-itis sounds amateurish: If you want to achieve scientific respectability for this condition and inspire others to conduct research, you have to develop the idea, cast it into a more conceptual framework, and give it a fancier title. Martin Seligman (1975) did this in his influential "Theory of Learned Helplessness" (which we described briefly in Chapter 7 as part of a cognitive perspective).

The basic idea is a simple one. Imagine a situation in which a person cannot control the outcome, no matter what he or she does. This person might be a child who is totally ignored by her parents, an adult in an unbending job, or a person in a scientific laboratory facing uncontrollable noise. Very often, that individual learns to be helpless. That is, he or she will not make any efforts at controlling his or her surroundings, even when subsequently placed in a controllable environment.

In the early 1940s, a number of healthy young Harvard undergraduates entered a study in which they underwent a physical examination and completed a battery of personality tests. Many of these men were then followed for the next forty years. In light of recent developments in the area of psychology and health, researchers dug the old questionnaires out of a closet and analyzed responses given by the men in 1946. The responses were categorized as indicating either a negative and pessimistic explanatory style or a positive, optimistic outlook. For example, one pessimistic man wrote, "I have symptoms of fear and nervousness . . . similar to those my mother has had." What were the relations to subsequent health? Starting at about age forty-five, a clear difference in the health and longevity of these men emerged. The men with the pessimistic explanatory style were less likely to be alive and healthy (Peterson, Seligman, & Vaillant, 1988).

When the comedian George Burns was eighty years old, he said that he would never retire: "I think the only reason you should retire is if you can find something you enjoy doing more than what you're doing now. I don't see what age has to do with retirement" (1976). Burns was right (and kept working all his life). Sociologists have shown that retirement is healthy for some but not all. If retirement means giving up an interesting daily routine, losing economic status, and moving away from friends, then retirement is likely to be unhealthy (Antonovsky, 1979). In other words, it is an unfortunate oversimplification to think that health will improve when people retire and take it easy. In 1996, George Burns died at the ripe old age of one hundred. Renowned cellist Pablo Casals put his view this way: "To stop, to retire even for a short time, is to begin to die" (Kirk, 1974, p. 504). In short, hard work is not unhealthy, but excessive hostility or excessive depression can be very bad for physical as well as mental health.

Other Diseases

Although the most rigorous research has focused on heart disease, scattered studies during the past fifty years have explored personality and proneness to other diseases, such as ulcers. To place these various studies into a single conceptual framework, a meta-analysis was conducted (Friedman & Booth-Kewley, 1987). **Meta-analysis** is a statistical technique of combining the results of various studies to see what they say when taken together.

Some of the most widespread speculation about health concerns the effects of emotional states on arthritis and asthma. Other attention focuses on headaches and ulcers. Fortunately, there is also a reasonable amount of scientific research on these health problems, and the meta-analysis included them as well. For comparison purposes, coronary heart disease was also included; as we have seen, there is overwhelming evidence that psychosocial factors play a role there. The researchers first examined every relevant study published between 1945 and the mid-1980s, but some of these studies could not be included in statistical analyses. For example, some of the research reports were only case studies in which a clinician reports that the patient's asthma seems to have come from emotional repression. But in total, over one hundred studies were included in the statistical meta-analyses. These studies in turn had included many thousands of people. They contained almost all the relevant published scientific work on the question, "Why are some people more likely to become ill?"

The results revealed associations between various psychological disturbances (like chronic anger or anxiety or depression) and several diseases. In other words, it was not the case that anxiety was related only to ulcers and repression exclusively to asthma. Rather, there was evidence for a generic "disease-prone personality."

Remember again that disease is not necessarily nor solely caused by unhealthy emotional patterns. Some emotionally imbalanced people live long and healthy lives. It is only when the right measures are applied to large numbers of the right people in the right situations that the findings clearly emerge. In order to clarify matters, it is necessary to follow large numbers of people throughout their lives. This was done in the study of the so-called human Termites.

The Human Termites

The psychologist Lewis Terman was one of the leading intelligence researchers of the twentieth century. Among other contributions, he developed the well-known Stanford-Binet IQ test. In 1921, Terman began one of the most comprehensive studies in psychology. To investigate his genetic theories of intelligence, Terman recruited bright California schoolchildren—856 boys and 672 girls—intensively studied their psychosocial and intellectual development, and followed them into adulthood. These clever participants nicknamed themselves Terman's "Termites."

Although, as we have seen, there is little doubt that psychosocial factors play some role in the onset or progression of many chronic diseases and in premature death, there is uncertainty about the nature of the causal pathways. In what ways are aspects of personality related to longevity in general and to heart disease or cancer in particular, across the life span? To address this question in a direct manner, we need to follow people for a lifetime. Obviously, this assignment is impossible for any single researcher, but we have been able to approximate just such a lifetime study, based on the Terman archives. By the 1990s, more than half of Terman's participants have died, and we (your textbook coauthor and colleagues) have gathered their death certificates and coded their dates and causes of death (Friedman et al., 1995).

The Terman Life-Cycle study began in 1921–22, when most of the children were preadolescent (Terman & Oden, 1947). Terman's aim was to secure a reasonably random sample of bright California children, and so most public schools in the San Francisco and Los Angeles areas were searched for bright kids, nominated by their teachers and tested by Terman to have an IQ of at least 135. They have been followed at five- to ten-year intervals ever since. In this remarkable study, only small percentages (less than 10 percent) of participants are unaccounted for. Analyses by Terman's researchers as well as our own comparisons indicate that those lost from the study do not differ systematically from those who remained, so there is not a bias due to dropouts.

The Termites were a bright, well-educated group, integrated into American society, and they maintained regular contact with Stanford University. This eliminates certain problems, or confounds, common to other psychosocial health studies. For example, the Termites could understand medical advice and prescription, had adequate nutrition, and had access to medical care. Explanations of poor health involving poverty, ignorance, or discrimination are generally not applicable to this sample, and so the sample is valuable for focusing on personality. The sample is not, however, representative of the U.S. population as a whole, but it is a good sample of bright, white children who lived during the twentieth century. In the sample, as in the general population, the women significantly outlive the men—in this sample, by about six years longer.

Is there evidence that resilient personalities—high in stability, responsibility, sociability, and optimism—are prone to health, whereas aggressive, excitable, impulsive, or neurotic people are prone to disease and mortality? In 1922, when the average Termite was about eleven years old, Terman collected trait ratings about the participants from their parents and teachers. The scales he used are remarkably modern in their appearance and provide a better assessment than the primitive personality tests that were available at the time. A sample page from one of Terman's scales was illustrated in Chapter 2 (Figure 2.1). It is reasonable to expect that parents and teachers have a good idea of whether an eleven-year-old child is a sociable, popular child, is conscientious, is self-confident, and so on. Howard Friedman and his collaborators constructed six personality dimensions from Terman's scales and used them to predict longevity and cause of death through 1986, using a statistical technique called *survival analysis* (Friedman et al., 1993; Friedman et al., 1995). We will now examine the intriguing findings in some detail.

Conscientiousness

Does childhood personality predict premature mortality decades later? The most striking finding is that childhood social dependability or "conscientiousness" is predictive of longevity. Children, especially boys, who were rated as prudent, conscientious, truthful, and free from vanity (four separate ratings,

In the Terman sample, children who were rated by their parents and teachers as high in conscientiousness lived longer than their less conscientious peers.

which were averaged) live significantly longer throughout the life span. They are about 30 percent less likely to die in any given year. Personality did indeed predict longevity.

This finding that personality predicts survival across the life span raises many fascinating questions concerning causal mechanisms. Why are conscientious, dependable children who live to adulthood more likely to reach old age than their less conscientious peers? Further survival analyses suggest that the protective effect of conscientiousness is not primarily due to a reduction in the risk of injury. How does it operate? Although there is some tendency for the unconscientious to be more likely to die a violent death, conscientiousness is also protective against early death from cardiovascular disease and cancer. Furthermore, a focus on unhealthy behaviors such as smoking and drinking shows them to be somewhat relevant as explanatory mechanisms, but a significant effect of conscientiousness remains after controlling for drinking and for smoking and other aspects of personality. In other words, a person who was conscientious as a child is less likely to suffer an early death from injury, and less likely to engage in unhealthy habits, but also stays healthier and lives longer for other reasons as well.

Sociability

Although some theories of psychosocial factors and health generally predict effects of sociability, this research found no evidence that the personality trait of sociability or other elements of extroversion are strongly related to health and longevity. Rather, the locus of health-relevant effects seems to be centered in such traits as impulsivity, egocentrism, tough-mindedness, and undependability. For example, childhood ratings on such variables as popularity and preference for playing with other people did not predict longevity.

To further explore the lifelong effects of sociability, Friedman followed up on Terman's (1954) study of scientists. Terman had found that the Termites who grew up to be scientists had been much less sociable early in life than the nonscientists. (Only male scientists were studied by Terman.) In fact, Terman considered the differences in sociability to be quite remarkable. We recreated Terman's groups and compared their longevity through 1991. However, our survival analyses found that the scientists did not die sooner. In fact, the scientists tended to live longer (Friedman et al., 1994). So here again, having a very sociable personality did not by itself forecast a long life.

Cheerfulness

Another interesting finding concerned childhood cheerfulness—that is, rated optimism and a sense of humor. Contrary to expectation, we found that childhood cheerfulness is inversely related to longevity. The cheerful kids grew up to be adults who died somewhat sooner.

Puzzled, we have followed up on those Termites rated as cheerful in childhood. We found that they grew up to be more likely to smoke, drink, and take risks, although these habits do not fully explain their increased risk of premature mortality (Martin et al., submitted). It might be the case that cheerfulness is helpful when facing a stress such as surgery, but harmful if it leads one to be careless or carefree throughout one's life (Tennen & Affleck, 1987; Weinstein, 1984). For example, they might say to themselves, "It doesn't matter if I smoke; it won't affect me."

Stressed Termites

In terms of relevant social factors, this project also looked at those children who faced the divorce of their parents. It is well known that divorce of one's parents during childhood can have ill effects on one's future mental health. For example, children of divorce, especially boys, are at greater risk for observable behavior and adjustment problems (Amato & Keith, 1991; Block, Block, & Gjerde, 1986, 1988; Hetherington, 1991; Jellinek & Slovik, 1981; Shaw, Emery, & Tuer, 1993; Zill, Morrison, & Coiro, 1993). Here too the explanations often concern a lack of social dependability or ego control—that is, impulsivity and nonconformity—although neuroticism or low emotional stability are also often implicated. But there had never before been a lifelong prospective study of family stress predictors of mortality and cause of death, although family stress (particularly parental divorce) has been found to predict unhealthy behaviors such as smoking and drug use in adolescence as well as poor psychological adjustment (Amato & Keith, 1991; Block, Block, & Keyes, 1986, 1988; Chassin et al., 1984; Conrad, Flay, & Hill, 1992; Hawkins, Catalano, & Miller, 1992). Would these detrimental effects of parental divorce reach across the life span and affect longevity and cause of death?

Friedman and his colleagues looked at the children whose parents either did or did not divorce before the child reached age 21. Children of divorced parents faced a one-third greater mortality risk than people whose parents remained married at least until the children reached age 21. Among males, for those whose parents divorced while they were children, the predicted median age of death is 76; for those whose parents remained married, the predicted median age of death is 80. For females, the corresponding predicted ages of death are 82 and 86 (Schwartz et al., 1995).

Only 13 percent of the people in the Terman sample had faced divorce of their parents during childhood, a situation different from that faced by children today. Still, in light of the overwhelming evidence from other studies indicating damaging psychological impacts of parental divorce, this finding does provoke serious concern. Death of a parent had very little effect, consistent with other research indicating that parental strife and divorce is a greater influence on subsequent psychopathology than is parental death (Tennant, 1988).

Using the information gathered and coded from the death certificates, we then examined whether divorce of one's parents relates differentially to cause of death. We found that parental divorce is not associated with whether one is more likely to die of cancer or heart disease or other disease. Also, the overall higher mortality risk cannot be explained away by a higher injury rate, although the possibility of an especially increased risk of injury death cannot be ruled out. In addition, personality and parental divorce were shown to be independent predictors of longevity. Figure 12.4 shows the effects of conscientiousness and parental divorce on longevity in males; the effects are analogous for females. It is interesting to note that the size of the combined effect of conscientiousness and parental divorce is equal to the effect of gender on longevity, which is one of the largest known effects on that variable.

Figure 12.4

Personality, Stress, and Longevity in the Terman Sample. Note that the probability of dying by age seventy is greater than .40 (more than 40 percent) for high-risk males, less than .30 for low-risk males, and only about .20 for low-risk females.

(© Howard S. Friedman and Joseph Schwartz.)

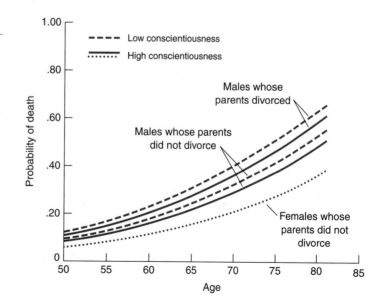

Is the increased mortality risk of children of divorce due in part to these people's own subsequent divorce? People whose parents divorced were indeed more likely to divorce their own partners. Further, individuals who were divorced or remarried reported that their childhoods were significantly more stressful than did those who got and stayed married. In other words, Terman study participants who experienced a marital breakup were more likely to have seen the divorce of their own parents, and they were more likely to report having experienced a stressful home environment as children (such as "marked friction among family members"). Given that parental divorce is associated with one's own future divorce, and that one's divorce is predictive of increased mortality risk, it is indeed the case that one's unstable adult relations "explain" some of the detrimental effect of parental divorce. However, after controlling for one's (adult) divorce, parental divorce during childhood remains a significant predictor of premature mortality, suggesting that it has some additional adverse consequences in adulthood.

Mental Health

What about personality and mental state in adulthood? In 1950 (when they were about forty years old), the Termites were asked about tendencies toward nervousness, anxiety, or nervous breakdown. Based on their responses, on personal conferences with participants and with family members, and on previous related information in the files dating back a decade, Terman's team then categorized each participant on a three-point scale of mental difficulty: satisfactory adjustment, some maladjustment, or serious maladjustment. Almost one-third experienced at least some mental difficulty by this stage. For males, mental difficulty as of 1950 significantly predicted mortality risk through 1991, with unstable males at high risk of premature mortality (Martin et al., 1995).

All in all, undependability, impulsivity, and family instability (parental and one's own divorce) are predictive of premature mortality. It may be the case that such psychosocial factors affect a whole host of health behaviors—drinking and smoking, exercise patterns, diet, use of prophylactics, adherence to medication regimens, avoidance of environmental toxins, and more—which, when put together, may explain a lot of the associations between psychology and longevity.

It is also likely that psychosomatic explanations involving stress often step into play. There are increasingly well-documented associations of stress with both cardiovascular disease mechanisms and effects on the immune system, or psychoneuroimmunology (Baum & Dougall, 1998; Temoshok, 1998). It is thus probable that there are multiple pathways linking personality to longevity.

Although both personality and stress variables have direct (psychosomatic) and behaviorally mediated effects on health, we do not yet know their relative importance. Overall, there is reliable confirmation in the physical health arena of the importance of what psychologists have typically called mental stability or ego strength—dependability, trust, and lack of impulsivity. How large are these effects? These effects are smaller than the influences of gender or smoking on longevity, but they are comparable to common biological risk factors such as systolic blood pressure and serum cholesterol, and to common behavioral risks such as exercise and diet, as they affect all-cause mortality.

Lewis Terman died in 1956, having almost reached age eighty. When he had set out in 1921 to study the simple bases of intelligence and success, he had no idea that his extensive data set would eventually be used to tell us so much about how personality is related to health and longevity across the life span.

Blaming the Victim

The social critic Susan Sontag (1978) has pointed out that tuberculosis (TB) was once thought to be the result of a weak or romantic personality. That is, tuberculosis used to be seen as caused by the character of the afflicted. That viewpoint changed dramatically when the TB-causing tubercle bacillus was discovered. Sontag argues that the same misperception is currently applied to seriously ill patients like cancer patients: they are unfairly blamed for causing their illness.

This (illogical) tendency to blame victims for their own illnesses is strong for two reasons. First of all, most of us have some concrete concerns about our own health and mortality. If our best friend could develop breast cancer, aren't we also vulnerable? It is psychologically more appealing for us to answer no—to assume that we are different from her and that our friend was somehow responsible for her own illness. That way, we distance and protect ourselves from feeling personally threatened. Or, put in religious terms, our friend must have done something bad or wrong to bring on this terrible scourge. The second reason we tend to blame people for their own disease has to do with our desire for a predictable world. We like to believe that if we work hard and take care of ourselves, things will work out reasonably well. But illness arises suddenly and progresses unpredictably. Blaming the victim reestablishes cause-and-effect predictability, and our own world view is safe again.

There is a danger that an undiscerning student will conclude that people with disease have brought it on themselves. Aside from the inhumanity and lack of compassion for suffering people that this view entails, it may lead to further problems and suffering for the victim, as others withdraw financial or emotional support. On the other hand, it is a disservice to both the healthy and the ill to pretend that they can have no effect on their prognosis. It is a big problem that about half of Americans agree with the statement, "There is not much a person can do to prevent cancer." Quite the contrary, there are indeed things that make disease and early death more likely. We must walk this fine line between blaming patients on the one hand and absolving them of any role in their health on the other hand. Cancer and other stigmatized diseases are not punishment for past sin, but just as we know that there are healthful and unhealthful foods to eat and beverages to drink, so too there are healthy and unhealthy personalities.

If there are links between personality and disease, then it makes sense that there are also personalities that tend to stay well. Yet physicians do relatively little to keep people healthy in terms of psychological and social influences. Although there are important exceptions, the medical research establishment (with a conventional medical model of disease) is similarly focused on a single issue: curing disease. This orientation has interfered with proper attention to the question of health maintenance.

The Self-Healing Personality

Mohandas K. Ghandi (also called Mahatma, which means the "Great Soul") was one of the greatest workaholics of all time. He was not sickly even though he spent over 2,300 days in prison and endured numerous self-imposed fasts. On the contrary, he had the personal strength and commitment to be one of the most influential leaders of the twentieth century, perhaps of all time. He pioneered nonviolent political resistance (*satyagrapha*), instituted numerous social reforms, and won political freedom for India. He was assassinated in his seventy-eighth year. What defined Ghandi's life was a commitment to principle. As he aged, he grew more and more content with his life, but he remained humble. He certainly was not blindly optimistic. People who are constructively challenged find it easier to remain healthy.

Although thousands of pages are published each year debating the question, "Why did Ms. X become ill, and how can she be treated?" little is asked about "Why did Ms. Y remain healthy?" Fortunately, personality researchers studying health have drawn much inspiration from the humanistic and existential approaches, which do indeed consider positive aspects (Friedman, 1991).

Control, Commitment, and Challenge

More than a decade ago, an extensive analysis by Salvatore Maddi and Suzanne Ouellette Kobasa (1984) of business executives under stress in a large midwestern firm examined the psychological differences between those who became ill and those who did not. Over a period of eight years, several key factors emerged. First, the executives' feeling of control was a significant factor in terms of health. Those who remained healthier did not feel powerless in the face of external challenges but instead had a sense of power. They tended to believe that challenging situations could be influenced by their personal efforts. For example, an executive named Andy clearly lacked this sense of control. He appeared polite and eager to please despite feeling increasing pressures of job responsibilities. He carefully transmitted job orders from his superiors to his subordinates but exerted little authority himself. He worried that his workload was getting out of control. At home, trouble was developing with his wife and children. Andy developed an ulcer and was on a restricted diet. He experienced sleeplessness, appetite loss, and heart palpitations. Although only in his forties, he had a tendency toward high blood pressure. He lacked the strength of personality to cope with his job stress.

The second characteristic of executives who remained healthy was their commitment to something they felt was important and meaningful. Those individuals who felt committed to their work, their communities, and their families were less likely to become ill. One executive, Bill, was seen as especially successful and healthy, even though his wife had been killed in an accident seven years earlier. He had a twinkle in his eye and a zest for his work. He enjoyed learning from his work, felt its social importance, and welcomed changes in the company as interesting and worthwhile.

Third, executives who remained healthy were those who responded to life with excitement and energy. They welcomed change and innovation while remaining true to the fundamental life goals that they had already established. One of the successful, healthy executives, Chuck, was involved in difficult customer relations work. As his company began reorganizing, Chuck reported feeling more challenge but said that it made his work that much more interesting and exciting. He was not threatened. Chuck is the kind of executive who views every problem as an opportunity to improve on the status quo. Contrary to some pop psychology theories, happy-go-lucky, lackadaisical people are not especially healthy.

Trust and Devotion

These ideas about self-healing have been confirmed by many other sorts of studies, though often indirectly. For example, the personality psychologist Julian Rotter is well known for work on the idea and measurement of *locus of control*. (This concept was dealt with in detail in Chapter 7 on cognitive approaches.) Some people feel pushed around by external forces, whereas other people feel the locus (the location) of control over their lives is within themselves. We have seen that this is relevant to health and coping. Unfortunately, an equally incisive analysis that Rotter (1980) wrote about *trust* has been overlooked by most personality psychologists. In it, Rotter asserts and presents evidence that people who trust others are less likely to be unhappy, conflicted, or maladjusted. They are more dependable and have more friends. They are not necessarily more gullible; they are just less cynical. In brief, they are healthier. This is not a moral judgment; it is merely a summary of the empirical evidence. Trust is a motivation directly relevant to the healing personality.

In 1978, Anatoly (now Natan) Sharansky was convicted of treason in communist Moscow and was sentenced to many years at hard labor. His real crime was that he was a Jewish activist who was trying to emigrate to Israel. At the end of his trial, the outcome of which had been predetermined, Sharansky stood up in court and expressed his faith and determination to be free. Sharansky survived many years in Soviet prison and was eventually permitted to emigrate, in good health. Although few westerners face the challenges Sharansky faced, almost everyone is subject to environmental pressures. Yet many hard workers thrive anyway, even in arduous or hectic circumstances. In precise opposition to what writers about workaholism and the Type A personality often claim, living life to the fullest seems to provide protection from disease. A key element of this healthy style, however, is a commitment to an ideal greater than oneself.

It is useful to think about two major types of self-healing personalities. The first is the more active, zealous type. This includes the busy but confident lawyer, and the hard-working, productive executive. These people actively seek out stimulation, are highly extroverted, and tend to be spontaneous and fun-loving.

The second main type of self-healing personality is the more calm, relaxed type. In American society, it is the image projected by a droll, jocular co-

Famous Personalities

Self-Healing or Doomed?

As an exercise to encourage thinking about self-healing and disease-prone personalities, sort the following public figures into the two personality–health categories, and try to defend your choices based on information from this chapter.

Prince Charles	Whoopi Goldberg	Sean Penn
Cesar Chavez	Tom Hanks	Richard Pryor
Hillary Clinton	Jesse Helms	Dennis Rodman
Curt Cobain	Jesse Jackson	Jerry Seinfeld
Bill Cosby	David Letterman	Donald Trump
Leonardo DiCaprio	Nelson Mandela	Mike Tyson
Albert Einstein	Dennis Miller	Robin Williams
Jodi Foster	Willie Nelson	Oprah Winfrey
Bill Gates	Dolly Parton	Tiger Woods

median such as Bob Hope or Bob Newhart or Chevy Chase—active, alert, involved, and responsive, but calm, philosophical, and bemused. Although these people also enjoy the presence of others, they are more likely to prefer the company of a few close friends. (See the Famous Personalities box.)

These two types of healthy people have different optimal levels of stress. For the second, more reserved and content type of person, it is better to have conflicts resolved and stimulation under control. For the first, more excitement-seeking type of healing personality, a higher level of challenge is healthier; unsolved dilemmas are not a bother for this person. In line with this thinking, research suggests that in similar situations these two types of people have different tendencies toward negative emotions and stress hormones. The low-key, goal-oriented individuals show more distress and greater release of stress hormones when challenges remain unresolved. The more spontaneous and arousal-seeking individuals, on the other hand, are especially likely to be distressed by a lack of stimulation and are threatened only when challenges become overwhelming. Thus, here again we see that blanket health recommendations for the whole population can lead to serious problems. The individual must also be considered.

Helpful Placebos

For several decades of the twentieth century, Harry Hoxsey, a former coal miner, sold a "successful" cure for cancer. Hoxsey's clinics spread to seventeen states as patients testified to the miraculous cures brought on by his potions. Hoxsey's cure for cancer "worked" for some people because it stimulated their bodies' own self-healing systems. The Hoxsey potion was an extraordinary placebo. Unfortunately for Mr. Hoxsey, it did not work on him—the miracle worker succumbed to cancer.

Almost everyone has heard about placebo effects, but few people understand their nature or power. Simply stated, a **placebo** is any intervention that does not have a specific, expected, direct physiological effect on the body. For example, a sugar pill may be compared to a morphine extract for pain control. Because the sugar has no direct pharmacologic action on the nervous system, any effects of the sugar pill on pain are placebo effects. But placebo effects, operating through psychological rather than directly pharmacological mechanisms, are very real; indeed they can be substantial. Self-healing personalities in particular benefit by these effects, and they also benefit from the healthy lifestyles, social relations, habits, and behaviors that often accompany a stable, well-integrated personality.

In sum, it is probably not a coincidence that performers like Katherine Hepburn, Vladimir Horowitz, and Pablo Casals, all successful late in life, also retained that magical spark and joie de vivre that audiences find so appealing. There is increasing evidence that the fulfillment and playfulness are key aspects of the self-healing personality.

The Influence of Humanistic and Existential Aspects on Understanding Self-Healing

As we saw in our discussion of humanistic and existential aspects of personality, the influential humanistic psychologist Carl Rogers was one of the first to call scientific attention to personal growth and fulfillment—the joy of being alive. Rogers saw each person as having an inherent tendency to grow and enhance his or her being (discovering a true self that may be hidden) in order to produce more positive inner feelings. The fully functioning person lives up to his or her potential and completely develops and uses any talents.

Rogers was primarily concerned with psychological health, but we now see that it turns out that his description applies to general, overall health. This is not so surprising because the many patients Rogers saw in therapy were facing major emotional imbalances, which are associated with neuronal and hormonal disruptions. Rogerian therapy involves helping patients to clarify their feelings so that they can integrate their unique life experiences into their self-concept.

An example from our own research is a male heart attack victim who worked very hard at his job but did little more than lie on the couch at home. He was not satisfied with his occupational level, and he would have preferred to live and work in a more relaxed environment. For him, the beginning of the road to recovery came in his recognizing that he was in the wrong line of work and should really be pursuing his love of the outdoors. Once this insight was achieved, his other problems began to resolve. This line of thinking supports the idea that a healing personality is necessarily somewhat different for each individual.

Growth Orientation

Like Rogers, the humanistic psychologist Abraham Maslow also spent a good part of his influential career focused on the positive, growth-oriented aspects of human beings. We saw that Maslow recognized that healthy people first need to achieve balance in their basic biological needs, and then they need to obtain affection and self-respect; finally, he emphasized self-actualization. People with this growth orientation are spontaneous and creative, are good problem solvers, have close relationships to others, and have a playful sense of humor.

As people become more self-actualized, they become more concerned with abstract issues of beauty, justice, and understanding. They develop a sense of humor that is philosophical rather than hostile. They become more independent and may march to the beat of a different drummer. They become more ethical and more concerned with the harmony among members of the human race. These characteristics of the self-healing personality are not merely the opposite of such disease-prone characteristics as suspiciousness, bitter cynicism, despair and depression, or repressed conflicts. Rather, they are positive, meaningful motives, behaviors, and goals in their own right. (See Self-Understanding.)

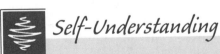

Self-Understanding

Assessing the Self-Healing Personality through Nonverbal Expressive Style

One way to assess personality aspects of health-proneness is to observe a friend and then have a friend observe you for an hour a day for two weeks. Simply count up the number of expressive behaviors that indicate a healthy psychoemotional state, and compare them to those indicating a possible problem. Of course, the following checklist is only a rough guide, but it illustrates the kinds of cues used by experienced clinicians (Chesney, Eagleston, & Rosenman, 1980; Friedman, 1991; Hall, Friedman, & Harris, 1986).

Nonverbal Cues Usually Associated with a Self-Healing Personality

- Calm, well-modulated, even speech
- Even hand gestures directed away from one's body
- Natural smiles; natural enthusiasm
- Open, relaxed body position (when sitting)
- Good mutual gaze with others
- Smooth body movements
- Seems charismatic and optimistic

Nonverbal Cues Usually Associated with a Disease-Prone Personality

- Uneven or accelerating speech; interruptions
- Loud voice with explosive words; too quick to answer
- Sighs, stutters, "ums"
- Clenched fists; clenched teeth
- Touching, scratching, picking one's body
- "Closed" body position of arms and legs (when sitting)
- Fidgeting and shifting; tapping or drumming with fingers
- Shifty-eyed; downcast gaze
- Facial grimaces of anxiety or anger
- Vocal or body gestures of impatience or intolerance
- Over-controlled unexpressiveness; looks repressed or too calm

Identity and Purpose

Talking to victims of serious illness, it is intriguing to note the ways many of them have changed their philosophies of life after their brushes with death. A reasonable expectation is that recognition of the fragility of life might lead to a callous and hedonistic rampage—"I might as well maximize my fun because I won't live forever." In fact, such reactions are rare. For people who make changes (many do not), the direction is almost always toward greater self-fulfillment. Here are some representative comments:

"I try to spend more time with my family."

"I stop to smell the roses."

"I try to see the other guy's side of things."

"I spend more time reading."

"I do volunteer work at the hospital."

"I've taken up painting."

Ironically, many of the illnesses could have been postponed or avoided if these people had made such changes sooner in their lives. Note also that these changes are hard to understand without an appreciation of existential personality psychology.

Remember that Viktor Frankl, the existential philosopher and therapist, developed his theories of a healing personality as a prisoner in a Nazi concentration camp. Although most inmates died, the quickest to go were those who were stripped of their sense of identity and purpose. On the other hand, survival was more likely for those who tried living in a meaningful way, even in dire straits. A person's sense of dignity has more than psychological and ethical importance. It is also an aspect of health. Lack of attention to this crucial factor during medical treatment seems to be what angers cancer patients the most. Much more distressing than the cancer itself is the sense of *being* a "cancer," a "tumor," a "disease." Thousands of writers with cancer, representing millions and millions of cancer sufferers, have pleaded, "Don't talk to my spouse about

Victor Frankl, although an inmate in a Nazi concentration camp, showed that a person's sense of dignity has more than ethical importance—it is also an aspect of health.

me as if I'm not here"; "Don't pretend that everything is OK"; "Don't be afraid to look at me and touch me"; "Treat me as a person, not as a disease." Once a sense of dignity and meaning is gone, the will to live disappears as well.

Sense of Coherence

The medical sociologist Aaron Antonovsky (1979, 1987) has led efforts to shift research attention from matters of disease to matters of health. He has proposed a general theory of how people stay healthy that he calls **salutogenesis.** Central to health, says Antonovsky, is a **sense of coherence**—a person's confidence that the world is understandable, manageable, and meaningful.

According to this approach, the world must not necessarily be controllable but controlled or ordered, in the grand scheme of things. For example, someone with a strong perception that she was carrying out God's purpose might have a high sense of coherence. Antonovsky describes the case of a male survivor of the Nazi holocaust, now living in Israel (Antonovsky, 1987). As a Jewish teenager in Nazi Europe, this individual was quite pessimistic, doubting that he would survive. Yet he had no sense of personal affront or distress. He saw all the Jews in the same sinking ship and carried on with his life as best he could, including participating in resistance efforts. After the war, it seemed natural to him that he would go to Israel and start a new life. This healthy man was hardly an optimist; rather he had a remarkable ability to take extraordinary challenges in stride.

This understanding of meaning and dignity, more common among anthropologists and European thinkers than among American psychologists (who tend to be more ethnocentric), adds an important new twist to our comprehension of health maintenance. For self-healing personalities, life matters. In their own ways, individuals come to a view of life as ordered and clear, rather than as chaotic and inexplicable. In their own ways, they are intact, thriving protagonists, not isolated, alienated drifters. This does not mean that the phenomenon of self-healing should not be investigated with scientific rigor. Rather, as we have said throughout this text, each of the basic approaches to understanding personality provides insight that can prove useful in coming to a full understanding of human personality.

Summary and Conclusion

Much insight into the complexities of personality can be gained by studying an applied area such as stress, illness, and health. By considering personality in an applied sphere such as health, we are following the advice of Kurt Lewin,

Gordon Allport, and other great theorists that the individual is best understood when studied in a real-world social context. Not only do we better understand health by studying personality, but we also better understand personality by studying health.

There are a number of ways in which personality has been shown to be linked to health. One key link between personality and health involves health behaviors. Certain types of people, because of their biology or socialization, are more likely to engage in risky behaviors, ranging from cigarette smoking to sky diving. A second key association between personality and illness comes from society's idea of the sick role and the rewards that it conveys. The third set of associations between personality and health involves disease affecting personality—a somatopsychic effect in which the body affects the mind. The fourth and most fascinating connection between personality and health is the diathesis–stress link.

Diathesis is the predisposition (often hereditary) of the body to a disease or disorder. However, the illness does not surface unless and until it is elicited by the environment. For example, someone might be prone to mental illness, and may have had a previous episode, but may not have another episode of mental illness until the environmental conditions are ripe. This model of illness has much in common with the idea of personality interacting with the situation.

There is now strong evidence that people who lead hostile, competitive, and driven lives are more likely to suffer heart disease than are more easygoing people. But it is not *hard work, activity, or a challenging job* per se that is the key problem. Rather it is the struggle that is the problem. On the other hand, if you are in a situation in which you cannot control the outcome, no matter what you do, you may learn to be helpless, a condition that can lead to depression and ill health. There are associations between various psychological disturbances (like chronic anger or anxiety or depression) and several diseases. In other words, it is not the case that anxiety is related specifically to ulcers and repression solely to asthma. Rather, there is evidence for a generic "disease-prone personality."

The Terman Life-Cycle study, which began in 1921–22, provides a means of seeing the effects of personality on health across the life span. It was found that childhood social dependability, or conscientiousness, is predictive of longevity. Children, especially boys, who were rated as prudent, conscientious, truthful, and free from vanity live significantly longer. A person who was conscientious as a child is less likely to suffer an early death from injury, and less likely to engage in unhealthy habits, but also stays healthier and lives longer for other psychosocial reasons as well.

In studying self-healing, personality researchers have drawn much inspiration from the humanistic and existential approaches, which consider positive aspects of human functioning. There are two major types of self-healing personalities. The first is the more active, "gung-ho" type. This category includes the busy lawyer and the hard-working executive. These people actively seek out stimulation, are highly extroverted, and tend to be spontaneous and fun-loving. The second main type of self-healing personality is the more calm, relaxed type. Both types achieve a balance that is appropriate for themselves. There is increasing evidence that the fulfillment and playfulness of living are key aspects of the self-healing personality.

Key Theorists

Franz Alexander

Flanders Dunbar

Marvin Zuckerman

Frank H. Farley

Bernard Lown

Ray Rosenman and Meyer Friedman

David Glass

Lewis Terman

Aaron Antonovsky

Key Concepts

psychosomatic medicine

sensation-seeking scale

Type T theory

sick role

somatopsychic effect

diathesis–stress model

Type A behavior pattern

Terman Life-Cycle study

self-healing personalities

placebo effects

salutogenesis

sense of coherence

Suggested Readings

Friedman, H. S. (1991). *The self-healing personality: Why some people achieve health and others succumb to illness.* New York: Henry Holt.

Friedman, H. S., & Booth-Kewley, S. (1987). "The disease-prone personality": A meta-analytic view of the construct. *American Psychologist, 42,* 539–555.

Friedman, H. S., Tucker, J. S., Schwartz, J. E., Tomlinson-Keasey, C., Martin, L. R., Wingard, D. L., & Criqui, M. H. (1995). Psychosocial and behavioral predictors of longevity: The aging and death of the "Termites." *American Psychologist, 50,* 69–78.

Friedman, H. S., Tucker, J. S., Tomlinson-Keasey, C., Schwartz, J. E., Wingard, D. L., & Criqui, M. H. (1993). Does childhood personality predict longevity? *Journal of Personality and Social Psychology, 65,* 176–185.

Kobasa, S. C. (1979). Stressful life events, personality, and health: An inquiry into hardiness. *Journal of Personality and Social Psychology, 37*, 1–11.

Payer, L. (1966). *Medicine and culture: Varieties of treatment in the United States, England, West Germany, and France.* New York: Henry Holt.

Pennebaker, J. W. (1990). *Opening up: The healing power of confiding in others.* New York: Morrow.

Chapter 13

Cultural and Ethnic Differences

It is sometimes said that American psychology is the study of white college sophomores and white laboratory rats. This indictment of the failures of some psychologists to reach out to study other cultures and subcultures does not apply directly to personality psychology. Many influential personality theorists were born in Europe and were heavily affected by European culture. Europeans, with their close contact of many different nations and cultures (and their many ethnic wars), have tended to be quite sensitive to cultural influences on personality. For example, Freud thought deeply about the bases of culture, religion, and literature; Jung studied Far Eastern philosophy and mysticism; and Lewin experimented on intergroup relations. So, personality psychology has a rich tradition of cultural awareness, even though such matters are sometimes ignored in modern personality research.

Personality psychologists have been less attentive, however, to cultural and ethnic influences on personality in groups that have been the object of social and economic discrimination, such as Asian Americans, African Americans, and Native Americans. One important exception was Gordon Allport, who wrote extensively about anti-Semitism and about American racial prejudice and discrimination toward African Americans (then referred to as Negroes). Allport believed that the behavior of Americans could not be understood without knowledge of black–white relations in America. But Allport's (1954) insightful work in this area (from the 1950s) has been followed up only infrequently by other personality psychologists, even those who pursue other of Allport's ideas.

There are many reasons for this gap in knowledge about ethnic and cultural aspects of personality. In part it is because laboratory studies do not easily lend themselves to cross-cultural approaches; it is more convenient simply to study college students. It is also the case that American universities do not yet have large numbers of professors who were raised in certain minority group cultures, and so there is a lack of intimate familiarity. A final key source for the narrowness of certain areas of American psychology is simply tradition; that is, most young researchers study what their professors (advisors) have studied, and it can take a long time for nonmainstream orientations such as a cross-cultural emphasis to enter forcefully into the arena of ideas.

*S*ince culture is one key determinant of what it means to be a person, the systematic study of these cultural influences should be, as Allport noted, an essential part of personality psychology. Modern personality psychology should draw on its rich traditions of cultural awareness. These influences are the subject of this chapter.

Layers of Group Influence

The poet John Donne told us that "No man is an island." He meant that the course of everyone's life is related to that of everyone else. Each person is embedded in a complex social system—families, friends, neighbors, communities, and societies.

The most direct and immediate influence on personality development is of course the family, which is why personality theorists give so much attention to the effects of our parents. But we are also heavily influenced by our peers. Harry Stack Sullivan emphasized the importance of "chums," especially around the time of adolescence, and the teen years also are important to forming an ethnic identity (Phinney, 1993). Yet even as adults, the ways we think about ourselves depend on our friends and associates. For example, imagine that we have a cocktail party to which we invite ten lawyers, ten surgeons, and ten psychology professors. Very likely, it would be relatively easy to pick out who is who (perhaps even before they congregate together) on the basis of mannerisms or politics or even shoe styles or other articles of apparel and aspects of appearance! In other words, each social (in this case occupational) grouping influences its members.

Beyond these direct social influences are the pressures of societal institutions. For most people, who they are is influenced by religious upbringing, the educational system, and government and nationality. A person raised in private Catholic schools in Boston is likely to have quite different patterns of responses than a person raised in communist schools in Beijing. These influences go beyond genetic differences and differences in family relations. They are **cultural effects**—the shared behaviors and customs we learn from the institutions in our society.

There are also dramatic differences within each culture that result from the effects of ethnicity and class. Even within the same city, within the same high school, individuals may develop strikingly different reaction patterns as a function of the history of their ethnic group (e.g., cultural traditions) and class (e.g., economic and educational status). For example, in the same Boston classroom, a middle-class African American will often have different experiences than an immigrant Latin American or a wealthy German American. This is not to minimize the fact that all are human beings and all are Americans. Rather, it is important to understand that cultural as well as biological and social influences profoundly shape personality.

History of Research on Personality and Culture

To a fish, the whole world is aquatic because that is the only world a fish can know. A similar problem challenges our knowledge of culture: it is difficult to see the peculiarities of our culture without an outside perspective. Things that seem natural and normal to us can often only be identified as culture-specific through comparison with other cultures. To many Americans, it is unusual and repulsive to eat insects; but to many Africans, insects are tasty but it is unusual and repulsive to eat pigs (ham, bacon). Even complex behaviors are culture-specific. For example, Europeans traditionally recorded their history in books, whereas Africans relied heavily on oral traditions; each method seems odd (and inadequate) to the other culture.

An ancient Olmec figure from Mexico. Culture influences what we find appealing versus ugly, as well as what we regard as acceptable for public display. In American culture, many men buy and enjoy pornography, and that behavior is seen as normal in many segments of our society—but it would generally be seen as deviant to display it on the coffee table or work desk.

All people have a biological sex drive. Yet culture and religion can influence people to refrain from premarital sex, to avoid adulterous relations during marriage, and even to refrain from sexual activity completely, as in the cases of monks, priests, and nuns. Preferred sexual positions vary cross-culturally, as do masturbation objects, homosexual practices, display of nudity, and bestiality (sexual relations with animals) (Kluckhohn, 1954). The habits—including prescriptions and proscriptions—of other cultures may often appear quite strange and even abhorrent to a naive and unsophisticated observer. During the colonial era, Europeans often described other peoples as heathen, uncivilized, and perverse (and prescribed the "missionary position" for sex). Evaluating others from one's own point of view is termed **ethnocentrism.** It was not until the twentieth century that cultures began to be seriously studied and compared rather than degraded and dismissed.

Contributions from Cultural Anthropology

Earlier this century, as the field of cultural anthropology began to develop, many insightful researchers such as Margaret Mead traveled to exotic locales and observed the native customs, families, and societies. In the 1920s, Mead violated expectations for educated young women in American society and took off to observe children and adolescents in Samoa (an island chain in the South Pacific). One particular focus of Mead's study was child-rearing. For example, Mead found that the difficulties of adolescence are not the same in all cultures. Although adolescence in the United States is a time of rebellion, in some cultures adolescents experience a smooth transition into adulthood. Of course all teenagers everywhere undergo the hormonal changes of puberty. But the *effects* of the biological (hormonal) changes can vary dramatically as a function of society's response. Modern-day American researchers are still concerned with the "problems" of adolescence—substance abuse, promiscuity, violence. Are these the result of innate processes of development? Not necessarily. It is important to remember Mead's pioneering point that the full story cannot be located inside each individual; rather, the dramatic effects of society are equally relevant (Mead, 1929, 1939).

Cultural anthropologists Beatrice Whiting and John W. Whiting (1975) also extensively studied child-rearing in different societies. In some cultures, such as Mexican and Filipino societies, children must help care for their younger siblings and also must cooperate with many family chores. These children tend to grow up to be prosocial—in other words, they are helpful to others. In contrast, in the dominant American culture (and now in the Asian American subculture), most children grow up learning to achieve success, to "fulfill their potential" by participating in sports, artistic performances, academic endeavors; in sum, to become number one. Such children are often less altruistic and more competitive. These ideas, derived from cross-cultural research, are still quite important, as modern researchers endeavor to understand how children thrive or fail in public schools. For example, a student of Hispanic background might not thrive in a classroom in which cutthroat competition is the norm.

Other anthropological studies, in attempts to prove or disprove Freudian psychoanalytic notions, began to examine exposure of children to sexual behavior. For example, one analysis concluded that some societies do not hide sexual matters as Americans do. Children may have opportunities to see adults copulate (for example, where the whole family sleeps together in one room); or, they may receive explicit instruction at a young age (Ford & Beach, 1951). On the other hand, in the Victorian Europe of Freud's time (and in much of American society today), children may hear about sexual behavior as a dirty little secret, and they may be severely punished or humiliated for sexual curiosity. Because it is these negative encounters that may lead to repression, anthropological study suggested that key aspects of Freudian theory needed substantial modification or outright rejection. In other words, the Freudian idea of sexual repression probably cannot be directly applied to a society that encourages open sexual expression.

In 1945, the anthropologist Ralph Linton wrote an influential book called *The Cultural Background of Personality.* Linton pointed out that any boy from a hunting tribe who finds himself alone in the woods after dark will know how to build a shelter and survive the night, even if he has never been alone and done this before. Linton's point was that a person comes to situations armed with much knowledge derived from culture. We share many of our reactions with those who live in our culture (such as current American culture) or subculture (such as American teenagers of Hispanic background). For example, the daily behaviors of many American college students have much in common—awakening to a radio tuned to pop music, washing, brushing teeth, eating bagels or cereal, putting on jeans, greeting friends, visiting campus clubs or houses, and so on. It would be a mistake to try to show how the individual's personality explains all these behaviors. Rather, people are shaped by their cultures and subcultures and so, in many ways, are like those in the same culture or subculture but different from those in other cultures.

Sometimes, when encountering people from a different cultural environment from our own, the culturally consistent aspects of their behavior are so salient to us that we are blind to the individual differences in personality among the members of the group. For example, anthropologist Bradd Shore (1996) found in his fieldwork in Samoa that it was only after becoming familiar with the culture of the community he studied that he was able to recognize personality differences among the Samoans he encountered. He was initially so overwhelmed by the striking *shared* (culturally determined) aspects of the Samoans' personalities that he was not initially able to detect that the individuals within that cultural differed from one another just as much as did individuals within his own culture (Shore, 1996).

Lewin's Experiments on Political Culture

In the late 1930s, as fascism spread through Europe and world war loomed, Kurt Lewin conducted a series of studies of different styles of leadership effectiveness. Lewin was a genius in capturing real-world psychological influences in a controlled laboratory setting. What he did was to create groups based either on democratic principles and leadership or on autocratic (fascist-like) ones (Lewin, Lippitt, & White, 1939; Lewin, 1947). For example, in one study, leaders of a youth club led with either an autocratic or democratic style. The members of the democratic club liked the club more (had higher morale). But effects of leadership style on task performance were less clear. Similarly, Lewin argued that democratic group discussions were more effective than autocratic lectures in changing the shopping habits of American housewives and the work habits of American workers. Although subsequent studies have not always confirmed Lewin's findings, he had shown that cultural issues can and should be studied, even in rigorously controlled laboratory research.

Emic versus Etic Approaches

Cross-cultural personality psychologists often distinguish between emic and etic approaches. An **emic** approach is culture-specific; it focuses on a single culture, understood on its own terms—for example, the ways that Americans toilet train their children. An **etic** approach is cross-cultural; it searches for generalities across cultures—for example, all cultures have ways of saying hello and good-bye. By the way, the terms emic and etic derive from a distinction made in the field of linguistics between language-specific versus universal ways of describing speech sounds.

Why is this relevant to personality? Problems arise when concepts, measures, and methods developed in one culture are carelessly transferred to another culture in an attempt to make cross-cultural generalizations about personality. For example, consider the F-scale, developed in Berkeley, California, to measure a person's proneness to being rigid and authoritarian. It works fairly well in detecting Americans prone to be prejudiced. But this scale cannot be validly and directly used in other cultures. In a study in South Africa, scores did not predict antiblack prejudiced behavior among white South Africans (Pettigrew, 1958). Does this mean that an analogous authoritarian personality cannot be isolated in other cultures? Not at all. Rather, various culture-specific variables must also be considered.

Carl Gustav Jung, the Swiss psychoanalyst, searched mythology, religion, ancient rituals, and dreams for the roots of personality. As we mentioned in Chapter 4, Jung described a **collective unconscious,** which is the depository of memories of human evolution. In other words, people evolved to share certain guiding thoughts and motivations. For example, take the case of the mother. All people through all generations had mothers. Jung (1959) suggests that just as it is clear that the infant has evolved to suck milk from the breast, it is also the case that all children have inborn tendencies to react in certain ways to their mothers. It is thus not surprising that all societies have myths and images that involve mothers. Jung termed these universal forms archetypes. **Archetypes** are the universal structures of the collective unconscious. All people are born expecting (psychologically) to have a mother. But the role of the mother varies from culture to culture in many respects. Jung thus pointed to ways that personality psychology must be universal while at the same time allow for important cultural variations.

Collectivist versus Individualistic

There have also been attempts to see how cultures differ from each other on dimensions relevant to personality. One key dimension involves the centrality of the autonomous individual versus the centrality of the collective. More **individualistic** themes tend to be found in Western cultures but more **collectivist** themes in Eastern cultures (Markus & Kitayama, 1991; Triandis, 1994). Americans admire the lone cowboy or the all-star athlete, whereas Asians may prefer a group leader or a winning team. Many Asian cultures have conceptions that insist on the fundamental relatedness of individuals; Americans, on the contrary, prize doing one's own thing.

Visiting a teeming city like collectivist Calcutta, India, you might find great hospitality, but visiting New York City might leave you very conscious of the meaning of rugged individualism. It is not an accident that New York is a world center of capitalism. Thus, differences in behavior might be badly misjudged if the surrounding cultural milieu were not considered.

Cultural effects, however, are not necessarily so simple. For example, one study compared decision-making strategies among 1,123 adolescents who grew up in Finland experiencing Western, individualistic educational practices to 428 adolescents who grew up in Estonia during the period of Soviet collectivist culture. The teenagers were asked to solve problems about such matters as teasing and stealing. The researchers found that the (collectivist) Estonian adolescents were more aggressive and showed lower levels of social responsibility than their Finnish peers; they also tended more to withdraw from the problem. The researchers argue that personal responsibility is not likely to develop if a focus on collective identity interferes with the initial development of personal identity and responsibility (Keltikangas-Jarvinen & Terav, 1996). Thus it is understandable that many Americans, who grow up in close-knit families that emphasize individual accomplishment but also justice and decency, mature into charitable, religious, and peace-minded adults, despite the strongly individualistic society.

Errors of Scientific Inference: The Case of Race

A chapter in this textbook on ethnic and cultural influences on personality is important as a means of helping us to be accurate and scientifically rigorous. We have seen throughout this book that an ignorance of social and cultural influences leads even the most brilliant scientists to errors of judgment. For example, Galton and many other ability and intelligence researchers convinced themselves that white males had the highest intelligence and thus it was only fitting that they occupied the leading positions in universities, businesses, and governments. Freud viewed a healthy woman as one who would be a good wife and mother, and who would be most satisfied sexually by sexual intercourse with her husband. Indeed, for many years, psychologists, like other leaders, rarely questioned the idea that a president, a senator, a surgeon, a corporate executive, a judge, or a professor should be a wealthy white male.

It is important to understand that these were not the views of ignorant or malicious bigots. They were the views of many thoughtful, educated people. In an interesting book called *Joining the Club: A History of Jews and Yale,* the author documents the reactions of Yale College's leaders in the 1920s, as the numbers of Jewish immigrant students began increasing at top colleges (Oren, 1985). For example, the book describes the comment of a psychologist—and dean of freshman—who advised that, though the Jewish students were doing very well academically, they should be excluded from Yale because of personal flaws: "I feel they are in the nature of a foreign body in the class organism. They contribute very little to class life" (Oren, 1985, p. 43). In other words, they came from a different culture.

Such prejudiced feelings led to exclusionary quotas that allowed only small numbers of nonmainstream students (and no women) to attend Yale College until the late 1960s. Most other elite colleges likewise limited or excluded many talented students (and most excluded all women) throughout most of the twentieth century. Subtle cultural prejudices and influences were distorting the judgments of even the most educated men in America.

Race as an Approach to Grouping People

Humans form groups based on many different sorts of criteria. Many groups are based on professed beliefs, such as political or religious beliefs. Political parties are examples. It is usually possible for a person to change between such groups (that is, convert) by adopting new beliefs.

Other groups are based primarily on cultural habits or customs, such as eating spaghetti or tacos, or dressing in kilts or beads or kaffiyehs (Arab head-dress), perhaps in addition to religious beliefs. These groupings are generally termed ethnic groups. Irish Catholics are an example.

Finally, some large groupings are based on physical characteristics tied to geographical origin, such as skin color or eye shape or height. Such groupings are often called races. But racial groupings are the source of much confusion and scientific misunderstanding because they are the most closely tied to biology. People can change religion or eating habits but cannot easily change skin color. Further, we can readily see if someone is "black," "white," or "yellow," but not if she is Catholic or Buddhist.

Because physical characteristics are so obvious, we often overgeneralize and overattribute personality characteristics based on them. An Arab man living in Saudi Arabia might have a large nose, dark hair, speak Arabic, wear a kaffiyeh, have conservative politics, follow traditional Arab customs, and, if a Muslim, not eat pork. But how about a grandson of such an Arab, who was born and grew up in Los Angeles and worked as an actor? He also might have a large nose and dark hair but otherwise might not be at all like his grandfather. It would not be logical to generalize on the basis of a few physical characteristics and assume that these two men would have similar behavior patterns. Yet this sort of confusion and overgeneralization is common, especially on the basis of skin color.

The Influence of Race in the United States

In America, black–white differences are the most significant such grouping, largely because of American history. The United States was founded on the principle that "All men are created equal," yet the U.S. Constitution allowed slavery (and counted slaves as three-fifths of a man for purposes of taxation and representation). Gunnar Myrdal (1944) called this problem the **American Dilemma.** How could we have a country in which all men are created equal but many were slaves (until the time of Lincoln)? How could we have a society in which all men are created equal but some cannot use restrooms or water fountains or sit at the front of the bus (until the civil rights legislation of the 1960s)? The thorn is so deeply embedded in American history and culture that it remains a significant issue in the understanding of personality.

In 1933, racial stereotyping was studied among male undergraduates at Princeton (Katz & Braly, 1933). The students were asked to select those traits that they believed most characterized ten so-called racial groups (such as Americans, Chinese, Irish, and so on). "Americans" (like the students themselves) were seen as industrious, intelligent, and progressive, but prejudiced judgments of other groups were pervasive. For example, "Negroes" were viewed as superstitious, lazy, happy-go-lucky, and musical. It is remarkable how illogical these distorted perceptions can be. For example, California imported Asian workers as manual laborers, forced them to live in segregated areas, and then often stereotyped them as ignorant and clannish.

As we discussed in detail in Chapter 5 on biological aspects of personality, it is clear that genetic make-up can have an important influence on per-

Self-Understanding

The Bell Curve

In 1994, Richard Herrnstein and Charles Murray published a controversial treatise called *The Bell Curve*. They claimed that they had compiled evidence for an inherited general factor of intelligence that is responsible for most categories of success and failure. This factor, they contend, is quite accurately and fairly measured by currently available IQ tests. The authors assert that IQ ("native intelligence") is highly correlated with success in our culture, including income level (poverty versus financial success), amount of schooling, employment (versus unemployment), job success (and one's position within one's company), laziness, receiving public assistance (welfare), out-of-wedlock births, divorce, quality of parenting, involvement in criminal activities, political and civil participation, and voting behavior (Herrnstein & Murray, 1994).

Although such a broad and sweeping attribution of personality to genetics should make us suspicious in the first place (given all we know about the complexity of personality), our suspicions are confirmed by the next claim: These authors additionally contend that genetically transmitted intelligence is the primary factor causing differences in success between ethnic groups. That is, rather than looking to social and cultural advantages and traditions as possible causes of differential levels of success among certain ethnic groups, Herrnstein and Murray claim that these differences are primarily due to group differences in IQ.

This argument has also been adopted uncritically by less-informed others. We read an editorial in a major newspaper arguing that society shouldn't worry so much about providing educational enrichment to students because "scientists have proven" that abilities and success are genetically determined. As a student of personality psychology, would you accept such a vague assertion?

sonality, but it does so in complicated ways. Skin color is just one particular observable manifestation of genes, as are eye color, height, build, foot size, eye shape, nose shape, and on and on. As we have seen, such physical attributes are poor substitutes for a more sophisticated biological, social, cognitive, existential, and cultural analysis of individuals. And a focus on skin color leads to needless controversial political conflict, which produces more heat than light (Klineberg, 1935; Yee, Fairchild, & Weizman, 1993; Spearman, 1925; Rushton, 1995). In the case of Nazi Germany, a focus on physical differences and so-called race differences led to mass murder of groups ranging from children in wheelchairs to Jews and Gypsies, all in the name of "scientific improvement" of society. In current American society, simplistic categorization into race ignores or distorts analysis of such more promising concepts such as temperamental differences among individuals or cultural influences on behavior and development. (See Self-Understanding.)

Most basically, we should be suspicious and even alarmed when someone tries to make policy conclusions based on ethnic group. Even if it were the case that such differences were biologically based, so what? There is tremendous variation with each group. When considering an *individual* applicant to a school or for a job, of what relevance is this person's ethnicity or gender if he or she may be the next Picasso or Einstein or Marie Curie (the first person to win two Nobel prizes)?

Are achievement and failure due primarily to allegedly "race-based" innate (in)ability? Many psychologists have countered these arguments by pointing out inaccuracies in the evidence and inconsistencies in the reasoning that nullify any conclusions about an inherited component of achievement. For example, it is known that high heritability values do not eliminate, or even often limit, the strong effects of environmental change on outcome (Wahlsten, 1995). This means that even to the extent that intelligence is highly inherited, a relatively minor environmental change (such as strong, well-educated parents) can still significantly change the achievement level of an individual with a particular IQ. Errors in *The Bell Curve* authors' use of statistics have also been criticized (Fancher, 1995; Fraser, 1995; Bateson, 1995; Krishnan, 1995).

Because of cultural influences, IQ tests have frequently been demonstrated to be inaccurate if misused. Although they are accurate about certain skills for many people of similar backgrounds, they have routinely been found to lead to the mistaken placement of intelligent students in special (remedial) education classes (Siegel, 1995; Barrow, 1995). Thus, for some, *The Bell Curve* is simply a racist polemic. As we have emphasized throughout this textbook, personality theories bring with them assumptions about human nature, assumptions that can have the most dramatic implications.

Should personality psychologists study "race"? On the one hand, it certainly makes sense to take into account that personality is influenced by the reactions of others, and that others often react to us based on perceived physical characteristics. (In the United States, this is often skin color.) Relatedly, it sometimes makes sense to study narrow biological similarities (such as genetic proneness to certain diseases) among subgroups of people, although many Americans have mixed ancestry. On the other hand, there is no known scientific advantage in trying to categorize all Americans into one of several races. Rather, it is more fruitful to study the effects of ethnic identification, history, family, subculture, religion, and social class as they interact with temperament and affect personality. These classifications are more readily definable and less susceptible to scientific and social distortion.

Socioeconomic Influences on Personality

There is a fascinating phenomenon in public health called the **SES gradient.** This term refers to the fact that the higher a person's socioeconomic status is, the lower is that person's risk of getting sick and of dying prematurely. (Socioeconomic status is a measure of one's level of education and income.) This relation has been found in various times and places (Adler et al., 1994). It holds at all ages and at all income levels. For example, old women who are rich live longer than old women who are merely affluent.

There are many sorts of explanations for this gradient, but none of them is fully adequate. For example, less educated people might be unable to earn as much and might also engage in more unhealthy behaviors like smoking; or, people who are sickly might drift down to lower socioeconomic status; or, poor people might have poorer nutrition and poorer medical care; or, wealthier people may be able to live in healthier environments. All of these possibilities would account for a relationship between socioeconomic status and health. Each of these mechanisms surely operates in some cases, but the overall phenomenon is still not well understood.

What is interesting about this phenomenon for personality psychologists is that social class can have such sweeping effects on individuals. The corresponding effects on personality are not yet as well documented. But if social class can affect one's likelihood of getting sick and how long one is likely to live, it probably also has significant effects on one's usual patterns of psychological reactions (e.g., Pearson, Lankshear, & Francis, 1989). In other words, class effects on personality are indisputable; even among the middle class, there are differences among the well-off middle class, the average middle class, and the working class (blue collar or lower middle class). Such issues are obvious to investigators in countries like India, which has a clear history of social classes or castes (e.g., Dubey, 1987). But in American academic settings, studies of social structure and personality appear primarily in the field of sociology (House, 1990). Personality psychologists have had little to say.

Karl Marx and Alienation

In a related field of study, some scholars emphasize the effects of the economic system on individual behavior. This type of approach took formal shape with the work of the German social philosopher Karl Marx (1818–1883). Marx, a student of history and economic oppression, concluded that many societal institutions (including religion) served mainly to maintain the economic power of the elite (1872). His ideas led to modern socialism and communism. Socialists believe in a society structured so that people work directly for the benefit of the society rather than for themselves. Communists believe in the use of revolutions by the working class to eliminate private property because property is thought to encourage a selfish and dehumanized society.

How is Marxist thought relevant to personality? Marx contended that psychosocial attributes such as alienation could be traced directly to the economic structure of a capitalist society. He thus saw strong socioeconomic influences on what it means to be a person. The socialist and communist revolutions of the twentieth century did not confirm Marxist predictions: the abolition of private property and the enforcement of economic equality did not lead to a workers' paradise of psychological fulfillment. However, the basic orientation of Marx and his followers—that socioeconomic class is a key concept in understanding human behavior—has indeed been adopted in many modern analyses in sociology, social psychology, and political science. In personality psychology, Marx's greatest influence was on Erich Fromm and his associates, as they thought deeply about existential alienation in modern society (discussed in Chapter 9).

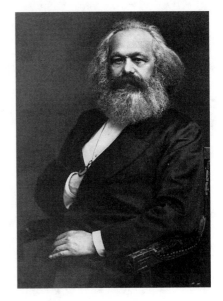

Karl Marx thought that individual attributes such as alienation could be traced directly to the economic structure of a capitalistic society rather than to biology or the unique history of the individual.

Like Marx, Fromm struggled to determine what is the basic nature of a human being and what kind of culture best promotes human fulfillment. Interestingly, Fromm accepted and extended the idea that the socioeconomic basis of society will shape its culture, but he was not deterministic or pessimistic. Fromm believed that capitalist societies must create, by their nature, a culture of consumption. If people are not shaped to crave and constantly consume newer and fancier products, then the capitalist society cannot function. (For example, think of the businesses that would collapse if most people most valued study, neighborhood sports, and good conversation, and were satisfied with simple clothes, simple foods, and simple means of transportation). On the other hand, Fromm believed that societies could be created that promoted self-fulfillment through an emphasis on community, love, and mutuality.

Language as a Cultural Influence

Language is one of the most central and influential features of any culture. In Canada, the French speakers of Quebec have had many cultural clashes with the English speakers of the rest of the country in their push toward complete political independence. In the United States, people from Spanish-speaking cultures, such as Mexican Americans, Cuban Americans, and Puerto Ricans, have been remarkably successful in maintaining key aspects of their subculture by maintaining their culture's language. Many other American subcultures also strive to treasure and preserve the original language of their culture.

Speaking and listening—that is, language in its oral form—are a pervasive mode of interpersonal interaction in all human societies, and a central part of who we are. Every natural human language ever studied is remarkably complex but, at the same time, has many features in common (referred to as "linguistic universals") with all other known languages, regardless of the level of technological development of the social group that uses it (Hockett, 1966). Thus, language makes us human, and particular characteristics of a particular language make us a particular type of human.

Language and Identity

Language is one of the defining features of a person's identity—you are what you speak. In the words of Martiniquan psychiatrist Frantz Fanon, "To speak means to be in a position to use a certain syntax, to grasp the morphology of this or that language, but it means above all to assume a culture, to support the weight of a civilization" (1952/1967). This role of language is a double-edged sword in its effects on social identity, keeping out those who do not proficiently speak a group's defining language, and reinforcing the ties among those who do.

Idiolects and Dialects

Because we each have different experiences, each individual speaks a unique version of his or her native language, called an **idiolect** (with the prefix *idio* referring to the "self"). The idiolect is a form of self-expression and thus a part of personality (Johnstone & Bean, 1997). This peculiarity has allowed historians and literary critics to attempt to determine whether all the Shakespearean plays were written by the same person and which books of the Bible come from one voice. Of course, the greater the similarities between any two people in terms of factors such as where they have lived, where they were educated, their social class, religion, and interests, the greater the similarity is likely to be between their idiolects. Variations between groups of people who share regional characteristics or cultural characteristics create distinct **dialects.** When two groups speak related but distinguishable dialects, dialect can be an important aspect of group identity. Within some African American communities, for example, group identity is supported by speaking Black English—and members who "talk white" are viewed as abandoning their roots.

Regional variation in the way people speak, which nonlinguists ordinarily consider a variation in accent, is more accurately viewed as an example of variation in dialects. The everyday concept of "accent" focuses on pronunciation, but the concept of dialect is much more comprehensive, encompassing variations in vocabulary and unique syntactic forms as well. For example, there are many subcultural differences in slang terms. Certain dialecticians are as skilled as the fictitious Professor Henry Higgins (from *My Fair Lady/Pygmalion*) who could listen to someone speak and pinpoint that person's neighborhood or tiny village, and thus know something important about personal identity.

The question of how much difference is enough difference to merit calling two regional variants separate dialects can be viewed as analogous to the question of how much difference there must be between two dialects to merit calling them separate languages. In practice, determining whether two variants are different dialects versus different languages is not just a linguistic issue. Some languages are so similar that people who know one language can, to a degree anyway, understand someone speaking the other. Examples of such pairs are Spanish and Portuguese, and Swedish and Danish. In other cases, some dialects of one language are so different as to allow no mutual intelligibility (such as variants of Chinese). Why are the pairs in the first case considered different languages and in the second case considered different dialects of the same language? Because nonlinguistic features are influencing the determination. National identity is a major determinant (Spaniards are not Portuguese, but all Chinese are Chinese), as are historical relationships (in the United States, we think of the language most of us speak as English, but many Britons would charge that we speak American).

In any case, language allows people to maintain a strong identification with their group; the dialect of a subcultural group like a street gang serves many of the same social functions as the technical jargon used within a narrow scientific specialty. In both cases, members of the group use words and expressions that are unique to the group or have special meanings within the group; language can therefore be used both to assert the speaker's membership in the group and to prevent outsiders from understanding communications among members.

Creating a Culture through Shared Language

An interesting example of the importance of shared language in creating a culture comes from the deaf community. There is a culture of the deaf to a much greater extent than there is a culture of the blind, at least partially because deafness seriously interferes with the ability of most deaf individuals to communicate with the larger society (that is, with those who cannot communicate in sign). People who are blind also face many extra difficulties in everyday life, but they are not especially impaired in using the common language of the community at large. This difference can account for the necessity and appropriateness of a strong deaf culture and community. Like any other group that shares a language within the group but not outside it, these people become a linguistic and social community. This community differs from the more common ethnic and regional social and linguistic communities because often the hearing families of the deaf community's members are not fully part of the same community.

Language as Politics: The "English Only" Movement

The "English Only" movement in the United States provides striking evidence of the psychological importance that most people attach to the idea of their mother tongue as part of who they are. Consider first those people who favor limiting all governmental communication to English (including government documents, election materials, and all information provided over the phone by government employees). One interpretation of their position is that they believe that immigrants and their children cannot become full participants and contributors to the society at large unless they are forced to become proficient in the language of the majority. An alternative interpretation of their position is that this country was established by speakers of English and that the English language thus embodies the essence of public life here. Out of respect for the heritage of this nation, they believe, English must remain the only "official" language.

People on the other side of the dispute want the government to continue to offer services in the languages preferred by the recipients of the services. Many of them view the "English Only" movement as a racist, exclusivist, bigoted attempt to undermine the cultures of minority-language groups—a movement intended to take away the rights of non–English-speaking people to live their lives and conduct their public business in their own native languages. What is clear from looking at both positions is how deeply people care about what language is used in the public sphere, and how important they think this issue is in defining the nature of public life and national identity.

Language and Thought

Why should it matter what language people speak, as long as all the parties to a conversation can understand and express themselves? As noted, the issue of identity is central, with language functioning as an expression of cultural solidarity. But language also functions as an influence on how people communicate and, to some extent, as an expression of the world view of their culture. What can be easily expressed, and what must be included in an utterance, varies among languages. For example, the Swedish language has a limited vocabulary for emotion words (relative to English). Hebrew, the oldest language revived for modern use, makes relatively little use of abstract terms, requiring its speakers to use concrete ones. In some Native American languages, the form (shape) of an object being acted on changes the form of the verb used. In all of these cases, the requirements of the language become part of how the speaker casts an intended communication into words, as well as how those words are interpreted by the listener. Anyone who has ever tried to translate a prose passage (or, worse yet, a poem) from one language to another soon becomes aware of how enormously difficult it is to preserve the meaning while shifting the language. Words in different languages rarely have identical meanings, and their degree of overlap (in both denotation and connotation) varies.

An even stronger role can be afforded to specific features of individual languages in shaping communication: Our language influences not only how we say things, but even how we think about and understand and perceive the world. That is, the specifics of your language not only determine how your thought is transformed into words, but also shape the very nature of the thoughts you can think. One well-known statement of this idea is often referred to as the Whorfian hypothesis or the Sapir-Whorf hypothesis (after anthropologists Benjamin Lee Whorf, who promoted it in the 1950s, and Edward Sapir, who had promulgated it ten years earlier). Their idea, often termed *linguistic relativity*, claims that our interpretation of the world is to a large extent dependent on the linguistic system by which we classify it. Imagine, for example, that your language has many familiar words for different types of clouds (terms like "nimbus" and "cumulus") but lacks a generic word for "cloud." The linguistic relativity hypothesis claims that you would then think about clouds very differently from the way a native speaker of English (who has the generic term "cloud") does.

The empirical data on this question are mixed, though. The methodological complexity of operationalizing the linguistic relativity hypothesis into an actual experiment makes it difficult to do research on this question. Still, there is scattered evidence about the relevance of language-influenced thought processes to personality. For example, one study found that people who tend to use active verbs also tend to have field-independent personalities (Doob, 1958); their perceptions are less passive. Other evidence can be found in literature: as Roger Brown pointed out (1970), one of the most powerful features in George Orwell's fictional totalitarian civilization in *Nineteen Eighty Four* is that Newspeak—the language invented by the dictatorship—makes it impossible to express or even to think rebellious thoughts (Orwell, 1949). There is little doubt that some aspects of who we are derive from the words and phrases we use to understand and communicate about things and ideas.

Language and Social Interaction

Imagine a world in which, before you can speak to another person, you first have to determine where that person stands relative to you in the social hierarchy. If you determine that you are lower in the "pecking order," you will speak differently than if you are higher, and differently again if you are equals. For such a system to work smoothly, of course, the social ranking has to be unambiguous—you have to be able to tell where each of you stands. What makes for high rank varies somewhat among societies but frequently includes factors of wealth, age, sex, occupation, family or clan, ethnicity, and education. In many traditional societies, social rank is obvious from visible signs (such as tattoos, hairstyles, or clothing). In a society like the present-day United States, the hierarchy can sometimes be more difficult to determine. Fortunately for us, though, American English doesn't require us to have as finely calibrated a gauge of status as many other languages do. You probably do make some adjustments, though, in both style and content when you talk to a peer versus a social superior (for example, your roommate as opposed to the president of your school).

The situation is quite different in many other language communities. One very clear example of this phenomenon is in the use of personal pronouns (Brown, 1970). In languages originally derived from Latin (e.g., French, Italian, Spanish) as well as in German, there is no generic "you." Instead, one form is used toward intimates and subordinates, and a different form for those to whom respect is due. In French, one says *tu* or *vous;* in Spanish, *tu* or *usted;* in German, *du* or *Sie.* While there is some variation among languages in exactly who receives the familiar versus the polite form (and under what circumstances), making the distinction correctly is always extremely important. English uses a generic "you," and without even the option of different forms. So,

The same behavior or attribute can be seen very differently from differing cultural perspectives. Business negotiations in Japan involve communication that is more indirect (in both verbal content and nonverbal style) than most Americans are accustomed to. Conversational statements that Americans view as appropriately bold, frank, and direct may be viewed by their Japanese hosts as pushy, tactless, and rude.

for many monolingual English speakers, incorporating this distinction when learning another language requires substantial effort. But look out if you address a superior with the wrong pronoun, such as addressing your Spanish father-in-law with the subordinate *tu*. Further, you had better not address your Japanese boss by his first name. Each language community enforces norms of politeness that are reflective of its view on proper conversational interaction (Brown & Levinson, 1987).

Gender and Language

Gender is a very important domain where many of these issues of status, power, and identity profoundly influence how we use language. Many languages include distinctions between word forms that are used by females versus males (and *about* females versus males). English makes very few such distinctions that are purely linguistic. We have male and female pronouns for the third person singular (he and she), with their associated forms (his/hers and him/her). Other than that, I am just "I" whether I am male or female, you are just "you" of either sex, or status or even number, and so on. Many other languages have different pronouns for each sex for first, second, and third person (e.g., we, you, they) and also put distinctive endings on many words that denote gender. A cousin in French is either *un cousin* (male) or *une cousine* (female); your professor in Spanish is either *un profesor* (male) or *una profesora* (female). The psychological impact of being forced to make this distinction is probably substantial. If I say "I am an American," my statement is the same whether I am male or female, and perhaps what it means (to speaker and listener) refers to a truly gender-neutral concept. Compare that to a French person, who must say either *Je suis Français* or *Je suis Française;* these are two different terms, and they may denote rather different underlying concepts—different types of personalities.

In recent years, most of the formal guidelines about English usage (for example, the *New York Times* style book, the APA manual) have required gender-neutral reference unless only one group is included in the reference. That is, we shouldn't say, "Each Senator should vote according to his own conscience" or "Scientists and their wives . . . ." For centuries though, the formal guidelines promoted the use of he/him/his for both all-male and mixed groups. Thus, it was considered proper to say "Each student should print his name at the top and sign his name at the bottom" as long as the instruction was not given at a girls' school. This notion of the male pronoun as the default or generic has sometimes led to almost comical phrasing, such as the biology textbook statement, "Like all mammals, the human bears his young alive."

From a psychological perspective, the masculine pronoun is (not surprisingly) closely linked to males. Thus, the politically and ethically motivated move toward more inclusive language is supported by evidence that the male as a generic pronoun is not generic at all. Experiments have demonstrated (in a variety of ways) that when people hear "he" and "his," they are not likely to think of female examples (e.g., Gastil, 1990; McConnell & Fazio, 1996). But most of the people who have had significant influence in the codification of language rules (especially rules for written language) over the centuries have been male and have reflected the male experience. Going back to the linguistic relativity hypothesis, it is informative to note that even for writers and speakers committed to egalitarian language, it can be a challenge to phrase certain ideas

Given what is known about the psychology of language, it is clear that terms such as "freshman," which is often used to refer to a first-year college student of either sex, are not truly gender-neutral.

in ways that are gender-neutral but not awkward. The absence of a gender-neutral third person singular pronoun (for "he or she") in English makes some things hard to say gracefully. Feminist critic Andrea Dworkin (1981) put it this way: "Male supremacy is fused into the language, so that every sentence both heralds and affirms it" (p. 17). While this statement is more extreme than most would endorse, it does capture the resistance of the English language to comfortable gender-neutrality. The language we use reflects and influences how we think and behave.

Culture and Testing

Like any intellectual endeavor, psychological testing rests on a number of assumptions. To the extent that the assumptions are met, the test may yield valuable information. However, when the assumptions are not met and the tester does not recognize the problem, then the testing can prove not only unhelpful but quite harmful.

One assumption of much psychological testing is that certain (high) scores are somehow better than other (low) scores; that is, they indicate better psychological adjustment or better intellectual understanding or better abilities to deal with other people (see Chapter 2). This is often true. For example, people with mental illnesses such as bipolar disorder (manic-depressive illness) cannot cope well, are in personal pain, and score "poorly" on psychological tests of adjustment.

The problem arises when the assumptions underlying the test are culturally biased. Most obviously, the item content of a test may not adequately capture some cultural experiences. For example, someone growing up on a farm will have different experiences than someone growing up in an inner city, and so certain general knowledge questions or psychological reaction questions could be appropriate for one group but totally inappropriate for the other group. Similarly, "hearing the voices of angels" may be seen as a valuable religious experience in some cultures but as a sign of psychopathology (schizophrenia) in another culture. Test scores are also known to be affected by such things as motivation, previous test-taking experience, the qualities of the examiner (test administrator), and socioeconomic status.

Culture-Free Tests

One attempt to deal with such problems was the development of what were called culture-free tests. For example, in an intelligence test called the Raven Progressive Matrices test (Raven, 1938), people analyze geometric figures. The test-taker has to identify recurring patterns in drawings. Since all children develop perceptual abilities—learn to see the world—it is hoped that such tests are not dependent on culture. However, more sophisticated analysis of this issue makes it clear that some cultural assumptions creep into every such test. (For example, children in some cultures have more experience in taking tests.) So, researchers turned to trying to develop tests that are culture-fair.

Culture-Fair Tests

Culture-fair tests attempt to control for or rule out effects that result from culture rather than from individual differences. So, for example, an intelligence test might see how quickly individuals respond to presentation of a stimulus such as a sound or a picture. The idea is that response time is more biological than influenced by environment. However, we have seen that all biological processes unfold in some environment. Some cultures value quick responses and others encourage slower, more deliberate responses. And, frankly, some cultures are more motivated regarding test-taking.

Another way to approach the issue is to include some subscales that are known to be culturally biased and other subscales that are thought to be more culture-fair (Cattell's Culture Fair Intelligence Test takes this approach). Then, if an individual scores differently on the two types of subscales, we have an indication that standard testing may be inappropriate for this individual. This is, of course, what teachers do naturally when they observe that a student of an unusual background performs well on most tasks but has trouble on others.

Some tests now try explicitly to take culture into account. For example, the **System of Multicultural Pluralistic Assessment** (SOMPA) developed by Jane Mercer (1979) assumes that test results cannot be divorced from the culture. Therefore, the focus of comparisons is among individuals within a cultural group rather than between cultural groups. Such ideas have been mostly applied to ability and intelligence testing because of a concern about misclassification of disadvantaged minority students as having less intellectual potential. Matters of fairness are often obvious when issues of education and jobs are at stake. There has been much less attention to such matters in the assessment of personality constructs like conscientiousness and extroversion, but the same sorts of errors will be made if cultural matters are not deliberately considered.

When tests are constructed, the thorny issue arises as to which items are culturally biased and which indicate valid cultural differences. For example, let us say that Group A scores higher than Group B on an item thought to indicate tendency toward depression. Should this item be included in the scale? If Group A is truly more prone to depression, then it should be. If the groups are not truly different in this way, then the item is the result of a cultural bias and should be excluded. Note that the only way to resolve such an issue is to look at the validating criterion—that is, to look at other sources of information about the two groups. This is almost always true: tests have no value outside the contexts in which they are created, but they may be quite useful when the context is well understood.

Consider now this more practical issue: Suppose a paper-and-pencil problem-solving test is used as an employment test to choose firefighters. Such a test is certainly not predictive of courage, or stamina, or of ability to carry a 150-pound person down a rescue ladder. However, this test might be relevant to the directing of a firefighting team's strategy or to making the correct split-second decision. In short, there are no simple rules that can be developed to ensure the complete validity of all tests.

One of the main problems with testing is not that the tests are culturally biased but rather that they are used inappropriately. For example, it does not much matter if a Japanese psychologist develops a test that shows that Americans are "too extroverted." What matters is what is done with this conclusion. Is an attempt made by the Japanese psychologist to change Americans because of their "deficiency"? Is an attempt made to exclude Americans from visiting Japan or from buying Japanese products or from reading Japanese scientific journals?

Even the testing situation, with its accompanying social expectations, can be relevant. Psychologist Claude Steele (1997) has shown that people faced with a difficult evaluative challenge such as an SAT test may react poorly if they see themselves as identified with a group that is expected to do poorly. For example, a woman taking an advanced math test and an African American taking a GRE test before graduate school may become anxious and do poorly if they believe that "women don't do as well as men on advanced math" or "blacks don't do as well as whites in graduate school." This is termed **stereotype threat**—the threat that others' judgments or their own actions will negatively stereotype them. If, however, they come to believe that the test or evaluation is not relevant to these characteristics (that the test is not gender-relevant or race-relevant), then their performance improves. In other words, this theory combines ego approaches, cognitive approaches, and interactionist ap-

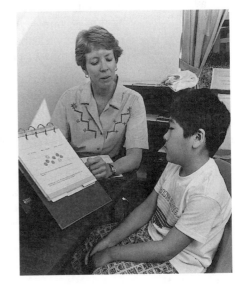

An additional factor when considering cultural issues in testing goes beyond the content of the test to the context of the testing: the relationship between the test administrator and the test-taker can also play a role in test performance.

Spanish actor Antonio Banderas. Despite the international dominance of the United States in cinema, sometimes people from other cultures can break the cultural barriers and achieve success.

proaches, in which the individual's identity in a specific situation depends on how he or she construes that challenge and affects behavior in predictable ways.

What about more general implications? Imperialism is the extension of one's own rule to other countries, and cultural imperialism is extending one's own cultural approaches over those of another culture or subculture. Some have condemned American schools as imperialistic in teaching the history of minority groups; for example, the cultures of Native Americans have often been disparaged or ignored. More recently, there have been countercharges that so-called multiculturalism (which, for example, might insist on non-Western books in literature and philosophy courses) has gone too far in attacking traditional Western forms of scholarship.

As a social science, psychology has an interesting role in this debate. In physical sciences such as chemistry, there can be no sincere debate: the laws of molecular structure are the same in all cultures. Conversely, in the humanities, no scientific standards can be applied: literature and philosophy operate in a different sphere of discourse. But a social science such as personality psychology is subject to cultural distortions while at the same time it is held to the standard of scientific methods. A fully valid personality psychology must take into account cultural variations, but must simultaneously construct theories that are verifiable through the collection of data. This is a significant challenge for the future of personality psychology.

A More General Model of Personality and Culture

Imagine a case in which the police in San Francisco picked up a five-year-old boy wandering in the park. When the officers questioned him, he refused to respond. When they served him food, he refused utensils and ate with his fingers. When they went out for a walk, he stopped and urinated behind a tree. For a child raised in San Francisco, this would indicate a very unusual personality. But suppose you discovered that the child had just immigrated with his refugee mother from a poverty-stricken, war-torn region of the world? Our judgments about his personality would change—and soften—dramatically. The point is that ideas of personality and predictable behavior are meaningless outside of a framework—a cultural context—in which they are to be understood (Betancourt & Lopez, 1993).

Some of the saddest examples of the results of failures to understand the role of culture in personality arose from relations between representatives of the U.S. government and Native Americans. In addition to the unsavory history of wars, betrayals, and misunderstandings, even twentieth-century relations have often been characterized by misinformation because Indian cultural assumptions are often so radically different. Interest was spurred in such matters when Erik Erikson (1950) undertook a study of the Sioux in South Dakota. He found that white teachers viewed the Indians as having a fundamental personality "flaw." In other words, the Indians didn't cooperate with or do well in traditional American classrooms.

Erikson traced the problem to a long history of contradictory government policies: Independent Indian reservations were established, but the inhabitants were made dependent on the government for their livelihood. Trust and cooperation were preached, but agreements were often broken. Indian culture was conceded to be distinct, yet government policies often tried to force the norms of the dominant culture onto the reservations. Not surprisingly, the children did not behave like white Americans. However, only in recent years have such matters of cultural clashes and personality begun to be explicitly studied. To fully understand personality stability and change as people age, it seems wise to consider their early predispositions, their developmental stage, and the culture in which this unfolds (Whitbourne et al., 1992).

Incorporating Culture into Personality Theory

One solution to the problems of cultural ignorance in approaches to personality is not to try to eliminate culture (or "control for" culture) but rather to bring culture into key consideration as a basic element of personality. Everyone grows up in some culture. And culture is certainly part of what it means to be a person—there are no people without cultures. So it makes sense to incorporate culture into personality theories and personality research.

When Gordon Allport (1954) studied prejudice, he saw that it was a mistake to locate prejudice totally inside an individual's personality. Which sociocultural conditions foster prejudice? Allport proposed a mix of societal, economic, historical, and communication factors as complementary to internal personality dynamics. For example, prejudice was more likely during times of social change, when economic rivalries exist (such as for jobs), when government authorities sanction scapegoating, when societal traditions support hostility, and when the society has unfavorable attitudes toward assimilation and pluralism. In this century, such conditions occurred when the First World War swept away many of the socioeconomic and geographic divisions of the late nineteenth century, and again when the Great Depression (beginning in 1929) produced worldwide economic hardship and chaos. Indeed, fascism grew in power and popularity in the 1930s, especially in countries that did not have a long history of democracy and freedom.

Culture and Humanness

It has been noted that culture provides the individual with basic information about what it means to be a human being, even though the specific content may vary (Shweder, 1990). Things that no child is born knowing but all cultures teach include answers to these fundamental questions: What does society value and expect of me? Who is like me, on my side, in my family? What should a man do versus what should a woman do? What is mature, rational behavior, and what is childish, impulsive behavior? It is interesting to recall that these are the same questions that Sigmund Freud asked a century ago. Personality psychology has come full circle in the understanding of the importance of culture.

Some of the most modern approaches to personality and culture focus on roles and cognitive sets. Culture, by influencing what roles we are likely to assume, likewise influences our behavior. For example, in modern American culture, success in competitive sports is highly valued for boys, and so the attributes of a successful competitive athlete are adopted by many. Furthermore, culture helps the growing child determine the ways or dimensions in which to think about the world. For example, if an adolescent girl is socialized to think primarily in terms of families and children and domestic chores, she may be more likely to leave school and start a family at a young age (Caspi, Bem, & Elder, 1989). Culture thus helps us set our goals. With a knowledge of cultural influences on personality, we are more hesitant to accept universal proclamations about, and more willing to look for socioenvironmental influences on, the nature of human beings (Shweder & Sullivan, 1990).

Modern approaches also understand that historical and socioeconomic influences on personality make it unwise to overgeneralize the concepts that emerge from the dominant or mainstream culture (DuBois, 1969; Gaines & Reed, 1995). As noted, a white, Italian American child growing up in a Catholic suburban school may have dramatically different experiences from a black child attending an inner-city school that emphasizes African culture. It may be difficult to compare the personalities of these students without taking culture directly into account. This does not mean that there cannot be universal theories of personality; it only means that the theories must not ignore these cultural, historical, and socioeconomic factors.

Culture is also important for understanding personality's effects on applied fields such as physical health. The Seventh-Day Adventist (SDA) church is a group of individuals whose doctrines center around their beliefs in the seventh-day sabbath (Saturday, not Sunday) and the physical return (advent) of Jesus. Interestingly, they are one of the healthiest groups of Americans. Since the earliest days of the SDA church, their "health message" has been of paramount importance. This message directs church members to abstain from smoking, drinking, and the eating of flesh (although in recent years, more SDAs have begun to eat meat). Because Seventh-Day Adventists believe their bodies to be sacred and dedicated to God, church members also are encouraged to pursue good health in other ways, such as through regular exercise and a wholesome diet. Their supportive social structure may also be health promoting. Furthermore, Adventists believe in abstaining from premarital sex, although the reasons for this are primarily moral rather than health-related. In total, these strong cultural beliefs help shape the personalities of most of the church's members, and the striking result is that Adventists are among the healthiest and longest-living groups in the United States (Fraser, Beeson, & Phillips, 1991). An explanation of the personality and health behavior of an Adventist that disregards this religious and cultural milieu would be superficial, if not totally inadequate.

Culture and Theory

An understanding of cultures also affects how we develop theories. When Kurt Lewin was a student and then a researcher and teacher in Berlin in the 1920s, he naturally adopted ideas from the Gestalt psychologists with whom he worked. Rather than focusing on specific stimuli and responses as the behaviorists did, Lewin tried to understand complex applied situations such as behavior in restaurants, leadership in groups, and people's motivations and aspirations (Ash, 1992). He knew that personality was not located solely inside a person but also depended on the social and cultural environment. When the Nazis came to power in Germany in 1933, Lewin fled to the United States.

As a psychologist who moved from the autocratic and obedient culture of Germany to the relatively democratic and free culture of America, Lewin began thinking about cultural differences in child-rearing, education, leadership, and societal expectations. Rather than being oblivious to the environment in which he was immersed, Lewin was forced to focus even more on the environment itself and was able to exert a tremendous influence on American social and personality psychology. In other words, this type of analysis suggests that the kinds of personality theories that are developed by a researcher will depend in part on the researcher's culture. Culture influences theory (Bond & Smith, 1996).

Does this mean that the theories cannot be scientifically valid? Not necessarily. Human behavior is so complex that it is natural that different but overlapping theories will emerge to try to explain it. As we have advocated throughout this book, each theory and explanation of what it means to be a person should be rigorously evaluated on logical and empirical grounds; some theories are better than others. However, we also believe that it is helpful to understand each theory in its context and to be open-minded about differing points of view.

Some Current Research Developments

The Individual and the Group

One interesting focus of current research on cultural aspects of personality involves the nature of self. Of particular interest are differences between Western and Eastern (Asian) cultural views of the self. In America, the underlying assumptions about people grow out of the idea of the unlimited potential of the divinely inspired free man or woman. In America, it is assumed that each person should strive to be independent and self-reliant. We have seen that this view, in its extreme, leads American psychologists to underestimate or overlook the importance of biological factors to personality. Ironically, because the focus is on the individual, not on the social context, this view also leads to an underemphasis on cultural factors.

In contrast, in a society such as Japan, the success of the society (rather than the success of the individual) is seen as of utmost importance. Selflessness and even self-sacrifice of one's life is admired in Japanese culture but often scorned in American society. For Americans, heroes are often those people who rebel against and overcome social expectations, such as a suffragist such as Susan B. Anthony, a civil rights leader such as Martin Luther King, Jr., or an entrepreneur such as Apple computer co-inventor Steven Jobs.

Consider then people's emotional reactions across cultures (Kitayama, Markus, & Matsumoto, 1995). For example, when does a person feel embarrassment or shame? In Japanese society, making a faux pas (false step) at work, say by violating or overlooking an expected ritual of greeting or honor, could be a source of extreme embarrassment. In contrast, in certain aspects of American business (or American football), triumphing brazenly over an opponent might be cause for celebration of individual accomplishment. Note that attributing these different reactions to the individual's personality would be a mistake if culture is not also taken into account.

Many African subcultures are likewise focused on the success of the group rather than the victory of the individual. A Muslim in a Holy War who charges into battle on the front lines would delight in being assured of a place in heaven, whereas to Americans, the front line troops are akin to "cannon fodder." Asian Americans and African Americans who are in touch with their cultural roots may face a degree of personal conflict as they attempt to reconcile the pressures to be both social and individual.

How the Situation Affects Cultural Differences

As we have seen in Chapter 10 on the interactions of persons and situations, there are times when ethnic identity must be elicited from the social situation. In an experimental demonstration of this phenomenon, Anglo (European American) students and Hispanic undergraduates were exposed to either cooperative or competitive feedback while working together in small (six-person) same-sex groups. When the experimental situation was a competitive one, the response patterns of the two ethnic groups were quite similar. However, the ethnic composition of the group had a dramatic impact on the behavior of Hispanics when the situation was cooperative. Hispanics were intensely competitive when they were in a minority in the small group; but they cooperated when they were in the majority. (In contrast, the behavior of Anglos exposed to the cooperative feedback was not affected by changes in the ethnic balance of the group.) In other words, the Hispanic students functioned like the Anglos, except when the cooperative norms of their culture were salient; in that case, the ethnically influenced aspect of their personality emerged (Garza & Santos, 1991).

How Should Discrimination Be Faced?

The personality development of African Americans faces special challenges because black skin has so long been seen as a sign of inferiority by the dominant culture. They are Americans but yet not mainstream Americans. African American parents must socialize their children to understand that they will likely face discrimination (Allen & Boykin, 1992; Bowman & Howard, 1985; DuBois, 1969). Should parents explicitly talk about racial issues? Should they emphasize the unique aspects of African American culture or should they minimize differences in the hope that their children will then have an easier time dealing with—or merging into—the mainstream society? Of course, such matters face parents of many ethnic groups, though perhaps to a lesser degree. Is it good for children to know that sometimes they will fail through no fault of their own but rather due to prejudice and discrimination? Is it better to minimize such potential obstacles but at the risk that the child will not have a firm ethnic identity? Such complex matters have no simple answers but are starting to attract significant research interest as the United States and many other countries increasingly try to face up to the conflicts that exist in their multiethnic societies. A broad and deep understanding of personality, which includes cultural aspects of personality, will be necessary for significant progress to occur on these issues. (See the Famous Personalities box on page 446.)

Famous
Personalities

The Model Minority?

Should Asian Americans appreciate or deplore their status as a "model minority" group? Consider this analysis, written by an Asian American college student—undergraduate honors student Patricia Ja Lee:

> Mental health institutions, counseling centers, and community psychological services agencies rarely treat Asian Americans. Does this mean that Asian Americans are all mentally and emotionally secure and untroubled? Do Asian Americans as a group have personality characteristics that protect them from psychological problems?
>
> A popularly held stereotype of Asian Americans is encompassed in the term "the model minority." The model minority is believed to have adjusted and assimilated into the majority group's mainstream way of life, and they are thought of as well educated and financially prosperous. Being recognized for such traits as passivity, hard work, not complaining, obedience, and emotional rigidity, Asian Americans have been regarded by the dominant culture as possessing the traits that other minorities should have in order to succeed in American society.
>
> Are Asian Americans really so successful financially and psychologically? Research data show that Asian Americans (like other Americans) have a multitude of psychological disturbances that could be relieved through treatment, some of which may result from the false attributions of their "model minority" status, and the resulting differential treatment of Asian Americans.
>
> Although Asian Americans may be highly educated, this does not guarantee financial success. Once they enter professional fields, Asian Americans often find themselves held back from upward mobility within the hierarchy of their companies. Because of personality traits attributed to the model minority, such as passivity, Asian Americans are often denied positions involving interpersonal relations. Often kept from reaching managerial positions, Asian Americans are frustrated by a glass ceiling.
>
> Traditionally held attitudes contribute to the tolerance of discrimination. As a whole, Asian Americans generally believe that hard work under harsh or unfair conditions will eventually pay off. Biting their tongues and not complaining, they believe that perseverance is a virtue for which they will eventually be compensated. This attitude is reflected in their lack of activism and could also be one reason they do not seek psychological treatment for the effects of their frustrations. Asian American culture also stigmatizes the use of psychological services—such services are viewed as being for people who are crazy and have no strength to persevere. Therefore, seeking psychological help would be an admission of weak will, and would result in embarrassment to the person and to his or her family.
>
> Therefore, although Asian Americans may be suffering and may be in just as much need of psychological treatment as other members of society, they are less likely to seek help both for social reasons and for cultural reasons. So, Asian Americans' underutilization of psychological services may not be a result of their being psychologically healthier, but rather a result of their greater reluctance to seek psychological services.

Summary and Conclusion

Understanding cultural influences is important to understanding all eight of the basic aspects of personality that we have been discussing in this book. Cultural differences involve the shared behaviors and customs we learn from the institutions in our society, and they are an essential component of who we are.

Many influential personality theorists were born in Europe and were heavily affected by European culture, and so personality psychology has a rich tradition of cultural awareness even though such matters are sometimes ignored in modern personality research. Since culture is one key determinant of what it means to be a person, the systematic study of these cultural influences should be, as Gordon Allport noted, an essential part of personality psychology. A person raised in private Catholic schools in Boston is likely to have patterns of responses quite different from those of a person raised in communist schools in Beijing.

It would be a mistake to try to show how the individual's personality explains all these behavioral variations. Rather, people are shaped by their cultures. More individualistic themes tend to be found in Western cultures, more collectivist themes in Eastern cultures (Triandis, 1994). In America, black–white differences are the most significant cultural grouping, because of American history. The United States embraced principles of both equality and racial stratification, a problem Gunnar Myrdal called the American Dilemma. It should now be clear that rather than studying the vague notion of "race," it is more fruitful to study the effects of ethnic identification, history, family, subculture, religion, and social class as they interact with temperament and affect personality. These classifications are more readily definable and less susceptible to scientific and social distortion.

The effects of social class—social and economic status—on personality can be dramatic. Such issues are obvious to investigators in countries like India, which have a clear history of social classes or castes, but in America, personality psychologists typically have had little to say about social structure and personality. Karl Marx argued that psychosocial attributes such as alienation could be traced directly to the economic structure of a capitalist society, and his writings greatly influenced Erich Fromm and his associates as they thought deeply about existential alienation in modern society.

Language is one of the defining features of a person's identity. Because we each have different experiences, each individual speaks a unique version of his or her native language, called an idiolect. The "English Only" movement in the United States provides striking evidence of the psychological importance that most people attach to the idea of their mother tongue as part of who they are. Not only does our language influence how we say things, it also impacts how we think about and understand and perceive the world. Gender is one important domain where many issues of status, power, and identity profoundly influence how we use language.

A major problem with psychological testing is not simply that the tests are culturally biased but rather that the test results are used inappropriately. A fully valid personality psychology must take into account cultural variations and must simultaneously construct theories that are verifiable through the scientific collection of data. One solution to the problems of cultural ignorance in approaches to personality is not to try to eliminate culture (or "control for" culture) but rather to bring culture into key consideration as a basic element of personality.

Key Theorists

Margaret Mead   Karl Marx
Beatrice and John Whiting   Jane Mercer
Ralph Linton   Claude Steele
Harry Triandis

Key Concepts

culture   idiolect and dialect
ethnocentrism   linguistic relativity
emic approach versus etic approach   pronouns and status
archetypes   "English Only" movement
individualistic versus collectivist cultures   System of Multicultural Pluralistic
American Dilemma   Assessment
SES gradient   stereotype threat

Suggested Readings

Allport, G. W. (1954). *The nature of prejudice.* Cambridge, MA: Addison-Wesley.

Lonner, W. J., & Berry, J. W. (Eds.) (1986). *Field methods in cross-cultural research.* Beverly Hills: Sage Publications.

Matsumoto, D. R. (1996). *Culture and psychology.* Pacific Grove, CA: Brooks/Cole.

Mead, M. (1963). *Sex and temperament in three primitive societies.* New York: Morrow. (Originally published in 1935.)

Stigler, J. W., Shweder, R. A., & Herdt, G. (Eds.) (1990). *Cultural psychology: Essays on comparative human development.* New York: Cambridge University Press.

Triandis, H. C. (1995). *Individualism & collectivism.* Boulder, CO: Westview Press.

Chapter 14

Love and Hate

Legend tells us of beautiful Helen of Troy, the daughter of Zeus, whose abduction by Paris caused the terrible Trojan War. Love and beauty led to death and destruction. Or, consider Cleopatra, the seductive ancient Egyptian queen, who was the lover of Julius Caesar and then the wife of Mark Antony. She combined love, lust, and power, and ultimately killed herself as her intrigues collapsed.

The young lovers Romeo and Juliet (of Shakespeare's play) faced the hatred and opposition of their feuding parents. When Juliet's father insists that she marry someone else, she takes a potion that makes her appear dead, so that Romeo will come and rescue her. When Romeo returns, he thinks

Shakespeare's Romeo and Juliet *captures the central themes of the human drama: love and hate. After four hundred years, audiences are still drawn to the play's portrayal of the intensity, passion, and recklessness of young love, and the power of group hatred to destroy the lives of individuals.*

she is really dead and in despair, kills himself with poison. Juliet awakens, sees her lover dead, and kills herself. Here, however, the love tragedy has a positive aspect: when the families see what has happened, they put an end to their fighting.

It certainly seems that many of the most central aspects of what it means to be a person revolve around issues of love and attraction. It is difficult to find better insights than those in Homer's epics or Shakespeare's plays, but personality psychology endeavors to be scientific. As we have seen, modern personality psychology takes ancient insights and intuitions and tries to evaluate them in systematic, testable ways. Is love really the most potent motivator of people's behavior, both negative and positive?

Or is hate the greatest force underlying human endeavor? Why would an Adolf Hitler or a Joseph Stalin order the murders of millions of innocent people? Why would so many people cooperate in the annihilation of their fellow citizens?

Adolf Hitler was born in April, 1889, and killed himself in the same month in the year 1945, as his Third Reich collapsed around him. During his lifetime, he exuded a hatred so potent that he was able to mobilize an amazing enmity in his countrymen. It resulted in the implementation of a policy culminating in the death of over 11,000,000 of those he hated. Millions of children were butchered, starved, shot, and burned. Hitler said, "It is not by the principles of humanity that man lives or is able to preserve himself above the animal world, but solely by means of the most brutal struggle" (Bullock, 1962).

How can someone come to hate so much? Hitler's father died when Hitler was still a young boy, and his mother was said to be overindulgent. Hitler was a poor student and a failed artist. Even in his youth, he had a temperament that led him to be passionate, intolerant, and unable to form the usual types of social ties. (These events are not that uncommon and so of course do not fully explain his later behavior; they are *part* of the picture.) Hitler welcomed his participation in the First World War, in which he repeatedly risked his life (Davidson, 1977). Yet Hitler was one of the world's shrewdest politicians, outmaneuvering the leaders of other countries. Despite his own unusual nature, he often well understood the nature of others.

We are also fascinated by so-called serial killers like David Berkowitz, the "Son of Sam," who crept up on young men and women sitting in parked cars and shot them. And consider this: why would a serial killer like Jeffrey Dahmer, a seemingly handsome and intelligent young man, strangle a series of male lovers, have sexual relations with their dead bodies (necrophilia), keep their heads in his freezer, mummify a penis, and eat his victims' dead flesh (using a meat tenderizer when it was too tough)? Can personality psychology explain this kind of apparently unprovoked hostility?

*A*s in the other chapters of the third section of this book, this chapter examines specific applications of personality psychology to individual differences. We believe that although personality psychology should be scientifically rigorous, it also must confront head-on the basic issues of human nature.

The Personality of Hate

For many years, love and hate were viewed as divinely inspired. For example, the ancient Roman god Cupid appeared as a winged infant carrying a bow and a quiver of arrows; if he shot you, the wound inspired love. Hate was often seen as the result of possession by the devil. For example, parts of the Christian church persecuted witches for several centuries, and in 1692, twenty so-called witches were cruelly executed after the famous witch trials in Salem, Massachusetts. The goal was to drive away the devil. However, when Charles Darwin turned attention to the "animal" nature of humans, the centuries-old stories of angels and devils were reinterpreted into psychological and psychobiological

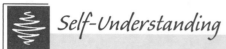

The Authoritarian Personality

At various times and places in history, the world is troubled by extremely militaristic and repressive leaders who act against what most of us consider to be ethical and moral. The fascist leaders of the 1930s and 1940s are notorious examples. Does personality psychology have anything to say about this? How can we assess a tendency toward fascism?

After World War II, a number of social scientists tried to make sense of the brutal deaths of millions of people. One research group, based at the University of California, Berkeley, conducted a large study of what they came to term the "authoritarian personality" (Adorno et al., 1950). Drawing heavily on Freud's theories (but also considering ego notions and social learning), these social scientists profiled a typical person with antidemocratic tendencies.

The authoritarian personality has a strong id but a weak ego, and so sexual and aggressive urges are not dealt with in a rational manner. Rather, there is a very strong superego, evidenced in the person's holding very conventional values and an uncritical acceptance of and admiration for authority. The authoritarian personality typically deals with sexual urges by projecting them onto the external world. To deal with anxieties and inadequacies about power and sexuality, the authoritarian blames and scapegoats others. In the case of a psychologically weak, threatened white man, this may result in stereotyping such as that blacks are uncontrollably oversexed, that Jews are plotting to grab world power, that handicapped people are immoral polluters, that Orientals are untrustworthy scavengers, and so on. The out-groups, who in reality lack much power, are portrayed as immoral, dangerous, power-hungry, and worthless, so that the authoritarian personality can feel good.

Authoritarians usually grow up in very strict homes, in which there is typically physical punishment from a domineering father intolerant of ambiguity and change. Or, the father may be absent altogether. Authoritarians cope with their own uncertainties and problems in relationships by believing that wild happenings and orgies are going on somewhere out there in the world around them, especially among members of the stereotyped out-group. They have a high respect for authority and believe in severe punishment for lawbreakers, such as castration for rapists. They desire to look tough and avoid dealing with inner feelings. These characteristics are measured with the **F-scale** (F for fascist).

Although the concept of authoritarianism is not problem-free, the main idea has survived the test of time. It may not be the source of most prejudice, but there is little doubt that this syndrome can be useful in understanding the behaviors of certain repressed individuals. Prejudice does form patterns. For example, such individuals are attracted to symbols of adolescent masculinity, such as wearing imposing uniforms or carrying weapons.

The prejudice, narrow-mindedness, and defensiveness of many people can be better addressed by understanding the personality dynamics that often underlie such patterns. It should be remembered, however, that the actions taken by authoritarians will be heavily influenced by the society and the precise social situations in which they find themselves.

theories. Personality theory and theorists provide varying explanations for these motivations—for why we hate. (See Self-Understanding.)

Why did Hitler, on a massive scale, and Dahmer, with his own hands, hurt others? What about serial killer Ted Bundy, an outwardly attractive, normal man who physically and sexually tortured young women? Women liked him and he gained their trust by faking injuries (such as wearing a cast). He viciously killed at least twenty.

How did these killers come to have such aggressive, hateful personalities? What makes a person hateful? Is it innate, inborn, part of the person? Is hate the by-product of a biological defect of some kind? Does it emerge from what the individual has learned or witnessed? Is hate the result of one's cognitive interpretation? Or, does some aspect of the situation in which the person finds himself or herself trigger his or her hateful behavior?

Explanations of Hate: The Different Perspectives

Biological Explanations of Hate

Several personality perspectives see aggression, and its internal manifestation in hatred, as a natural, biologically based aspect of humanity. That is, we are biologically predisposed to hate by our genetic heritage. The psychoanalytic and neo-analytic views are part of this tradition but they have been surpassed by more modern biological theorizing. Perhaps most influential of these today is the ethological perspective and we will begin there.

Ethological Explanations

Ethologists study animal behavior in natural environments and draw inferences about the function of the behavior for survival. The ethologists Konrad Lorenz (1967) and Eibl-Eibesfeldt (1971, 1979) characterized aggression as the product of adaptive evolutionary processes. According to this argument, hatred is innate because aggression was adaptive in the evolution of our species. Just as brightly colored male fish attack and kill their fellow fish in tropical waters to protect territorial and mating rights, so too humans defend their beachfront property to the death. A "Son of Sam" may kill young dating couples in part because he himself does not have access to a date. Consistent with evolutionary theory, mass murderers are usually men rather than women, and they are usually men of prime mating age rather than old men. Further, despots like Hitler and Stalin and their henchmen are always expansionist—seeking new territories for their empire.

Ethologists view aggression in animals (and by extension, in humans) as innate and adaptive. Does that perspective shed any light on why cultural differences (across time and locale) and individual differences (within a cultural group) are so strikingly great?

These ethological theories also state that natural aggressive tendencies may be distorted and sometimes expressed inappropriately. For example, because our modern society restrains aggressive actions, this frustrating of natural aggression may result in modern individuals' experiencing a buildup of aggressiveness, which requires some kind of expression or outlet. Consistent with this view, there is some evidence that serial killers often have unusually strict parents, who may foster a buildup of aggressive feelings.

Or, on a larger scale, Hitler may have been expressing his territorial aggressions, accumulated through years of societal repression and intensified when Germany was forced to give up territory after losing the First World War. So, he ordered the extinction of all individuals who, he believed, should not remain in his territory, especially Gypsies and Jews. According to this view, the handicapped, the disfigured, and the homosexuals were "naturally" repellent to Hitler because of a biologically based aversion to deviancy; it follows that they too had to be eliminated. Ethologists point out that mutant members of a species are often destroyed. (Ethologists acknowledge that such notions are repugnant to our sensibilities but reply that nature is cruel.)

There are, however, serious problems with these ethological explanations when we try to utilize them in a scaled-down way to explain the hateful actions of an individual. This theoretical orientation helps us understand why people have a deep-rooted capacity for aggression, but why do we find so many individual and cross-cultural differences in aggressiveness? Many people who grow up with strict parents do not have an explosion of hostile aggression. They do not murder their neighbors or wage war against children. Many cultures and subcultures have a very low incidence of aggression (like Japan, or like Madison, Wisconsin, and western Pennsylvania), while in others it is sky-high (as in the United States overall, or in Miami and New Orleans). Similarly, although evolutionary psychologists would not be surprised that invading Bosnian Serbs would want to rape and impregnate Bosnian Muslims, why would some soldiers relish this pillage but others refuse?

Furthermore, ethological solutions to aggression have often proved ineffective. For example, Lorenz suggests organized sports as a safe means for people to release inner aggressive tendencies. Yet sports matches (such as soccer matches and hockey games) regularly inspire fistfights among players and spectators, and sometimes even lead to stadium riots. (And the armed forces engage in war games to *encourage* toughness and aggression in their troops.) If anything, competition often seems to bring out aggressive tendencies rather than dissipate them. Finally, ethological explanations generally bring with them a sense of inevitability about aggression: if it is in our genes, then it cannot be halted (Silverberg & Gray, 1992; Stoff & Cairns, 1996). This fatalism is a problem we have discussed throughout this book.

Brain Disorders

Another biological explanation for individuals with particularly aggressive, hateful personalities involves structural and drug-induced brain disorders. For example, many homicides are committed under the influence of alcohol or amphetamines (Brain, 1986). It is well known from experiments on laboratory animals that stimulation of certain brain centers can produce intense, unremitting rage (Adams et al., 1993). Indeed, some people who have evidenced fits of rage or intense hatred have been found to have abnormalities of brain structures involving lesions on and near the hypothalamus and amygdala (temporal lobe). Might Hitler have been the victim of such a brain abnormality? There is some anecdotal evidence that Hitler did indeed blow up in violent outbursts at times. Obviously without post-mortem access to his central nervous system, we will never know for sure, but note that Hitler and his associates often functioned quite rationally in a sophisticated German society. Brain disorder is usually associated with sudden, uncontrollable rages rather than with the cold, calculated planning of the deaths of millions.

Recent studies using brain positron emission tomography (PET) scans hint that people with a low density of dopamine receptors (D2 receptors) in the basal ganglia area of the brain are more likely to have a detached, aloof personality (Farde, Gustavsson, & Jonsson, 1997). Dopamine, a key neurotransmitter (chemical messenger), is known to be related to mood. Here again we have a piece of the basis for unraveling the biological correlates of personality, but the biology is only small part of the picture.

In the mid-1960s, one mass murderer, Charles Whitman, took possession of the campus tower at the University of Texas and shot (killing or injuring)

Sniper Charles Whitman, shown here (back row, right) with his family in earlier days, was found to have had a malignant brain tumor. Does this explain (or excuse) the murderous behavior of this clean-cut All-American?

dozens of people. A post-mortem examination determined that Whitman had a malignant brain tumor near the amygdala. Was that lesion responsible for his sudden rage? Or, did it merely contribute to other influences? If so, should a killer like Whitman be excused from his actions because of his "illness"? Such questions illustrate ways in which the study of personality psychology is relevant to many matters of societal concern.

Psychoanalytic Approaches to Hate

After viewing the destruction caused by the First World War, Sigmund Freud more fully developed his ideas of the aggressive, destructive side of the id as a counter force to the lustful urges of the libido. Remember that Freud was heavily influenced by Darwin and was trained as a biologist, so Freudian explanations of hate have a distinctly biological flavor, although they also draw from other wells.

Freud postulated the existence of an aggressive instinct or drive. In fact, he theorized that all people have a death instinct: **thanatos** is the drive toward death and self-destructive behavior. Self-destructive behavior is, however, unacceptable in modern society (Weininger, 1996). As with socially unacceptable sexual impulses, this energy must either be released or be dealt with in another, more socially appropriate manner. Whereas some, maybe even most, individuals repress this instinct and are not conscious of it, other people may utilize other defense mechanisms to deter thanatos.

One such likely mechanism involves projecting the unacceptable death impulse onto the hated object(s)—that is, attributing the hatred to others. For example, they might see others as aggressive, hateful, and dangerous. According to this line of thinking, projection of aggressive impulses results in hatred and paranoia toward the object of the projection. Alternatively, if an individual feels hatred toward a dangerous, unsuitable object such as his father, he might displace that hostility to a more suitable and less threatening object—

perhaps toward a disadvantaged social group. Thus, Freudian theory can lead to the prediction that a dictator's scapegoating of out-group members (blaming them for all the ills of his society) results from his own problems and the consequent use of defense mechanisms. In fact, a study that examined the defense mechanisms of violent individuals found that they were more likely to use projection as a defense mechanism and that the use of displacement differentiated violent and nonviolent individuals (Apter et al., 1989).

In modern psychiatric terminology, many of these hateful people, including many serial killers, would be diagnosed as having an antisocial personality disorder (Meyer et al., 1998). (Such people are also called "psychopaths.") They violate rules even as children; for example, a thirteen-year-old boy who pulls the wings off insects, carries a knife to bully his classmates, likes to destroy property, and generally lies to and cons others would be so diagnosed. Not surprisingly, serial killer Ted Bundy tortured animals as a teenager.

Neo-Analytic Views of Hate

Neo-analytic theorists go beyond Freud's description of an innate death instinct when explaining aggression. Jung hypothesized that of the personality elements that are common to all human personality—the archetypes—one particular archetype, the shadow, is where the primitive, animal instincts reside. Thus, according to Jung, inappropriate or uncontrolled expression of one's shadow could result in the type of primal hatred and aggression evidenced by Hitler. Additionally, remember that Jung described psychological types based on the individual's placement on personality trait typologies: introversion/extroversion and thinking/feeling/sensing/intuiting. The thinking-extroverted type is described as stubborn, intolerant and opinionated, aspiring to tough, unyielding principles—a type not incompatible with dictators.

Jung also discussed the manner in which individuals combine their experiences and memories into personality. A power complex, for example, may increasingly influence an individual's perceptions and actions until it seems that the complex is in control. It is certainly possible to conceive of Hitler as controlled by a power complex. To sum up in Jungian terms: a Hitler might be seen as a man for whom one particular archetype, the shadow, dominates other archetypes in his personality, emphasizing his animal, aggressive nature; with a thinking-extroverted (rigid and obstinate) type; and a power complex driving him to seek ever-increasing territory.

Alfred Adler and Karen Horney also believed (along with Freud and Jung) that hostile, hateful personalities developed during childhood, but these neo-analysts did not claim that they arose directly from a biological instinct or drive. (This is in line with the neo-analytic emphasis on the role of society.) When explaining the etiology of hostility in the individual, Adler focused on

Famous Personalities

The Murder of Cara Knott

Cara Knott was a bright, blond, energetic twenty-year-old college student in San Diego when her battered and strangled body was found beneath a well-traveled freeway overpass. What was so surprising about her murder was that Cara was an extremely careful and conscientious person who always took the utmost precautions. She would never have associated with strangers.

What was even more surprising, however, was the identity of her murderer. Craig Peyer was a distinguished officer of the California Highway Patrol (CHP) with a spotless record. Married with three children, Peyer was known as friendly and a "straight arrow."

When Cara's body was discovered near a little-used freeway off-ramp, the police were at first stumped. But then an increasing number of young women—dozens of them—alerted by the publicity, called in to say that they previously had been pulled over on the same off-ramp at night and detained by a CHP officer. These women likewise were pretty and had been driving alone. Evidently, Officer Peyer liked to use his authority to force conversations with women, until something went very wrong when he tried to do this with Cara Knott.

Although this case is certainly unusual, many people thought it to be impossible. How could such a man, sworn to law enforcement and with a perfect record, be a murderer?

As we have seen throughout this book, surface consistencies in personality may spring from a deeper set of forces. Should we be suspicious when someone is too "perfect"? It was reported that Craig Peyer was a super-responsible officer; the district attorneys loved to work with him on cases. The CHP sometimes used him as their television spokesman because of his confident and friendly manner. Other officers even liked to use his patrol car on the next shift because he kept it so clean! Yet remember that this super-straight officer was also attracted to and professionally trained in the use of authority and, when necessary, deadly force.

Such unusual cases remind us of the complexity of evil. No simple explanations will suffice. But some level of understanding is possible.

If you travel I-15 in San Diego today, you drive over the Cara Knott Memorial Bridge.

early social experiences, especially coping with rejection. Children who are rejected by their parents may come to view the world as inhospitable and hostile. These children are more likely to grow up to be criminals. Remember that Adler emphasized that although it is a natural part of childhood to experience feelings of inferiority, most of us learn to compensate for these inferior feelings by succeeding in a variety of endeavors. However, individuals who develop an inferiority complex (including feelings of helplessness and incompetence) may sometimes overcompensate (developing a superiority complex), which leads them to attack and denigrate others in an attempt to increase their own feelings of importance. Hitler and Stalin seem to fit the type that Adler called dominant or ruling—the kind of person who proceeds for his or her own gain without consideration of others. (See Famous Personalities.)

Why did twenty-eight-year-old Timothy McVeigh blow up the federal building in Oklahoma City, sending body parts of nineteen small children flying? Was he the popular class president in high school? No, he was small, thin, the son of divorced parents, did not date, and had a strong, early fascination with guns. Was he a family man with a loving wife and four kids? No, he wanted to join the army's Special Forces (Green Berets) but didn't make it. He read racist, anti-Semitic literature and admired terrorists for their individualism.

Karen Horney also looked to childhood as the time of life when an individual becomes hateful, arguing that children must feel safe during childhood to develop properly. When children experience an extended time when they do not feel safe (for example, when they repeatedly experience undue punishment or when parents embarrass or shame them), their security is undermined. Repressed anxiety becomes basic anxiety, and neurosis.

Horney proposed self-protective measures to which the abused child might turn. One of these mechanisms is to achieve power and superiority over others, which counteracts the feeling that one is impotent or being mistreated. She called these personality characteristics neurotic trends and specified one of these trends to be an aggressive personality (moving against people). A person with an aggressive personality sees most others as being hostile and believes that only the most competent and cunning survive; so he behaves accordingly—is hateful and hostile, denigrating and abusing others (and in this manner maintains his feelings of control and power). As a child, Joseph Stalin (who became the ruthless Soviet dictator) was savagely beaten by his drunken father. He was physically strong but short, and his face was severely scarred by a childhood bout with smallpox. Like Hitler, he became strong-willed and revenge-minded. Stalin even scorned his own son as a "weakling." Millions of peasants died under his policies of forced collectivization of farming and production, and his political purges.

Under Stalin's rule, millions of citizens (peasants, military leaders, politicians, and industrialists) disappeared during the "Great Terror," killed by starvation, execution, or forced labor. Here, members of Stalin's Communist Youth League dig up bags of grain that had been hidden in a cemetery by farmers trying to protect their harvest from confiscation by Stalin's totalitarian state. Is Horney right that aggressive personalities arise from abuse in childhood?

Erik Erikson, in his theory that people are presented with conflicts to overcome during each stage of life, viewed individual aggression as emerging during the social interactions of early childhood. According to Erikson, three unsuccessfully resolved psychosocial stages may result in an individual who is angry, hostile, and hateful: (1) The child who does not develop an adequate trust during infancy will likely develop a pattern of continuing to be distrustful later in life. (2) The child who is treated in a hostile manner when pursuing autonomy may become destructive and angry. (3) Finally, if the child's initiative is punished and thwarted rather than realistically channeled, the child may fail to develop an adequate superego. This individual, whose parents are so woefully lacking during these three important stages of psychosocial development, may become a hateful, aggressive adult.

In sum, the neo-analytic perspective spans both biological and nonbiological explanations for hate. Neo-analysts see hate as arising from improper channeling of drives and from failures to resolve the conflicts of childhood. Although powerful instincts exist, aggression is not inevitable but rather is the result of poor parenting and an unstable social environment. This view is commonly seen today in explanations of inner-city violence committed by children of immature single mothers.

Hate and Authoritarianism: Erich Fromm

Like many social scientists, Erich Fromm struggled to understand why many Germans willingly accepted Nazi totalitarianism. Fromm emphasized the cultural milieu as well as the individual's personal history as sources of hostility and hatred. Fromm theorized that individuals feel more and more alone and isolated as civilization advances and as people attain more and more individual freedom. In order to counteract these feelings of loneliness and alienation, he theorized, some people renounce their freedom, surrendering their individuality and principles in order to belong to the group, at any cost.

However, Fromm, a psychoanalyst, additionally emphasized the importance of early relationships. He accepted psychic mechanisms within the individual similar to the neurotic trends defined by Horney. People with an authoritarian personality type often have a cruel penchant for exerting power over others, abusing them, and taking their possessions. That is, the authoritarian person actually wants to cause the suffering of others. This personality characteristic, according to Fromm, is generated by a particularly negative relationship with one's parents. Thus Fromm straddles the line between biological and nonbiological determinants of hate. He accepts that we have a biological heritage that yields the capacity for violence, and he accepts that improper channeling of drives during childhood can create lifelong problems; but he places the bulk of the blame on our failure to find meaning in an empty society. He thereby incorporates elements of an existential and humanistic view of hate.

Interestingly, the British actor Anthony Hopkins was able to overcome a lonely childhood and alcohol problems as an adult, to star as the psychopath Hannibal Lecter in the chilling film *The Silence of the Lambs* (1991). Lecter (the character) was a seemingly charming and intelligent gentleman but one who would bite off the nose of someone who got too close. Hopkins (the actor) was able to relate to the dark forces of personality that might motivate such vile behavior, yet Hopkins himself was able to overcome the forces that had afflicted him.

The Humanistic Perspective on Hate

Humanistic psychologists take a viewpoint nearly opposite to the biological approaches to hatred. In contrast to the ethologists, humanistic theorists emphasize the many ways in which people are different from animals. They underscore the importance of morality, justice, and commitment, which involve complex thought and self-awareness. In contrast to the psychoanalysts and neo-analysts, humanistic psychologists focus more on the mature self-actualizer than on the inordinately hateful individual. They look at what can go right rather than what can go wrong during upbringing. However, humanistic explanations for individual hatred can be derived from the theories.

The humanistic psychologist Carl Rogers believed that negative emotion stems from a lack of positive regard in the individual's life, particularly from parents during childhood. Rogers emphasized the individual's need for unconditional positive regard, acceptance, and love from others, especially from one's mother. Parents who place conditions on their positive regard for their child (such as a mother who coldly withdraws her love each time her child misbehaves) will likely have an anxious child. Such children grow up afraid to realize their full potential; they are threatened by experiences that challenge their self-concept. As the amount of discrepancy (incongruence) between one's perceptions of oneself and one's real experiences increases, the greater is the tendency to distort reality and possibly even become psychotic. For example, someone who hoped to be a friendly, well-liked, and well-respected leader but had to deny or distort negative reactions from peers because of inner fears and insecurities cannot become a self-confident, fully functioning, and growing individual. Instead, such a person might be stagnating, cruel, and antisocial. However, Rogers (1961) was so optimistic that he believed *all* persons—regardless of their circumstances—could unleash their internal tendencies toward positive growth.

Abraham Maslow (1968) also pointed out that our fears and doubts about ourselves are at the root of immaturity and hate. He focused on unmet safety needs as afflicting the neurotic adult. Like Rogers, Maslow insisted that evil and hatred are not a basic part of people's personalities but instead result from experiencing a deficient environment. In a world without child abuse, poverty, divorce, and discrimination, the incidence of children growing into hating adults presumably would plummet. Yet Maslow, unlike Rogers, did not urge unconditional acceptance of others. Rather, he argued that children (and adults) need structure and regulation as well as love and feelings of safety. Further, Maslow, reflecting on Hitler's atrocities, did not share Rogers's optimistic view that every person could be redeemed.

Hatred as a Trait

Starting in 1979, a number of women were ambushed and murdered while hiking in the San Francisco Bay area. Eventually, David Carpenter was arrested. He had suffered under an emotionally abusive father, a physically abusive mother, and childhood peers who made fun of his stuttering. He was cruel to animals and had a violent temper and a strong sex drive (Douglas, 1995). Remember that trait theorist Gordon Allport (1961) described cardinal traits as personality characteristics that are ubiquitous and highly influential in an individual's personality and which dominate the individual's day-to-day actions. When we consider Carpenter and similar others filled with hatred and aggression (like Ted Bundy), it seems clear that these are cardinal traits, defining characteristics of their personalities.

For trait theorists, traits like aggression are part of the dynamic organization of personality, parts of personality that incline an individual to behave in certain ways. Raymond Cattell (1966), using factor analysis to extract the common human traits, isolated those source traits that, if manifest to an extreme degree, seem to characterize a killer. Individuals low on factor A are aloof and critical; people low on factor C are emotionally unstable; people high on factor E are dominant and aggressive; those low on Factor I are tough-minded; and those high on factor L are suspicious. Extreme scores on these factors could conceivably combine to describe a cold-blooded killer. Since these traits are descriptive (derived from factor analysis), they are not incompatible with other theoretical formulations. They are merely a different view of the same phenomenon.

For Hans Eysenck, the personality dimension most relevant to hate is psychoticism. As we have seen (Chapter 8), a person high on this dimension is impulsive, cruel, tough-minded, and antisocial. (In terms of the Big Five scheme, the counterpart would be low Agreeableness and low Conscientiousness.) For Eysenck, these dispositional differences are assumed to be based in differences in neurophysiology (and often hereditary). However, no one has yet discovered the physiological pattern that may underlie this orientation.

In applied research on aggression, psychologist Seymour Feshbach (1971) viewed anger as an emotional reaction that culminates in hateful behavior. Feshbach found that other emotional responses such as empathy and altruism could counter aggression. That is, Feshbach says that empathy inhibits one's response to the social contexts that elicit aggressive feelings and behaviors. Children who are more empathic are less aggressive, and low-empathy children are more aggressive (Feshbach & Feshbach, 1969). Interestingly, participation in an empathy training program reduced aggression in both aggressive and relatively nonaggressive children (Feshbach & Feshbach, 1982).

Cognitive Approaches to Hate

Remember that cognitive approaches to personality pay little direct attention to biology and the actual events of childhood. Rather, they emphasize that it is not an individual's real experiences, but the manner in which a person interprets (construes) his or her relationships and experiences that determines his or her actions. According to this view, hatred and aggression depend on the ways we learn to explain the world.

George Kelly, for example, looked at personal constructs toward others. He found that some people do not make many distinctions among others—they are more likely to perceive other people as similar to one another. People who are more authoritarian are like this, exhibiting what Kelly (1963) called cognitive simplicity. This permits one to dismiss whole groups of people as "enemies."

Kelly additionally explained that hostility may result when an individual's construal of others is not supported by experience. Well-adjusted people evaluate others realistically and alter their concepts if evidence indicates they are incorrect; maladjusted people do not. Instead, hostile people try to constrain others to fit their construal, rather than changing their interpretation of reality. Hitler attempted to alter the composition of an entire nation to fit his construal of it. Did Berkowitz perhaps "eliminate" those who did not meet his view of reality? Indeed, differences have been found in the manner in which violent people perceive threat compared to people who are not hostile. For example, violent criminals are more likely to perceive events as threatening and to see other people as having hostile intentions. It is believed that psychopaths have deficits in the processing of both social and cognitive tasks (Serin & Kuriychuk, 1994).

These distortions of the meaning of social interactions begin at an early age. Dodge and his colleagues have found that preadolescent and young adolescent boys who are aggressive are more likely to misperceive hostility in a variety of aspects of their social engagements (Lochman & Dodge, 1994). Therefore, according to these cognitive models, extreme hostility and hatred result from the individual's misconstrual of situations, frequently attributing malevolent intentions to events and people that are actually benign.

Learning Theory: Hate as Learned Behavior

B. F. Skinner held that we gain little except confusion by arguing that someone has hatred, or aggressive tendencies, or a motivation to aggress. Instead, we should simply note if and when someone (or some pigeon) actually does aggress. By focusing directly on the behavior, we can begin to see which environmental contingencies make the aggressive act more likely to occur. Learning theories state that aggression is acquired through the same mechanisms as all behavior.

Classic learning theory says that hateful emotions are conditioned responses, whereas operant learning theory emphasizes the role of reinforcements and punishments in shaping learned aggressiveness. Social learning theory incorporates the point that the hateful behavior of others is modeled, observed, imitated, and vicariously reinforced.

What about the serial killer who murders only women? A series of events, such as violent abuse by one's mother during childhood, would, according to the theory of conditioned learning, result in the eventual pairing of the conditioned response of hatred and aggression to women, even when the abuse was not occurring. This hatred might be quite specific to women who look like, or have some specific characteristics similar to, the original unconditioned stimulus—Mom. Or, the hateful emotions might generalize to a larger group of individuals, for example, all middle-aged women. That is, the sight of the conditioned stimulus (any woman) would elicit hateful feelings and would provoke the behaviors that accompany them. Examination of the childhoods and life histories of several mass murderers indicates that many of them indeed did suffer at the hands of individuals who are similar to their victims, lending some credence to the premise that, in at least some cases, hatred is a conditioned response.

It is certainly true that if hateful behavior (toward a group) is reinforcing, either because it attracts attention to an otherwise ignored individual, or because it evokes the adulation of others, or because it brings material possessions (booty), then the person will continue to behave in a hostile manner, and in fact, the aggression may actually escalate.

When Dollard and Miller further expanded the conditioned response paradigm, they demonstrated that defense mechanisms such as projection, and one's thoughts (including angry and hostile ones), can be conditioned. Some of these may become secondary drives that motivate much of the individual's actions. Hatred can thus be learned and become a drive that impels one to behave in an aggressive, hostile manner.

Children who live in homes filled with hate (fighting parents) often grow up to be hateful themselves, learning hostility from their parents' example. Further, a person who was abused as a child is more likely to become an abusive parent. These social learning processes—vicarious learning and modeling—can be quite powerful.

Cultural Differences in Hatred

Anthropologists have provided a significant amount of evidence that there are huge societal differences in the average (and the culturally acceptable) level of hostility in a society (Goldstein & Segall, 1983). Whereas some societies have been characterized as extremely aggressive, others demonstrate little interpersonal hatred or hostility. Obviously, something in the social structure must be relevant.

Even within the boundaries of the United States, cultural differences have been found to predict differential levels of hostility. Nisbett and Cohen (1996) compared the northern part of the United States to the southern states and found that the higher rate of homicide in the South seems to be due to a culture of honor that advocates violent responses to perceived insults.

Interestingly, there is little regional difference in the North/South homicide rates for African Americans, suggesting that it is something about white southern culture that causes the violence, instead of just living below the Mason-Dixon line (Nisbett & Cohen, 1996). Also, a widespread presence of guns contributes to a cycle of violence in which arguments lead to deadly retri-

Within the United States, the states of the deep South have a higher rate of homicide among whites than in the northern states. Specific cultural beliefs or practices in the region may produce this effect.

bution. With dramatic cultural and subcultural differences in aggression, personality theories that focus solely on characteristics of the individual are clearly inadequate. Thus, some sort of person-by-situation interactionist approach is needed (as described in Chapter 10).

Evaluation: Hate

In sum, there is usually no simple explanation of hatred and aggression. Just as we have seen throughout this book, the different personality perspectives make different assumptions and collect differing evidence about what it means to be a person—in this case, what it means to be an evil, hateful person.

Occasionally, a brain tumor or other severe provocation is the simple explanation for hate, but those cases are extremely rare. Rather, hate and aggression often seem to arise from a combination of forces. Most basically, there does seem to be an innate capacity for hate and aggression. Many animals defend their offspring, their territories, and their mates through vicious aggression. And specific parts of the brain are central to rage. The evidence supports the idea that we have a capacity but not an inevitability for hate and aggression in our natures.

Several perspectives agree that hate and aggression are especially likely if one faces an abusive and unstable childhood environment. These orientations take the emphasis away from biology and place it in the identities and patterns that are set in motion through parent–child relations. Children who are treated with abuse and contempt by their parents or their society are likely to become abusive and contemptuous adults. Further, the ways we learn to interpret events, and the rewards we see and receive, can have dramatic effects on our likelihood of aggression. Even whole societies differ markedly in the amount of hate and aggression they contain and display. The specific situation also matters, as certain people in certain situations are more likely to aggress.

It is interesting to consider the supposed simple "cures" for hate and aggression that our complex analysis tells us will generally *not* work as a comprehensive solution: medications or brain surgery for violent offenders; school education programs; threats of whipping or death; organized intensive sports competitions; or hoping the inherent good inside each person will eventually surface or prevail. Such simple solutions are often proposed by politicians, but they are too narrow to be generally effective. Rather, tendencies toward hatred and aggression can be minimized by serious efforts to create a society with physically healthy individuals (who also avoid substance abuse) who develop good relations with their parents; a society that models and rewards only cooperative behavior; a society that fosters justice and guides its citizens along a disciplined and productive life path. However, even in such a stable, well-balanced society, certain individuals will still need more intensive interventions.

The Personality of Love

Is love the counterpart of hatred? Are they opposite sides of the same coin? Or is love, in its own right, the most potent motivator of behavior? How do the personality theorists explain love?

Ethological Explanations of Love

The British journalist Woodrow Wyatt (1981) said, "A man falls in love through his eyes, a woman through her ears." He meant that a man is attracted by a woman's beauty but a woman is attracted by what she hears about a man's status. Evolutionary psychology explains that love through the millennia developed because of its adaptive consequences. Attraction to members of the opposite sex is obviously necessary if we are to reproduce. In addition, for our genes to produce offspring that will themselves grow to reproduce, two basic elements must immediately come into play: (1) characteristics that ensure that a healthy offspring is born and (2) characteristics that ensure that the helpless child will survive (to reproductive age).

Such arguments underlie the research of evolutionary psychologists like David Buss, who draws on the work of biologist Robert Trivers (1996) and psychologists Martin Daly and Margo Wilson (Daly, Wilson, & Weghorst, 1982). Buss hypothesizes that there are different characteristics for which males and females look when selecting a mate because of their different biological roles during reproduction. The male, according to this argument, is attracted to females who have physical characteristics indicating their suitability to conceive and carry a healthy offspring through a successful pregnancy. Thus, the male should be attracted to females who are young, fit, and healthy—characteristics represented, in part, by the degree of physical attractiveness.

Females are also somewhat attracted to males based on their physical attractiveness because of the ability of physical attractiveness to indicate potential fertility and genetic health. (Males with disease and infirmity are less likely to be suitable gene carriers.) Females, however, must invest nine months during gestation, and a long period of time during the child's helpless infancy and childhood, taking care of the child. Since the female's energies are concentrated on child care, she requires a male who can provide her with the necessities of life, such as food and shelter, while her offspring are children. Thus, females prefer men who are able to provide for these needs. According to Buss, this means that females are attracted to men who have skills required to successfully acquire resources (Buss & Schmitt, 1993; Buss et al., 1998). Evolutionary considerations are seen to be as salient today as they were in earlier times.

The evolutionary perspective claims that the optimal mate has different characteristics for males than for females. A male should prefer females who appear young and fertile, whereas a female should prefer males who appear able to provide resources for her offspring.

Buss has supported his theoretical perspective with several empirical studies. For example, in one study, German and American men and women demonstrated dependable sex differences in attraction: men routinely emphasized physical attractiveness as important for mate selection, whereas women consistently highlighted earning ability as important when choosing a partner (Buss & Angleitner, 1989).

Are these differences just due to gender role expectations? Cross-cultural evidence yields some support to the contention that these preferences reflect inherent, genetic characteristics. Reviewing studies in thirty-three countries, representing an array of different cultural orientations, Buss found that, irrespective of culture, women are more likely to prefer mates who have an ability to acquire resources. Ambitious, hard-working men were consistently valued by women, across cultures (Buss, 1989). Moreover, men in all cultures were more likely to value youth and physical attractiveness in females.

Where does love come into this picture? From the male perspective, it is necessary for males (but not females) to ensure the paternity of their offspring. (Females know that their infant is theirs, but males cannot be certain.) Emotional commitment between sexual partners has adaptive value as it bolsters monogamy, helping to ensure that the female will not mate with others. From the female perspective, love, and the commitment that accompanies it, helps ensure that the male will stick around, providing resources, until the child is grown (Buss & Schmitt, 1993).

One of the problems with confirming these ideas is that we do not know for sure what specific evolutionary pressures were faced by our ancestors. Furthermore, most of us know that men are attracted to healthy and sexy young women and that women like men who are stable and have talents and resources. So the evolutionary "prediction" was not a difficult or intriguing one to make or confirm. Women are also attracted to men with a sense of humor. What evolutionary pressures could be relevant to that? In other words, this line of reasoning holds great promise but is far from proven.

Psychoanalytic Explanations for Love

Freud viewed love as arising from the sexual instincts. During the oral stage of development, mothers provide one's first erotic pleasure—that involved in oral gratification. As a result, mother becomes the child's first object of love. Much later, during the genital stage, the individual learns that sexual satisfaction can be provided by a sexual partner. The strong feeling accompanying mature sexual attraction, according to Freud, is love. That is, love is a result of the fact that one's sexual partner is responsible for sexual satisfaction. Love arises out of adult sex, just as love first arose out of oral gratification. This perspective suggests that "what I do for love," I am really doing for sex, a somewhat limited and pessimistic outlook (Miller & Siegel, 1972).

Freud's followers adapted this theoretical outlook. Melanie Klein and the object relations theorists noted that for almost all children the mother is the nurturer, and therefore mother is the first and most salient love object. Object relations theory digresses from Freudian theory at this point, avoiding Freud's use of the Oedipal stage to explain the transfer of affection to the parent of the same sex. Instead, object relations theorists emphasize the importance of this first mother/child relationship, stating that the child internalizes the nature of this relationship, which becomes, in a sense, the prototype or

Psychoanalytic and neo-analytic theories stress the lasting influence of the mother as the first love object. Is it just a coincidence that when the little boy on the left grew up to become the young man on the right, he chose to marry a woman who resembles what his mother looked like as a young woman?

template for future loves. Our adult love is based on our mother love, perhaps being imitative, perhaps opposite. If mother teases with her breast, we may seek a teasing lover in adulthood (or may avoid teases). Some theorists highlight the feeding and drive-reduction elements of the early relationship, while others emphasize the attachment aspects—the tactile comfort and feelings of safety and security offered by one's mother.

Neo-Analytic Explanations for Love

Erik Erikson (1963) focused on the sixth stage of psychosocial development, when the individual is in his or her early twenties (and has established an adult identity) as the time at which mature love develops. Erikson noted that during this stage, Intimacy versus Isolation, the young adult is ready to commit to another, forming an intimate relationship and experiencing love. According to Erikson, only those who have found their identity will be able to experience true intimacy—and love—whereas those whose ego identity is not complete will either remain isolated or will engage in false relationships by being sexually promiscuous or by having shallow relationships. Thus Erikson saw love as the result of healthy, normal development.

A modern approach by psychologist Phillip Shaver and his associates also relies on understanding a child's development, but Shaver uses models of attachment learned during childhood to account for differences in the quality of adult relationships. The idea is that the nature of one's childhood attachment relationship is reflected to some extent in later romantic relationships (Brennan & Shaver, 1995; Hazan & Shaver, 1987; Shaver, Collins, & Clark, 1996). Note that this way of thinking derives directly from the neo-analytic theory of Karen Horney (1945), involving unresolved basic anxiety, and from related studies of the biological bases of infant attachment (Ainsworth, 1979; Ainsworth & Bowlby, 1991; Bowlby, 1969).

There are three romantic attachment styles, according to Shaver and colleagues: (1) **secure lovers,** who easily form close relationships with others and let others become close to them; (2) **avoidant lovers,** who feel uncomfortable when they are close to another or when others are close to them, and who have trouble trusting and being trusted by others (adult children of alcoholics may often fall into this group); (3) **anxious-ambivalent lovers,** who want to get close but are insecure with the relationship and may scare away partners by being desperate about the relationship. About half of people studied were found to be secure, but unfortunately the rest were found to be avoidant and anxious-ambivalent. An individual's adult attachment style was found to be predicted by the quality of their relationships with their parents, further supporting the theory that people form models of these early relationships that influence later attachments.

Cognitive Approaches to Love

Can we count the ways we can love? The cognitive approach to love tries to classify the different types of loving and, further, to distinguish our passions from our thoughts. It seems clear that there are some good friends whom we like a lot but would not want to be intimate with; some we are very self-disclosing to but not physically attracted to; some we are madly passionate about but don't really like that much; and so on.

Unfortunately, love has eluded any simple classification scheme. Most approaches distinguish liking and respect from love and passion. Some distinguish a respectful, companionate love from an emotional devotion. Still others try to use several such dimensions simultaneously, comparing infatuation to sexual exploitation to true love, and so on. What is clear from these analyses is that our thoughts are very much involved with our feelings. There are so many different kinds of love because there are so many different ways that we reflect on and interpret our drives, motivations, and interpersonal relations (Beall & Sternberg, 1995; Berscheid, 1994; Fehr & Russell, 1991; Rubin, 1973; Sternberg & Barnes, 1988).

Humanistic/Existential Perspectives on Love

The humanistic personality psychologists have devoted a considerable amount of energy to explaining the etiology of love. They disdain the simple behaviorist view that we love someone who provides us with reinforcements. Their theories emphasize that people who realize their potential, becoming the best that they can be, are the people who can have the truest love. They also focus on the idea that a person must accept (and love) him- or herself before he or she can give real love to others. For example, Carl Rogers argued that children who learn to accept themselves can grow up to be fully functioning individuals, able truly to love others.

Maslow's View on the Need for Love

Abraham Maslow placed the need for love on the third rung of his need pyramid. He meant that only after one's physiological needs (as for food) and one's safety needs (as for order) are met can one work on satisfying needs for love and affiliation (belongingness). As the individual moves successfully up the need pyramid, satisfying belongingness and esteem needs, he or she can become more able to fully love and self-actualize.

Maslow (1968) described two types of love, B-love (short for "being" love) and D-love ("deficiency" love). D-love is selfish and needy, whereas B-love is unselfish and cares for the needs of the other. B-lovers are more self-actualized and help their partners toward self-actualization. This perspective implies that people bring different personality orientations to loving—self-actualizing people love unselfishly (B-love), but needy, immature people experience D-love. We all know some immature people seeking selfish D-love.

Erich Fromm's Theory of Love

Erich Fromm combines the humanistic/existential and psychoanalytic perspectives in his theory of love. Remember that Fromm believes that modern man suffers from a societally induced sense of alienation and loneliness (see Chapter 9). Unlike Freud, who saw love and sex as expressions of the instinctual, animalistic nature of humans, Fromm sees love as a special characteristic that actually humanizes men and women. In order to alleviate feelings of loneliness, people seek contact with the world around them and, in particular, with other individuals. Love is the positive result of individuals striving to join with others.

Fromm goes on to describe characteristics that discriminate between different qualities of and types of love. For example, love is immature when the taking of love overwhelms the giving of love, which may occur in (immature) adult–adult, as well as adult–child, unions. But when an individual's personality is mature, the person is capable of true giving and therefore of genuine, mature love.

In mature love, each partner is caring for the other. In addition, mature lovers feel a sense of responsibility toward each other, not out of obligation, but freely given (Miller & Siegel, 1972). Mature love also encompasses respect for the development of the partner. Finally, in order to love maturely, each person must have knowledge of his or her partner. Thus, Fromm sees love as much more complex than simply a means of reducing sexual tension. Fromm's view of mature love has been adopted by most modern marriage counselors.

For Fromm, **motherly love** is completely one-sided and unequal—the mother gives unconditional love, asking for nothing. From this love the child acquires a sense of stability and security. **Brotherly love** involves loving all others—all of mankind. This kind of love reunites the isolated individual with others. **Erotic love** is, however, directed toward a single individual; erotic love is a momentary, short-lived intimacy. In such cases (when this dominates), the individual may move from one lover to the next fairly rapidly. People who engage solely in erotic love do not experience true mature love but rather satisfy sexual needs, alleviate anxiety, or control or are controlled. Real **mature love,** according to Fromm, is much more than pure sex, and it incorporates elements of brotherly love and self-love. One must be able to love oneself and one must have the sense of devotion that accompanies brotherly love before one can successfully and maturely love another. Interestingly, in contrast to Freud, Fromm believed that immediate sexual satisfaction did not presage love but rather that sexual satisfaction would follow true love. This is the idea that the best sex comes in the most loving relationships.

If a woman is seeking the relationship she never had with her father, or if the man is seeking childish motherly love, neither will ever be fully satisfied. These are examples of neurotic love. Similarly, if an individual gives up his or her own identity and worships the partner, the result is a form of pseudo-love.

Rollo May: Types of Love

Because Fromm saw love as crucial to addressing questions of meaning and existence, his can be thought of as an existentialist point of view. In the 1970s, Rollo May, the existentialist psychotherapist and author, followed Fromm and published influential books that described modern humans as depersonalized by modern culture and technology. He believed that this resulted in the numbing of the individual's ability to love. Violence and dehumanization may be the result (May, 1972).

In particular, Rollo May described various types of love. These are sex (lust, tension release); **eros** (procreative love—savoring, experiential); brotherly love (**"philia,"** liking); **agape,** or devotion (to the welfare of others; unselfish love); and **authentic love,** which incorporates the other types of love. May argued that modern society unfortunately promotes the dividing up of the different types of love. But he believed that love has different aspects and should be seen from different perspectives, just as we have repeatedly argued in this textbook.

May developed these ideas during and after the sexual revolution of the 1970s, at the height of the hippie subculture. May suggested that our technological age has had important negative consequences for love, resulting in people who are obsessed with sex, independent of other aspects of love. As a result, tenderness and closeness are missing from many sexual unions. (It was also not surprising that the divorce rate rose dramatically in the 1970s.)

Love and Will

In addition, as an existentialist, May emphasized the importance of will. He noted that love and will are intertwined—that love needs will (or effort, volition) to be lasting and meaningful. He noted that the difficulty with the hippies was that although love was given freely, it lacked will. It was too unrestrained and irre-

According to Rollo May, "free love" as practiced by the hippies was not an ideal form of love—it lacked the discipline and will that characterize meaningful and lasting love.

sponsible (May, 1969). The hippie culture overthrew the sexual hang-ups that resulted from sexual repression, but it sometimes went too far by eliminating all discipline and commitment. It is apparent that Rollo May's perception of the impact of will is similar to Fromm's inclusion of knowledge, accomplishment, and development in mature love.

Cultural Differences in Love

Just as cultural context influences aggressive tendencies, there are cultural differences in the experience and expectations for love. This again suggests that love cannot simply be a biological phenomenon or an instinctual (id-dominated) phenomenon, nor even simply a family-based concept.

In many cultures and in many times throughout history, marriages were arranged by the bride's and groom's parents. Economic, religious, and social factors played a key role. Matchmakers were important forces in society. Yet few American college students would want their parents to find their mates for them. We often assume that there is an ideal partner out there for us, and all we have to do is find this person and fall deeply in love. However, to the extent that the neo-analysts and the humanists/existentialists are correct, it might make more sense to allow some forms of matchmaking to return. Rather than choosing on the basis of immediate sexual attraction or fulfillments of immature needs, an experienced matchmaker might choose pairings on the basis of respect, maturity, and the potential for a deep, integrative love, as well as physical compatibility. The result might be better marriages and deeper love. This is another example of how understanding the assumptions about human nature that accompany the different approaches to personality can help us become more sophisticated in understanding many key issues in our lives.

Most American college students would not want their parents (or a matchmaker, shown here with the mother of the prospective bride) to select their mates for them, as happens in many traditional cultures. Young adults selecting their own partners may use different criteria from those used by parents and matchmakers.

A recent study of eighty married Mexican American and Euro American volunteers found that practical attitudes about love, and less idealism about sex, were related to level of acculturation in the Mexican American group—with more Hispanically oriented individuals being more pragmatic. However, passionate love was correlated with marital satisfaction for all groups (Contreras, Hendrick, & Hendrick, 1996). In other words, we certainly would not want to carry the argument too far and assert that passionate love and attraction are unimportant. A balance of the two approaches is needed. Other studies have found that members of individualistic cultures tend to place more emphasis on romance and personal fulfillment than people from collectivistic societies, but they are not necessarily more loving (Dion & Dion, 1993; Levine et al., 1995).

Fromm was distressed by the modern capitalist structure in which the highest goals of life often seem to be consumption and "having fun." The result of this lifestyle is often loneliness.

Where Has Love Gone?

Loneliness

Let us consider the case of Joe, a twenty-year-old college student who is somewhat of a loner. He keeps to himself, has difficulty relating to others, and does not much share his thoughts or feelings with others. Although Joe is uncomfortable about his lack of social interactions, he rarely talks about being lonely.

A significant number of people have difficulty finding love and forging meaningful relationships. They feel lonely and isolated. Is there a relationship between personality and loneliness? The study of loneliness has provided an informative picture of the typical personality of the lonely individual.

Lonely people have trouble forming relationships, trusting others, and getting close. They have difficulty talking about themselves, disclosing their feelings to others, forming social relationships, and feeling comfortable in social interactions (Berg & Peplau, 1982; Peplau & Caldwell, 1978). They may be generally less sociable (Perlman & Joshi, 1987). In trait terms, they may be very low on extroversion and somewhat low on agreeableness and emotional stability. In other words, loneliness is a common and stable condition. Cognitive personality theorists point out that lonely people often have a negative explanatory style—they see things as beyond their control and tend to view others in a negative light (Snodgrass, 1987).

Other personality characteristics that are not as intuitively obvious have also been shown to be related to loneliness. People who are high in both masculine and feminine traits (androgynous people) seem to be the least lonely, possibly because they feel comfortable in a variety of social situations and are able to make friends with an assortment of people with different interests and outlooks (Berg & Peplau, 1982). They may have better social skills and higher self-esteem.

A study of elderly adults found that loneliness was associated both with psychosocial problems like social inadequacy and social isolation, and also with instrumental problems like health ailments and lower incomes (Perlman, Gerson, & Spinner, 1978). As Erik Erikson would expect, different issues affect loneliness as we age. This information suggests that environmental character- istics might take a significant toll as well. In fact, for a behaviorist like Skinner, the loneliness of college results from having to move to an environment in which one cannot emit one's usual responses to obtain rewards. This line of thinking suggests that loneliness can be overcome by developing skills and changing environments. That is why many counselors (treating lonely people) suggest their getting involved with social groups and clubs related to their in- terests, knowledge, and skills, even if they feel awkward at first. Loneliness cannot be considered only a personality trait; rather, an interactionist view that takes the situation fully into account is needed (Rook, 1988; 1991). Lone- liness occurs when there is a mismatch between a person's actual relationships and needed relationships (Perlman & Peplau, 1998).

Love Gone Wrong: Violent or Risky Sexual Behavior

What personality traits may encourage one to participate in risky sexual prac- tices? This question is receiving increasing attention as a result of the spread of AIDS (acquired immuno-deficiency syndrome). Even more seriously, what is it about an individual's personality that drives her or him to engage in violent sexual acts?

Many investigators have been interested in determining the relations be- tween personality and sexual behavior—in particular, between personality and unsafe sex. Most basically, extroverts are more sexually adventurous be- cause they seek extra stimulation. Extroverts have even been found to be more apt to engage in "French kissing" and to engage in a wider variety of sexual ac- tivities (Fontaine, 1994; Barnes, Malamuth, & Check, 1984). People who are dispositionally impulsive also tend to act impulsively in their sexual encoun- ters. People who are less controlled and more outgoing take more sexual risks. For example, a study of college students found that those who were likely to make impulsive decisions and take risks in their daily lives were also more likely to take more risks in their sexual behaviors. This was true regardless of their understanding of safe sex, so risk-taking is not primarily a cognitive factor (Seal & Agostinelli, 1994). These students were also more sensitive to situa- tional cues, suggesting that they might be more likely to be carried away by the moment, a response that is associated with not using condoms.

Such people are generally more extroverted, less restrained, and more likely to have sex earlier in relationships, to have more than one sexual partner at a time, and to be in relationships that are less committed (Simpson & Gangestad, 1991). According to an ethological explanation, such people prefer physical attractiveness and are more sexually active, compared to people who care more about partner *investment* and so are more sexually selective (and inhibited). The people who are more sexually active and indiscriminate do not necessarily have a greater sex drive or greater sexual satisfaction, however.

Psychoticism is also related to sexual risk. Indeed, as Eysenck conceived the dimension, this is one of the core components of psychoticism. Fontaine (1994) used the Eysenck Personality Questionnaire to examine the personalities of men aged eighteen to thirty-five and their sexual activities. He did find that high scores on psychoticism were related to risky sexual practices such as having unprotected sex and having sex with bisexual, intravenous drug-using, or multiple partners.

How is it that sex, which we most often identify with love (or at the very least, with caring), becomes a venue of anger, force, and violence? Neil Malamuth and his associates have investigated the type of personality characteristics that are associated with sexual aggression toward women and with sexual violence such as rape. They have found that men's level of dominance, hostility toward women, favorable attitudes toward violence against women, and higher levels of psychoticism predict sexual aggression (Malamuth, 1986; Barnes, Malamuth, & Check, 1984). In other words, sexual aggressors tend to be cold, impulsive, tough, and cruel. They may be odd but even charming like Ted Bundy. Serial killers are often found to have collections of pornography (but of course most people with pornography are not predators or killers).

A scale, the Attraction to Sexual Aggression scale (Malamuth, 1989), is somewhat capable of identifying men who are apt to engage in sexual violence toward women. Such men tend to believe in rape myths, such as that women enjoy rape, and they have a strong need for dominance. They have positive attitudes toward sexual aggression. For Freud, it was clear that such men had not resolved their Oedipal complex nor developed an adequate superego; and for the neo-analysts, it was clear that such men faced deficient parenting. From a cognitive viewpoint, such men may lack an understanding of the humanness of others. From a trait point of view, they lack empathic abilities and are oblivious to many of the rules that govern society. To a humanist, they are simply immoral. In all these cases, there is agreement that it is difficult to change a sexual predator. Increasingly, when they are convicted of felonies, these men are being sentenced to life in prison. Society's views are coming into line with psychology's views.

In sum, most perspectives on love agree that it has a biological basis, presumably one that is related to the benefits for reproductive success of being sexually attracted to and supportive of a mate. This explanation, however, is a long way from saying that love is predominantly biology. And the precise influences of biology on love are poorly understood.

In American society, the romantic ideal tells us that we should marry someone with whom we fall passionately in love. Yet there is also much evidence that love can grow out of a meaningful friendship. Many of the wisest personality psychologists have emphasized that true love, long-lasting love, thrives best when it is part of an unselfish, mature concern for another.

Summary and Conclusion

This chapter attempts to bring to life the eight basic aspects of personality by considering some of their implications for understanding love and hate. We are shocked but fascinated by serial killers, who kill their victims one by one, and by brutal dictators, who murder by the thousands. They show us the truly evil side of humanity. Yet we are also inspired by the devotion and true love of which people are capable. We have seen that a simple explanation of these complex motivations and behaviors is not possible.

Ethological approaches characterize aggression as the product of adaptive evolutionary processes. That is, hatred is innate because aggression was adaptive in the evolution of our species. These natural aggressive tendencies may be distorted and sometimes expressed inappropriately and grotesquely due to biological aberrations, or drug abuse, or unusual environmental circumstances. However, why are there so many individual and cross-cultural differences in aggressiveness? All people have a capacity for hatred but the capacity is usually not realized to any significant degree.

For Freud, aggression is ultimately traced to defense mechanisms against the death instinct—thanatos. It may be displaced onto others, projected onto others, or repressed, only to emerge in drastic or dramatic ways. But for the neo-analysts, hatred arises from the insecurities, anxieties, and traumas of childhood, especially in parent–child relations. In a world of stable parenting and emotional health, aggression would be rare. For trait theorists, aggressive or domineering patterns become defining styles of how the individual interacts with his or her world.

In the humanistic/existential view, aggression results from the thwarting of the natural tendencies toward fulfillment, as a result of the combination of failures in family life, societal life, and individual choices. Also nonbiological are the learning approaches, which examine the reward structures and models of aggression that show and sustain violence.

In the cognitive approach, hateful people are often characterized by cognitive simplicity. This leads them to dismiss whole groups of people as "enemies." Violent criminals are more likely to perceive events as threatening and to see other people as having hostile intentions; psychopaths have deficits in the processing of both social and cognitive tasks. These views imply that aggression can be lessened as people are taught to take a more accurate and benign view of their worlds. Given the dramatic cultural differences in aggression, nonbiological influences must play an important role.

Is love, not hate, the most potent motivator of behavior? Evolutionary psychologists propose that there are different characteristics for which males and females look when selecting a mate because of their different biological roles during reproduction. The male is attracted to females who have physical characteristics indicating their suitability to conceive and carry a healthy offspring through a successful pregnancy. But because the female's energies are concentrated on child care, she requires a male who can and will provide her with the necessities of life, such as food and shelter, while her offspring are children. Love derives from its adaptive value in promoting survival.

For Freud, what we do for love is really a fulfillment of the sexual drives of the id. Freud's successors, such as the object relations theorists, emphasize the importance of the first mother–child relationship, stating that the child internalizes the nature of this relationship, which becomes in a sense the prototype or template for future loves. But according to Erikson and other ego psychologists, only those who have found their identity will be able to experience true intimacy—and love. Those whose ego identity is not complete will either remain isolated or will engage in false relationships—promiscuous or shallow.

The humanistic personality psychologists devote considerable energy to explaining love, and they disdain the simple behaviorist view that we love someone who provides us with reinforcements. In mature love, each partner is caring for the other. Mature lovers feel a sense of responsibility toward each other, but love is freely given, without selfish conditions. For Maslow, "being" lovers (but not "deficiency" lovers) help their partners toward self-actualization. The existentialists like Rollo May emphasize the importance of will: love needs will (or effort, volition) to be lasting and meaningful.

Customs and feelings about love and marriage vary significantly across time and culture, warning us against simple acceptance of our own common views about love. Loneliness, sexual promiscuity, and sexual violence are complex issues at the intersection of love and hate, and they are fruitfully viewed from multiple perspectives to be fully comprehended.

In sum, in this section of this book—Chapters 11, 12, 13, and 14—we have endeavored to apply the eight basic perspectives on personality to important topics of individual differences: male–female differences, health differences, cultural differences, and love–hate differences. We have seen that personality is by no means a dry academic exercise or a historical curiosity. Rather, as we have maintained throughout this book, the study of personality goes to the heart of what it means to be a person.

In the final chapter of this book, we look toward the future of personality.

Key Theorists

Seymour Feshbach
David Buss
Melanie Klein

Phillip Shaver
Neil Malamuth

Key Concepts

ethological theories
thanatos
antisocial personality disorder
ruling type
neurotic trends
authoritarian personality type
cognitive simplicity

evolutionary psychology
romantic attachment styles
"being" love versus "deficiency" love
Erich Fromm's types of love
Rollo May's types of love
Attraction to Sexual Aggression scale

Suggested Readings

Douglas, J. E. (1995). *Mindhunter: Inside the FBI's elite serial crime unit* (J. Douglas & M. Olshaker, Eds.). New York: Scribner's.

Fromm, E. (1956). *The art of loving.* New York: Harper & Row.

Fromm, E. (1973). *The anatomy of human destructiveness.* New York: Fawcett Crest.

Herrnstein, R. J., & Murray, C. (1994). *The bell curve: Intelligence and class structure in American life.* New York: Free Press.

Lifton, R. J. (1986) *The Nazi doctors: Medical killing and the psychology of genocide.* New York: Basic Books.

Peplau, L. A., & Perlman, D. (Eds.) (1982). *Loneliness: A sourcebook of current theory, research, and therapy.* New York: Wiley Interscience.

Silverberg, J., & Gray, J. P. (Eds.) (1992). *Aggression and peacefulness in humans and other primates.* New York: Oxford University Press.

Where Will We Find Personality?

Why would anyone want to study personality psychology? Why would students take a course about personality when they could spend time learning useful computer or accounting or engineering skills, or becoming culturally enriched through the study of literature, music, or art? Who is interested in what makes people tick?

Although there is not much research directly on this topic, some related findings have emerged from the California Psychological Inventory (CPI), a well-constructed personality test developed by the University of California, Berkeley, psychologist Harrison Gough (Gough, 1987). One of the CPI scales is termed "Psychological-mindedness"; it identifies individuals interested in the needs, motives, and experiences of others. Such people also may be good judges of what others feel. There is some evidence that this tendency toward psychological-mindedness can be improved through study (perhaps through taking courses in personality!) and that it is predictive of a more mature and wise adulthood (Donohue, 1995; Gough, Fox, & Hall, 1972; Helson & Roberts, 1994; Staudinger, Lopez, & Baltes, 1997). On the other hand, it is sometimes the case that people with psychological problems gravitate toward the study of psychology.

What about the demographic characteristics of personality students? Although documentation on this issue is scant, it appears that the dominant and powerful people in society are typically not formal students of personality. For example, in American society, no U.S. presidents, senators, governors, or cabinet secretaries were elected or chosen from the ranks of personality psychologists, although there aren't that many personality psychologists to choose from. Students of personality and social psychology currently are likely to be women; females now fill most graduate school student slots in this field. Historically, they often have been likely to be immigrants or Jewish Americans or Catholic Americans—persons who faced prejudice and who worried about their place in the larger society. Increasingly, they are other victims of societal discrimination, such as Hispanic Americans. Those members of the dominant culture who do enter the field may have strong philosophical or religious yearnings, or spiritual aches, or an unusual desire to look inward, as did Jung and Allport and Rogers. They turn to personality psychology for a better understanding of life and its meaning.

*T*he type of analysis in this book reinforces a comprehensive view of personality. Personality psychology is not merely a dry academic exercise, but it includes a wider philosophical view of what it means to be a person. In this book, we have considered many basic and age-old issues of human nature, but we have done so in terms of the conceptual and empirical advances of twentieth-century psychology. In this vein, it is not at all surprising that many of the leading contributors to the field of personality were not content to limit their writings to probing individual differences, or processes of change, or enlightening psychotherapies; but rather, they went on to articulate visions for creating restructured societies, utopias, and new worlds. The process continues.

The Brave New World of Personality

Three dramatic scientific developments of the new century are likely to change the way psychologists think about what it means to be a person. First, better understanding of brain biochemistry will raise the possibility of **designer personalities.** Second, more accurate control of environmental contingencies will improve society's ability to control individual behavior. Third, better understanding of the human genetic code may lead to a dramatic change in our understanding of the genetic bases of personality.

Designer Personalities

Since the beginnings of humankind, people have used psychoactive substances such as alcohol and opium to influence the brain and thereby influence behavior. For example, the Aztecs and other early and native Americans used peyote, a small spineless psychedelic cactus native to Texas and Mexico. How and why such substances affected personality were not of much concern; they were consumed either as part of a religious experience or for recreation. Now, however, breakthroughs in understanding brain chemistry—the **neurotransmitters** through which brain cells communicate—are making possible drugs that scientifically change the nature of who we are, in a targeted fashion.

The research began as an attempt to help people suffering from mental illnesses such as depression, chronic anxiety, and schizophrenia. A century ago, Freud highly recommended the use of cocaine and used it himself (it was even one of Coca-Cola's original ingredients), until its addictive qualities became recognized. Amphetamines to treat depression, and tranquilizers like Valium to treat anxiety, have been available for almost half a century. They are heavily prescribed legally, and heavily abused illegally. But now, designer drugs are being synthesized to create designer personalities. Perhaps the best example of this new type of drug is Prozac (fluoxetine).

Prozac blocks the reabsorption of the neurotransmitter serotonin in the brain and thus enhances the user's mood and alters emotional reaction patterns. Prozac was created to treat severe depression. It is now being used, however, by people who want to overcome a wide range of perceived problems ranging from shyness and moodiness to a tendency to be obsessive. Because Prozac seems to interfere with obsessive-compulsive tendencies, it is even being tried as a treatment for gambling and for lack of concentration. Although the number of people taking Prozac in an attempt to "improve" their usual personality is not well documented, the number seems substantial as millions of prescriptions are written for Prozac every year. A popular book, *Listening to Prozac,* describes how Prozac works wonders as a mood enhancer for grumpy people (Kramer, 1993).

Around 1960, Timothy Leary was a well-established psychology professor at Harvard University, making important contributions to our understanding of the interpersonal nature of personality. Turned on by an anthropologist to "magic mushrooms," Leary and others then began studying and advocating the use of the psychedelic drug lysergic acid diethylamide (LSD) for its potential to expand the mind and promote creativity and well-being. A fungus derivative, LSD is a hallucinogenic drug that evokes dreamlike changes in perception and thought. Hollywood psychiatrists jumped on the bandwagon; one of the more famous patients to use LSD during therapy was actor Cary Grant (Psyche in 3-D, 1960). Unfortunately, many users jumped out windows. As

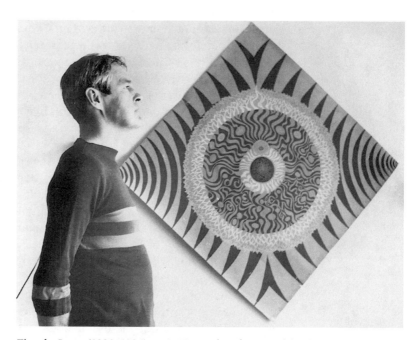

Timothy Leary (1920–1996) was a Harvard professor studying interpersonal dimensions of personality when, in 1960, he began taking and exploring and then promoting the use of psychedelic drugs. Leary claimed that he was able to reach a higher level of consciousness by contemplation of mandalas—Oriental religious symbols representing the universe—such as the one shown here with him. He was fired from Harvard, dubbed the "high priest of LSD," and became involved in a variety of leftist political causes. Leary abandoned the scientific study of mind-altering drugs, but many scientists are now carefully studying (and often succeeding in) systematically changing people's patterns of behavior.

LSD's effects—among them, delusions and bizarre behaviors—became better understood, Harvard fired Leary (who was still promoting it widely) and LSD was outlawed.

Most people agree that mind-altering drugs should indeed be used to treat patients with long-term clinical depression, who sit in their rooms crying miserably, incapacitated, unable to work or to lead anything approaching a normal life. But what about treating unhappiness, or poor concentration, or shyness? There is evidence that 10–30 percent of the population have a biological tendency toward shyness. Should we boost their sociability with pills?

With the sophisticated understanding of personality developed in the preceding chapters, we can see that such a simple approach to the person is naive and uninformed—such treatments will not prove effective over the long term. Personality is much more than the release of chemicals in the brain, although such elements of biology are surely very important. Personality is a function of many brain systems and has a cognitive aspect and a skill aspect. Personality depends heavily on learning, and on socialization, and on the social situation. And, who we are has an important spiritual element of freedom, consciousness, and nobility, which is overlooked at our peril.

What kind of world would it be if everyone had their brain chemistries continually adjusted so that no one would yell at you, no one would rush to get ahead of you, no one would cry, and no one would worry whether she had turned the oven off? For every psychosocial problem, a pill would be there. Further, artists could take creativity pills for enhanced performance, and academics, intelligence pills for clear thinking. Even if such a world does not sound so appealing, the issues will not simply go away. Drugs that alter our thinking and feeling are now being created at a rapid pace; and society will have to decide if, when, and how to use them.

A Utopian World versus Abuse of Reward and Punishment

Henry David Thoreau (1854) emphasized the freedom and dignity of the individual, arguing that each person should march in step with the music that he hears, seeking simplicity, integrity, and individuality. In B. F. Skinner's version of utopia, the perfect community is one in which convention and coercive societal restrictions are likewise eliminated, but are replaced by a reward system that shapes peoples' desires to fit the community's needs. Since freedom and dignity are seen to be only illusions, Skinner can move beyond them to a place where society pleasantly manipulates the work force through positive reinforcement. All tasks are willingly done because cleaning sewers is more highly rewarded than tending community flower gardens.

Skinner's ideas have sometimes made their way into the modern work force, where the threat of being fired for low-quality work has been superseded by enticing incentives for high-quality work—bonus resort meetings for high sales output, special health-club or bathroom privileges, or even written notes of praise from the boss. Inner-city schoolchildren at high risk of academic failure may be paid for reading books. Preschoolers may be given candies or trinkets when their behavior conforms to teacher desires. Advertising campaigns are designed on the basis of extensive studies of social learning. Especially effective rewards can be offered as more and more is known about the individual's earlier inclinations and past experiences. Corporate computer banks are rapidly filling with such information about each person in the country.

However, less effective means of control—coercion, fear, and punishment—are still a popular force to contend with, as there is strong public support for high-security prisons with hard labor, long prison terms, the death penalty, corporal (physical) punishment of unruly students, fines and taxes, and spread of sophisticated guns and other weapons of self-defense. Although much is known about shaping personality through learning and rewards, it remains to be seen which approach will come to dominate society.

In our discussion of designer personalities, we posed some questions about what a world ruled by drugs would look like. What if everyone's behavior were continually shaped by environmental contingencies? For every psychosocial problem, a new conditioning regimen would be there. Even if such a world does not seem appealing, the issues that arise must still be confronted. We must become and remain educated about personality.

Genetic Superhumans

We saw in our chapter on biological aspects of personality that at least some manic-depressive personalities clearly have a strong genetic basis. Further, some of the genetic bases for diseases such as Huntington's disease, Tay-Sachs disease, breast cancer, cystic fibrosis, amyotrophic lateral sclerosis (Lou Gehrig's disease), and others are being documented (International Conference, 1996; Palmer, 1996; Sharp & Ross, 1996). As more is discovered about the human genome, there will inevitably be implications for our understanding of the genetic bases of personality. For example, genetic deficiencies in the regulation of the neurotransmitter serotonin seem to play a role in some forms of depression. For some researchers, the ultimate goal of the research is human genetic therapy—manipulation of the genes—just as is now commonplace with certain crop plants.

As we have seen, the biological approach to personality is often misunderstood. Much of this confusion can be traced back to the perceived separation between the mind and the body, forcefully analyzed in the early seventeenth century by René Descartes. The separation, known as Cartesian dualism, grew out of a world view in which the life of the spirit, derived from God, was distinct from the goings-on of the earthly world. However, since the time of Darwin, we have known that the "mind" must have a physical basis. As we have seen, this does not mean that personality is biology; it does not mean that personality can be "reduced" to biology. Take, for example, the case of people who have gene-based mood swings. There must be physiological correlates of these mood swings in the person's brain. This does not in any way mean that the person's moods are not affected by her perceptions, her interactions with her friends and family, her early childhood experiences, her religious beliefs, her learning experiences in specific situations, and many other influences that we have discussed throughout this book.

The genetic code affects the development of our brains, the rest of our nerves, and our hormones and neurotransmitters. In other words, the genetic code affects the biological bases of our consistencies in behavior. The activity levels of our nervous systems, in turn, likely account for much of the temperamental differences seen in infants and young children. This does not mean that personality is inherited. It does seem likely, however, that the biological tendencies that underlie some of our traits will increasingly be documented as more and more of the human genome is mapped and explored. Presumably, some of these tendencies will soon be changeable through genetic engineering; but who will decide which, and whose?

What kind of world would it be if all fetuses had their future behavior programmed by genetic engineering? For every psychosocial problem, a new genetic intervention would be designed, just as we now engineer corn seeds to be healthier and more productive. Even if a genetically engineered world sounds no more appealing than a world of designer personalities or a world of conditioning-shaped utopias, the issues will not just disappear. We must be educated about what it means to be a person.

In our rapidly changing world, other dramatic new conceptions of personality will also undoubtedly arise. For example, there is increasing computer modeling of brain function and behavior, and there are of course many computer-based technologies that change our daily behaviors. However, all these changes can be thoughtfully evaluated and understood if one has a good understanding of the basic aspects of personality.

The Eight Perspectives Revisited

In this book, we have studied personality in terms of eight basic perspectives. We believe that to fully appreciate modern understandings of personality, it is important to be well grounded in the rich intellectual history of the field. We have looked at the psychoanalytic aspects of personality, which focus on the complex inner workings of the mind; the ego aspects, which focus on the self; the biological perspective, which is currently witnessing great advances in the understanding of evolution and neuroscience; the behaviorist approach, which brings to bear the insights of learning theories; the cognitive perspective, which relies on the insights of modern experimental psychology; the trait approach, which looks for overall consistencies in the individual; the humanistic and existential approach, which draws on the rich traditions of the humanities in understanding human existence; and the interactionist perspective, which looks at the person in the environment. Table 15.1 on pages 490–491 reviews these perspectives.

Is There One Correct Perspective?

Which perspective is most correct? There is no simple answer to this question. Theories that lead to testable hypotheses can be evaluated by collecting data; but the eight basic perspectives are more nearly philosophies than they are scientific theories. So, proving a perspective is rather like proving the existence of God. It is not a strictly scientific matter. It is very important to note, however, that the theories that grow out of these perspectives can indeed be tested, and as we have seen, some theories about particular aspects of personality are preferable to others. Empirical data show that some predictions and hypotheses about personality are false, some are true, and many need further evaluation.

Do we need to choose our favorite perspective, the way we might choose a religious affiliation or political philosophy? Not necessarily. It is important to understand the dangers and weaknesses of each perspective, so that when we hear about a "new" idea regarding personality, we can thoughtfully evaluate (in an informed way) its potential for good or bad, success or failure. For example, we might be suspicious of a new "miracle" drug that claims to cure school-behavior problems in children, and we might be equally suspicious of a "miracle" behavior therapy for curing marital conflict. We should be skeptical of a questionnaire that claims to assess our "money personality" and advises us how to invest, and we should wonder about a "dream and consciousness" seminar that promises to erase our neuroses and heal our diseases. To be sure, we should not dismiss all such approaches as inherently valueless. Rather, we should be able to evaluate such ideas and techniques from the perspective of a highly educated and sophisticated person who has achieved an advanced and complex understanding of what it means to be a person.

Are There Exactly Eight Perspectives?

Are eight basic perspectives too few, or too many? This is a matter of personal preference. Rather than arguing about the correct number of perspectives, and about which theorists should be grouped together into a given perspective, it is more important to understand what each perspective has to offer, and its strengths and weaknesses. To convey this broad view, fully and fairly, has been our guiding principle throughout this book.

Since all the perspectives are trying to explain patterns in people's lives, they necessarily will have some overlap with one another. It is interesting to note that some early reviewers who saw only parts of this textbook wrote comments like, "I knew they (the authors) were really Freudians at heart"; or, "The text is sympathetic to the humanistic approaches"; or, "Great knowledge of and influence by the biological perspective"; and so on. In other words, readers could detect that we find something very valuable in each perspective. But to those who read this book as a whole it should be clear that we do not believe that any single perspective provides the royal road to understanding personality.

Can the Perspectives Be Merged?

Should we try to merge these eight perspectives into one grand approach? There are certainly ways in which this could be attempted. For example, we could search for the evolutionary and biological bases of psychoanalytic defense mechanisms like repression (Nesse, 1990). Indeed, Freud was trained as a biologist and would probably feel quite at home today in a modern biological or evolutionary perspective. We saw also (in Chapter 3) how notions of the unconscious have much in common with modern cognitive approaches.

Or, we might search for the cognitive or biological bases for the Big Five or Big Three trait approaches to personality. Traits are presumably based in inherent perceptual or temperamental differences. Or, the social learning approaches might be integrated with the cognitive approaches. Both emphasize experimental study of thinking and learning.

Work from the learning and behaviorist perspective fits nicely into current notions that personality manifests itself differently in different situations. Similarly, work from the ego perspective overlaps with modern interactionist approaches that propose we have different selves in different situations. Humanistic and existential notions of freedom and self-fulfillment echo notions of motives and skills, not only elevating human dignity and free will but also

Table 15.1   **The Eight Basic Aspects of Personality**

Perspective	Free will?	Structures	Key Concepts	Key Methods
Psychoanalytic	No	Id, ego, superego	Psychosexual stages, Oedipus complex, defense mechanisms	Free association, dream analysis
Ego	Usually no	Unconscious, conscious self, social self	Identity, sociocultural influences on self-esteem, life goals	Varies from free association to situational and autobiographical, with an emphasis on self-concept
Biological	No	Genes, instincts, brain structure	Evolution, hormones, and neurotransmitters	Neuroscience, heritability studies
Behaviorist	No	External regularities in rewards	Reinforcement, conditioning, learning, extinction	Experimental analysis of animal learning
Cognitive	Sometimes yes	Constructs, expectancies, cognitions, schemas	Perception, observation, human as scientist/ decision maker	Decision tasks, biographical analysis
Trait	Sometimes yes	Traits, motives, skills	Basic dimensions of personality, unique personal styles/ dispositions	Factor analysis, self-reports, testing of styles and skills
Humanistic	Yes	Spirit, being-in-the-world	Self-actualization, alienation	Interviews, self-exploration, art, biographical analysis of creativity
Interactionist	Usually yes	Predispositions, situations	Person-in-situation	Observation and testing of cross-situational consistency, classifying situations

Vision of Utopia	Some Leading Theorists	Key Strength	Key Weakness
Unconflicted psycho-sexual development, mature socialization of id instincts	S. Freud	Attention to unconscious influences, importance of sexual drives even in nonsexual spheres	Many ideas superseded by more modern research on the brain, speculations often unverified or unverifiable, influenced by sexist assumptions of the times
Mature self, adapted to the many situations to be faced	A. Adler, K. Horney, E. Erikson	Emphasis on the self as it struggles to cope with emotions and drives on the inside and the demands of others on the outside	Sometimes a hodgepodge of ideas from different traditions, difficult to test in rigorous manner
Improvement through medication of the brain and gene manipulation or selection, understanding how our biological inheritance affects society	I. Pavlov, R. Plomin, H. Eysenck, S. Scarr, M. Daly	Focuses on tendencies and limits imposed by biological inheritance, can be combined with other approaches	Tends to minimize human potential for growth and change, serious danger of misuse by politicians who oversimplify its findings
Conditioning and reinforcing of individual behaviors so the person wants to do what benefits society	B. F. Skinner, J. Dollard, N. Miller	Can force a more scientific analysis of the learning experiences that shape personality	May dehumanize unique human potentials through comparisons to rats and pigeons, may ignore advances from cognitive and social psychology
Rational decision making through understanding thought processes, computer simulation of personality	G. Kelly, A. Bandura	Captures active nature of human thought and uses modern knowledge from cognitive psychology	Often ignores unconscious and emotional aspects of personality
Understanding unity of each individual, accurate assessment of abilities	G. Allport, R. B. Cattell, H. Eysenck	Good individual assessment techniques	May reach too far in trying to capture individual in a few ways, may label people on the basis of test scores
Self-actualization, overcoming existential crises, love and dignity	A. Maslow, C. Rogers, E. Fromm	Appreciates the spiritual nature of a person, emphasizes struggles for self-fulfillment and dignity	May avoid quantification and scientific method needed for science of personality
Understanding how the individual creates and maintains appropriate or inappropriate roles and identities	H. Murray, H. S. Sullivan, W. Mischel	Understands that we are different selves in different situations	No good ways to define situations or to study the many complexities of interactions

in forcefully attacking the behaviorist ideas of Skinner. The existential perspective is also of course concerned with concepts of the self. In short, there is plenty of overlap among perspectives.

The Value of Retaining Multiple Perspectives

However, often these various perspectives cannot and perhaps should not be merged; it may be that personality is too complex to be understood from any single perspective. Just as biology needs different levels of scientific analysis—the biochemical level, the cellular level, the organ level, the organism level, and the population level—so too personality psychology needs different sorts of analyses to understand different sorts of issues. As we have seen, this does not mean that each theory or idea or hypothesis is equally valid or true. Within each issue or topic, scientific analysis based on data shows that some hypotheses are true and some are false. There is no superego section of the brain, but the brain does derive from different evolutionary pieces and contains many specialized functions. The phenomenon of infantile amnesia (having no conscious access to early memories) does exist, but it is not brought on by sexual repression. And so on. Early concepts can be refined, not totally discarded, as new insights emerge from research.

In studying personality, we have seen that there is no simple understanding of the self (ego). There are aspects of ourselves that are hidden from our view, but yet our conscious self-concept is an important element of who we are. Furthermore, although extroverts can act in an introverted fashion and vice versa, people do maintain a certain consistency over time. Although there are striking differences across cultures and culture must be considered when studying personality, the nature of an individual can be understood across great reaches of time and place. It is also now clear that, to some extent, we are different people in different situations. That is, our social self continually redefines and recreates itself as we take on new roles and negotiate new social identities throughout life.

In studying personality, there is a constant tension between notions of self-fulfillment and notions of deterministic control. We have seen that there are many ways in which who we are and what we do is affected by forces beyond our control and often beyond our knowledge—by our genes, and by our early socialization and rewards, and by our thoughts and inclinations, and by the demands of the situation. On the other hand, there is good reason to assume that people have a creative and spiritual nature, and sometimes make conscious choices toward spiritual self-fulfillment or acts of nobility. Perhaps the actress Mae West expressed this unresolved tension best in the film *My Little Chickadee* (1940): "I generally avoid temptation unless I can't resist it."

In studying personality, we have seen that it is necessary to study both the individual and the group. For example, women share some qualities mostly with other women, but each woman is different from all other women. Both nomothetic and idiographic analyses prove useful. As Gordon Allport (1955) noted, most of psychology searches for general processes and laws of behaviors, but personality psychology places major emphasis on individual differences—the individual is central. As Allport repeatedly asked, "How shall a life history be written?"

Summary and Conclusion

Why would anyone take a course about personality? As we have seen, our knowledge of "human nature" affects many of the most important decisions we make as individuals and as a society. Further, the questions of personality derive from fascinating, age-old intellectual puzzles. But where philosophers relied on theology, observation, and logical analysis, personality psychologists turn to systematic empirical investigations of the correlates and causes of individual differences.

Many people interested in personality will think about ways to improve society, or even to create a utopia. The goal may be designer personalities or brave new worlds. We've postulated about what the world would look like if everyone had their brain chemistries continually adjusted by medications, behavior was continually shaped by environmental contingencies, and all fetuses had their future behaviors programmed by genetic engineering. Such notions are not so far-fetched. Some politicians around the world are toying with these concepts even now. Other dramatic new conceptions of personality will also undoubtedly arise, such as using computer modeling of brain function and behavior to "improve" society. These changes can be thoughtfully evaluated and understood if and only if one has a good understanding of the basic aspects of personality.

We have studied personality in terms of eight basic perspectives. We have seen that there is no simple answer as to which perspective is correct—each has its strengths and weaknesses. To some extent, the eight perspectives overlap. This is not surprising because all are attempting to explain the same thing—personality.

Some of you might be more comfortable integrating various ideas and findings into your own theory of what it means to be human and why each person is unique. In our view, the most important caution is that the shortcomings and dangers of each approach not be overlooked; there is a significant chance of harmful, or even evil, results when the college-educated among us do not fully appreciate the implications of each view of humankind.

Personality has not yet yielded all its secrets. They will be unearthed only as the best personality students demand the integration of complex theory and solid empirical data. For these reasons, personality psychology can be one of the most challenging yet rewarding areas of academic study.

Suggested Readings

Hogan, R., Johnson, J., & Briggs, S. (Eds.) (1997). *Handbook of personality psychology.* San Diego: Academic Press

Kramer, P. D. (1993). *Listening to Prozac.* New York: Viking.

Pervin, L. A. (1985). Personality: Current controversies, issues, and directions. *Annual Review of Psychology, 36*, 83–114.

Pervin, L. A. (1990). Personality theory and research: Prospects for the future. In L. A. Pervin (Ed.), *Handbook of personality theory and research.* New York: Guilford.

References

Abelson, R. P. (1981). Psychological status of the script concept. *American Psychologist, 36,* 715–729.

Abramson, L. Y., Metalsky, G. I., & Alloy, L. B. (1989). Hopelessness depression: A theory-based subtype of depression. *Psychological Review, 96*(2), 358–372.

Adams, D. B., Boudreau, W., Cowan, C. W., & Kokonowski, C. (1993). Offense produced by chemical stimulation of the anterior hypothalamus of the rat. *Physiology & Behavior, 53,* 1127–1132.

Adams, H. E., Wright, L. W. & Lohr, B. A. (1996). Is homophobia associated with homosexual arousal? *Journal of Abnormal Psychology, 105,* 440–445.

Adler, A. (1930). *The neurotic constitution; outlines of a comparative individualistic psychology and psychotherapy* (B. Glueck & J. E. Lind, Trans.). New York: Dodd, Mead.

Adler, N. E., Boyce, T., Chesney, M. A., & Cohen, S. (1994). Socioeconomic status and health: The challenge of the gradient. *American Psychologist, 49,* 15–24.

Adorno, T. W., Frenkel-Brunswik, E., Levinson, D., & Sanford, N. (1950). *The authoritarian personality.* New York: Harper.

Ainsworth, M. S. (1979). Infant-mother attachment. *American Psychologist, 34,* 932–937.

Ainsworth, M. S., & Bowlby, J. (1991). An ethological approach to personality development. *American Psychologist, 46,* 333–341.

Albright, L., Kenny, D. A., & Malloy, T. E. (1988). Consensus in personality judgments at zero acquaintance. *Journal of Personality and Social Psychology, 55,* 387–395.

Alessandri, S. M., Sullivan, M. W., Bendersky, M., & Lewis, M. (1995). Temperament in cocaine-exposed infants. In M. Lewis & M. Bendersky (Eds.), *Mothers, babies, and cocaine: The role of tox-ins in development* (pp. 273–286). Hillsdale, NJ: L. Erlbaum Associates.

Alexander, F. (1950). *Psychosomatic medicine.* New York: W. W. Norton.

Allen, B. A., & Boykin, A. W. (1992). African-American children and the educational process: Alleviating cultural discontinuity through prescriptive pedagogy. *School Psychology Review, 21,* 586–596.

Allport, G. W. (1937). *Personality: A psychological interpretation.* New York: Holt, Rinehart & Winston.

Allport, G. W. (1954). *The nature of prejudice.* Cambridge, MA: Addison-Wesley.

Allport, G. W. (1955). *Becoming: Basic considerations for a psychology of personality.* New Haven, CT: Yale University Press.

Allport, G. W. (1965). *Letters from Jenny.* New York: Harcourt Brace.

Allport, G. W. (1961). *Pattern and growth in personality.* New York: Holt, Rinehart & Winston.

Allport, G. W. (1968). *The person in psychology.* Boston: Beacon Press.

Allport, G. W., & Odbert, H. S. (1936). Trait names: A psycho-lexical study. *Psychological Monographs, 47*(211), 171.

Allport, G. W., & Vernon, P. E. (1933). *Studies in expressive movement.* New York: Macmillan.

Amato, P. R., & Keith, B. (1991). Parental divorce and the well-being of children: A meta-analysis. *Psychological Bulletin, 110,* 26–46.

Ambady, N., & Rosenthal, R. (1993). Half a minute: Predicting teacher evaluations from thin slices of nonverbal behavior and physical attractiveness. *Journal of Personality and Social Psychology, 64,* 431–441.

American Psychiatric Association (1994). *Diagnostic and Statistical Manual of Mental Disorders* (4th ed.). Washington, DC: Author.

Antonovsky, A. (1979). *Health, stress, and coping*. San Francisco: Jossey-Bass.

Antonovsky, A. (1987). *Unraveling the mystery of health: How people manage stress and stay well*. San Francisco: Jossey-Bass.

Appelbaum, P. S., Uyehara, L. A., & Elin, M. R. (Eds.). (1997). *Trauma and memory: Clinical and legal controversies*. New York: Oxford University Press.

Apter, A., Plutchik, R., Sevy, S., Korn, M. L., & others. (1989). Defense mechanisms in risk of suicide and risk of violence. *American Journal of Psychiatry, 146*(8), 1027–1031.

Ardrey, R. (1966). *The territorial imperative: A personal inquiry into the animal origins of property and nations*. New York: Atheneum.

Arenberg, I. K. (1990). Van Gogh had Meniere's disease and not epilepsy. *Journal of American Medical Association, 264*, 491–493.

Aronson, E. (1978). *The jigsaw classroom*. Beverly Hills, CA: Sage.

Asch, S. E., (1952). *Social psychology*. New York: Prentice-Hall.

Ash, M. G. (1992). Cultural contexts and scientific change in psychology: Kurt Lewin in Iowa. *American Psychologist, 47*, 198–207.

Atkinson, J. W. (Ed.) (1958). *Motives in fantasy, action, and society*. Princeton, NJ: Van Nostrand.

Auden, W. H. (1970). Behaviorism. *A certain world*. New York: Viking Press.

Bacon, F. (1625). *The essayes or counsels, civill and morall of Francis Lo. Verulam, Viscount St. Alban*. Newly enlarged. London: Printed by Iohn Haviland for Hanna Barret and Richard Whitaker.

Baddeley, A. (1990). *Human memory: Theory and practice*. Boston: Allyn and Bacon.

Bailey, J. M., & Pillard R. C. (1991). A genetic study of male sexual orientation. *Archives of General Psychiatry, 48*, 1089–1096.

Baker, L. A., & Daniels, D. (1990). Nonshared environmental influences and personality differences in adult twins. *Journal of Personality & Social Psychology, 58*, 103–110.

Balch, R. W. (1995). Waiting for the ships: Disillusionment and the revitalization of faith in Bo and Peep's UFO cult. In J. R. Lewis (Ed.), *The gods have landed: New religions from other worlds* (pp. 137–166). Albany, NY: State University of New York Press.

Bales, R. F. (1958). Task roles and social roles in problem-solving groups. In E. E. Maccoby, T. M. Newcomb, & E. L. Hartley (Eds.), *Readings in social psychology* (3rd ed.). New York: Holt.

Bandura, A. (1969). *Principles of behavior modification*. New York: Holt, Rinehart & Winston.

Bandura, A. (1973). *Aggression: A social learning analysis*. Englewood Cliffs, NJ: Prentice-Hall.

Bandura, A. (1977). Self-efficacy: Toward a unifying theory of behavioral change. *Psychological Review, 84*(2), 191–215.

Bandura, A. (1978). The self system in reciprocal determinism. *American Psychologist, 33*, 344–358.

Bandura, A. (1982). Self-efficacy mechanism in human agency. *American Psychologist, 37*(2), 122–147.

Bandura, A. (1992). Exercise of personal agency through the self-efficacy mechanism. In R. Schwarzer (Ed.), *Self-efficacy: Thought control of action* (pp. 3–38). Washington, DC: Hemisphere.

Bandura, A. (1997). *Self-efficacy: The exercise of control*. New York: W. H. Freeman.

Bandura, A., & Walters, R. H. (1963). *Social learning and personality development*. New York: Ronald Press.

Barkley, R. A., & Edwards, G. H. (1998). Attention Deficit/Hyperactivity Disorder (ADHD). In H. S. Friedman (Ed.), *Encyclopedia of mental health* (Vol. 1, 169–182). San Diego, CA: Academic Press.

Barnes, G. E., Malamuth, N. M., & Check, J. V. (1984). Personality and sexuality. *Personality and Individual Differences, 5*(2), 159–172.

Barrick, M. R., & Mount, M. K. (1991). The Big Five personality dimensions and job performance: A meta-analysis. *Personnel Psychology, 44*(1), 1–26.

Barrow, R. (1995). Keep them bells a-tolling [Special issue: Canadian perspectives on *The Bell Curve*]. *Alberta Journal of Educational Research, 41*(3), 289–296.

Bartlett, F. C. (1932). *Remembering: A study in experimental and social psychology*. Cambridge, UK: Cambridge University Press.

Bateson, D. J. (1995). How can *The Bell Curve* be taken seriously? [Special issue]. *Alberta Journal of Educational Research, 41*(3), 271–273.

Baum, A., & Dougall, A. L. (1998). Stress. In H. S. Friedman (Ed.), *Encyclopedia of mental health* (Vol 3. 599–606). San Diego, CA: Academic Press.

Baumeister, R. F., & Leary, M. R. (1995) The need to belong: Desire for interpersonal attachments as a fundamental human motivation. *Psychological Bulletin, 117*(3), 497–529.

Bayne, R. (1995). *The Myers-Briggs type indicator: A critical review and practical guide.* New York: Chapman and Hall.

Beall, A. E., & Sternberg, R. J. (1995). The social construction of love. *Journal of Social and Personal Relationships, 12*(3), 417–438.

Beck, A. T., & Freeman, A. (1989). *Cognitive therapy of personality disorders.* New York: Guilford.

Becker, B. J. (1986). Influence again: An examination of reviews and studies of gender differences in social influence. In J. S. Hyde & M. C. Linn (Eds.), *The psychology of gender: Advances through meta-analysis.* Baltimore: Johns Hopkins University Press.

Bellak, L. (1993). *The Thematic Apperception Test, the Children's Apperception Test, and the Senior Apperception Technique in clinical use* (5th ed.). Boston: Allyn and Bacon.

Bem, D. J. (1996). Exotic becomes erotic: A developmental theory of sexual orientation. *Psychological Review, 103*, 320–335.

Bem, D. J., & Allen, A. (1974). On predicting some of the people some of the time: The search for cross-situational consistencies in behavior. *Psychological Review, 81*, 506–520.

Bem, D. J., & Funder, D. C. (1978). Predicting more of the people more of the time: Assessing the personality of situations. *Psychological Review, 85*(6), 485–501.

Bem, S. L. (1974). The measurement of psychological androgyny. *Journal of Consulting and Clinical Psychology, 42*(2), 155–162.

Bem, S. L. (1981). Gender schema theory: A cognitive account of sex typing. *Psychological Review, 88*(4), 354–364.

Benassi, V. A., Sweeney, P. D., & Dufour, C. L. (1988). Is there a relation between locus of control orientation and depression? *Journal of Abnormal Psychology, 97*, 357–367.

Benjamin, L. S. (1996). A clinician-friendly version of the Interpersonal Circumplex: Structural Analysis of Social Behavior (SASB). *Journal of Personality Assessment, 66*(2), 248–266.

Berg, J. H., & Peplau, L. A. (1982). Loneliness: The relationship of self-disclosure and androgyny. *Personality and Social Psychology Bulletin, 8*(4), 624–630.

Bernstein, A. (1976). Freud and Oedipus: A new look at the Oedipus complex in the light of Freud's life. *Psychoanalytic Review, 63*, 393–407.

Berscheid, E. (1994). Interpersonal relationships. *Annual Review of Psychology, 45*, 79–129.

Bertini, M., Pizzamiglio, L., & Wapner, S. (Eds.). (1986). *Field dependence in psychological theory, research, and application: Two symposia in memory of Herman A. Witkin.* Hillsdale, NJ: L. Erlbaum Associates.

Betancourt, H., & Lopez, S. R. (1993). The study of culture, ethnicity, and race in American psychology. *American Psychologist, 48*, 629–637.

Betancourt, H., & Weiner, B. (1982). Attributions for achievement-related events, expectancy, and sentiments: A study of success and failure in Chile and the United States. *Journal of Cross-Cultural Psychology, 13*(3), 362–374.

Betz, B., & Thomas, C. (1979). Individual temperament as a predictor of health or premature disease. *Johns Hopkins Medical Journal, 144*, 81–89.

Binet, A., & Simon, T. (1916). The development of intelligence in children (E. S. Kite, Trans.). Baltimore: Williams and Wilkins.

Blass, T. (1991). Understanding behavior in the Milgram obedience experiment: The role of personality, situations, and their interactions. *Journal of Personality & Social Psychology, 60*(3), 398–413.

Blatt, S. J., Cornell, C. E., & Eshkol, E. (1993) Personality style, differential vulnerability, and clinical course in immunological and cardiovascular disease. *Clinical Psychology Review, 13*, 421–450.

Block, J. (1993). Studying personality the long way. In D. C. Funder, R. D. Parke, C. Tomlinson-Keasey, & K. Widaman (Eds.), *Studying lives through time: Personality and development* (pp. 9–41). Washington, DC: American Psychological Association.

Block, J. (1995a). A contrarian view of the five-factor approach to personality description. *Psychological Bulletin, 117*(2), 187–215.

Block, J. (1995b). Going beyond the five factors given: Rejoinder to Costa and McCrae (1995) and Goldberg and Saucier (1995). *Psychological Bulletin, 117*(2), 226–229.

Block, J. H. (1984). *Sex role identity and ego development.* San Francisco: Jossey-Bass.

Block, J. H., Block, J., & Gjerde, P. F. (1986). The personality of children prior to divorce: A prospective study. *Child Development, 57,* 827–840.

Block, J., Block, J. H., & Gjerde, P. F. (1988). Parental functioning and the home environment in families of divorce: Prospective and concurrent analyses. *Journal of the American Academy of Child & Adolescent Psychiatry, 27,* 207–213.

Block, J., Block, J. H., & Keyes, S. (1988). Longitudinally foretelling drug usage in adolescence: Early childhood personality & environmental precursors. *Child Development, 59,* 336–55.

Block, J. H., Gjerde, P. F., Block, J. H. (1991). Personality antecedents of depressive tendencies in 18-year-olds: A prospective study. *Journal of Personality & Social Psychology, 60,* 726–738.

Bohan, J. S. (Ed.). (1992). *Seldom seen, rarely heard: Women's place in psychology.* Boulder, CO: Westview Press.

Bond, M. H., & Smith, P. B. (1996). Cross-cultural social and organizational psychology. *Annual Review of Psychology, 47,* 205–235.

Borkenau, P., & Liebler, A. (1993). Convergence of stranger ratings of personality and intelligence with self-ratings, partner ratings, and measured intelligence. *Journal of Personality and Social Psychology, 65,* 546–553.

Borys, S., & Perlman, D. (1985). Gender differences in loneliness. *Personality and Social Psychology Bulletin, 11*(1), 63–74.

Bouchard, T. J., Lykken, D. T., McGue, M., & Segal, N. L. (1990). Sources of human psychological differences: The Minnesota study of twins reared apart. *Science, 250*(4978), 223–228.

Bowman, P. J., & Howard, C. (1985). Race-related socialization, motivation, and academic achievement: A study of Black youths in three-generation families. *Journal of the American Academy of Child Psychiatry, 24,* 134–141.

Bowlby, J. (1969). *Attachment and loss.* New York: Basic Books.

Brain, P. F. (Ed.). (1986). *Alcohol and aggression.* London: Croom Helm.

Brennan, K. A., & Shaver, P. R. (1995). Dimensions of adult attachment, affect regulation, and romantic relationship functioning. *Personality and Social Psychology Bulletin, 21*(3), 267–283.

Breuer, J., & Freud, S. (1957). *Studies on hysteria.* New York: Basic Books.

Briggs, S. R., & Cheek, J. M. (1988). On the nature of self-monitoring: Problems with assessment, problems with validity. *Journal of Personality & Social Psychology, 54,* 663–678.

Broverman, I. K., Vogel, S. R., Broverman, D. M., Clarkson, F. E., & Rosekrantz, P. S. (1972). Sex-role stereotypes: A current appraisal. *Journal of Social Issues, 28,* 59–78.

Brown, P., & Levinson, S. C. (1987). *Politeness: Some universals in language usage.* Cambridge, UK: Cambridge University Press.

Brown, R. (1965). *Social psychology.* New York: Free Press.

Brown, R., et al. (1970). *Psycholinguistics: Selected papers by Roger Brown.* New York: Free Press.

Brown, R. I. (1986). Arousal and sensation-seeking components in the general explanation of gambling and gambling addictions. *International Journal of the Addictions, 21*(9–10), 1001–1016.

Bruner, J. S., Goodnow, J. J., & Austin, G. A. (1956). *A study of thinking.* New York: Wiley.

Buber, M. (1937). *I and thou* (R. G. Smith, Trans.). Edinburgh: T. & T. Clark.

Buck, R. (1979). Individual differences in nonverbal sending accuracy and electrodermal responding: The externalizing-internalizing dimension. In R. Rosenthal (Ed.), *Skill in nonverbal communication* (pp. 140–170). Cambridge, MA: Oelgeschlager, Gunn, & Hain.

Buck, R. (1984). *The communication of emotion.* New York: Guilford Press.

Buhrich, N., Bailey, J. M., & Martin, N. G. (1991). Sexual orientation, sexual identity, and sex-dimorphic behaviors in male twins. *Behavior Genetics, 21,* 75–96.

Bullock, A. (1962). *Hitler, a study in tyranny* (Rev. ed.). Harmondsworth, UK: Penguin.

Burns, G. (1976). *Living it up.* New York: Putnam.

Burnstein, E., Crandall, C., & Kitayama, S. (1994). Some neo-Darwinian decision rules for altruism: Weighing cues for inclusive fitness as a function of the biological importance of the decision. *Journal of Personality & Social Psychology, 67,* 773–789.

Burwick, S., & Knapp, R. R. (1991). Advances in research using the Personal Orientation Inventory. *Journal of Social Behavior and Personality, 6,* 311–320.

Buss, A. H., & Plomin, R. (1984). *Temperament : Early developing personality traits.* Hillsdale, NJ : L. Erlbaum Associates.

Buss, D. M. (1989). Sex differences in human mate preferences: Evolutionary hypotheses tested in 37 cultures. *Behavioral and Brain Sciences, 12*(1), 1–49.

Buss, D. M. (1990). Toward a biologically informed psychology of personality. *Journal of Personality, 58,* 1–16.

Buss, D. M. (1994). *The evolution of desire: Strategies of human mating.* New York: Basic Books.

Buss, D. M. (1995a). Evolutionary psychology: A new paradigm for psychological science. *Psychological Inquiry, 6,* 1–30.

Buss, D. M. (1995b). Psychological sex differences: Origins through sexual selection. *American Psychologist, 50,* 164–168.

Buss, D. M., & Angleitner, A. (1989). Mate selection preferences in Germany and the United States. *Personality and Individual Differences, 10*(12), 1269–1280.

Buss, D. M., Haselton, M. G., Shackelford, T. K., Bleske, A. L., & Wakefield, J. C. (1998). Adaptations, exaptations, and spandrels. *American Psychologist, 53,* 533–548.

Buss, D. M., & Schmitt, D. P. (1993). Sexual Strategies Theory: An evolutionary perspective on human mating. *Psychological Review, 100*(2), 204–232.

Butcher, J. N. (1990). *MMPI-2 in psychological treatment.* New York: Oxford University Press.

Bylsma, W. H., & Major, B. (1994). Social comparisons and contentment: Exploring the psychological costs of the gender wage gap. *Psychology of Woman Quarterly, 18*(2), 241–249.

Cacioppo, J. T., Crites, S. L., Berntson, G. G., & Coles, M. G. (1993). If attitudes affect how stimuli are processed, should they not affect the event-related brain potential? *Psychological Science, 4,* 108–112.

Campbell, D. T. (1988). *Methodology and epistemology for social science: Selected papers* (E. S. Overman, Ed.). Chicago: University of Chicago Press.

Campbell, D. T., & Fiske, D. W. (1959). Convergent and discriminant validation by the multitrait-multimethod matrix. *Psychological Bulletin, 56,* 81–105.

Campbell, J. M., Amerikaner, M., Swank, P. R., & Vincent, K. (1989). The relationship between the Hardiness Test and the Personal Orientation Inventory. *Journal of Research in Personality, 23,* 373–380.

Camras, L. (1982). Ethological approaches to nonverbal communication. In R. S. Feldman (Ed.), *Development of nonverbal behavior in children* (pp. 3–28). New York: Springer-Verlag.

Cantor, N. (1994). Life task problem solving: Situational affordances and personal needs. *Personality & Social Psychology Bulletin, 20*(3), 235–243.

Cantor, N., Norem, J. K., Niedenthal, P. M., Langston, C. A., et al. (1987). Life tasks, self-concept ideals, and cognitive strategies in a life transition [Special Issue]. *Journal of Personality & Social Psychology, 53*(6), 1178–1191.

Cantor, N., & Kihlstrom, J. F. (1987). *Personality and social intelligence.* Englewood Cliffs, NJ: Prentice-Hall.

Carlson, R. (1980). Studies of Jungian typology: II. Representations of the personal world. *Journal of Personality & Social Psychology, 38*, 801–810.

Carver, C. S., & Scheier, M. F. (1981). *Attention and self-regulation: A control-theory approach to human behavior.* New York: Springer-Verlag.

Cash, T. F., Mikulka, P. J., & Brown, T. A. (1989). Validity of Millon's computerized interpretation system for the MCMI: Comment on Moreland and Onstad. *Journal of Consulting and Clinical Psychology, 57*(2), 311–312.

Caspi, A., & Bem, D. J. (1990) Personality continuity and change across the life course. In L. A. Pervin (Ed.), *Handbook of personality: Theory and research* (pp. 549–575). New York: Guilford Press.

Caspi, A., Bem, D. J., & Elder, G. H. (1989). Continuities and consequences of interactional styles across the life course [Special Issue: Long-term stability and change in personality]. *Journal of Personality, 57*, 375–406.

Cattell, R. B. (1966). *The scientific analysis of personality.* Chicago: Aldine.

Cattell, R. B. (1990). Advances in Cattellian personality theory. In L. A. Pervin (Ed.), *Handbook of personality: Theory and research* (pp. 101–110). New York: Guilford Press.

Chapman, A. H. (1976). *Harry Stack Sullivan: His life and his work.* New York: Putnam.

Chassin, L., et al. (1984). Predicting the onset of cigarette smoking in adolescents: A longitudinal study. *Journal of Applied Social Psychology, 14,* 224–243.

Chassin, L., Presson, C. C., Sherman, S. J., & Edwards, D. A. (1991a). Four pathways to young-adult smoking status: Adolescent social-psychological antecedents in a midwestern community sample. *Health Psychology, 10,* 409–418.

Chassin, L., Rogosch, F., & Barrera, M. (1991b). Substance use and symptomatology among adolescent children of alcoholics. *Journal of Abnormal Psychology, 100,* 449–463.

Cheek, J. M. (1989). *Conquering shyness: The battle anyone can win.* New York: Putnam.

Cheek, J. M., & Melchior, L. A. (1990). Shyness, self-esteem, and self-consciousness. In H. Leitenberg (Ed.), *Handbook of social and evaluation anxiety* (pp. 47–82). New York: Plenum Press.

Chesney, M. A., Eagleston, J. R., & Rosenman, R. H. (1980). The Type A Structured Interview. *Journal of Behavioral Assessment, 2,* 255–272.

Chesney, M. A., & Rosenman, R. H. (Eds.). (1985). *Anger and hostility in cardiovascular and behavioral disorders.* Washington, DC: Hemisphere.

Chipuer, H. M., Plomin, R., Pedersen, N. L., McClearn, G. E., & Nesselroade, J. (1993). Genetic influence on family environment: The role of personality. *Developmental Psychology, 29,* 110–118.

Chomsky, N. (1973). *For reasons of state* (1st ed.). New York: Pantheon.

Chua-Eoan, H. (1997, April 7). Imprisoned by his own passions. *Time, 149,* 40–43.

Clapper, R. L., Martin, C. S., & Clifford, P. R. (1994). Personality, social environment, and past behavior as predictors of late adolescent alcohol use. *Journal of Substance Abuse, 6*(3), 305–313.

Clark, L. A., & Halford, G. S. (1983). Does cognitive style account for cultural differences in scholastic achievement? *Journal of Cross-Cultural Psychology, 14*(3), 279–296.

Cohen, J., Nuttin, J., & Maslow, A. (1968). The psychology of man: Today. *Psychological Scene, 2,* 5–16.

Cohen, J. D., & Schooler, J. W. (Eds.) (1997). *Scientific approaches to consciousness.* Mahwah, NJ: L. Erlbaum Associates.

Commons, M. L., Nevin, J. A., & Davison, M. C. (1991). *Signal detection: Mechanisms, models and applications.* Hillsdale, NJ: L. Erlbaum Associates.

Conley, J. J. (1984). Longitudinal consistency of adult personality: Self-reported psychological characteristics across 45 years. *Journal of Personality and Social Psychology, 47*(6), 1325–1333.

Conrad, K. M., Flay, B. R., & Hill, D. (1992). Why children start smoking cigarettes: Predictors of onset. *British Journal of Addiction, 87,* 1711–1724.

Contreras, R., Hendrick, S. S., & Hendrick, C. (1996). Perspectives on marital love and satisfaction in Mexican American and Anglo-American couples. *Journal of Counseling and Development, 74*(4), 408–415.

Conway, M. A. (Ed.). (1996). *False and recovered memories*. Oxford, UK: Oxford University Press.

Costa, P. T, & McCrae, R. R. (1987a) On the need for longitudinal evidence and multiple measures in behavioral-genetic studies of adult personality. *Behavioral & Brain Sciences, 10,* 22–23.

Costa, P. T., Jr., & McCrae, R. R. (1987b). Role of neuroticism in the perception and presentation of chest pain symptoms and coronary artery disease. In J. W. Elias & P. H. Marshall (Eds.), *Cardiovascular disease and behavior* (pp. 39–66). Washington, DC: Hemisphere Publishing.

Costa, P. T., & McCrae, R. R. (1992a). Four ways five factors are basic. *Personality & Individual Differences, 13,* 653–665.

Costa, P. T., & McCrae, R. R. (1992b). Normal personality assessment in clinical practice: The NEO Personality Inventory. *Psychological Assessment, 4,* 5–13.

Costa, P. T., Jr., & McCrae, R. R. (1994). Set like plaster: Evidence for the stability of adult personality. In T. F. Heatherton & J. L. Weinberger (Eds.), *Can personality change?* (pp. 21–40). Washington, DC: American Psychological Association.

Costa, P. T., & McCrae, R. R. (1995a). Primary traits of Eysenck's P-E-N system: Three- and five-factor solutions. *Journal of Personality & Social Psychology, 69*(2), 308–317.

Costa, P. T., & McCrae, R. R. (1995b). Solid ground in the wetlands of personality: A reply to Block. *Psychological Bulletin, 117*(2), 216–220.

Costa, P. T., Zonderman, A. B., McCrae, R. R., Cornoni-Huntley, J., et al. (1987). Longitudinal analysis of psychological well-being in a national sample: Stability of means levels. *Journal of Gerontology, 42*(1), 50–55.

Coyne, J. C., & Whiffen, V. E. (1995). Issues in personality as diathesis for depression: The case of sociotropy–dependency and autonomy–self-criticism. *Psychological Bulletin, 118*(3), 358–378.

Craig, R. J. (Ed.) (1993). *The Millon Clinical Multiaxial Inventory: A clinical research information synthesis.* Hillsdale, NJ: L. Erlbaum Associates.

Crews, F. (1996). Forward to 1896? Commentary on papers by Harris and Davies. *Psychoanalytic Dialogues, 6*(2), 231–250.

Crider, A., & Lunn, R.(1971). Electrodermal lability as a personality dimension. *Journal of Experimental Research in Personality, 5,* 145–150.

Crockett, L. (1994). *The Turing test and the frame problem: AI's mistaken understanding of intelligence.* Norwood, NJ: Ablex.

Cross-National Collaborative Group. (1992). The changing rate of major depression: Cross-national comparisons. *Journal of the American Medical Association, 268,* 3098–3105.

Csikszentmihalyi, M. (1990). The domain of creativity. In M. A. Runco & R. S. Albert (Eds.), *Theories of creativity* (pp. 190–212). Newbury Park, CA: Sage Publications.

Csikszentmihalyi, M. (1996). *Creativity : Flow and the psychology of discovery and invention.* New York: HarperCollins.

Cunningham, M. R. (1977). Personality and the structure of the nonverbal communication of emotion. *Journal of Personality, 45,* 564–584.

Dabbs, J. M., Jr. (1993). Salivary testosterone measurements in behavioral studies. In D. Malamud & L. A. Tabak (Eds.), *Annals of the New York Academy of Sciences, Vol. 694, Saliva as a diagnostic fluid* (pp. 177–183). New York: New York Academy of Sciences.

Daly, M., & Wilson, M. (1988). Evolutionary social psychology and family homicide. *Science, 242,* 519–524.

Daly, M., & Wilson, M. (1988). *Homicide.* Hawthorne, NY: Aldine de Gruyter.

Daly, M., Wilson, M. I., & Weghorst, S. J. (1982). Male sexual jealousy. *Ethology and Sociobiology, 3*(1), 11–27.

Daniel, D. (1997, April 14). The beginning of the journey. *Newsweek, 129,* 36–37.

Darwin, C. (1859). *The origin of species by means of natural selection: or, The preservation of favored races in the struggle for life.* London: J. Murray.

Davidson, E. (1977). *The making of Adolf Hitler.* New York: Macmillan.

Davidson, R. J., & Fox, N. A. (1989). Frontal brain asymmetry predicts infants' response to maternal separation. *Journal of Abnormal Psychology, 98*(2), 127–131.

Deaux, K., & Major, B. (1987). Putting gender into context: An interactive model of gender-related behavior. *Psychological Review, 94,* 369–389.

DeGiustino, D. (1975). *The conquest of mind: Phrenology and Victorian social thought.* Totowa, NJ: Rowman and Littlefield.

Dell, G. S. (1995). Speaking and misspeaking. In L. Gleitman & M. Liberman (Eds.), *Language: An invitation to cognitive science,* Vol. 1 (2nd ed.) (pp. 183–208). Cambridge, MA: MIT Press.

DePaulo, B. M., Blank, A. L., Swain, G. W., & Hairfield, J. G. (1992). Expressiveness and expressive control. *Personality and Social Psychology Bulletin, 18,* 276–285.

DePaulo, B. M., & Friedman, H. S. (1997). Nonverbal communication. In D. Gilbert, S. Fiske, & G. Lindzey (Eds.), *Handbook of Social Psychology,* (4th ed.). New York: McGraw-Hill.

Derlega, V. J., Winstead, B. A., & Jones, W. H. (1991). *Personality: Contemporary theory and research.* Chicago: Nelson-Hall.

Descartes, R. (1961). *Essential works.* New York: Bantam.

Diener, C. I., & Dweck, C. S. (1980). An analysis of learned helplessness: The processing of success. *Journal of Personality and Social Psychology, 39*(5), 940–952.

DiLalla, D. L. (1998). Genetic contributors to mental health. In H. S. Friedman (Ed.), *Encyclopedia of mental health* (Vol. 2, 277–287). San Diego, CA: Academic Press.

Dion, K. K. (1972). Physical attractiveness and evaluation of children's transgressions. *Journal of Personality & Social Psychology, 24,* 207–213.

Dion, K. K. (1973) Young children's stereotyping of facial attractiveness. *Developmental Psychology, 9,* 183–188.

Dion, K. L., & Dion, K. K. (1993). Gender and ethnocultural comparisons in styles of love [Special issue]. *Psychology of Women Quarterly, 17*(4), 463–473.

Dole, A. A. (1995). Why not drop race as a term? *American Psychologist, 50*(1), 40.

Dollard, J., & Miller, N. E. (1950). *Personality and psychotherapy; an analysis in terms of learning, thinking, and culture.* New York: McGraw-Hill.

Dollard, J., Doob, L. W., Miller, N. E., & Mowrer, O. H. (1961). *Frustration and aggression.* New Haven, CT: Yale University Press.

Dollard, J., Miller, N. E., Doob, L. W., Mowrer, O. H., Sears, R. R., et al. (1939). *Frustration and aggression.* New Haven, CT: Yale University Press.

Donohue, M. V. (1995). A study of the development of traits of entry-level occupational therapy students. *American Journal of Occupational Therapy, 49*(7), 703–709.

Doob, L. W. (1958). Behavior and grammatical style. *Journal of Abnormal and Social Psychology, 56,* 398–401.

Douglas, J. E. (1995). *Mindhunter: Inside the FBI's elite serial crime unit* (J. Douglas & M. Olshaker, Eds.). New York: Scribner.

Dubey, S. N. (1987). Personality characteristics of the socioculturally deprived class. *Perspectives in Psychological Researches, 10*(2), 51–53.

DuBois, W. E. B. (1969). *The souls of black folk.* New York: Signet.

Dunbar, Flanders. (1955). *Mind and body: Psychosomatic medicine.* New York: Random House.

Dunn, J., & Plomin, R. (1990). *Separate lives: Why siblings are so different.* New York: Basic Books.

Dworkin, A. (1981). *Pornography: Men possessing women.* New York: Perigee Books/G. Putnam.

Eagly, A. H. (1987). *Sex differences in social behavior: A social-role interpretation.* Hillsdale, NJ: L. Erlbaum Associates.

Eagly, A. H. (1995). The science and politics of comparing women and men. *American Psychologist, 50*(3), 145–158.

Eagly, A. H., & Crowley, M. (1986). Gender and helping behavior: A meta-analytic review of the social psychological literature. *Psychological Bulletin, 100*(3), 283–308.

Eagly, A. H. (1978). Sex differences in influence ability. *Psychological Bulletin, 85,* 86–116.

Eagly, A. H., & Carli, L. L. (1981). Sex of researchers and sex-typed communications as determinants of sex differences in influenceability: A meta-analysis of social influence studies. *Psychological Bulletin, 90*, 1–20.

Eagly, A. H., & Johnson, B. T. (1990). Gender and leadership style: A meta-analysis. *Psychological Bulletin, 108*(2), 233–256.

Eagly, A. H., Karau, S. J., & Makhijani, M. G. (1995). Gender and the effectiveness of leaders: A meta-analysis. *Psychological Bulletin, 117*(1), 125–145.

Eagly, A. H., Makhijani, M. G., & Klonsky, B. G. (1992). Gender and the evaluation of leaders: A meta-analysis. *Psychological Bulletin, 111*(1), 3–22.

Eagly, A. H., & Steffen, V. J. (1986). Gender and aggressive behavior: A meta-analytic review of the social psychological literature. *Psychological Bulletin, 100*(3), 309–330.

Ehrlichman, H., & Eichenstein, R. (1992). Private wishes: Gender similarities and differences. *Sex Roles, 26*, 399–422.

Eibl-Eibesfeldt, I. (1971). *Love and hate: The natural history of basic behaviour patterns* (G. Strachan, Trans.). London: Methuen.

Eibl-Eibesfeldt, I. (1979). *The biology of peace and war: Men, animals, and aggression* (E. Mosbacher, Trans.). New York: Viking Press.

Eisenman, R. (1995). Why psychologists should study race. *American Psychologist, 50*(1), 42–43.

Elder, G. H., Jr., & Caspi, A. (1988). Human development and social change: An emerging perspective on the life course. In N. Bolger, A. Caspi, G. Downey, & M. Moorehouse (Eds.), *Persons in context: Developmental processes. Human Development in cultural and historical contexts* (pp. 77–113). New York: Cambridge University Press.

Eliot, G. (1859). *Adam Bede.* New York: Harper & Brothers.

Elliot, A. J., Sheldon, K. M., & Church, M. A. (1997). Avoidance personal goals and subjective well-being. *Personality and Social Psychology Bulletin, 23*, 915–927.

Elliott, E. S., & Dweck, C. S. (1988). Goals: An approach to motivation and achievement. *Journal of Personality and Social Psychology, 54*(1), 5–12.

Ellis, H. (1913). *Analysis of the sexual impulse, love, and pain* (2nd ed.). Philadelphia: F. A. Davis.

Ellis, H. (1936). *Studies in the psychology of sex.* New York: Random House. (Originally published 1899.)

Emde, R. N., Plomin, R., Robinson, J., Corley, R., De-Fries, J., Fulker, D. W., Reznick, J. S., Campos, J., Kagan, J., & Zahn-Waxler, C. (1992). Temperament, emotion, and cognition at fourteen months: The MacArthur Longitudinal Twin Study. *Child Development, 63*(6), 1437–1455.

Emmons, R. A. (1986). Personal strivings: An approach to personality and subjective well-being. *Journal of Personality and Social Psychology, 51*, 1058–1068.

Emmons, R. A. (1992). The repressive personality and social support. In H. S. Friedman (Ed.), *Hostility, coping, & health* (pp. 141–150). Washington, DC: American Psychological Association.

Engler, B. (1991). *Personality theories: An introduction* (3rd ed.). Boston: Houghton Mifflin.

Erdelyi, M. H. (1996). *The recovery of unconscious memories: Hypermnesia and reminiscence.* Chicago: University of Chicago Press.

Erikson, E. H. (Ed.). (1978). *Adulthood.* New York: W. W. Norton.

Erikson, E. H. (1950). *Childhood and society.* New York: W. W. Norton.

Erikson, E. H. (1958). *Young man Luther: A study in psychoanalysis and history.* New York: W. W. Norton.

Erikson, E. H. (1963). *Childhood and society* (2nd ed.). New York: W. W. Norton.

Erikson, E. H. (1969). *Gandhi's truth: On the origins of militant nonviolence.* New York: W. W. Norton.

Evidence found for a possible aggression gene [Research News]. (1993). *Science, 260,* 1722–1723.

Exline, R. V. (1972). Visual interaction: The glances of power and preference. *Nebraska Symposium on Motivation, 19*, 163–206.

Exline, R. V., Ellyson, S. L., & Long, B. (1975). Visual behavior as an aspect of power role relationships. In P. Pliner, L. Krames, & T. Alloway (Eds.), *Nonverbal communication of aggression* (pp. 21–52). New York: Plenum.

Exner, J. (1986). *The Rorschach: A comprehensive system* (2nd ed.). New York: Wiley.

Eysenck, H. J. (1967). *The biological basis of personality*. Springfield, IL: Charles C. Thomas.

Eysenck, H. J. (1990). Biological dimensions of personality. In L. A. Pervin (Ed.), *Handbook of personality: Theory and research* (pp. 244–276). New York: Guilford Press.

Eysenck, H. J. (1992). Four ways five factors are not basic. *Personality and Individual Differences, 13*(6) 667–673.

Eysenck, H. J. (1994). The Big Five or giant three: Criteria for a paradigm. In C. F. Halverson, Jr., G. A. Kohnstamm, & R. P. Martin (Eds.), *The developing structure of temperament and personality from infancy to adulthood* (pp. 37–51). Hillsdale, NJ: L. Erlbaum Associates.

Eysenck, H. J., & Eysenck, M. W. (1985). *Personality and individual differences: A natural science approach*. New York: Plenum.

Fagala, G. E., & Wigg, C. L. (1992). Psychiatric manifestations of mercury poisoning. *Journal of the American Academy of Child and Adolescent Psychiatry, 31*(2), 306–311.

Fancher, R. E. (1995). The Bell Curve on separated twins. *Alberta Journal of Educational Research, 41* (3), 265–270.

Fanon, F. (1952/1967). *Black skin, white masks* (C. L. Markmann, Trans.). New York: Grove Press. (Original work published in 1952 as *Peau noire, masques blancs.*)

Farde, L., Gustavsson, J. P., & Jonsson, E. (1997, Feb. 13). D2 dopamine receptors and personality traits [letter]. *Nature, 385,* 590.

Fausto-Sterling, A. (1985). *Myths of gender: Biological theories about women and men*. New York: Basic Books.

Fehr, B., & Russell, J. A. (1991). The concept of love viewed from a prototype perspective. *Journal of Personality and Social Psychology, 60*(3), 425–438.

Feingold, A. (1994). Gender differences in personality: A meta-analysis. *Psychological Bulletin, 116* (3), 429–456.

Feingold, A. (1995). The additive effects of differences in central tendency and variability are important in comparisons between groups. *American Psychologist, 50*(1), 5–13.

Fernandez, E., & Turk, D. C.(1995). The scope and significance of anger in the experience of chronic pain. *Pain, 61,* 165–175

Feshbach, N. D., & Feshbach, S. (1969). The relationship between empathy and aggression in two age groups. *Developmental Psychology, 1,* 102–107.

Feshbach, N. D., & Feshbach, S. (1982). Empathy training and the regulation of aggression: Potentialities and limitations. *Academic Psychology Bulletin, 4,* 399–413.

Feshbach, S. (1971). Dynamics and morality of violence and aggression: Some psychological considerations. *American Psychologist, 26,* 281–292.

Feshbach, S. (1984). The catharsis hypothesis, aggressive drive, and the reduction of aggression. *Aggressive Behavior, 10,* 91–101.

Findley, M. J., & Cooper, H. M. (1983). Locus of control and academic achievement: A literature review. *Journal of Personality & Social Psychology, 44,* 419–427.

Fisher, M., & Pressley, S. A. (1997, March 29). Crisis of sexuality launched strange journey. *Washington Post,* p. A1.

Fisher, S., & Greenberg, R. P. (1996). *Freud scientifically reappraised: Testing the theories and therapy*. New York: John Wiley & Sons.

Flannery, W. P., Reise, S. P., & Widaman, K. F. (1995). An item response theory analysis of the general and academic scales of the Self-Description Questionnaire II. *Journal of Research in Personality, 29*(2), 168–188.

Fontaine, K. R. (1994). Personality correlates of sexual risk-taking among men. *Personality and Individual Differences, 17*(5), 693–694.

Ford, C. S., & Beach, F. A. (1951). *Patterns of Sexual Behavior*. New York: Harper & Paul B. Hoeber.

Frank, A. (1952). *The diary of a young girl* (B. M. Mooyaart, Trans.; Eleanor Roosevelt, Intro.). Garden City, NY: Doubleday.

Frankl, V. E. (1962). *Man's search for meaning: An introduction to logotherapy* (Rev. ed.; I. Lasch, Trans.). Boston: Beacon Press.

Franklin, B. (1906). *The autobiography of Benjamin Franklin, with illustrations.* Boston: Houghton Mifflin.

Fraser, G. E., Beeson, W. L., & Phillips, R. L. (1991). Diet and lung cancer in California Seventh-day Adventists. *American Journal of Epidemiology, 133,* 683–693.

Fraser, S. (Ed.). (1995). *The Bell Curve wars: Race, intelligence, and the future of America.* New York: Basic Books.

Freedman, M. B., Ossorio, A. G., & Coffey, H. S. (1951). The interpersonal dimension of personality. *Journal of Personality, 20,* 143–161.

Freud, A. (1942). *The ego and the mechanisms of defense* (C. Baines, Trans.). London: Hogarth Press.

Freud, A. (1981). *The writings of Anna Freud.* New York: International Universities Press.

Freud, S. (1913). *The interpretation of dreams* (3rd ed.; A. A. Brill, Trans.). New York: Macmillan.

Freud, S. (1924). *Collected papers.* (Trans.). London: Hogarth Press.

Freud, S. (1947). *Leonardo da Vinci: A study in psychosexuality.* New York: Random House.

Freud, S. (1952). *Totem and taboo: Some points of agreement between the mental lives of savages and neurotics.* New York: Norton.

Freud, S. (1966). *On the history of the psycho-analytic movement.* New York: W. W. Norton.

Freud, S. (1966). Character and anal eroticism. In J. Strachey (Ed. & Trans.), *The standard edition of the complete psychological works of Sigmund Freud,* Vol. 9. London: Hogarth Press. (Original work published 1908).

Freud, S. (1967). Analysis of a phobia in a five-year-old boy. In J. Strachey (Ed. & Trans.), *The standard edition of the complete psychological works of Sigmund Freud,* Vol. 10. London: Hogarth Press. (Original work published in 1909.)

Freud, S. (1963). Introductory lectures on psychoanalysis. In J. Strachey (Ed. & Trans.), *The standard edition of the complete psychological works of Sigmund Freud,* Vol. 16. London: Hogarth Press. (Original work published 1916–1917).

Friedan, B. (1963). *The feminine mystique.* New York: Norton.

Friedman, H. S. (1979). The concept of skill in nonverbal communication: Implications for understanding social interaction. In R. Rosenthal (Ed.), *Skill in nonverbal communication* (pp. 2–27). Cambridge, MA: Oelgeschlager, Gunn, & Hain.

Friedman, H. S. (1991). *The self-healing personality: Why some people achieve health and others succumb to illness.* New York: H. Holt.

Friedman, H. S., & Booth-Kewley, S. (1987a). "The disease-prone personality": A meta-analytic view of the construct. *American Psychologist, 42,* 539–555.

Friedman, H. S., & Booth-Kewley, S. (1987b). Personality, Type A behavior, and coronary heart disease: The role of emotional expression. *Journal of Personality and Social Psychology, 53,* 783–792.

Friedman, H. S., DiMatteo, M. R., & Taranta, A. (1980). A study of the relationship between individual differences in nonverbal expressiveness and factors of personality and social interaction. *Journal of Research in Personality, 14,* 351–364.

Friedman, H. S., & Miller-Herringer, T. (1991). Nonverbal display of emotion in public and private: Self-monitoring, personality, and expressive cues. *Journal of Personality and Social Psychology, 61,* 766–775.

Friedman, H. S., Prince, L. M., Riggio, R. E., & DiMatteo, M. (1980). Understanding and assessing nonverbal expressiveness: The Affective Communication Test. *Journal of Personality & Social Psychology, 39,* 333–351.

Friedman, H. S., & Riggio, R. E. (1981). Effect of individual differences in nonverbal expressiveness on transmission of emotion. *Journal of Nonverbal Behavior, 6,* 96–104.

Friedman, H. S., Riggio, R. E., & Casella D.F. (1988). Nonverbal skill, personal charisma, and initial attraction. *Personality and Social Psychology Bulletin, 14,* 203–211.

Friedman, H. S., Riggio, R. E., & Segall, D. O. (1980). Personality and the enactment of emotion. *Journal of Nonverbal Behavior, 5,* 35–48.

Friedman, H. S., Tucker, J. S., Martin, L. R., Tomlinson-Keasey, C., Schwartz, J. E., Wingard, D. L., & Criqui, M. H. (1994). Do non-scientists really live longer? *The Lancet, 343,* 296.

Friedman, H. S., Tucker, J. S., Schwartz, J. E., Tomlinson-Keasey, C., Martin, L. R., Wingard, D. L., & Criqui, M. H. (1995). Psychosocial and behavioral predictors of longevity: The aging and death of the "Termites." *American Psychologist, 50,* 69–78.

Friedman, H. S., Tucker, J. S., Tomlinson-Keasey, C., Schwartz, J. E., Wingard, D. L., & Criqui, M. H. (1993). Does childhood personality predict longevity? *Journal of Personality and Social Psychology, 65,* 176–185.

Friedman, M., & Rosenman, R. H. (1974). *Type A behavior and your heart.* New York: Knopf.

Fromm, E. (1947). *Man for himself: An inquiry into the psychology of ethics.* New York: Rinehart.

Fromm, E. (1956). *The art of loving.* New York: Harper & Row.

Fromm, E. (1973). *The anatomy of human destructiveness.* New York: Fawcett Crest.

Funder, D. C. (1987). Errors and mistakes: Evaluating the accuracy of social judgment. *Psychological Bulletin, 101,* 75–90.

Funder, D. C., & Colvin, C. R. (1988). Friends and strangers: Acquaintanceship, agreement, and the accuracy of personality judgments. *Journal of Personality and Social Psychology, 55,* 149–158.

Funder, D. C., & Colvin, C. R. (1991). Explorations in behavioral consistency: Properties of persons, situations, and behaviors. *Journal of Personality and Social Psychology, 60*(5), 773–794.

Funder, D. C., & Dobroth, K. M. (1987). Differences between traits: Properties associated with interjudge agreement. *Journal of Personality and Social Psychology, 52,* 409–418

Funder, D. C., & Sneed, C. D. (1993). Behavioral manifestations of personality: An ecological approach to judgmental accuracy. *Journal of Personality and Social Psychology, 64*(3), 479–490.

Funder, D. C., Kolar, D. C., & Blackman, M. C. (1995). Agreement among judges of personality: Interpersonal relations, similarity, and acquaintanceship. *Journal of Personality and Social Psychology, 69*(4), 656–672.

Funder, D. C., & Ozer, D. J. (1983). Behavior as a function of the situation. *Journal of Personality and Social Psychology, 44*(1), 107–112.

Furnham, A., & Saipe, J. (1993). Personality correlates of convicted drivers. *Personality and Individual Differences, 14*(2), 329–336.

Gaines, S. O., & Reed, E. S. (1995). Prejudice: From Allport to DuBois. *American Psychologist, 50,* 96–103.

Gale, A. (1983). Electroencephalographic studies of extraversion-introversion: A case study in the psychophysiology of individual differences. *Personality & Individual Differences, 4,* 371–380.

Gallaher, P. E. (1992). Individual differences in nonverbal behavior: Dimensions of style. *Journal of Personality and Social Psychology, 63,* 133–145.

Galton, F. (1869). *Hereditary genius: An inquiry into its laws and consequences.* London: MacMillan.

Galton, F. (1907). *Inquiries into human faculty and its development* (2nd ed.). London: J. M. Dent.

Gangestad, S. W. (1989). The evolutionary history of genetic variation: An emerging issue in the behavioral genetic study of personality. In D. M. Buss & N. Cantor (Eds.), *Personality psychology: Recent trends and emerging directions* (pp. 320–332). New York: Springer-Verlag.

Garcia, J., & Koelling, R. A. (1966). Relation of cue to consequence in avoidance learning. *Psychonomic Science, 4*(3), 123–124.

Gardner, H. (1983). *Frames of mind.* New York: Basic Books.

Garza, R. T., & Santos, S. J. (1991). Ingroup/outgroup balance and interdependent interethnic behavior. *Journal of Experimental Social Psychology, 127,* 124–137.

Gastil, J. (1990). Generic pronouns and sexist language: The oxymoronic character of masculine generics. *Sex Roles, 23,* 629–643.

Gay, P. (1988). *Freud: A life for our time.* New York: W. W. Norton.

Geary, D. C. (1995). Reflections of evolution and culture in children's cognition: Implications for mathematical development and instruction. *American Psychologist, 50*(1), 24–37.

Gifford, R. (1994). A lens-mapping framework for understanding the encoding and decoding of interpersonal dispositions in nonverbal behavior. *Journal of Personality and Social Psychology, 66,* 398–412.

Glass, D. C., Krakoff, L. R., Contrada, R., Hilton, W. F., Kehoe, K., Mannucci, E. G., Collins-Snow, B., & Elting, E. (1980). Effect of harassment and competition upon cardiovascular and plasma catecholamine responses in type A and type B individuals. *Psychophysiology, 17,* 453–463.

Glick, P., Gottesman, D., & Jolton, J. (1989). The fault is not in the stars: Susceptibility of skeptics and believers in astrology to the Barnum effect. *Personality & Social Psychology Bulletin, 15*(4), 572–583.

Glick, S. D. (Ed.) (1985). *Cerebral lateralization in non-human species.* New York: Academic Press.

Goffman, E. (1967). *Interaction ritual: Essays in face-to-face behavior.* Chicago: Aldine.

Goldberg, L. R. (1990). An alternative "description of personality": The Big-Five factor structure. *Journal of Personality and Social Psychology, 59*(6), 1216–1229.

Goldberg, L. R., & Saucier, G. (1995). So what do you propose we use instead? A reply to Block. *Psychological Bulletin, 117*(2), 221–225.

Goldsmith, H. H. (1989). Behavior-genetic approaches to temperament. In G. A. Kohnstamm, J. E. Bates, & M. K. Rothbart (Eds.), *Temperament in childhood* (pp. 111–132). Chichester, England: John Wiley & Sons.

Goldstein, A. P., & Segall, M. H. (1983). *Aggression in global perspective.* New York: Pergamon Press.

Goldstein, K. (1963). *The organism, a holistic approach to biology derived from pathological data in man.* (Foreword, K. S. Lashley.) Boston: Beacon Press.

Goleman, D. (1995). *Emotional intelligence.* New York: Bantam.

Gottesman, I. I. (1991). *Schizophrenia genesis: The origins of madness.* New York: Freeman.

Gottlieb, B. (1998). Support groups. In H. S. Friedman (Ed.), *Encyclopedia of mental health* (Vol. 3, 635–648). San Diego: Academic Press.

Gough, H. G. (1987). *CPI, California Psychological Inventory: Administrator's guide.* Palo Alto, CA: Consulting Psychologists Press.

Gough, H. G., Fox, R. E., & Hall, W. B. (1972). Personality inventory assessment of psychiatric residents. *Journal of Counseling Psychology, 19*(4), 269–274.

Gould, S. J. (1981). *The mismeasure of man.* New York: W. W. Norton.

Gould, S. J. (1996). *The mismeasure of man* (2nd ed.). New York: W. W. Norton.

Graf, P., Mandler, G., & Squire, L. R. (1984). The information that amnesic patients don't forget. *Journal of Experimental Psychology: Learning, Memory, & Cognition, 10,* 164–178.

Gray, J. (1992). *Men are from Mars, women are from Venus: A practical guide for improving communication and getting what you want in your relationships.* New York: HarperCollins.

Graziano, W. G., & Eisenberg, N. (1997). Agreeableness: A dimension of personality. In R. Hogan, J. Johnson, & S. Briggs (Eds.), *Handbook of personality psychology* (pp. 795–824). San Diego: Academic Press.

Greenbaum, C. W., Auerbach, J. G., Guttman, R. (1989). Fathers' and mothers' perceptions of temperament in Israeli neonates: Effects of adoption and social class. *Israel Journal of Psychiatry and Related Sciences, 26*(1–2), 85–95.

Greer, G. (1971). *The female eunuch.* New York: McGraw-Hill.

Grunberg, N. E., Klein, L. C., & Brown, K. J. (1998). Psychopharmacology. In H. S. Friedman (Ed.), *Encyclopedia of mental health.* San Diego, CA: Academic Press, Vol. 3, 335–344.

Guilford, J. P. (1940). Human abilities. *Psychological Review, 47,* 367–394.

Haier, R. J. (1998). Brain scanning and neuro-imaging. In H. S. Friedman (Ed.), *Encyclopedia of men-*

tal health (Vol. 1, 317–329). San Diego: Academic Press.

Halberstadt, A. (1991). Family patterns of nonverbal development. In R. S. Feldman & B. Rime (Eds.), *Fundamentals of nonverbal behavior*. Cambridge, UK: Cambridge University Press.

Hall, J. A. (1990). *Nonverbal sex differences: Accuracy of communication and expressive style*. Baltimore: Johns Hopkins University Press.

Hall, J. A., Friedman, H. S., & Harris, M. J. (1986). Nonverbal cues, the Type A behavior pattern, and coronary heart disease. In P. D. Blanck, R. Buck, & R. Rosenthal (Eds.), *Nonverbal communication in the clinical context* (pp. 144–168). University Park, PA: Pennsylvania State University Press.

Hall, J. A., & Halberstadt, A. G. (1986). Smiling and gazing. In J. S. Hyde & M. C. Linn (Eds.), *The psychology of gender: Advances through meta-analysis*. Baltimore: Johns Hopkins University Press.

Hall, J. A., & Veccia, E. M.(1990). More "touching" observations: New insights on men, women, and interpersonal touch. *Journal of Personality & Social Psychology, 59*, 1155–1162.

Hall, M. H. (1967). An interview with "Mr. Behaviorist": B. F. Skinner. *Psychology Today, 1*, 68–71.

Halpern, D. F. (1992). *Sex differences in cognitive abilities* (2nd ed.). Hillsdale, NJ: L. Erlbaum Associates.

Hamilton, D. L., & Sherman, J. W. (1994). Stereotypes. In R. S. Wyer, Jr., & T. K. Srull (Eds.), *Handbook of social cognition* (pp. 1–68). Hillsdale, NJ: L. Erlbaum Associates.

Hammer, A. L. (Ed.). (1996). *MBTI applications: A decade of research on the Myers-Briggs Type Indicator*. Palo Alto, CA: Consulting Psychologists Press.

Hansen, K. (1983). The anals of history: Unintentional humor from freshman composition. *English Journal, 72*.

Hare, A. P., & Blumberg, H. H. (1988). *Dramaturgical analysis of social interaction*. New York: Praeger.

Hargreaves, D. J. (1987). Psychological theories of sex-role stereotyping. In D. J. Hargreaves & A. M. Colley (Eds.), *The psychology of sex roles* (pp. 27–44). Cambridge, UK: Hemisphere.

Hargreaves, D. J., & Colley, A. M. (Eds.). (1987). *The psychology of sex roles*. Cambridge, UK: Hemisphere.

Harlow, H. F. (1986). *From learning to love: The selected papers of H. F. Harlow* (Clara Mears Harlow, Ed.). New York: Praeger.

Harlow, H. F., & Mears, C. (1979). *The human model: Primate perspectives*. Washington, DC: V. H. Winston.

Harsch, N., & Neisser, U. (1989). *Substantial and irreversible errors in flashbulb memories of the Challenger explosion*. Poster presented at the meeting of the Psychonomic Society, Atlanta, GA.

Hartmann, H. (1958). *Ego psychology and the problem of adaptation* (D. Rapaport, Trans.). New York: International Universities Press.

Hartshorne, H., & May, M. A. (1928). *Studies in the nature of character*, Vol. 1. New York: Macmillan.

Hatfield, E., & Sprecher, S.(1986). Measuring passionate love in intimate relationships. *Journal of Adolescence, 9*, 383–410.

Hawkins, J. D., Catalano, R. F., & Miller, J. Y. (1992). Risk and protective factors for alcohol and other drug problems in adolescence and early adulthood: Implications for substance abuse prevention. *Psychological Bulletin, 112*, 64–105.

Hazan, C., & Shaver, P. (1987). Romantic love conceptualized as an attachment process. *Journal of Personality & Social Psychology, 52*(3), 511–524.

Heath, A. C., Eaves, L. J., & Martoin, N. G. (1989). The genetic structure of personality: Multivariate genetic item analysis of the EPQ. *Personality and Individual Differences, 10*, 877–888.

Heatherton, T. F., & Hebl, M. R. (1998). Body image. In H. S. Friedman (Ed.), *Encyclopedia of mental health* (Vol. 1, 257–266). San Diego, CA: Academic Press.

Heidegger, M. (1962). *Being and time* (J. Macquarrie & E. Robinson, Trans.). New York: Harper.

Helson, R., & Roberts, B. W. (1994). Ego development and personality change in adulthood. *Journal of Personality and Social Psychology, 66*(5), 911–920.

Helzer, J. E., Robins, L. N., & McEvoy, L. (1987). Post-traumatic stress disorder in the general population. *New England Journal of Medicine, 317,* 1630–1634.

Henley, N. (1977). *Body politics: Power, sex, and non-verbal communication.* Englewood Cliffs, NJ: Prentice-Hall.

Herman, J. L. (1992). *Trauma and recovery.* New York: Basic Books.

Hermans, H., Kempen, H., & van Loon, R. (1992). The dialogical self. *American Psychologist, 47,* 23–33.

Herrnstein, R. J., & Murray, C. A. (1994). *The bell curve: Intelligence and class structure in American life.* New York: Free Press.

Herschberger, S. L. (1998). Homosexuality. In H. S. Friedman (Ed.), *Encyclopedia of mental health* (Vol. 2, 403–420). San Diego, CA: Academic Press.

Hetherington, E. M. (1991). Families, lies, and videotapes. *Journal of Research on Adolescence, 1,* 323–348.

Hines, M., & Sandberg, E. C. (1996). Sexual differentiation of cognitive abilities in women exposed to diethylstilbestrol (DES) prenatally. *Hormones & Behavior, 30,* 354–363.

Hockett, C. F. (1966). The problem of universals in language. In J. H. Greenberg (Ed.), *Universals of language,* 2nd ed. Cambridge, MA: MIT Press.

Hoeller, K. (Ed.). (1990). *Readings in existential psychology and psychiatry.* Seattle: Review of Psychology and Psychiatry.

Hofstadter, R. (1959). *Social Darwinism in American thought* (Rev. ed.). New York: G. Braziller.

Horner, M. S. (1972). Toward an understanding of achievement-related conflicts in women. *Journal of Social Issues, 28*(2), 157–175.

Horney, K. (1945). *Our inner conflicts: A constructive theory of neurosis.* New York: W. W. Norton.

Horney, K. (1968). *Self-analysis.* New York: W. W. Norton.

Horney, K. (1987). *Final lectures* (D. H. Ingram, Ed.). New York: W. W. Norton.

Horney, K. (1991). The goals of analytic therapy [Special issue] (A. Dlaska, Trans.). *American Journal of Psychoanalysis, 51*(3), 219–226.

Horowitz, L. M., Rosenberg, S. E., Baer, B. A., Ureno, G., et al. (1988). Inventory of interpersonal problems: Psychometric properties and clinical applications. *Journal of Consulting & Clinical Psychology, 56*(6), 885–892.

Horowitz, M. J. (1998). Psychoanalysis. In H. S. Friedman (Ed.), *Encyclopedia of mental health* (Vol. 3, 299–313). San Diego, CA: Academic Press.

House, J. S. (1990). Social structure and personality. In M. Rosenberg & R. H. Turner (Eds.), *Social psychology: Sociological perspectives* (pp. 525–561). New Brunswick, NJ: Transaction.

Howells, K. (1987). Sex roles and sexual behavior. In D. J. Hargreaves & A. M. Colley (Eds.), *The psychology of sex roles* (pp. 268–286). Cambridge, UK: Hemisphere.

Huesmann, L. R., Eron, L. D., & Yarmel, P. W. (1987). Intellectual functioning and aggression. *Journal of Personality & Social Psychology, 52*(1), 232–240.

Hull, C. L. (1940). *Mathematico-deductive theory of rote learning.* New Haven, CT: Yale University Press.

Hull, C. L. (1943). *Principles of behavior: An introduction to behavior theory.* New York: D. Appleton-Century.

Hyde, J. S. (1986a). Gender differences in aggression. In J. S. Hyde & M. C. Linn (Eds.), *The psychology of gender: Advances through meta-analysis.* Baltimore: Johns Hopkins University Press.

Hyde, J. S. (1986b). Introduction: Meta-analysis and the psychology of gender. In J. S. Hyde & M. C. Linn (Eds.), *The psychology of gender: Advances through meta-analysis.* Baltimore: Johns Hopkins University Press.

Hyde, J. S. (1991). *Half the human experience: The psychology of women* (4th ed.). Lexington, MA: D. C. Heath.

Hyde, J. S., & Linn, M. C. (1986). *The psychology of gender: Advances through meta-analysis.* Baltimore: Johns Hopkins University Press.

International Conference on Carcinogenesis and Risk Assessment (1996). Genetics and cancer susceptibility: Implications for risk assessment. *Proceedings of the Eighth International Conference on*

Carcinogenesis and Risk Assessment. New York: Wiley-Liss.

Izard, C. E. (1992). Basic emotions, relations among emotions, and emotion-cognition relations. *Psychological Review, 99,* 561–565.

Jacklin, C. N., Wilcox, K. T., & Maccoby, E. E. (1988). Neonatal sex-steroid hormones and intellectual abilities at six years. *Developmental Psychobiology, 21*(6), 567–574.

Jackson, D. N., & Messick, S. (Eds.). (1967). *Problems in human assessment.* Huntington, NY: R. E. Krieger.

Jaeger, J. (1992). 'Not by the chair of my hinny hin hin': Some general properties of slips of the tongue in young children. *Journal of Child Language, 19,* 335–366.

James, W. (1890). *Principles of psychology.* New York: Henry Holt.

Janet, P. (1907). *The major symptoms of hysteria: Fifteen lectures given in the Medical School of Harvard University.* New York: Macmillan.

Jaycox, L. J., & Foa, E. B. (1998). Posttraumatic stress. In H. S. Friedman (Ed.), *Encyclopedia of mental health* (Vol. 3, 209–218). San Diego: Academic Press.

Jellinek, M. S., & Slovik, L. S. (1981). Current concepts in psychiatry. Divorce: impact on children. *New England Journal of Medicine, 305*(10), 557–560.

Jensen, A. R. (1995). Psychological research on race differences. *American Psychologist, 50*(1) 41–42.

Jensen, M. R. (1987). Psychobiological factors predicting the course of breast cancer. *Journal of Personality, 55,* 317–342.

John, O. P. (1990). The "Big Five" factor taxonomy: Dimensions of personality in the natural language and in questionnaires. In L. A. Pervin (Ed.), *Handbook of personality: Theory and research* (pp. 66–100). New York: Guilford Press.

Johnstone, B., & Bean, J. M. (1997). Self-expression and linguistic variation. *Language in Society, 26,* 221–246.

Jones, E. (1953). *The life and work of Sigmund Freud.* New York: Basic Books.

Jones, E. E., & Nisbett, R. E. (1987). The actor and the observer: Divergent perceptions of the causes of behavior. In E. E. Jones, D. E. Kanouse, H. H. Kelley, R. E. Nisbett, S. Valins, & B. Weiner, (Eds.), *Attribution: Perceiving the causes of behavior* (pp. 79–94). Hillsdale, NJ: L. Erlbaum Associates.

Jones, M. C. (1924). The elimination of children's fears. *Journal of Experimental Psychology, 7,* 383–390.

Jung, C. G. (1921/1967). Psychological types. In *Collected works of C. G. Jung,* Vol. 6. Princeton, NJ: Princeton University Press. (Original work published 1921.)

Jung, C. G. (1933). *Modern man in search of a soul.* New York: Harcourt, Brace.

Jung, C. G. (1959). Psychological aspects of the mother archetype. In *Collected works of C. G. Jung,* Vol. 9, Part I. Princeton, NJ: Princeton University Press.

Jung, C. G. (1961a). *Memories, dreams, reflections* (A. Jaffe, Ed.). New York: Pantheon.

Jung, C. G. (1961b). The psychogenesis of mental disease. In *Collected Works,* Vol. 3. New York: Pantheon.

Jung, C. G. (1961c). On psychological understanding. In *Collected Works,* Vol. 3. New York: Pantheon.

Jung, C. G. (1990). *The basic writings of C. G. Jung* (R. F. C. Hull, Trans.). Princeton, NJ: Princeton University Press.

Kagan, J., Snidman, N., & Arcus, D. (1995). The role of temperament in social development. In G. P. Chrousos, R. McCarty, K. Pacak, G. Cizza, E. Sternberg, P. W. Gold, & R. Kvetnansky (Eds.), *Stress: Basic mechanisms and clinical implications. Vol. 771, Annals of the New York Academy of Sciences* (pp. 485–490). New York: New York Academy of Sciences.

Kagan, J., & Moss, H. A. (1962). *From birth to maturity.* New York: Wiley.

Kagan, J., Reznick, J. S., Snidman, N., Gibbons, J., & Johnson, M. O. (1988). Childhood derivatives of inhibition and lack of inhibition to the unfamiliar. *Child Development, 59,* 1580–1589.

Kagan, S., & Madsen, M. C. (1972). Experimental analyses of cooperation and competition of Anglo-American and Mexican children. *Developmental Psychology, 6*(1), 49–59.

Kagan, S., & Zahn, B. L. (1975). Field dependence and the school achievement gap between Anglo-American and Mexican-American children. *Journal of Educational Psychology, 67*(5), 643–650.

Kamarck, T. W., & Jennings, J. R. (1991). Biobehavioral factors in sudden cardiac death. *Psychological Bulletin, 109,* 42–75.

Kaplan, H. S. (1983). *The evaluation of sexual disorders: Psychological and medical aspects.* New York: Brunner/Mazel.

Katz, D., & Braly, K. (1933). Racial stereotypes of one hundred college students. *Journal of Abnormal & Social Psychology, 28,* 280–290.

Keebler, J. (1996, November). A feature-packed family hauler. *Motor Trend,* 101.

Kelly, G. A. (1955). *The psychology of personal constructs: A theory of personality.* New York: Norton.

Kelly, G. A. (1963). *A theory of personality: The psychology of personal constructs.* New York: Norton.

Kelly, O. E. (1979). *Until tomorrow comes.* New York: Everst House.

Keltikangas-Jarvinen, L., & Terav, T. (1996). Social decision-making strategies in individualist and collectivist cultures: A comparison of Finnish and Estonian adolescents. *Journal of Cross-Cultural Psychology, 27,* 714–732.

Kenny, D. A., Horner, C., Kashy, D. A., & Chu, L. C. (1992). Consensus at zero acquaintance: Replication, behavioral cues, and stability. *Journal of Personality and Social Psychology, 62*(1), 88–97.

Kenrick, D. T., Neuberg, S. L., Zierk, K. L., & Krones, J. M. (1994). Evolution and social cognition: Contrast effects as a function of sex, dominance, and physical attractiveness. *Personality & Social Psychology Bulletin, 20,* 210–217.

Key, S. (1995). The definition of race. *American Psychologist, 50*(1), 43–44.

Kihlstrom, J. F. (1987). The cognitive unconscious. *Science, 237,* 1445–1452.

Kihlstrom, J. F. (1998). Hypnosis and the psychological unconscious. In H. S. Friedman (Ed.), *Encyclopedia of mental health* (Vol. 2, 467–487). San Diego, CA: Academic Press.

Kihlstrom, J. F., & Barnhardt, T. M. (1993). The self-regulation of memory: For better and for worse, with and without hypnosis. In D. M. Wegner & J. W. Pennebaker (Eds.), *Handbook of mental control* (pp. 88–125). Englewood Cliffs, NJ: Prentice-Hall.

Kihlstrom, J. F., & Glisky, E. L. (1998). Amnesia. In H. S. Friedman (Ed.), *Encyclopedia of mental health* (Vol. 1, 83–93). San Diego, CA: Academic Press.

Kinsey, A. C., Pomeroy, W. B., & Martin, C. E. (1948). *Sexual behavior in the human male.* Philadelphia: W. B. Saunders.

Kirk, H. L. (1974). *Pablo Casals: A biography.* New York: Holt, Rinehart & Winston.

Kitayama, S., Markus, H. R., & Matsumoto, H. (1995). Culture, self, and emotion: A cultural perspective on "self-conscious" emotions. In J. P. Tangney & K. W. Fischer (Eds.), *Self-conscious emotions: The psychology of shame, guilt, embarrassment, and pride* (pp. 439–464). New York: Guilford Press.

Klein, M. (1975). *The writings of Melanie Klein.* London: Hogarth Press.

Klineberg, O. (1935). *Race differences.* New York: Harper.

Kluckhorn, C., & Murray, H. A. (Eds.). (1948). *Personality in nature, society, and culture.* New York: Alfred A. Knopf.

Koestler, A. (1967). *The ghost in the machine.* London: Hutchinson.

Kohler, W. (1947). *Gestalt psychology: An introduction to new concepts in modern psychology.* New York: Liveright.

Kohut, H. (1971). *The analysis of the self: A systematic approach to the psychoanalytic treatment of narcissistic personality disorders.* New York: International Universities Press.

Koss, M. P., & Harvey, M. R. (1991). *The rape victim: Clinical and community interventions* (2nd ed.). Newbury Park, CA: Sage Publications.

Krahe, B. (1990). *Situation cognition and coherence in personality.* New York: Cambridge University Press.

Kramer, P. D. (1993). *Listening to Prozac.* New York: Viking.

Kretschmer, E. (1925). *Physique and character; an investigation of the nature of constitution and of the theory of temperament.* New York: Harcourt, Brace.

Kretschmer, E. (1934). *Medizinische psychologie* [Medical psychology]. Translated with an introduction by E. B. Strauss. London: Oxford University Press.

Krishnan, P. (1995). *The Bell Curve:* Some statistical concerns [Special issue]. *Alberta Journal of Educational Research, 41*(3), 274–276.

Kuhn, T. S. (1962). *The structure of scientific revolutions.* Chicago: University of Chicago Press.

Ladd, C. O., Owens, M. J., & Nemeroff, C. B. (1996). Persistent changes in corticotropin-releasing factor neuronal systems induced by maternal deprivation. *Endocrinology, 137,* 1212–1218.

LaFrance, M., & Mayo, C. (1976). Racial differences in gaze behavior during conversations: Two systematic observational studies. *Journal of Personality & Social Psychology, 33,* 547–552.

Lagerspetz, K. M. J., & Bjorkqvist, K. (1994). Indirect aggression in boys and girls. In L. R. Huesmann (Ed.), *Aggressive behavior: Current perspectives. Plenum series in social/clinical psychology* (pp. 131–150). New York: Plenum.

Larrance, D. T., & Zuckerman, M. (1981). Facial attractiveness and vocal likeability as determinants of nonverbal sending skills. *Journal of Personality, 49,* 349–362.

Larsen, R. J. (1989). A process approach to personality. In D. M. Buss & N. Cantor (Eds.), *Personality psychology: Recent trends and emerging directions* (pp. 177–193). New York: Springer-Verlag.

LeVay, S. (1991). A difference in hypothalamic structure between heterosexual and homosexual men. *Science, 253,* 1034–1037.

LeVay, S. (1993). *The sexual brain.* Cambridge, MA: MIT Press.

Levenson, H. (1981). Differentiating among internality, powerful others, and chance. In H. Lefcourt (Ed.), *Research with the locus of control concept.* New York: Academic Press.

Levesque, M. J., & Kenny, D. A. (1993). Accuracy of behavioral predictions at zero acquaintance: A social relations analysis. *Journal of Personality and Social Psychology, 65,* 1178–1187.

Levine, R., Sato, S., Hashimoto, T., & Verma, J. (1995). Love and marriage in eleven cultures. *Journal of Cross-Cultural Psychology, 26*(5), 554–571.

Lewin, K. (1935). *A dynamic theory of personality: Selected papers* (D. K. Adams & K. E. Zener, Trans.). New York: McGraw-Hill.

Lewin, K. (1947). Group decision and social change. In T. M. Newcomb & E. L. Hartley (Eds.), *Readings in social psychology* (pp. 330–344). New York: Holt.

Lewin, K., Lippitt, R., & White, R. K. (1939). Patterns of aggressive behavior in experimentally created "social climates." *Journal of Social Psychology, 10,* 271–299.

Lewis, C. (1987). Early sex-role socialization. In D. J. Hargreaves & A. M. Colley (Eds.), *The psychology of sex roles* (pp. 95–117). Cambridge, UK: Hemisphere.

Lewis, C. A. (1996). Examining the specificity of the orality-depression link: Anal personality traits and depressive symptoms. *Journal of Psychology, 130,* 221–223.

Lifton, R. J. (1986) *The Nazi doctors: Medical killing and the psychology of genocide.* New York: Basic Books.

Lindzey, G. (1961). *Projective techniques and cross-cultural research.* New York: Appleton-Century-Crofts.

Linton, R. (1945). *The cultural background of personality.* New York: Appleton-Century.

Lips, H. M., & Colwill, N. L. (1978). *The psychology of sex differences.* Englewood Cliffs, NJ: Prentice-Hall.

Little, B. R. (1993). Personal projects and the distributed self: Aspects of a conative psychology. In J. M. Suls (Ed.), *The self in social perspective* (pp. 157–185). Hillsdale, NJ: Erlbaum.

Lochman, J. E., & Dodge, K. A. (1994). Social-cognitive processes of severely violent, moderately aggressive, and nonaggressive boys. *Journal of Consulting and Clinical Psychology, 62*(2), 366–374.

Locke, J. (1690/1964). *An essay concerning human understanding* (A. D. Woozley, Ed.). Cleveland: Meridian Books, 1964.

Loehlin, J. C. (1992). *Genes and environment in personality development.* Newbury Park, CA: Sage Publications.

Loevinger, J. (1996). The meaning and measurement of ego development. *American Psychologist, 21,* 195–206.

Loevinger, J. (1997). Stages of personality development. In R. Hogan, J. A. Johnson, & S. R. Briggs (Eds.), *Handbook of personality psychology.* San Diego, CA: Academic Press, pp. 199–208.

Loevinger, J., et al. (1985). Ego development in college. *Journal of Personality and Social Psychology, 48*(4), 947–962.

Loewald, H. W. (1988). *Sublimation: Inquiries into theoretical psychoanalysis.* New Haven, CT: Yale University Press.

Loftus, E. F., & Ketcham, K. (1991). *Witness for the defense: The accused, the eyewitness, and the expert who puts memory on trial.* New York: St. Martin's Press.

Lord, C. G. (1982). Predicting behavioral consistency from an individual's perception of situational similarities. *Journal of Personality & Social Psychology, 42,* 1076–1088.

Lorenz, K. (1937). The companion in the bird's world. *Auk, 54,* 245–273.

Lorenz, K. (1967). *On aggression* (M. Kerr, Trans.). Toronto: Bantam Books.

Lown, B. (1987). Sudden cardiac death. *Circulation, 76*(Suppl. 1), 186–196.

Lown, B. (1988). Reflections on sudden cardiac death: Brain and heart. *Transactions and Studies of the College of Physicians of Philadelphia, 10*(1–4), 63–80.

Lyon, D., & Greenberg, J. (1991). Evidence of codependency in women with an alcoholic parent: Helping out Mr. Wrong. *Journal of Personality and Social Psychology, 61,* 435–439.

Maccoby, E. E., & Jacklin, C. N. (1974). *The psychology of sex differences.* Stanford, CA: Stanford University Press.

MacDonald, K. (1995). Evolution, the five-factor model, and levels of personality. *Journal of Personality, 63,* 525–567.

Maddahian, E., Newcomb, M. D., & Bentler, P. M. (1986). Adolescents' substance use: Impact of ethnicity, income, and availability. *Advances in Alcohol & Substance Abuse, 5,* 63–78.

Maddi, S. R. (1970). Alfred Adler and the fulfillment model of personality theorizing. *Journal of Individual Psychology, 26,* 153–160.

Maddi, S. R., & Kobasa, S. (1984). *The hardy executive.* Chicago: Dorsey.

Madigan, S., & O'Hara, R. (1992). Initial recall, reminiscence, and hypermnesia. *Journal of Experimental Psychology: Learning, Memory, & Cognition, 19,* 421–425.

Magnus, K., Diener, E., Fujita, F., & Payot, W. (1993). Extraversion and neuroticism as predictors of objective life events: A longitudinal analysis. *Journal of Personality & Social Psychology, 65,* 1046–1053.

Magnusson, D. (1990). Personality development from an interactional perspective. In L. A. Pervin (Ed.), *Handbook of personality: Theory and research* (pp. 193–222). New York: Guilford Press.

Magnusson, D., & Endler, N. S. (Eds.). (1997). *Personality at the crossroads: Current issues in interactional psychology.* Hillsdale, NJ: L. Erlbaum Associates.

Mahler, M. S. (1979). *Infantile psychosis and early contributions.* New York: J. Aronson.

Major, B. (1993). Gender, entitlement, and the distribution of family labor. *Journal of Social Issues, 49*(3), 141–159.

Major, B., Schmidlin, A. M., & Williams, L. (1990). Gender patterns in social touch: The impact of setting and age. *Journal of Personality and Social Psychology, 58*(4), 634–643.

Malamuth, N. M. (1986). Predictors of naturalistic sexual aggression. *Journal of Personality and Social Psychology, 50*(5), 953–962.

Malamuth, N. M. (1989). The Attraction to Sexual Aggression scale: II. *Journal of Sex Research, 26*(3), 324–354.

Mansfield, E. D., & McAdams, D. P. (1996). Generativity and themes of agency and communion in adult autobiography. *Personality & Social Psychology Bulletin, 22,* 721–731.

Manstead, A. (1991). Expressiveness as an individual difference. In R. S. Feldman & B. Rime (Eds.), *Fundamentals of nonverbal behavior.* Cambridge, UK: Cambridge University Press.

Markus, H. R., & Kitayama, S. (1991). Culture and the self: Implications for cognition, emotion, and motivation. *Psychological Review, 98,* 224–253.

Martin, L. R., Friedman, H. S., et al. (Submitted). Optimism and longevity: Examination of the inverse relation in Terman's gifted group.

Martin, L. R., Friedman, H. S., Tucker, J. S., Schwartz, J. E., Criqui, M. H., Wingard, D. L., & Tomlinson-Keasey, C. (1995). An archival prospective study of mental health and longevity. *Health Psychology, 14,* 381–387.

Marx, K. (1872). *Das kapital: Kritik der politischen oekonomic.* Hamburg, Germany: O. Meissner.

Maslow, A. H. (1942). Self-esteem (dominance-feeling) and sexuality in women. *Journal of Social Psychology, 16,* 259–294.

Maslow, A. H. (1968). *Toward a psychology of being* (2nd ed.). Princeton, NJ: VanNostrand.

Maslow, A. H. (1987). *Motivation and personality* (3rd ed.). New York: Harper & Row.

Masters, W. H., & Johnson, V. E. (1966). *Human sexual response* (1st ed.). Boston: Little, Brown.

Matarazzo, J. D. (1992). Psychological testing and assessment in the 21st century. *American Psychologist, 8,* 1007–1018.

Mathews, A., & MacLeod, C. (1986). Discrimination of threat cues without awareness in anxiety states. *Journal of Abnormal Psychology, 95,* 131–138.

May, R. (1969). *Love and will.* New York: W. W. Norton.

May, R. (1972). *Power and innocence.* New York: W. W. Norton.

May, R. (1977). *The meaning of anxiety* (Rev. ed.). New York: W. W. Norton.

Mayr, E. (1991). *One long argument: Charles Darwin and the genesis of modern evolutionary thought.* Cambridge, MA: Harvard University Press.

McAdams, D. P. (1991). Self and story. In D. J. Ozer, J. M. Healy, Jr., & A. J. Stewart (Eds.), *Perspectives in personality* (pp. 133–159). London: Jessica Kingsley Publishers. .

McCartney, K., Harris, M. J., & Bernieri, F. (1990). Growing up and growing apart: A developmental meta-analysis of twin studies. *Psychological Bulletin, 107,* 226–237.

McClelland, D. C. (1961). *The achieving society.* Princeton, NJ: Van Nostrand.

McClelland, D. C. (1984). *Motives, personality, and society.* New York: Praeger.

McClelland, D. C., Atkinson, J. W., Clark, R. A., & Lowell, E. L. (1953). *The achievement motive.* New York: Irvington.

McClintock, M. K., & Herdt, G. (1996). Rethinking puberty: The development of sexual attraction. *Current Directions in Psychological Science, 5,* 178–186.

McConnell, A. R., & Fazio, R. H. (1996). Women as men and people: Effects of gender-marked language. *Personality & Social Psychology Bulletin, 22,* 1004–1013.

McCrae, R. R., & Costa, P. T., Jr. (1985). Updating Norman's "adequacy taxonomy": Intelligence and personality dimensions in natural language and in questionnaires. *Journal of Personality and Social Psychology, 49,* 710–721.

McCrae, R. R., & Costa, P. T., Jr. (1987). Validation of the five-factor model of personality across instruments and observers. *Journal of Personality and Social Psychology, 52,* 81–90.

McCrae, R. R., & Costa, P. T., Jr. (1989). Reinterpreting the Myers-Briggs Type Indicator from the perspective of the five-factor model of personality. *Journal of Personality, 57,* 17–40.

McCrae, R. R., & Costa, P. T., Jr. (1997a). Conceptions and correlates of openness to experience. In R. Hogan, J. Johnson, & S. Briggs (Eds.), *Handbook of personality psychology* (pp. 825–847). San Diego: Academic Press.

McCrae, R. R., & Costa, P. T., Jr. (1997b). Personality trait structure as a human universal. *American Psychologist, 52,* 509–516.

McCrae, R. R., & John, O. P. (1992). An introduction to the five-factor model and its applications [Special issue]. *Journal of Personality, 60,* 175–215.

McDougall, W. (1908). *Introduction to social psychology.* London: Methuen.

McGue, M., & Lykken, D. T. (1992). Genetic influence on risk of divorce. *Psychological Science, 3,* 368–373.

McMahon, R. C., & Richards, S. K. (1996). Profile patterns, consistency and change in the Millon Clinical Multiaxial Inventory-II in cocaine abusers. *Journal of Clinical Psychology, 52,* 75–79.

Mead, G. H. (1968). *George Herbert Mead: Essays on his social philosophy* (J. W. Petras, Intro.). New York: Teachers College Press.

Mead, M. (1929). *Coming of age in Samoa: A psychological study of primitive youth for Western civilisation* (F. Boas, Foreword). London: Jonathan Cape.

Mead, M. (1935). *Sex and temperament in three primitive societies.* New York: William Morrow.

Mead, M. (1939). *From the South Seas; Studies of adolescence and sex in primitive societies.* New York: W. Morrow.

Mechanic, D. (1968). *Medical sociology: A selective view.* New York: Free Press.

Mehrabian, A. (1969). Significance of posture and position in the communication of attitude and status relationships. *Psychological Bulletin, 71,* 359–372.

Melburg, V., & Tedeschi, J. T. (1989). Displaced aggression: Frustration or impression management? *European Journal of Social Psychology, 19,* 139–145.

Mencius. (1898). *The four books; or, The Chinese classics in English compiled from previous works.* Hong Kong: Man Yu Tong.

Menninger, K. A., & Menninger, W. C. (1936). Psychoanalytic observations in cardiac disorders. *American Heart Journal, 11,* 1–12.

Menza, M. A., Forman, N. E., Goldstein, H. S., & Golbe, L. I. (1990). Parkinson's disease, personality, and dopamine. *Journal of Neuropsychiatry and Clinical Neurosciences, 2,* 282–287.

Mercer, J. R. (1979). In defense of racially and culturally non-discriminatory assessment. *School Psychology Review, 8,* 89–115.

Meyer, R. C., Wolverton, D., & Deitsch, S. E. (1998). Antisocial personality disorder. In H. S. Friedman (Ed.), *Encyclopedia of mental health* (Vol. 1, 119–128). San Diego, CA: Academic Press.

Meyer-Bahlburg, H. F. L., Ehrhardt, A. A., Rosen, L. R., & Gruen, R. S. (1995). Prenatal estrogens and the development of homosexual orientation. *Developmental Psychology, 31*(1), 12–21.

Milgram, S. (1974). *Obedience to authority,* New York: Harper & Row.

Miller, H. L., & Siegel, P. S. (1972). *Loving: A psychological approach.* New York: Wiley.

Miller, N. E., & Dollard, J. (1941). *Social learning and imitation.* New Haven, CT: Yale University Press.

Millon, T. (1997). (Ed.) *The Millon inventories: Clinical and personality assessment.* New York: Guilford Press.

Milner, B. (1962). Les troubles de la memoire accompagnant des lesions hippocampiques bilaterales. In P. Passonant (Ed.), *Physiologie de l'hippocampique.* Paris: Centre National de la Recherche Scientifique.

Mischel, W. (1968). *Personality and assessment.* New York: Wiley.

Mischel, W., & Shoda, Y. (1995). A cognitive-affective system theory of personality: Reconceptualizing situations, dispositions, dynamics, and invariance in personality structure. *Psychological Review, 102,* 246–268.

Mishnah, Torah, Hilchot Teshuva, 5.1.

Moir, A., & Jessel, D. (1991). *Brain sex: The real difference between men & women.* London: Mandarin.

Moore, T., & Merikle, P. (1991). *In the mind's eye: Enhancing human performance.* Washington, DC: National Academy Press.

Morawski, J. G. (1985). The measurement of masculinity and femininity: Engendering categorical realities [Special Issue]. *Journal of Personality, 53*(2), 196–223.

Morehouse, R. E., Farley, F. H., & Youngquist, J. V. (1990). Type T personality and the Jungian classification system. *Journal of Personality Assessment, 54,* 231–235.

Moreland, K. L., Eyde, L. D., Robertson, G. J., Primoff, E. S., et al. (1995). Assessment of test user qualifications: A research-based measurement procedure. *American Psychologist, 50*(1), 14–23.

Morell V. (1993). Evidence found for a possible "aggression gene." *Science, 260* (5115), 1722–1723.

Mowrer, O. H., & Mowrer, W. A. (1928). Enuresis: A method for its study and treatment. *American Journal of Orthopsychiatry, 8,* 436–337.

Murray, H. A. (1938). *Explorations in personality: A clinical and experimental study of fifty men of college age, by the workers at the Harvard Psychological Clinic.* New York: Oxford University Press.

Murray, H. A. (1948). *Assessment of men.* New York: Rinehart.

Murray, H. A. (1962). *Explorations in personality.* New York: Science Editions.

Murther, T. C., Kanfer, R., & Ackerman, P. L. (1996). Toward an interactionist taxonomy of personality and situations: An integrative situational-dispositional representation of personality traits. *Journal of Personality & Social Psychology, 71,* 193–207.

Mussell, M. P., & Mitchell, J. E. (1998). Anorexia nervosa and bulimia nervosa. In H. S. Friedman (Ed.), *Encyclopedia of mental health* (Vol. 1., 111–118). San Diego, CA: Academic Press,

Myers, I. B. (1962). *The Myers-Briggs type indicator.* Princeton, NJ: Educational Testing Service.

Myers, I. B., & McCaulley, M. H. (1985). *Manual, a guide to the development and use of the Myers-Briggs type indicator* (R. Most, Ed.). Palo Alto, CA: Consulting Psychologists Press.

Myrdal, G. (1944). *An American dilemma: The Negro problem and modern democracy.* New York, London: Harper & Brothers.

Nakano, K. (1990). Effects of two self-control procedures on modifying Type A behavior. *Journal of Clinical Psychology, 46*(5), 652–657.

Needleman, H. L., & Bellinger, D. (1991). The health effects of low level exposure to lead. *Annual Review of Public Health, 12,* 111–140.

Nelson, K. (1993). The psychological and social origins of autobiographical memory. *Psychological Science, 4,* 7–14.

Nesse, R. M. (1990). The evolutionary functions of repression and the ego defenses. *Journal of the American Academy of Psychoanalysis, 18,* 260–285.

Neubauer, P. B. (1994). The role of displacement in psychoanalysis. *Psychoanalytic Study of the Child, 49,* 107–119.

Newcomb, M. D., Maddahian, E., & Bentler, P. M. (1986). Risk factors for drug use among adolescents: Concurrent and longitudinal analyses. *American Journal of Public Health, 76,* 525–531.

Newman, L. S., Duff, K. J., & Baumeister, R. F. (1997). A new look at defensive projection: Thought suppression, accessibility, and biased person perception. *Journal of Personality & Social Psychology, 72,* 980–1001.

Newsweek, 1993, p. 7.

Nicholson, J. (1993). *Men and women: How different are they?* Oxford: Oxford University Press.

Nisbett, R. E., & Cohen, D. (1996). *Culture of honor: The psychology of violence in the South.* Boulder, CO: Westview Press.

Noel, J. G., Forsyth, D. R., & Kelley, K. N. (1987). Improving the performance of failing students by overcoming their self-serving attributional biases. *Basic & Applied Social Psychology, 8,* 151–162.

Norem, J. (1989). Cognitive strategies as personality: Effectiveness, specificity, flexibility, and change. In D. M. Buss & N. Cantor (Eds.), *Personality psychology: Recent trends and emerging directions* (pp. 45–60). New York: Springer-Verlag.

Norman, W. T. (1963). Toward an adequate taxonomy of personality attributes: Replicated factor structure in peer nomination personality ratings. *Journal of Abnormal and Social Psychology, 66*(6), 574–583.

Norman, W. T., & Goldberg, L. R. (1966). Raters, ratees, and randomness in personality structure. *Journal of Personality and Social Psychology, 4*(6), 681–691.

Oakley, A. (1972). *Sex, gender and society.* New York: Harper & Row.

Omoto, A. M.., & Snyder, M. (1995). Sustained helping without obligation: Motivation, longevity of service, and perceived attitude change among AIDS volunteers. *Journal of Personality & Social Psychology, 68,* 671–686.

Oren, D. A. (1985). *Joining the club: A history of Jews and Yale.* New Haven, CT: Yale University Press.

Orwell, G. (1949). *Nineteen eighty-four.* New York: Harcourt Brace.

Orgler, H. (1963). *Alfred Adler: The man and his work.* New York: Capricorn.

Otten, C. M. (1985). Genetic effects on male and female development and on the sex ratio. In R. L. Hall (Ed.), *Male–female differences: A biocultural perspective.* New York: Praeger.

Overmier, J. B., & Seligman, M. E. (1967). Effects of inescapable shock upon subsequent escape and avoidance responding. *Journal of Comparative and Physiological Psychology, 63,* 28–33.

Owens, J., Bower, G. H., & Black, J. B. (1979). The "soap opera" effect in story recall. *Memory and Cognition, 7,* 185–191.

Ozer, D. J. (1986) *Consistency in personality: A methodological framework.* New York: Springer-Verlag.

Ozer, D. J. (1993). The Q-sort method and the study of personality development. In D. C. Funder, R. D. Parke, C. Tomlinson-Keasey, & K. Widaman (Eds.), *Studying lives through time: Personality and development* (pp. 147–168). Washington, DC: American Psychological Association.

Palmer, J. P. (Ed.). (1996). *Prediction, prevention, and genetic counseling in IDDM.* New York: Wiley.

Panksepp, J. (1991). Affective neuroscience: A conceptual framework for the neurobiological study of emotions. In K. Strongman (Ed.), *International reviews of studies in emotions* (pp. 59–99). New York: Wiley.

Parsons, J. E. (1980). Psychosexual neutrality: Is anatomy destiny? In J. E. Parsons (Ed.), *The psychobiology of sex differences and sex roles.* Cambridge, UK: Hemisphere.

Pavlov, I. P. (1927). *Conditioned reflexes: An investigation of the physiological activity of the cerebral cortex.* London: Oxford University Press.

Pearce, J. (1985). Harry Stack Sullivan: Theory and practice. *American Journal of Social Psychiatry, 5* (4), 5–13.

Pearson, P. R., Lankshear, D. W., & Francis, L. J. (1989). Personality and social class among eleven-year-old children. *Educational Studies, 15* (2), 107–113.

Pederson, N. L., Plomin, R., McClearn, G. E., & Friberg, L. (1988). Neuroticism, extraversion, and related traits in adult twins reared apart and reared together. *Journal of Personality & Social Psychology, 55,* 950–957.

Pennebaker, J. W. (1982). *The psychology of physical symptoms.* New York: Springer-Verlag.

Pennebaker, J. W. (1990). *Opening up: The healing power of confiding in others.* New York : W. Morrow.

Pennebaker, J. W., Burnam, M. A., Schaeffer, M. A., & Harper, D. C. (1997). Lack of control as a determinant of perceived physical symptoms. *Journal of Personality & Social Psychology, 35,* 167–174.

Peplau, L. A., & Caldwell, M. A. (1978). Loneliness: A cognitive analysis. *Essence, 2*(4), 207–220.

Perlman, D., Gerson, A. C., & Spinner, B. (1978). Loneliness among senior citizens: An empirical report. *Essence, 2*(4), 239–248.

Perlman, D., & Joshi, P. (1987). The revelation of loneliness. *Journal of Social Behavior and Personality, 2*(2, Pt. 2), 63–76.

Perlman, D., & Peplau, L. A. (1998). Loneliness. In H. S. Friedman (Ed.), *Encyclopedia of mental health* (Vol. 2, pp. 571–581). San Diego, CA: Academic Press.

Perry, H. S. (1982). *Psychiatrist of America: The life of Harry Stack Sullivan.* Cambridge, MA: Belknap Press.

Perry, H. S. (1985). Using participant observation to construct a life history. In D. N. Berg & K. K. Smith (Eds.), *Exploring clinical methods for social research* (pp. 319–332). Beverly Hills, CA: Sage Publications.

Persky, H. (1987) *Psychoendocrinology of human sexual behavior.* New York: Praeger.

Persky, V., Kempthorne-Rawson, J., & Shekelle, R. (1987). Depression was a general risk factor for early death. *Psychosomatic Medicine, 49*(5), 435–449.

Peterson, C., & Barrett, L. C. (1987). Explanatory style and academic performance among university freshmen. *Journal of Personality and Social Psychology, 53,* 603–607.

Peterson, C., & Seligman, M. E. (1987). Explanatory style and illness. *Journal of Personality, 55,* 237–265.

Peterson, C., Seligman, M., & Vaillant, G. E. (1988). Pessimistic explanatory style is a risk factor for physical illness: A thirty-five year longitudinal study. *Journal of Personality and Social Psychology, 55*(1), 23–27.

Peterson, R. (1978). Review of the Rorschach. In O. Buros (Ed.), *The eighth mental measurements yearbook.* Hyland Park, NJ: Gryphon.

Petrinovich, L. F. (1995). *Human evolution, reproduction, and morality.* New York: Plenum.

Pettigrew, T. (1958). Personality and sociocultural factors in intergroup attitudes: A cross-national comparison. *Journal of Conflict Resolution, 2,* 29–42.

Pezdek, K., & Banks, W. P. (Eds.). (1996). *The recovered memory/false memory debate.* San Diego, CA: Academic Press.

Phares, E. J. (1991). *Introduction to personality* (3rd ed.). New York: HarperCollins.

Phillips, D. P., Van Voorhees, C. A., & Ruth, T. E. (1992). The birthday: Lifeline or deadline? *Psychosomatic Medicine, 54*(5), 532–542.

Phinney, J. S. (1993). A three stage model of ethnic identity development in adolescence. In M. E. Bernal & G. P. Knight (Eds.), *Ethnic identity: Formation and transmission among Hispanics and other minorities* (pp. 61–79). New York: State University of New York Press.

Piaget, J. (1952). *The origins of intelligence in children.* New York: International University Press.

Pillemer, D. B., & White, S. (1989). Childhood events recalled by children and adults. In H. W. Reese (Ed.), *Advances in child development and behavior,* Vol. 21 (pp. 297–340). New York: Academic Press.

Pinizzotto, A. J., & Finkel, N. J. (1990). Criminal personality profiling. *Law and Human Behavior, 14,* 215–233.

Plomin, R., & Neiderhiser, J. M. (1992). Genetics and experience. *Current Directions in Psychological Science, 1*(5), 160–163.

Plomin, R., & Nessselroade, J. R. (1990). Behavioral genetics and personality change. *Journal of Personality, 58,* 191–220.

Plutchik, R., & Conte, H. R. (1997). *Circumplex models of personality and emotions.* Washington, DC: American Psychological Association.

Porter, C.A., & Suedfeld, P. (1981). Integrative complexity in the correspondence of literary figures: Effects of personal and societal stress. *Journal of Personality and Social Psychology, 40,* 321–330.

Posner, M. I., Petersen, S., Fox, P., & Raichle, M. E. (1988). Localization of cognitive operations in the human brain. *Science, 240,* 1627–1631.

Prince, R. J., & Guastello, S. J. (1990). The Barnum effect in a computerized Rorschach interpretation system. *Journal of Psychology, 124*(2), 217–222.

Psyche in 3-D. (1960, March 28). *Time.*

Rabin, A. I., Zucker, R. A., Emmons, R. A., & Frank, S. (Eds.). (1990). *Studying persons and lives.* New York: Springer-Verlag.

Rausch, M. L. (1977). Paradox, levels, and junctions in person–situation systems. In D. Magnusson & S. S. Endler (Eds.), *Personality at the crossroads* (pp. 287–303). Hillsdale, NJ: L. Erlbaum Associates.

Raven, J. C. (1938). *Progressive matrices.* London: Lewis.

Reder, L. M. & Gordon, J. S. (1997). Subliminal perception: Nothing special, cognitively speaking. In J. D. Cohen & J. W. Schooler (Eds.), *Scientific approaches to consciousness* (pp. 125–134). Mahwah, NJ: L. Erlbaum Associates.

Riggio, R. E. (1986). Assessment of basic social skills. *Journal of Personality and Social Psychology, 51,* 649–660.

Riggio, R. E. (1992). Social interaction skills and nonverbal behavior. In R. S. Feldman (Ed.), *Applications of nonverbal behavioral theories and research* (pp. 3–30). Hillsdale, NJ: L. Erlbaum Associates.

Riggio, R. E., & Friedman, H. S. (1986). Impression formation: The role of expressive behavior. *Journal of Personality and Social Psychology, 50,* 421–427.

Rippl, S., & Boehnke, K. (1995). Authoritarianism: Adolescents from East and West Germany and the United States compared. In J. Youniss (Ed.), *After the wall: Family adaptations in East and West Germany* (pp. 57–70). San Francisco: Jossey-Bass.

Rogers, C. (1951). *Client-centered therapy: Its current practice, implications, and theory.* Boston: Houghton Mifflin.

Rogers, C. (1961). *On becoming a person: A therapist's view of psychotherapy.* Boston: Houghton Mifflin.

Rogers, C., & Dymond, R. F. (Eds.). (1954). *Psychotherapy and personality change.* Chicago: University of Chicago Press.

Rook, K. S. (1988). Toward a more differentiated view of loneliness. In S. Duck, D. F. Hay, S. E.

Hobfoll, W. Ickes, & B. M. Montgomery (Eds.), *Handbook of personal relationships: Theory, research and interventions* (pp. 571–589). Chichester, UK: John Wiley.

Rook, K. S. (1991). Facilitating friendship formation in late life: Puzzles and challenges. *American Journal of Community Psychology, 19,* 103–110.

Rose, R. J., Koskenvuo, M., Kaprio, J., Sarna, S., & Langinvainio, H. (1988). Shared genes, shared experiences, and similarity of personality. *Journal of Personality and Social Psychology, 54,* 161–171.

Rosenman, R. H. (1978). Role of type A behavior pattern in the pathogenesis of ischemic heart disease, and modification for prevention. *Advances in Cardiology, 25,* 35–46.

Rosenthal, R. (Ed.). (1979). *Skill in nonverbal communication: Individual differences.* Cambridge, MA: Oelgeschlager, Gunn & Hain.

Rosenthal, R., & Rosnow, R. L. (1991). *Essentials of behavioral research: Methods and data analysis* (2nd ed.). New York: McGraw-Hill.

Rothbart, M. K. (1981). Measurement of temperament in infancy. *Child Development, 52,* 569–578.

Rotter, J. B. (1954). *Social learning and clinical psychology.* Englewood Cliffs, NJ: Prentice-Hall.

Rotter, J. B. (1966). Generalized expectancies for internal versus external control of reinforcement. *Psychological Monographs, 80*(1, Whole No. 609).

Rotter, J. B. (1980). Interpersonal trust, trustworthiness, and gullibility. *American Psychologist, 35*(1), 1–7.

Rotter, J. B. (1982). *The development and applications of social learning theory: Selected papers.* New York: Praeger.

Rotter, J. B., Chance, J. E., & Phares, E. J. (Eds.). (1972). *Applications of a social learning theory of personality.* New York: Holt, Rinehart & Winston.

Rubin, Z. (1973). *Liking and loving: An invitation to social psychology.* New York: Holt, Rinehart & Winston.

Rumelhart, D. E. (1980). Schemata: The building blocks of cognition. In R. Spiro, B. Bruce, & W. Brewer (Eds.), *Theoretical issues in reading comprehension.* Hillsdale, NJ: L. Erlbaum Associates.

Rushton, J. P. (1995). Construct validity, censorship, and the genetics of race. *American Psychologist, 50*(1), 40–41.

Rychlak, J. F. (1997). *In defense of human consciousness.* Washington, DC: American Psychological Association.

Sabatelli, R. M., & Rubin, M. (1986). Nonverbal expressiveness and physical attractiveness as mediators of interpersonal perceptions. *Journal of Nonverbal Behavior, 10,* 120–133.

Salinger, J. D. (1951). *The catcher in the rye.* Boston: Little, Brown.

Sapir, E. (1956). *Culture, language and personality.* Berkeley, CA: University of California Press.

Sartre, J. P. (1956). *Being and nothingness: A phenomenological essay on ontology* (H. E. Barnes, Trans.). New York: Washington Square Press.

Saudino, K. J. (1997). Moving beyond the heritability question: New directions in behavioral genetic studies of personality. *Current Directions in Psychological Science, 6,* 86–90.

Saudino, K. J., Pedersen, N. L., Lichtenstein, P., & McClearn, G. E. (1997). Can personality explain genetic influences on life events? *Journal of Personality and Social Psychology, 72,* 196–206.

Scarr, S., & McCartney, K. (1990). How people make their own environments: A theory of genotype to environment effects. *Child Development, 54,* 424–435.

Schacter, D. L. (1987). Implicit memory: History and current status. *Journal of Experimental Psychology: Learning, Memory, and Cognition, 13,* 501–518.

Scheier, M. F., & Carver, C. S. (1985). Optimism, coping, and health: Assessment and implications of generalized outcome expectancies. *Health Psychology, 4,* 219–247.

Scheier M. F., & Carver, C. S. (1988). A model of behavioral self-regulation. In L. Berkowitz (Ed.), *Advances in Experimental Social Psychology,* Vol. 21 (pp. 303–346). New York: Academic Press.

Scherer, K. R. (1978). Personality inference from voice quality: The loud voice of extroversion. *European Journal of Social Psychology, 8,* 467–487.

Scherer, K. R. (1982). Methods of research on vocal communication: Paradigms and parameters. In K. R. Scherer & P. Ekman (Eds.), *Handbook of methods in nonverbal behavior research* (pp. 136–198). Cambridge, UK: Cambridge University Press.

Schiffman, J., & Walker, E. (1998). Schizophrenia. In H. S. Friedman (Ed.), *Encyclopedia of mental health* (Vol. 3, 399–410). San Diego, CA: Academic Press.

Schultz, D. P. (1986). *Theories of personality* (3rd ed.). Monterey, CA: Brooks/Cole.

Schuster, B., Forsterling, F., & Weiner, B. (1989). Perceiving the causes of success and failure: A cross-cultural examination of attributional concepts. *Journal of Cross-Cultural Psychology, 20*(2), 191–213.

Schwartz, J. E., Friedman, H. S., Tucker, J. S., Tomlinson-Keasey, C., Wingard, D. L., & Criqui, M. H. (1995). Sociodemographic and psychosocial factors in childhood as predictors of adult mortality. *American Journal of Public Health, 85*(9), 1237–1245.

Scott, S. G., & Bruce, R. A. (1995). Decision-making style: The development and assessment of a new measure. *Educational and Psychological Measurement, 55*, 818–831.

Seal, D. W., & Agostinelli, G. (1994). Individual differences associated with high-risk sexual behaviour: Implications for intervention programmes. *AIDS Care, 6*(4), 393–397.

Sears, R. R. (1951). A theoretical framework for personality and social behavior. *American Psychologist, 6*, 476–483.

Sears, R. R., Maccoby, E. E., & Levin, H. (1957). *Patterns of child rearing*. Evanston, IL: Row, Peterson.

Sears, R. R., Rau, L., & Alpert, R. (1966). *Identification and child rearing*. Stanford, CA: Stanford University Press.

Sears, R. R., Whiting, J. W. M., Nowlis, V., & Sears, P. S. (1953). Some child-rearing antecedents of aggression and dependency in young children. *Genetic Psychology Monographs, 47*, 135–234.

Segall, M. H., Dasen, P. R., Berry, J. W., & Poortinga, Y. H. (1990). *Human behavior in global perspective: An introduction to cross-cultural psychology*. New York: Pergamon Press.

Seligman, M. E. P. (1975). *Helplessness: On depression, development, and death*. San Francisco: W. H. Freeman.

Seligman, M. E. P., Reivich, K., Jaycox, L., & Gillham, J. (1995). *The optimistic child*. Boston: Houghton Mifflin.

Serin, R. C., & Kuriychuk, M. (1994). Social and cognitive processing deficits in violent offenders: Implications for treatment. *International Journal of Law and Psychiatry, 17*(4), 431–441.

Shaffer, J., Graves, P. L., Swank, R. T., & Pearson, T. A. (1987). Clustering of personality traits in youth and the subsequent development of cancer among physicians. *Journal of Behavioral Medicine, 10*(5), 441–444.

Sharp, A. H., & Ross, C. A. (1996). Neurobiology of Huntington's disease. *Neurobiological Disease, 3*(1), 3–15.

Shaver, P. R., Collins, N., & Clark, C. L. (1996). Attachment styles and internal working models of self and relationship partners. In G. J. O. Fletcher & J. Fitness (Eds.), *Knowledge structures in close relationships: A social psychological approach* (pp. 25–61). Mahwah, NJ: L. Erlbaum Associates.

Shaw, D. S., Emery, R. E., & Tuer, M. D. (1993). Parental functioning and children's adjustment in families of divorce: A prospective study. *Journal of Abnormal Child Psychology, 21*, 119–134.

Sheldon, W. H., & Stevens, S. S. (1942). *The varieties of temperament: A psychology of constitutional differences* (4th ed.). New York: Harper.

Shields, S. A. (1975). Darwinism and the psychology of women: A study in social myth. *American Psychologist, 30*(7), 181–195.

Shoda, Y., Mischel, W., & Wright, J. C. (1994). Intraindividual stability in the organization and patterning of behavior: Incorporating psychological situations into the idiographic analysis of personality. *Journal of Personality and Social Psychology, 67*(4), 674–687.

Shore, B. (1996). *Culture in mind: Cognition, culture, and the problem of meaning*. New York: Oxford University Press.

Shostrom, E. L. (1974). *Manual for the Personal Orientation Inventory*. San Diego: EdITS/Educational and Industrial Testing Service.

Shweder, R. A. (1990). In defense of moral realism: Reply to Gabennesch. *Child Development, 61,* 2060–2067.

Shweder, R. A., & Sullivan, M. A.(1990). The semiotic subject of cultural psychology. In L. A. Pervin (Ed.), *Handbook of personality: Theory and research* (pp. 399–416). New York: Guilford Press.

Siegel, L. S. (1995). Does the IQ god exist? [Special issue]. *Alberta Journal of Educational Research, 41*(3), 283–288.

Silverberg, J., & Gray, J. P. (Eds.). (1992). *Aggression and peacefulness in humans and other primates.* New York: Oxford University Press.

Simonton, D. K. (1994). *Greatness: Who makes history and why.* New York: Guilford Press.

Simpson, J. A., & Gangestad, S. W. (1991). Personality and sexuality: Empirical relations and an integrative theoretical model. In K. McKinney & S. Sprecher (Eds.), *Sexuality in close relationships* (pp. 71–92). Hillsdale, NJ: L. Erlbaum Associates.

Simpson, J. A., & Kenrick, D. T. (Eds.). (1997). *Evolutionary social psychology.* Mahwah, NJ: L. Erlbaum Associates.

Skinner, B. F. (1938). *The behavior of organisms: An experimental analysis.* New York: Appleton-Century-Crofts.

Skinner, B. F. (1948). *Walden Two.* New York: Macmillan.

Skinner, B. F. (1971). *Beyond freedom and dignity.* New York: Knopf.

Skinner, B. F. (1974). *About behaviorism* (1st ed.). New York: Knopf.

Smith, C. P. (1992). Reliability issues. In C. P. Smith, J. W. Atkinson, D. C. McClelland, & J. Veroff (Eds.), *Motivation and personality: Handbook of thematic content analysis* (pp. 126–139). New York: Cambridge University Press.

Snodgrass, M. A. (1987). The relationships of differential loneliness, intimacy, and characterological attributional style to duration of loneliness. *Journal of Social Behavior and Personality, 2,* 173–186.

Snyder, C. R., Shenkel, R. J., & Lowery, C. R. (1977). Acceptance of personality interpretations: The "Barnum effect" and beyond. *Journal of Consulting & Clinical Psychology, 45*(1), 104–114.

Snyder, D. K., Wills, R. M., & Grady-Fletcher, A. (1991). Long-term effectiveness of behavioral versus insight-oriented marital therapy: A 4-year follow-up study. *Journal of Consulting & Clinical Psychology, 59,* 138–141.

Snyder, M. (1974). Self-monitoring of expressive behavior. *Journal of Personality and Social Psychology, 30*(4), 526–537.

Snyder, M. (1987). *Public appearances/Private realities: The psychology of self-monitoring.* New York: Freeman.

Sommer, R. (1969). *Personal space: The behavioral basis of design.* Englewood Cliffs, NJ: Prentice-Hall.

Sommer, R. (1971). *Design awareness.* San Francisco: Rinehart Press.

Sontag, S. (1978). *Illness as metaphor.* New York: Farrar, Straus and Giroux.

Spearman, C. (1925). The new psychology of "shape." *British Journal of Psychology, 15,* 211–225.

Srull, T. K., & Wyer, R. S., Jr. (1989). Person memory and judgment. *Psychological Review, 96,* 58–83.

Stabler, B., Surwit, R. S., Lane, J. D., Morris, M. A., et al. (1987). Type A behavior and blood glucose control in diabetic children. *Psychosomatic Medicine, 49,* 313–316.

Stagner, R. (1937). *Psychology of personality.* (1st ed.). New York: McGraw-Hill.

Staudinger, U. M., Lopez, D. F., & Baltes, P. B. (1997). The psychometric location of wisdom-related performance. *Personality and Social Psychology Bulletin, 23,* 1200–1214.

Stavraky, K. M., Donner, A. P., Kincade, J., & Stewart, M. A. (1988). The effect of psychosocial factors on lung cancer mortality at one year. *Journal of Clinical Epidemiology, 41,* 75–82.

Steele, C. M. (1997). A threat in the air: How stereotypes shape intellectual identity and performance. *American Psychologist, 52,* 613–629.

Stelmack, R. M. (1990). Biological bases of extraversion: Psychophysiological evidence [Special Issue]. *Journal of Personality, 58,* 293–311.

Stelmack, R. M., & Pivik, R. T. (1996). Extraversion and the effect of exercise on spinal motoneuronal excitability. *Personality & Individual Differences, 21,* 69–76.

Sternberg, R. J., & Barnes, M. L. (Eds.). (1988). *The psychology of love*. New Haven, CT: Yale University Press.

Stockard, J., & Johnson, M. M. (1992). *Sex and gender in society* (2nd ed.). Englewood Cliffs, NJ: Prentice-Hall.

Stoff, D. M., & Cairns, R. B. (Eds.). (1996). *Aggression and violence: Genetic, neurobiological, and biosocial perspectives*. Mahwah, NJ: L. Erlbaum Associates.

Stone, A. A., Kessler, R. C., & Haythornthwaite, J. A. (1991). Measuring daily events and experiences: Decisions for the researcher [Special issue]. *Journal of Personality, 59*(3), 575–607.

Storms, M. D. (1981). A theory of erotic orientation development. *Psychological Review, 88,* 340–353.

Strelau, J., & Eysenck, H. J. (Eds.). (1987). *Personality dimensions and arousal*. New York: Plenum.

Strube, M. J. (1989). Evidence for the Type in Type A behavior: A taxometric analysis. *Journal of Personality & Social Psychology, 56,* 972–987.

Suddath, R. L., Christison, G. W., Torrey, E. F., & Casanova, M. F. (1990). Anatomical abnormalities in the brains of monozygotic twins discordant for schizophrenia. *New England Journal of Medicine, 322*(12), 789–794.

Suinn, R. M. (1995). Schizophrenia and bipolar disorder: Origins and influences. *Behavior Therapy, 26,* 557–571.

Sullins, E. S. (1989). Perceptual salience as a function of nonverbal expressiveness. *Personality and Social Psychology Bulletin, 15,* 584–595.

Sullivan, H. S. (1953). *The interpersonal theory of psychiatry*. New York: Norton.

Sullivan, K. T., & Christensen, A. (1998). Couples therapy. In H. S. Friedman (Ed.), *Encyclopedia of mental health* (Vol. 1, 595–606). San Diego, CA: Academic Press.

Sulloway, F. J. (1996). *Born to rebel: Birth order, family dynamics, and creative lives*. New York: Pantheon.

Swann, W. B., & Read, S. J. (1981). Acquiring self-knowledge: The search for feedback that fits. *Journal of Personality and Social Psychology, 41*(6), 1119–1128.

Swets, J. A. (1996). *Signal detection theory and ROC analysis in psychology and diagnostics: collected papers*. Mahwah, NJ: L. Erlbaum Associates.

Tangney, J. P., & Fischer, K. W. (Eds.). (1995). *Self-conscious emotions: The psychology of shame, guilt, embarrassment, and pride*. New York: Guilford Press.

Tangney, J. P., Wagner, P. E., Hill-Barlow, D., & Marschall, D. E. (1996). Relation of shame and guilt to constructive versus destructive responses to anger across the lifespan. *Journal of Personality & Social Psychology, 70*(4), 797–809.

Tavris, C. (1992). *The mismeasure of woman*. New York: Simon & Schuster.

Taylor, S. E., & Crocker, J. (1981). Schematic bases of social information processing. In E. T. Higgins, C. P. Herman, & M. P. Zanna (Eds.), *Social cognition: The Ontario symposium*, Vol. 1. Hillsdale, NJ: L. Erlbaum Associates.

Temoshok, L. (1998). HIV and AIDS. In H. S. Friedman (Ed.) *Encyclopedia of mental health* (Vol. 2, 375–392). San Diego, CA: Academic Press.

Tennant, C. (1988). Parental loss in childhood: Its effect in adult life. *Archives of General Psychiatry, 45,* 1045–1050.

Tennen, H., & Affleck, G. (1987). The costs and benefits of optimistic explanations and dispositional optimism. *Journal of Personality, 55,* 377–393.

Terman, L. M. (1917). The intelligence quotient of Francis Galton in childhood. *American Journal of Psychology, 28,* 208–215.

Terman, L. M. (1921). *Suggestions for the education and training of gifted children*. Stanford, CA: Stanford University Press.

Terman, L. M. (1954). Scientists and nonscientists in a group of 800 gifted men. *Psychological Monographs, 68,* No. 7.

Terman, L. M. and Oden, M. H. (1947). *The gifted child grows up: Twenty-five years' follow-up of a superior group*. Stanford, CA: Stanford University Press.

Thomas, A., Chess, S., & Korn, S. J. (1982). The reality of difficult temperament. *Merrill-Palmer Quarterly, 28,* 1–20.

Thompson, R. F. (1993). *The brain: A neuroscience primer* (2nd ed.). New York: Freeman.

Thoreau, H. D. (1854). *Walden: or, Life in the woods*. Boston: Ticknor and Fields.

Thorne, A. (1987). The press of personality: A study of conversations between introverts and extraverts. *Journal of Personality & Social Psychology, 53,* 718–726.

Torestad, B., Magnusson, D., & Olah, A. (1990). Coping, control, and experience of anxiety: An interactional perspective. *Anxiety Research, 3*(1), 1–16.

Triandis, H. C. (1989). The self and social behavior in differing cultural contexts. *Psychological Review, 96*(3), 506–520.

Triandis, H. C. (1994). *Culture and social behavior.* New York: McGraw-Hill.

Triesman, A. M. (1964). Selective attention in man. *British Medical Bulletin, 20,* 12–16.

Trivers, R. L. (1996). Parental investment and sexual selection. In L. D. Houck & L. C. Drickamer (Eds.), *Foundations of animal behavior: Classic papers with commentaries* (pp. 795–838). Chicago: University of Chicago Press.

Tucker, L. A. (1983). Muscular strength and mental health. *Journal of Personality and Social Psychology, 45,* 1355–1360.

Tucker, J., Friedman, H. S., Tomlinson-Keasey, C., Schwartz, J. E., Wingard, D. L., & Criqui, M. H. (1995). Childhood psychosocial predictors of adulthood smoking, alcohol consumption, and physical activity. *Journal of Applied Social Psychology, 25,* 1884–1899.

Tulving, E., & Osler, S. (1968). Effectiveness of retrieval cues in memory for words. *Journal of Experimental Psychology, 77,* 593–601.

Ullian, D. Z. (1976). The development of conceptions of masculinity and femininity. In B. Lloyd & J. Archer (Eds.), *Exploring sex differences* (pp. 25–47). London: Academic Press.

Ulrich, R. E., Stachnik, T. J., & Stainton, N. R. (1963). Student acceptance of generalized personality interpretations. *Psychological Reports, 13,* 831–834.

Vaillant, G. E. (Ed.). (1986). *Empirical studies of ego mechanisms of defense.* Washington, DC: American Psychiatric Press.

Vaillant, G. E., Bond, M., & Vaillant, C. O. (1986). An empirically validated hierarchy of defense mechanisms. *Archives of General Psychiatry, 43* (8), 786–794.

Vandenberg, B. (1991). Is epistemology enough? An existential consideration of development. *American Psychologist, 46*(12), 1278–1286.

von Helmholtz, H. L. F. (1866/1925). *Handbuch der physiologischen optik,* Vol. III. Liepzig. In Southall, J. P. C. (Trans.), *Helmholtz's Treatise on Physiological Optics,* Vol. III. Rochester, NY: Optical Society of America. (Original work published in 1866.)

Wahlsten, D. (1995). Increasing the raw intelligence of a nation is constrained by ignorance, not its citizens' genes [Special issue]. *Alberta Journal of Educational Research, 41*(3), 257–264.

Waller, N. G., Kojetin, B. A., Bouchard, T. J., & Lykken, D. T. (1990). Genetic and environmental influences on religious interests, attitudes, and values: A study of twins reared apart and together. *Psychological Science, 1,* 138–142.

Wang, A. Y. (1994). Passionate love and social anxiety of American and Italian students. *Psychology: A Journal of Human Behavior, 31*(3–4), 9–11.

Warrington, E. K., & Weiskrantz, L. (1978). Further analysis of the prior learning effect in amnesic patients. *Neuropsychologia, 16,* 169–176.

Wason, P. C., & Johnson-Laird, P. N. (1972). *Psychology of reasoning: Structure and content.* Cambridge, MA: Harvard University Press.

Watson, D. (1989). Strangers' ratings of five robust personality factors: Evidence of a surprising convergence with self-report. *Journal of Personality & Social Psychology, 57,* 120–128.

Watson, J. B. (1914). *Behavior.* New York: Holt, Rinehart & Winston.

Watson, J. B. (1919). *Psychology from the standpoint of a behaviorist.* London: Routledge/Thoemmes Press.

Watson, J. B. (1925). *Behaviorism.* New York: People's Institute.

Watson, J. B., & Rayner, R. (1920). Conditioned emotional reactions. *Journal of Experimental Psychology, 3,* 1–14.

Watts, A. (1961, April 21). *Life Magazine,* p. 21.

Webb, J. A., Baer, P. E., McLaughlin, R. J., McKelvey, R. S., et al. (1991). Risk factors and their relation to initiation of alcohol use among early adolescents. *Journal of the American Academy of Child & Adolescent Psychiatry, 30,* 563–568.

Wegner, D.M. (1994). Ironic processes of mental control. *Psychological Review, 101,* 34–52.

Weiner, B. (1985). An attributional theory of achievement motivation and emotion. *Psychological Review, 92*(4), 548–573.

Weininger, O. (1996). *Being and not being: Clinical applications of the death instinct.* Madison, CT: International Universities Press.

Weinstein, N. (1984). Why it won't happen to me: Perceptions of risk factors and susceptibility. *Health Psychology, 3,* 431–457.

Weiss, A. S. (1991). The measurement of self-actualization: The quest for the test may be as challenging as the search for the self. *Journal of Social Behavior and Personality, 6,* 265–290.

Whalen, R. E., Geary, D. C., & Johnson, F. (1990). Models of sexuality. In D. P. McWhirter, S. A. Sanders, & J. M. Reinisch (Eds.), *Homosexuality/heterosexuality: Concepts of sexual orientation* (The Kinsey Institute Series, Vol. 2). New York: Oxford University Press.

Whitbourne, S. K., Zuschlag, M. K., Elliot, L. B., & Waterman, A. S. (1992). Psychosocial development in adulthood: A 22-year sequential study. *Journal of Personality & Social Psychology, 63,* 260–271.

White, R. W. (1959). Motivation reconsidered: The concept of competence. *Psychological Review, 66,* 297–333.

Whiting, B. B., & Edwards, C. P. (1988). *Children of different worlds: The formation of social behavior.* Cambridge, MA: Harvard University Press.

Whiting, B. B., & Whiting, J.W. (1975). *Children of six cultures: A psychocultural analysis.* Cambridge, MA: Harvard University Press.

Whitman, W. (1871). *Democratic Vistas.* New York: J. S. Redfield.

Whitney, K., Sagrestano, L. M. & Maslach, C. (1994). Establishing the social impact of individuation. *Journal of Personality and Social Psychology, 66,* 1140–1153.

Whitson, E. R., & Olczak, P. V. (1991). The use of the POI in clinical situations: An evaluation. *Journal of Social Behavior and Personality, 6,* 291–310.

Williams, M. D., & Hollan, J. D. (1982). The process of retrieval from very long-term memory. *Cognitive Science, 5,* 87–119.

Wilson, E. O. (1975). *Sociobiology: The new synthesis.* Cambridge MA: Belknap Press.

Windholz, G. (1991). I. P. Pavlov as a youth. *Integrative Physiological and Behavioral Science, 26,* 51–67.

Winter, D. G. (1973). *The power motive.* New York: Free Press.

Winter, D. G. (1987). Leader appeal, leader performance, and the motive profiles of leaders and followers. *Journal of Personality and Social Psychology, 52,* 196–202.

Winter, D. G. (1992). Power motivation revisited. In C. P. Smith, J. W. Atkinson, D. C. McClelland, & J. Veroff (Eds.), *Motivation and personality: Handbook of thematic content analysis* (pp. 301–310). New York: Cambridge University Press,

Winter, D. G. (1993). Power, affiliation, and war: Three tests of a motivational model. *Journal of Personality & Social Psychology, 65,* 532–545.

Witelson, S. F. (1991). Neural sexual mosaicism: Sexual differentiation of the human temporo-parietal region for functional asymmetry. *Psychoneuroendocrinology, 16,* 131–153.

Witkin, H. A. (1949). Perception of body position and of the position of the visual field. *Psychological Monographs, 63* (7, Whole No. 302).

Witkin, H. A., & Berry, J. N. (1975). Psychological differentiation in cross-cultural perspective. *Journal of Cross-Cultural Psychology, 6,* 4–87.

Witkin, H. A., & Goodenough, D. R. (1977). Field dependence and interpersonal behavior. *Psychological Bulletin, 84,* 661–689.

Wolpe, J., & Plaud, J. J. (1997). Pavlov's contributions to behavior therapy: The obvious and the not so obvious. *American Psychologist, 52,* 966–972.

Wood, P. B., Cochran, J. K., Pfefferbaum, B., & Arneklev, B. J. (1995). Sensation-seeking and delinquent substance use: An extension of learning theory. *Journal of Drug Issues, 25*(1), 173–193.

Wood-Sherif, C. (1980). A social psychological perspective on the menstrual cycle. In J. E. Parsons (Ed.), *The psychobiology of sex differences and sex roles.* Cambridge, UK: Hemisphere.

Woodworth, R. S. (1919). *Personal data sheet.* Chicago: Stoelting.

Woodworth, R. S. (1934). *Psychology* (3d ed.). New York: H. Holt.

Wyatt, W. (1981). *To the point.* London: Weidenfeld and Nicolson.

Yee, A. H., Fairchild, H. H., Weizmann, F., & Wyatt, G. E. (1993). Addressing psychology's problem with race. *American Psychologist, 48,* 1132–1140.

Yerkes, R. M. (Ed.). (1921). *Psychological examining in the United States Army. Memoirs of the National Academy of Sciences.* Washington, DC: U. S. Government Printing Office.

Zill, N., Morrison, D. R., & Coiro, M. J. (1993). Long-term effects of parental divorce on parent-child relationships, adjustment, and achievement in young adulthood. *Journal of Family Psychology, 7,* 91–103.

Zivin, G. (1982). Watching the sands shift: Conceptualizing development of nonverbal mastery. In R. S. Feldman (Ed.), *Development of nonverbal behavior in children* (pp. 63–98). New York: Springer-Verlag.

Zori, R. T., Hendrickson, J., Woolven, S., & Whidden, E. M. (1992). Angelman syndrome: Clinical profile. *Journal of Child Neurology, 7,* 270–280.

Zuckerman, M. (Ed.). (1979). *Sensation seeking: Beyond the optimal level of arousal.* Hillsdale, NJ: L. Erlbaum Associates.

Zuckerman, M. (Ed.). (1983a). *Biological bases of sensation seeking, impulsivity, and anxiety.* Hillsdale, NJ: L. Erlbaum Associates.

Zuckerman, M. (1983b). Sensation seeking and sports. *Personality and Individual Differences, 4*(3), 285–292.

Glossary

achievement motivation according to David McClelland, the disposition to strive for success.

acquiescence response set a bias in which people are more likely to agree than disagree with anything that is asked of them.

agape according to Rollo May, a type of unselfish love characterized by devotion to the welfare of others.

aggression drive Alfred Adler's concept that an individual is driven to lash out against the inability to achieve or master something, as a reaction to perceived helplessness.

aggressive personality according to Karen Horney, a neurotic trend to see most others as being hostile, to believe that only the most competent and cunning survive, and to behave hatefully and hostilely toward others in order to maintain a feeling of control and power.

aggressive style according to Karen Horney, a mode of adapting to the world used by those who believe in fighting to get by.

agreeableness according to the Big Five approach, the personality dimension that includes friendliness, cooperation, and warmth; people low in this dimension are cold, quarrelsome, and unkind.

Alzheimer's disease a disease of the brain's cerebral cortex, primarily affecting the elderly, which causes quirks of behavior and memory loss.

American Dilemma Gunnar Myrdal's term for the paradoxical idea that slavery was allowed and endorsed despite the claim that the United States was founded on the principle that all men are created equal.

anal stage Freud's stage of psychosexual development around age two during which children are toilet trained.

androgenized females genetically female individuals who were prenatally exposed to excessive levels of androgens and are born with either masculine or ambiguous external genitalia.

androgyny the consolidation of both female and male traits.

anima according to Carl Jung, the archetype representing the female element of a man.

animus according to Carl Jung, the archetype representing the male element of a woman.

anterograde amnesia the inability to form new conscious memories.

antisocial personality disorder a personality disorder in which an individual is excessively impulsive, violates the rules of society, and lacks anxiety or guilt for his or her behavior.

anxious-ambivalent lovers according to Phillip Shaver, people who have a romantic attachment style in which they want to get close but are insecure with the relationship.

approach–approach conflict a term used by Dollard and Miller to describe a conflict in which a person is drawn to two equally attractive choices.

approach–avoidance conflict   a term used by Dollard and Miller to describe a conflict between primary and secondary drives that occurs when a punishment results in the conditioning of a fear response to a drive.

archetypes   in Carl Jung's neo-analytic theory, emotional symbols that are common to all people and have been formed since the beginning of time.

attention deficit/hyperactivity disorder (ADHD)   a disorder in which a person has atypical attentional processes.

attribution theories   theories that examine the ways in which individuals draw inferences about other people's behavior.

authentic love   according to Rollo May, a type of love that incorporates all other types of love.

authoritarian personality type   according to Erich Fromm, a person who has a cruel penchant for exerting power over others, abusing them, and taking their possessions; such a personality characteristic may result from a particularly negative relationship with one's parents.

authoritarian personality   a person with antidemocratic tendencies; such a person tends to be narrow-minded, rigid, defensive, and tends to show prejudice against minority groups.

avoidance–avoidance conflict   a term used by Dollard and Miller to describe a conflict in which a person is faced with two equally undesirable choices.

avoidant lovers   according to Phillip Shaver, people who have a romantic attachment style in which they feel uncomfortable being close to others or having others close to them and have trouble trusting and being trusted by others.

Barnum effect   the tendency to believe vague generalities about one's personality.

basic anxiety   according to Karen Horney, a child's fear of being alone, helpless, and insecure that arises from problems with one's parents.

behavior potential   a term used by Julian Rotter to describe the likelihood that a particular behavior will occur in specific situation.

behavioral signature   according to Walter Mischel, the set of situation–behavior relationships that are typical of an individual and that contribute to the apparent consistency of an individual's personality.

behaviorism   the learning approach to psychology introduced by John Watson that emphasizes the study of observable behavior.

being love   according to Abraham Maslow, love that is unselfish and cares for the needs of others; a person who is involved in being love is more self-actualized and helps his or her partner toward self-actualization.

being-in-the-world   the existential idea that the self cannot exist without a world and the world cannot exist without a person or being to perceive it.

Bem Sex Role Inventory   a measure designed by Sandra Bem to classify individuals as masculine, feminine, androgynous, or undifferentiated (low in both masculinity and femininity).

Big Five   the trait approach to personality that is supported by a great deal of research and suggests that the most common trait approaches to personality can be captured in five dimensions: extroversion, agreeableness, conscientiousness, neuroticism, and openness.

biological determinism   the belief that an individual's personality is completely determined by biological factors (and especially by genetic factors).

brotherly love   according to Erich Fromm, the type of love that involves loving all of mankind and that reunites isolated individuals with one another.

cardinal dispositions a term used by Gordon Allport to describe personal dispositions that exert an overwhelming influence on behavior.

Cartesian dualism the concept proposed by René Descartes that there is a separation of the mind and body.

castration anxiety according to Sigmund Freud, an unconscious fear of castration that results from a boy's struggle to deal with his love for his mother while knowing that he cannot overcome his father.

categorization the perceptual process by which highly complex ensembles of information are filtered into a small number of identifiable and familiar objects and entities.

central dispositions a term used by Gordon Allport to describe the several personal dispositions around which personality is organized.

choleric a personality type based on the ancient Greek humors discussed by Hippocrates and Galen in which one is angry against the arbitrary controls of one's life and has generally poor interpersonal relations.

chumship Harry Stack Sullivan's idea, derived from the sociological concept of the social self, that a preadolescent's chums serve as a social mirror for forming his or her identity.

classical conditioning the concept that after the repeated pairing of an unconditioned stimulus that elicits an unconditioned response and a neutral stimulus, the previously neutral stimulus can come to elicit the same response as the unconditioned stimulus.

cognitive intervention teaching people to change their thought processes.

cognitive simplicity according to George Kelly, the tendency for some people to fail to make distinctions among other people and to perceive other people as similar to one another.

cognitive style an individual's distinctive, enduring way of dealing with everyday tasks of perception and problem solving.

collective unconscious according to Carl Jung, the component of the mind that contains a deeper level of unconsciousness made up of archetypes that are common across all people.

common traits the term used by Gordon Allport to describe organizing structures that people in a population share.

competencies according to Walter Mischel, a person's abilities and knowledge.

complex a group of emotionally charged thoughts, feelings, and ideas that are related to a particular theme.

conscientiousness according to the Big Five approach, the personality dimension that includes dependability, cautiousness, organization, and responsibility; people low in this dimension are impulsive, careless, disorderly, and undependable.

construct validity the extent to which a test truly measures a theoretical construct.

contemporaneous causation Kurt Lewin's concept that behavior is caused at the moment of its occurrence by all the influences that are present in the individual at that moment.

content validity the extent to which a test is measuring the domain it is supposed to be measuring.

control group a comparison group that provides a standard by which to evaluate a theory or technique.

controllability of causality according to Bernard Weiner, the perception that events are due either to controllable factors or to influences beyond an individual's control.

convergent validation the extent to which an assessment is related to what it should be related to.

corpus callosum the fibers that connect the two brain hemispheres.

correlation coefficient a mathematical index of the degree of agreement or association between two measures.

criterion-related validation   the extent to which an assessment predicts to outcome criteria of different assessment methods.

critical period   the point during development when an organism is optimally ready to learn a particular response pattern.

cultural imperialism   the extending of one's own cultural approaches over those of another culture or subculture.

declarative memory   memory for facts about a task or event.

deductive approach   an approach to psychology in which the conclusions follow logically from the premises or assumptions.

defense mechanisms   in psychoanalytic theory, the processes that distort reality to protect the ego.

deficiency love   according to Abraham Maslow, love that is selfish and needy.

deficiency needs   according to Abraham Maslow, needs that are essential for survival including physiological, safety, belonging, love, and esteem needs.

delay of gratification   a specific aspect of self-control that occurs when an individual chooses to forgo an immediate reinforcer in order to wait for a later, better reinforcer.

demographic information   information relevant to population statistics such as age, cultural group, place of birth, religion, and the like.

demon   according to Carl Jung, the archetype that embodies cruelty and evil.

denial   a defense mechanism in which one refuses to acknowledge anxiety-provoking stimuli.

designer personalities   personalities that are altered in a targeted fashion through the use of drugs.

dialect   regional variations in vocabulary and syntactic forms.

dialectical humanism   Erich Fromm's approach to personality, which tries to reconcile the biological, driven side of human beings and the pressures of societal structure by focusing on the belief that people can rise above or transcend these forces and become spontaneous, creative, and loving.

dialectical tension   concept used by Mihaly Csikszentmihalyi for the idea that creative people tend to have traits that are seemingly contradictory but that play a role in their creativity.

diathesis–stress model   model of disease that suggests that although a predisposition to illness exist because of genetics or upbringing, the illness itself will not appear unless or until it is elicited by the environment.

diathesis   the often hereditary predisposition of the body to disease or disorder.

discriminant validation   the extent to which an assessment is not related to what it should not be related to.

discrimination   the concept that a conditioned response will not occur for all possible stimuli, indicating that an animal can learn to tell the difference between different stimuli.

displacement   a defense mechanism in which the target of one's unconscious fears or desires is shifted away from the true cause.

document analysis   a method of assessing personality by applying personality theories to the study of diaries, letters, and other personal records.

ectomorph   according to W. H. Sheldon, a somatotype describing thin, slender, bookworm types of people.

effect size   a statistical index of the magnitude of a measured effect, capturing how much difference a variable makes.

ego crisis   in Erik Erikson's theory of identity, each of the series of eight "crises" (conflicts or choices) that must be resolved, in sequence, for optimal psychological development.

ego in psychoanalytic theory, the personality structure that develops to deal with the real world; in neo-analytical theory, this term refers to the individuality of a person that is the central core of personality; and specifically for Carl Jung, it is the aspect of personality that is conscious and embodies the sense of self.

ego-development an individual's level of psychological maturity.

ego-resilient a term used to describe people who are calm, socially at ease, insightful, and not anxious.

egoistic dominance according to Whiting and Edwards, trying to control the behavior of others in order to meet one's own needs.

electrodermal measures measures that monitor the electrical activity of the skin with electrodes.

electroencephalography a measurement of electrical brainwave activity using electrodes attached to the outside of the skull.

emic approach an approach that is culture-specific, focusing on a single culture on its own terms.

encoding strategies according to Walter Mischel, the schema and mechanisms one uses to process and encode information.

endomorph according to W. H. Sheldon, a somatotype describing overweight, good-natured types of people.

environmental press the push of the situation emphasized in Henry Murray's approach to personality; it is a directional force on a person that arises from other people and events in the environment.

eros according to Rollo May, a type of procreative love that is experiential and savoring.

erotic love according to Erich Fromm, the type of love that is directed toward a single individual; it is a short-lived intimacy that satisfies sexual needs and alleviates anxiety.

error variance variations of a measurement that are the result of irrelevant, chance fluctuations.

estrogen a sex hormone, typically considered the female sex hormone.

ethnic bias a type of bias in which a test fails to take into account the relevant culture or subculture of the person being tested.

ethnic group a group whose membership is based primarily on shared cultural habits or customs.

ethnocentrism evaluating others from one's own cultural point of view.

ethology the study of animal behavior in natural environments.

etic approach an approach that is cross-cultural, searching for generalities across cultures.

eugenics the movement begun by Francis Galton that encouraged preserving or purifying the gene pool of the elite in order to improve human blood lines.

evolution the theory in which individual characteristics that evolve are those that enable the organism to pass on genes to offspring.

existentialism an area of philosophy concerned with the meaning of human existence.

experience sampling method of assessment a method in which participants record their current activity or thought processes when they are paged by the experimenter at various intervals during the day.

experiencing person in Carl Rogers's phenomenological view, important issues are defined by each person for him- or herself in the context of the total range of things the person experiences.

explanatory style a set of cognitive personality variables that captures a person's habitual means of interpreting events in his or her life.

explicit memory a memory that can be consciously recalled or recognized.

expressive behavior behavior that involves the emotional well-being of one's social or family group; contrasts with instrumental behavior.

expressive style a term used to describe nonverbal social skills such as vocal characteristics, facial expressions, body gestures, and movements.

external locus of control according to Julian Rotter, the belief that things outside of the individual determine whether desired outcomes occur.

extinction the process by which the frequency of the organism's producing a response gradually decreases when the response behavior is no longer followed by the reinforcement.

extroversion a term used by Carl Jung to describe the directing of the libido, or psychic energy, toward things in the external world. In Hans Eysenck's biologically based theory the term is used to describe people who are generally sociable, active, and outgoing and who are thought to have a relatively lower level of brain arousal and who thus tend to seek stimulation. According to the Big Five approach, this term refers to the personality dimension that includes enthusiasm, dominance, and sociability; people low on this dimension are considered introverted.

F-scale a scale developed at the University of California, Berkeley, to measure a person's proneness to being rigid and authoritarian.

factor analysis a statistical technique in which correlations among a number of simple scales are reduced to a few basic dimensions.

femininity the qualities associated with being a woman.

fictional goals according to Alfred Adler, strivings for self-improvement that vary from person to person but that reflect an individual's view of perfection.

field dependence the extent to which an individual's problem solving is influenced by salient but irrelevant aspects of the context in which the problem occurs.

field independence the extent to which an individual's problem solving is *not* influenced by salient but irrelevant aspects of the context in which the problem occurs.

field theory Kurt Lewin's approach to personality, suggesting that behavior is determined by complex interactions among a person's internal psychological structure, the forces of the external environment, and the structural relationships between the person and the environment.

fixed interval reinforcement schedule a pattern of reinforcement occurring after a regular interval of time.

fixed ratio reinforcement schedule a pattern of reinforcement occurring after a regular number of responses by the organism.

forced choice recognition a procedure in which a person studies a word list and then chooses which word appeared on the list from pairs of words.

free association a method used in psychoanalysis in which an individual reports everything that comes into awareness.

free recall a procedure in which a person studies a word list and then writes down as many words as he or she can remember from the list.

Freudian slip a psychological error in speaking or writing that reveals something about the person's unconscious.

functionalism the approach to psychology that declares that behavior and thought evolve as a result of their functionality for survival.

functionally autonomous   a term used by Gordon Allport to describe the idea that in adulthood many motives and tendencies become independent of their origins in childhood and that finding out where such tendencies originated therefore is not important.

functionally equivalent   Gordon Allport's concept that many behaviors of individuals are similar in their meaning because the individuals tend to view many situations and stimuli in the same way; for Allport, the trait is the internal structure that causes this regularity.

gender roles   social roles based on gender.

gender schema theory   the theory that argues that our culture and gender-role socialization provide us with gender schemas.

gender schemas   organized mental structures that delineate our understanding of the abilities of, appropriate behavior of, and appropriate situations for males and females.

gender typed   describes an individual whose conception of self and of others is unusually strongly organized around gender schemas.

generalization   the tendency for similar stimuli to evoke the same response.

generalized expectancy   according to Julian Rotter, expectancies that are related to a group of situations.

generalized reinforcement   according to Dollard and Miller, a secondary reinforcement that becomes associated with a variety of primary reinforcers.

genetic sex   whether an individual has XX chromosomes (female) or XY chromosomes (male).

genital stage   Freudian stage of psychosexual development beginning at adolescence in which attention is turned toward heterosexual relations.

Gestalt psychology   an approach to psychology that emphasizes the integrative and active nature of perception and thought suggesting that the whole may be greater than the sum of its parts.

gestalt   a German word for pattern or configuration.

habit hierarchy   in social learning theory, a learned hierarchy of likelihoods that a person will produce particular responses in particular situations.

habits   simple associations between a stimulus and a response.

hemispheric activity   the level of activity within one cerebral hemisphere (left or right).

hero   according to Carl Jung, the archetype that represents a strong and good force that does battle with the enemy in order to rescue another from harm.

human genome project   an effort to identify each of the thousands of genes in our chromosomes.

human potential movement   a existential-humanistic movement in which people are encouraged to realize their inner potentials through small group meetings, self-disclosure, and introspection.

humanism   a philosophical movement that emphasizes the personal worth of the individual and the importance of human values.

hydraulic displacement model   Sigmund Freud's concept that suggests that during displacement, pressure builds up like steam in a boiler and must be released.

hypermnesia   a situation in which a later attempt to remember something yields information that was not reportable on an earlier attempt to remember.

hypnosis   a process by which a person is induced into a trance state where action is partially under the control of another person.

hysteria   a term used for various forms of mental illness for which no organic cause could be found and which could sometimes be cured by psychological and social influences.

I-It monologue a phrase used by philosopher Martin Buber to describe a utilitarian relationship in which a person uses others but does not value them for themselves.

I-thou dialogue a phrase used by philosopher Martin Buber to describe a direct, mutual relationship in which each individual confirms the other person as being of unique value.

id in psychoanalytic theory, the undifferentiated, unsocialized core of personality that contains the basic psychic energy and motivations.

identity crisis a term proposed by Erik Erikson to describe uncertainty about one's abilities, associations, and future goals.

identity formation the process of developing one's individual personality and concept of one's self.

idiographic involved in the study of individual cases.

idiolect each individual's own unique version of his or her native language.

illusion of individuality according to Harry Stack Sullivan, the idea that a person has a single, fixed personality is just an illusion.

immature love according to Erich Fromm, the type of love in which the taking of love overwhelms the giving of love.

implicit memory a memory that is not consciously recalled but that nevertheless influences behavior or thoughts.

implicit personality theory a type of biasing tendency for people to, perhaps erroneously, see certain traits as going together and to perceive consistencies when viewing the personalities of others.

imprinting a term used by ethologists to describe a type of learning that occurs at a particular early point in an organism's life and cannot be changed later on.

Individual Psychology Alfred Adler's theory of personality that stresses the unique motivations of individuals and the importance of each person's perceived niche in society.

inductive approach an approach to psychology in which observations are systematically collected and concepts are developed based on what the data reveal.

infantile amnesia the phenomenon of adults being unable to remember what happened to them before age three or four.

inferiority complex according to Alfred Adler, an individual's exaggerated feelings of personal incompetence that result from an overwhelming sense of helplessness or some experience that leaves him or her powerless.

instrumental behavior behavior that is oriented to objectives that are task-focused and beyond our interpersonal system; contrasts with expressive behavior.

internal consistency reliability degree of consistency between subparts or equivalent parts of a test.

internal locus of control according to Julian Rotter, the generalized expectancy that an individual's own actions lead to desired outcomes.

interpersonal theory of psychiatry Harry Stack Sullivan's approach to personality that focuses on the recurring social situations faced by an individual.

intimacy motive the need to share oneself with others in intimate ways as studied by Dan P. McAdams.

introversion a term used by Carl Jung to describe the directing of the libido, or psychic energy, toward things in the internal world. In Hans Eysenck's biologically based theory the term describes people who are generally quiet, reserved, and thoughtful, and who are thought to have a relatively higher level of brain arousal, which causes them to shy away from stimulating social environments. According to the Big Five approach, this term is used to describe those who are low on the personality dimension of extroversion; people who are introverted are shy, submissive, retiring, and quiet.

Inventory of Interpersonal Problems a scale that measures distress arising from the interpersonal problems that people experience.

item intercorrelation the extent to which test items are related to one another.

Item Response Theory a mathematical approach to choosing test items in which the probability of a positive response for a particular item is examined given the person's overall position on the underlying trait being measured by the test as estimated by other answers.

Judgment-Perception scale subclassification of the Myers-Briggs Type Indicator that reflects whether a person is oriented toward evaluating or perceiving things.

kin selection the idea that increasing the likelihood for the family members of an individual to survive increases the likelihood that the individual's genes will be carried on to the next generation even if the individual did not reproduce him- or herself.

L-data the term used by R. B. Cattell to describe data gathered about a person's life from school records or similar sources.

latency period according to Sigmund Freud, the period between age five and eleven in which no important psychosexual developments take place and during which sexual urges are not directly expressed but instead are channeled into other activities.

latent content the part of dreams or other aspects of psychological experience that underlies the conscious portion and reveals hidden meaning.

Law of Effect Edward Thorndike's concept that the consequence of a behavior will either strengthen or weaken the behavior; that is, when a response follows a stimulus and results in satisfaction for the organism, this strengthens the connection between stimulus and response; however, if the response results in discomfort or pain, the connection is weakened.

learned helplessness the term used by Martin Seligman to describe a situation in which repeated exposure to unavoidable punishment leads an organism to accept later punishment even when it *is* avoidable.

libido in Sigmund Freud's psychoanalytic theory, the sexual energy that underlies psychological tension; in Carl Jung's neo-analytic theory, the term is used to describe a general psychic energy that is not necessarily sexual in nature.

life-course approach approach to personality by Avshalom Caspi that emphasizes that patterns of behavior change as a function of age, culture, social groups, life events, and so forth, as well as because of internal drives, motives, and traits.

life space in Kurt Lewin's theory, all the internal and external forces that act on an individual.

life tasks a term used by Nancy Cantor to describe age-determined issues on which people are currently concentrating.

linguistic relativity the idea of Benjamin Lee Whorf and Edward Sapir that claims that our interpretation of the world is to a large extent dependent on the linguistic system by which we classify it.

linguistic universals common features among all known languages.

locus of causality according to Bernard Weiner, the perception that situations are caused either by some internal factor within an individual or by external situational issues.

locus of control   In Julian Rotter's theory, the variable that measures the extent to which an individual habitually attributes outcomes to factors internal to the self versus external to the self.

longitudinal study   according to Jack Block, the close, comprehensive, systematic, objective, sustained study of individuals over significant portions of the life span.

love tasks   according to Alfred Adler, the fundamental social issue of finding a suitable life partner.

LSD (lysergic acid diethylamide)   a hallucinogenic drug derived from a fungus that evokes dreamlike changes in perception and thought.

manic-depression   a disorder in which an individual swings regularly between bouts of wildly enthusiastic energy and bouts of hopeless depression.

manifest content   the part of dreams or other aspects of psychological experience that is remembered and consciously considered.

masculine protest   according to Alfred Adler, an individual's attempt to be competent and independent rather than merely an outgrowth of his or her parents.

masculinity   the qualities associated with being a man.

maternal instinct   according to the functional school of psychology, an inborn emotional tendency toward nurturance that is triggered by contact with a helpless infant.

mature love   according to Erich Fromm, the type of love in which each partner cares for the other, feels responsibility to the other, and gives love freely.

Meniere's disease   an inner-ear disorder that can produce disabling dizziness, nausea, and auditory disturbances.

mesomorph   according to W. H. Sheldon, a somatotype describing muscular, large-boned, athletic types of people.

meta-analysis   a statistical technique for combining the results of multiple research studies.

Minnesota Multiphasic Personality Inventory (MMPI)   a comprehensive, self-report personality test that is focused on assessing psychopathology.

mother   according to Carl Jung, the archetype that embodies generativity and fertility.

motherly love   according to Erich Fromm, the type of love that is completely one-sided and unequal, in which the mother gives love and asks for nothing, and from which a child acquires a sense of security and stability.

motives   internal psychobiological forces that induce behavior or push for expression.

multiple intelligences   Howard Gardner's theory that claims that all human beings have at least seven different ways of knowing about the world and that people differ from one another in the relative strengths of each of these seven ways.

multitrait–multimethod perspective   the use of multiple assessment methods and various traits in order to determine test validity.

Myers-Briggs Type Indicator   a widely used instrument that attempts to measure introversion and extroversion and several other subclassifications as defined by Carl Jung.

narcissistic personality disorder   a disorder in which one feels powerless and dependent yet appears to be authoritative and self-aggrandizing.

narrative approach   Dan P. McAdams' approach to personality that involves studying motivations through biographies in order to understand the full life context of the whole person.

natural selection   the process by which certain adaptive characteristics emerge over generations.

need for achievement   according to Henry Murray, the need to succeed on tasks that are set out by society.

need for affiliation   according to Henry Murray, the need to draw near to and win the affection of others.

need for exhibition   according to Henry Murray, the need to show one's self before others and to entertain, amuse, shock, and excite others.

need for power   according to Henry Murray, the need to seek positions and offices in which one can exert control over others.

need   term used by Henry Murray to describe a readiness to respond in a certain way under given conditions.

negative reinforcement   an aversive event that ends if a behavior is performed, making it more likely for that behavior to be performed in the future.

neo-analytic approach   the approach to personality psychology that is concerned with the individual's sense of self (ego) as the core of personality.

neurotic trend   according to Karen Horney, a self-protective measure to achieve power and superiority over others, which counteracts the feeling that one is impotent or being mistreated.

neuroticism   according to the Big Five approach, the personality dimension that includes nervousness, tension, and anxiety; people low in this dimension are emotionally stable, calm, and contented. This term is also one of Hans Eysenck's three personality dimensions and includes emotional instability and apprehensiveness.

neurotransmitter   a chemical used by nerves to communicate.

nomothetic   seeking to formulate laws.

nondeterministic   the idea that it is an oversimplification to view people as controlled by fixed physical laws.

normal symbiotic   according to Margaret Mahler, the forming of ties between a child and mother in which the child develops empathy and the sense of being a separate but loving person.

nuclear quality   Gordon Allport's term for describing personal dispositions in terms of a person's unique goals, motives, or styles.

object relations theories   The approach to personality that focuses on the objects of psychic drives and the importance of relations with other individuals in defining ourselves.

objective assessment   measurement that is not dependent on the individual making the assessment.

observational learning   learning by an individual that occurs by watching others perform the behavior, with the individual neither performing the behavior him- or herself, nor being directly rewarded or punished for the behavior.

occupational tasks   according to Alfred Adler, a fundamental social issue in which one must choose and pursue a career that makes one feel worthwhile.

Oedipus conflict   a term used by Sigmund Freud to describe a boy's sexual feelings for his mother and rivalries with his father.

openness   according to the Big Five approach, the personality dimension that includes imagination, wit, originality, and creativity; people low on this dimension are shallow, plain, and simple.

operant conditioning   the changing of a behavior by manipulating its consequences.

oral stage   Freudian stage of psychosexual development before age one, when infants are driven to satisfy their drives of hunger and thirst.

organ inferiority   Alfred Adler's concept that everyone is born with some physical weakness at which point incapacity and disease are most likely to take place, but the body attempts to make up for the deficiency in another area.

organismic   a term sometimes used to describe theories that focus on the development that comes from inside the growing organism and that assume a natural unfolding, or life course, for each organism.

outcome expectancy the expected consequences of a behavior that is the most significant influence on whether or not an individual will reproduce an observed behavior, in the view of Albert Bandura. Also, the extent to which an individual expects his or her performance to have a positive result.

partial reinforcement   a large, unpredictable reward.

passive style   according to Karen Horney, a mode of adapting to the world used by those who believe that they can get along best by being compliant.

patterns   the basic underlying mechanisms of personality that dynamically direct activity and remain relatively stable.

peak experiences according to Abraham Maslow, powerful, meaningful experiences in which people seem to transcend the self, be at one with the world, and feel completely self-fulfilled; Mihaly Csikszentmihalyi describes them as the "flow" that comes with total involvement in an activity.

penis envy   a term used by Sigmund Freud to describe the phenomenon in which a girl develops feelings of inferiority and jealousy over her lack of a penis.

perfection striving   according to Alfred Adler, an individual's attempt to reach fictional goals by eliminating his or her perceived flaws.

persona   according to Carl Jung, the archetype representing the socially acceptable front that is presented to others.

personal construct theory   the approach to personality proposed by George Kelly that emphasizes the idea that people actively endeavor to construe or understand the world and construct their own theories about human behavior.

personal dispositions   a term used by Gordon Allport to describe traits that are peculiar to an individual.

Personal Orientation Inventory   a self-report questionnaire that asks people to classify themselves on a number of dimensions for the various characteristics of self-actualization or mental health.

personal projects   a term used by Brian Little to describe specific tasks that people are currently working on that motivate them on a daily basis.

personal strivings   a term used by Robert Emmons to describe abstract, overarching goals that may be satisfied by a number of different behaviors.

personal unconscious   according to Carl Jung, the component of the mind that contains thoughts and feelings that are not currently a part of conscious awareness.

personality psychology   the scientific study of the psychological forces that make people uniquely themselves.

Personality Research Form (PRF)   a self-report test that assesses needs by forced responses to short, standardized items.

personality test   a standardized stimulus that evokes different responses in different individuals and assesses these differences.

personological system   Henry Murray's term for his theory of personality that emphasizes the richness of the life of each person and the dynamic nature of the individual as a complex organism responding to a specific environment.

phallic stage   Freudian stage of psychosexual development around age four in which a child's sexual energy is focused on the genitals.

phenomenology   the concept that people's perceptions or subjective realities are considered valid data for investigation.

philia   according to Rollo May, a type of brotherly love or liking.

phlegmatic   a personality type based on the ancient Greek humors discussed by Hippocrates and Galen in which one is apathetic and conforming on the outside but tense and distraught on the inside.

phobia   an excessive or incapacitating fear.

placebo   any intervention that does not have a specific, expected physiological effect on the body.

pleasure principle   the operating principle of the id to satisfy pleasure and reduce inner tension.

positivism   the philosophical view of the world that focuses on the laws that govern the behavior of objects in the world.

post-traumatic stress   anxiety, nightmares, and flashbacks that result when the conscious mind cannot deal with overwhelmingly disturbing memories.

primary drive   a fundamental innate motivator of behavior, specifically hunger, thirst, sex, or pain.

primary reinforcement   according to Dollard and Miller, an event that reduces a primary drive.

principle of reinforcement   the theory that the frequency of a behavior depends on its consequences or the types of outcomes that follow it.

procedural memory   memory for how to do a task.

projection   a defense mechanism in which anxiety-arousing impulses are externalized by placing them onto others.

projective test   an assessment technique that attempts to study personality through use of a relatively unstructured stimulus, task, or situation.

prolactin   the hormone that causes lactation.

proprium   Gordon Allport's term for the core of personality that defines who one is; Allport believed that the proprium has a biological counterpart.

prospective design   using early measures to predict later outcomes.

Prozac   a drug that blocks reabsorption of the neurotransmitter serotonin in the brain and thus elevates moods and alters emotional reaction patterns.

psyche   the essence of the human mind or spirit or soul; in Carl Jung's theory, personality as the dynamic sum of its parts.

psychoanalysis   Sigmund Freud's approach to understanding human behavior; also, Freud's psychotherapeutic techniques.

psychological situation   according to Julian Rotter, the individual's unique combination of potential behaviors and the value of these behaviors to the individual.

psychopharmacology   the study of the role of drugs and other toxic substances in causing and treating psychiatric disturbance.

psychosomatic medicine   treatment that is based on the idea that the mind affects the body.

psychosurgery   operating on the brain in an attempt to repair personality problems.

psychotherapeutic interview   an interview in which a client talks about the important or troubling parts of his or her life.

psychoticism   one of Hans Eysenck's three personality dimensions; it includes a tendency toward psychopathology, involving impulsivity and cruelty, tough-mindedness, and shrewdness.

punishment   an unpleasant consequence to a behavior that decreases the likelihood of performing the behavior in the future.

Q-data   the term used by R. B. Cattell to describe data gathered from self-reports and questionnaires.

Q-sort   a method of personality assessment in which a person is given a stack of cards naming various characteristics and is asked to sort them into piles.

race   large groupings based upon physical characteristics, such as skin color, eye shape, or height, tied to geographical origin.

radical determinism   the belief that all human behavior is caused and that humans have no free will.

rationalization   a defense mechanism in which post-hoc logical explanations are given for behaviors that were actually driven by internal unconscious motives.

reaction formation   a defense mechanism that pushes away threatening impulses by overemphasizing the opposite in one's thoughts and actions.

readiness   the extent to which individuals are likely to respond appropriately in a given situation, as a function of their prior experiences with that situation.

reality principle   in Freudian psychoanalytic theory, the operating force of the ego to solve real problems.

regression   a defense mechanism in which one returns to earlier, safer stages of one's life in order to escape present threats.

reinforcement   an event that strengthens a behavior and increases the likelihood of repeating the behavior in the future.

reinforcement schedules   the frequency and the interval of reinforcement that may be based on time or responses.

reinforcement value   the extent to which an individual values the expected reinforcement of an action.

relative self   the philosophical idea that there is no underlying self but that the true self is composed merely of masks.

reliability   the consistency of scores that are expected to be the same.

repression   a defense mechanism that pushes threatening thoughts into the unconscious.

response set   a bias in responding to test items that is unrelated to the personality characteristic being measured.

Rogerian therapy   the client-oriented psychotherapy developed by Carl Rogers in which the therapist tends to be supportive, nondirective, and empathetic, and gives unconditional positive regard.

Role Construct Repertory Test   an assessment instrument designed by George Kelly to evoke a person's own personal construct system by making comparisons among triads of important people in the life of the person being assessed.

romantic attachment style   according to Phillip Shaver, one's style of adult romantic relationships, which is modeled on and reflects the nature of one's childhood attachment relationships to the parents or caregivers.

ruling type   according to Alfred Adler, a type of person who proceeds for his or her own gain without consideration of others.

salutogenesis   Aaron Antononvsky's theory of how people stay healthy; according to this approach, the world must not necessarily be controlled or ordered for the healthy individual, but the individual must have a sense of coherence.

schema   a cognitive structure that organizes knowledge and expectations about one's environment.

schizophrenia   a condition whose symptoms include distorted reality, odd emotional reactions, and sometimes paranoia and/or delusions.

scientific inference   the use of systematically gathered evidence to test theories.

script   a schema that guides behavior in social situations.

secondary drives   in social learning theory, drives that are learned by association with the satisfaction of primary drives.

secondary reinforcement   according to Dollard and Miller, a conditioned reinforcement; a previously neutral stimulus that becomes a reinforcer following its pairing with a primary reinforcer.

secure lovers   according to Phillip Shaver, people who have a romantic attachment style in which they easily form close relationships with others and let others be close to them.

self-actualization   the innate process by which one tends to grow spiritually and realize one's potential.

self-efficacy   an expectancy or belief about how competently one will be able to enact a behavior in a particular situation.

self-monitoring   Mark Snyder's concept of self-observation and self-control guided by situational cues to the social appropriateness of behavior.

self-presentation   a term used by Mark Snyder to describe doing what is socially expected.

self-regulation   monitoring one's own behavior as a result of one's internal processes of goals, planning, and self-reinforcement.

self-system   according to Albert Bandura, the set of cognitive processes by which a person perceives, evaluates, and regulates his or her own behavior so that it is appropriate to the environment and effective in achieving goals.

Sensation-Intuition scale   subclassification of the Myers-Briggs Type Indicator that reflects whether a person is more prone to realism or imagination.

sensation-seeking scale   a scale developed by Marvin Zuckerman to measure an individual's level of susceptibility to excitement or boredom.

sense of coherence   a person's confidence that the world is understandable, manageable, and meaningful.

SES gradient   a phenomenon in public health in which the higher a person's socioeconomic status, the lower is that person's risk of getting sick and dying prematurely.

shadow   according to Carl Jung, the archetype representing the dark and unacceptable side of personality.

shaping   the process in which undifferentiated operant behaviors are gradually changed or shaped into a desired behavior pattern by the reinforcement of successive approximations, so that the behavior more and more resembles the target behavior.

sick role   a set of societal expectations about how a person should behave when ill.

signal detection theory   an approach to analyzing a person's memory for an event (or their comprehension of a message) that is sensitive to the fact that responses are biased by the rewards and penalties for correct and incorrect yes and no answers.

Skinner box   an enclosure in which an experimenter can shape the behavior of an animal by controlling reinforcement and accurately measuring the responses of the animal.

Social Darwinism   the idea that societies and cultures naturally compete for survival of the fittest.

social desirability response set   a bias in which people are likely to want to present themselves in a favorable light or to try to please the experimenter or test administrator.

social intelligence   the idea that individuals differ in their level of mastery of the particular cluster of knowledge and skills that are relevant to interpersonal situations.

social learning theory   a theory that proposes that habits are built up in terms of a hierarchy of secondary drives.

social roles theory   Alice Eagly's theory that the social behaviors that differ between the sexes are embedded in social roles; that is, the different roles in which men and women find themselves specify their behaviors.

social roles   gender roles and many other roles pertaining to work and family life that involve expectations applied to a category of people.

social self   George Herbert Mead's idea that who we are and how we think of ourselves arise from our interactions with those around us. Also, having an identity in a social world.

societal tasks   according to Alfred Adler, a fundamental social issue in which one must create friendships and social networks.

socioeconomic status   a measurement of one's level of education and income.

sociobiology   the study of the influence of evolutionary biology on individual responses regarding social matters.

somatopsychic effect   disease or genetic predispositions to illness that affect personality.

somatotypology   W. H. Sheldon's theory relating body type to personality characteristics.

specific expectancy   according to Julian Rotter, the expectancy that a reward will follow a behavior in a particular situation.

stability of causality   according to Bernard Weiner, the perception that the causes of occurrences are either long-lasting across time or of the moment and changing across time.

stereotype   a schema or belief about the personality traits that tend to be characteristic of members of some group.

stereotype threat   the threat that others' judgments or one's own actions will negatively stereotype an individual.

strategies   according to Walter Mischel, individual differences in the meanings people give to stimuli and reinforcement that are learned during experiences with situations and their rewards.

structured interview   a systematic interview in which the interviewer follows a definite plan so that similar types of information are elicited from each interviewee.

subjective assessment   measurement that relies on interpretation by the individual making the assessment.

sublimation   a defense mechanism in which dangerous urges are transformed into positive, socially acceptable motivations.

subliminal perception   the perception and processing of weak stimuli without conscious awareness that any stimulus has occurred.

superego   in Freudian psychoanalytic theory, the personality structure that develops to internalize societal rules and guide goal-seeking behavior toward socially acceptable pursuits.

superiority complex   according to Alfred Adler, an exaggerated arrogance that an individual develops in order to overcome an inferiority complex.

survival of the fittest   the concept that species evolve because those individuals who cannot compete well in the environments in which they live tend to be less successful in growing up and producing offspring.

symbiotic psychotic   according to Margaret Mahler, the forming of emotional ties that are so strong that a child is unable to form a sense of self.

System of Multicultural Pluralistic Assessment (SOMPA) a system developed by Jane Mercer that assumes that test results cannot be divorced from the culture and focuses on comparisons among individuals within a cultural group rather than between cultural groups.

systematic desensitization gradually extinguishing a phobia by causing the feared stimulus to become dissociated from the fear response.

systems according to Henry Murray, dynamic influences with feedback.

T-data the term used by R. B. Cattell to describe data gathered from placing a person in a controlled test situation and noting or rating responses.

teleology the idea that there is a grand design or purpose to one's life.

temperament stable individual differences in emotional reactivity.

test–retest reliability the degree of consistency between the results of the same test taken on different occasions.

testosterone a sex hormone, typically considered the male sex hormone.

thanatos according to Freud, the drive toward self-destructive behavior or death.

The Despised Self Karen Horney's concept of the part of personality consisting of perceptions of our inferiority and shortcomings, often based on others' negative evaluations of us and our resulting helplessness.

The Ideal Self Karen Horney's concept of the self that we view as perfection and hope to achieve, as molded by perceived inadequacies.

The Real Self Karen Horney's concept of the inner core of personality that we perceive about ourselves, including our potential for self-realization.

thema according to Henry Murray, a typical combination of needs and presses.

Thematic Apperception Test (TAT) a projective test in which a participant is asked to make up a story (including what will happen in the future) about a picture that is presented.

Thinking-Feeling scale subclassification of the Myers-Briggs Type Indicator that reflects whether a person is logical and objective or personal and subjective.

trait according to Gordon Allport, a generalized neuropsychic structure or core tendency that underlies behavior across time and situations.

transcend to overcome biological drives and societal pressures.

Turing Test a standard test by which to judge whether a computer can adequately simulate a human; in this test, first proposed by Alan Turing, a human judge interacts with two hidden others and tries to decide which is the human and which is the computer.

Turner's syndrome an anomaly in which an individual is born with only a single X chromosome; such a person has female external genitals but no ovaries.

Type A behavior pattern/Type A personality a tense, competitive style that is especially likely to be asssociated with coronary heart disease.

Type T theory Frank H. Farley's theory that suggests a psychobiological need for stimulation due to an internal arousal deficit; Type T stands for "Thrill Seeking."

types a theoretical approach to personality in which people are divided into discrete categories or classes as opposed to being placed along a continuum.

unconscious the portion of the mind that is not accessible to conscious thought.

validity   the extent to which a test measures what it is supposed to be measuring.

variable interval reinforcement schedule   a pattern in which reinforcement occurs at irregularly spaced intervals of time.

variable ratio reinforcement schedule   a pattern in which reinforcement occurs after a varying number of responses by the organism.

withdrawn style   according to Karen Horney, a mode of adapting to the world used by those who believe that it is best not to engage emotionally at all.

zero acquaintance   observation and judgment of someone with whom one has never interacted.

Name Index

Subject Index

Photo Credits

Chapter 1:   p. 6, © Alan Carey/The Image Works;   p. 13, © Chris Wahlberg/Gamma Liaison;   p. 15, Corbis-Bettmann.

Chapter 2:   p. 26, © Roger Viollet/Gamma Liaison;   p. 27, The Granger Collection, New York;   p. 42, © Hank Morgan/Science Source/Photo Researchers;   p. 44, The Granger Collection, New York;   p. 47, AP/Wide World Photos;   p. 49, The Granger Collection, New York;   p. 53, © Francis/Gamma Liaison;   p. 54, UPI/Corbis-Bettmann.

Chapter 3:   p. 62, Mary Evans Picture Library;   p. 64, The Granger Collection, New York;   p. 65, The Granger Collection, New York;   p. 70, © Eric A. Wessman/Stock Boston;   p. 70, © Hans Namuth/Photo Researchers;   p. 72, © Ruth Dixon/Stock Boston;   p. 77(l), © Shahn Kermani/Gamma Liaison;   p. 77(r), © Shahn Kermani/Gamma Liaison;   p. 79, © Catherine Bauknight/Gamma Liaison;   p. 83, The Granger Collection, New York;   p. 93, UPI/Corbis-Bettmann.

Chapter 4:   p. 114, The Granger Collection, New York;   p. 117, The Granger Collection, New York;   p. 124, Corbis-Bettmann;   p. 128, The Granger Collection, New York;   p. 135, © Elizabeth Crews/Stock Boston;   p. 136, © Jean-Claude Lejeune/Stock Boston;   p. 137(t), Reuters/Corbis-Bettmann;   p. 137(b), Reuters/Corbis-Bettmann;   p. 139, UPI/Corbis-Bettmann.

Chapter 5:   p. 150, © Gale Zucker/Stock Boston;   p. 153, © Peter Menzel/Stock Boston;   p. 155, Corbis-Bettmann;   p. 156, © George W. Gardner/Stock Boston;   p. 158, © T. K. Wanstal/The Image Works;   p. 159, Reuters/Corbis-Bettmann;   p. 162, © Gary Wagner/Stock Boston;   p. 165, Corbis-Bettmann;   p. 171, © William Thompson/The Picture Cube.

Chapter 6:   p. 185, © David Stoecklein/Adstock Photos;   p. 190, Used with permission of the Fear of Flying Clinic;   p. 193, © Ken Robert Buck/Stock Boston;   p. 195, Ann Mercer/Twin Oaks Community;   p. 197, © Michael Dwyer/Stock Boston;   p. 200, Dr. Robert Epstein. Reprinted by permission.

Chapter 7:   p. 214, The Granger Collection, New York;   p. 221, © Joseph Schuyler/Stock Boston;   p. 237, © Bob Daemmrich/The Image Works;   p. 239, © Michael Siluk/The Image Works.

Chapter 8:   p. 262, (first) AP/Wide World Photos;   p. 262, (second) © Larry Kolvoord/The Image Works;   p. 262, (third) AP/Wide World Photos; p. 262, (fourth) © Mark Reinstein/The Image Works;   p. 262, (fifth) © Gilles Mermet/Gamma Liaison;   p. 269, Archives of the History of American Psychology; p. 275, Rapho/Photo Researchers;   p. 281, © Topham/The Image Works.

Chapter 9:   p. 292, © Peter Simon/Stock Boston;   p. 297, Corbis-Bettmann; p. 300, The Granger Collection, New York;   p. 302, © James Wilson/Woodfin Camp & Associates;   p. 304, Corbis-Bettmann;   p. 306(l), © DPA/MKG/The Image Works;   p. 306(m), UPI/Corbis-Bettmann;   p. 306(r), Agence France Presse/Corbis-Bettmann.

Chapter 10:   p. 319, © Jean-Claude Lejeune/Stock Boston;   p. 321, © Joseph Schuyler/Stock Boston;   p. 325, © Jean-Claude Lejeune/Stock Boston; p. 334, Corbis-Bettmann.

Chapter 11:   p. 354, © Margot Granitsas/The Image Works;   p. 355, © Hazel Hankin/Stock Boston;   p. 357, © Suzanne Arms/The Image Works;   p. 361, © Gale Zucker/Stock Boston;   p. 362(r), © Fredrik D. Bodin/Stock Boston; p. 362(l), © Judity Kramer/The Image Works;   p. 364, © W. Marc Bernsau/ The Image Works;   p. 372, © John Chiasson/Gamma Liaison;   p. 374, © Andy Levin/Photo Researchers;   p. 382, AP/Wide World Photos.

Chapter 12:   p. 389, © Michael Siluk/The Image Works;   p. 390, © Jim Mahoney/The Image Works;   p. 392, The Granger Collection, New York; p. 401, Corbis-Bettmann;   p. 412, Reuters/Jacqueline Godany/Archive Photos.

Chapter 13:   p. 420, © Mark Godfrey/The Image Works;   p. 429, The Granger Collection, New York;   p. 435, © K. Kai/Fujiphotos/The Image Works;   p. 439, © Bob Daemmrich/The Image Works;   p. 440, © J. Echeveria/The Image Works.

Chapter 14:   p. 450, 20th Century Fox (Courtesy Kobal);   p. 454, © Boyd Norton/The Image Works;   p. 456, UPI/Corbis-Bettmann;   p. 459, UPI/Corbis-Bettmann;   p. 465, © Michael Dwyer/Stock Boston;   p. 468(l), © Brian Yarvin/The Image Works;   p. 468(r), © Michael A. Dwyer/Stock Boston; p. 469(l), © Peter Vandermark/Stock Boston;   p. 469(r), © Chuck Fishman/ Woodfin Camp & Associates;   p. 473, © Abigail Heman/Stock Boston; p. 474, United Artists (Courtesy Kobal).

Chapter 15:   p. 484, UPI/Corbis-Bettmann.